MATHEMATICS FOR ELEMENTARY SCHOOL TEACHERS

JAMES E.
SCHULTZ

MATHEMATICS FOR ELEMENTARY SCHOOL TEACHERS

Charles E. Merrill Publishing Company
A Bell & Howell Company
Columbus Toronto London Sydney

Published by Charles E. Merrill Publishing Co.
A Bell & Howell Company
Columbus, Ohio 43216

This book was set in Times Roman
Copy editor: Nancy Tenney
Text design and cover design coordination: Ann Mirels
Production coordination: Carnes Publication Services
                        and Ben Shriver

Acknowledgements

Red Is for Apples by Beth Greiner Hoffman, copyright © 1966 by Random House, Inc., is reprinted by permission of Random House, Inc.

"An Agenda for Action," copyright 1980, is reprinted by permission of the National Council of Teachers of Mathematics.

"A Magic Number," from Adventures in Good Music (Radio Show) by Karl Haas is discussed with permission of Karl Haas.

Excerpt from *The Messenger* by R.V.C. Bodley, copyright 1946 by Ava Waverley, The Viscountess Waverly. Reprinted by permission of Doubleday & Company, Inc.

Excerpts in Chapter 6 from copyrighted articles in *U.S. News & World Report* of February 16, 1981, and July 14, 1980, are reprinted with permission.

Excerpt from "The Human Need to Break Records," copyright 1980, Time, Inc. All rights reserved. Reprinted by permission.

"100 and out" game in Chapter 3 is reprinted with permission from Carol Winner's *Make It, Take It Math Games*.

Problems from *A Source of Applications of School Mathematics* in Chapters 2 and 11 are reprinted with the permission of The National Council of Teachers of Mathematics and the Mathematical Association of America.

Odds of becoming a millionaire, being killed on a plane, becoming pregnant in Chapter 12 are reprinted by permission of G. P. Putnam's Sons from *The Odds* by the Editors of Heron House. Copyright © 1980 by Heron House, Inc.

The visibility formula in Chapter 8 is reprinted with the permission of Delta Air Lines.

The problem referring to *Twelve Little Pieces* in Chapter 11 is based on William Hugh Miller's *Everybody's Guide to Music*, copyright 1961 by Chilton Company, Philadelphia.

Photo of Nepalese woman by Michael A. Nilson; all other photographs by the author.

Library of Congress Catalog Card Number: 81-85086
International Standard Book Number: 0–675–09860-2
Printed in the United States of America
1 2 3 4 5 6 7 8 9 10—87 86 85 84 83 82

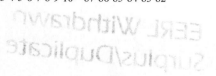

To my mother

Preface

Like the 1977 edition of *Mathematics for Elementary School Teachers*, this revision emphasizes a problem solving approach to understanding mathematics. Changes from the first edition include the following:

1. Over 500 new problems have been added.
2. Problems are grouped to facilitate instruction.
3. Problems suitable for microcomputers or programmable calculators, and more problems involving calculators, have been added.
4. Problem solving strategies are woven throughout the book and receive special emphasis in three new sections.
5. Geometry and measurement have been expanded from four sections to twelve.
6. Probability has been more thoroughly developed and expanded with abundant examples.
7. Longer sections have been subdivided for convenience.
8. References to current events, worldwide travel, mathematics history, assessment tests, and classroom games are now included, as well as error diagnosis and laboratory activities.
9. A bibliography keyed to the text has been added.
10. Logic is now included in a separate appendix.
11. Relevant photos have been added to stimulate interest.

As in the previous edition, we seek an approach that is mathematically sound without being pedantic, stimulating yet accessible. This is founded on the following considerations, based on the author's involvement with different approaches:

1. Prospective teachers should experience success while doing some genuine mathematics.
2. Not all of the mathematics that should be included in these courses can be rigorously developed in the time allotted, yet the presentation must be mathematically accurate.
3. The content should relate to the teaching of elementary school mathematics, both in terms of topics covered and (as much as is feasible) in method of presentation.

We do *not* assume that instructors using this book are experienced in teaching mathematics in the elementary school or that extensive laboratory facilities or concurrent field experience opportunities are available, though each of these aspects could enhance a course taught from this text.

Exercises range from straightforward computations to more challenging problems to accommodate the variety of individual backgrounds and abilities typically found among students in these courses. The instructor may design an individual course by emphasizing different proofs, lab activities, or calculators in the problem sections and by selecting topics from Chapters 6 through 12. Suggestions and further details are provided in the Solution Manual, available to instructors from the publisher.

While little prerequisite knowledge is assumed, students are expected to become actively involved in the learning process by working problems. The emphasis is on "What is true, and why?" rather than "Show that this is true."

The author wishes to thank the following people for their various contributions: Professors Harry Allen, Joe Ferrar, Jim Leitzel, Joan Leitzel, John Riedl, and Bert Waits (Ohio State University); Jim Boone (Texas A. & M. University); Michael Bowling (Stephens College); Tom Butts (University of Texas at Dallas); Jay Graening (University of Arkansas); Ken Hashasaki (Western Washington State College); Tom Hill (University of Oklahoma); Alan Hoffer (University of Oregon); Wallace Judd; Glenda Lappan, John Wagner, and Mary Winter (Michigan State University); Ann Miller (Southern Illinois University at Carbondale); Ronald Pierce (Eastern Kentucky University); Tom Obremski (University of Denver); Zbigniew Semadeni (Institute of Mathematics, Warszawa, Poland); J. Michael Shaughnessy (Oregon State University); Larry Sowder (Northern Illinois University); Raymond Stock (Warren Wilson College); Diane Thiessen (University of Northern Iowa); Irv Vance (New Mexico State University); Jerry Young (Boise State College); Steve Meiring (The Ohio State Department of Education); Alice Hart and Lauren Woodby; students Linda Jones, Myrna Moore, and Amy Pike; and classroom teachers and educators from many lands with whom I have been fortunate to work.

The author is also grateful to Nancy Tenney for her careful editing and to Jerry Martin and Barb Bartow for their assistance in preparing the Solution Manual.

Special thanks are due to William Burger and Gary Musser (Oregon State University), John Dossey (Illinois State University), and Chris Conty (Charles E. Merrill Publishing Company) for offering their valuable services so unselfishly; to Susan Schultz—fantastic elementary school teacher, typist, critic, aide, and understanding wife; and finally to son Scott for his patience.

To the Student

Mastery of this text may require considerable involvement on your part. You will not find this to be a "Turn the crank to get the answer" approach. The main objective is to have you *think* about mathematics. Just as learning history should not be memorizing dates, learning mathematics should not be memorizing formulas or rules. The aim of this text is not so much to add to what you must know about mathematics as to increase your understanding by giving you greater insight into topics you may already have studied.

This book emphasizes a problem solving approach, with problems ranging from fairly easy to fairly difficult. An asterisk or italicized letter prefixed to a problem number indicates the following:

*   Special challenge (may involve advanced ideas.)
C Use a calculator if available.
P Programming problem. Use a computer or programmable calculator.
L Requires special laboratory materials.

There may be some problems you cannot do quickly and even some you may not be able to do at all. With good effort (and perhaps a little help) you will probably be able to do most of them.

To help you further, useful books and articles are cited in the text. A number in brackets indicates a publication identified in the Bibliography at the end of the book.

Contents

Problem Solving

1-1

THE IMPORTANCE OF PROBLEM SOLVING

Problem solving touches our lives in many ways. Selecting the best buy in shampoo, finding a way to get a child's ball down from a tree, or determining why a car won't start are just a few examples of problems we may face in our everyday lives. Even when relaxing during a card game we may enjoy solving problems such as "How should I play my cards to take as many tricks as possible?"

Seldom are we faced directly with a question like "How much is 140 divided by 6?" except of course in the classroom. In our everyday lives, we are more likely to require answers to questions such as "How many 2-by-3 rectangles can be cut from a 10-by-4 piece of cardboard?" Questions like "How much is 140 divided by 6?" are usually called exercises, while questions like "How many 2-by-3 rectangles can be cut from a 10-by-14 piece of cardboard?" are usually called problems. Exercises merely require carrying out a known procedure; problems require determining *what* procedure to carry out or — in some cases — inventing a new procedure. In the words of G. Polya, author of *How to Solve It* [15], a classic on the subject of problem solving, "Solving a problem is finding the unknown means to a distinctly conceived end" [13].

A problem solving approach to mathematics is especially relevant in the 1980s, because routine computations can be made and solutions to common exercises found by using readily available calculators and computers. For most people, the important issue in mathematics becomes "*Which* computations should I make to solve the problem?" Happily, the effect of this change is that we can devote more time to the creative aspects of mathematics. Most educators would agree that there is less need for pages and pages of drill exercises and more need for posing and solving interesting problems. The artificial barriers between mathematics and other subjects, such as science, social studies, industrial arts, and home economics, melt away as we consider applications of mathematics to these areas. For most students, mathematics now becomes more useful and more enjoyable.

One aim of this book is to help you to become a better problem solver, not by having you merely read about problem solving, but more important, by giving you many problems to help improve your problem solving ability. Your capacity for problem solving hinges largely on the extent to which you get involved. In short, the best way to learn to solve problems is to solve problems. The National Council of Teachers of Mathematics, North America's foremost professional organization of teachers of mathematics in the schools, recommended in its *An Agenda for Action* [66] that "problem solving be the focus of school mathematics in the 1980s."

Just one further comment before we give you some problems to try: Problem solving is more challenging than exercise solving, so don't be surprised if you have some difficulty with the six problems that follow. Consider yourself successful if you try them all and solve a few.

Solve as many of these problems as you can. Keep a record of all your work, explaining what you did, both for the problems you solve and for those you attempt.

1. Farmer Watson always plants square cabbage patches, like those illustrated.

```
                                                    O   O   O   O

                              O   O   O             O   O   O   O

              O   O           O   O   O             O   O   O   O

    O         O   O           O   O   O             O   O   O   O
    1             4               9                      16
```

This year his square cabbage patch contains 23 more cabbages than his square patch last year. How many cabbages does he have this year?

2. Write a different digit in each of the boxes so that the three horizontal equations and the one vertical equation are all correct. Use each of the digits 1 through 9. (In filling in the boxes, notice how this puzzle uses each of the nine digits and each of the four basic operations exactly once.)

$$\square - \square = \square$$
$$\times$$
$$\square \div \square = \square$$
$$=$$
$$\square + \square = \square$$

3. There were eight people at a party. If each person shook hands with everyone else, how many handshakes were there?

4. Suppose you overheard the following conversation:

Ann: I have three children.
Bob: What are their ages?
Ann: The product of their ages is 36.
Bob: I can't determine their ages.
Ann: The sum of their ages is your apartment number.
Bob: I still can't do it.
Ann: The oldest has red hair.
Bob: OK, now I know their ages.

It is possible to determine the ages of the three children from this information. What are they?

5. We can connect five straight lines to touch all nine dots in a 3-by-3 array without lifting our pencil from the paper. (See Figure A.) Can you do it with only four straight lines, again without lifting your pencil from the paper?

Figure A

Figure B

6. Complete the table up to seven points, in each case indicating the *maximum* number of regions formed by joining points around a circle. (Don't "lose" regions by having more than two lines intersect at the same point.)

Points	1	2	3	4	5	6	7
Regions	1	2	4	8			

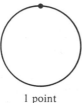

1 point
1 region

2 points
2 regions

3 points
4 regions

4 points
8 regions

1-2
PROBLEM SOLVING STRATEGIES

We recommend that before you read this section, you try to solve the six problems at the end of Section 1-1. We will use these problems and their solutions as a way of introducing some problem solving strategies, or as they are often called, "**heuristics**."

One or more solutions will be given for each of the problems. You may have arrived at a correct answer in a different way. Fine! This is precisely what we meant in Section 1-1 when we mentioned the creative aspect of mathematics. Good problems often can be solved by more than one approach.

Three solutions are given for Farmer Watson's square cabbage patch problem:

EXAMPLE 1-1

Farmer Watson always plants square cabbage patches. This year his square cabbage patch contains 23 more cabbages than his square patch last year. How many cabbages does he have this year?

SOLUTION I
(Make a table.)

Since his cabbage patch last year was *square*, we know that the number of cabbages it contained was one of the numbers 1, 4, 9, 16, ...
His cabbage patch this year is 23 larger, so it is one of the numbers 24, 27, 32, 39, ...

$$1 + 23 = 24, \quad 4 + 23 = 27, \quad 9 + 23 = 32, \quad 16 + 23 = 39, \quad \text{etc.}$$

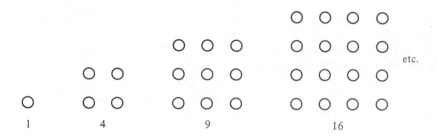

etc.

1   4   9   16

We make a table, hoping to find one of the possibilities for this year's cabbage patch which is itself a perfect square.

Last year	1	4	9	16	25	36	49	64	81	100	121
This year	24	27	32	39	48	59	72	87	104	123	144

Not perfect squares   A perfect square

Since 144 is 12 times 12, we have found an answer that meets all the given conditions. Farmer Watson has 144 cabbages this year.

SOLUTION II
(Draw a sketch.)

We start by drawing a square to represent last year's cabbage patch. Since we don't know how many cabbages it contains, we'll leave it blank (Figure A).

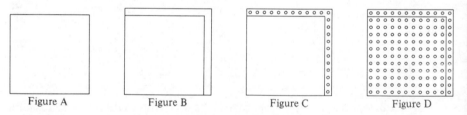

Figure A   Figure B   Figure C   Figure D

Now we build a larger square that contains the previous one. The larger square represents this year's cabbage patch (Figure B).

We are told that the difference is 23 cabbages. We see that we can fill in the region with 23 cabbages, as shown in Figure C, so that we arrive at a square cabbage patch. As a check, we draw Figure D. Now we must be sure to answer the original question. Farmer Watson has 144 cabbages this year.

We provide still another solution, based on elementary algebra.

SOLUTION III
(Write an open sentence.)

Let a^2 be the number of cabbages this year and let b^2 be the number of cabbages last year. Then

$$a^2 - b^2 = 23 \quad \text{or, factoring,}$$
$$(a + b)(a - b) = 23$$

Now, $a + b$ and $a - b$ are whole numbers whose product is 23, where $a + b$ is bigger than $a - b$. The only factors of 23 are 1 and 23, so

$$a + b = 23 \quad \text{and} \quad a - b = 1$$

Solving these equations by the addition/subtraction method gives $2a = 24$, or $a = 12$. This tells us that Farmer Watson has 144 cabbages this year (and 121 cabbages last year).

The three solutions provide an interesting contrast. Roughly speaking, they represent a numerical approach, a geometric approach, and an algebraic approach. The first solution lends itself nicely to the use of a calculator or computer, which is especially appropriate if the numbers are larger. (See, for instance, Problem 3 at the end of this section.)

Each of the solutions to our first problem also illustrates the use of a problem solving strategy. Our first three strategies are:

1. Make a table.
2. Draw a sketch or diagram.
3. Write an open sentence.

We will extend our list of problem solving strategies considerably in this section.

EXAMPLE 1-2

Write a different digit in each of the boxes so that the three horizontal equations and the one vertical equation are all correct. You may use the digits 1 through 9 each once. (Notice how this puzzle uses each of the nine digits and each of the four basic operations.)

$$\square - \square = \square$$
$$\times$$
$$\square \div \square = \square$$
$$=$$
$$\square + \square = \square$$

SOLUTION

(Identify a subgoal, Guess and check.)

As we will see in Section 3-4, there are 362,880 ways to fill in the boxes with the nine digits, so we would like to restrict the possibilities. Of the four problems, the multiplication and division problems have the fewest solutions. In fact, the only possibilities for the multiplication problem are $2 \times 3 = 6$ (or $3 \times 2 = 6$) and $2 \times 4 = 8$ (or $4 \times 2 = 8$). Can you explain why this is true? All other choices would put the same digit in more than one box (such as $1 \times 4 = 4$ or $3 \times 3 = 9$) or require a number of more than one digit (such as $2 \times 5 = 10$).

Our subgoal will be to satisfy both the multiplication problem and the division problem, since these have the fewest possibilities. The possible division problems are $6 \div 2 = 3, 6 \div 3 = 2, 8 \div 2 = 4$, and $8 \div 4 = 2$. Since *every* possibility for multiplication and for division involves 2, the digit 2 must appear in both the multiplication problem and the division problem; there is only one box where it can go, as shown at the top of the next page. The possibilities for the multiplication problem are now reduced to either $3 \times 2 = 6$ or $4 \times 2 = 8$.

$$\boxed{} - \boxed{} = \boxed{}$$
$$\times$$
$$\boxed{} \div \boxed{} = \boxed{2}$$
$$=$$
$$\boxed{} + \boxed{} = \boxed{}$$

We now employ the "Guess and check" strategy. For each of these choices there is only one way to fill in the division problem, so we must have either

$$\boxed{} - \boxed{} = \boxed{3} \qquad\qquad \boxed{} - \boxed{} = \boxed{4}$$
$$\times \qquad\qquad\qquad\qquad\qquad \times$$
$$\boxed{8} \div \boxed{4} = \boxed{2} \quad \text{or} \quad \boxed{6} \div \boxed{3} = \boxed{2}$$
$$= \qquad\qquad\qquad\qquad\qquad =$$
$$\boxed{} + \boxed{} = \boxed{6} \qquad\qquad \boxed{} + \boxed{} = \boxed{8}$$

Now the only place the 9 can go is in the upper left-hand corner. (Why?) Consequently, we must have

$$\boxed{9} - \boxed{5} = \boxed{4}$$
$$\times$$
$$\boxed{6} \div \boxed{3} = \boxed{2}$$
$$=$$
$$\boxed{1} + \boxed{7} = \boxed{8}$$

Except for reversing the positions of the 1 and 7, this is the only solution.

We can now add "Identify a subgoal" and "Guess and check" to our list of strategies:

    4. Identify a subgoal.
    5. Guess and check.

Together with the previously mentioned strategy "Make a table," our next example can be solved by combining the following strategies:

    6. Act it out.
    7. Solve a simpler problem.
    8. Look for a pattern.

EXAMPLE
1-3

There were eight people at a party. If each person shook hands with everyone else, how many handshakes were there?

SOLUTION
(Act it out,
Solve a simpler
problem, Make
a table, Look
for a pattern.)

If we "act it out," we clarify the question. For instance, we observe that no one shakes hands with himself (or herself) and that if I shake hands with you, then you have shaken hands with me. We try simpler problems (for two, three, four, and five people) and look for a pattern.

People	2	3	4	5
Handshakes	1	3	6	10

This suggests the pattern that the increase in the number of handshakes grows by one each time. Using this information, we extend the chart up to eight people.

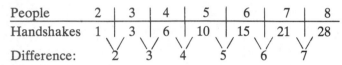

We must be careful, however, because some problems (like Example 1-6) lead to false patterns! Beginning with two people acting it out, we see that each time a new person is added to the group, new handshakes arise as he or she shakes hands with each of the old members of the group. Thus, for example, if we count ten handshakes for five people there will be five more handshakes (for a total of 15) when a sixth person joins the group. There are numerous other ways to solve the problem.

Our next example may seem a bit whimsical, but it nicely illustrates two more strategies:

9. Systematically account for all possibilities.
10. Consider all of the given information.

EXAMPLE
1-4

Suppose you overheard the following discussion:

Ann: I have three children.
Bob: What are their ages?
Ann: The product of their ages is 36.
Bob: I can't determine their ages.
Ann: The sum of their ages is your apartment number.
Bob: I still can't do it.
Ann: The oldest has red hair.
Bob: OK, now I know their ages.

Determining the ages of the three children is possible from this information. What are they?

SOLUTION
(Systematically
account for all

At first glance there seems to be no connection between the children's ages and the unknown apartment number or the color of their hair. There is, however, plenty of information to get us started. Let's systematically write down all the possible ways that three ages could give a product of 36, beginning with the youngest being one year old. We also list the sums of the ages:

Youngest	Middle	Oldest	Product	Sum
1	1	36	36	38
1	2	18	36	21
1	3	12	36	16
1	4	9	36	14
1	6	6	36	13
2	2	9	36	13
2	3	6	36	11
3	3	4	36	10

We have systematically accounted for all of the possibilities. Have we considered all of the given information? Since we don't know Bob's apartment number, the remark about the sum seems to be of no apparent help. The breakthrough comes when we realize that Bob *still* couldn't determine their ages. This would be true only if the sum of their ages were 13, since this can happen two ways. (For instance, if the sum were 14 he could readily determine the ages at 1, 4, and 9.) The fact that "the oldest has red hair" suggests that of the two choices that sum to 13 (1, 6, and 6; or 2, 2, and 9), the latter is correct.

possibilities, Consider all of the given information.)

Though some may question the analysis in Example 1-4 on technical grounds, this well-known problem colorfully illustrates the importance of considering all of the given information. The next example provides a contrasting bit of advice:

11. Don't make any unwarranted assumptions.

We can connect five straight lines to touch all nine dots in a 3-by-3 array without lifting our pencil from the paper. (See Figure A.) Can you do it with only four straight lines, again without lifting your pencil from the paper?

EXAMPLE

1-5

Figure A   Figure B

Many people falsely assume that they can't extend any lines beyond the given grid. The problem is suddenly much easier if you start like this:

SOLUTION
(Don't make any unwarranted assumptions.)

With this rather strong hint the solution is not difficult.

Our last example stresses the importance of our twelfth principle:

12. Check your answer.

EXAMPLE
1-6

Complete the table of Problem 6, Section 1-1, up to seven points, in each case indicating the *maximum* number of regions formed by joining points around a circle. (Don't "lose" regions by having more than two lines intersect at the same point.)

SOLUTION
(Check your
answer.)

It is tempting when we see the doubling pattern 1, 2, 4, 8, . . . to continue with 16, 32, 64, especially since the 16 is correct. However, actual verification by drawing the circle shows a maximum of 31 regions when 6 points are connected:

6 points
31 regions

Careful counting yields the following table:

Points	1	2	3	4	5	6	7
Regions	1	2	4	8	16	31	57

Actually 1, 2, 4, 8, 16, 31, 57, . . . is a perfectly good pattern, though it is hardly obvious what comes next. This problem will be revisited later. It is also discussed in detail in [6].

Our next example calls attention to a mathematical technique which can be used to solve problems. The same technique is called upon several times in the book and can be used to solve one of the problems at the end of this section. We won't tell you which problem, because we want you to keep the strategy

13. Think of a similar problem.

in mind when you consider the problems. This example also illustrates the power of deductive thinking over mere trial and error. Try the following problem before reading the solution.

EXAMPLE
1-7

Two squares are removed from opposite corners of a checkerboard as shown. If one domino exactly covers two adjacent squares, can you cover the 62 remaining squares with 31 dominoes? Explain your solution.

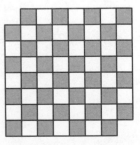

We can show a domino covering
two adjacent squares like this:

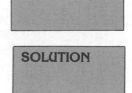

SOLUTION

There are 30 light squares and 32 dark squares. Each domino covers one
light square and one dark square. Thus 31 dominoes will cover 31 light
squares and 31 dark squares, so it is impossible to cover 30 light squares and
32 dark squares with 31 dominoes.

We close the chapter by summarizing the thirteen strategies you can use
with the problems that follow. You or your instructor may wish to add to the
list, especially if you're superstitious! Several references are given in the
bibliography. An extended list of references can be found in the 1980 Yearbook
of the National Council of Teachers of Mathematics, *Problem Solving in
School Mathematics* [13].

Problem Solving Strategies ☐

1. Make a table.
2. Draw a sketch or diagram.
3. Write an open sentence.
4. Identify a subgoal.
5. Guess and check.
6. Act it out.
7. Solve a simpler problem.
8. Look for a pattern.
9. Systematically account for all possibilities.
10. Consider all of the given information.
11. Don't make unwarranted assumptions.
12. Check your answer.
13. Think of a similar problem.

EXERCISES AND PROBLEMS 1-2

1. It is often recommended that students make up their own problems (or exercises) from a
given set of information. Make up and solve (a) several exercises and (b) one problem
based on the following information:
   Scott, David, and Melissa collected fossils. Scott found 7 fossils, David found 9
   fossils, and Melissa found 12 fossils.

2. Solve the problem of Example 1-3 using the "Draw a sketch or diagram" strategy. (Hint:
Draw eight points around a circle to represent the eight people and symbolize a handshake
by connecting two points.)

3. Repeat the problem from Example 1-1 where this year's cabbage patch has (a) 51 more
than last year; (b) 401 more than last year.

4. A woman bought a horse for $100, sold it for $110, then bought it back for $120, and finally sold it for $130. How much money did she make or lose?

5. When Al and Bob ran a 100-meter dash, Al won by 10 meters. When Bob ran a 100-meter dash against Cal, Bob won by 10 meters. If Al and Cal raced in a 100-meter dash, by how many meters would Al win? (Assume their speed does not vary from race to race.)

6. Jody is driving on the interstate highway. After a while she passes a milepost with a two-digit number. Exactly one hour later she passes a milepost with the same two digits, but they are reversed. In another hour she passes a third milepost with the same two digits (backward or forward) separated by a 0. If she drove at a constant speed the whole time, what was her speed?

7. Once upon a time, a woman noticed on her birthday that when she multiplied her age by itself, the answer equaled the year at that time. How old was she on her birthday in 1980?

8. Using the digits 1, 2, 3, 4, 5, 6, 7, 8, 9 only once each, which two whole numbers multiply to give the largest product? To clarify, 7463×98512 uses the nine digits each once but it isn't the solution, because another pair fulfilling the conditions gives a larger product.

9. If it takes 858 digits to number the pages of a book, (a) how many pages are there? (b) How many times is "4" used? (The number 44 uses 4 twice.)

10. Each of the letters in this **cryptarithm** represents a different digit, but a repeated letter has the same value each time it is used. Find a solution.

$$\begin{array}{r} S\,E\,N\,D \\ +\ M\,O\,R\,E \\ \hline M\,O\,N\,E\,Y \end{array}$$

11.

   A   B   C

   Three playing cards are face down on the table. With the help of the following clues, find the value of each card:
   1. No card is a 7 or has a value higher than 9.
   2. The total value of A and B is 15.
   3. The total value of B and C is 17.

12. A two-volume set of books is placed on a shelf in the usual way. A worm bores directly from the first page of Volume I to the last page of Volume II. If the paper in each volume is 2 centimeters thick and the front and back covers of each volume are each 1/2 centimeter thick, how far did the worm travel?

13. The *odd numbers* are 1, 5, 5, 7, 9, 11, ... Find the sum of the first 1000 odd numbers.

14. Each day at 6 A.M. and every five minutes thereafter until midnight, a subway train leaves Station A and travels to Station B. Trains leave Station B and travel to Station A on the same schedule. The trip takes one hour either way. How many trains does the noon train pass after leaving Station A and before arriving at Station B?

15. Eight Girl Scouts and three leaders want to cross a river using an inflatable raft that will carry either two scouts or one leader.
   (a) Describe a way for the 11 people to cross.
   (b) How many crossings will it take? (A round trip equals two crossings.)

16. In how many ways is it possible to make change for 50 cents using pennies, nickels, dimes, and/or quarters?

17. In a certain classroom, the 25 seats are arranged in a square of 5 rows with 5 seats in each row. The teacher announces that students are to change their seats by going either to the seats in front of them, in back of them, or to the left or right of them. Can this be done?

18. A bear walks 1 kilometer south, 1 kilometer east, and 1 kilometer north and is back in his original position. (**a**) What color is the bear? *(**b**) Describe how the bear could do this in the Southern Hemisphere.

19. (True Story.) The author, being an absent-minded professor, once recorded his mileage when he left home on a business trip but forgot to check it when he returned. He noticed his mistake the first time he used his car after the business trip when he was on his way to a distant shopping center. Tell how he was able to determine his mileage for the business trip without doing any extra driving.

20. Using six matches or toothpicks, show how to form four equilateral triangles. (All sides and angles are the same.)

21. Use three upright pop bottles and three table knives to build a platform to hold the fourth pop bottle in an upright position above the others. Your platform must also satisfy the condition that no two of the three bottles in the platform are close enough together to be touched by the same knife. (Also, no bottle should rest directly above another.)

22. We can use three 9's to make 10, 11, or 18, as shown below. Can we use three 9's to make 20?

$$\text{\textit{Permissible}} \qquad\qquad \text{\textit{Not Permissible}}$$

$$9 + \frac{9}{9} = 10 \qquad\qquad \frac{90}{9} + 9 = 19$$

$$\frac{99}{9} = 11 \qquad\qquad \frac{6 \times 6}{9} = 4$$

$$\sqrt{9} \times 9 - 9 = 18$$

(You may use any mathematical symbols known to eighth graders. Hint: Work backwards.)

Whole Numbers and Place Value

2

2-1
DEFINING WHOLE NUMBERS

Though arithmetic is only one facet of the elementary school curriculum (even the mathematics component involves others, such as geometry), it unquestionably accounts for a significant portion of the teacher's responsibility. Successful teaching of arithmetic requires thorough understanding of the processes, and this understanding begins with a good knowledge of the idea of "number" itself. We begin with a discussion of whole numbers, 0, 1, 2, 3, 4, etc., looking at these familiar numbers in terms of even more basic concepts.

The way in which children learn the meaning of "three" is not unlike the way they learn the meaning of "red." For example, a children's book, *Red Is for Apples,* contains this rhyme along with the appropriate pictures:

Red is for apples, Grandma's roses,
Healthy cheeks and sunburned noses,
Fire trucks and cherry pop.
At the corner, red says: STOP.

Red is, of course, the outstanding common property of all the objects mentioned in the rhyme. Numbers are learned in much the same way. "Three" might be suggested by the sets of objects in Figure 2-1, though other interpretations, such as "things I would like to play with," are possible. The question of interpretation arises because only a limited number of sets are provided, and they may, in fact, share properties other than the one we are defining. Of course, normal learners with exposure to more examples will overcome this obstacle in due time, yet it is interesting that this problem can be avoided altogether.

FIGURE 2-1

The somewhat formal development that follows is intended to give a fuller understanding beneficial to you as a teacher. It is certainly *not* the approach you would use with children. We argue simply that to be an effective teacher of first graders, for example, you need to know more than first grade subject matter. The approach to use should be provided by the elementary school laboratory and text materials and the teachers' manuals which accompany them.

Let's direct our attention to the matter of more carefully defining the concept of "three." The sets given in Figure 2-1 are only a few of those which share the desired property. Since we cannot write down all possible sets of three objects, we need a way to specify them by some other method. To do this, it will be convenient to first develop some vocabulary about sets.

We will not define the notion of **set** itself. Instead we accept it as a primitive idea (starting point) used to define other terms. However, we insist in our work that there be no ambiguity about what constitutes any particular set. For example, we would refrain from speaking of the set of all "big numbers," since not everyone would agree on which numbers qualify.

There are two common techniques for specifying sets — rosters and rules. A **roster** is merely a listing of all the members separated by commas and within braces. Here are some examples (notice that we name sets using capital letters):

$$A = \{r, \ s, \ t, \ u\}$$
$$B = \{a, \ b, \ c, \ d, \ z\}$$
$$C = \{a, \ b, \ c, \ d, \ ..., \ z\}$$
$$D = \{1, 3, 5, 7, 9, \ ...\}$$
$$E = \{ \ \}$$

Set A contains the four members listed, also called **elements**; and set B contains the five elements a, b, c, d, and z (and no others). Set C contains all the letters of the English alphabet and has 26 elements; set D is the set of all odd (whole) numbers; and set E, called the **empty set**, is the set containing no elements. In sets C and D, we use exactly three dots to mean *et cetera*. Some of these sets could also be conveniently defined by a **rule**:

$$A = \{\text{letters in the word "rust"}\}$$
$$C = \{\text{letters of the English alphabet}\}$$
$$D = \{\text{odd (whole) numbers}\}$$
$$E = \{\text{women U.S. presidents prior to 1900}\}$$

We will usually use whichever method is easier. Thus for $\{1, 3, 12, 89\}$ the roster method is more appropriate, while {real numbers} is given better by rule.

To express the fact that r is an element of set A and that f is not an element of set A, we use the following notation:

$$r \in A \quad \text{or} \quad r \in \{r, \ s, \ t, \ u\}$$
$$f \notin A \quad \text{or} \quad f \notin \{r, \ s, \ t, \ u\}$$

Thus each of the following is a true statement for the above sets:

$$u \in A$$
$$d \in C$$
$$f \notin A$$
$$f \in C$$
$$2 \notin D$$
$$13 \in D$$
$$0 \notin E$$

Since {*r*, *s*, *t*, *u*} and {letters of the word "rust"} are precisely the same set, we write

$$\{r, \ s, \ t, \ u\} = \{\text{letters of the word "rust"}\}$$

and say that these sets are **equal**. For two sets to be equal, they must contain exactly the same members; that is, each member of the first set must belong to the second set, and each member of the second set must belong to the first set. Here is another example:

$$\{r, \ s, \ t, \ u\} = \{u, \ t, \ s, \ r\}$$

Note that it follows from this definition of equal sets that it makes no difference in which order you write down the members.

It is clear from the definition of equal sets that {*a*, *b*, *c*} ≠ {*r*, *s*, *t*}; namely, these sets are not equal. Yet they do have the same *number* of members. Can you argue that they have the same number of members *without counting*? One way to do this is suggested in Figure 2-2. We can see that each member of the first set is paired with exactly one member of the second set and that each member of the second set is paired with exactly one member of the first set. Such a pairing is called a **one-to-one correspondence** (usually written **1-1 correspondence**). Figure 2-3 shows another 1-1 correspondence for the same sets. Can you find any others?

FIGURE 2-2

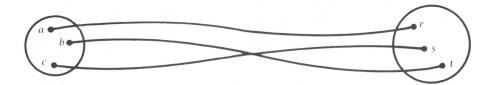

FIGURE 2-3

When we are able to find a 1-1 correspondence between two sets, we say that they **match** or that they are **equivalent**. Thus,

{Ann, Tom, Joe, Betty} matches {autumn, summer, winter, spring}
{*r*, *s*, *t*, *u*} matches {*r*, *s*, *t*, *u*}, but
{*r*, *s*, *t*, *u*} does not match {*r*, *s*, *t*}

Notice that if two sets are equal they must match, but if two sets match they are not necessarily equal.

We are now (at last!) in a position to define "three." "Three" is the property common to all sets that match the set {cat, dog, bird} in number of elements. Of course, instead of {cat, dog, bird} we could have used {a, b, c} or {red, white, blue} or any other set of three. Similarly, we can define "four" as the property common to all sets that match the set {autumn, summer, winter, spring}. We can use this technique to define *any* whole number, because a **whole number** is the property common to all sets that match some finite set. We call whole numbers greater than zero the **natural numbers**. Thus the set of whole numbers is {0, 1, 2, 3, . . .} and the set of natural numbers is {1, 2, 3, 4, . . .}.

Children learn the *names* of the first twenty or so whole numbers much as they learn the letters of the alphabet. It is interesting that children usually know names for many of the whole numbers before they comprehend the numbers themselves. For example, the author's son could correctly say all the numbers up to 20 before he could count a set of 8 pennies. Thus, children can usually "count" in the sense of saying the numbers before they can "count" in the sense of determining how many objects are in a given set. If this observation is correct, then it is quite possible that a child who could "count" (that is, *say* the numbers) to ten would not know that seven is more than six. "Seven is more than six" would make no more sense to this child than "*g* is more than *f*."

This leads us to an important property of the whole numbers: the whole numbers are **ordered**. Since whole numbers are defined in terms of sets, it should be no surprise that sets play a role in ordering them.

We first need to extend our vocabulary of sets to include the notion of subset, which may already be familiar to you. Given two sets, when each element of the first set is also an element of the second set, we say that the first set is a **subset** of the second. Here are some examples:

(a) {1, 2, 3} is a subset of {1, 2, 3, 4, 5}
(b) {girls in your class} is a subset of {students in your class}
(c) {even whole numbers} is a subset of {whole numbers}
(d) {vowels} is a subset of {letters of the alphabet}
(e) {1, 2, 3} is a subset of {1, 2, 3}
(f) {0, 1} is *not* a subset of {1, 2, 3}

The symbol $\subseteq$ is frequently used to mean "is a subset of." Thus, a shorter notation for some of the preceding examples is:

(a) {1, 2, 3} $\subseteq$ {1, 2, 3, 4, 5}
(b) {girls in your class} $\subseteq$ {students in your class}
(f) {0, 1} $\not\subseteq$ {1, 2, 3}

One special case occurs in example (e), where we see that a set is considered to be a subset of itself. This concept follows immediately from the definition, since surely each member of {1, 2, 3} (the first set) is a member of {1, 2, 3} (the second set). The subset which consists of *all* the members of a given set is called the **improper subset**. All other subsets are called **proper** subsets. Another special case arises when we ask if the empty set is a subset of a given set. For example, is { } a subset of {1, 2, 3}? To see why we answer this question affirmatively, see Problem 30.

The following example summarizes many of these ideas. (Notice how we *systematically account for all possibilities*.)

EXAMPLE 2-1

(a) Find all subsets of {1, 2, 3}.
(b) Which ones are proper subsets?

SOLUTION

(a) To satisfy the definition of subset, the only elements which can be used to form subsets are 1, 2, and 3.

Using all three of these, we get {1, 2, 3}.

Using exactly two of these, we get {1, 2}, {1, 3}, and {2, 3}.

Using exactly one of these, we get {1}, {2}, and {3}.

Using none of these, we get { }.

Thus, the subsets are {1, 2, 3}, {1, 2}, {1, 3}, {2, 3}, {1}, {2}, {3}, and { }.

(b) {1, 2, 3} is the improper subset, so the proper subsets are {1, 2}, {1, 3}, {2, 3}, {1}, {2}, {3}, and { }.

We now turn to the concept of comparing whole numbers. Suppose that you were trying to *teach* the idea that seven is more than six. Is the best approach, "It just is" or "Seven is greater because it comes after six"? A more convincing argument might be to stack up seven pennies and six pennies and compare the piles. Notice that this justification that seven is more than six lies in the comparison of sets. A step-by-step solution is outlined in Figure 2-4.

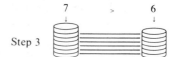

FIGURE 2-4

In Step 1, we associate with each number a set of pennies. The next step shows a comparison of the sets using the idea of matching. Note that it takes only part of the first stack to match all of the second stack, or, in set vocabulary (which we probably would *not* use with very young children), a proper subset of the first set matches the second set. In Step 3, we arrive at a corresponding decision about the numbers and conclude that seven is greater than six. Note that we took what may have been inaccessible (to the child) and converted it to a more familiar situation.

All this may seem rather stilted to you since comparing numbers seems like such a simple idea, but consider the following problem. In a lecture room, each student has his own seat and some seats remain empty. Are there more students or more seats? This problem is simple to answer even though you don't know the number of students or the number of seats! It is only necessary to know that the students matched a proper subset of the seats.

The one remaining goal in this section is to establish the general procedure for comparing *any* two whole numbers.

Recall that whole numbers are defined in terms of finite sets. Exactly one of the following three things must happen when we compare any two finite sets:

1. The sets match.
2. The first set matches a proper subset of the second set.
3. A proper subset of the first set matches the second set.

A situation in which exactly one of three alternatives must hold is called a **trichotomy**, so the preceding statement is often called the **trichotomy property for matching finite sets**.

Thus, to compare any two whole numbers, we associate them with sets and determine which one of the preceding three choices holds for these sets. These choices then respectively suggest that exactly one of the following conclusions must hold for any two whole numbers:

1. The numbers are equal.
2. The first number is less than the second number.
3. The first number is greater than the second number.

This principle is called the **trichotomy property for comparing whole numbers**. We will use the familiar symbols < for "less than" and > for "greater than." Occasionally we write ≤ for "less than or equal to" and ≥ for "greater than or equal to." Hence all the following statements are true:

$$3 < 5$$
$$1 > 0$$
$$2 \leq 3$$
$$5 \geq 5$$

EXERCISES AND PROBLEMS 2-1

ONE-TO-ONE CORRESPONDENCE

1. Show *two* different 1-1 correspondences between $\{x, y, z, w\}$ and $\{a, b, c, d\}$.

2. Show *all* 1-1 correspondences between $\{a, b, c\}$ and $\{1, 2, 3\}$.

3. (a) *How many* 1-1 correspondences are possible between $\{r, s, t\}$ and $\{a, e, i, o, u\}$?
   (b) $\{r, s, t\}$ matches a proper subset of $\{a, e, i, o, u\}$ in at least two ways:

$$r \leftrightarrow a \qquad r \leftrightarrow u$$
$$s \leftrightarrow e \quad \text{and} \quad s \leftrightarrow o$$
$$t \leftrightarrow i \qquad t \leftrightarrow e$$

   How many ways are there in all?

4. How many 1-1 correspondences are there between
   (a) two two-member sets?   (b) two three-member sets?
   (c) two four-member sets?   (d) a four-member set and six-member set?
   (e) two six-member sets?

5. Explain which ideas from this section are involved in playing dominoes.

6. A primitive tribe kept a record of how many hunters left camp each day by placing a stone in a pile for each hunter who departed. A stone was removed from this pile for each hunter who returned. Could it be determined whether all the hunters returned? Did this depend on knowing the actual *number* of hunters?

7. At a Girl Scout camp, each swimmer had a tag which she transferred from the "on shore" to the "in the water" portion of a bulletin board and back again according to her location. At the close of each swimming period, the lifeguards checked the board to see if all swimmers were accounted for. What idea from this chapter was involved? What assumptions were being made?

8. Is there a 1-1 correspondence between English words and French words? And German words? What are idioms?

9. Consider the following game. We deal an ordinary deck of 52 cards, and each of us gets 26 cards. We simultaneously turn up a card. If both cards are black, you get them. If both cards are red, I get them. If they are different colors, they are discarded. The process is repeated until all the cards are used. You get $5 if you have won more cards; I get $1 if you haven't. Is it profitable for you to play the game with me? Try to analyze the results in terms of ideas presented in this section.

10. Define each of the following numbers in a way similar to the way we defined "three" and "four" in this section. (Hint: A correct answer may be "impossible.")
    (a) 5   (b) 2   (c) 1   (d) 0   (e) −1   (f) 2/3

11. Is there a least whole number? A greatest?

12. A secretary types ten letters and addresses ten envelopes. How many ways are there to pair the letters with the envelopes?

*13. (a) Can you show a 1-1 correspondence between {0, 1, 2, 3, 4} and a proper subset of itself?
    (b) Can you show a 1-1 correspondence between {0, 1, 2, 3, 4, ...} and a proper subset of itself?

*14. Can you show a 1-1 correspondence between arc XY and segment XY?

*15. Can you show a 1-1 correspondence between the points on the given triangle and the circle which circumscribes it?

*16. Let $C = \{0, 2, 4, 6, 8 \ldots\}$ and $D = \{1, 3, 5, 7, 9, \ldots\}$. Show that *all* of these are true:
    (a) C matches D.   (b) C matches a proper subset of D.
    (c) D matches a proper subset of C.

ATTRIBUTES AND COMMON PROPERTIES

17. Different denominations of U.S. currency are distinguishable by the numbers (1, 2, 5, 10, etc.) and by pictures (Washington, Franklin, Lincoln, Hamilton, etc.). Some foreign currencies further distinguish by other attributes. Give examples.

18. Is the idea of "learning lessons from history" dependent upon recognizing common properties? Discuss.

19. Have someone in your class who knows *The True Believer* [73] by Eric Hoffer give an example of a property common to mass movements.

20. Can you think of any examples in which music (without words) depicts a story?

21. What common properties are preserved between each of the following and what they represent in real life?
    (a) sewing patterns   (b) house floor plans
    (c) pictures   (d) recipes
    (e) newspaper articles

SETS

22. Indicate the following sets by the roster method:
    (a) {whole numbers between 6 and 10}
    (b) {positive odd numbers less than 10}
    (c) {positive odd numbers less than 100}
    (d) {whole numbers greater than 6}
    (e) {whole numbers less than 0}

23. Indicate the following sets by rule:
    (a) {1, 3, 5, 7, 9, 11}   (b) {0, 1, 4, 9, 16, 25, ...}
    (c) {0, 1}   (d) {   }

24. Though the notation of set is quite basic, certain difficulties can arise in set notation. Give two possible interpretations for each of the following:
    (a) {101,102}   (b) {whole numbers}

25. Which of the following sets equal {0, 1, 2}?
    (a) {1, 2}
    (b) {2, 1, 0}
    (c) {whole numbers less than 3}
    (d) {a, b, c}
    *(e) {0, 1, 2, 2}

26. Does {s, a, l, e} = {l, e, a, s, e}? Why?

27. Which of the sets in Problem 25 match {0, 1, 2}?

28. (a) Can you give two sets that match but are not equal?
    (b) Can you give two sets that are equal but do not match?

29. True or False?
    (a) $2 \in \{1, 2, 3\}$ (b) $1/2 \in \{0, 1, 2\}$
    (c) $6 \notin \{1, 2, 3\}$ (d) $3 \notin \{1, 2, 3\}$
    (e) $\{1, 2\} \subseteq \{1, 2, 3\}$ (f) $\{1, 2, 3\} \subseteq \{1, 2, 3\}$
    (g) $\{   \} \subseteq \{1, 2, 3\}$ (h) $\{0, 1\} \subseteq \{1, 2, 3\}$
    (i) $\{3\} \not\subseteq \{1, 2, 3\}$ (j) $\{1\} \in \{1, 2, 3\}$
    (k) $1 \subseteq \{1, 2, 3\}$ (l) $5 < 2$
    (m) $3 \leq 3$ (n) $\{1\} \leq \{1, 2, 3\}$

30. Observe the following pattern:

$\{a, b, c, d, e\} \not\subseteq \{a, b, c\}$ $\{a, b\} \subseteq \{a, b, c\}$

$\{a, b, c, d\} \not\subseteq \{a, b, c\}$ $\{a\} \subseteq \{a, b, c\}$

$\{a, b, c\} \subseteq \{a, b, c\}$

Based on this pattern, would you expect the following statement to be true or false?

$$\{ \ \} \subseteq \{a, b, c\}$$

Is the statement true or false?

31. A set is called **finite** when there is a whole number n such that there is a set of the form $\{1, 2, 3, ..., n\}$ which matches it. We also say the empty set is finite. Sets which are not finite are called **infinite**.

Examples: is finite since it matches $\{1, 2, 3, 4\}$. ($n = 4$)

$\{a\}$ is finite since it matches $\{1\}$. ($n = 1$)

$\{$letters of the English alphabet$\}$ is finite since it matches $\{1, 2, 3, ..., 26\}$. ($n = 26$)

$\{$whole numbers$\}$ is infinite.

Which of the following sets are finite? For those which are finite, what is n?

(a) $\{$cat, dog, bird, fish, horse$\}$ **(b)** $\{1, 2, 3, 4, ..., 1000\}$

(c) $\{10, 11, 12, 13, 14, ..., 100\}$ **(d)** $\{100, 101, 102, 103, ...\}$

(e) $\{$points belonging to a line segment$\}$

Which of the following sets are finite?

(f) $\{ \ \}$ **(g)** $\{$hairs on your head$\}$

TRICHOTOMY AND ORDER

32. One of the three alternatives for the trichotomy of matching finite sets might be restated, "The first set has more elements than the second set." Which one? Make up similar restatements for the other two alternatives.

33. It is known that the number of members in set A is less than the number of members in set B. Which of the three alternatives for the trichotomy of matching sets holds in this case?

34. Which sports have outcomes which are trichotomies? Dichotomies?

35. Suppose a, b, and c are whole numbers. In each case, replace $\square$ by $<$, $=$, or $>$. (In some cases, you may wish to write a question mark to indicate that no conclusion can be drawn.)

(a) If $a < b$ and $b < c$, then $a \square c$. (**transitive** for $<$)

(b) If $a > b$ and $b > c$, then $a \square c$. (transitive for $>$)

(c) If $a = b$ and $b = c$, then $a \square c$. (transitive for $=$)

(d) If $a < b$ and $a < c$, then $b \square c$.

(e) If $a < c$ and $b < c$, then $a \square b$.

(f) If $a < b$, then $b \square a$. (**antisymmetric** for $<$)

(g) If $a > b$, then $b \square a$. (antisymmetric for $>$)

(h) If $a = b$, then $b \square a$. (**symmetric** for $=$)

36. Suppose a set P has 79 members and a set Q has 43 members. Which one of the three possibilities of the trichotomy property for matching (finite) sets holds? (Write out the conclusion in full.)

COUNTING SUBSETS. PASCAL'S TRIANGLE

37. List *all* subsets of $\{a, b\}$. Which are proper subsets?

38. How many subsets does a set with
    (**a**) 0 members have?   (**b**) 1 member have?
    (**c**) 2 members have?   (**d**) 3 members have?
    (**e**) 4 members have?   (**f**) n members have?

39. Explain why $\{\star, a, b, c, d, e, f, g, h\}$ has twice as many subsets as $\{a, b, c, d, e, f, g, h\}$ has.

40. Observe that a three-member set has:

    1 subset with zero members
    3 subsets with one member
    3 subsets with two members, and
    1 subset with three members

Extend this list up to five-member sets.

has	subsets with 0 members	subsets with 1 member	subsets with 2 members	subsets with 3 members	subsets with 4 members	subsets with 5 members
0-member set	1					
1-member set	1	1				
2-member set	1	2	1			
3-member set	1	3	3	1		
4-member set						
5-member set						

41. In Pascalville the streets are laid out according to the following map:

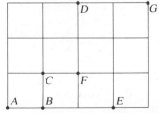

    Note that if you travel only along the streets, then you find one "shortest route" from A to B, two "shortest routes" from A to C, and ten "shortest routes" from A to D. How many "shortest routes" are there from A to
    (**a**) E?   (**b**) F?   (**c**) G?

*42. Compute each of these. (The first two are done for you.)

$$(x + y)^1 = x + y$$

$$(x + y)^2 = x^2 + 2xy + y^2$$

$$(x + y)^3 =$$
$$(x + y)^4 =$$
$$(x + y)^5 =$$

43. (a) Compare Problems 40, 41, and 42. What do they have in common?

(b) The configuration suggested by these problems is called **Pascal's triangle**. It is unbelievably rich in number patterns and is an ideal topic for middle school mathematics programs. We will search for patterns after extending Pascal's triangle to ten rows. To make the job easier we make an important observation:

EXAMPLE 2-2

Let $\binom{8}{5}$ (read "8 choose 5") be the number of five-member subsets of an eight-member set, and in general let $\binom{n}{r}$ (read "n choose r") be the number of r-member subsets of an n-member set. Show that $\binom{8}{5} = \binom{7}{4} + \binom{7}{5}$.

SOLUTION

We have eight objects and wish to choose five. Let us identify any one of the objects as "special" and call it "☆". Thus we have ☆ and seven other objects from which to form a five-member set. Either ☆ is chosen as a member of our five-member set or it isn't. If it is a member, we must choose the remaining four members from the other seven elements. This can be done in $\binom{7}{4}$ ways. If ☆ is not a member of our five-member set, we must choose all five members from the other seven elements. This can be done in $\binom{7}{5}$ ways. Thus $\binom{8}{5} = \binom{7}{4} + \binom{7}{5}$.

Similarly, $\binom{10}{3} = \binom{9}{2} + \binom{9}{3}$, and in general, $\binom{n}{r} = \binom{n-1}{r-1} + \binom{n-1}{r}$. This last result is called the **Pascal triangle relationship** and can be proven by the method of Example 2-2. Notice how it makes it possible to find a member of one row of Pascal's triangle by adding together two members of the previous row. Use this idea to extend Pascal's triangle to ten rows.

(c) Find at least three patterns or properties of Pascal's triangle.

44. Use Pascal's triangle to do the following:

(a) How many four-member subsets does a six-member set have?

(b) How many four-member subsets does a ten-member set have?

(c) Determine $\binom{10}{3}$, $\binom{9}{2}$, and $\binom{9}{3}$ and verify that $\binom{10}{3} = \binom{9}{2} + \binom{9}{3}$.

(d) Prove that $\binom{57}{23} = \binom{56}{22} + \binom{56}{23}$.

*(e) Prove that $\binom{n}{r} = \binom{n-1}{r-1} + \binom{n-1}{r}$.

(f) Write $\binom{83}{49}$ as the sum of two other numbers from Pascal's triangle.

(g) Argue without computing that $\binom{57}{47} = \binom{57}{10}$.

(h) Argue that $\binom{n}{r} = \binom{n}{n-r}$.

(i) Solve Problem 3, Section 1-1.

45. A teacher wishes to select three students for the safety patrol out of a group of eight students. In how many ways may the choice be made? (Order is immaterial.)

46. The middle school chess club plans to have a tournament in which each of its ten members plays each other member once. How many games will be played?

47. Terri likes five new records but can only buy at most three. In how many ways can she make the choice if she buys 0, 1, 2, or 3 records?

2-2
NUMERATION

Numeration is one of the most important underlying ideas in the arithmetic of whole numbers. Many of the mistakes that children make when adding, subtracting, multiplying, and dividing whole numbers can be traced back to misunderstandings in numeration. In this section, we will examine the process used to name numbers in our ordinary numeration system as well as in others. Our reason for considering other numeration systems will be to isolate the intrinsic ideas of place value in a fresh setting, so that we can study them independently of any misconceptions we may have ourselves developed in ordinary arithmetic. By way of analogy, an average tennis player who has developed bad habits that inhibit his play might benefit from concentrating for a while on fundamentals to eliminate these weaknesses. While he might temporarily be less effective, he would stand to improve considerably in the long run.

We will first discuss the distinction between a number and its name. Many of the curricula developed in the 1960s were characterized by an overt effort to emphasize this difference.

Recall from the preceding section that we defined the number three as a *property*. The symbols we use to represent this number, such as "3," "three," and "III," are called **numerals**. Thus, for example, the statement "3 is half of 8" is false if we are speaking of numbers, but it is true if we are speaking of numerals, for the configuration of the numeral 3 is the right "half" of 8! As fanciful as this may seem to you, children occasionally confuse numbers and numerals in this way. Following are a few incidents which have actually been observed in the elementary schools:

A first grade teacher was teaching some subtraction concepts, using a ruler. She asked questions like "How many numbers are there between two and seven?" She didn't seem to understand why so many children responded "four." They were, of course, telling how many *numerals* there were between two and seven on the ruler while she was thinking of numbers (units).

An amusing situation occurred in a third grade class when a teacher asked the children to show "two times three" using bottle caps. While most of the students made two rows of three bottle caps, one little boy worked tediously to construct an answer similar to Figure 2-5.

The discussion of number vs. numeral should be recognized for what it is, a warning to teachers to be aware of *why* in certain situations a pupil fails to understand. It is not intended to suggest that teachers insist on the distinction between the words *number* or *numeral* when the context is clear. Don't be like

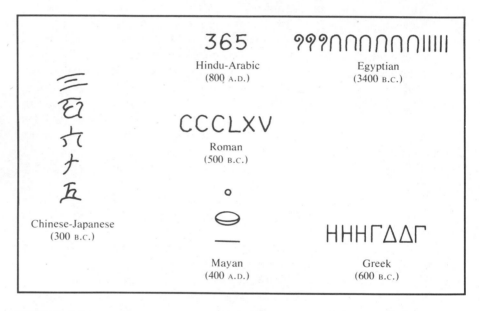

FIGURE 2-5

the teacher who corrected a student who had used the word *number* by saying, "No, Fred, give me a different word *which means the same thing.*"

Throughout history, various ways of naming numbers have been employed in different countries. All the numerals in Figure 2-6 represent the same number. In most instances the Hindu-Arabic system is the simplest one to

365
Hindu-Arabic
(800 A.D.)

ϙϙϙ∩∩∩∩∩∩ΙΙΙΙΙ
Egyptian
(3400 B.C.)

CCCLXV
Roman
(500 B.C.)

Chinese-Japanese
(300 B.C.)

Mayan
(400 A.D.)

ΗΗΗΓΔΔΓ
Greek
(600 B.C.)

FIGURE 2-6

use, not just because we are accustomed to it but because of its ingenious use of place value. Without engaging in a detailed discussion of the various systems alluded to, we observe that the Hindu-Arabic system represents most quantities with a minimum number of characters used a minimum number of times. Examples involving the other systems appear in the problems. Good accounts of the history of numeration can be found in *Historical Topics for the Mathematics Classroom*, the Thirty-first Yearbook of the National Council of Teachers of Mathematics [42], and in *Numbers and Numerals* by David Eugene Smith and Jekuthiel Ginsburg (also available from the National Council of Teachers of Mathematics) [44].

A subtle use of numbers is shown in the photograph of Figure 2-7. The picture, taken at the Sultan's Palace in Yogyakarta, Indonesia, shows the date 1853 of the Japanese calendar using a crown (a symbol for the one highest) for '1," a serpent (which can cross itself to form an 8) for "8," a face (with the five

FIGURE 2-7

senses: sight, hearing, smell, taste, and feeling) for "5," and a leech (of which there are three varieties) for "3."

An interesting discussion of number symbolism in music was given by the noted musicologist Karl Haas in an hour-long program called "A Magic Number." He cited examples in which the number three played a role in the works of Verdi, Mozart, Gluck, Puccini, Richard Strauss, Offenbach, and Mahler. For example, in discussing Mozart's opera *The Magic Flute*, he pointed out the occurrence of three prominent chords; the use of three instruments; the mention of three ladies-in-waiting, three geniuses, three pillars (wisdom, strength, beauty), and three doors (logic, wisdom, nature); and the three attempts of Tamino to gain entry.

Historically, cultures have used clever means to suggest large numbers. Figure 2-8 shows a Hindu temple at Bhaktapur, Nepal. The strength of a god was depicted using the following symbolism:

The human figure is ten times as strong as an ordinary man.
The elephant is ten times as strong as the human figure.
The lion is ten times as strong as the elephant.
The griffin (body of lion, head of bird) is ten times as strong as the lion.
The tigress is ten times as strong as the griffin.
The god figure is ten times as strong as the tigress.

FIGURE 2-8

The god is how many times as strong as the ordinary man?

According to legend, an even larger number is being measured using rings and spindles, like those in the puzzle shown below.

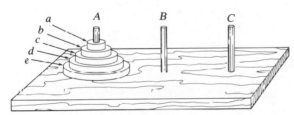

The object of the puzzle is to move the rings from spindle A to spindle B according to the following rules:

1. only one ring may be moved at a time,
2. the rings can only be moved to one of the three spindles, and
3. a ring may never be placed on top of a smaller ring.

For example, if the rings are labeled a, b, c, d, and e as shown, the first few moves might be as follows:

1. ring a to spindle B
2. ring b to spindle C
3. ring a to spindle C (on top of ring b)
4. ring c to spindle B

It is told that an order of monks is moving 64 such rings, one move per second. When all 64 rings have been moved according to these rules, it is said that the world will end! You can explore this puzzle, often called the *Towers of Hanoi*, in the problems.

We now return to the number system now in use in Europe and the Americas, the Hindu-Arabic system. According to Smith and Ginsburg (*Numbers and Numerals*), the system came to us by means of a book on arithmetic written in India about twelve hundred years ago. It was translated into Arabic soon afterward and by chance carried to Europe, where it was translated from Arabic to Latin. The "Arabic" numerals as we know them were never in fact used by the Arabs. They actually took their present shapes in Europe.

The Hindu-Arabic system is based on a "ten-for-one" trading principle which we shall develop shortly. We begin, however, with a "five-for-one" trading principle simply because it conveys all the same ideas about place value with less cluttered pictures, and again because it is free of biases we may have about base ten.

A familiar setting for a five-for-one basis of trading involves exchanging a given number of pennies for an appropriate number of pennies, nickels, and quarters. Suppose we begin with the pennies shown:

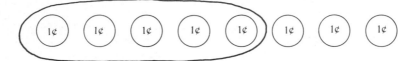

We could trade five for one (five pennies for a nickel) to get:

Similarly, we can trade five nickels for a quarter as in this example:

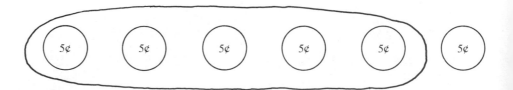

Trading gives:

A problem which involves several trades is:

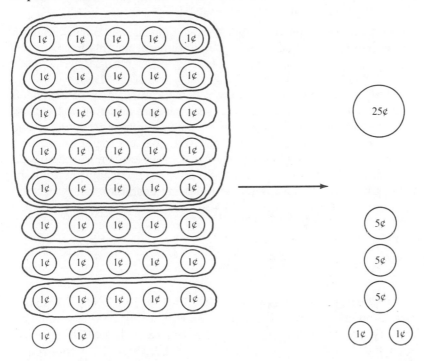

A convenient symbol for this configuration is 132_{five}, which is read "one, three, two, base five" and represents 1 quarter, 3 nickels, and 2 pennies. The "five" indicates a five-for-one trading scheme. 132_{five} is called a **base five numeral**.

(a) Draw a sketch of 34 pennies and trade for nickels and quarters. Write the corresponding base five numeral.

(b) Write the base five numeral for 53.

EXAMPLE
2-3

SOLUTION

(a)

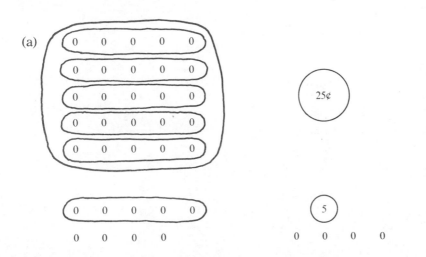

Hence the base five numeral is 114_{five}. (Don't forget the subscript "five," or else it is indistinguishable from the ordinary (base ten) 114.)

(b) We recognize that we could trade for two quarters and no nickels, with three pennies left over. The base five numeral for this is 203_{five}.

Of course, this five-for-one trading scheme could easily be extended beyond quarters. While it is not consistent with our own monetary system, we might invent new denominations so that we could continue the five-for-one exchange pattern indefinitely. For example, five quarters might be worth a "gold," and five "golds" might be worth a "gem." While we might be pressed to come up with appropriate names, we could carry out the scheme as far as we wanted. We illustrate this idea with the following example:

EXAMPLE 2-4

(a) Write 365 as a base five numeral.

(b) Write 1492 as a base five numeral.

SOLUTION

(a) 365 will be a certain number of 1's, 5's, 25's, 125's, 625's, etc. We do not have enough to trade for denominations higher than 125's, so we begin by trading for two 125's. This uses up 250 and leaves us with 115, which is enough for four 25's, three 5's, and no 1's. All this may be summarized as follows:

$$365 = \overline{}_{125\text{'s}} \, \overline{}_{25\text{'s}} \, \overline{}_{5\text{'s}} \, \overline{}_{1\text{'s}} \, {}_{\text{five}}$$

$$
\begin{array}{r}
365 \\
-250 \\ \hline
115 \\
-100 \\ \hline
15 \\
-\;15 \\ \hline
0
\end{array}
\begin{array}{l}
= 2 \times 125 \\[1.2em]
= 4 \times 25 \\[1.2em]
= 3 \times 5
\end{array}
$$

$$365 = 2430_{\text{five}}$$

(b)
$$1492 = \overline{}_{625\text{'s}} \, \overline{}_{125\text{'s}} \, \overline{}_{25\text{'s}} \, \overline{}_{5\text{'s}} \, \overline{}_{1\text{'s}} \, {}_{\text{five}}$$

$$
\begin{array}{r}
1492 \\
-1250 \\ \hline
242 \\
-\;125 \\ \hline
117 \\
-\;100 \\ \hline
17 \\
-\;15 \\ \hline
2 \\
-\;2 \\ \hline
0
\end{array}
\begin{array}{l}
= 2 \times 625 \\[1.2em]
= 1 \times 125 \\[1.2em]
= 4 \times 25 \\[1.2em]
= 3 \times 5 \\[1.2em]
= 2 \times 1
\end{array}
$$

$$1492 = 21432_{\text{five}}$$

Since we trade whenever we have five or more, it is impossible to have any digit greater than four. Thus the only permissible digits in base five numerals are 0, 1, 2, 3, and 4. (There is no single character for 5 itself.) This is quite agreeable with base ten, where the only permissible digits are 0, 1, 2, 3, 4, 5, 6, 7, 8, and 9. (There is no single character for 10 itself.) Note that if we had a twelve-for-one trading scheme, we would expect to have 12 different characters, perhaps 0, 1, 2, 3, 4, 5, 6, 7, 8, 9, T, E. It turns out that we need individual symbols for 10 and 11 since no grouping occurs until we get to 12.

With this behind us, it is easy to see the workings of the base ten (decimal) system. Since it is a ten-for-one trading scheme, the denominations are 1's, 10's, 100's, 1000's, etc. Thus 873 represents eight 100's, seven 10's, and three 1's. We often say the eight is in "the hundreds place," the seven is in "the tens place," and the three is in "the ones place."

That 37 represents three 10's and seven 1's is not necessarily obvious to children in the primary grades. In one instance, each pupil in a second grade class counted out 37 counting sticks and was then asked how many groups of ten he or she could form. Guesses ranged from two to five! Only after determining by actual count that 37 was three groups of ten with seven left over and repeating this for numerous examples did many of the children begin to see any connection between the numerals and the grouping principle. Yet knowledge of this principle is essential when adding and subtracting two-digit numbers. We will discuss this in later sections.

There are many manipulative devices which we can use to strengthen place value concepts. Among these are Dienes' multibase blocks, chips, beansticks, counting sticks, abaci, and bead frames. Activities involving these materials are highly recommended for teaching children. A few examples occur in the problems.

We close this section with additional examples to reinforce your understanding of place value.

(a) Change 136 to a base five numeral.

(b) Change 114 to a base four numeral.

(c) Change 57 to a base twelve numeral.

(d) Change 3012_{five} to a base ten numeral.

(e) Change TOE_{twelve} to a base ten numeral.

(f) $25 = 34_\square$. (Find the base.)

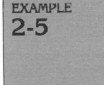

EXAMPLE
2-5

(a)
$$136 = \overline{}\ \overline{}\ \overline{}\ \overline{}\ _{\text{five}}$$
$$ \text{125's } \text{25's } \text{5's } \text{1's}$$

$$
\begin{array}{r}
136 \\
-125 = 1 \times 125 \\
\hline
11 \\
- \ 10 = 2 \times 5 \\
\hline
1 \\
- \ \ 1 = 1 \times 1 \\
\hline
0
\end{array}
$$

$$136 = 1021_{\text{five}}$$

SOLUTION

(b)
$$114 = \overline{}_{64\text{'s}} \; \overline{}_{16\text{'s}} \; \overline{}_{4\text{'s}} \; \overline{}_{1\text{'s}} \;^{\text{four}}$$

$$
\begin{array}{l}
114 \\
\underline{- \;\; 64} = 1 \times 64 \\
 50 \\
\underline{- \;\; 48} = 3 \times 16 \\
  2 \\
\underline{- \;\; 2} = 2 \times 1 \\
  0
\end{array}
$$

$$114 = 1302_{\text{four}}$$

(c)
$$57 = \overline{}_{12\text{'s}} \; \overline{}_{1\text{'s}} \;^{\text{twelve}}$$

$$
\begin{array}{l}
57 \\
\underline{-48} = 4 \times 12 \\
 9 \\
\underline{- \;9} = 9 \times 1 \\
 0
\end{array}
$$

$$57 = 49_{\text{twelve}}$$

(d) Since this is a base five numeral, we recognize that it represents two 1's, one 5, no 25's, and three 125's. We can summarize this as follows:

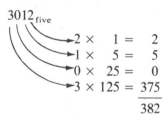

$$
\begin{array}{rcl}
2 \times & 1 = & 2 \\
1 \times & 5 = & 5 \\
0 \times & 25 = & 0 \\
3 \times & 125 = & 375 \\
\hline
& & 382
\end{array}
$$

Hence $3012_{\text{five}} = 382$. (Note that when no base is indicated it is assumed to be base ten.)

(e) Here T means ten and E means eleven.

$$
\begin{array}{rcl}
\text{TOE}_{\text{twelve}} & & \\
11 \times & 1 = & 11 \\
0 \times & 12 = & 0 \\
10 \times & 144 = & 1440 \\
\hline
& & 1451
\end{array}
$$

Hence $\text{TOE}_{\text{twelve}} = 1451$.

(f) Note that the numeral $34_\square$ represents three groups of $\square$ with four ones left over. In other words,

$$3 \times \square + 4 = 25, \text{ so}$$

$$3 \times \square = 21, \text{ so}$$
$$\square = 7.$$

EXERCISES AND PROBLEMS 2-2

NAMING NUMBERS

1. Which number is larger, 3 or 7?
   Which numeral is larger?

2. Tell whether the word in parentheses is being used in the "number sense" (as an entity) or in the "numeral sense" (as a symbol for an entity):
   (a) Cat is a three-letter word. (cat)
   (b) A cat is a furry animal that says "meow." (cat)
   (c) Angela is pretty. (Angela)
   (d) Angela is a pretty name. (Angela)

3. In geometry we say that a "line" has no thickness and extends indefinitely in two directions, but when we draw a "line" it necessarily has thickness and necessarily ends. Comment on these two interpretations of "line" in light of the number-numeral distinction.

4. What troublesome inconsistency (for children learning to count) occurs in the naming of Hindu-Arabic numbers? (Hint: Is it easier to learn the names of the numbers from ten through nineteen or from sixty through sixty-nine?) Suppose you could alter the names to alleviate this difficulty. How would you do it?

5. The symbol 3^2 (read "three squared" or "three to the second power") means 3×3. Similarly 2^5 (read "two to the fifth power") means $2 \times 2 \times 2 \times 2 \times 2$. Thus $3^2 = 9$ and $2^5 = 32$. Compute the following:
   (a) 4^2 (b) 2^6 (c) 3^4 (d) $2^3 \times 3^2 \times 5$ (e) 10^4

6. Using the notation of Problem 5, we can write 200 as 2×10^2, 50 as 5×10^1, 6 as 6×1, and hence 256 as $2 \times 10^2 + 5 \times 10^1 + 6 \times 1$. We call this the **expanded form** for 256. Write each of these in expanded form:
   (a) 50   (b) 900   (c) 958   (d) 842   (e) 8,000,040   (f) 920,300
   Write each of these in ordinary form:
   (g) $3 \times 10^2 + 2 \times 10^1 + 9 \times 1$
   (h) $6 \times 10^3 + 5 \times 10^2 + 1 \times 10^1 + 3 \times 1$
   (i) $8 \times 10^6 + 3 \times 10^2 + 5 \times 1$
   (j) $4 \times 10^7 + 9 \times 10^4$

7. The word "one" originates with the Latin *unus*. This can be found in words like "uniform" or "unicorn."

Number	Root	Found in
one	*unus* (Latin)	uniform, unicorn
two	*duo* (Latin)	duplicate
three	*tri* (Latin & Greek)	tricycle

   Give additional examples of words using these roots.

8. The names for September, October, November, and December suggest the (consecutive) numbers of the months on the old calendar. (a) Which month was November on the old calendar? (b) Give more examples of words which contain "*sept*," "*oct*," or "*dec*," in each case relating the word to the appropriate number.

9. Discover the pattern and complete this chart.

Word	Latin Root	Meaning of Root	Power of 10
billion	bi-	2	9
trillion	tri-	3	12
quadrillion	quater	4	(a)
quintillion	quintus	(b)	18
sextillion	(c)	6	21
(d)	septem	7	24
octillion	octo	(e)	(f)
nonillion	novem	(g)	(h)
(i)	decem	(j)	(k)
undecillion	undecim	11	36
. . .			
quindecillion	quindecim	15	48
sexdecillion	sexdecim	16	(l)
. . .			
novemdecillion	novemdecim	(m)	(n)

10. Use the chart from the previous problem to write these numerals in words:
    (a) 1,000,000,000   (b) 53,000,000,000,000
    (c) 84,039,531,207,531   (d) 23,000,000,000,000,000,000

11. According to geological estimates the earth is about 3¼ billion years old. Write this number (without words).

12.

In Circleland, people write when they mean 58, and

they write when they mean 834. What do they mean

when they write   (a)   or   (b) ?

Write each of these in this system: (c) 93   (d) 256   (e) 2003

13. (a) Make up an arithmetic problem in which we prefer to think of 82 as 7 tens and 12 ones (rather than as 8 tens and 2 ones).
    (b) 256 names 2 hundreds, 5 tens, and 6 ones. It also names 1 hundred, 15 tens, and 6 ones. Give some more possibilities.

14. (a) 406 is usually thought of as _____ hundreds, _____ tens, and _____ ones. However, to subtract 79 from 406 we regroup and think of 406 as _____ hundreds, _____ tens, and _____ ones.
    (b) To divide 834 by 6 we regroup and think of 834 as _____ hundreds, _____ tens, and _____ ones.

15. A second grade child writes 3005 for "three hundred five" and 600207 for "six hundred twenty-seven." How can you help him?

16. If we let t represent the tens place of a number and let u represent the ones place of a number, then this two-digit number can be written "$10t + u$." How can we write a three-digit number whose hundreds place is p, whose tens place is q, and whose ones place is r?

HISTORICAL

17. The god on the steps of the Hindu temple mentioned on page 29 would be how many times as strong as an ordinary man?

18. The basic characters in Roman numerals are:

Roman	Hindu-Arabic
I	1
V	5
X	10
L	50
C	100
D	500
M	1000

Examples: VI = 6, IV = 4, MDCCXXXII = 1732, CMXLIX = 949

Change each of these to Hindu-Arabic numerals:
(a) VIII   (b) IX   (c) MCMLXXXII

Change each of these to Roman numerals:
(d) 62   (e) 43   (f) 2001
(g) What is the trading principle of the Roman system? Five-for-one? Two-for-one?

19. Given that ??????∩∩∩∩∩∩IIIII in the Egyptian system represents 365, what would ?????∩∩I represent?

L20. Refer to the Towers of Hanoi puzzle on page 29. Figure out the minimum number of moves required if you have
(a) two rings   (b) three rings
(c) four rings   (d) ten rings
C(e) 64 rings. (Use a calculator to carry out the arithmetic.)
(f) If moves are made once each second, how long will it take to move 64 rings? Answer in appropriate units.

21. In *The Messenger* [37], a biography of Mohammed, Bodley writes of Mohammed's journey into the seventh heaven:

> Abraham bowed Mohammed into this blissful abode, which was made of divine light and beyond the powers of description of any human voice. Its size alone could not be expressed. It was infinite. And here too was another angel unlike anything Mohammed had seen before. His magnitude was such that it made the angels of the four preceding heavens seem like dwarfs. He was bigger than the whole of the world. He had seventy thousand heads, and each head had seventy thousand mouths. In each mouth were seventy thousand tongues, and each tongue spoke seventy thousand different languages.

Express *in words* our modern numerals for the approximate number of (a) mouths (b) tongues   (c) languages.

Bodley compares this description with this declaration attributed to Christ by St. Irenius, a bishop of Lyons in the Second Century:

> Days shall come in which there will be vines which shall each have ten thousand branches, and every one of these branches shall have ten thousand lesser branches, and every one one of these lesser branches shall have ten thousand twigs, and every one of these twigs shall have ten thousand clusters of grapes, and in every one of these clusters shall be ten thousand grapes, and every one of these grapes being pressed shall yield two hundred and seventy five gallons of wine.

Express *in words* our modern numerals for the approximate number of (**d**) lesser branches   (**e**) twigs   (**f**) grapes   (**g**) gallons of wine.

OTHER BASES

22. (**a**) Write out the base five numerals in order from 1 to 100_{five}.
    (**b**) Write out the base three numerals in order from 1 to 1000_{three}.
    (**c**) What base five number follows 204_{five}?
    (**d**) In base seven the next numbers after 365_{seven} are _____$_{\text{seven}}$, _____$_{\text{seven}}$, _____$_{\text{seven}}$, and _____$_{\text{seven}}$.

23. True or False?
    (**a**) $2_{\text{three}} = 2$ (**b**) $20_{\text{three}} = 20$ (**c**) $2_{\text{three}} = 2_{\text{four}}$ (**d**) $20_{\text{three}} = 20_{\text{four}}$

24. What is the largest three-digit base five number? What base five number follows it?

25. How many characters would be needed in a base fifteen system?

26. What is wrong with the numerals 37_{six} and 23_{three}?

27. Change each of the following to base ten numerals:
    (**a**) 234_{five} (**b**) 1002_{four} (**c**) 98_{twelve}
    (**d**) $EIEIO_{\text{twelve}}$ (Old MacDonald's number)

28. Write each of the following in base three and in base twelve: (**a**) 87   (**b**) 128

29. Find the base:
    (**a**) $37 = 45_\square$ (**b**) $37 = 31_\square$ (**c**) $37_{\text{nine}} = 31_\square$

30. Write as a base ten numeral: (**a**) 2310_{four} (**b**) 23.2_{four} (**c**) 1.231_{four}

31. In Dotland, people use the following numeration system:

Example:

Use this system to represent: (**a**) 57   (**b**) 67.

Change each to base ten numerals: (**c**)   0   (**d**)   0

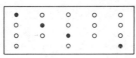      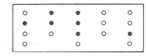

*32. Change each of the numbers 9, 19, and 486 to base two (**binary**) and to base eight (**octal**). Then look for a relationship between the representations in these two bases. The following sample may serve as a hint:

$$110,001,111_{two}$$

$$6\quad 1\quad 7_{eight}$$

Change $11011101100000110101000111100111101001110_{two}$ to base eight by this method. Can you invent a similar procedure for any other bases?

33. Explain how "Dec. 25 = Oct. 31." (Hint: See Problem 32.)

34. A rather unusual (and expensive) clock indicates the time by using base two representations by means of a series of lights that are either on or off. Here are some examples, where a solid dot means the light is on:

is 1:24 and 8 seconds   is 10:59 and 46 seconds

(**a**) What time is shown in the third box?

(**b**) Show the clock's representation for 11:36 and 50 seconds.

(**c**) Why are some columns shorter than others?

MATERIALS AND CALCULATORS

35. (**a**) Group this set (by ringing the x's) in base three:

xxx   xxx   xxx   xxx
xxx   xxx   xxx   xxx
xxx   xxx   xxx   x

(**b**) Write the base three numeral for the set.

36. Write a base four numeral for the set of Dienes' blocks shown below. (Perform all possible trades first.)

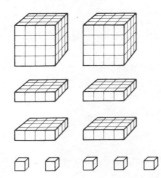

37. We illustrate representations for 23 using Dienes' blocks, chips, and bundling sticks. Which is most concrete? Which is most abstract?

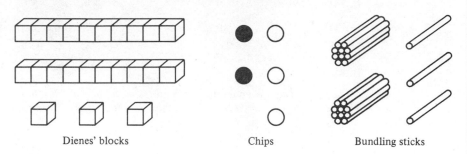

Dienes' blocks   Chips   Bundling sticks

*L*38. (a) Count out 38 sticks. Form as many bundles of ten as you can.
Record your results:

10's	1's
3	8

Write a base ten numeral for this amount: _____
(b) Use the sticks from part (a) to form as many bundles of eight as you can (starting over).
Record your results:

8's	1's

Write a base eight numeral for this amount: _____
(c) Form as many bundles of six as you can. Form "super bundles" out of each six bundles of six.
Record your results:

6 of 6's	6's	1's

Write a base six numeral for this amount: _____
(d) Form as many bundles of five as you can. Form "super bundles" out of each five bundles of five.
Record your results:

5 of 5's	5's	1's

Write a base five numeral for this amount: _____
(e) Fill in: 38_{ten} = _____ $_{eight}$ = _____ $_{six}$ = _____ $_{five}$
(f) Form one "super bundle" of five bundles of five, two more bundles of five, and four left over. This can be recorded as follows:

5 of 5's	5's	1's
1	2	4

Write a base five numeral for this amount: _____
(g) Use the sticks from part (f) to form bundles of ten.
Record your results:

10's	1's

Fill in from parts (f) and (g): _____ $_{five}$ = _____ $_{ten}$

*L*39. Represent each of the following with bundling sticks, with Dienes' blocks, and with chips.

    (**a**) 53   (**b**) 43_{five} (**c**) 124_{five}

40. (**a**) Draw a sketch of 58 pennies and trade for nickels and quarters. Write the corresponding base five numeral.

    (**b**) Write the base five numeral for 89.

    (**c**) Write the base five numeral for 1776.

*C*41. Most calculators have a repeated multiplication feature. By pressing the

    sequence of buttons   2 ⊠ ⊟ ⊟ ⊟ ⊟ . . .
    the output is respectively   2, 2, 4, 8, 16, 32, . . .

Use this feature to determine 2^{10} and 2^{20}. (Be careful, it's easy to be off by one entry. Note that pressing the ⊟ button four times in the example above gives 2^5.)

*C*42. In the game of "Wipeout" described by Wallace Judd in the *Arithmetic Teacher* [56], children are asked to determine what number to subtract from a given number on the calculator so as to "wipe out" a certain digit (replace it by 0). What number must be subtracted from 987,654,321 to "wipe out" the 4 — that is, to give an answer of 987,650,321?

PROBLEM SOLVING EXTENSIONS

43. Light travels about 186,000 miles per second. How far does it travel in one year? This *distance* is called a **light-year**.

44. (**a**) The numbers 1, 4, 9, 16, 25, . . . are called **squares**, since $1 = 1^2, 4 = 2^2, 9 = 3^2, 16 = 4^2, 25 = 5^2$, etc. (See Problem 5.) The year 1936 was a square. What is the next year that will be a square?

    (**b**) The numbers 1, 8, 27, 64, 125, . . . are called **cubes**, since $1 = 1^3, 8 = 2^3, 27 = 3^3, 64 = 4^3, 125 = 5^3$, etc. The year 1728 was a cube. What is the next year that will be a cube?

    (**c**) What is the next year that will be both a square and a cube?

45. It takes 2977 digits to number the pages of a large book consecutively. (**a**) How many pages are there?   (**b**) How many times is the digit 4 used? (The number 44 uses 4 twice.)

46. In a non-leap year, what is the greatest number of Friday the 13ths that can occur? The least number?

47. Don was buying something in the hardware store. He noticed that the cost of 1 was $1, the cost of 3 was $1, the cost of 38 was $2, and the cost of 1338 was $4. What was he buying?

48. Consider the sequence 2, 3, 10, 12, 13, 20, 21, 22, 23, 24, 25, 26, ... What number in the sequence follows

    (**a**) 26?   (**b**) 29?

    (**c**) 39?   (**d**) 399?

    (Warning: This is a tricky problem!)

49. (From NCTM/MAA *Sourcebook on Applications* [14], p. 286.)
A digital display shows the numbers 0 through 9 by lighting certain segments in the figure shown at right. (Each segment is like a small, elongated light bulb.) For example, the digits 0, 1, 6, 7, and 9 are respectively

(a) Show the segments which must be lit to form each of the digits 2, 3, 4, 5, and 8. If a battery can keep one segment lit for 1000 hours (or two segments lit for 500 hours, etc.) how long can it keep each of the following lit?

(b) 0   (c) 8   (d) 2   (e) 349

(f) Assume that each digit is displayed equally often. (0 is displayed the same amount as 1, as 2, etc.) Which of the segments will be lit most often?

Operations
with Whole Numbers

3-1
ADDITION OF WHOLE NUMBERS — DEFINITION AND PROPERTIES

Do you remember *Alice in Wonderland* and *Through the Looking Glass*?

"Can you do Addition?" the White Queen asked. "What's one and one and one and one and one and one and one and one and one and one?"

"I don't know," said Alice. "I lost count."

"She can't do Addition," the Red Queen interrupted. "Can you do Subtraction? Take nine from eight."

"Nine from eight I can't, you know," Alice replied very readily: "but—"

"She can't do Subtraction," said the White Queen. "Can you do Division? Divide a loaf by a knife—what's the answer to *that?*"

Poor Alice. While her problems with arithmetic are unique, we hope in this chapter to provide a firm basis for *understanding* the concepts involved in the four basic operations on whole numbers — addition, subtraction, multiplication, and division — so that you as a teacher may help children avoid some of the obstacles they might otherwise meet.

Our specific goals in Sections 3-1 and 3-2 are to become familiar with the basic language needed to define addition, to understand the definition of addition, to become acquainted with the basic properties of addition and their applications, and to understand the addition algorithm and know how to use it in base ten and other bases.

Let's begin by looking at an example. When first learning to add, a child might add three and two like this:

"If I have one, two, *three* white blocks and one, *two* black blocks, then I have one, two, three, four, *five* blocks."

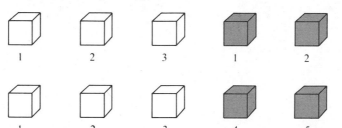

Note that the child associates a set of blocks with each of the numbers three and two, then combines the sets, and finally counts the elements of this new set.

Since whole numbers themselves are defined in terms of sets, it follows that addition of whole numbers involves sets. Before actually defining addition, we need to clarify the underlying process of combining sets.

In the previous example, the set of five blocks consists of all the blocks that are either white or black. In general, if we start with any two sets A and B and form a new set consisting of exactly those elements that belong to either set A *or* set B (or both), we denote this new set by $A \cup B$, which is read "A **union** B." Here are several examples:

$\{1, 2, 3\} \cup \{4, 5\} = \{1, 2, 3, 4, 5\}$

$\{6, 7, 8, 9\} \cup \{8, 9, 10\} = \{6, 7, 8, 9, 10\}$

$\{$odd whole numbers$\} \cup \{$even whole numbers$\} = \{$whole numbers$\}$

$\{a, b, c\} \cup \{\ \ \} = \{a, b, c\}$

The meaning of "union" with regard to sets is quite consistent with our ordinary use of the word for an association of workers from several different plants.

It is sometimes convenient to picture the union of two sets with a **Venn diagram**. Figure 3-1 suggests that $A = \{6, 7, 8, 9\}$, $B = \{8, 9, 10\}$, and $A \cup B = \{6, 7, 8, 9, 10\}$.

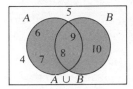

FIGURE 3-1

Observe that the union of two sets is a set. This is our first example of an **operation**. In this case, we have an operation which takes two sets and gives us another set.

Another set operation which we will have use for is intersection. For any two sets A and B, $A \cap B$, which is read "A **intersection** B," is the set consisting of exactly those elements that belong to both set A *and* set B simultaneously. (Think of the intersection of two streets.) The following examples are intended to clarify the situation:

$\{6, 7, 8, 9\} \cap \{8, 9, 10\} = \{8, 9\}$

$\{1, 2, 3\} \cap \{4, 5\} = \{\ \ \}$

$\{$odd whole numbers$\} \cap \{$even whole numbers$\} = \{\ \ \}$

$\{$multiples of 2$\} \cap \{$multiples of 3$\} = \{$multiples of 6$\}$

Whenever the intersection of two sets is the empty set, we say the sets are **disjoint**. Thus $\{1, 2, 3\}$ and $\{4, 5\}$ are disjoint sets, while $\{$multiples of 2$\}$ and $\{$multiples of 3$\}$ are not disjoint sets.

Again we can illustrate intersection of sets with a Venn diagram. Figure 3-2 tells us that $A = \{6, 7, 8, 9\}$, $B = \{8, 9, 10\}$ and $A \cap B = \{8, 9\}$.

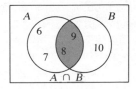

FIGURE 3-2

To reinforce these ideas and to show how more than two sets can be involved, we provide one more example:

EXAMPLE
3-1

If $A = \{1, 3, 5\}$, $B = \{1, 5, 7\}$, and $C = \{1, 2, 3\}$, then find
(a) $A \cup B$ (b) $B \cap C$ (c) $(A \cup B) \cap C$ (d) $A \cup (B \cap C)$

SOLUTION

(a) $A \cup B = \{1, 3, 5\} \cup \{1, 5, 7\} = \{1, 3, 5, 7\}$

(b) $B \cap C = \{1, 5, 7\} \cap \{1, 2, 3\} = \{1\}$

(c) $(A \cup B) \cap C = \{1, 3, 5, 7\} \cap \{1, 2, 3\} = \{1, 3\}$

(d) $A \cup (B \cap C) = \{1, 3, 5\} \cup \{1\} = \{1, 3, 5\}$

Going back to our example with black and white blocks, we can say that adding two whole numbers involves taking the union of two disjoint sets according to these steps:

☐ Steps in Adding Two Whole Numbers

1. Associate with the first number, a, a set A which has a members. Associate with the second number, b, a set B which has b members (none of which belongs to set A).
2. Combine the sets to form $A \cup B$.
3. $a + b$ is then the number of members in $A \cup B$.

Once again we move from the world of abstractions, in this case whole numbers, to the world of concrete objects (step 1). We manipulate these concrete objects, in this case by taking the union of two sets (step 2), and then move back to the world of abstractions with our answer (step 3). The three-step process is shown in Figure 3-3. We suggest you compare it with Figure 2-3.

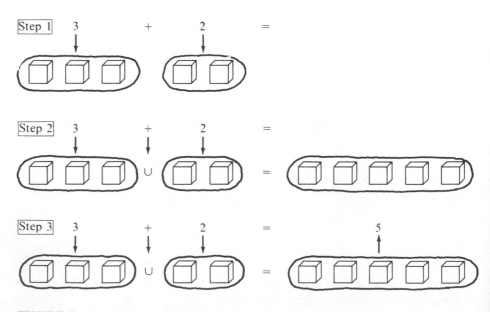

FIGURE 3-3

Since we will often be counting the elements of a set, we introduce the notation $n(A)$, read "n of A," which means simply "the number of elements in (finite) set A." For instance, $n(\{a, b, c\}) = 3$. If $A = \{$odd whole numbers less than 10$\}$, then $n(A) = 5$.

With these ideas to guide us, we can now define addition of whole numbers:

Definition of Addition of Whole Numbers

If a and b are whole numbers, then the **sum** of a and b denoted $a + b$ is the number of members in $A \cup B$, where A and B are any disjoint sets such that $n(A) = a$ and $n(B) = b$.

Addition is an operation defined for numbers; it takes two numbers (called **addends**) and gives us another number (called their sum). We wish to emphasize that the two sets A and B mentioned in the definition of addition must be *disjoint*, as Example 3-2 shows.

Let $A = \{r, s, t\}$ and $B = \{t, u\}$. Does $n(A \cup B) = n(A) + n(B)$?

Recall that $A \cup B$ is the set of all objects which are in either A or B (or both). Thus $A \cup B = \{r, s, t, u\}$. Since $n(A \cup B)$ refers to the number of members in $A \cup B$, we have $n(A \cup B) = 4$, and since A has three members and B has two members, we have $n(A) + n(B) = 3 + 2 = 5$. Thus it is *not* true that $n(A \cup B) = n(A) + n(B)$ for these sets A and B. A Venn diagram shows this procedure well. In Figure 3-4 we can readily see that set A has three members, set B has two members, but $A \cup B$ has four members. Observe

SOLUTION

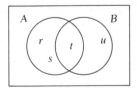

FIGURE 3-4

that the element t was counted once in determining $n(A)$ and once in determining $n(B)$. Thus t was counted twice in determining $n(A) + n(B)$, though it was counted only once in determining $n(A \cup B)$. This is why in this case $n(A) + n(B) > n(A \cup B)$.

A very nice model for addition is provided by a number line. We draw a line, mark some point 0, and then place copies of a fixed unit end to end to mark off equal distances to the right to indicate one, two, three, and so forth as shown in Figure 3-5. (The point paired with 0 is called the **origin**.) The first time a child sees this, it might be marked off on the floor in units equal to his or her steps.

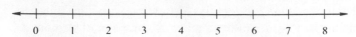

FIGURE 3-5

Thus 3 + 2 would mean "take three steps, then two steps." Of course, the result is taking a total of five steps, as Figure 3-6 shows. Later, the number line can be drawn on the chalkboard and on paper. One of the best features of the number line is that it generalizes to numbers that are not whole numbers and helps to display operations other than addition as well.

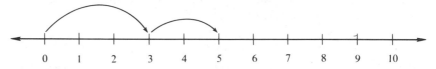

FIGURE 3-6

Another closely related model is provided by Cuisenaire rods, or centimeter rods. For example, a "train" consisting of a yellow rod (5) together with a red rod (2) is the same as a black rod (7), as shown in Figure 3-7.

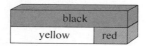

FIGURE 3-7

While the definition of addition is useful for developing an understanding of the operation, it is simply not reasonable to appeal to it every time we need to solve an addition problem. For instance, we use the fact that 7 + 9 = 16 so often that it eventually becomes unnecessary to rely on the physical interpretation using sets. We simply memorize it as a fact.

This collection of facts which we find convenient to memorize is summarized in Figure 3-8 and is, as you already know, referred to as the **addition table.**

FIGURE 3-8
Base Ten Addition Table

+	0	1	2	3	4	5	6	7	8	9
0	0	1	2	3	4	5	6	7	8	9
1	1	2	3	4	5	6	7	8	9	10
2	2	3	4	5	6	7	8	9	10	11
3	3	4	5	6	7	8	9	10	11	12
4	4	5	6	7	8	9	10	11	12	13
5	5	6	7	8	9	10	11	12	13	14
6	6	7	8	9	10	11	12	13	14	15
7	7	8	9	10	11	12	13	14	15	16
8	8	9	10	11	12	13	14	15	16	17
9	9	10	11	12	13	14	15	16	17	18

We will find that though the table contains 100 addition facts, the numbers that need to be memorized can be sharply reduced with the knowledge of certain properties of addition.

What about the problem 236 + 589? It would be awkward to rely on our set interpretation, nor does it appear in our addition table. To solve problems like this one, we use an **algorithm** (computation process) which is also based on certain properties of addition. This will be covered in the next section.

We will now concentrate on the development of these properties to facilitate use of the table and the algorithm. The first property we state is an immediate consequence of the definition for the addition of whole numbers. Recall that $a + b$ is the number of members in $A \cup B$ where A and B are disjoint sets with a and b members respectively. Thus the sum of the whole numbers a and b is the number of members in the union of two finite sets. Since the union of two finite sets is a finite set, the number of members it contains is a whole number. We summarize this property, called the **closure** property for addition of whole numbers, by saying that the sum of two whole numbers is a whole number. Sometimes we will use the terminology "the set of whole numbers is closed under addition."

To give you a better idea of what closure means, we offer Example 3-3.

EXAMPLE 3-3

Which of these sets is (are) closed under addition?
(a) {even whole numbers}   (b) {odd whole numbers}
(c) {0, 1, 2, 3, 4}

SOLUTION

(a) Since the sum of any two even whole numbers is necessarily an even whole number, we say that the set of even whole numbers is closed under addition.

(b) Since the sum of two odd whole numbers is an even whole number, and not an odd whole number (for instance, 1 + 3 = 4), this set is not closed under addition.

(c) While the sum of two members of this set *may* be a member of the set, it does not happen in all cases (for instance 2 + 3 = 5), so this set is not closed under addition.

While the closure property is important since it guarantees that we can add any two whole numbers and get a whole number for an answer, the next three properties are often helpful in telling us how to find the answer.

The **commutative** property of addition, usually referred to in elementary school texts as the **order** property of addition, is a powerful tool. A glance at the addition table (Figure 3-8) reveals a kind of symmetry in that, for example, the problems 2 + 3 and 3 + 2 have the same answer, as do 4 + 8 and 8 + 4, and 9 + 1 and 1 + 9. In fact we have for any two whole numbers a and b that $a + b = b + a$. This property is an immediate consequence of the definition and the fact that $A \cup B = B \cup A$ (see exercises). We caution you as a future teacher, however, that this is not necessarily obvious to children who are just learning to add. Do you see why it is easier for them to compute one more than eight than it is to compute eight more than one, and that they may therefore know the sum of $8 + 1$ without knowing the sum of $1 + 8$?

This one property reduces the number of facts to 55, for any entry above the main diagonal of the table can be obtained by finding the sum of the corresponding members in the portion of the table below the main diagonal.

Another useful property is the **associative** property of addition, or as it is called in some elementary school texts, the **grouping** property of addition. The associative property of addition of whole numbers tells us for any whole numbers a, b, and c that $(a + b) + c = a + (b + c)$. Our first application of this property is in learning the addition facts involving 9. The problem $10 + 4$ happens to be particularly easy to solve in our base ten place value system, for clearly 1 ten and 4 ones is 14. We borrow this idea to solve the problem $9 + 5$. First we think of the 5 as being $1 + 4$, so that $9 + 5$ becomes $9 + (1 + 4)$. Now if we *regroup* we have the "easier" problem $9 + 1$ or 10 added to 4, so our answer is 14. Any time the sum of two one-digit numbers is greater than ten, we can apply the associative property to help find the answer. The proof of the associative property is dealt within the exercises.

Together, the commutative and associative properties tell us that given an addition problem involving several numbers, we can reorder and regroup the numbers in any fashion to obtain the answer. We will use these properties more when discussing the addition algorithm.

Now examine the first column of the addition table. The fact that 0 added to any number gives the other number is referred to as the **identity** property (or **zero** property) of addition. This one property then replaces 10 separate addition facts, or 19 if we also count the first row.

These four properties are summarized as follows:

☐ Properties for Addition of Whole Numbers

1. (Closure) For any whole numbers a and b, $a + b$ is a whole number.
2. (Commutative) For any whole numbers a and b, $a + b = b + a$.
3. (Associative) For any whole numbers a, b, and c, $(a + b) + c = a + (b + c)$.
4. (Identity) For any whole number a, $a + 0 = a$ and $0 + a = a$.

We now summarize how these properties help in learning the 100 basic addition facts. In Figure 3-9 the addition table has been divided into four regions. Region F contains the basic facts that need to be memorized initially. Region Z consists of the addition facts involving zero, all of which can be replaced by using the single property that zero added to any number gives that number. Region A is made up of all those addition facts that can conveniently be determined by using the associative property. Region C comprises those addition facts that can be obtained by applying the commutative property. Instead of 100 facts to learn by rote we have only 25, together with the identity, associative, and commutative properties.

Additional practice involving the properties is provided in Example 3-4.

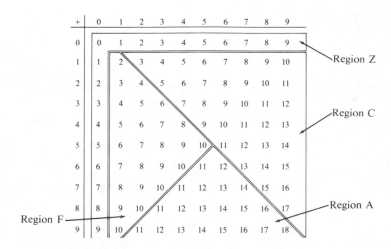

FIGURE 3-9

Which property or properties of addition justify each of these statements?

(a) $7 + 0 = 7$

(b) $25,689,813 + 83,000,251,611$ is a whole number

(c) $(5 + 2) + 0 = (2 + 5) + 0$

(d) $(30 + 4) + (20 + 5) = (30 + 20) + (4 + 5)$

(e) $3 + (5 + 8) = (5 + 8) + 3$

(a) This is clearly the identity property, or zero property.

(b) The property which guarantees that the sum of two whole numbers is a whole number is the closure property.

(c) While at a glance this may look like an illustration of the associative property, it is the *order* that was changed and not the grouping, so it is the commutative property.

(d) Here both the order and the grouping were changed, so the properties involved are the commutative and associative properties.

(e) Since the order of addition (not the grouping) was changed, this is an application of the commutative property of addition. One difficulty that some students have is in recognizing the *two* numbers being reordered, namely 3 and (5 + 8). That (5 + 8) is simply a whole number depends (rather inconspicuously) on the closure property for addition of whole numbers.

Our table, even with its 100 facts, doesn't give us the answers to relatively simple problems like $34 + 25$. Is this another fact to be memorized? What about $863 + 792$? Our remaining goal is to understand the addition algorithm and learn how it is used to solve problems like these as well as similar problems in other bases. We address this goal in the next section.

EXERCISES AND PROBLEMS 3-1

DEFINITION AND SETS

1. A farmer has $3\frac{1}{2}$ haystacks in one corner of the field and $5\frac{1}{2}$ haystacks in another corner of the field. If he puts them all together, how many haystacks will he have?

2. If $A = \{1, 2, 3, 4, 5\}$, $B = \{4, 5, 6, 7\}$, and $C = \{1, 5, 7, 9\}$, find
   (a) $A \cup B$ (b) $A \cap B$
   (c) $(A \cup B) \cap C$ (d) $A \cup (B \cap C)$

3. A hotel advertises that it is located in a secluded area, at the intersection of the Pennsylvania Turnpike and U.S. Interstate 80. Do you believe the advertisement? Why?

4. Devise a way to help someone learn which of the symbols $\cup$ and $\cap$ means union and which means intersection.

5. Explain why each of the following is true for all sets A and B (and C).
   (a) $A \cup B = B \cup A$ (b) $A \cap B = B \cap A$
   (c) $(A \cup B) \cup C = A \cup (B \cup C)$ (d) $(A \cap B) \cap C = A \cap (B \cap C)$
   (e) $A \cup \{\ \} = A$ (f) $A \cap \{\ \} = \{\ \}$
   (g) $A \cap B \subseteq A$ (h) $A \subseteq A \cup B$
   (i) $A \cap B \subseteq A \cup B$ (j) $A \cap (B \cup C) = (A \cap B) \cup (A \cap C)$

6. When does $A \cap B = A$? When does $A \cup B = A$?

7. In the drawing below, C is the interior of the circle, T is the interior of the triangle, and R is the interior of the rectangle. Copy the drawing on a sheet of paper and then shade in each of the following regions:
   (a) $C \cup R$ (b) $C \cap R$
   (c) $(C \cup R) \cup T$ (d) $C \cup (R \cup T)$
   (e) $(C \cap R) \cup T$ (f) $C \cap (R \cup T)$

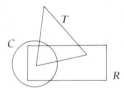

8. Draw a Venn diagram for the three sets A, B, and C and fill it in for the sets given in Problem 2.

9. True or False? Venn diagrams are named after the famous logician Joe Diagram.

10. Are $\{0, 1\}$ and $\{0, 2\}$ disjoint sets?

11. Find sets V and W such that $n(V) = 127$, $n(W) = 562$, and V and W are disjoint.

12. Find sets (when possible) satisfying each of the following:
    (a) $n(D) + n(E) > n(D \cup E)$ (b) $n(P) + n(Q) = n(P \cup Q)$
    (c) $n(H) + n(J) < n(H \cup J)$

13. For which of the following pairs of sets is it true that $n(A \cup B) = n(A) + n(B)$?
    (a) $A = \{p, q, r, s, t\}$ $B = \{u, v, w, x\}$
    (b) $A = \{\ \}$ $B = \{\ \}$
    (c) $A = \{p, q, r\}$ $B = \{r, q, p\}$

PROPERTIES

14. Which of the following sets are closed under addition?
    (a) {10, 20, 30, . . .}   **(b)** {1}
    (c) {1, 4, 9, 16, 25, . . .}   **(d)** {1, 2, 3}
    (e) {3, 6, 9, 12, . . .}   **(f)** {whole numbers less than 10}
    (g) {whole numbers greater than 10}   **(h)** {0}

15. Is the set of whole numbers closed under
    (a) subtraction?   **(b)** multiplication?   **(c)** division?

16. Tell which property or properties are being illustrated:
    (a) $1492 + 1776$ must be a whole number
    (b) $8 + 3 = 3 + 8$ **(c)** $53 + 99 = 52 + 100$
    (d) $0 + 0 = 0$ **(e)** $5 + 0 = 0 + 5$

17. Which property or properties justify that you get the same answer to the problem

$$\begin{array}{r} 2 \\ 3 \\ +4 \\ \hline \end{array}$$

whether you add "up" (starting $4 + 3$) or "down" (starting $2 + 3$)?

18. In this section, we stated that the zero property "replaces 10 separate addition facts, or 19 if we also count the first row" (of the addition table). Since there are 10 facts in the first column and 10 facts in the first row, shouldn't this be a total of 20 facts involving zero? Why? Explain in five words or less why the union of the set of 10 facts in the first row with the set of 10 facts in the first column isn't a set of 20 facts.

19. Prove that for any whole number a, $a + 0 = a$. (Hint: You may wish to use one of the results from Problem 5.)

20. **(a)** Prove that for any whole numbers a and b, $a + b = b + a$. (Hint: You may wish to use one of the results from Problem 5.)
    (b) Prove that for any whole numbers a, b, and c, $(a + b) + c = a + (b + c)$.

21. Does this statement hold for all whole numbers a, b, and c? "If $a < b$, then $a + c < b + c$." Explain.

MATERIALS AND CALCULATORS

22. Draw a figure similar to Figure 3-3 to illustrate the problem $5 + 1 = 6$.

23. Illustrate the problem $5 + 2 = 7$ on the number line.

C24. **(a)** Use your calculator to add 8 sevens together. You can probably do this by pressing "7 ⊞ ⊟ ⊟ ⊟ ⊟ ⊟ ⊟ ⊟." (Watch the display as you do it.)
    (b) Repeat the procedure for 11 nines.
    (c) This "repeated addition" process is effectively what other familiar operation? (Do additional examples if necessary.)
    (d) Could this technique be useful in teaching children? Explain.

C25. **(a)** Play this calculator version of "Nim" described by Wallace Judd in the November 1976 *Arithmetic Teacher* [56]:

    For: Two players and one calculator
    Object of the game: To get 67 on the display
    How to play: The first player pushes a single digit key (not zero), then pushes the ⊞ key. The next player takes his turn by pushing a single digit key (again not zero), then

pushing the ⊞ key. Players take turns until a player pushes the ⊞ key and the display reads 67. The player who pushes ⊞ and gets the display to show 67 wins. If a player pushes ⊞ and the display shows a number larger than 67, that player has gone "bust" and loses.

Variations for primary grades. Use only the first row of digits — the 1, 2, or 3 keys — and 21 as the goal.

Variations for junior high. Use the first column of digits — the 1, 4, or 7 keys — and go to 47.

(b) Determine a strategy for the first player to win the first version of the game every time.

(c) Determine a strategy for the first player to win the junior high version of the game every time.

3-2
ADDITION OF WHOLE NUMBERS — ALGORITHM

You would probably solve the problem $34 + 25$ something like this: $3 + 2 = 5$ and $4 + 5 = 9$, so the answer is 59. While this procedure seems quite natural to us now, it would not be obvious to children first learning to add even if they knew their addition facts. Actually, there are many other ways which make just as much sense to children who are not grounded in the concepts which underlie the correct algorithm. If you teach second or third grade, you are almost sure to see some of these ways.

How could we use the definition of addition of whole numbers along with place value concepts to give meaning to the solution? The definition tells us to determine the number of members in the union of a set with 34 members and a set with 25 members. If we think of 34 as being 3 tens and 4 ones and of 25 as being 2 tens and 5 ones, then the problem has been reduced to adding $3 + 2$ (to find out how many tens we have) and $4 + 5$ (to find out how many ones we have). In so doing, we of course arrive at the correct answer: 59.

Figure 3-10 shows how the three-step process used earlier is applied to this problem.

After children actually work with bundling sticks as suggested in Figure 3-10, they can begin to abbreviate the process first by

tens	ones
3	4
+2	5
5	9

and finally in the familiar form

$$\begin{array}{r} 34 \\ + 25 \\ \hline 59 \end{array}$$

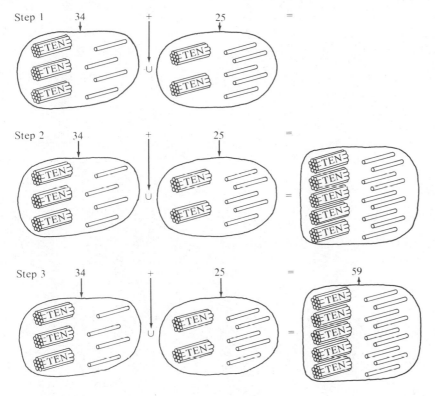

FIGURE 3-10

A mathematical justification of this process might look like this:

$$34 + 25 = (30 + 4) + (20 + 5) \tag{1}$$
$$= (30 + 20) + (4 + 5) \tag{2}$$
$$= 50 + 9 \tag{3}$$
$$= 59 \tag{4}$$

Note that we used first the idea of place value (to replace 34 by 30 + 4 and 25 by 20 + 5, then both reordering and regrouping in step 2, then addition facts (where it is understood that 30 + 20 means 3 tens + 2 tens), and finally place value concepts again in the last step. Even though we don't write out justifications such as this for elementary school children, we should realize that the ideas listed here are inherent in the problem, so that *understanding* the algorithm as more than a rote process depends upon understanding these underlying concepts, particularly place value.

As you know, some two-digit addition problems involve more steps, as shown in Figure 3-11. Consider the problem 18 + 26. What lies behind this harmless-looking calculation? First we think of each number in terms of tens and ones. Upon summing the tens and ones, we get 3 tens and 14 ones. The 14 ones are then regrouped as 1 ten and 4 ones. You have probably heard this referred to as "carrying a one." At last we see that we have 4 tens and 4 ones.

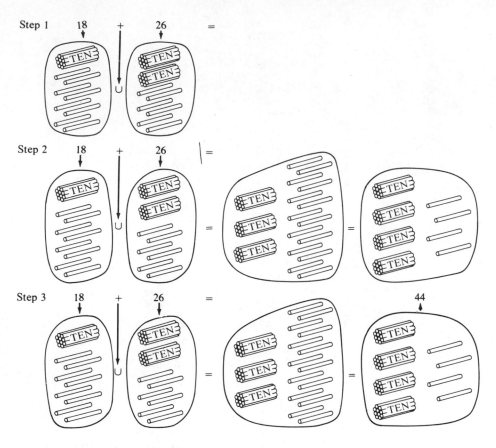

FIGURE 3-11

Again after manipulating physical objects, the children are able to represent the process first as

tens	ones	
1	8	
+2	6	
3̸	1̸4	(add)
4	4	(trade)

where 3 tens and 14 ones were replaced by 4 tens and 4 ones as a result of a ten-for-one trade. Later they can write simply

$$\begin{array}{r} 1 \\ 18 \\ +26 \\ \hline 44 \end{array}$$

A step-by-step justification for this problem could take the form

$$18 + 26 = (10 + 8) + (20 + 6) \qquad \text{place value concept}$$
$$= (10 + 20) + (8 + 6) \qquad \begin{array}{l}\text{commutative and associative} \\ \text{properties of addition}\end{array}$$

$= 30 + 14$ addition facts (note: 1 ten + 2 tens = 3 tens)

$= 30 + (10 + 4)$ place value concept

$= (30 + 10) + 4$ associative property of addition

$= 40 + 4$ addition fact

$= 44$ place value concept

Again it is apparent that place value concepts and knowledge of the properties are involved. Examples are provided in the exercises to suggest what can happen when understanding fails to accompany use of the algorithm.

Some educators advocate the use of **flowcharts** to describe the basic algorithms. Figure 3-12 provides a flowchart for adding two 2-digit numbers.

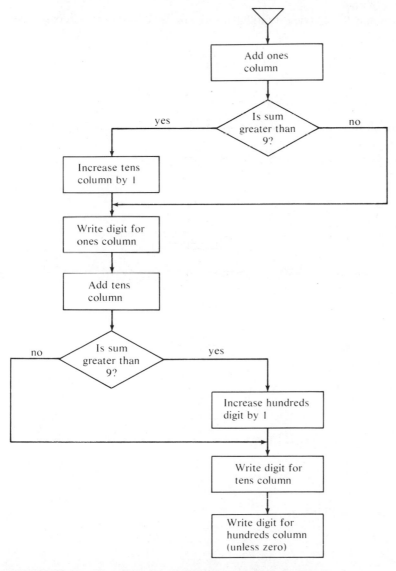

FIGURE 3-12   Flowchart for Adding Two 2-Digit Numbers

You are probably so accustomed to using the addition algorithm that you hardly even think about how and why it works. It can be instructive for you as a future teacher to examine the algorithm in different number bases where you cannot lean on years of experience. In a way, this will put you in the shoes of an elementary school pupil who is first being introduced to these concepts.

We will begin by considering addition problems in base five of the following types:

    (1) one-digit addends without regrouping
    (2) one-digit addends with regrouping
    (3) two-digit addends without regrouping
    (4) two-digit addends with regrouping

(We remind you that addends are merely the numbers that are to be added in an addition problem.)

The problem $2 + 2$ (type 1) still gives an answer of 4 — even in base five:

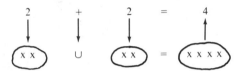

(Even though this is base five, we can write "2" for "2_{five}," since "2" means "2 ones" in any base.)

However, solving $4 + 3$ requires regrouping:

$23_{five} + 11_{five}$ is an example of the third type:

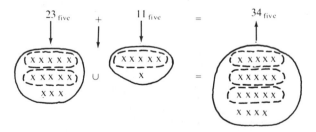

Our next example involves regrouping with two-digit addends:

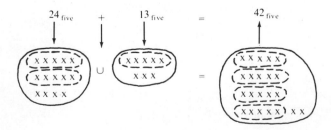

Once you have tried a few examples using pictures (or better yet bundling sticks or other manipulatives), you are ready for the algorithm, first in this form:

fives	ones
2	4
+1	3
$\not{3}$	$\not{12}_5$
4	2

(add in base five)
(trade)

Note that in adding 4 + 3 we write 12 (base five), since 4 ones + 3 ones is one group of five with 2 left over. (This is the same problem we did in our second example of addition problems in base five. You may wish to refer to it.) Then we regroup to get 4 fives and 2 ones.

A complete table for base five addition is given in Figure 3-13. We will use it to solve one last example.

FIGURE 3-13
Base Five Addition Table

+	0	1	2	3	4
0	0	1	2	3	4
1	1	2	3	4	10
2	2	3	4	10	11
3	3	4	10	11	12
4	4	10	11	12	13

(All entries are base five.)

Calculate $243_{\text{five}} + 431_{\text{five}}$.

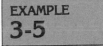

We will use the preliminary form of the algorithm.

one hundred twenty-fives	twenty-fives	fives	ones	
	2	4	3	
+	4	3	1	
	11_5	12_5	4	(add in base five)
	12_5	2	4	(trade)
1	2	2	4	(trade)

We add each column using the base five addition table (Figure 3-13) and then make five-for-one trades (regroup) whenever possible. The sum is 1224_{five}.

You can develop considerable insight into the teaching of addition by doing some addition problems with manipulatives such as bundling sticks or Dienes' blocks.

EXERCISES AND PROBLEMS 3-2

ALGORITHM

1. Can you tell without performing the addition which sum is greater?

$$
\begin{array}{r}
12345 \\
12340 \\
12300 \\
12000 \\
+\,10000 \\
\end{array}
\qquad\qquad
\begin{array}{r}
00001 \\
00021 \\
00321 \\
04321 \\
+\,54321 \\
\end{array}
$$

2. Find a solution to this cryptarithm. (See Problem 10, Section 1-2.)

$$
\begin{array}{r}
\text{A B C D E F G H I J} \\
+\ \text{A B C D E F G H I J} \\
\hline
\text{B D F I A C E G H J}
\end{array}
$$

3. Copy the flowchart given in Figure 3-12 and draw a heavy line indicating the path followed to solve the problem $23 + 58$.

4. Write a flowchart for adding one-digit numbers.

5. Modify the flowchart given in Figure 3-12 to add two two-digit numbers in base five.

OTHER BASES

6. Solve each of the following base five addition problems:
   (a) $2 + 1$ (b) $2 + 4$
   (c) $12_{five} + 31_{five}$ (d) $23_{five} + 13_{five}$
   (e) $432_{five} + 304_{five}$ (f) $342_{five} + 423_{five}$
   (g) $2403_{five} + 2113_{five}$ (h) $4324_{five} + 3412_{five}$

7. Write out a base six addition table. Use this table to solve $35_{six} + 24_{six}$ and to solve $25314_{six} + 32143_{six}$.

8. For each part, draw a sketch to show the sum in the indicated base and write the numeral:

Example: $6 + 4$ (base eight) $\rightarrow$ (X X X X X X   X X)X X $\rightarrow 12_{eight}$

   (a) $4 + 6$ (base seven)   (b) $8 + 5$ (base twelve)
   (c) $5 + 5$ (base twelve)   (d) $1 + 1$ (base two)

9. $\begin{array}{r} 23 \\ +\,45 \\ \hline 101 \end{array}$ is a correct problem in what base?

MATERIALS AND CALCULATORS

10. (a) Sketch the solution of $23 + 16$ using bundling sticks as in Figure 3-10.
   (b) Sketch the solution of $28 + 35$ using bundling sticks as in Figure 3-11.

L11. Use the following manipulative devices to illustrate the problem $34 + 58$:
   (a) bundling sticks   (b) Dienes' multibase arithmetic blocks
   (c) chips   (d) abacus

L12. Repeat the previous problem for $24_{five} + 32_{five}$.

13. Examine one or more elementary textbook series to see how and when addition is introduced.

P14. (a) Write a program summing the whole numbers from 1 up to n. For example, when n = 5, it adds $1 + 2 + 3 + 4 + 5$ and answers 15.

   (b) Use your program from part (a) to sum the whole numbers from 1 to 100.

   (c) Write a program summing the odd numbers from 1 up to $2n - 1$. For example, when $n = 5$, it adds $1 + 3 + 5 + 7 + 9$ and answers 25.

   (d) Use your program from part (c) to sum the first 100 odd whole numbers (1 to 199).

   (e) Write a program to sum the squares of the first n whole numbers. For example, when $n = 5$, it adds $1^2 + 2^2 + 3^2 + 4^2 + 5^2$ and answers 55.

   (f) Use your program from part (e) to sum the squares of the first 20 positive whole numbers.

   (g) Write a program to sum the cubes of the first n odd whole numbers. For example, when $n = 3$ it adds $1^3 + 2^3 + 3^3$ and answers 36.

   (h) Use your program from part (g) to sum the cubes of the first 20 positive whole numbers. (See also Problems 22-24.)

PROBLEM SOLVING EXTENSIONS

15. The Department of Agriculture listed the following number of calories in certain fast foods:

Item	Calories
hamburger	235
fish sandwich	447
french fries	238
chocolate shake	298
apple turnover	269

Andy wants to order as much as possible without exceeding 1000 calories. Find a reasonable combination he can order.

16. Assuming that Al, Betty, and Cal do all their addition problems as they did the example below,

	Al:	26	Betty:	1 26	Cal:	2 26
		+55		+55		+55
		711		810		99

what would each of them get when adding $38 + 24$? (These examples are patterned after actual examples taken from the elementary schools.)

17. (Source: Carol Winner [55].)

   (a) Play this addition game with someone:

   Make a deck of 36 cards, four each of the numbers 1 through 9. (Use part of an ordinary deck of playing cards with the ace as "1" or make your own cards.) Two players draw alternately from the deck, placing the card drawn in either the tens column or the ones column. The player closest to 100 after five draws wins. For example, suppose you drew 2, 6, 5, 3, and 5. By placing them as follows, your total would be 102:

tens	ones
6	2
3	5
	5

(**b**) What is the best possible score for each of the following?

Ann	1, 4, 1, 5, 9
Bob	2, 6, 5, 3, 5
Cora	8, 9, 7, 9, 3
Don	2, 3, 8, 4, 6

(**c**) What does this game teach? At what grade level?

18. Circle three numbers whose sum is 22.

$$
\begin{array}{ccc}
1 & 1 & 1 \\
3 & 3 & 3 \\
5 & 5 & 5 \\
7 & 7 & 7 \\
9 & 9 & 9
\end{array}
$$

19. (**a**) Circle any 3-by-3 block of digits on a calendar. Find a way to determine the sum just by looking at the middle number.

Example:

						1	2
3	4	5	6	7	8	9	
10	11	12	13	14	15	16	
17	18	19	20	21	22	23	
24	25	26	27	28	29	30	

Middle number is 21.
Sum is 189.

(**b**) Repeat part (a) for any one complete row (such as 10 through 16).
(**c**) Repeat part (a) for any three complete rows (such as 10 through 30).

20. Copy and complete each of these magic squares taken from a grades 6-8 supplementary text.

(**a**)

9	2	
	6	8
5	10	

(**b**)

23	12			9
4		7	21	15
10		13		16
	5	19	8	
17	6		4	3

(A **magic square** is an array in which the sum of each row, each column, and each main diagonal is the same.)

21. We know that

8	1	6
3	5	7
4	9	2

is a magic square.

Complete this magic square using the numbers 1 through 9.

6		
1		
8		

Complete this magic square using nine different numbers of your choice.

22. We can count the x's in half of each figure in two ways:

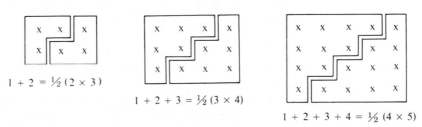

$1 + 2 = \frac{1}{2}(2 \times 3)$

$1 + 2 + 3 = \frac{1}{2}(3 \times 4)$

$1 + 2 + 3 + 4 = \frac{1}{2}(4 \times 5)$

(a) Draw a similar figure for $1 + 2 + 3 + 4 + 5$.
(b) Use your figure to express the sum $1 + 2 + 3 + 4 + 5$ in a manner similar to the examples above.
(c) Evaluate your expression of part (b) and compare your answer with $1 + 2 + 3 + 4 + 5$.
(d) Use this idea to determine the sum of the whole numbers from 1 to 100.

23. (a) Complete this chart and look for a pattern:

Problem	Sum
1	1
1 + 3	4
1 + 3 + 5	
1 + 3 + 5 + 7	
1 + 3 + 5 + 7 + 9	
1 + 3 + 5 + 7 + 9 + 11	

(b) What is the tenth odd whole number? Use the results of part (a) to guess the sum of the first ten odd whole numbers. Check your work by adding them.
(c) What is the 100th odd whole number? What do you think the sum of the first 100 odd whole numbers would be? (Don't add them!)
*(d) Use the technique of Problem 22 to find the sum of the first ten odd whole numbers, and to find the sum of the first 100 odd whole numbers. Compare with parts (b) and (c).

C24. (a) Complete this chart and look for a pattern:

Problem	Sum
1^3	1
$1^3 + 2^3$	9
$1^3 + 2^3 + 3^3$	
$1^3 + 2^3 + 3^3 + 4^3$	
$1^3 + 2^3 + 3^3 + 4^3 + 5^3$	

(b) Use the results of part (a) to guess the sum or the cubes of the first ten positive whole numbers.

3-3
SUBTRACTION OF WHOLE NUMBERS

We'll start this section with a brief quiz: Which of the following story problems can be solved by doing the subtraction problem $8 - 1 = 7$?

(a) Eight crows were perched on a telephone wire. Farmer Jones shot one of them. How many crows were left on the wire?

(b) Debbie had eight pieces of candy. Kathy took one. How many did Debbie have left?

(c) Frank wants to buy a shirt which costs $8. He has $1. How many more dollars does he need to buy the shirt?

(d) Sue has eight boyfriends; Ann has one. Sue has how many more boyfriends than Ann?

Did you recognize that exactly three of the choices were correct? Choice (b) is the familiar "take-away" interpretation of subtraction. Choice (c) is sometimes called the "missing addend" description of subtraction. Choice (d) illustrates the "comparison" interpretation of subtraction. If you are in doubt about choice (a), we offer the additional information that the crows were not slow learners.

Among other things that the above example illustrates is that subtraction problems are not necessarily "take-away" problems. In problems (c) and (d) we subtract, even though "take-away" is not involved. Each of these interpretations is illustrated in Figure 3-14 for the problem $6 - 2 = 4$. We will

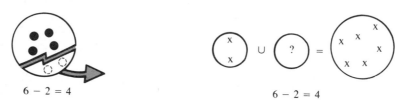

I. Take-away description of subtraction

$6 - 2 = 4$

II. Missing addend description of subtraction

$6 - 2 = 4$

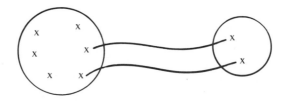

$6 - 2 = 4$

III. Comparison description of subtraction

FIGURE 3-14

focus on the first two interpretations, as they are the ones that appear most often in the elementary school setting. Our goals will be similar to our goals for addition.

To facilitate the take-away description of subtraction, we require a process for removing some of the members of a given set. We can accomplish this quite readily by introducing a new operation for sets. We define $A \setminus B$ (read "A **complement** of B") as follows: Let A be any set which contains B as one of its subsets. Then $A \setminus B$ is the set of all elements which belong to A and *not* to B. (This definition holds even when B is not a subset of A, but we have no need for such cases in this text.) The set $A \setminus B$ is illustrated in Figure 3-15.

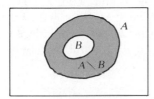

FIGURE 3-15

Here are some examples:

$\{1, 2, 3, 4, 5\} \setminus \{1, 2, 3\} = \{4, 5\}$

$\{\text{whole numbers}\} \setminus \{\text{even whole numbers}\} = \{\text{odd whole numbers}\}$

$\{a, b, c\} \setminus \{\ \ \} = \{a, b, c\}$

Before defining subtraction, we offer an example that involves counting the number of members in the difference of two sets.

Determine $n(A \setminus B)$ for $A = \{r, s, t, u, v\}$ and $B = \{r, s, t\}$.

EXAMPLE 3-6

$$n(A \setminus B) = n(\{r, s, t, u, v\} \setminus \{r, s, t\})$$
$$= n(\{u, v\})$$
$$= 2$$

SOLUTION

Based on our take-away description we make the following definition:

Definition of Subtraction of Whole Numbers □

If a and b are whole numbers with $a \geq b$, then the **difference** of a and b, denoted $a - b$, is the number of members in $A \setminus B$, where A is any set such that $n(A) = a$ and B is any subset of A such that $n(B) = b$. a is called the **minuend** and b is called the **subtrahend**.

(Observe that we have defined $a - b$ only when $a \geq b$.)

As an example of how our definition works, consider Figure 3-14, where we illustrated the problem $6 \doteq 2$ like this:

The picture suggests that we begin with a set of six objects and remove two of them, leaving a set of four objects. In this instance we have $a = 6$, $b = 2$. A is the set of all six objects; B is the subset consisting of the two light-colored objects; and $A \setminus B$ is the set of dark-colored objects. Thus our definition could be paraphrased in this case to read:

> If 6 and 2 are whole numbers with $6 \geq 2$, then the difference of 6 and 2, denoted $6 - 2$, is the number of members in the set we obtain by removing from a set of six objects a subset consisting of two objects.

We will consider the definition of subtraction given above for the take-away description to be *the* definition of subtraction. However, using the missing addend description, we can give what we will refer to as the alternative definition of subtraction.

A very good example of the missing addend description of subtraction is provided by a common method for making change. Suppose you buy something for 58¢ and hand the clerk a dollar. He may figure your change, which is $100 - 58$ cents, by adding to 58 until he reaches 100. As he gives you two pennies, a nickel, a dime, and a quarter, he may in fact say, "58, 59, 60, 65, 75, 100." (He would probably say "one dollar" rather than "100.") Thus what is clearly a subtraction problem, $100 - 58$, is solved using addition. We could say $100 - 58$ is the answer to the question "What do you add to 58 to get 100?" We use this example to introduce our alternative definition of subtraction.

☐ Alternative Definition of Subtraction of Whole Numbers

> If a and b are whole numbers with $a \geq b$, then the difference of a and b, denoted $a - b$, is the answer to the question $b + \square = a$.

Since addition was defined using the union of sets, we can picture the problem $6 - 2$ using this interpretation as in Figure 3-14 by

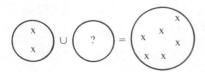

It may also be helpful to paraphrase the alternative definition of subtraction for the example $6 - 2$:

> If 6 and 2 are whole numbers with $6 \geq 2$, then the difference of 6 and 2, denoted $6 - 2$, is the answer to the question $2 + \square = 6$.

As shown in Figure 3-16, we can use a number line to illustrate each of the interpretations of subtraction. The matter of showing that the two definitions necessarily agree will be investigated in the problems.

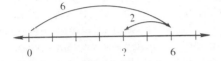

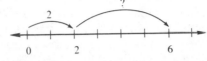

Take-away description of $6 - 2$ illustrated on the number line.

Missing addend description of $6 - 2$ illustrated on the number line.

FIGURE 3-16

Once again it will be convenient to develop basic subtraction facts and a subtraction algorithm for problems involving larger numbers, just as we did for addition. Actually all the basic facts we need for subtraction are already displayed for us in the addition table, particularly if we think in terms of missing addends. Look at Figure 3-17, where a portion of the addition table is repeated. Since $6 - 2$ is the number which added to two gives six, we need only look across from 2 in the addition table until we see a sum of 6. Since the 6 is in the column headed by the 4, we conclude that $6 - 2 = 4$.

+	0	1	2	3	4	5	6	7	8	9
0	0	1	2	3	4	5	6	7	8	9
1	1	2	3	4	5	6	7	8	9	10
2	2	3	4	5	(6)	7	8	9	10	11
3	3	4	5	6	7	8	9	10	11	12

FIGURE 3-17

One interesting (and sometimes troublesome) feature of subtraction is that some of the basic facts involve two-digit numbers. For instance, we can see from Figure 3-18 that $11 - 2$ is a basic subtraction fact, even though 11 is a two-digit number.

+	0	1	2	3	4	5	6	7	8	9
0	0	1	2	3	4	5	6	7	8	9
1	1	2	3	4	5	6	7	8	9	10
2	2	3	4	5	6	7	8	9	10	(11)
3	3	4	5	6	7	8	9	10	11	12

FIGURE 3-18

Yet $2 - 6$, a problem involving only one-digit numbers, is not a subtraction fact at all; it is not even defined for whole numbers. In terms of the language developed in Section 3-1, the fact that $2 - 6$ is not a whole number shows that the set of whole numbers is *not* closed under subtraction. (Recall that since the sum of any two whole numbers is a whole number, we said that the set of whole numbers is closed under addition.) We will inquire about other properties of subtraction in the exercises.

Our next goal is to develop the subtraction algorithm to handle problems involving larger numbers. The need for careful examination of the subtraction algorithm is suggested by the examples in Figure 3-19, which are actual problems taken from children's papers. Note that each child was consistent in the errors he made. Unfortunately, these examples are all too representative of the way many children solve subtraction problems, and they suggest how errors may occur when the algorithm is not fully understood.

	John's Work			Greg's Work

$$\begin{array}{cc}
& ^{4}\cancel{8}11 ^{5}\cancel{6}^{}\cancel{7}111\\
\begin{array}{r}40\\-19\\\hline 39\end{array} \quad
\begin{array}{r}423\\-235\\\hline 212\end{array} \quad
\begin{array}{r}605\\-237\\\hline 432\end{array} \quad
\begin{array}{r}\cancel{6}05\\-237\\\hline 278\end{array} \quad
\begin{array}{r}\cancel{8}002\\-236\\\hline 5876\end{array}
\end{array}$$

FIGURE 3-19

The following five subtraction problems represent some of the common types. They are listed in increasing order of difficulty:

$$(1)\ \begin{array}{r}6\\-2\\\hline\end{array} \quad (2)\ \begin{array}{r}60\\-20\\\hline\end{array} \quad (3)\ \begin{array}{r}67\\-23\\\hline\end{array} \quad (4)\ \begin{array}{r}65\\-28\\\hline\end{array} \quad (5)\ \begin{array}{r}605\\-237\\\hline\end{array}$$

Problem 1 is solved at first by appealing to the definition (or alternative definition) of subtraction and is eventually learned as a basic fact. We have already discussed this problem. Problem 2 uses the same basic fact (that $6 - 2 = 4$) but represents 2 *tens* subtracted from 6 *tens* to give 4 *tens*, or 40. The third problem is pictured with bundling sticks in Figure 3-20. We are subtracting 2 tens and 3 ones (23) from 6 tens and 7 ones (67), leaving 4 tens and 4 ones (44). In Problem 4 (Figure 3-21) we must remove 2 tens and 8 ones (28) from 6 tens and 5 ones (65). Since there are only 5 ones, we will have to regroup by "unbundling" a group of 10 ones — namely, by trading 1 ten for 10 ones as shown in the figure.

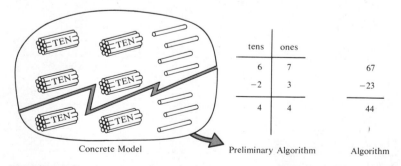

Concrete Model   Preliminary Algorithm   Algorithm

tens	ones	
6	7	67
−2	3	−23
4	4	44

FIGURE 3-20

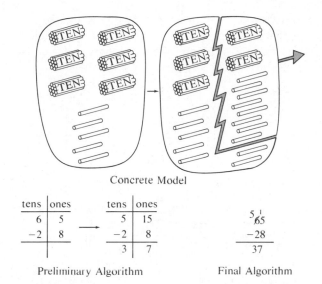

Concrete Model

tens	ones		tens	ones
6	5		5	15
−2	8	→	−2	8
			3	7

Preliminary Algorithm

$$5^{\,1}\!\!\!\!\!/\!6\,5$$
$$-28$$
$$\overline{37}$$

Final Algorithm

FIGURE 3-21

In each of these problems, we show a model using physical objects, then a preliminary form of the algorithm where we carefully record the number of tens and ones, and finally the concise form of the algorithm. It is worth noting that the teaching of the subtraction algorithm should evolve as shown from the actual manipulation of objects.

Problem 5 is perhaps the most difficult type of subtraction problem because several trades are involved in the regrouping process. In order to account for the ones column, we must subtract 7 ones from a number which has only 5 ones. A special problem occurs when there are no tens available to trade for ones, so we must look to the hundreds column. We can exchange 1 hundred for 10 tens, then 1 of these tens for 10 ones. What we are saying is that

$$6 \text{ hundreds } + 5 \text{ ones } = 5 \text{ hundreds } + 10 \text{ tens } + 5 \text{ ones}$$

$$= 5 \text{ hundreds } + 9 \text{ tens } + 15 \text{ ones}$$

We choose for our physical embodiment of this problem Dienes' multibase arithmetic blocks, which perhaps are more appropriate than bundling sticks when larger numbers are involved. The denominations for ones, tens, hundreds, and thousands are termed "units," "flats," "longs," and "blocks," respectively, as shown in Figure 3-22.

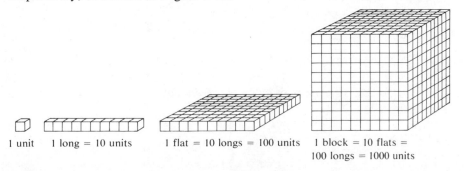

1 unit   1 long = 10 units   1 flat = 10 longs = 100 units   1 block = 10 flats = 100 longs = 1000 units

FIGURE 3-22 Dienes' Multibase Arithmetic Blocks

As shown in Figure 3-23, the 605 would be represented by 6 flats and 5 units. The trading process would involve trading one of the flats for 10 longs and then one of the longs for 10 units. From this remove 2 flats, 3 longs, and 7 units, leaving 3 flats, 6 longs, and 8 units.

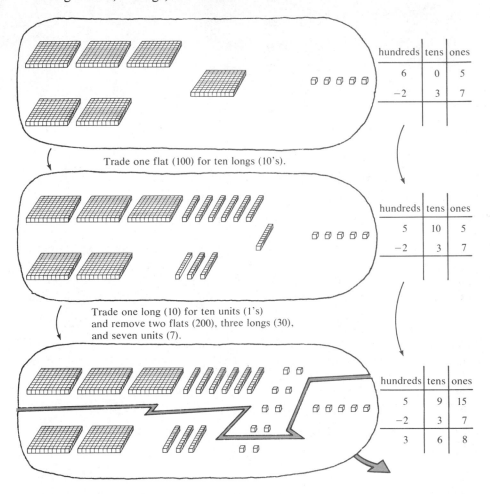

FIGURE 3-23

You may wish to consider using the missing addend interpretation, especially in problems like the last one. Simply write it out as an addition problem, leaving out one of the addends:

$$\begin{array}{r} 237 \\ + \\ \hline 605 \end{array}$$

Then, beginning with the ones place, fill in the missing addend that makes the statement true:

$$\begin{array}{r} 237 \\ + 368 \\ \hline 605 \end{array} \quad \leftarrow \quad \text{fill in}$$

As we did for addition, we will do subtraction in base five in hopes of bettering our understanding. We will again progress from one-digit problems to problems that require regrouping. You may wish to consult the base five addition table, Figure 3-13, to help you remember the basic facts, although they can easily be derived from sketches, as shown by our first two problems given below.

Problems like $3 - 1$ are the same in base five as in base ten, for $3 - 1$ still means 3 ones minus 1 one.

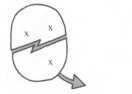

$$
\begin{array}{r}
3 \\
-1 \\
\hline
2
\end{array}
$$

Concrete Model   Algorithm

Next we will do the problem $12_{\text{five}} - 4$. We are to take 4 ones from 1 five and 2 ones. (Recall that 12_{five} means 1 five and 2 ones.)

$$
\begin{array}{r}
12_{\text{five}} \\
-\ 4 \\
\hline
3
\end{array}
$$

Concrete Model   Algorithm

You can see that we must "break up" the five and think of it as 5 ones rather than as 1 five.

Two-digit problems without regrouping appear much as they would in base ten. For instance, $44_{\text{five}} - 21_{\text{five}} = 23_{\text{five}}$, though the answer, 23_{five}, now means 2 fives and 3 ones.

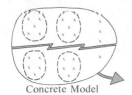

fives	ones
4	4
−2	1
2	3

$$
\begin{array}{r}
44_{\text{five}} \\
-21_{\text{five}} \\
\hline
23_{\text{five}}
\end{array}
$$

Concrete Model   Preliminary   Algorithm
                      algorithm

Of course, when regrouping is involved, we will be making five-for-one trades as the example $42_{\text{five}} - 14_{\text{five}}$ shows:

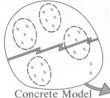

fives	ones
4	2
−1	4

fives	ones
3	12_{five}
−1	4
2	3

$$
\begin{array}{r}
{}^{3}{}^{1} \\
\not{4}2 \\
-14 \\
\hline
23_{\text{five}}
\end{array}
$$

Concrete Model   Preliminary algorithm   Algorithm

Here we trade 1 five for 5 ones to accommodate removing 4 ones. Then we have to do the two individual problems $3 - 1$ (in the five column) and $12_{\text{five}} - 4$ (in the ones column). These are the first two problems we did in the discussion of base five subtraction.

We conclude by solving the problem $401_{five} - 234_{five}$ using the preliminary form of the algorithm:

twenty-fives	fives	ones		twenty-fives	fives	ones		twenty-fives	fives	ones
4	0	1	→	3	10_{five}	1	→	3	4	11_{five}
−2	3	4		−2	3	4		−2	3	4
								1	1	2

Answer: 112_{five}

After becoming proficient with the preliminary form of the algorithm (this may take some practice!), you may wish to use this more condensed form:

$$\begin{array}{r} 3\,4\,1\,1 \\ \not{4\,0\,1}_{five} \\ -\,234_{five} \\ \hline 112_{five} \end{array}$$

Facts like $11_{five} - 4 = 2$ can be determined from the base five addition table, or you can think of 11_{five} as 1 five and 1 one, which is 6. It may also help to go back to our original example of base five numbers on page 30 and think of 11_{five} as 1 nickel and 1 penny. Thus "$11_{five} - 2$" could be thought of as "a nickel and a penny take away two pennies."

EXERCISES AND PROBLEMS 3-3

DEFINITION AND SETS

1. Which interpretation of subtraction does each of the following problems suggest?
   (a) John lost two of his seven marbles. How many did he have left?
   (b) Elise drove the first 23 kilometers of a 70-kilometer trip. How many more kilometers did she have to drive?
   (c) Marilyn has 24 students in her class this year. Last year there were 22. How many more students does she have this year?
   (d) Ms. March had a net income of $9800 after $3200 was taken away by taxes. How much did she earn originally, assuming there were no other deductions? (Be careful!)

2. Find each of the following:
   (a) $\{a, b, c, d, e\}\backslash\{a, e\}$
   (b) {whole numbers}\{whole numbers greater than 6}
   (c) {books}\{dictionaries}
   (d) {children}\{boys}
   (e) $n(\{$letters of the English alphabet$\}\backslash\{a, e, i, o, u\})$

3. Make up some statements like the following (all are true):
   $\{w, o, m, a, n\}\backslash\{m, a, n\} = \{o, w\}$
   $\{b, a, t, h, r, o, b, e\}\backslash\{r, o, b\} = \{h, a, t, e\}$
   $\{c, h, e, a, t\}\backslash\{h, e,\} = \{c, a, t\}$

$\{b, e, a, r, s, k, i, n\}\backslash\{s, k, i, n\} = \{b, a, r, e\}$

$\{o, r, c, h, e, s, t, r, a\}\backslash\{h, e, a, r\} = \{c, o, s, t\}$

Hint: Recall that $\{a, b, c\} = \{c, b, a\} = \{a, a, b, c\}$, etc. (See Problem 25, Section 2-1.)

4. (a) Following the examples in this section, paraphrase both the definition and the alternative definition of subtraction for the problem $9 - 3$.
   (b) Illustrate the take-away description of $9 - 3$, using a set model as in Figure 3-14.
   (c) Do the same for the missing addend description. (See part b.)
   (d) Illustrate the take-away description of $9 - 3$, using the number line as in Figure 3-16.
   (e) Do the same for the missing addend description. (See part d.)

5. Figure 3-7 illustrates the addition problem $5 + 2 = 7$ using Cuisenaire rods. It also illustrates what two subtraction problems? Which interpretation of subtraction is this?

6. (a) If $B \subseteq A$ and $A\backslash B = C$, then $B \cup C = ?$
   (b) If $2 \leq 7$ and $7 - 2 = 5$, then $2 + 5 = ?$
   (c) Compare parts (b) and (c).

7. Construct enough of the addition table to display the basic subtraction fact $8 - 3 = 5$.

8. Which of these subtraction problems are basic facts; which are done by the algorithm; and which are not defined?

$$
\begin{array}{ccccc}
7 & 3 & 15 & 11 & 237 \\
-3 & -7 & -2 & -8 & -182 \\
\end{array}
$$

9. We know that the addition table contains 100 facts. Display the corresponding 100 basic subtraction facts $0 - 0 = 0, 1 - 0 = 1, 2 - 0 = 2, \ldots, 18 - 9 = 9$ in a table that can be read directly. Part of the table is given below:

$-$	0	1	2	3	4	5	6	7	8	9
0	0	*	*	*					*	
1	1	0	*				*			
2										
3										
4			1	0						
17	#							#	9	8
18			#					#	#	9

*10. Verify each of the following for sets A and B:
   (a) $B \cap (A\backslash B) = \{ \ \}$.
   (b) $B \cup (A\backslash B) = A \cup B$.
   (c) If $B \subseteq A$, then $A \cup B = A$.
   (d) Now let $B \subseteq A$, $n(A) = a$, and $n(B) = b$ and show that $b + n(A\backslash B) = a$.
   (e) Argue from part (d) that the two definitions given for subtraction are equivalent.

PROPERTIES

11. Find these differences:

   (a) $\begin{array}{r} 83 \\ -57 \end{array}$ and $\begin{array}{r} 93 \\ -67 \end{array}$ (b) $\begin{array}{r} 528 \\ -283 \end{array}$ and $\begin{array}{r} 628 \\ -383 \end{array}$

(c)   490,763,844,219,027   and   27
    − 490,763,844,219,013   − 13

(d) State a general principle illustrated by these examples.

(e) Marcia owes $36,457.87 on her home mortgage. If she pays $42.19 of it, what is her new balance? If Marcia uses a calculator, can she use a shortcut to avoid entering all seven digits of the $36,457.87?

12. Pick the best answer to this question from an eighth grade assessment test:
$17 - 3 + 4 =$ _____.

A. $3 - 17 + 4$
B. $4 - 3 + 17$
C. $17 - 4 + 3$
D. $17 + 3 + 4$

13. Is subtraction of whole numbers commutative? Associative? Is there an identity? (See page 50, where these properties are listed for addition.) Give some evidence to support your answers.

14. (a) For which values of a, b, and c is $(a - b) - c$ defined?
    (b) For which values of a, b, and c is $(a - c) - b$ defined?
    (c) When both $(a - b) - c$ and $(a - c) - b$ are defined, does $(a - b) - c$ necessarily equal $(a - c) - b$?

*15. True or False? "Any set which is closed under subtraction is closed under addition." (Support your answer.)

ALGORITHM

16. 8003 is usually thought of as 8 thousands and 3 ones, but in subtracting $8003 - 4879$ by the usual algorithm we regroup and think of 8003 as _____ thousands, _____ hundreds, _____ tens, and _____ ones.

17. Solve this cryptarithm. (See Problem 10, Section 1-2.)

R O B E R T
− D O N A L D
G E R A L D

18. Write a flowchart for subtracting two-digit numbers.

19. (a) Do this subtraction problem using Roman numerals: CCCXXVIII
    (b) Did you use any subtraction facts?   − CCXXI

20. Solve $9001 - 4826$ by the missing addend method; namely, find the missing number:
4826
+ ☐
9001

Repeat part (a) for the following:
(b)   875   (c)   628   (d)   8004   (e) 42_{five}
    − 431   − 573   − 4567   − 13_{five}

(f) Do you think subtraction ought to be taught this way to children? Defend your answer.

21. The **Austrian algorithm** (or **equal addends algorithm**) is widely used. Study these examples.

Example 1:

		tens	ones	
83	becomes	8	13	, which is abbreviated
−57		−6	7	
		2	6	

which is abbreviated:
$$\begin{array}{r} 8\overset{1}{}3 \\ -\overset{6}{5}\,7 \\ \hline 2\ 6 \end{array}$$

Example 2:

		h	t	o	
528	becomes	5	12	·8	, which is abbreviated
−283		3	8	3	
		2	4	5	

which is abbreviated:
$$\begin{array}{r} 5\overset{1}{2}\,8 \\ -\overset{3}{2}\,8\,3 \\ \hline 2\ 4\ 5 \end{array}$$

Example 3:

		th	h	t	o	
2003	becomes	2	10	10	13	, which is abbreviated
− 896		−1	9	10	6	
		1	1	0	7	

which is abbreviated:
$$\begin{array}{r} 2\overset{1}{0}\,\overset{1}{0}\,\overset{1}{3} \\ -1\,\overset{9}{8}\,\overset{10}{9}\,6 \\ \hline 1\ 1\ 0\ 7 \end{array}$$

(a) What is added to each number in Example 2?
(b) In Example 3?

Do the following subtraction problems by this method.

(c) $\begin{array}{r} 62 \\ -48 \\ \hline \end{array}$ (d) $\begin{array}{r} 219 \\ -182 \\ \hline \end{array}$ (e) $\begin{array}{r} 87 \\ -24 \\ \hline \end{array}$ (f) $\begin{array}{r} 812 \\ -459 \\ \hline \end{array}$ (g) $\begin{array}{r} 6221 \\ -4227 \\ \hline \end{array}$ (h) $\begin{array}{r} 42_{\text{five}} \\ -13_{\text{five}} \\ \hline \end{array}$

(i) Do you think subtraction ought to be taught this way to children? Defend your answer.

OTHER BASES

22. Solve each of the following base five subtraction problems:
(a) $4 - 3$ (b) $11_{\text{five}} - 3$ (c) $43_{\text{five}} - 12_{\text{five}}$
(d) $31_{\text{five}} - 12_{\text{five}}$ (e) $312_{\text{five}} - 123_{\text{five}}$ (f) $2001_{\text{five}} - 413_{\text{five}}$

23. Solve the following problems:
(a) $10_{\text{six}} - 2$ (b) $10_{\text{twelve}} - 2$ (c) $36_{\text{twelve}} - 19_{\text{twelve}}$
(d) $3002_{\text{six}} - 1205_{\text{six}}$

24. $\begin{array}{r} 40 \\ -24 \\ \hline 15 \end{array}$ is a correct problem in what base?

*25. Observe these examples of "subtraction by adding the complement" done in base two:

Example 1

$$\begin{array}{r} 1011_{\text{two}} \\ -101_{\text{two}} \\ \hline \end{array} \rightarrow \begin{array}{r} 1011_{\text{two}} \\ +1010_{\text{two}} \\ \hline \overset{\frown}{1}0101_{\text{two}} \\ \hookleftarrow +1 \\ \hline 110_{\text{two}} \end{array}$$

Example 2

$$\begin{array}{r} 1010001_{\text{two}} \\ -110111_{\text{two}} \\ \hline \end{array} \rightarrow \begin{array}{r} 1010001_{\text{two}} \\ +1001000_{\text{two}} \\ \hline \overset{\frown}{1}0011001_{\text{two}} \\ \hookleftarrow +1 \\ \hline 11010_{\text{two}} \end{array}$$

(a) Devise a similar algorithm for base ten subtraction.
(b) Explain why this process works (in base ten).

MATERIALS AND CALCULATORS

26. Sketch solutions to the following problems, using bundling sticks:

    (a) $\begin{array}{r} 40 \\ -30 \\ \hline \end{array}$ (b) $\begin{array}{r} 48 \\ -32 \\ \hline \end{array}$ (c) $\begin{array}{r} 43 \\ -29 \\ \hline \end{array}$

L27. Illustrate the problem $9 - 3$, using Cuisenaire rods.

L28. Use the following manipulative devices to illustrate the problem $45 - 28$:

    (a) bundling sticks   (b) Dienes' multibase arithmetic blocks
    (c) chips   (d) abacus

L29. Repeat the previous problem for $32_{\text{five}} - 14_{\text{five}}$.

30. Examine one or more elementary textbook series to see how and when subtraction is introduced.

C31. (a) Use your calculator to subtract as many sevens as you can, one at a time, from 56. Count how many times you are able to subtract 7 before getting a negative number. How much is left?

    (b) Repeat the procedure, counting how many sixes can be subtracted from 43. How much is left?

    (c) This "repeated subtraction" process is effectively what other familiar operation? (Do additional examples if necessary.)

PROBLEM SOLVING EXTENSIONS

32. Assuming that John's and Greg's work is consistent with their work in Figure 3-19, what answer would each get for the problem $507 - 269$?

33. Arrange the following problems in increasing order of difficulty:

     $\begin{array}{r} 48 \\ -26 \\ \hline \end{array}$ $\begin{array}{r} 8 \\ -6 \\ \hline \end{array}$ $\begin{array}{r} 303 \\ -254 \\ \hline \end{array}$ $\begin{array}{r} 8974 \\ -5231 \\ \hline \end{array}$ $\begin{array}{r} 800 \\ -200 \\ \hline \end{array}$

34. Farmer Jones's only son, Peter, stayed home with his father during the crow hunting trip. Who shot the crows?

35. Joan and Betty had a combined time of 5 minutes and 18 seconds in a relay where they each swam 200 meters. If Joan's time was 2 minutes and 36 seconds, what was Betty's time?

36. What is the least number of coins needed to make any amount from 1¢ to $1.00? (We have coins available in the following denominations: 1¢, 5¢, 10¢, 25¢, 50¢.)

37. Suppose you buy something for $12 and the clerk gives your change for a $20 bill saying, "Thirteen, fourteen, fifteen, and five is twenty." Which interpretation of subtraction is this?

*38. (Method of **Finite Differences**.) In many instances it is possible to determine a pattern in a sequence of numbers by examining the differences between consecutive terms.

EXAMPLE

Find the next three terms of each of the following sequences:
(a) 7, 11, 15, 19, 23, 27, . . .

(b) 10, 17, 31, 52, 80, 115, . . .

(c) 1, 1, 13, 73, 241, 601, 1261, . . .

(a) We write the sequence and underneath it the difference of consecutive terms:

Recognizing a difference of 4, we conclude that the sequence continues in this fashion:

(b) First we find the differences:

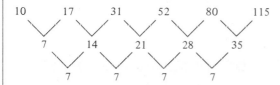

At this point we may recognize that the *differences* are increasing by 7 each time. Another way of looking at this is to consider the *differences of the differences*:

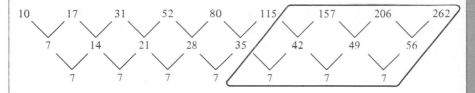

Continuing this pattern gives

(c) We find differences, then differences of the differences, etc., until we arrive at a constant:

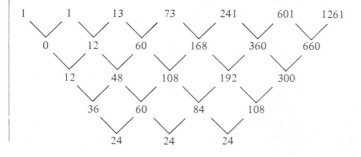

SOLUTION

Continuing this pattern gives

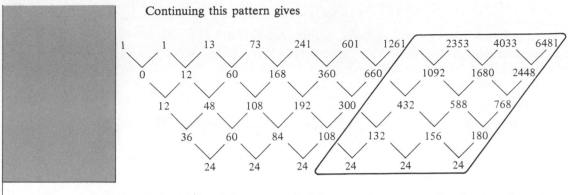

Use the method of finite differences to find the next three terms of each of the following sequences:

(a) 2, 21, 40, 59, 78, 97

(b) 3, 9, 17, 27, 39, 53

(c) 7, 8, 11, 16, 23, 32

(d) 4, 18, 48, 100, 180, 294

(e) 1, 2, 4, 8, 16, 31, 57. (This is the circle problem of Example 1-6.)

3-4
MULTIPLICATION OF WHOLE NUMBERS — DEFINITION AND PROPERTIES

These eight different solutions to a multiplication problem on an arithmetic achievement test all came from the same class of about thirty sixth graders:

346	346	346	346	346	346	346	346
×30	×30	×30	×30	×30	×30	×30	×30
000	000	000	000	000	000	10440	1220
738	91218	1258	1038	10380	1012		
738	912180	12580	1038	10380	10120		

Careful examination of these solutions reveals that in each case a computational process much like the usual algorithm was used — yet only one is correct. One of the aims of this section and the next section is to provide a clear understanding of the multiplication process — in brief, to make it meaningful.

Specifically, we wish to become familiar with the basic language needed to define multiplication, to understand the definition of multiplication, to become acquainted with the basic properties of multiplication and their applications, and to understand the multiplication algorithm and to know how to use it — even in other bases.

Because of similarities between multiplication and addition, it will in some ways be easier to accomplish these objectives for multiplication. For example, we will again encounter the commutative, associative, and other properties. Since you will be relying on concepts developed earlier, it is imperative that you understand them. As a simple example, multiplying 23 times 42 in the usual way requires adding 46 and 920. Thus knowledge of the addition algorithm is prerequisite for understanding the multiplication algorithm.

Some of the occurrences of multiplication are revealed by the following contrasting examples:

(a) If three teams each have four players, how many players are there in all?
(b) A garden is three meters by four meters. Find its area.
(c) If you have three kinds of ice cream and four kinds of toppings, how many kinds of sundaes can be made consisting of one of each?

In each case, the answer is 3×4, but we can note an interesting difference in the units. In problem (a), the unit for the answer is the same as one of the given units (players). In problem (b), we begin with meters and give the answer in square meters, a new unit. In problem (c), the unit for the answer is again a new one. Problems like (a), where a given unit is repeated, can be considered to be *one-dimensional;* problems like (b) and (c), where new units are derived from given units, can be considered to be *two-dimensional.* This means of classification will suggest two interpretations of multiplication, each of which can be thought of in terms of sets.

The set interpretation for the one-dimensional case, illustrated by problem (a), is reminiscent of the interpretation of addition. Here three times four arises as the number of members in the union of three disjoint sets (teams), each with four members (players). One popular elementary school text introduces multiplication in this way in the third grade with examples of three sets of four keys each. Thus three times four is illustrated by three disjoint sets of four objects.

We can generalize this interpretation as follows:

Definition of Multiplication of Whole Numbers ☐

If a and b are whole numbers, then the **product** of a and b, denoted $a \times b$, is the number of members in the union of a disjoint sets each with b members. a and b are called **factors**.

The two-dimensional case can be facilitated by a new operation for sets which involves taking pairs of elements. In problem (c), for instance, suppose that the kinds of toppings are butterscotch, fudge, marshmallow, and pineapple, and the kinds of ice cream are vanilla, strawberry, and chocolate. Then, some of the pairs consisting of one kind of topping with one flavor of ice cream are (butterscotch, vanilla), (fudge, vanilla), and (pineapple, chocolate). Here we have used the customary notation, writing each pair separated by a comma and within parentheses. We refer to these pairs as **ordered pairs**. In the ordered pair (butterscotch, vanilla), butterscotch is the **first coordinate** and vanilla is the

second coordinate. We regard two pairs to be equal (the same) only if they have the same first coordinate and the same second coordinate. Thus

(butterscotch, vanilla) $\neq$ (fudge, vanilla) and

(butterscotch, vanilla) $\neq$ (vanilla, butterscotch)

All the possible ordered pairs are shown in Figure 3-24. Note that for each of the three kinds of ice cream there are four kinds of toppings, so that we have 3×4 kinds of sundaes.

The principle involved here is so important we will refer to it as

☐ The Fundamental Counting Principle

> If for each of the *m* ways of making a first choice there are *n* ways of making a second choice, then there are $m \times n$ pairs of choices.

Given any two sets *A* and *B*, it is always possible to form a set of ordered pairs. This is called the **Cartesian product** (or **cross product**) of *A* and *B*. Denoted by $A \times B$, it is the set consisting of all ordered pairs whose first coordinate comes from *A* and whose second coordinate comes from *B*.

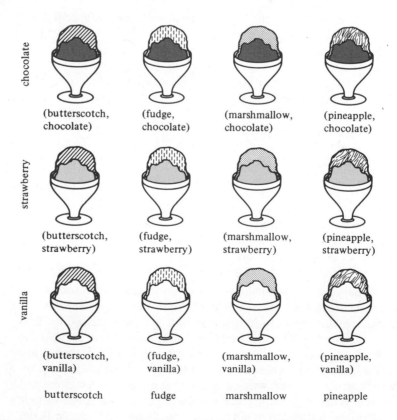

FIGURE 3-24

If $X = \{1, 2, 3\}$, $Y = \{a, b\}$, and $Z = \{\ \}$, find $X \times Y$, $Y \times X$, and $Y \times Z$.

EXAMPLE

3-7

SOLUTION

$X \times Y$ will be the set of all ordered pairs whose first coordinate comes from X and whose second coordinate comes from Y. Thus $X \times Y = \{(1, a), (1, b),$ $(2, a), (2, b), (3, a), (3, b)\}$. Similarly, $Y \times X = \{(a, 1), (a, 2), (a, 3), (b, 1),$ $(b, 2), (b, 3)\}$. Since Z is the empty set, there can be no ordered pairs whose second coordinate comes from Z, so $Y \times Z$ is the set that contains no ordered pairs; namely, $Y \times Z = \{\ \}$.

The garden problem, (b) in our introductory examples, can also be interpreted in terms of Cartesian products. Suppose we label the four one-meter pieces that constitute the length 1, 2, 3, 4, and the three one-meter pieces that constitute the width $a, b, c,$ as shown in Figure 3-25a. It is easy to see that exactly 12 square meters will cover the garden. The 12 square meters can be labeled using ordered pairs as shown in Figure 3-25b. The ordered pairs which result are precisely the members of $\{1, 2, 3, 4\} \times \{a, b, c\}$. There are 12 ordered pairs, the same as the number of square meters in the area.

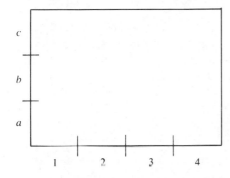

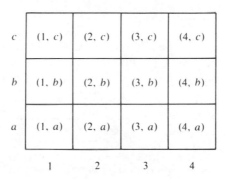

FIGURE 3-25a   **FIGURE 3-25b**

The systematic tabulation of objects in rows and columns as in Figures 3-24 and 3-25b is called an **array**. Arrays and Cartesian products suggest two more possible definitions for multiplication:

Alternative Definitions of Multiplication of Whole Numbers ☐

> If a and b are whole numbers, then the product of a and b is the number of objects in an array with a rows and b columns:
> or,
> If a and b are whole numbers, then the product of a and b is the number of elements in $A \times B$, where A and B are any sets with a and b elements respectively.

Number lines and Cuisenaire rods are again among the devices we can use to illustrate simple problems. Of course, the number line provides the one-dimensional interpretation of multiplication. Three times four can be interpreted as "three jumps of four," as shown in Figure 3-26.

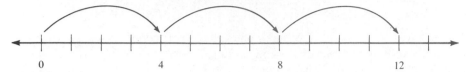

FIGURE 3-26

Cuisenaire rods can be used to illustrate both the one- and two-dimensional interpretations. In the one-dimensional case shown in Figure 3-27, three times four is the answer to the question "How long is a train consisting of three purple rods?" By making a train of white blocks alongside the purple train, we can see that three times four is twelve.

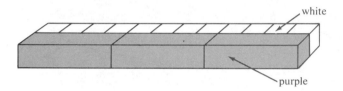

FIGURE 3-27

In the two-dimensional case shown in Figure 3-28, three times four can be interpreted as "build a rectangle whose width equals a light green rod (three) and whose length equals a purple rod (four)."

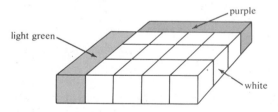

FIGURE 3-28

The five descriptions of multiplication are reviewed in Example 3-8.

EXAMPLE 3-8

Illustrate 2×3 using

(a) the definition,   (b) arrays,   (c) Cartesian products,

(d) the number line,   (e) Cuisenaire rods.

SOLUTION

(a) Take the union of two disjoint sets of three members each:

$$(x\ x\ x) \cup (x\ x\ x) = (x\ x\ x\ x\ x\ x)$$

(b) Form an array with two rows and three columns.

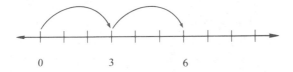

(c) Let $A = \{r, s\}$, $B = \{u, v, w\}$. Then $A \times B = \{(r, u), (r, v), (r, w), (s, u),$ $(s, v), (s, w)\}$, so $n(A \times B) = 6$.

(d) Take two jumps of three.

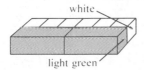

(e) Form a train consisting of two light-green rods.

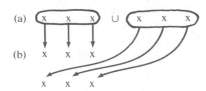

With so many interpretations of multiplication, it is natural to ask if they will always all give the same answer. We respond with an enthusiastic yes, but are limited here to a somewhat sketchy explanation of why this is true. We do this in Figure 3-29 in terms of the previous example, where the arrows indicate one possible 1-1 correspondence. We see that each set from (a) corresponds to a row from (b) and that each element of a given set corresponds to exactly one entry in the appropriate row. Thus for each element of (a) there corresponds precisely one member of the array in (b). This same procedure would work regardless of the number of sets or the number of elements per set. This is the essence of an argument that interpretations (a) and (b) will always yield the same answer, though many details would have to be provided for a complete proof of the general case.

To see that (b) is equivalent to (c), it helps to write out the Cartesian product set in an array so that all the pairs with r as first coordinate appear in the first row and so that all the pairs with u as second coordinate appear in the first column, etc., as shown in Figure 3-30. The resulting array of ordered pairs in (c) will have the same number of rows and columns, and thus the same number of entries, as the array for (b). A similar argument could be made for any number of rows and columns.

Since the products for interpretations (a) and (b) are equal and the products for interpretations (b) and (c) are equal, it follows that the products

(a) ⟨ x   x   x ⟩ ∪ ⟨ x   x   x ⟩

(b) x   x   x

      x   x   x

Suggested 1-1 correspondence between (a) and (b).

FIGURE 3-29

(b)

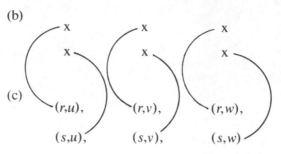

Suggested 1-1 correspondence between (b) and (c).

(c)

(r,u),   (r,v),   (r,w),

(s,u),   (s,v),   (s,w)

FIGURE 3-30

for interpretations (a) and (c) are equal. The models involving the number line and the Cuisenaire rods are actually special cases of interpretation (a).

Our next example reviews some of our problem solving strategies.

EXAMPLE 3-9

Boss Dogg, the campus hot dog vendor, sells hot dogs with a choice of ketchup, mustard, onions, relish, kraut, or coney sauce. (a) How many versions of the hot dog are possible? (b) How many of these have exactly four condiments?

SOLUTION

(a) We will use the strategies *Solve a simpler problem*, *Make a table*, and *Look for a pattern*.

0 condiments: If we have no condiments, there is one version: plain.

1 condiment: Suppose only ketchup were available. Then there would be two versions: plain or with ketchup.

2 condiments: Suppose ketchup and mustard were available. Then we would have the same two versions we had before (plain or ketchup) and two new versions (mustard or both mustard and ketchup).

3 condiments: Suppose now we have ketchup, mustard, and onions. We can have any of the previous four versions by declining onions, and we can create four new versions by adding onions to each of the former versions. Thus we have eight possibilities. Next we make a table and look for a pattern:

Condiments	0	1	2	3
Versions	1	2	4	8

The table suggests that the number of versions doubles each time we add a new condiment, but in light of the false pattern in the circle problem (Example 1-6), we must be careful! When considering three condiments we saw why the numbers do, in fact, double each time. (When adding another condiment we still have all of the old versions, plus an equal number of new versions created by adding the new condiment to a former version.) With confidence in our supporting argument, we extend the table and answer the original question:

Condiments	0	1	2	3	4	5	6
Versions	1	2	4	8	16	32	64

There are 64 possible combinations.

(b) A useful strategy for this problem is *Think of a similar problem*. Do you see how we have a set of six condiments from which we are to choose four? This is the same as asking "How many four-member sets does a six-member set have?," which is precisely Problem 44(a) of Section 2-1. According to Pascal's triangle, there are 15 four-member subsets of a six-member set.

Next in our development of multiplication is the consideration of properties. We will test multiplication of whole numbers for closure, commutativity, associativity, and identity. Another property, distributivity, which combines addition and multiplication, will also be investigated.

According to one of the alternative definitions of multiplication of whole numbers, the product of two whole numbers — say, a and b — is the number of objects in an array with a rows and b columns. Now, the number of objects in an array is either a whole number or infinite. But certainly an array with a finite number, a, of rows and a finite number, b, of columns cannot have an infinite number of entries, so we can safely conclude that we get a whole number. To say that the product of whole numbers is a whole number is to say that the set of whole numbers is *closed* under multiplication.

What about the order property, commutativity? We are asking if $a \times b = b \times a$ for all whole numbers a and b, or in terms of the alternative definition, whether an array with a rows and b columns has the same number of entries as an array with b rows and a columns. This is illustrated in Figure 3-31 for $a = 4$ and $b = 8$.

```
x  x  x  x  x  x  x  x
x  x  x  x  x  x  x  x
x  x  x  x  x (x) x  x
x  x  x  x  x  x  x  x

         Array I
```

```
x   x   x   x
x   x   x   x
x   x   x   x
x   x   x   x
x   x   x   x
x   x  (x)  x
x   x   x   x
x   x   x   x

    Array II
```

FIGURE 3-31

One obvious way to set up a 1-1 correspondence between the arrays, and thereby show that they contain the same number of entries, is to pair the elements of the first row of Array I with the elements of the first column of Array II, etc. Thus the entry in the third row and sixth column of I is paired with the entry in the sixth row and third column of II. This method will work for any number of rows and columns.

We can visualize an alternative 1-1 correspondence by thinking of the arrays as a marching band at two different times during a parade. Imagine the band first in position I and then later in position II after turning a corner, as shown in Figure 3-32. The desired 1-1 correspondence is the one that pairs the original and the new positions of each "band member." For example, the circled entries would be paired. These arguments help us to conclude that multiplication of whole numbers is commutative — namely, $a \times b = b \times a$ for any whole numbers a and b.

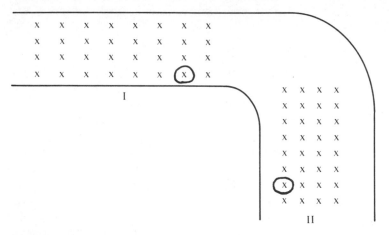

FIGURE 3-32

Proofs of associativity tend to be cumbersome. We will trace one approach through a simple case. Recalling that associativity is the grouping property, we will compare $(2 \times 3) \times 4$ and $2 \times (3 \times 4)$. We are interested in more than the fact that each product equals 24, for we are trying to sketch an argument that will work for any choice of factors.

First consider $(2 \times 3) \times 4$. The parentheses indicate that we start by computing 2×3, which by definition means "count the members in the union of two disjoint sets each with three members." So far, we have:

— namely, we have 2×3 objects. Now this number (six) tells us how many sets of four to take, so we have six sets of four, or pictorially:

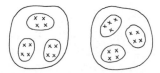

Now consider $2 \times (3 \times 4)$. This might be translated as "count the members in the union of two disjoint sets each with 3×4 members," so we begin by picturing 3×4:

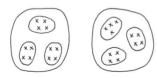

Now, $2 \times (3 \times 4)$ instructs us to take the union of two such collections, so we get:

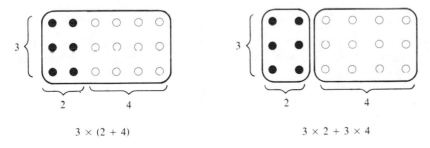

arriving at the same result. We will not provide a general argument here, but we will record the fact that multiplication is indeed associative — namely, $(a \times b) \times c = a \times (b \times c)$ for all whole numbers a, b, and c.

We found that zero is the identity for addition. You are asked in the exercises to establish the role of zero in multiplication. Is there an identity for multiplication, a fixed whole number which, multiplied by any whole number, yields the other whole number? Clearly, 1 is the candidate. Can you show this in terms of the definition or one of the alternative definitions?

An extremely important property is the **distributive** law of multiplication over addition, which says that for any whole numbers a, b and c, $a \times (b + c) = a \times b + a \times c$. (Another form of the distributive law is $(b + c) \times a = b \times a + c \times a$.) This is quite easy to visualize through the two-dimensional interpretation of multiplication. Figure 3-33 demonstrates the distributive property for the case $3 \times (2 + 4) = 3 \times 2 + 3 \times 4$. We can count entries in either of the two ways suggested by the grouping.

$$3 \times (2 + 4) \qquad\qquad 3 \times 2 + 3 \times 4$$

FIGURE 3-33

The distributive property is important enough to merit another example, this one using the area model. Suppose a realtor is selling two adjacent lots, each 200 meters deep and with frontages of 70 meters and 80 meters respectively, as shown in Figure 3-34. Then the total area could be found either by considering this to be a single plot of land $200 \times (70 + 80)$ or by considering it to be separate plots 200×70 and 200×80. Either way, we necessarily get the same area, so $200 \times (70 + 80) = 200 \times 70 + 200 \times 80$.

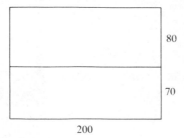

FIGURE 3-34

Unlike our previous properties, the distributive property involves two operations. We sometimes say "multiplication distributes over addition." You will have the opportunity to investigate other distributive properties in the problems.

In the summary of properties that follows, notice the similarity to the properties for addition of whole numbers on page 50.

☐ Properties for Multiplication of Whole Numbers

1. (Closure) For any whole numbers a and b, $a \times b$ is a whole number.
2. (Commutative) For any whole numbers a and b, $a \times b = b \times a$.
3. (Associative) For any whole numbers a, b, and c, $(a \times b) \times c = a \times (b \times c)$.
4. (Identity) For any whole number a, $a \times 1 = a$ and $1 \times a = a$.
5. (Distributive) For any whole numbers a, b, and c, $a \times (b + c) = a \times b + a \times c$. (This is the distributive property of multiplication over addition.)

Once again the properties are used to help develop a table of facts for problems involving one-digit numbers and an algorithm for problems involving larger numbers. Development of the multiplication table is in many respects analogous to the development of the addition table and is outlined in the exercises. We will concentrate on the multiplication algorithm in the next section.

EXERCISES AND PROBLEMS 3-4

DEFINITION AND SETS

1. Which of the following interpretations for multiplication "generalize to" (will also work for) multiplying fractions?
   (a) union of disjoint sets
   (b) area
   (c) cross-product
   (d) array
   (e) number line
   (f) Cuisenaire rods

2. True or False?
   (a) $\{(1, 2), (3, 4)\} = \{(3, 4), (1, 2)\}$
   (b) $\{(1, 2), (3, 4)\} = \{(2, 1), (4, 3)\}$
   (c) $\{(1, 2), (3, 4)\} = \{(1, 4), (2, 3)\}$
   (d) $\{(1, 2), (3, 4)\} = \{1, 2, 3, 4\}$
   (e) For any sets A and B, $A \times B = B \times A$
   (f) For any sets A and B, $n(A \times B) = n(B \times A)$

3. Find
   (a) $\{1\} \times \{r, s, t\}$ (b) $\{1, 2\} \times \{r, s, t\}$
   (c) $\{r, s, t\} \times \{1, 2\}$ (d) $\{\ \} \times \{1, 2\}$

4. Find sets R and S so that $R \times S$ has
   (a) 4 members   (b) 5 members

5. If T has three members, then how many members does V have if $n(T \times V)$ is
   (a) 3   (b) 9   (c) 10   (d) 900   (e) 0

6. (a) If $D = \{1, 2\}$ and $E = \{a\}$, find $D \times E$ and $E \times D$. Are they equal?
   (b) Is $\times$ commutative?
   (c) Does $n(D \times E) = n(E \times D)$?

7. (a) If $D = \{1, 2\}$, $E = \{a\}$, and $F = \{\triangle, \square, \bigcirc\}$, find $(D \times E) \times F$ and $D \times (E \times F)$. Are they equal?
   (b) Is $\times$ associative?
   (c) How would you define $A \times B \times C$ for any sets A, B, and C?

8. (a) Why does the definition of multiplication require disjoint sets?
   (b) Do the sets in the second alternate definition of multiplication have to be disjoint?

COUNTING

9. (a) How many ways are there to connect one dot from row A with one dot from row B?

   row A • • • •

   row B • • •

   (b) What multiplication problem does this suggest?
   (c) Which interpretation of multiplication is represented here?

10. (a) The card game euchre uses four suits (clubs, diamonds, hearts, spades) and six cards per suit (9, 10, jack, queen, king, ace). How many cards are in a euchre deck? What set operation is involved here?
    (b) If a new car comes in a choice of six exterior and three interior colors, how many color combinations are possible?
    (c) How many pairs of words can be formed if we choose a word from the adjective list and a word from the noun list? (Examples: timid brontosaurus, wanton albatross, etc.)

adjectives	*nouns*
timid	albatross
unattached	brontosaurus
virginal	choreographer
wanton	do-gooder
	exorcist

11. If John owns 15 shirts and 8 sweaters, then how many shirts and sweaters does he have in all?

12. (a) Bill and Jean and their three children from New York call Carl and Carol and their four children, who live in Wisconsin. During the call, each of the five members of the New York family talks for half a minute to each of the six members of the Wisconsin family. If the rates are $1.05 per minute, how much does the call cost?
    (b) If Grandma is visiting Carl and Carol at the time, how much will it cost if she also talks a half-minute to each of the callers?

13. (a) If you can order a hamburger with or without each of eight condiments, how many ways are there to order?
    (b) How many of them contain exactly four condiments?
    (c) Five condiments?
    (d) Six condiments?
    (e) Seven condiments?
    (f) Eight condiments?
    (g) If pizzas come in three sizes and with or without each of six ingredients, how many ways are there to order a pizza?
    (h) How many ways are there to order a large pizza with three of six ingredients?

14. Show each of the following using the Fundamental Counting Principle (without using Pascal's triangle):

   (a) $\binom{6}{2} = \dfrac{6 \times 5}{2 \times 1}$

   (b) $\binom{8}{3} = \dfrac{8 \times 7 \times 6}{3 \times 2 \times 1}$

   (c) $\binom{21}{4} = \dfrac{21 \times 20 \times 19 \times 18}{4 \times 3 \times 2 \times 1}$

   (d) $\binom{10}{2} = \dfrac{10 \times 9}{2 \times 1}$

   (e) $\binom{100}{3} = \dfrac{100 \times 99 \times 98}{3 \times 2 \times 1}$

15. (a) How many different five-card poker hands can be dealt from a 52-card deck?
    (b) If we dealt one hand per minute, how long would it take to deal all of the hands? (Answer in appropriate units.)

PROPERTIES

16. Write out examples of the closure, commutative, associative, and identity properties for multiplication using specific whole numbers. Do the same for the distributive property of multiplication over addition.

17. What multiplication problem is suggested by each of the following arrays?

What property do these two problems (taken together) suggest?

18. Invent "the zero property for multiplication."

19. Show that 1 is the identity for multiplication using the definition (or one of the alternative definitions) for multiplying whole numbers.

20. Which of the following sets are closed under multiplication?
    (a) {0}
    (b) {1}
    (c) {0, 1}
    (d) {0, 2}
    (e) {odd whole numbers}
    (f) {even whole numbers}
    (g) {multiples of 3}
    (h) {powers of 3} = {1, 3, 9, 27, 81, . . .}

21. We know that W, the set of whole numbers, is closed under addition and that it is closed under multiplication. Is the set {0, 1, 2, 3, 4, 6, 7, 8, 9, 10, 11, 12, . . .} (the whole numbers with 5 removed)
    (a) closed under addition? Why?
    (b) closed under multiplication? Why?

22. In the marching band example of Figure 3-32, we saw that the entry in the fourth row and seventh column of array I, let's call it (4, 7), was paired with (7, 1) of array II. What would (4, 5) of array I be paired with? What would (p, q) of array I be paired with?

23. Which entries in the multiplication table (0×0 through 9×9) can be obtained using
    (a) the zero property?   (b) the identity property?
    (c) the commutative property (together with another entry)?

24. Are the associative and distributive properties used in developing the multiplication table?

25. Do these statements hold for all whole numbers a, b, and c? Explain.
    (a) "If $a < b$, then $ac < bc$."   (b) "If $ac < bc$, then $a < b$."

26. Explain how the following figure can be used to provide a specific illustration of the distributive property. (Be sure to tell what specific example is being illustrated.)

    o   o   o   o   o

    o   o   o   o   o

    o   o   o   o   o

    o   o   o   o   o

27. Do the following problem two ways, using the distributive property: George goes to the hardware store to buy eight bolts, eight washers, and eight nuts that he needs to assemble some shelves. If bolts cost 24¢ each, washers cost 3¢ each, and nuts cost 5¢ each, how much will he spend?

28. Use the distributive law to compute $(546 \times 9827637) + (454 \times 9827637)$.

29. Mr. James was to be reimbursed 15¢ per mile for the following mileage:

January 4	182 miles
January 5	256 miles
January 7	23 miles
January 8	292 miles
January 10	269 miles

    How much should he be reimbursed? (Hint: You need to do only one multiplication problem if you apply the distributive law.)

30. (a) Does $\times$ distribute over $\setminus$? Namely, does

$$A \times (B \setminus C) = (A \times B) \setminus (A \times C)?$$

(b) Does $+$ distribute over $\times$?   **(c)** Does $\times$ distribute over $-$?
(d) Does $\times$ distribute over $\cup$?   **(e)** Does $\cup$ distribute over $\cap$?

MATERIALS AND CALCULATORS

31. Repeat Example 3-8 for 3×2.

L32. (a) Using base ten Dienes' blocks, form three piles each containing one flat, two longs, and four units. Record the contents of the first pile as pile A. Combine the piles and exchange. Record the results of the new pile as "Product." Write out the corresponding multiplication problem in base ten.

> Pile A: _____ flats, _____ longs, _____ units
>
> $\times\ 3$
>
> Product: _____ flats, _____ longs, _____ units

(b) Repeat part (a) using base five blocks.
(c) Repeat part (a) using base six blocks.

C33. (a) Use a calculator to generate a times table through 9×9 *without using the* $\boxtimes$ *button.* Describe your procedure.
(b) In particular, tell how 7×9 can be obtained (without using the $\boxtimes$ button).

C34. Some calculators have a $\boxed{x^2}$ key which squares the number in the display. For example, pressing "3 $\boxed{x^2}$" gives 9. **(a)** Tell how to use this key to compute 13^4. **(b)** What other powers of a number can be found using this key? Explain.

C35. (a) Suppose you are using a calculator to compute an answer and that you inadvertently press $\boxplus$ instead of $\boxtimes$. What number can you add so as not to change the display? **(b)** If you inadvertently press $\boxtimes$ instead of $\boxplus$, what number can you multiply by so as not to change the display?

P36. Write a program to compute $\binom{n}{r}$; for example, to compute $\binom{8}{3}$ or $\binom{52}{5}$.

3-5
MULTIPLICATION OF WHOLE NUMBERS — ALGORITHM

We begin our discussion of the multiplication algorithm with problems of the type 3×20. How does this differ from 3×2? Only that instead of 3×2 we have 3×2 tens, or 6 tens. This can be shown nicely using bundling sticks:

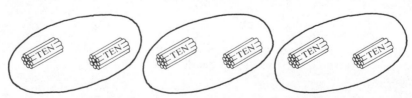

Thus
$$3 \times 20 = 3 \times (2 \times 10)$$
$$= (3 \times 2) \times 10$$
$$= 6 \times 10$$
$$= 60$$

Hopefully, you recognize that the justification for the preceding steps depends upon place value and the associative property for multiplication. Similarly,

$$7 \times 90 = 7 \times (9 \times 10)$$
$$= (7 \times 9) \times 10$$
$$= 63 \times 10$$
$$= 630$$

Here we justify the last step, namely $63 \times 10 = 630$, by interpreting "63×10" as "63 groups of ten." Since each 10 tens is 100, 60 tens is 600, and 63 tens is 630. We can also show directly that $63 \times 10 = 630$ using the properties. (See Problem 6.)

These techniques can be used for all problems of the form $c \times d$, where c is a one-digit number and d is one of the numbers 10, 20, 30, 40, . . . , 90. By the commutative principle (for multiplication) we have also taken care of 20×3, 90×7, and all problems of the form $d \times c$, where d and c are defined as above. Extensions of these ideas can be made to show why, for instance,

$$20 \times 30 = 600,$$
$$60 \times 800 = 48000, \text{ and}$$
$$500 \times 6000 = 3000000$$

We will call this the

Multiplying by Multiples of Ten Principle □

The product that can be represented as a whole number p followed by m 0's times a whole number q followed by n 0's is the whole number represented by $p \times q$ followed by $(m + n)$ 0's.

Thus for the preceding examples,

$$3 \times 2\underline{0} = 6\underline{0}$$
$$7 \times 9\underline{0} = 63\underline{0}$$
$$2\underline{0} \times 3\underline{0} = 6\underline{00}$$
$$6\underline{0} \times 8\underline{00} = 48\underline{000}$$
$$5\underline{00} \times 6\underline{000} = 3\underline{00000}$$

We still haven't taken care of problems like 32×47. Mathematically, we have all the necessary machinery:

$$32 \times 47 = 32 \times (40 + 7)$$
$$= 32 \times 40 + 32 \times 7$$
$$= (30 + 2) \times 40 + (30 + 2) \times 7$$
$$= 30 \times 40 + 2 \times 40 + 30 \times 7 + 2 \times 7$$
$$= 1200 + 80 + 210 + 14$$
$$= 1504$$

We leave it to you to justify each step, emphasizing that place value and the associative and distributive properties play an important role.

While the above solution to 32×47 has the advantage of displaying the properties involved, it is certainly not the most desirable format for doing ordinary multiplication. Before writing down the usual algorithm, we suggest an intermediate form of the algorithm that shows all of the important steps without being excessively long:

```
      32
    × 47
    ─────
      14      (2 × 7)
     210      (30 × 7)
      80      (2 × 40)
    1200      (30 × 40)
    ─────
    1504
```

Note that the multiplying by multiples of ten principle is used to compute $30 \times 7, 2 \times 40$, and 30×40. These three "little problems" along with 2×7 are called **partial products** for the "big problem" 32×47. After children have considerable practice with the algorithm in this form, it can be shortened to:

```
      32
    × 47
    ─────
     224
    1280
    ─────
    1504
```

by combining some of the partial products. While you may be more familiar with the notation

```
      32                          32
    × 47                        × 47
    ─────       than with       ─────
     224                         224
     128                        1280
    ─────                       ─────
    1504                        1504
```

we strongly feel that the inclusion of the 0 in writing 1280 is quite helpful to children. Errors children make (as shown in the exercises) suggest the desirability of filling in the 0's.

EXAMPLE 3-10

Illustrate the solution to 402×56 using

(a) the step-by-step mathematical justification,

(b) the intermediate form of the algorithm, and

(c) the shortened form of the algorithm.

(a) $402 \times 56 = 402 \times (50 + 6)$

$= 402 \times 50 + 402 \times 6$

$= (400 + 2) \times 50 + (400 + 2) \times 6$

$= 400 \times 50 + 2 \times 50 + 400 \times 6 + 2 \times 6$

$= 20000 + 100 + 2400 + 12$

$= 22512$

(b)
```
    402
  × 56
    12    (2 × 6)
     0    (0 × 6)
  2400    (400 × 6)
   100    (2 × 50)
     0    (0 × 50)
 20000    (400 × 50)
 22512
```

(c)
```
    402
   × 56
   2412
  20100
  22512
```

Problems such as 32×26 can be illustrated graphically using the area model on squared paper (or dot paper), as demonstrated in Figure 3-35. The total area represented by 32×26 is divided into four regions separated by the darker lines. Region A has dimensions 30×20, so it covers 600 square units. (Do you see the 6 hundreds?) Region B is 30×6 and has area 180. (Do you see

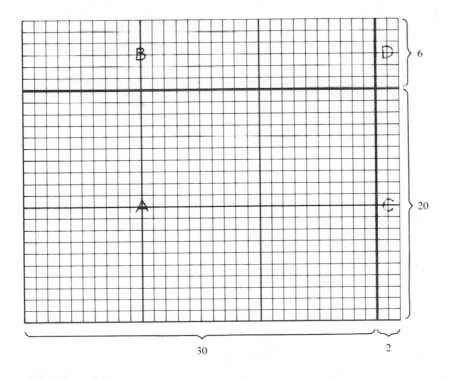

FIGURE 3-35

96

the 18 tens?) Region C is $2 \times 20 = 40$. (Do you see the 4 tens?) Region D is $2 \times 6 = 12$. The four partial products in the intermediate algorithm

$$
\begin{array}{r}
32 \\
\times 26 \\
\hline
12 \\
180 \\
40 \\
600 \\
\hline
832
\end{array}
$$

    (2×6)
    (30×6)
    (2×20)
    (30×20)

are evident in Figure 3-35 as regions D, B, C, and A respectively.

And now, are you ready? Yes, we're going to do multiplication in base five. First we need our basic multiplication facts. Here are a few:

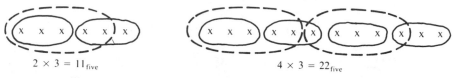

$2 \times 3 = 11_{five}$ $4 \times 3 = 22_{five}$

Here the solid loops indicate the original sets, and the dashed loops indicate the grouping in base five. Thus 2×3 (in base five) gives us enough objects for 1 five and 1 left over; 4×3 (in base five) gives us enough objects for 2 fives and 2 left over. A complete base five multiplication table is given in Figure 3-36.

FIGURE 3-36
Base Five Multiplication Table

$\times$	0	1	2	3	4
0	0	0	0	0	0
1	0	1	2	3	4
2	0	2	4	11_5	13_5
3	0	3	11_5	14_5	22_5
4	0	4	13_5	22_5	31_5

The properties for base five multiplication are analogous to the properties for base ten multiplication. We will reinforce these ideas with a fairly detailed example:

EXAMPLE 3-11

Illustrate the solution to $24_{five} \times 32_{five}$ using (a) the step-by-step mathematical justification, (b) the intermediate form of the algorithm, and (c) the shortened form of the algorithm.

SOLUTION

(a) $24_5 \times 32_5 = 24_5 \times (30_5 + 2)$

            $= 24_5 \times 30_5 + 24_5 \times 2$

            $= (20_5 + 4) \times 30_5 + (20_5 + 4) \times 2$

            $= 20_5 \times 30_5 + 4 \times 30_5 + 20_5 \times 2 + 4 \times 2$

            $= 1100_5 + 220_5 + 40_5 + 13_5$

            $= 1423_5$

In the second-to-last step, we used the basic fact from the base five multiplication table (Figure 3-36) that $2 \times 3 = 11_5$ to infer that $20_5 \times 30_5 = 1100_5$. This is like the "multiplying by multiples of ten" principle except that in this case it involves multiples of five. Similarly, $4 \times 30_5 = 220_5$. We leave it to you to supply the justification for the other steps.

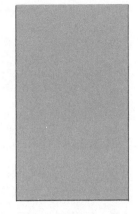

(b)
$$
\begin{array}{r}
24_5 \\
\times 32_5 \\
\hline
13_5 \\
40_5 \\
220_5 \\
1100_5 \\
\hline
1423_5
\end{array}
$$

(4×2)
$(20_5 \times 2)$
$(4 \times 30_5)$
$(20_5 \times 30_5)$

(c)
$$
\begin{array}{r}
24_5 \\
\times 32_5 \\
\hline
103_5 \\
1320_5 \\
\hline
1423_5
\end{array}
$$

EXERCISES AND PROBLEMS 3-5

ALGORITHM

1. Play the role of each of the eight children mentioned in the opening of Section 3-4 and do the problem 253×40 as each of them might do it.

2. Estimate the answer to 346×30 by doing 300×30 in your head. According to this estimate, which of the eight answers (see Problem 1) are obviously wrong? Is this a high estimate or a low estimate? What kind of estimate is 400×30?

3. Solve this cryptarithm. (See Problem 10, Section 1-2.)

$$
\begin{array}{r}
NORA \\
\times \quad L \\
\hline
ARON
\end{array}
$$

4. The **Russian peasant algorithm** is illustrated below:

~~68 × 51~~	27 × 320	~~28 × 119~~
~~34 × 102~~	13 × 640	~~14 × 238~~
17 × 204	~~6 × 1280~~	7 × 476
~~8 × 408~~	3 × 2560	3 × 952
~~4 × 816~~	1 × 5120	1 × 1904
~~2 × 1632~~	8640	3332
1 × 3264		
3468		

$\therefore 68 \times 51 = 3468$ $\therefore 27 \times 320 = 8640$ $\therefore 28 \times 119 = 3332$

Observe that numbers in the first column are halved (dropping any remainder), and that numbers in the second column are doubled. Entries where the first column is even are crossed out. Remaining entries in the second column are summed. Use the Russian peasant algorithm to compute

(a) 35×201 (b) 48×31 (c) 29×206

*(d) Explain why it works. (Hint: $68 \times 51 = (4 + 64) \times 51 = 204 + 3264 = 3468$.)

*(e) Relate Russian peasant multiplication to writing numbers in base two.

5. Squared paper works well in showing certain products.

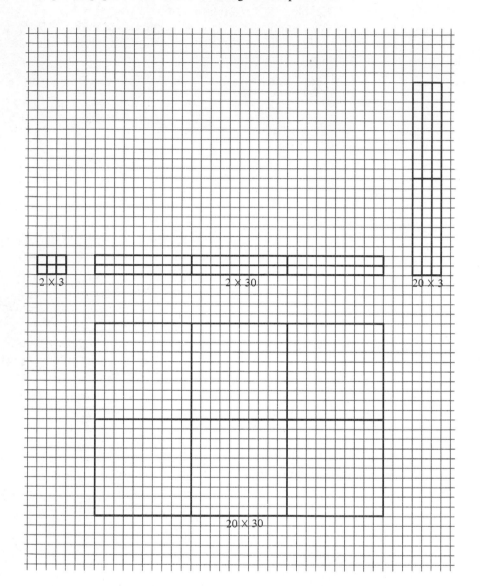

(a) What do 2×3, 2×30, 20×3, and 20×30 as illustrated on the squared paper have in common?

(b) The answer to 2×3 is 6 *units*, while the answer to 2×30 is 6 *tens*. What is the answer to 20×3? to 20×30?

(c) Use squared paper to show 2×4, 2×40, 20×4, and 20×40 in a similar way. (For example, show 2×40 as 8 tens.)

(d) Use squared paper to show these base five multiplications. Shade fives and twenty-fives when appropriate: 2×3, $2 \times 30_{\text{five}}$, $20_{\text{five}} \times 3$, $20_{\text{five}} \times 30_{\text{five}}$.

(e) Use squared paper to show these base five multiplications. Shade fives and twenty-fives when appropriate: 3×4, $3 \times 40_{\text{five}}$, $30_{\text{five}} \times 4$, $30_{\text{five}} \times 40_{\text{five}}$.

(f) Use squared paper to show 3×4, 3×40, 30×4, and 30×40. Shade to show that 3×4 is 1 ten and 2 ones, and that 3×40 is 1 hundred and 2 tens, etc.

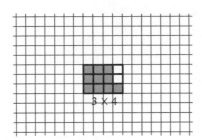

(g) The tens and hundreds or fives and twenty-fives give the same effect as Dienes' blocks. Which ones are longs? flats?

6. Show 17×41 on squared paper.

7. Lattice multiplication takes this form:

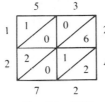 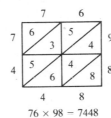 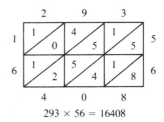

$$53 \times 24 = 1272 \qquad 76 \times 98 = 7448 \qquad 293 \times 56 = 16408$$

Study the examples to uncover the method. Use it to solve these problems:

(a) 42×65 (b) 21×13 (c) 46×35

(d) 259×37 (e) 816×974

8. Give a reason for each step in the following justification that $63 \times 10 = 630$:

$$
\begin{aligned}
63 \times 10 &= (60 + 3) \times 10 \\
&= 60 \times 10 + 3 \times 10 \\
&= (6 \times 10) \times 10 + 3 \times 10 \\
&= 6 \times (10 \times 10) + 3 \times 10 \\
&= 6 \times 100 + 3 \times 10 \\
&= 600 + 30 \\
&= 630
\end{aligned}
$$

9. Justify each step of 32×47 as it was written out on page 93-94.

10. State the values of p, q, m, and n in the multiplying by multiples of ten principle for the example 500×6000.

11. Draw a flowchart for multiplying a two-digit number by a one-digit number.

12. Order the problems below in increasing difficulty:

$$
\begin{array}{cccccc}
9 & 12 & 16 & 90 & 82 & 900 \\
\times 2 & \times 4 & \times 3 & \times 2 & \times 46 & \times 20
\end{array}
$$

13. Multiply in the given bases:

(a) 40_5 (b) 43_5 (c) 43_5 (d) 204_5
     $\times 3$ $\times 11_5$ $\times 23_5$ $\times 43_5$

(e) 32_4 (f) 32_{12} (g) $T6_{12}$ (h) 11001_2
     $\times 12_4$ $\times 12_{12}$ $\times 49_{12}$ $\times 1011_2$

(For more problems related to other bases see Problems 4 and 16.)

CALCULATORS

C14. This is a modification of a game described by Glenda Lappan and Mary Winter in the April 1978 *Arithmetic Teacher* [57]. Two players alternate turns. For each turn a player selects a pair of numbers from those on a grid like the one shown below. A calculator is used to find the product of the numbers. The player then covers the box containing that number with a marker. If it is already covered by a marker his turn is over. The first player to get five in a row (horizontally, vertically, or diagonally) wins. (The game can be modified so that the winner must have four or six in a row, but experience in the classroom shows that six in a row is difficult.)

368	91	1652	299	161	437
364	304	301	2537	644	592
688	247	2183	532	767	112
1591	1121	703	133	1204	208
259	1357	413	1036	481	944
817	559	851	448	196	989

FACTOR LIST: 7   23   43   59   16   13   37   19   28

(a) Play the game with someone a few times.

(b) How many boxes are in the grid?

(c) How many products are possible for the given list of numbers? Are they all different? How can you tell?

(d) Suppose the factor list were $1, 2, 3, 4, 5, 6, 7, 8, 9$. Note that 2×6 and 3×4 give the same product. Find another pair of problems that give the same product.

*(e) Find the nine smallest positive whole numbers that can be used so that all the products are different.

(f) How many different products are possible if the list has ten numbers? (We do not multiply a number by itself.)

(g) Suppose you wanted to capture the box with the 1036. List all pairs of factors on the list which when multiplied give a product ending in 6. Use estimation to pick the right pair. Multiply. Were you correct?

(h) This game is appropriate for what grade level?

(i) Modify it so that it is suitable for first graders.

P15. Note that $153 = 1^3 + 5^3 + 3^3$; namely, 153 equals the sum of the cubes of its digits. Find another three-digit number with this property.

C16. Consult the article "Using a Calculator to Do Arithmetic in Bases Other Than 10" by J. Schultz [60] and solve these problems using a calculator. In each case write out the problems and answers using the block notation described in the article. Then give the answer in the usual form. (For bases greater than ten, A = 10, B = 11, C = 12, etc.)

(a) $\begin{array}{r} 23_5 \\ +14_5 \\ \hline \end{array}$ **(b)** $\begin{array}{r} 43_5 \\ +34_5 \\ \hline \end{array}$ **(c)** $\begin{array}{r} 324_5 \\ +\ 43_5 \\ \hline \end{array}$ **(d)** $\begin{array}{r} 34_7 \\ +25_7 \\ \hline \end{array}$

(e) $\begin{array}{r} 43_5 \\ -24_5 \\ \hline \end{array}$ **(f)** $\begin{array}{r} 402_5 \\ -231_5 \\ \hline \end{array}$ **(g)** $\begin{array}{r} 322_4 \\ -133_4 \\ \hline \end{array}$ **(h)** $\begin{array}{r} 204_{17} \\ -1B1_{17} \\ \hline \end{array}$

(i) $\begin{array}{r} 32_5 \\ \times 12_5 \\ \hline \end{array}$ **(j)** $\begin{array}{r} 62_8 \\ \times 35_8 \\ \hline \end{array}$ **(k)** $\begin{array}{r} 5A_{11} \\ \times 67_{11} \\ \hline \end{array}$ **(l)** $\begin{array}{r} A4_{20} \\ \times CF_{20} \\ \hline \end{array}$

C17. (a) Find the last four digits of $257{,}987{,}601{,}389{,}572 \times 255{,}783{,}429{,}942$ (even though your calculator probably can't handle numbers this large).

(b) Repeat part (a) for $793{,}872{,}030{,}817 \times 422{,}891{,}776{,}034$.

(c) Find the first four digits of the two products given in parts (b) and (c).

(d) Use a strategy similar to the one you used to do parts (a)-(c) to find *all* the digits of $814{,}203{,}916 \times 423{,}116{,}904$. (Hint: Split each of the numbers into blocks of three and multiply the blocks.)

PROBLEM SOLVING EXTENSIONS

18. Diagnose the error pattern and tell what you think each student will get for the last problem. (These examples are based on actual examples from children's papers.)

Art:

$2 \times 2 \times 3 = 46$
$4 \times 3 \times 5 = 1215$
$2 \times 4 \times 7 = $

Becky:

$\begin{array}{r} 22 \\ \times\ 4 \\ \hline 28 \end{array}$ $\begin{array}{r} 313 \\ \times\ 2 \\ \hline 316 \end{array}$ $\begin{array}{r} 43 \\ \times 27 \\ \hline 101 \end{array}$ $\begin{array}{r} 82 \\ \times 35 \\ \hline 250 \end{array}$ $\begin{array}{r} 94 \\ \times 26 \\ \hline \end{array}$

Cindy:

$\begin{array}{r} 346 \\ \times\ 30 \\ \hline 10440 \end{array}$ $\begin{array}{r} 65 \\ \times\ 3 \\ \hline 255 \end{array}$ $\begin{array}{r} 61 \\ \times 32 \\ \hline 122 \\ 243 \\ \hline 2552 \end{array}$ $\begin{array}{r} 46 \\ \times 23 \\ \hline \end{array}$

19. Show that there are 362,880 ways to fill in the nine boxes in Problem 2, Section 1-1, with the nine different digits 1 through 9. (Of course only two ways are correct.)

20. Suppose a lock combination consists of three numbers from 1 to 20 inclusive.

(a) How many combinations are possible if there are no further restrictions?

(b) How many are possible if the middle number must be different from the other two?

21. **(a)** Solve the handshake problem (Problem 3, Section 1-1) using the Fundamental Counting Principle.   **(b)** Solve the problem if there were 100 people at the party.

22. The symbol 4! (read "four **factorial**") means $4 \times 3 \times 2 \times 1$. Similarly 6! (read "six factorial") means $6 \times 5 \times 4 \times 3 \times 2 \times 1$. Thus 4! = 24 and 6! = 720. Compute the following: **(a)** 3!   **(b)** 5!   **(c)** 7!

23. Certain multiplication problems lend themselves to a special trick. Here are some examples:

$$
\begin{array}{ccccc}
87 & 52 & 19 & 75 & 94 \\
\times 83 & \times 58 & \times 11 & \times 75 & \times 96 \\
\hline
7221 & 3016 & 209 & 5625 & 9024 \\
\end{array}
$$

   (a) Make up three other problems which can be done using this trick.
   (b) Find three which can't.
   (c) Describe the necessary conditions for applying the trick.
   *(d) Prove that the trick works.

24. Kim: I like the number 12,345,679. What one-digit number do you like?
   Mary: 8.
   Kim: Fine. I like the number 72. Would you multiply 12,345,679 by 72, please, and tell me how you like the answer?
   Mary: I got 888,888,888. How did you do that?!
   (a) Kim was ready for any one-digit number Mary might have given her. What would she have used instead of the 72 if Mary had chosen 6?
   (b) How *did* Kim do it?!

25. Find these products:

   $1 \cdot 1 =$
   $11 \cdot 11 =$
   $111 \cdot 111 =$
   $1111 \cdot 1111 =$

   Based on the pattern, guess at:

   $111111111 \cdot 111111111 =$

26. Suppose we use $2 \wedge 3$ to represent 2^3. (Some computer languages use this notation.) Then $2 \wedge 3 = 2^3$ or 8, and $3 \wedge 2 = 3^2$ or 9.
   (a) Find $5 \wedge 2$.
   (b) Find $2 \wedge 5$.
   (c) Is the operation "$\wedge$" commutative?
   (d) Is the operation "$\wedge$" associative?

27. **(a)** The numbers $1, 3, 6, 10, \ldots$ are called **triangular numbers** for reasons suggested by the following figures:

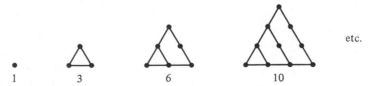

   Find the next three triangular numbers.
   (b) Find the triangular numbers in Pascal's triangle (Problem 43 of Section 2-1).

(c) Bowling pins are arranged in a triangle. How many are there? What sport or game uses 15 balls arranged in a triangle?

(d) The numbers 1, 4, 9, 16, . . . are called square numbers.

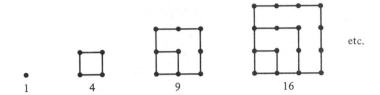

Find the next three square numbers.

(e) Add pairs of consecutive triangular numbers. Describe the resulting numbers.

(f) Find the smallest number (greater than 1) which is both a triangular number and a square number.

*P***(g)** Find the next two numbers which are both triangular numbers and square numbers.

28. (a) Express 365 as the sum of two consecutive squares. **(b)** Express 365 as the sum of three consecutive squares. **(c)** 365 is the smallest whole number that can be expressed in both of these ways. Why else is 365 a well-known number?

29. Show $(a + b)^2 = a^2 + 2ab + b^2$ using the rectangle model. (Hint: See Figure 3-35.)

3-6
DIVISION OF WHOLE NUMBERS

Now that you have thought carefully about addition, subtraction, and multiplication in the first five sections of this chapter, it is appropriate for you to try to anticipate what kinds of questions need to be answered about division, the fourth of the major operations defined for whole numbers. Think about this and then compare your thoughts with those on the following list:

How is division defined? What is the algorithm (process) to be used for dividing one arbitrary whole number by another; how and why does it work? Are there properties that help to make things easier?

We will examine these questions and others in light of our earlier work. With respect to each of these inquiries, would you expect division to behave most like addition, subtraction, or multiplication? By the end of this section, you not only ought to understand each of the operations individually, but you also should be aware of the relationships between them. It is no coincidence that the definition, algorithm, and properties for division will emerge in a way similar to that for the other operations.

We will begin with a model for the problem $12 \div 3 = 4$ and generalize the definition from it. Suppose we wish to divide 12 marbles among three children so that each child gets the same number of marbles. How many marbles should be given to each child? Let's pretend we don't know the answer and look for a procedure that will find it. We could begin by distributing one marble to each child. We would then see that there were enough marbles left to give each of them another, and would do so. In the same way, we would repeat the distribution twice more until the supply was exhausted. We would have split the set of 12 marbles into three sets each containing four marbles. Thus $12 \div 3$ is the number of members in each of three disjoint matching sets whose union has 12 members. The generalization of this example is our

☐ Definition of Division of Whole Numbers

> If a and b are whole numbers (and b is not 0), then the **quotient** of a and b, denoted $a \div b$, is the number of members in each of b disjoint matching sets whose union has a members. The number a is called the **dividend** and the number b is called the **divisor**.

Consistent with the definitions of the other operations, we also find that the quotient is the number of members in some set (or sets). It is most like the definition of multiplication. In fact, going back to the example, if we knew how to multiply (but not necessarily how to divide) we could easily anticipate the outcome without physically distributing the marbles. We would do this by realizing that

Giving Each Child	Would Require
1 marble	3 marbles
2 marbles	6 marbles
3 marbles	9 marbles
4 marbles	12 marbles

Thus $12 \div 3$ is the missing factor in a multiplication problem, $3 \times \square = 12$. This generalizes into our "missing factor"

☐ Alternative Definition of Division of Whole Numbers

> If a and b are whole numbers (and b is not 0), then the quotient of a and b, denoted $a \div b$, is the (whole number) answer to the question $b \times \square = a$.

Attempting to apply the definitions to division by 0 has unsatisfactory results. For instance, the alternative definition applied to $5 \div 0$ says that $5 \div 0 = \square$ is equivalent to $0 \times \square = 5$, which has no solution. Clearly $p \div 0 = \square$, which is equivalent to $0 \times \square = p$, would have no solution unless p were 0. Now $0 \div 0 = \square$ means $0 \times \square = 0$. The trouble this time is that *any* whole number is a solution. So we exclude 0 as a divisor because it behaves so badly, giving either no solution or too many solutions.

Not only does each of these definitions exclude division by 0, but each severely limits division among the other whole numbers. Even in so simple a case as $2 \div 3$ there is no solution (among the whole numbers). Moreover, the problem $3 \div 2$ has no solution either, so things are even worse than with subtraction where it was simply a matter of subtracting smaller numbers from larger ones. You will find that among the whole numbers 0 through 9, only 32 division problems are defined, and more than half of those are trivial instances involving 0 or 1. Thus in many cases (actually in *most* cases), these definitions do not permit division of one arbitrary whole number by another.

Fortunately there are ways of modifying the definition of division to obtain meaningful results in most cases. For instance, if we had 13 marbles to distribute equally among three children, we could pass out 12 of them as before and withhold the odd marble. Or if we were dividing two pizzas among three people, we could use fractions to provide them with equal amounts. We will discuss the first of these options (division with remainder) now, and the second (use of fractions) in a later chapter. Each of these approaches will resolve most of the shortcomings, so that it will be possible to divide one arbitrary whole number by another — except that division by 0 will remain undefined.

To provide a setting for the discussion of our modified form of division (division with remainder), we will consider some representative problems. It would not be inappropriate to think in terms of dividing marbles among children, though of course the mathematics is valid independent of any physical objects.

To Divide	By	You Get	With This Left Over
12	3	4	0
13	3	4	1
14	3	4	2
15	3	5	0
16	3	5	1
17	3	5	2
18	3	6	0

The main idea to note here is that each of these represents the best of several alternatives. For example, here are the alternatives for $16 \div 3$:

To Divide	By	You Get	With This Left Over
16	3	0	16
16	3	1	13
16	3	2	10
16	3	3	7
16	3	4	4
16	3	5	1

One of our goals in mathematics is to avoid ambiguities, so we will select a single outcome from these choices, the one in which the number left over (the remainder) is minimal. Hence we will agree that in doing division with remainder, $16 \div 3$ is 5 with remainder 1.

A natural question arises at this point. In doing this modified division, following the rule of selecting the quotient and remainder such that the remainder is minimal, is there always exactly one answer to each problem? It turns out that we can be quite specific and state what we will call

☐ The Quotient-Remainder Theorem

> Given any whole numbers a and b (b cannot be 0), there is exactly one whole number q (called the **quotient**) and exactly one whole number r (called the **remainder**) such that $r < b$ and $b \times q + r = a$.

(When we apply this theorem to find the values of q and r, we will often refer to it as the **division algorithm**.) We choose not to give a formal proof, but will instead provide some illustrative examples.

Determining q and r can be visualized readily in terms of the marble distribution problem. Suppose that the number of marbles we have is a, and we wish to distribute them to b children. If there are more marbles than children, we give everybody one. If there are still enough marbles left, we give everyone another one. This continues until the number left (perhaps none) is less than the number of children. The number of marbles each child receives is q; the number of marbles remaining is r. Surely there is ultimately only one value of q (for if we had two or more choices of how many marbles to distribute, we would always opt for the greatest possible amount that does not exceed our supply and thus arrive at a single value for q) and only one value of r (exactly the amount of marbles left over). Moreover $r < b$ (for if the number of marbles left over equaled or exceeded the number of children we would distribute at least one more round).

Next we will consider some numerical examples. Situations for which the definition of division given earlier applied (such as $12 \div 3$, $14 \div 7$, etc., but *not* $3 \div 2$) are special cases of the quotient-remainder theorem and will be dealt with first. By the alternate form of the definition, we have, for example, that $12 \div 3 = 4$ since $3 \times 4 = 12$. The number 4, which we called the "quotient" in the earlier definitions is also the desired "quotient" in the quotient-remainder theorem. In this problem the "remainder" is 0, which certainly satisfies the conditions of being a whole number less than 3, the value of b. Thus given that $a = 12$ and $b = 3$, we see that $q = 4$ and $r = 0$, so that the quotient-remainder thorem says in this case that

> Given whole numbers 12 and 3 (3 is not 0) there is exactly one whole number 4 (called the quotient) and exactly one whole number 0 (called the remainder) such that $0 < 3$ and $3 \times 4 + 0 = 12$.

We have clearly found whole numbers q and r (4 and 0 respectively) that satisfy the conditions $r < b$ and $b \times q + r = a$, but the theorem proclaims more than the existence of such numbers. It further says that these are the *only* whole numbers satisfying these conditions. How can we be sure that there are no others? First we see that if q is 4, we have $3 \times 4 + r = 12$ so r must be 0; namely, no other remainder is possible. Now suppose that q is not 4. Then either $q < 4$ or $q > 4$. (What property is this?) If $q < 4$, then $3 \times q$ is at most 9, and since $3 \times q + r = 12$, r would have to be at least 3. This violates the condition that $r < b$. If $q > 4$, then $3 \times q$ is at least 15, so there can be no whole number r such that $3 \times q + r = 12$. Roughly speaking, this says that if you find a q and r which work, a smaller choice of q will force r to be too large, and a larger choice of q will force r to be "too small" (smaller than any whole number).

The preceding argument is representative of what happens when we are given numbers a and b for which $a \div b$ is defined. Now suppose we are given numbers a and b for which $a \div b$ is not defined (though we still insist that $b \neq 0$). For example, suppose $q = 16$ and $b = 3$. You will recall that we listed six pairs of numbers q and r such that $b \times q + r = a$. Once again, these were

$$q = 0, \; r = 16, \qquad 3 \times 0 + 16 = 16$$
$$q = 1, \; r = 13, \qquad 3 \times 1 + 13 = 16$$
$$q = 2, \; r = 10, \qquad 3 \times 2 + 10 = 16$$
$$q = 3, \; r = 7, \qquad 3 \times 3 + 7 = 16$$
$$q = 4, \; r = 4, \qquad 3 \times 4 + 4 = 16$$
$$q = 5, \; r = 1, \qquad 3 \times 5 + 1 = 16$$

Note that among all of the possibilities, there is only one q and one r (5 and 1 respectively) such that $r < b$ and $b \times q + r = a$ are both true. Once again, smaller values of q force r to be too large, larger values of q force r to be too large, and larger values of q make it impossible to satisfy $b \times q + r = a$ for any whole number r.

To further clarify the relationship among the dividend (a), the divisor (b), the quotient (q), and the remainder (r), we paraphrase the quotient-remainder theorem as it applies to this example:

> Given whole numbers 16 and 3 (3 is not 0), there is exactly one whole number 5 (called the *quotient*) and exactly one whole number 1 (called the *remainder*) such that $1 < 3$ and $3 \times 5 + 1 = 16$.

A few additional examples show, among other things, that the quotient-remainder theorem applies even when the divisor is larger than the dividend.

Find the quotient and remainder for

(a) $5\overline{)19}$ (b) $3\overline{)2}$ (c) $15\overline{)15}$

(We will use the symbol "$a\overline{)b}$" to represent "dividing (with remainder) b by a.")

EXAMPLE 3-12

SOLUTION

(a) $5 \times 0 = 0,$ $r = 19$
    $5 \times 1 = 5,$ $r = 14$
    $5 \times 2 = 10,$ $r = 9$
    $5 \times 3 = 15,$ $r = 4$
    $5 \times 4 = 20,$ (too big)

So the quotient is 3 and the remainder is 4.

(b) $3 \times 0 = 0,$ $r = 2$
    $3 \times 1 = 3,$ (too big)

So the quotient is 0 and the remainder is 2.

(c) $15 \times 0 = 0$, $\qquad r = 15$
$15 \times 1 = 15$, $\qquad r = 0$
$15 \times 2 = 30$, $\qquad$ (too big)

So the quotient is 1 and the remainder is 0.

Of course, after we gain experience in multiplying, we could more directly predict the quotient. In part (a) of the example we might immediately recognize that 19 is between 15 (which is 3×5) and 20 (which is 4×5), so we could immediately conclude that $q = 3$.

The procedure of Example 3-12 works fine for numbers like those given, but what about problems involving larger numbers, such as $592\overline{)20225}$? The process which begins testing

$592 \times 0 = 0$, $\qquad r = 20225$
$592 \times 1 = 592$, $\qquad r = 19633$
$592 \times 2 = 1184$, $\qquad r = 19041$

would eventually yield the right answer, but it is far too tedious. Our next goal is to build a version of the customary algorithm that helps us arrive at the answer with less effort.

Our "passing out marbles" model tends to be a bit unrealistic here, but the idea of how it might be done is still somewhat suggestive of how to attack the problem. It would be quite natural if we were faced with this problem to pass out more than one marble at a time. Suppose that we pass out 10 marbles at a time as many times as possible.

Original amount:	20225	
Distribute 10 to each:	-5920	$= 592 \times 10$
Amount left:	14305	
Distribute 10 to each:	-5920	$= 592 \times 10$
Amount left:	8385	
Distribute 10 to each:	-5920	$= 592 \times 10$
Amount left:	2465	

At this point, the number left would be insufficient to distribute 10 more to each. We could get a clue to our next step by observing that 592×4 is less than $600 \times 4 = 2400$, so there would be enough marbles left to give everyone four more.

Amount left (from above):	2465	
Distribute 4 to each:	-2368	$= 592 \times 4$
Amount left:	97	

The balance of 97 is insufficient to permit further handouts, so we have a remainder of 97. Since each person would receive a total of $10 + 10 + 10 + 4$, the quotient is 34.

When students are at the introductory stage of doing long division, this would not be an unreasonable approach to doing the problem. As multiplication skills were improved, students might correctly estimate that the original supply would be sufficient to distribute 30 the very first time. This might be apparent from the fact that 592×30 is less than $600 \times 30 = 18000$. Then, the organization of the solution might look like this:

Original amount:	20225	
Distribute 30 to each:	-17760	$= 592 \times 30$
Amount left:	2465	
Distribute 4 to each:	-2368	$= 592 \times 4$
	97	$q = 34,\ r = 97$

Once the students understood the process, it could be further abbreviated to

$$592\overline{)20225}$$
$$\underline{-17760} \qquad = 592 \times 30$$
$$2465$$
$$\underline{-2368} \qquad = 592 \times 4$$
$$97 \qquad\qquad q = 34,\ r = 97$$

which is the algorithm used in many elementary school texts, and which in any case resembles most of the common algorithms now in use. This approach, called the **scaffold** method (in that we "build up" to the quotient) has at least three advantages. First, every entry is meaningful in that it can be visualized in terms of the distribution process illustrated above. Second, the position of each number is automatically accounted for. The 0 which appears on the end of 17760 as a result of multiplying by 30, for instance, helps students to write

$$592\overline{)20225}$$
$$-17760$$

rather than

$$592\overline{)20225}$$
$$-1776$$

as is often done with less meaningful algorithms. Third, this format does not severely penalize students who might incorrectly estimate that there are only twenty 592's in 20225 (or in terms of the older algorithm first learned by the author, "592 goes into 2022 two times"). Compare this old approach with the one described above:

2	$592\overline{)20225}$
$592\overline{)20225}$	$\underline{-11840} \quad = 592 \times 20$
$\underline{1184}$	8385
838	$\underline{-5920} \quad = 592 \times 10$
	2465
(Erase and start over, since $838 > 592$.)	

Old Approach   *Repeated Subtraction Approach*

So long as the estimates are *low* estimates, we can continue the process without backtracking.

We now consider the matter of finding low estimates and give several examples.

For the last time, we will consider our overworked example of distributing marbles. If we wished to guard against distributing too many marbles (so that there would not be enough to go around), we could protect ourselves a bit by acting either as if we had fewer marbles or as if there were more children. Thus, to get a low estimate, we could round *down* the dividend and round *up* the divisor. Some examples follow:

Original Problem	Round Off to	Low Estimate of q
$2465 \div 592$	$2400 \div 600$	4
$20225 \div 592$	$18000 \div 600$	30
$4321 \div 76$	$4000 \div 80$	50
$66591 \div 136$	$60000 \div 200$	300

In each case, the estimate was arrived at through the following procedure:

(1) Round *up* the divisor so all but the first digit are 0's.
(2) Round *down* the dividend to a number whose first digits are a multiple of the first digit of the divisor and whose remaining digits are 0.
(3) Use the missing factor interpretation for division to determine the estimate.

These rules for estimating should not be regarded as inflexible. In many cases, better estimates can be obtained with slight alterations. For example, in estimating $66591 \div 136$, a better low estimate is obtained by rounding to $60000 \div 150$. The nice feature of these rules is, however, that they will always lead to the correct answer without backtracking.

A suggestion about determining the number of zeros in the answers to

$$2400 \div 600$$
$$18000 \div 600$$
$$4000 \div 80$$
$$60000 \div 200$$

may be in order.

Think of	As	Which Is
$2400 \div 600$	$24 \div 6$	4
$18000 \div 600$	$180 \div 6$	30
$4000 \div 80$	$400 \div 8$	50
$60000 \div 200$	$600 \div 2$	300

To build up this ability, students might be convinced through prior exercises of this type:

$$6 \times 4 = 24, \qquad so \qquad 24 \div 6 \ = 4$$

$$60 \times 4 = 240, \qquad \text{so} \qquad 240 \div 60 \ \ = 4$$
$$600 \times 4 = 2400, \qquad \text{so} \qquad 2400 \div 600 \ \ = 4$$
$$6000 \times 4 = 24000, \qquad \text{so} \qquad 24000 \div 6000 = 4$$

From this, students could generalize a rule.

We are now ready for further examples of the division algorithm.

Use the scaffold form of the division algorithm to compute

(a) $76\overline{)4321}$ (b) $136\overline{)66591}$

EXAMPLE 3-13

SOLUTION

(a)
$$
\begin{array}{r}
76\overline{)4321} \\
-3800 \\
\hline
521 \\
-456 \\
\hline
65
\end{array}
$$
$= 76 \times 50$ (Estimate $4000 \div 80 = 50$.)

$= 76 \times 6$ (Estimate $480 \div 80 = 6$.)

$q = 56, \quad r = 65$

(b)
$$
\begin{array}{r}
136\overline{)66591} \\
-54400 \\
\hline
12191 \\
-8160 \\
\hline
4031 \\
-2720 \\
\hline
1311 \\
-816 \\
\hline
495 \\
-408 \\
\hline
87
\end{array}
$$
$= 136 \times 400$ (Estimate $60000 \div 150 = 400$.)

$= 136 \times 60$ (Estimate $12000 \div 200 = 60$.)

$= 136 \times 20$ (Estimate $4000 \div 200 = 20$.)

$= 136 \times 6$ (Estimate $1200 \div 200 = 6$.)

$= 136 \times 3$ (Estimate $450 \div 150 = 3$.)

$q = 489, \quad r = 87$

Notice that in doing part (b), some judgment was exercised in forming estimates. In two cases 136 was rounded up to 150, and in three cases it was rounded up to 200. Other alternatives are also possible. For the student who doesn't feel good about making these choices, the three-step procedure outlined earlier will always apply, though it may require more steps in some problems.

Clearly, use of the algorithm described above, or almost any form of the division algorithm, depends to a great extent on proficiency with multiplication and subtraction. This is likely to be more apparent when we practice using the algorithm in other bases.

We will illustrate the repeated subtraction algorithm for some base five problems. Much like the way each addition fact corresponds to a subtraction fact, we now know that each multiplication fact corresponds to some division fact. Here are two examples based on the multiplication table for base five given in Figure 3-36, page 96:

$$2 \times 3 = 11_{\text{five}}, \quad \text{so} \quad 11_{\text{five}} \div 2 = 3$$
$$4 \times 3 = 22_{\text{five}}, \quad \text{so} \quad 22_{\text{five}} \div 4 = 3$$

From the problem $24_{\text{five}} \times 32_{\text{five}} = 1423_{\text{five}}$ of Example 3-11, we get the corresponding division problem $1423_{\text{five}} \div 24_{\text{five}} = 32_{\text{five}}$. We will use this as our first example of applying the division algorithm in other bases.

EXAMPLE 3-14

Use the scaffold form of the division algorithm to compute

(a) $24_{\text{five}}\overline{)1423_{\text{five}}}$ (b) $33_{\text{five}}\overline{)2414_{\text{five}}}$

SOLUTION

(All numbers are in base five.)

(a) $24\overline{)1423}$ (Estimate $1400 \div 30 = 30$)
$$\underline{-1320} = 24 \times 30$$
$$103$$ (Estimate $30 \div 30 = 1$)
$$\underline{-24} = 24 \times 1$$
$$24$$
$$\underline{-24} = 24 \times 1$$

$$q = 32_{\text{five}}, \quad r = 0$$

In estimating $1423_{\text{five}} \div 24_{\text{five}}$, we round the divisor to 30_{five}. The multiplication table shows that 14_{five} is a multiple of 3, so we round 1423_{five} to 1400_{five}. This gives an estimate of 30_{five}, so we subtract $24_{\text{five}} \times 30_{\text{five}}$. Of course, the multiplication and subtraction are done in base five. The 103_{five} which remains is sufficient to subtract 24_{five} twice more.

(All numbers are in base five.)

(b) $33\overline{)2414}$ (Estimate $2200 \div 40 = 30$.)
$$\underline{-2040} = 33 \times 30$$
$$324$$ (Estimate $310 \div 40 = 4$.)
$$\underline{-242} = 33 \times 4$$
$$32$$ $q = 34_{\text{five}}, \quad r = 32_{\text{five}}$

Division problems in other bases follow the same procedure shown in the examples. The complexity of the division algorithm may render it obsolete as calculators gain popularity.

Following are some of the ways the four basic operations are interrelated.

1. Subtraction can be defined in terms of addition. Division can be defined in terms of multiplication.
2. Multiplication is repeated addition. Division is repeated subtraction. (See calculator exercises.)
3. Addition and multiplication of whole numbers each satisfy properties of closure, commutativity, associativity, and identity. Subtraction enjoys none of these properties. (You will be asked to investigate which properties hold for division.)

Figure 3-37 summarizes some of these ideas.

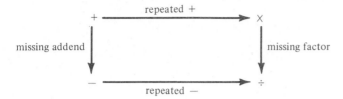

FIGURE 3-37

EXERCISES AND PROBLEMS 3-6

DEFINITION AND SETS

1. Write the missing addend definition of subtraction. What changes are necessary to reword this into the missing factor interpretation of division?

2. One definition of multiplication says that $a \times b$ is the number of objects in an array with a rows and b columns. Formulate an alternate definition of division based on this interpretation.

3. In our marbles example, $12 \div 3$ told "how many marbles per set." Approaching it from a different angle, suppose we had 12 marbles and gave three to each child. Then $12 \div 3$ would be "how many sets." Formulate an alternate definition of division based on this interpretation.

4. Which of these is (are) undefined? (a) $5 \div 0$ (b) $0 \div 5$ (c) $0 \div 0$

5. There are 32 division problems (without remainder) where one member of the set $\{0, 1, 2, 3, \ldots, 9\}$ is divided by another (possibly the same) member of this set. List them. How many problems are defined among the members of the set $\{2, 3, 4, 5, \ldots, 10\}$?

6. Suppose in doing the division algorithm that we permitted remainders larger than the divisor. List three possible answers (quotients and remainders) for the problem $19 \div 4$. How many such answers are possible?

7. Suppose we applied the division algorithm to the problem $3 \div 0$. How many answers (quotients and remainders) are possible? How many answers would be possible if we permitted remainders larger than the divisor?

8. How many possible remainders are there when dividing by 7? By 17? By 1? How many possible quotients are there when dividing by 7? By 17? By 1?

9. In discussing the quotient-remainder theorem, we said, "Now suppose q is not 4. Then either $q < 4$ or $q > 4$." What property tells us this?

10. Paraphrase the quotient-remainder theorem for the problem $29 \div 6$.

11. Find the quotient and remainder for (a) $5 \div 2$ (b) $2 \div 5$.

12. Explain how to find the answer to $72 \div 9$ in a multiplication table.

13. We know that $100 \div 10 = 10$. What can you say about the quotient when 100 is divided by a number larger than 10? Smaller than 10?

14. How many hours and how many minutes is 144 minutes?

15. (a) If we count one number per second, guess how long it will take to count to one million.
    (b) Now compute the answer, answering in appropriate units.

16. State an arithmetic problem (such as $6 \div 2 = 3$) that corresponds to each of the following statements about sets:
    (a) $\{r, s, t, u\} \setminus \{r, s\} = \{t, u\}$
    (b) $\{a, b\} \times \{d, e\} = \{(a, d), (a, e), (b, d), (b, e)\}$
    (c) $\{x, y\} \cup \{v, z\} = \{x, y, v, z\}$

PROPERTIES

17. Which of the properties (closure, commutative, associative, identity) hold for division (without remainder) of whole numbers?

18. Tell whether the given set has the property named for the given operation, where $W = \{whole\ numbers\}$.

Set	Operation	Closure	Commutative	Associative	(Two-Sided) Identity
W	$+$	Yes			
W	$-$				
W	$\times$				
W	$\div$				
$\{1\}$	$+$				
$\{1\}$	$\times$				
$\{1\}$	$\div$				

ALGORITHM

19. Use the method of this section to obtain a low estimate for
    (a) $206 \div 48$ (b) $331 \div 77$ (c) $293 \div 21$

20. Use the scaffold form of the division algorithm to compute
    (a) $48\overline{)1300}$ (b) $56\overline{)4091}$ (c) $72\overline{)42785}$

21. (a) 89,257 was divided by a certain number giving a quotient of 427 and a remainder of 14. What was the divisor?
    (b) A student accidentally erased a long-division example. He could only recall that the successive subtrahends starting from the top were 690, 2415, and 2070 and that the remainder was 1. With this information he restored the problem. Can you?

OTHER BASES

22. Use the scaffold form of the division algorithm to compute
    (a) $43_{five}\overline{)3034_{five}}$ (b) $21_{five}\overline{)4114_{five}}$ (c) $24_{five}\overline{)31022_{five}}$

Write out a base six multiplication table. Use it to help compute each of these by the scaffold form of the division algorithm.

(d) $35_{six}\overline{)4012_{six}}$ (e) $54_{six}\overline{)34512_{six}}$ (f) $45_{six}\overline{)24531_{six}}$

MATERIALS AND CALCULATORS

23. As a kindergarten teacher you have two children who are to split a set of 30 identical blocks evenly. Tell them how to do the task, given that neither of them can count dependably past 10.

L24. Illustrate each of the following problems using Cuisenaire rods:

(a) $2\overline{)8}$ (b) $3\overline{)15}$ (c) $4\overline{)11}$

L25. (a) Using base ten Dienes' blocks, start with pile A: four flats, two longs, and four units. Separate it unto three identical piles, exchanging whenever necessary. Record the results in the following chart and alongside as a division problem in base ten.

	Flats	Longs	Units
Pile A			
Quotient			
Remainder			

(b) Repeat part (a) using base five blocks.
(c) Repeat part (a) using base six blocks.

L26. Illustrate each of the following problems using Dienes' blocks; using chips:

(a) $3\overline{)38}$ (b) $3\overline{)502}$ (c) $7\overline{)297}$

27. Examine one or more elementary text series to see how and when division of whole numbers is introduced.

C28. (a) Use a calculator to compute $7\overline{)56}$ *without using the* $\div$ *button.* Describe your procedure.
(b) Do the same for $9\overline{)103.}$
(c) Do the same for $89\overline{)593.}$

C29. Describe a procedure for computing the quotient and remainder on a calculator that expresses answers (for problems like $4\overline{)21}$) as decimals.

C30. (Target Game.) Using *only* the $\boxplus$, $\boxminus$, $\boxtimes$, $\boxdiv$, $\boxminus$, and $\boxed{7}$ keys (no other numbers), tell how to obtain the following target numbers:

(a) 35   (b) 1   (c) 2   (d) 84   (e) 100

P31. Write a program that gives a quotient and a remainder for division (rather than a decimal). This program will be useful later on.

PROBLEM SOLVING EXTENSIONS

32. The L-1011 aircraft has a fuel capacity of over 23,000 gallons. (a) How many 15-gallon automobile gas tanks will this fill? (b) At 30 miles to the gallon, how many miles can a car travel on 23,000 gallons of fuel?

33. Scott consistently made errors on problems like these:

$$\underset{8)\overline{4824}}{63} \qquad \underset{5)\overline{1535}}{37} \qquad \underset{9)\overline{3645}}{45}$$

(a) What is his error pattern?   (b) How can you help him?   (c) Would estimation help Scott? Explain.

Tom worked the same problems but got these answers:

$$\underset{8)\overline{4824}}{630} \qquad \underset{5)\overline{1535}}{370} \qquad \underset{9)\overline{3645}}{450}$$

(d) What is his error pattern?   (e) How can you help him?   (f) Would estimation help Tom? Explain.

34. The following question appeared on a grade 8 mathematics assessment test with pupils responding as indicated:

If John drives his car at an average speed of 50 miles per hour, how long will it take him to drive 275 miles?	
A. 5 hours, 5 minutes	(21%)
B. 5 hours, 25 minutes	(38%)
C. 5 hours, 30 minutes	(36%)
D. 2 hours, 5 minutes	(3%)
E. I don't know	(3%)

(a) Which response is correct?   (b) Can you account for why students so often chose the two incorrect responses?

35. A certain car gets 23 miles per gallon and has a 27-gallon fuel tank. How many miles can it go on a tank of gasoline?

36. A certain "regular" brand of cigarettes contains 11 milligrams of tar per cigarette while a "low tar" brand contains 6 milligrams per cigarette.
   (a) How much more tar is contained in a package (20 cigarettes) of the "regular" cigarettes than in a package of "low tar" cigarettes?
   (b) How much more tar is contained in a package of the "low tar" cigarettes than in no cigarettes?
   (c) Sue smoked a package of regular cigarettes each day for a year. How much tar was contained in these cigarettes?
   (d) A nickel weighs 5000 milligrams (5 grams). Express your answer to part (c) in terms of nickels.

37. To avoid ambiguities, a set of rules has been established governing order of operations where there are no parentheses to indicate the sequence in which they should be done. First, do all multiplications and divisions in order from left to right. Then, do all additions and subtractions in order from left to right.

Examples:

$$2 + 3 \times 4 = 14$$
$$2 \times 3 + 4 = 10$$
$$(2 + 3) \times 4 = 20$$
$$8 \div 4 \times 2 = 4$$

$$8 \times 4 \div 2 = 16$$
$$10 - 5 - 2 = 3$$

Use these rules to compute the following:
(a) $3 \times 4 + 2$ (b) $3 + 4 \times 2$ (c) $24 \div 4 + 2$
(d) $24 + 4 \div 2$ (e) $100 \div 20 \div 5$

38. Observe the correspondence between the following two problems:

$$4 \quad + \quad 3 \quad = \quad 7$$
$$\updownarrow \quad\quad \updownarrow \quad\quad \updownarrow \quad\quad \updownarrow \quad\quad \updownarrow$$
$$2^4 \quad \times \quad 2^3 \quad = \quad 2^7$$

(Convince yourself that $2^4 \times 2^3 = 2^7$ by computing 2^4, 2^3, and 2^7.) Find a problem involving exponents which corresponds in the same way to $6 - 2 = 4$. Check your results.

39. Shirley is sewing a blouse. The front of the blouse is 52 centimeters from top to bottom. Buttons are to be placed 8 centimeters apart beginning 1 centimeter from the top of the blouse.   **(a)** How many buttons are needed?   **(b)** How far will the last button be from the bottom?

40. Solve the well-known "bellhop problem": Three men register for a room costing $30, so each pays $10. The desk clerk later discovers that the rate should have been $25 and instructs the bellhop to return the difference. Unable to split the $5 evenly, the men take back $1 each and tip the bellhop $2. Thus each man paid $9, which is $27 in all, and the bellhop got $2. What happened to the other dollar?

41. When a three-digit number is divided by the sum of its digits, the quotient is 26. Find the smallest number meeting this condition.

42. When possible, express each of these as a single power of 10:
(a) $10^2 \times 10^5$ (b) $10^6 \div 10^2$ (c) $10^2 + 10^5$ (d) $10^6 - 10^2$

43. (a) What is half of 2^4? Express your answer as a power of 2.
(b) What is half of 2^{27}? Express your answer as a power of 2.

Number Theory

4-1
DIVISIBILITY

You can imagine how surprised the author was when an experienced teacher revealed that he did not know the meanings of "greatest common factor" and "least common multiple," though these terms could be found repeatedly in the sixth grade mathematics text from which the teacher taught. Since these concepts belong (and are!) in the elementary school mathematics curriculum, we will present them, along with some other important ideas, in this chapter. Later we will see that comparing fractions, adding fractions, and reducing fractions are just some of the arithmetic problems that involve these concepts.

A useful technique to help in understanding number theory is to take given whole numbers and view them as products of smaller whole numbers. One illustration of how this can be of use is given in Example 4-1. Others will be given in Chapter 5.

| EXAMPLE 4-1 | Devise a way of multiplying 12×25 in your head. |

| SOLUTION | Observe that each four 25's make 100 and think as follows: |

$$12 \times 25 = 3 \times 4 \times 25$$
$$= 3 \times 100$$
$$= 300$$

(It may help to visualize 12 quarters. Each 4 quarters make a dollar, so 12 quarters make 3 dollars.)

Notice in Example 4-1 that it helps to think of 12 as 3 times 4. Central to the idea of expressing a given whole number as the product of smaller whole numbers is the following definition:

☐ Definition of Divisibility

> Given whole numbers a and b (a can't be 0), we say that b **divides** a if there is a whole number c such that $a = b \times c$. The symbol " $|$ " is used to indicate "divides" and " $\nmid$ " is used to indicate "does not divide."

| EXAMPLE 4-2 | Which are true? |

(a) $3 \mid 15$ (b) $8 \mid 4$ (c) $10 \mid 10$

(d) $2 \mid 7$ (e) $2 \nmid 3$ (f) $3 \mid 9$

(g) $17 \mid (23 \times 17 \times 73)$

(h) $(3^4 \times 5^2) \mid (2^{10} \times 3^{10} \times 5^{10})$

SOLUTION

(a) The problem says "three divides fifteen," which is true, since $15 = 3 \times 5$. (There is a whole number which when multiplied by 3 gives 15.)

(b) $8 \mid 4$ is false, since $4 = 8 \times c$ holds for no *whole number c*. There is no whole number which when multiplied by 8 gives 4.

(c) $10 \mid 10$ is true, since $10 = 10 \times 1$. (1 is a whole number.)

(d) $2 \mid 7$ is false, since $7 = 2 \times c$ holds for no *whole number c*.

(e) The problem says "two does *not* divide three," which is true, since $3 = 2 \times c$ holds for no *whole number c*.

(f) $3 \mid 9$ is true, since $9 = 3 \times 3$. (3 is a whole number.)

(g) $17 \mid (23 \times 17 \times 73)$ is true provided there is a whole number c which when multiplied by 17 gives $23 \times 17 \times 73$. Since $23 \times 17 \times 73$ can be thought of as $17 \times (23 \times 73)$ (after applying the commutative and associative properties of multiplication), the whole number c that we sought is 23×73.

(h) $(3^4 \times 5^2) \mid (2^{10} \times 3^{10} \times 5^{10})$ is true provided there is a whole number c which when multiplied by $3^4 \times 5^2$ gives $2^{10} \times 3^{10} \times 5^{10}$. What quantity, when multiplied by the product of four 3's and two 5's, gives the product of ten 2's, ten 3's, and ten 5's? We need the product of ten 2's, six more 3's, and eight more 5's, so $c = 2^{10} \times 3^6 \times 5^8$.

We can make two helpful observations from the examples. First, the whole numbers a, b, and c of the definition of "divides" need not be different, as can be seen in parts (c) and (f). Second, "$3 \mid 15$" is a *statement*, which in this case is true. Regarding this second point, note that

$$\text{"}3 \mid 15\text{" says "3 divides 15"}$$

which is a true statement, while the symbolism

$$\text{"}15 \div 3\text{" means "15 divided by 3"}$$

which is a number, namely 5.

If b divides a we also say that

$$b \text{ is a } \textbf{divisor} \text{ of } a$$
$$b \text{ is a } \textbf{factor} \text{ of } a \text{ and}$$
$$a \text{ is a } \textbf{multiple} \text{ of } b$$
$$a \text{ is } \textbf{divisible} \text{ by } b$$

For example, all the following statements are true:

$$\text{"8 is a divisor of 24,"}$$
$$\text{"8 is a factor of 24,"}$$

"24 is a multiple of 8," and

"24 is divisible by 8."

Two closely related facts are valuable both for reinforcing the basic notion of divisibility and for their usefulness later. They are the following:

☐ Divisibility Properties for Sums and Differences

> If $b \mid a$ and $b \mid d$, then $b \mid (a + d)$, and
> If $b \mid a$ and $b \mid d$, then $b \mid (a - d)$ (provided $a - d$ is defined).

We wish to show that these results hold for any whole numbers a, b, and d that satisfy the given conditions. To illustrate the method of proof, we will first consider a numerical example. Specifically, we will verify that since $11 \mid 99$ and $11 \mid 55$, $11 \mid (99 + 55)$. To argue that $11 \mid (99 + 55)$, we must find a whole number c such that $99 + 55 = 11 \times c$. How can we use our given information? We are given that $11 \mid 99$, so there is some whole number e (we have already used c to represent something else) such that $99 = 11 \times e$. Clearly e is 9; namely, $99 = 11 \times 9$. We are also given that $11 \mid 55$, so there is some whole number f such that $55 = 11 \times f$. Clearly f is 5; namely, $55 = 11 \times 5$. Thus $99 + 55 = 11 \times 9 + 11 \times 5$, which by the distributive property is $11 \times (9 + 5)$, or 11×14. So the number c which we sought is 14. Summarizing, we said that if 99 is 9 elevens and 55 is 5 elevens, then $99 + 55$ must be 9 elevens + 5 elevens, or 14 elevens.

We can do a proof for arbitrary whole numbers a, b, and d in exactly the same way. Let us prove that

If $b \mid a$ and $b \mid d$, then $b \mid (a + d)$.

To argue that $b \mid (a + d)$, we must find a whole number c such that $a + d = b \times c$. How can we use our given information? We are given that $b \mid a$, so there is some whole number e such that $a = b \times e$. We are also given that $b \mid d$, so there is some whole number f such that $d = b \times f$. Thus $a + d = b \times e + b \times f$, which by the distributive property is $b \times (e + f)$. Since e and f are whole numbers, their sum must be a whole number, according to the closure property for addition. So the number c which we sought is $e + f$.

This result can also be stated another way: If a number divides each of two numbers, then it divides their sum. You will have the opportunity to prove the companion result in the problems; namely, that if a number divides each of two numbers, then it divides their difference. The proof is quite similar.

These two divisibility properties will be called upon many times. One way in which they are helpful is shown in Example 4-3.

EXAMPLE 4-3

(a) Is 156 divisible by 13?   (b) Is 692 divisible by 7?

We could use long division (or a calculator) to answer each of these questions, but it is not necessary.

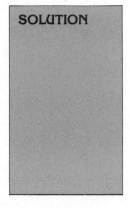

SOLUTION

(a) Look for a number about the size of 156 which is known to be divisible by 13. For instance, 156 is 26 more than 130, which is clearly divisible by 13. Since both 130 and 26 are divisible by 13, their sum, which is 156, is also divisible by 13.

(b) Look for a number about the size of 692 which is known to be divisible by 7. Observe that 692 is 8 less than 700, a known multiple of 7. If 692 were divisible by 7, then the difference $700 - 692$ (which is 8) would have to be divisible by 7. Since 8 is not divisible by 7, 692 cannot be divisible by 7.

Not all problems will work out this well, but there are enough instances where the method of Example 4-3 is helpful to make it worthwhile.

Another application of these two divisibility properties is establishing the validity of certain divisibility tests, such as the well-known **divisibility test for 2**, which says:

A number is divisible by 2 if and only if its last digit is 0, 2, 4, 6, or 8.

We will prove this result for three-digit numbers. Arguments for bigger or smaller numbers would be similar. Suppose we have a three-digit number n whose hundreds digit is p, whose tens digit is q, and whose ones digit is r. Then, recalling some facts about place value, we have $n = p \times 100 + q \times 10 + r$. Now

$$2 \mid (p \times 100), \text{ since } p \times 100 = 2 \times (50 \times p), \text{ and}$$

$$2 \mid (q \times 10), \text{ since } q \times 10 = 2 \times (5 \times q), \text{ so}$$

$$2 \mid (p \times 100 + q \times 10), \text{ by the sum property.}$$

It will be helpful to think of $(p \times 100 + q \times 10)$ as a single whole number that is divisible by 2. Using parentheses for emphasis we can write

$$n = (p \times 100 + q \times 10) + r.$$

Now it will be easy to see that if r is 0, 2, 4, 6, or 8, then $2 \mid n$; and if $2 \mid n$, then r is 0, 2, 4, 6, or 8. First, if r is 0, 2, 4, 6, or 8, then $2 \mid r$. But since $2 \mid (p \times 100 + q \times 10)$ and $2 \mid r$, it follows by the sum property that $2 \mid (p \times 100 + q \times 10) + r$; namely, $2 \mid n$. Conversely, if $2 \mid n$, rewrite

$$n = (p \times 100 + q \times 10) + r, \text{ as}$$

$$r = n - (p \times 100 + q \times 10).$$

Observe that $2 \mid n$ and $2 \mid (p \times 100 + q \times 10)$ implies $2 \mid n - (p \times 100 + q \times 10)$, so $2 \mid r$. But if the one-digit number r is divisible by 2, r must be 0, 2, 4, 6, or 8.

Is there a divisibility test for 3? Each of the numbers 30, 21, 12, 33, 24, 15, 36, 27, 18, and 39 is divisible by 3, so it doesn't seem to matter what the last digit is. Yet there *is* a good **divisibility test for 3**:

A number is divisible by 3 if and only if the sum of its digits is divisible by 3.

Notice that the sum of the digits of each of the numbers listed above is divisible by 3. Here are some examples:

The sum of the digits of 30 is $3 + 0 = 3$.

The sum of the digits of 21 is $2 + 1 = 3$.

The sum of the digits of 24 is $2 + 4 = 6$.

The sum of the digits of 39 is $3 + 9 = 12$.

In each case, the sum of the digits is divisible by 3.

We will sketch a proof for three-digit numbers. Other cases are similar. Suppose our three-digit number $n = p \times 100 + q \times 10 + r$ as in the previous proof. After applying some of the properties developed in the preceding chapter, we have

$$n = p \times 100 + q \times 10 + r$$
$$= p \times (99 + 1) + q \times (9 + 1) + r$$
$$= p \times 99 + p + q \times 9 + q + r$$
$$= p \times 99 + q \times 9 + p + q + r$$
$$= (p \times 99 + q \times 9) + (p + q + r)$$

where parentheses were added in the last step for emphasis. Now $(p \times 99 + q \times 9)$ is clearly divisible by 3, so if $(p + q + r)$ is divisible by 3, so is n; and, if n is divisible by 3, so is $(p + q + r)$, which can be expressed as the difference $n - (p \times 99 + q \times 9)$.

Other divisibility tests will be considered in the problems.

EXERCISES AND PROBLEMS 4-1

DEFINITION

1. Which are true?
   (a) $6 \mid 12$ (b) $12 \mid 6$ (c) $6 \mid 6$
   (d) 8 is a multiple of 4.   (e) 8 is a factor of 4.

2. Use the definition of "divides" (find c) to show
   (a) $5 \mid 120$ (b) $5 \mid 2^3 \times 3 \times 5$
   (c) $5 \mid 2^{11} \times 3^8 \times 5^7 \times 13^{87}$ (d) $10 \mid 2^{11} \times 3^8 \times 5^7 \times 13^{87}$
   (e) $1000000 \mid 2^{11} \times 3^8 \times 5^7 \times 13^{87}$
   (f) $p^2 q^3 \mid p^6 q^6 r^6$, where p, q, and r are whole numbers
   (g) $3 \mid 6 \times 4$ (h) $3 \mid (6 \times 4 + 3)$

3. If 12 divides n, what else must divide n?

4. (a) Obviously 2 divides 86. Why?
   (b) Find c (in the definition of "divides") to show that 2 divides 86.
   (c) Is the number c a divisor of 86? Prove it.

5. The previous problem illustrates how divisors occur "in pairs." This can be helpful in finding divisors of a number. For example, it is easy to see from the divisibility tests that 2 and 3 (and thus 6) are divisors of 222. From each of these divisors we obtain a "c" (from the definition of divides).

$$222 = 2 \times 111 \qquad (c = 111)$$
$$222 = 3 \times 74 \qquad (c = 74)$$
$$222 = 6 \times 37 \qquad (c = 37)$$

This technique tells us that 111, 74, and 37 are also divisors of 222, so a complete list of divisors of 222 is 1, 2, 3, 6, 37, 74, 111, 222. Use this technique to find a list of all divisors of **(a)** 78, **(b)** 170, **(c)** 266, **(d)** 36. **(e)** Which divisor of 36 is "paired with" 6?

6. **(a)** Find the smallest whole number divisible by all of the numbers 2, 3, 4, 5, and 6.
   (b) Describe the smallest whole number divisible by all of the numbers 2, 3, 4, 5, 6, 7, . . . , 20. (Do not do any computation.)

DIVISIBILITY TESTS AND PROPERTIES

7. You should be able to answer each of these questions without actually performing any divisions (or using a calculator) — just using divisibility ideas. Tell whether each is true or false and how you know:
   (a) $15 \mid 1000$ **(b)** $8 \mid 1000$ **(c)** $17 \mid 168$
   (d) $35 \mid 1092$ **(e)** $18 \mid 6372$ **(f)** $6 \mid 10,000,002$

8. **(a)** An employer promises to pay a new employee \$14,000 per year. For easy bookkeeping, the actual salary is to be the smallest whole number $\geq 14,000$ which is divisible by 12. (Why 12?) Find this number.
   (b) Repeat part (a) replacing \$14,000 by \$13,000.
   (c) The secretary in charge of payroll frequently faces similar problems. Devise a divisibility test for 12. (Hint: See Problem 3.)

9. **(a)** Devise a divisibility test for 9. Prove it works for three-digit numbers (of the form $100a + 10b + c$).
   (b) Do the same for 5. **(c)** Do the same for 4. **(d)** Do the same for 11.
   (Hint for part (d): $100a + 10b + c = 99a + a + 11b - b + c$.)

10. Which of the following are divisible by 3? by 4? by 9?
   (a) 225   **(b)** 348   **(c)** 31687452   **(d)** 7001936

11. Take any three-digit number. Rearrange the digits in any order. Subtract the smaller number from the larger. **(a)** Show that the result is divisible by 9. *(b)** Will this work for *all* three-digit numbers? *(c)** Prove it.

12. Give an example of each of the following properties. Use the example to find a proof that each is true for all non-zero whole numbers a, b, and c. (See the discussion and proof of the sum property given in this section to see how a numerical example can help to discover a general proof.)
   (a) If $b \mid a$ and $b \mid d$, then $b \mid (a - d)$ (provided $a - d$ is defined). (difference property of divisibility)
   (b) If $b \mid a$ and $a \mid d$, then $b \mid d$. (**transitive property of divisibility**)
   (c) If $b \mid a$, then $b \mid ad$.
   (d) If $b \mid a$ and $b \mid d$, then $b \mid (ra + sd)$ for any whole numbers r and s.
   (e) If $ab \mid d$, then $a \mid d$.

13. True or False? Give reasons.
    (a) If $b \mid a$ and $b \nmid d$, then $b \nmid (a + d)$.
    (b) If $b \nmid a$ and $b \nmid d$, then $b \nmid (a + d)$.

14. The sum $1^2 + 2^2 + 3^2 + 4^2 + \ldots \cdot n^2$ can be shown to equal $n(n + 1)(2n + 1)/6$. Verify this result for
    (a) $n = 1$ (b) $n = 2$ (c) $n = 3$ (d) $n = 4$
    *(e) Show that for every whole number n, 6 divides $n(n + 1)(2n + 1)$. (In other words, show that $[n(n + 1)(2n + 1)/6]$ is a whole number for each n.)

15. Prove every number of the form ABCABC, such as 957957 or 100100, is divisible by 7, by 11, and by 13.

*16. (a) Show that $3 \mid (n^3 - n)$ for each whole number n.
    (b) Show that $5 \mid (n^5 - n)$ for each whole number n.
    (c) Show that $9 \mid (n^9 - n)$ for each whole number n *is false*.

CALCULATORS

C17. Suppose we compute $p \div d$ using a dependable calculator. (a) If $p \div d$ gives an answer of 233, is it necessarily true that $d \mid p$?   (b) If $p \div d$ gives an answer of 3.8, is it possible that $d \mid p$?   (c) If $p \div d$ gives an answer of 3.8, is it possible that $p \mid d$?

PROBLEM SOLVING EXTENSIONS

18. Devise a way to multiply each of these mentally:
    (a) 15×18 (b) 15×42 (c) 25×32 (d) 25×33 (e) 25×34

19. In Example 4-1, the term $3 \times 4 \times 25$ is thought of both as 12×25 and as 3×100. Which of the basic properties of multiplication is being used implicitly here?

20. The symbol 5! is called five factorial (see Problem 22, Section 3-5) and means $5 \times 4 \times 3 \times 2 \times 1$; namely, $5! = 120$. Also $3! = 3 \times 2 \times 1 = 6$. Which of the following are true? If the statement is true, find the value of c in the definition of "divides."
    (a) $5 \mid 5!$ (b) $4 \mid 5!$ (c) $7 \mid 6!$ (d) $6 \mid 5!$
    (e) $5 \mid (5! + 1)$ (f) $4 \mid 7!$ (g) $50 \mid 50!$ (h) $50 \mid (50! + 1)$
    (Do not multiply out parts g and h.)

21. (Note: It is recommended that you do the parts to this question in sequence, since they are related. See Problem 20.)
    How many zeros are at the end of each of the following?
    (a) 4!   (b) 5!   (c) 9!   (d) 10!   (e) 11!   (f) 20!   (g) 100!

22. An old invoice showed that 72 turkeys had been purchased for $\$\_67.9\_$. The first and last digits were illegible. Assuming that the total amount (expressed in cents) is divisible a whole number of times by 72, what are the missing digits!

23. We say that 6 is a **perfect number**, since it equals the sum of its proper divisors (divisors other than 6 itself):

$$6 = 1 + 2 + 3$$

    (a) There is another perfect number less than 35. Find it.
    (b) Euclid knew that $N = (2^{n-1})(2^n - 1)$ is an even perfect number whenever $2^n - 1$ is prime. For example, if $n = 5$, then

$$N = (2^4) (2^5 - 1) = 16 \times 31 = 496,$$

which is a perfect number. Use Euclid's formula to find two more perfect numbers. (Verify that they are perfect numbers.)

(c) Perfect numbers are always triangular numbers. (See Problem 27, Section 3-5.) For example, 6 is a triangular number. Show that your answer to part (a) is a triangular number.

(d) Notice that $496 = 1^3 + 3^3 + 5^3 + 7^3$. Is $1^3 + 3^3$ a perfect number? Is $1^3 + 3^3 + 5^3$ a perfect number? Express your answer to part (a) as the sum of odd cubes.

For more information on perfect numbers see references [20] and [25].

4-2
PRIME NUMBERS

With this background in the concept of divisibility, we return to the question of expressing whole numbers as products of smaller whole numbers. An embodiment of this concept that is quite appropriate for elementary school children is the task of building rectangle-shaped "houses" with a specified number of blocks. For instance, children might be asked to build as many different kinds of (rectangular) "houses" as possible using exactly six blocks. The only possibilities (in which no block is placed on top of another) are given in Figure 4-1. Among the things a child might learn from this example is that the factors of six are one, two, three, and six.

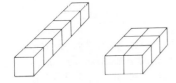

FIGURE 4-1

What rectangles are possible using exactly seven blocks? Since seven is not the product of two smaller whole numbers, the only possible rectangles are 1×7 (or 7×1). The classification of whole numbers according to which numbers can be expressed as the product of smaller factors leads us to the following definitions:

If a whole number can be expressed as the product of two smaller whole numbers, it is called **composite**.

If a whole number (other than 1 or 0) cannot be expressed as the product of two smaller whole numbers, it is called **prime**.

0 and 1 are exceptions and are not considered either prime or composite.

(a) List the first five composites.   (b) List the first five primes.

**EXAMPLE
4-4**

SOLUTION

0 is excluded from both categories.

1 is excluded from both categories.

2 is prime

3 is prime

$4 = 2 \times 2$

5 is prime

$6 = 2 \times 3$

7 is prime

$8 = 2 \times 4$

$9 = 3 \times 3$

$10 = 2 \times 5$

11 is prime

Thus (a) the first five composites are 4, 6, 8, 9, and 10, and (b) the first five primes are 2, 3, 5, 7, and 11.

Some composites can be written as the product of two smaller whole numbers in more than one way. For example, $12 = 2 \times 6$ and $12 = 3 \times 4$. If we continue the factoring process, observing that $6 = 2 \times 3$ and $4 = 2 \times 2$, we have

$$12 = 2 \times 6 = 2 \times 2 \times 3 \quad \text{and} \quad 12 = 3 \times 4 = 3 \times 2 \times 2.$$

In each case, we arrive at exactly the same list of factors (except for the order in which they appear). These factors are primes, so the process terminates. We choose to ignore factors of 1, for though it is true that $12 = 12 \times 1$ and that $12 = 2 \times 2 \times 3 \times 1 \times 1 \times 1$, the 1's don't provide any useful information about the number 12. This is why we do not consider 1 to be prime, for now we can make the following remark: there is exactly one way to write 12 as the product of primes, except for the order of the factors.

Is this true for other whole numbers? For all whole numbers? We shall investigate these interesting and important questions further.

First, we examine a few more examples, borrowing a technique often used in elementary school texts. We draw a **prime factor tree** to help factor numbers into primes. Figure 4-2 shows two of the possible prime factor trees for 12. In either case, we collect the prime factors from the ends of the branches. Some prime factor trees for 60 are shown in Figure 4-3. In each of the prime factor

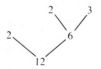

FIGURE 4-2

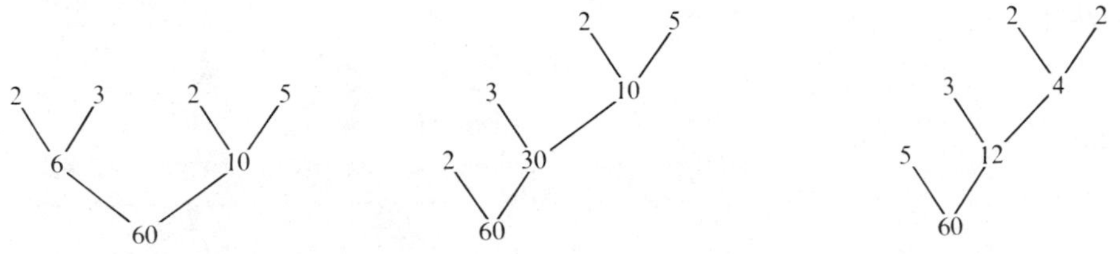

FIGURE 4-3

trees for 60, we arrived at the same prime factors: 2, 2, 3, and 5. (Are there other ways to factor 60? Do they lead to the same prime factors?)

While we are far from exhausting all the possibilities in determining which numbers factor into primes *in just one way* (except for the order of the factors), the prime factor trees suggest one conclusion:

A whole number (larger than 1) is either prime or can be written as the product of primes.

If the given whole number is larger than 1 and is not itself a prime, it can be written as the product of two smaller whole numbers. (In terms of our picture, if it is not the end of a branch, it will split into further branches.) Now if either (or both) of these two smaller whole numbers is not prime, then it (they) can be written as the product of two still smaller whole numbers. We continue until all the factors are primes. But since the supply of whole numbers smaller than the original number is limited, the process must eventually terminate. For instance, if we start with the whole number 1000, the first branches must consist of two numbers each not more than 999, the next branches must consist of two numbers each not more than 998, and so on, so there can be no more than 1000 "levels." (See Figure 4-4.) While the actual number is far less, the important thing is that the process must end. The preceding argument shows that a whole number (larger than 1) is either prime or can be written as the product of primes *in at least one way.*

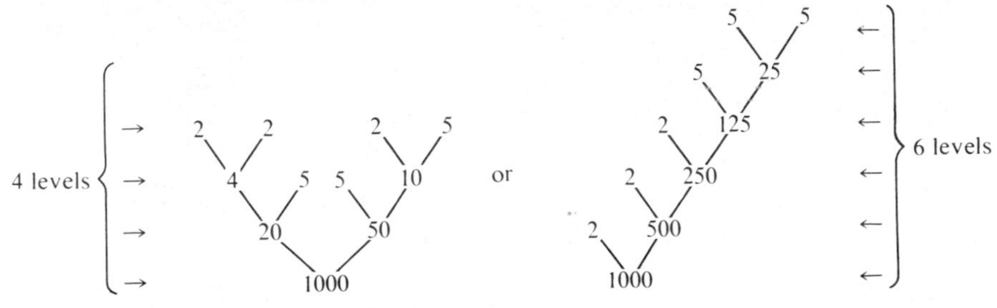

FIGURE 4-4

The problem of determining whether there is *at most one way* to do this, though it is quite interesting, is not presented here. You will be given ample opportunity to investigate whether this unique factorization into primes holds for certain subsets of the whole numbers. We will clarify the issue for the whole numbers themselves by stating the Unique Factorization Theorem (also called The Fundamental Theorem of Arithmetic):

☐ Unique Factorization Theorem

> Any whole number (greater than 1) is either prime or can be written as the product of primes in exactly one way, except for the order of the factors.

Oystein Ore in *Invitation to Number Theory* [23] provides a straightforward proof of this theorem for the interested reader.

The Unique Factorization Theorem tells us that numbers which are not already prime factor into primes in a unique way, but it doesn't tell us how to find them. Our next example provides a number of helpful hints for this process.

EXAMPLE 4-5

Write (a) 231, (b) 229, and (c) 279 each as a product of primes.

SOLUTION

(a) We try to find prime factors of 231 beginning with 2:

2 is not a factor, as the last digit is 1.

3 is a factor, since the sum of the digits is 6.

Write $231 = 3 \times 77$. We recognize 77 as 7×11, so $231 = 3 \times 7 \times 11$. Since 3, 7, and 11 are all primes, no further factorization is possible.

(b) We try to find prime factors of 229 beginning with 2:

2 is not a factor, as the last digit is 9.

3 is not a factor, since the sum of the digits is 13.

5 is not a factor. Why?

7 is not a factor, since 229 is 19 more than 210.

(We know $7 \mid 210$, so if $7 \mid 229$ it would have to divide the difference $229 - 210$, which is 19.)

11 is not a factor, since 229 is 9 more than 220.

(We know $11 \mid 220$, so if $11 \mid 229$ it would have to divide the difference $229 - 220$, which is 9.)

13 is not a factor, since 229 is 31 less than 260.

(We know $13 \mid 260$, so if $13 \mid 229$ it would have to divide the difference $260 - 229$, which is 31.)

The next prime is 17. We know 229 has no factors (other than 1) smaller than 17, because we have already tried all the primes less than 17. But multiplying two factors, each one at least 17, would give a product which is at least $17 \times 17 = 289$. Hence 229 is not the product of two smaller primes, so 229 must itself be a prime.

(c) We try to find prime factors of 279 beginning with 2:

> 2 is not a factor, as the last digit is 9.

> 3 is a factor since the sum of the digits is 18.

Write $279 = 3 \times 93$. Now we wish to check if 93 has any prime factors. We have already eliminated 2 as a possibility, but there could be another factor of 3. In fact there is, and we get $279 = 3 \times 3 \times 31$, or $3^2 \times 31$.

Some observations from this rather long example are in order.

(1) *We test only primes as divisors.* We didn't try 4 or 6. Why? If some composite divides the number, so would the prime factors of this composite number. For instance, if a number is divisible by 6, it is divisible by 2 and by 3. In part (a) of Example 4-5 it is true that $21 \mid 231$, but $21 = 3 \times 7$. Long before it would have been necessary to try 21 as a divisor, we found that $3 \mid 231$ and $7 \mid 231$.

(2) *There is no need to try primes which when squared exceed the given number.* This situation was dealt with in part (b). Another way of looking at it is like this: Suppose in factoring 229 that 31 is one of the prime factors. What would the other factor be? Since 31 goes into 229 about 7 or 8 times, the other factor would be about 7 or 8. But 7 is not a factor (we tried it), and 8 is not a factor (because a number divisible by 8 is divisible by 2, which we tried). In fact we accounted for all factors up to 17, and 17×31 is much too big.

(3) *A particular prime may occur more than once* in the factorization. This is clear in view of part (c).

We now turn to the question of how many primes there are. Example 4-6 will construct a sequence of four consecutive whole numbers, none of which is prime, in order to illustrate a technique to use to show that there are strings of consecutive composites which are as (finitely) long as we may like.

Construct a string of at least four consecutive composite numbers.

EXAMPLE 4-6

SOLUTION

Consider the number $1 \times 2 \times 3 \times 4 \times 5$, which is 120. Since it has factors of 2, 3, 4, and 5, clearly each of the numbers 2, 3, 4, and 5 divides 120. By the divisibility property for sums we have:

$$2 \mid 120 \quad \text{and} \quad 2 \mid 2, \quad \text{so} \quad 2 \mid 122$$
$$3 \mid 120 \quad \text{and} \quad 3 \mid 3, \quad \text{so} \quad 3 \mid 123$$
$$4 \mid 120 \quad \text{and} \quad 4 \mid 4, \quad \text{so} \quad 4 \mid 124$$
$$5 \mid 120 \quad \text{and} \quad 5 \mid 5, \quad \text{so} \quad 5 \mid 125$$

Now the numbers 122, 123, 124, and 125 each have a divisor other than 1 which is smaller than that number, so none of them is prime.

Actually this is only part of a longer sequence of consecutive composites 114, 115, 116, 117, . . . , 126, which might be easy to find by trial and error, but the method of the previous example can provide impressive results without trial and error, as shown in Example 4-7.

EXAMPLE
4-7

Construct a string of at least 100 consecutive composite numbers.

| SOLUTION |

Consider the number $1 \times 2 \times 3 \times 4 \times \ldots \times 100 \times 101$, which we will call m. Since m has factors of 2, 3, 4, . . . , 100, 101, clearly each of the numbers 2, 3, 4, . . . , 100, 101 divides m. By the divisibility property for sums, we have

$$2 \mid m \quad \text{and} \quad 2 \mid 2, \quad \text{so} \quad 2 \mid (m + 2)$$
$$3 \mid m \quad \text{and} \quad 3 \mid 3, \quad \text{so} \quad 3 \mid (m + 3)$$
$$4 \mid m \quad \text{and} \quad 4 \mid 4, \quad \text{so} \quad 4 \mid (m + 4)$$
$$. . .$$
$$100 \mid m \quad \text{and} \quad 100 \mid 100, \quad \text{so} \quad 100 \mid (m + 100)$$
$$101 \mid m \quad \text{and} \quad 101 \mid 101, \quad \text{so} \quad 101 \mid (m + 101)$$

Now the 100 consecutive numbers $m + 2, m + 3, m + 4, \ldots, m + 100, m + 101$ each have a divisor other than 1 which is smaller than that number, so none of them is prime.

Of course, the technique of Examples 4-6 and 4-7 could be used to find a string of composites of any desired (finite) length. It might appear that prime numbers would eventually vanish altogether. It may be surprising, therefore, that a proof using a similar technique shows that the list of primes never ends! In other words, we will show that

There is no largest prime.

To establish this result, we will argue, as Euclid did thousands of years ago, that as soon as we assume that there is a largest prime we can find another prime which is larger. Suppose there *were* a largest prime. Call it p. Let k be the product of all the primes including p. Then $k = 2 \times 3 \times 5 \times 7 \times 11 \times \ldots \times p$, so every prime number from 2 through p divides k. Now consider the number $k + 1$.

This number is not divisible by 2, for if 2 divided both k and $k + 1$ it would have to divide their difference, which is 1. But $2 \nmid 1$, hence $2 \nmid (k + 1)$. In the same way, 3 cannot divide $k + 1$, nor can 5, 7, 11, or any of the primes up to and including p. Thus, either $k + 1$ has no prime factors (other than itself) so it is a prime, or it has prime factors larger than those listed. Either way, there is a prime larger than p; hence, the assumption that there is a largest prime is impossible. Since there is no largest prime, it follows that the list of primes continues indefinitely; namely, the number of primes is infinite.

Methods of finding primes and other related questions have intrigued mathematicians for centuries. For instance, the deceptively simple statement (called **Goldbach's conjecture**) that every even number greater than 2 is the sum of two primes has yet to be proven true or false. It is easy to see that it holds for the first few even numbers greater than 2:

$$4 = 2 + 2$$
$$6 = 3 + 3$$
$$8 = 3 + 5$$
$$10 = 5 + 5$$
$$12 = 5 + 7$$

This and some other interesting queries will be raised in the problems.

EXERCISES AND PROBLEMS 4-2

DEFINITION

1. The process for finding primes described below, called the **sieve of Eratosthenes**, was in use thousands of years ago and is still used today in computer programs written to generate primes. To find all primes less than or equal to 100, list the numbers 1 through 100.

1	2	3	4	5	6	7	8	9	10
11	12	13	14	15	16	17	18	19	20
21	22	23	24	25	26	27	28	29	30
31	32	33	34	35	36	37	38	39	40
41	42	43	44	45	46	47	48	49	50
51	52	53	54	55	56	57	58	59	60
61	62	63	64	65	66	67	68	69	70
71	72	73	74	75	76	77	78	79	80
81	82	83	84	85	86	87	88	89	90
91	92	93	94	95	96	97	98	99	100

Cross off 1, since the definition of prime excludes it. Beginning with the number 4, cross off every second number, since these are each divisible by 2. Cross off every third number, beginning with 6. Then the first three rows will look like this:

~~1~~	2	3	~~4~~	5	~~6~~	7	~~8~~	~~9~~	~~10~~
11	~~12~~	13	~~14~~	~~15~~	~~16~~	17	~~18~~	19	~~20~~
~~21~~	~~22~~	23	~~24~~	25	~~26~~	~~27~~	~~28~~	29	~~30~~

(a) Which numbers are crossed off more than once?
(b) In continuing the process it is unnecessary, after doing the above, to cross off the multiples of 4; namely, 8, 12, 16, . . . , 100. Why?
(c) Cross off all multiples of 5 (except 5 itself). Do the same for multiples of other primes.

(d) What was the smallest prime for which you found all its multiples (other than itself) already crossed off? Compare this result with the observations which follow Example 4-5.

(e) Examine your sieve and list all primes less than 100.

2. Use the sieve method to find all primes less than 200.

3. The sieve of Eratosthenes is based on which divisibility property?

4. Find (if possible)
   (a) the smallest prime   (b) the largest prime
   (c) all primes between 90 and 100
   (d) $\{1, 2, 3, 4, \ldots, 10\}\backslash\{$primes less than 10$\}$

5. Mathematicians have long tried to find a formula which consistently yields primes. The formula $p(n) = n^2 - n + 41$ yields primes for $n = 0, 1, 2, 3, 4, \ldots, 40$. For instance $p(0) = 0^2 - 0 + 41 = 41$ is prime, $p(1) = 1^2 - 1 + 41 = 41$ is prime, $p(2) = 2^2 - 2 + 41 = 43$ is prime.
   (a) Find $p(3)$, $p(4)$, $p(5)$, $p(6)$, and $p(7)$.
   (b) Find $p(41)$. Is it prime? Support your answer.

6. (a) Show that the formula $f(n) = n^2 + n + 11$ yields primes for $n = 0, 1, 2$, and 3. (See Problem 5.) Find the smallest whole number n for which $f(n) = n^2 + n + 11$ is *not* a prime.
   (b) Repeat part (a) for $f(n) = n^2 + n + 17$.
   (c) $f(n) = n^2 - 79n + 1601$ yields primes for $n = 0, 1, 2, 3, \ldots, 79$. Show that $f(80)$ is *not* a prime. (Hint: It's a perfect square.)
   (Note: There is no known formula that consistently yields different primes for all values of n.)

PRIME FACTORIZATION

7. Find a factor tree for 60 different from those in Figure 4-3.

8. Find a factor tree for (a) 28   (b) 168.

9. When factoring a given number into primes, some students like to organize their work like this:

$$\begin{array}{r} 5 \\ 3\overline{)15} \\ 2\overline{)30} \\ 2\overline{)60} \end{array}$$

Divide by 2 as often as possible, then 3, then 5, and so on for each prime to conclude $60 = 2 \times 2 \times 3 \times 5$. This method is used below to factor 294 into primes:

$$\begin{array}{r} 7 \\ 7\overline{)\ 49} \\ 3\overline{)147} \\ 2\overline{)294} \end{array}$$

Thus $294 = 2 \times 3 \times 7 \times 7$.
Use this method to factor the following into primes:
(a) 66   (b) 72   (c) 153   (d) 459   (e) 1000.

10. Write the number whose prime factorization is given by
    (a) $2 \times 3 \times 5 \times 7$ (b) $2^3 \times 3^2$
    (c) $2^5 \times 5^5$ (d) $3^4 \times 7 \times 11$

11. Select the best answers from the choices given in parentheses: To test whether 149 is prime, one could divide by all (*whole numbers, primes, odd numbers*) less than (*11, 13, 15, 75, 149, 150*).

12. Factor each of the following into primes: (a) 143   (b) 151   (c) 493

13. Make a flowchart for factoring a given number into primes, using the observations which follow Example 4-5.

14. (a) Factor 100 into primes.   (b) Factor each divisor of 100 into primes.
    (c) What relationship exists between parts (a) and (b)?
    (d) Suppose $n = 17^5 \times 19^7$. If m is a divisor of n, what can you say about the prime factorization of m?

COUNTING DIVISORS

15. (a) How many divisors does 0 have?   (b) 0 divides how many numbers?

16. Complete the following chart:

Number	Prime Decomposition	Divisors	Number of Divisors
2	2	1, 2	2
3	3	1, 3	2
4	2^2	1, 2, 4	3
5			
6			
7			
8			
9			
10			
11			
12			
16			
20			
24	$2^3 \times 3$	1, 2, 3, 4, 6, 8, 12, 24	8
32			
60			
72			
100			

17. Which whole number from 1 through 100 has the most divisors? Which has the most prime factors?

18. Tell how many divisors each of the following numbers has:
    (a) $5^2 \times 3$ (b) $5^2 \times 3^2$ (c) $5^2 \times 3^3$ (d) $13^5 \times 17^{11}$
    (e) $2^3 \times 3^4 \times 5 \times 7^{30}$

19. Find the smallest whole number that has exactly
    (a) 1 divisor   (b) 2 divisors
    (c) 3 divisors   (d) 4 divisors
    (e) 5 divisors   (f) 6 divisors
    (g) 7 divisors   (h) 8 divisors.

20. Characterize (describe by some rule) all whole numbers which have exactly
    (a) 2 divisors   (b) 3 divisors   (c) 5 divisors
    *(d) 4 divisors   *(e) 6 divisors   *(f) 12 divisors.

PROPERTIES

21. Refer to the proof that there is no largest prime. Note that if p were assumed to be 5, $k = 2 \times 3 \times 5 = 30$, so $k + 1 = 31$, which is a prime larger than 5. Find $k + 1$ if p were assumed to be 7.

22. True or False? Support your answer. "Every whole number (greater than 1) is either prime or can be expressed as the *sum* of primes in exactly one way."

*23. Let $S = \{$whole numbers$\} \setminus \{2\}$; that is, S is the set of all whole numbers except 2. Then $S = \{0, 1, 3, 4, 5, 6, 7, 8, \ldots\}$. We will call a member of S an **S-prime** if it is greater than 1 and cannot be written as the product of two smaller members *of S*. Thus the first few S-primes are 3, 4, 5, 6, and 7. (Though $6 = 2 \times 3$ it is an S-prime since the factor 2 is not in S.)

    (a) Do the closure, commutative, associative, and identity properties for multiplication hold for the set S?

    (b) Find the smallest member of S which is not an S-prime.

    (c) Find a member of S which factors into S-primes in two ways. This shows that S fails to satisfy what property or theorem?

    (d) Find a member of S which factors into S-primes in three ways.

    (e) When does a member of S factor into S-primes in exactly one way?

    (f) Does the sum property of divisibility hold in S? Support your answer.

    (g) Does the difference property of divisibility hold in S? Support your answer.

    (h) What happens if instead of 2 some other prime, like 7, is removed?

    (i) What happens if two or more primes are simultaneously removed?

MATERIALS AND CALCULATORS

L24. Use a set of blocks (cubes) in this problem. Show all "houses" (rectangles) which can be made from up to 12 blocks, as in the examples below. (See also Figure 4-1.)

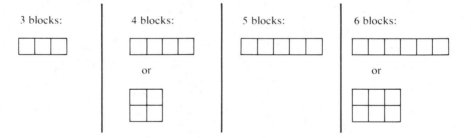

Which whole numbers will have more than one representation?

C25. Notice that for the first few values of n, the number obtained by adding 1 to the product of the first n primes is itself a prime.

n	(Product of First n Primes) $+ 1$
1	$2 + 1 = 3$
2	$2 \times 3 + 1 = 7$
3	$2 \times 3 \times 5 + 1 = 31$
4	$2 \times 3 \times 5 \times 7 + 1 = 211$

    (a) Determine the value when n is 5.

    (b) Determine the value when n is 6. Show that this value is not prime by finding a factor between 50 and 60.

C26. (Note: It is recommended that you do the parts to this question in sequence, since they are related.) Use repeated multiplication on a calculator to help answer these questions.
   (a) What are the last two digits of 2^{22}?
   (b) What are the last two digits of 2^{23}?
   (c) What are the last two digits of 2^{24}?
   (d) What are the last two digits of 102^{22}?
   (e) What are the last two digits of 12^{22}?
   (f) What are the last two digits of 372^{22}?
   (g) What is the last digit of $39,407^{99}$?
   (h) What are the last two digits of $39,407^{99}$?
   (i) What is the last digit of $83,903^{99}$?
   (j) What are the last two digits of $83,903^{99}$?

P27. Write a program that finds the first 50 prime numbers.

P28. Write a program that factors a given number into primes.

P29. Use your program of Problem 28 to factor these numbers into primes:
   (a) 221   (b) 441   (c) 899   (d) 907   (e) 99,299   (f) 2,893,443

PROBLEM SOLVING EXTENSIONS

30. Two primes whose difference is 2 are called **twin primes**. Thus 5 and 7, 11 and 13, and 29 and 31 are three pairs of twin primes. Find all pairs of twin primes less than 100.

31. 2 and 3 are primes whose difference is 1. Find all such pairs of primes less than 1,000,000.

32. An elusive result that mathematicians have been unable to prove either true or false is older than the U.S. Declaration of Independence. Called Goldbach's conjecture, it claims that each even number greater than 2 is the sum of two primes. Some examples were given on page 133.
   (a) Verify that it holds for even numbers through 50.
   (b) Assuming Goldbach's conjecture is true, prove that each odd whole number greater than 6 is the sum of three primes.

33. Can you find whole numbers m and n such that $3^m = 7^n$?

34. For what type of whole numbers n is it true that n divides $(n - 1)!$? For example, 8 divides $7 \times 6 \times 5 \times 4 \times 3 \times 2 \times 1$, but 5 does not divide $4 \times 3 \times 2 \times 1$. (See Problem 20, Section 4-1.)

35. Find a string of 1000 consecutive composite numbers.

36. Is it possible to make a magic square with the first nine prime numbers? (In a magic square all rows, columns, and main diagonals have the same sum. (See Problems 20 and 21, Section 3-2.) Do it or explain why it cannot be done.

4-3

GREATEST COMMON DIVISOR AND LEAST COMMON MULTIPLE

The discussion and problems of the previous section provide several techniques that enable us to split a given whole number into primes, the "building blocks" of the whole numbers with respect to multiplication. Once we have the prime factors, it is easy to find all the divisors of a given number.

With respect to our goals, finding common divisors (and multiples) of two or more numbers is most important. For instance, 18 and 24 have several common divisors:

$$\text{divisors of } 18 = 1, 2, 3, 6, 9, 18$$

$$\text{divisors of } 24 = 1, 2, 3, 4, 6, 8, 12, 24$$

$$\text{common divisors of } 18 \text{ and } 24 = 1, 2, 3, 6$$

Any two whole numbers will always have at least one common divisor. (What is it?) Among all the common divisors, there will always be a largest one, since the divisors cannot exceed the numbers themselves. For these reasons, it is meaningful to talk about a greatest common divisor for two (or more) numbers.

> The **greatest common divisor** of two (or more) whole numbers is the largest whole number which divides both (all) of them.

The greatest common divisor is usually abbreviated **GCD**. It is sometimes called the **greatest common factor (GCF)**.

EXAMPLE 4-8

Find each of the following:

(a) GCD (6, 8)   (b) GCD (20, 30)   (c) GCD (24, 28, 30)

(d) GCD (4, 9)   (e) GCD (153, 204)

SOLUTION

(a) divisors of 6 = 1, 2, 3, 6

divisors of 8 = 1, 2, 4, 8

common divisors of 6 and 8 = 1, 2

GCD (6, 8) = 2

(b) divisors of 20 = 1, 2, 4, 5, 10, 20

divisors of 30 = 1, 3, 5, 6, 10, 30

common divisors of 20 and 30 = 1, 2, 5, 10

GCD (20, 30) = 10

(c) divisors of 24 = 1, 2, 3, 4, 6, 8, 12, 24

divisors of 28 = 1, 2, 4, 7, 14, 28

divisors of 30 = 1, 2, 3, 5, 6, 10, 15, 30

common divisors of 24, 28, and 30 = 1, 2

GCD (24, 28, 30) = 2

(d) divisors of 4 = 1, 2, 4

divisors of 9 = 1, 3, 9

common divisors of 4 and 9 = 1

GCD (4, 9) = 1 (When no prime divides both of the given numbers, they are called **relatively prime**.)

(e) divisors of 153 = 1, 3, 9, 17, 51, 153

divisors of 204 = 1, 2, 3, 4, 6, 12, 17, 34, 51, 68, 102, 204

common divisors of 153 and 204 = 1, 3, 17, 51

GCD (153, 204) = 51

While the method of Example 4-8 is satisfactory for many problems, other procedures work better in some cases, especially for larger numbers. Among them is a process where the GCD is constructed from the prime factors. Another method is the Euclidean algorithm, where the GCD is calculated directly by successive applications of the division algorithm.

We introduce the construction method by recalling that the exercises of the previous section revealed a relationship between the prime factors of a number and the prime factors of its divisors. As one example (see also Problem 14, Section 4-2) consider the divisors of 84, whose prime factorization is $2^2 \times 3 \times 7$.

Divisor of 84	Prime Factorization of Divisor
1	1
2	2
3	3
4	2^2
6	2×3
7	7
12	$2^2 \times 3$
14	2×7
21	3×7
28	$2^2 \times 7$
42	$2 \times 3 \times 7$
84	$2^2 \times 3 \times 7$

Note that each divisor of 84 (except 1, the trivial divisor) is either a prime factor of 84 or it factors into a product consisting of some or all of the prime factors of 84. Suppose, to the contrary, that 84 had some other divisor d, and that d had a different prime factor, say 13. Then 13 would divide d and d would divide 84, so by the transitive property of divisibility 13 would divide 84. This means 84 would equal 13 multiplied by some other primes. But then 84 would factor into primes in two ways (with and without the prime factor 13), which is impossible according to the Unique Factorization Theorem. Thus it is absurd for any divisor of 84 to have a factor of 13. By a similar argument, each divisor of 84 (except 1) must have as its prime factors some choice from among 2, 3, and 7. What is argued here for 84 is valid as well for all whole numbers; namely, the divisors (other than 1) of a whole number w must either be prime factors of w or be products of some of the prime factors which give w itself.

This observation makes finding the GCD of two or more numbers considerably easier, for we can construct it from the common prime factors of the numbers.

EXAMPLE 4-9

Use prime factorization to find the GCD of

(a) 20 and 30   (b) 153 and 204

(c) $2^5 \times 3^6 \times 11^8$ and $2^3 \times 3^{17} \times 7^2 \times 11$ (d) 261 and 377

SOLUTION

(a) $20 = 2^2 \times 5$, so any divisor of 20 can have at most two 2's and one 5 (and no other primes) as prime factors. Since $30 = 2 \times 3 \times 5$, any divisor of 30 can have at most one 2, one 3, and one 5 (and no other primes) as prime factors. Thus a number which is a common factor of 20 and 30 must satisfy all these conditions and can have at most one 2 and one 5 (and no other primes) as prime factors, so the common factors are 1, 2, 5, and 10. To find the GCD, the *greatest* of the common divisors, we use both of the possible factors, 2 and 5, and obtain 10. As we would expect, the list of common divisors and the GCD are consistent with the results of Example 4-8.

(b) $153 = 3^2 \times 17$ and $204 = 2^2 \times 3 \times 17$. As before, to find the GCD we construct the number that uses as many of the common prime factors as possible. We may select no 2's, one 3, and one 17, so GCD $(153, 204) = 3 \times 17 = 51$.

(c) A common divisor of $2^5 \times 3^6 \times 11^8$ and $2^3 \times 3^{17} \times 7^2 \times 11$ can have at most three 2's, six 3's, no 7's, one 11, and no other prime factors. The greatest number satisfying these conditions is $2^3 \times 3^6 \times 11$, and we are content to leave our answer in this form.

(d) $261 = 3^2 \times 29$ is easy to factor by applying the divisibility test for 3 (or for 9). We could painstakingly factor 377, which is more difficult, but the only possible *common* prime factors (which are all we care about at this point) are 3 and 29. 377 fails the divisibility test for 3, but it does divide by 29 ($377 = 29 \times 13$). So GCD $(261, 377) = 29$.

These examples suggest a three-step procedure to construct the GCD of two (or more) numbers.

☐ To Construct the GCD of Two (or More) Numbers

1. Factor each number into primes.
2. Select each prime the least number of times that it appears on any of the lists.
3. Express the GCD as the product of the primes that result from step 2.

Our next example applies this process to finding the GCD of three numbers.

EXAMPLE 4-10

Use prime factorization to find

(a) GCD (54, 72, 90)   (b) GCD (36, 49, 56)

(a) $54 = 2 \times 3^3$

$72 = 2^3 \times 3^2$

$90 = 2 \times 3^2 \times 5$

GCD $(54, 72, 90) = 2 \times 3^2 = 18$

(b) $36 = 2^2 \times 3^2$

$49 = 7^2$

$56 = 2^3 \times 7$

The least number of times 2 occurs is zero (on the list for 49).

The least number of times 3 occurs is zero (on the list for 49).

The least number of times 7 occurs is zero (on the list for 36).

Thus there are no common prime factors, so GCD $(36, 49, 56) = 1$.

The **Euclidean algorithm** is a good method for finding the GCD of two numbers that are hard to factor. We will present an example and then analyze how and why it works.

Use the Euclidean algorithm to find the GCD $(493, 221)$.

EXAMPLE
4-11

SOLUTION

(1) $493 = 221 \times 2 + 51$

(2) $221 = 51 \times 4 + 17$

(3) $51 = 17 \times 3 + 0$

Therefore GCD $(493, 221) = 17$.

We now offer an explanation of what happened!

(1) Divide 493 by 221. Use the division algorithm to express 493 as a multiple of 221 plus a remainder that is less than 221.

(2) Divide 221 by 51. Use the division algorithm to express 221 as a multiple of 51 plus a remainder that is less than 51.

(3) Divide 51 by 17. Use the division algorithm to express 51 as a multiple of 17 plus a remainder that is less than 17. This time the remainder is 0, so the process terminates.

So why is 17 the GCD $(493, 221)$? We will answer this by examining the Euclidean algorithm one step at a time. In the first step we wrote

$$493 = 221 \times 2 + 51.$$

We show that the list of divisors of both 493 and 221 is precisely the same as the list of divisors of both 221 and 51:

Suppose $p \mid 493$ and $p \mid 221$. Then $p \mid (221 \times 2)$ (see Problem 12c, Section 4-1), and consequently $p \mid (493 - 221 \times 2)$ (see Problem 12a, Section 4-1). In other words, $p \mid 51$. This shows that any number that divides both 493 and 221 will also divide both 221 and 51.

Now suppose $s \mid 221$ and $s \mid 51$. Then $s \mid (221 \times 2)$ and consequently $s \mid (221 \times 2 + 51)$, by the divisibility of a sum property. In other words, $s \mid 493$. This shows that any number that divides both 221 and 51 will also divide both 493 and 221.

Summarizing, we see that the list of divisors of both 493 and 221 and the list of divisors of both 221 and 51 must be identical, so in particular, GCD (493, 221) = GCD (221, 51).

In this same way we can show that in general, if $a = b \times q + r$, then GCD (a, b) = GCD (b, r). Returning to our original example, we can apply this principle several times to obtain

$$\begin{aligned} \text{GCD } (493, 221) &= \text{GCD } (221, 51) \\ &= \text{GCD } (51, 17) \\ &= \text{GCD } (17, 0) \\ &= 17 \end{aligned}$$

Let's double our number of examples of the Euclidean algorithm by presenting another one:

EXAMPLE 4-12

Use the Euclidean algorithm to find the GCD (1776, 1492).

SOLUTION

$$\begin{aligned} 1776 &= 1492 \times 1 + 284 \\ 1492 &= 284 \times 5 + 72 \\ 284 &= 72 \times 3 + 68 \\ 72 &= 68 \times 1 + 4 \\ 68 &= 4 \times 17 + 0 \end{aligned}$$

Applying our new principle five times gives:

$$\begin{aligned} \text{GCD } (1776, 1492) &= \text{GCD } (1492, 284) \\ &= \text{GCD } (284, 72) \\ &= \text{GCD } (72, 68) \\ &= \text{GCD } (68, 4) \\ &= \text{GCD } (4, 0) \\ &= 4 \end{aligned}$$

With three methods of finding common divisors at our disposal, we will now investigate the topic of common multiples.

Finding the multiples of a single number is straightforward. For example, the multiples of 6 are

$$6 \times 0 = 0$$
$$6 \times 1 = 6$$
$$6 \times 2 = 12$$
$$6 \times 3 = 18$$
$$6 \times 4 = 24$$

We can find common multiples of two (or more) numbers by methods much like those used to find common divisors. For instance, to find common multiples of 18 and 24, we could list the multiples of each and search for common ones:

multiples of 18: 0, 18, 36, 54, 72, 90, 108, 126, 144, 162, . . .

multiples of 24: 0, 24, 48, 72, 96, 120, 144, 168, . . .

common multiples of 18 and 24: 0, 72, 144, . . .

One difference between these results and those for finding common divisors is immediately noticeable: the list of multiples is endless, as is the list of common multiples. To show that the list of common multiples never ends, we will show that every multiple of 72 is a common multiple of 18 and 24.

Let $72k$ be a multiple of 72, where k is a whole number. Then

$$72k = (18 \times 4)k = 18 \times 4k \text{ and}$$
$$72k = (24 \times 3)k = 24 \times 3k$$

Since k is a whole number, so are $4k$ and $3k$. Thus there is a whole number ($4k$) which multiplied by 18 gives $72k$, so 18 divides $72k$ ($72k$ is a multiple of 18). Also there is a whole number ($3k$) which shows that 24 divides $72k$ ($72k$ is a multiple of 24).

Clearly, there is no greatest common multiple of 18 and 24. If $72k$ is some multiple of 72, then $72(k + 1)$ will be a larger multiple. It so happens (as when finding lowest common denominators for fractions) that we are interested this time in the *least* common multiple. Since 0 is a multiple of each whole number, 0 is technically the least of all common multiples for any two (or more) numbers. This fact is of little use to us. So henceforth when we use the term "least common multiple" we exclude 0.

Is there always a least common multiple for any two whole numbers? Given some whole numbers, their product is always a common multiple. For instance, given 7 and 9, 63 is a multiple of 7 and 63 is a multiple of 9. Similarly, the product of any two whole numbers is a common multiple. Now, among all of the common multiples (we exclude 0), there will always be a smallest one, since every (non-empty) set of whole numbers has a least member. This makes the following definition meaningful:

The **least common multiple** of two (or more) whole numbers is the smallest whole number (other than 0) which is a multiple of both (all) of them.

The least common multiple is usually abbreviated **LCM**.

EXAMPLE
4-13

Find each of the following:

(a) LCM (6, 8)   (b) LCM (20, 30)   (c) LCM (24, 28, 30)

SOLUTION

(a) multiples of 6 = 0, 6, 12, 18, 24, 30, 36, 42, 48, 54, . . .

multiples of 8 = 0, 8, 16, 24, 32, 40, 48, 56, . . .

common multiples of 6 and 8 = 0, 24, 48, . . .

LCM (6, 8) = 24

(b) multiples of 20 = 0, 20, 40, 60, 80, 100, 120, . . .

multiples of 30 = 0, 30, 60, 90, 120, 150, 180, . . .

common multiples of 20 and 30 = 0, 60, 120, 180, . . .

LCM (20, 30) = 60

(c) multiples of 24 = 0, 24, 48, 72, 96, 120, 144, 168, 192, 216, 240, . . .

multiples of 28 = 0, 28, 56, 84, 112, 140, 168, 196, 224, 252, 280, . . .

multiples of 30 = 0, 30, 60, 90, 120, 150, 180, 210, 240, 270, 300, . . .

common multiples of 24, 28, and 30 = 0, ?, . . .

Writing out eleven multiples of each did not produce a single non-trivial common multiple. We do know that $24 \times 28 \times 30 = 20160$ is a common multiple, but is it the smallest?! We will defer the solution of this problem in hopes of finding a better way.

This last example shows the need for other methods. We found when considering the GCD that it was helpful to factor the given numbers into primes. Will this help us here? Let's go back to the easier example. We found LCM (6, 8) = 24. Factoring these three numbers into primes, we see

$$6 = 2 \times 3$$

$$8 = 2^3$$

$$24 = 2^3 \times 3$$

What is the relationship between the prime factors of 6 and 8 and the prime factors of 24, the LCM of 6 and 8? If you do not recognize the pattern at this point, you might try several more examples. Additional clues for determining how to construct the LCM from the prime factors will be given in the problems.

We know that the Euclidean algorithm always yields the GCD of two numbers. Once the GCD is known, a simple computation gives the LCM, but again we will give you the opportunity to discover this for yourself.

EXERCISES AND PROBLEMS 4-3

DEFINITION

1. Which are bigger, divisors of 12 or multiples of 12? Are there any exceptions? Which is bigger, GCD (12, 15) or LCM (12, 15)? If a and b are two different whole numbers, which is bigger, GCD (a, b) or LCM (a, b)?

2. Use the method of Example 4-8 to find
   (a) GCD (8, 10)   (b) GCD (40, 60)   (c) GCD (25, 36)
   (d) GCD (24, 36, 42)   (e) GCD (232, 261).

3. Any two whole numbers have one common divisor. What is it?

4. Find the GCD of each pair of numbers by any method. (This problem is adapted from a sixth grade text.)
   (a) 36, 42   (b) 20, 36   (c) 90, 315   (d) 72, 450
   (e) 175, 105   (f) 525, 441   (g) 152, 228

5. Find by any method:
   (a) GCD (14, 28)   (b) GCD (72, 90, 96)   (c) GCD (312, 468, 1092)

6. Determine a three-step procedure for constructing the LCM of two (or more) numbers based on factoring each of the numbers into primes. (Hint: Beginning with the three-step construction of the GCD given on page 140, few words need to be replaced to make this a method for finding the LCM.)

7. Use the method of construction from prime factorization that you have developed to find the LCM of each pair of numbers.
   (a) 15, 20   (b) 63, 72   (c) 98, 126   (d) 152, 228
   (e) 21, 6   (f) 20, 24   (g) 14, 28   (h) 136, 153

8. (a) Use this method to show LCM (24, 28, 30) = 840.
   (b) Find LCM (90, 105, 120).

9. True or False? The LCM of any two positive whole numbers m and n is the smallest positive multiple of m that has n as a factor.

10. (a) When does LCM $(a, b) = a \times b$?   (b) When does LCM $(a, b) = a$?
    (c) When does GCD $(a, b) = a \times b$?   (d) When does GCD $(a, b) = a$?

11. According to the definition of LCM, what is
    (a) LCM (0, 5)   (b) LCM (0, 0)?

EUCLIDEAN ALGORITHM

12. Use the Euclidean algorithm to find the GCD of each pair of numbers:
    (a) 36, 42   (b) 737, 871   (c) 4189, 4307
    (d) 89, 144   (e) 1746, 9846

13. The Euclidean algorithm works to find the GCD of two numbers. Is it possible to find the GCD of three (or four or five) numbers by finding the GCD's for two numbers at a time? Explain. (Hint: It may help to think in terms of the method of factoring into primes. Try some examples by this method.)

*14. Draw a flowchart for using the Euclidean algorithm to find the GCD of two numbers.

15. (a) If $493 = 221 \times 2 + 51$, show that GCD (493, 221) = GCD (221, 51).
    (b) If $a = b \times q + r$, show that GCD (a, b) = GCD (b, r).

PROPERTIES AND RELATIONSHIPS

16. (a) What are the prime factors of 10?
    (b) 10, 20, and 30 are some of the positive multiples of 10. List all of the positive multiples of 10 up to 100.
    (c) Factor each of these multiples of 10 into primes.
    (d) Which prime factors occur on every one of the lists?

17. As in the previous problem, examine the prime factors of 12 and the prime factors of the positive multiples of 12 (up to 120).

18. Based on the two preceding problems (and other examples, if you wish), state a relationship between the prime factors of a number and the prime factors of its multiples. Give an argument to show that this relationship is generally true.

19. (a) Complete the following chart:

a	b	GCD (a, b)	LCM (a, b)	GCD (a, b) × LCM (a, b)
2	3	1	6	6
3	4			
4	6			
8	12			
42	56			
50	60			

  (b) Look for a relationship between the last column and the first two.
  (c) Does this relationship hold for all whole numbers? Why?

20. Use the results of the preceding problem to answer the following:
  (a) If GCD (493, 221) = 17 (see Example 4-11), find LCM (493, 221).
  (b) If GCD (1492, 1776) = 4 (see Example 4-12), find LCM (1492, 1776).
  (c) Find LCM (737, 871). (See Problem 12b.)

21. The LCM of two numbers is $2^3 \times 3^2 \times 7 \times 11 \times 13$. The GCD of the same two numbers is $2 \times 3 \times 7$. If one of the numbers is $2^3 \times 3 \times 7 \times 11$, what is the other number?

22. We said earlier that two numbers are called relatively prime if their GCD is 1. Thus 4 and 9 are relatively prime (though neither is prime). Find all numbers less than 20 which are relatively prime with 12.

23. What property of multiplication justifies each of the following statements that were made in showing that 72 is a common multiple of 18 and 24?
  (a) $(18 \times 4) k = 18 \times 4k$
  (b) Since k is a whole number, so are $4k$ and $3k$.

24. Suppose we write "aLb" to mean LCM (a, b) and "aGb" to mean GCD (a, b). For example, $3L4 = 12$, $6L8 = 24$, $6G8 = 2$, $4G9 = 1$. Which of the following properties hold?
  (a) The set of whole numbers is closed under L.
  (b) The set of whole numbers is closed under G.
  (c) L is commutative.
  (d) G is commutative.
  (e) L is associative.
  (f) G is associative.
  (g) L distributes over G; namely, $aL(bGc) = (aLb) G (aLc)$.
  (h) G distributes over L; namely, $aG(bLc) = (aGb) L (aGc)$.

MATERIALS AND CALCULATORS

L25. Which "train" involving Cuisenaire rods represents each of the following?
  (a) GCD of a purple rod and a dark green rod.
  (b) LCM of a purple rod and a dark green rod.

(c) GCD of a dark green rod and a blue rod.

(d) Describe the rod (or "train") which is the GCD of any two rods (or "trains").

(e) Describe the rod (or "train") which is the LCM of any two rods (or "trains").

26. Read "Star Patterns," in the January 1978 *Arithmetic Teacher* [47] and answer these questions:

(a) How many paths are there for the star (10,4)? the star (15,6)?

(b) How many orbits will there be in completing one path of (10,4)? of (15,6)?

(c) Draw (10,4) and (15,6).

(d) Construct a star having three paths and four orbits for each path.

C27. (a) Use a calculator to list the first ten positive multiples of 56 and of 42. Use this process to find LCM (56, 42).

(b) Repeat for 133 and 209.

C28. Outline a systematic procedure for finding the GCD of two numbers on a calculator.

P29. Write a program which uses the Euclidean algorithm to find the GCD of two numbers. (Hint: See Problem 31, Section 3-6.)

P30. Use your program of Problem 29 to find the GCD of

(a) 664 and 747

(b) 65,039 and 78,091

(c) 323 and 493

(d) 9991 and 48,791

(e) 1597 and 2584

(f) 4,084,361 and 18,399,131

PROBLEM SOLVING EXTENSIONS

31.

A   B

You have a balance scale with an unlimited supply of 3-lb and 5-lb weights (but no other denominations). Examples: You can weigh 11 lb of potatoes on pan *A* by placing two 3-lb weights and one 5-lb weight on pan *B*. You can weigh 2 lb of potatoes by placing a 3-lb weight on one pan and a 5-lb weight on the other.

Is it possible to weigh the following amounts of potatoes? If so, tell how.

(a) 9 lb   (b) 22 lb   (c) 17 lb   (d) 1 lb   (e) 7 lb

(f) Describe all possible values which can be weighed, assuming there are no other limitations.

32. Repeat Problem 31 when there is an unlimited supply of 4-lb and 6-lb weights (but no other denominations).

33. Repeat Problem 31 when there is an unlimited supply of 6-lb and 9-lb weights.

34. Generalize the results of the three previous problems.

Fractions 5

5-1
DEFINING FRACTIONS

For a number of reasons, we can describe this chapter by saying, "The plot thickens." The whole numbers, though infinite in extent, are at times quite meager in applying to real-life situations. A vote requires a two-thirds majority; a car's gas tank is one-quarter full; three girls wish to divide two pizzas evenly. These examples do not represent even one-millionth of all the uses for fractions. The plot indeed thickens: we need more than just the whole numbers.

Our first of several extensions of the whole numbers is to the fractions. We extend first to the fractions because it is consistent with the historical development of numbers and, more important, it is consistent with our personal experiences. Young children usually encounter fractions in and out of school well before they encounter negative and irrational numbers, which we will discuss later. Moreover, fractions (including decimals and percentages) play a much more important role in the elementary school curriculum; so we choose to give them more attention.

Some changes are taking place. With the move towards the metric system, there is less need for arithmetic with ordinary fractions. We will always have some use for common fractions, like those cited in the opening paragraph of this section, but many of the settings that give rise to doing arithmetic with fractions (such as adding 3/8 inches + 5/16 inches) will vanish altogether with increased use of the metric system. As the old units are phased out and the metric units become more universally accepted, there will be an emphasis instead on decimals, which are in fact just a specific type of fraction. The popularity of hand calculators also dictates a greater stress on decimals. Mathematically, the idea is the same whether we divide our units into sixteenths and twelfths or into tenths, though of course computation is usually easier in the latter case because we have a base ten number system.

After introducing the fraction concept, we will consider their ordering and certain other properties. In the remaining two sections of this chapter, we will develop the arithmetic of fractions. Certain important applications of whole numbers and fractions will be investigated in the next chapter.

Among the ways in which fractions arise in real-life situations are circumstances in which we consider part of a whole and those in which we wish to divide one counting number by another, but find that no counting number is a solution. The voting and gas tank problems are examples of the "part of" interpretation, while the pizza problem is an example of the "division" interpretation.

Whole numbers were defined in terms of sets. (How?) One of our interpretations of fractions will also depend on sets. In Figure 5-1 is a set of five flowers, three of which are tulips. We say in this situation that three-fifths of the flowers are tulips. The fraction 3/5 is then a pair of whole numbers that compares part of a set with all of the set. Since the tulips are a subset of the entire set, we could say that the pair 3/5 stands for the number of members in a certain set *preceded* by the number of members in one of its subsets. Similar interpretations could be given for any symbol of the form p/q, where p is any whole number less than or equal to a non-zero whole number q.

FIGURE 5-1

Sometimes we interpret fractions in terms of what we call **area models**. To show 3/5 we would start with one unit, preferably a square, divide it into five parts having the same size and shape, and shade three of them, as shown in Figure 5-2. The shaded area would then represent 3/5. (Though children might have little or no knowledge of area at the time fractions are introduced, it is not difficult for them to recognize this as simply three parts out of five.) We will find the area model to be very useful later.

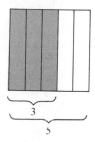

FIGURE 5-2

We alluded to another interpretation for fractions when we discussed division of whole numbers in Section 3-6. We saw that problems like $2 \div 3$ and $3 \div 2$ had no solution unless we introduced remainders. Yet the fact that when two pizzas are divided among three people each gets none with two left over (quotient = 0, remainder = 2) is of little help. In this case, it is more useful to know that each person gets two-thirds of a pizza. A practical way of accomplishing this is for each person to take one-third of each of the pizzas. If they were the same size, this would be equivalent to each person getting two-thirds of a pizza. The problem $3 \div 2$ also has a solution if we admit fractions. Assuming that two people are sharing three pizzas, each hungry person gets one pizza and half of the third one (1½ pizzas), or half of each one (which is three halves in all). By similar methods, we can introduce fractions to give an answer to any problem in which one whole number is divided by another (non-zero) whole number.

In the "part of" interpretation, the symbol p/q had meaning only when p was no bigger than q. This restriction is removed in the division interpretation. We require only that p and q are whole numbers and that q is not 0. We call expressions of this form **fractions**. The numbers p and q are called the **numerator** and **denominator** respectively. (We will often use the familiar notation $\frac{3}{5}$ and $\frac{p}{q}$ to represent what we have been calling 3/5 and p/q respectively.) Notice that the whole numbers have representations in this set since according to the division interpretation, 0/1 = 0, 1/1 = 1, 2/1 = 2, etc. Technically we have not explicitly defined fractions, but have merely given a name to a set of ordered pairs of whole numbers and have chosen to write the

ordered pair (p, q) either in the form p/q or in the form $\frac{p}{q}$.

We saw that the whole number 2 can be thought of as the fraction 2/1 in terms of the division interpretation. According to this interpretation, we also have 4/2 = 2, 6/3 = 2, 8/4 = 2, etc. Thus there are many fractions that represent the same whole number. The area model for fractions suggests that there are also many fractions that signify the same amount. This is shown in Figure 5-3, where we see that 2/3, 4/6, 6/9, and 8/12 each suggest the same part of the whole. Fractions like 2/3, 4/6, and 8/12, which name the same amount, are called **equivalent fractions**. Thus 2/1, 4/2, 6/3, and 8/4 are also equivalent fractions.

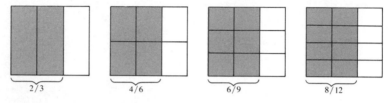

FIGURE 5-3

The area model strongly suggests, at least for fractions for which the numerator is less than or equal to the denominator, what we call

☐ The Reducing Fractions Principle

> If $\frac{p}{q}$ is any fraction and n is any whole number other than 0,
>
> then $\frac{p \times n}{q \times n}$ and $\frac{p}{q}$ are equivalent. $\left(\text{We will write } \frac{p \times n}{q \times n} = \frac{p}{q}.\right)$

For example, in saying that 8/12 = 2/3 we have $p = 2$, $q = 3$, and $n = 4$.

To argue that the reducing fractions principle also holds when p is larger than q, we can extend our area model. In order to represent an arbitrary fraction (like 13/5), we take a unit square, divide it into (five) parts of equal size and shape as before, and repeat this process successively until we have generated a number of parts equal to or greater than the numerator. Thus, in Figure 5-4, we see that three squares provide us with 15 fifths, of which we can take 13. Figures 5-4 and 5-5 then demonstrate that 13/5 is equivalent to 39/15.

According to the reducing fractions principle, the essential idea is to find a common factor of the numerator and denominator. A fraction is said to be **reduced** or **in lowest terms** when the numerator and denominator have no common factor other than 1. (If there were any other common factor, the

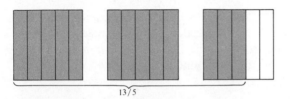

$13/5$

FIGURE 5-4

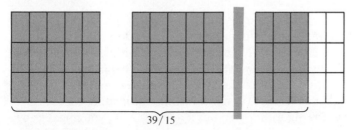

$39/15$

FIGURE 5-5

reducing fractions principle could be applied again to get an equivalent fraction in lower terms.) Hence we seek the greatest of all common factors of the numerator and denominator, which is precisely the greatest common divisor (GCD) of these two numbers as it was introduced in Chapter 4. Our next example shows how the techniques of Chapter 4 apply directly to reducing fractions.

Reduce (a) $\dfrac{20}{30}$ (b) $\dfrac{153}{204}$ (c) $\dfrac{2^5 \times 3^6 \times 11^8}{2^3 \times 3^{17} \times 7^2 \times 11}$ (d) $\dfrac{377}{261}$

EXAMPLE
5-1

SOLUTION

In Example 4-9 we found the GCD of each of these pairs of numbers. You may wish to refer to that example.

(a) Since $20 = 2 \times 2 \times 5$ and $30 = 2 \times 3 \times 5$, GCD $(20, 30) = 2 \times 5 = 10$. Thus $\dfrac{20}{30} = \dfrac{2\boxed{\times 2 \times 5}}{3\boxed{\times 2 \times 5}} = \dfrac{2}{3}$. (This may have been obvious. The next example is less obvious.)

(b) Common factors of 153 and 204 are not immediately apparent (except perhaps that each has a factor of 3), so we factor them into primes and learn that GCD (153, 204) is $3 \times 17 = 51$.

$$\frac{153}{204} = \frac{3\boxed{\times 3 \times 17}}{2 \times 2\boxed{\times 3 \times 17}} = \frac{3}{2 \times 2} = \frac{3}{4}$$

(c) By the method of Example 4-9, the GCD is $2^3 \times 3^6 \times 11$. Hence

$$\frac{2^5 \times 3^6 \times 11^8}{2^3 \times 3^{17} \times 7^2 \times 11} = \frac{(2^2 \times 11^7)\boxed{\times (2^3 \times 3^6 \times 11)}}{(3^{11} \times 7^2)\boxed{\times (2^3 \times 3^6 \times 11)}} = \frac{2^2 \times 11^7}{3^{11} \times 7^2}$$

(d) When we found GCD (377, 261) in Example 4-9, we commented that 261 is easy to factor ($261 = 3^2 \times 29$) and that 377 is not so easy to factor. We learned after factoring 261 that the only possible common prime factors are 3 and 29. We immediately found that 29 divided 377; namely, $377 = 29 \times 13$. Hence,

$$\frac{377}{261} = \frac{13 \times 29}{3 \times 3 \times 29} = \frac{13}{3 \times 3} = \frac{13}{9}$$

It is unlikely that in real-life situations you will need to reduce fractions like most of the ones in Example 5-1. The reason for their inclusion here is to give you further insight into the *method* involved. We have deliberately exposed you to unfamiliar fractions to avoid the biases you may have in working with the familiar ones, much as we did arithmetic in other bases to give you better insight into the algorithms. To put it another way, you might know that 6/8 = 3/4 without understanding why; but to solve problems like 377/261 = 13/9, it is more likely that you need to be aware of what is going on.

Our last remark on the topic of reducing fractions is that one does not always necessarily reduce a fraction just because it is possible. There are times, for instance, when 60/100 is a better form than 3/5. Can you think of such a time?

We saw in Figure 5-3 that two fractions can be equivalent though neither is a reduced form of the other. One such example is 6/9 and 8/12. We will now devise a test that applies to such cases as well. We will take the given fractions and replace them by equivalent fractions having the same denominator. By reducing 6/9 and 8/12 we see that they are each equivalent to 2/3, so they must be equivalent to each other:

$$\frac{6}{9} = \frac{2 \times 3}{3 \times 3} = \frac{2}{3} \quad \text{and} \quad \frac{8}{12} = \frac{2 \times 4}{3 \times 4} = \frac{2}{3}$$

Thus it worked in this example to reduce each fraction as far as possible and compare the reduced versions. Since *any* common denominator will facilitate direct comparison, there are other options. One number which is sure to be a common multiple of the two denominators is the least common multiple (LCM), which we investigated in Chapter 4. Since LCM (9, 12) = 36, we have

$$\frac{6}{9} = \frac{6 \times 4}{9 \times 4} = \frac{24}{36} \quad \text{and} \quad \frac{8}{12} = \frac{8 \times 3}{12 \times 3} = \frac{24}{36}$$

Finally, we mention that another common multiple of any two numbers is their product. Clearly 9×12 is a multiple of 9 and a multiple of 12. Hence,

$$\frac{6}{9} = \frac{6 \times 12}{9 \times 12} = \frac{72}{108} \quad \text{and} \quad \frac{8}{12} = \frac{8 \times 9}{12 \times 9} = \frac{72}{108}$$

While each of these options is quite acceptable, the last one is often the simplest to apply. Given 6/9 and 8/12, we see that one common denominator is simply 9×12 and the numerators are respectively 6×12 and 8×9. In general, given the fractions p/q and r/s, we have

$$\frac{p}{q} = \frac{p\boxed{\times s}}{q\boxed{\times s}} \quad \text{and} \quad \frac{r}{s} = \frac{r\boxed{\times q}}{s\boxed{\times q}} = \frac{r \times q}{q \times s}$$

Therefore, to compare $\frac{p}{q}$ and $\frac{r}{s}$ we need only compare $p \times s$ and $r \times q$. The fractions are equivalent if and only if $p \times s = r \times q$.

Test each pair of fractions to see if they are equivalent:

(a) $\frac{4}{5}$ and $\frac{7}{9}$ (b) $\frac{14}{91}$ and $\frac{23}{143}$

EXAMPLE

5-2

(a) Since $4 \times 9 \neq 7 \times 5$, the fractions are not equivalent. (The underlying idea is that

$$\frac{4}{5} = \frac{4\boxed{\times 9}}{5\boxed{\times 9}} = \frac{36}{45} \quad \text{and} \quad \frac{7}{9} = \frac{7\boxed{\times 5}}{9\boxed{\times 5}} = \frac{35}{45}.)$$

(b) Since $14 \times 143 = 2002 = 22 \times 91$, the fractions are equivalent. (This would be a convenient place to use a calculator.) (The underlying idea is that

$$\frac{14}{91} = \frac{14\boxed{\times 143}}{91\boxed{\times 143}} = \frac{2002}{3913} \quad \text{and} \quad \frac{22}{143} = \frac{22\boxed{\times 91}}{143\boxed{\times 91}} = \frac{2002}{3913}.)$$

It should be clear that any fraction is either in lowest terms or is equivalent to exactly one fraction which is in lowest terms. This is an immediate consequence of the Unique Factorization Theorem. The explicit process of factoring the numerator and denominator into primes and "canceling" the common factors necessarily arrives at a well-defined answer. Hence the collection of all possible fractions is partitioned into various (non-overlapping) sets of equivalent fractions which we will call **classes**. Some of the possible classes are:

$$\left\{ \frac{1}{2}, \frac{2}{4}, \frac{3}{6}, \frac{4}{8}, \frac{5}{10}, \cdots \right\}$$

$$\left\{ \frac{1}{3}, \frac{2}{6}, \frac{3}{9}, \frac{4}{12}, \frac{5}{15}, \cdots \right\}$$

$$\left\{\frac{2}{3}, \frac{4}{6}, \frac{6}{9}, \frac{8}{12}, \frac{10}{15}, \cdots\right\}$$

$$\left\{\frac{2}{13}, \frac{4}{26}, \frac{6}{39}, \frac{8}{52}, \cdots, \frac{14}{91}, \cdots, \frac{22}{143}, \cdots, \frac{2002}{13013}, \cdots\right\} \text{ (see Example 5-2)}$$

$$\left\{\frac{3}{1}, \frac{6}{2}, \frac{9}{3}, \frac{12}{4}, \frac{15}{5}, \cdots\right\}$$

$$\left\{\frac{4}{3}, \frac{8}{6}, \frac{12}{9}, \frac{16}{12}, \frac{20}{15}, \cdots\right\}$$

Up to now, we have thought of fractions as certain pairs of whole numbers. But our experience suggests that fractions themselves can be thought of as numbers which can be compared and which can be added, subtracted, multiplied, and divided. Since each member of a class represents the "same amount" (in terms of area models, such as Figure 5-3), an entire class gives us just one number. In accordance with common usage, we will call these numbers *fractions*. Thus the term *fraction* takes on both a numeral sense (as a representative for a number) and a number sense (as an amount). We do not wish to become overly concerned with the distinction between numerals and numbers. Consequently, we write "1/2 = 2/4" to mean both "the fractions (numerals) 1/2 and 2/4 are equivalent" and "the fractions (numbers) 1/2 and 2/4 are equal." (In other books you may encounter symbols like $\sim$, $\simeq$, or $\cong$ used to mean "is equivalent to.") It is important to remember that each number has (infinitely) many names.

Among the classes to which our new numbers have been assigned are the ones that correspond to whole numbers — that is, the classes for 0, 1, 2, . . . respectively:

$$\left\{\frac{0}{1}, \frac{0}{2}, \frac{0}{3}, \frac{0}{4}, \cdots\right\}$$

$$\left\{\frac{1}{1}, \frac{2}{2}, \frac{3}{3}, \frac{4}{4}, \cdots\right\}$$

$$\left\{\frac{2}{1}, \frac{4}{2}, \frac{6}{3}, \frac{8}{4}, \cdots\right\}$$

. . .

Thus the set of fractions includes the whole numbers as special cases. We will refer to this process of enlarging the set of whole numbers into a larger set as **extending** the whole numbers. We want to gain some new properties (like being able to divide 2 by 3) while preserving everything that worked for the whole numbers (ordering, addition and its properties, etc.).

One of the first things we did with whole numbers, even before we began to add and subtract them, was to order them. Given two whole numbers, the first was either less than, equal to, or greater than the second. (This was called the trichotomy property for comparing whole numbers.) Is there such a property for the fractions?

Given two fractions, they will be **equal** (the same number) if and only if their representatives come from the same class of equivalent fractions. Thus we can test to see if two such numbers are equal by checking if their representatives are equivalent fractions. To compare numbers which are not equal, we initiate the following definition:

The fraction $\frac{p}{q}$ is **less than** the fraction $\frac{r}{s}$, written "$\frac{p}{q} < \frac{r}{s}$," if and

only if $p \times s < r \times q$. $\frac{p}{q}$ is **greater than** $\frac{r}{s}$, written "$\frac{p}{q} > \frac{r}{s}$," if and

only if $p \times s > r \times q$.

Note that we have defined $<$ for fractions p/q and r/s in terms of $<$ for the whole numbers $p \times s$ and $q \times r$. The idea here is the same as what we do to determine whether two fractions are equivalent. We express them in a form where they have a common denominator and compare their numerators. It may not be immediately obvious which is greater, 4/5 or 7/9, but expressing them in terms of fractions having a common denominator, it is clear that 36/45 > 35/45 (so 4/5 > 7/9). It turns out that we compared 36, which is 4 × 9, with 35, which is 7 × 5. Just as the definition of $>$ says, 4/5 > 7/9 since 4 × 9 > 7 × 5.

In search of a trichotomy property for comparing fractions, suppose p/q and r/s are two such numbers. We compare them by looking at $p \times s$ and $r \times q$. Since p and s are whole numbers, so is $p \times s$. Similarly, $r \times q$ is a whole number. Now, by the trichotomy property for comparing *whole numbers*, exactly one of three things must be true about the whole numbers $p \times s$ and $r \times q$:

(1) $p \times s < r \times q$,

(2) $p \times s = r \times q$, or

(3) $p \times s > r \times q$.

But these three statements, respectively, tell us that

(1) $\frac{p}{q} < \frac{r}{s}$,

(2) $\frac{p}{q} = \frac{r}{s}$, or

(3) $\frac{p}{q} > \frac{r}{s}$.

Hence exactly one of these three statements about fractions must be true, and we have our **trichotomy property for comparing fractions**.

An interesting question arises because each non-negative rational number has many representations. We saw earlier that 4/5 > 7/9. Now suppose we represent the same numbers in other ways. Is it necessarily true that 8/10 > 21/27, for instance?! A check of this one case shows that 8 × 27 > 21 × 10. Can we depend on being this fortunate in every case? The answer turns out to be yes. (See Problem 29.) If we think in terms of area models, the statement seems reasonable enough. If one figure has more area than another, dividing each of them into more (or fewer) pieces will have no effect. (See Problem 15.) Figure 5-6 illustrates our special case, that if 4/5 > 7/9, then 8/10 > 21/27. We use the term **well-defined** to refer to a definition that holds regardless of the choice of representation. Thus "greater than" as applied to fractions is well-defined.

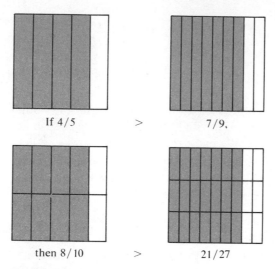

If 4/5   >   7/9,

then 8/10   >   21/27

FIGURE 5-6

Having begun an extension of the whole numbers, we want to check to see whether our new rules are consistent with the old ones. For instance, 2 < 3 if we think of them as whole numbers. It had better be the case that 2/1 < 3/1 when we think of these numbers as fractions. This is easy to check, since 2/1 < 3/1 is true if and only if $2 \times 1 < 3 \times 1$. Any time we have $p < q$, then $p/1 < q/1$ since $p \times 1 < q \times 1$. Making sure that definitions are well-defined and consistent is crucial throughout each of our extensions of the whole numbers.

In Chapter 3 it was helpful to pair the whole numbers with certain points on a line. We referred to this geometric representation as a number line and used it to illustrate addition and other operations with whole numbers. Is there a reasonable way to locate the fractions on a number line that will be suggestive later when we add, subtract, multiply, and divide them? We seek a way that would preserve order (1/5 should come "before 2/5," etc.) and would preserve distance (the distance from 1/5 to 2/5 should be the same as the distance from 2/5 to 3/5, etc.).

The fractions, whether interpreted on the number line or not, have a property not applicable to the whole numbers. Between any two consecutive whole numbers, such as 0 and 1, there is no other whole number, yet between two fractions there is always another. 37/100 and 38/100 may seem close together, but rewritten as 370/1000 and 380/1000 it is easy to see that 371/1000, 372/1000, 373/1000, . . . , 379/1000 are all between 37/100 and 38/100. Such is the case for any two fractions.

**EXAMPLE
5-3**

Find a fraction between 1/8 and 1/7.

First find a common denominator and express each of these fractions using the common denominator: 1/8 = 7/56 and 1/7 = 8/56. Now get equivalent fractions by multiplying numerators and denominators by 10. 1/8 = 7/56 = 70/560 and 1/7 = 8/56 = 80/560. Then 71/560 is an answer.

SOLUTION

We already have common *numerators*, but the denominators are "too close together." So, 1/8 = 2/16 and 1/7 = 2/14. Then 2/15 is an answer. In the problems at the end of this section we will show another way to get the answer 2/15.

ALTERNATIVE SOLUTIONS

Our number line as we would like to have it (so far) can be described as follows:

(1) We mark two points and identify them with the numbers 0 and 1. (1 is placed to the right of 0.) We lay off equally spaced points to the right using copies of the part of the line between 0 and 1 and match these points in the natural way with the numbers 2, 3, 4, ... These same points 0, 1, 2, 3, 4, . . . are also named 0/1, 1/1, 2/1, 3/1, ...

(2) We insert 1/2 halfway between 0/1 and 1/1 (by dividing the segment from 0 to 1 in half). Then we insert 1/3 and 2/3 one-third and two-thirds of the way between 0/1 and 1/1 respectively (by dividing the segment from 0 to 1 in thirds). Similarly, we insert 1/4, 2/4 = 1/2, and 3/4; then 1/5, 2/5, 3/5, 4/5, etc. A similar procedure is simultaneously carried out between 1/1 and 2/1, between 2/1 and 3/1, etc.

(3) By preserving order and distance, certain points to the right of the origin matched up with the fractions. It may seem as though we have completely used up all the points on this part of the line. However, there remain points to the right of the origin which have not been paired with any fractions. We will exhibit such points in Chapter 8. Thus the pairing of numbers and points is *not* yet complete. Of course, it is far from complete in that we have said nothing of the points to the left of the origin.

Though the story is not over yet, the plot has indeed thickened.

EXERCISES AND PROBLEMS 5-1

DEFINITION

1. Illustrate each of the following interpretations for 5/6:
   (a) set   (b) area model   (c) division   (d) number line

2. (a) Make up some "real-life" division problems where we would prefer to have the answers expressed as quotients and remainders.
   (b) Make up some "real-life" division problems where we would prefer to have the answers expressed as fractions.

3. A company advertises its product on sale for "a fraction of the original cost." What information does this provide about the sale price?

4. Why might a rectangle area model be better than a circle area model for children?

5. Tell how to fold a string into
   (a) two equal parts   (b) four equal parts   (c) three equal parts.

6. Describe how to locate (precisely) 3/5 on a number line.

7. Change to base ten fractions:

   (a) $\dfrac{1}{10_{\text{two}}}$ (b) $\dfrac{1}{10_{\text{three}}}$ (c) $\dfrac{1}{10_{\text{five}}}$ (d) $\dfrac{1}{10_{\text{twelve}}}$

8. Ann drank a 16-ounce bottle of pop and Joyce drank a 12-ounce bottle. "I drank 1/3 more," said Ann. "I drank 1/4 less," said Joyce. Who was right?

EQUIVALENT FRACTIONS

9. Give five different fractions which name the whole number 6. Give five different fractions equivalent to 3/8.

10. Use an area model to show that 5/9 = 20/36.

11. Which pairs of fractions are equivalent?
    (a) 9/12 and 15/20   (b) 17/4 and 13/3
    (c) 4/9 and 2/3   (d) 18/6 and 42/14

12. Show that 5/3 = 1⅔ by dividing five pizzas among three people in two different ways.

13. Give a real-life example of when it is more convenient to think of 3/5 as 60/100.

14. Figure 5-3 shows that 6/9 and 8/12 are equivalent, though neither is a reduced form of the other. Find another such pair of fractions in Figure 5-3.

15. A guy ordered a pizza. Asked if he wanted it cut into four pieces or six, he replied "Four, I'm not that hungry." He was obviously unaware that what two fractions are equivalent?

16. In a story for children involving fractions, the "bad guy" 2/3 assumes a disguise as 4/6. What other disguises can he assume?

17. Reduce each of these fractions to lowest terms: (a) 6/8   (b) 4/10   (c) 4/9
    (d) 34/51   (e) 52/65   (f) 253/207   (g) 477/1537   (h) 237/869

18. How many ways are there to reduce 18/24 (not necessarily completely)?

19. Use the Euclidean algorithm to reduce each to lowest terms: (a) 1007/1219
    (b) 8051/13,363

20. Does $\dfrac{3 \times 2}{4 \times 2} = \dfrac{3}{4}$? Does $\dfrac{3+2}{4+2} = \dfrac{3}{4}$? Draw a conclusion about "canceling."

21. Note that $\dfrac{1\cancel{6}}{\cancel{6}4} = \dfrac{1}{4}$. Find another such example.

22. When possible, write each of the following as a fraction whose denominator is a power of 10; namely, 1, 10, 100, 1000, 10000, etc. Explain those cases that won't work.

    (a) $\dfrac{1}{5}$ (b) $\dfrac{1}{3}$ (c) $\dfrac{4}{25}$ (d) $\dfrac{3}{80}$

    (e) $\dfrac{5}{18}$ (f) $\dfrac{7}{60}$ (g) $\dfrac{1}{90}$ (h) $\dfrac{1}{11}$

(i) $\dfrac{3}{40}$ (j) $\dfrac{5}{140}$ (k) $\dfrac{7}{140}$ (Careful!)

(l) $\dfrac{65}{64}$ (m) $\dfrac{64}{65}$

23. Generalize Problem 22, characterizing all fractions that can be written with a denominator which is a power of 10.

ORDER

24. (a) Which is greater, 9/11 or 4/5? How can you tell?
   (b) Find a fraction between 9/11 and 4/5.

25. Write in order, smallest to largest:

   (a) $\dfrac{1}{4}, \dfrac{1}{5}, \dfrac{1}{6}$ (b) $\dfrac{1}{5}, \dfrac{2}{5}, \dfrac{3}{5}$

   (c) $\dfrac{2}{7}, \dfrac{3}{10}, \dfrac{5}{17}$ (d) $\dfrac{3}{5}, \dfrac{5}{8}, \dfrac{11}{18}$

26. Find a fraction between:

   (a) $\dfrac{63}{100}$ and $\dfrac{64}{100}$ (b) $\dfrac{1}{12}$ and $\dfrac{1}{11}$

   (c) $\dfrac{5}{6}$ and $\dfrac{6}{7}$ (d) $\dfrac{p}{q}$ and $\dfrac{r}{s}$

27. When Melissa tried to find a fraction between $\dfrac{1}{8}$ and $\dfrac{1}{7}$, she noticed that $\dfrac{1+1}{8+7} = \dfrac{2}{15}$ worked, but she didn't know why. "Will this always work?" she asked.

   (a) Is $\dfrac{2+5}{7+9}$ between $\dfrac{2}{7}$ and $\dfrac{5}{9}$? Prove it.

   (b) Try several more examples. Does this method work?

   (c) Show that this works every time, or give an example to show it doesn't work.

28. For what values of p and q is $\dfrac{p}{q} < \dfrac{p+1}{q+1}$.

*29. Show that "greater than" (applied to fractions) is well-defined.

*30. Show that "greater than" (applied to fractions) is transitive.

MATERIALS AND CALCULATORS

31. If a purple rod equals 1, what is the value of
   (a) a white rod?
   (b) a red rod?
   (c) a yellow rod?

32. Repeat Problem 31 if a dark green rod equals 1.

33. Repeat Problem 31 if an orange rod equals 1.

34. (a) Explain how to use the rods to show that 1/2 is equivalent to 2/4.
   (b) To show that 6/9 is equivalent to 2/3, which rod should you choose to represent 1? Why?

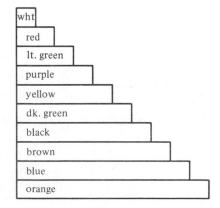

C35. Use the definition of "less than" for fractions and a calculator to determine which fraction in each pair is smaller:

(a) $\dfrac{243}{534}$ and $\dfrac{298}{654}$ (b) $\dfrac{79}{5464}$ and $\dfrac{119}{8231}$

(c) $\dfrac{87}{2842}$ and $\dfrac{3}{98}$ (d) $\dfrac{419}{2250}$ and $\dfrac{192}{1031}$

C36. Outline a procedure for comparing fractions using decimal notation. Use it to compare the fractions in the previous problem.

*P37. Write a program that reduces fractions to lowest terms.

PROBLEM SOLVING EXTENSIONS

38. Solve this cryptarithm, where C > 0 and all values are different from 0.

$$\frac{PORK}{CHOP} = C$$

39. (a) If pizzas can be ordered with or without each of five ingredients, in how many different ways may a pizza be ordered?
   *(b) Answer this question if each ingredient may be placed on all, half, or none of the pizza. For example, a pizza might be ordered with sausage and mushrooms, and anchovies on half.

*40. The **Farey sequence of order n** is the increasing sequence of all fractions $\dfrac{p}{q}$ such that $\dfrac{p}{q}$ is in lowest terms, $0 \le \dfrac{p}{q} \le 1$, and $q \le n$. For example, the Farey sequence of order 5 is $\dfrac{0}{1}, \dfrac{1}{5}, \dfrac{1}{4}, \dfrac{1}{3}, \dfrac{2}{5}, \dfrac{1}{2}, \dfrac{3}{5}, \dfrac{2}{3}, \dfrac{3}{4}, \dfrac{4}{5}, \dfrac{1}{1}$. Find the Farey sequence of order (a) 3   (b) 4   (c) 6   (d) 7.   (Hint: These properties may be helpful: If a/b, c/d, e/f, are consecutive terms of a Farey sequence, then $bc - ad = 1$ and $\dfrac{c}{d} = \dfrac{a + e}{b + f}$.)

41. The sequence $\dfrac{1}{3}, \dfrac{1 + 3}{5 + 7}, \dfrac{1 + 3 + 5}{7 + 9 + 11}, \dfrac{1 + 3 + 5 + 7}{9 + 11 + 13 + 15}, \cdots$ was discovered by Galileo while studying free-falling bodies. Verify that

(a) $\dfrac{1 + 3}{5 + 7} = \dfrac{1}{3}$.   (b) $\dfrac{1 + 3 + 5}{7 + 9 + 11} = \dfrac{1}{3}$.   (c) $\dfrac{1 + 3 + 5 + 7}{9 + 11 + 13 + 15} = \dfrac{1}{3}$.

(d) What is the next term in the sequence? Does it equal 1/3?
*(e) What is the 54th term in the sequence? Does it equal 1/3?

5-2
ADDITION AND SUBTRACTION OF FRACTIONS

We saw in the previous section how fractions help fill certain gaps in the whole numbers. By incorporating them into our system, we can solve more problems involving whole numbers, for we are assured of an answer when we divide one whole number by another (non-zero) whole number. But a new question arises: Can we divide (and add, subtract, and multiply) these new numbers themselves, or have we merely created a different breed of undefined problems?

Our experience with elementary school mathematics tells us that it is possible to perform these operations, so our next goal is to develop our mathematical structure to include the arithmetic of fractions. Again we investigate *why* things are done as they are, beginning with addition.

First among our objectives is finding a suitable definition for addition of fractions. Since the whole numbers are special cases of fractions, we know what must happen in certain instances. For one thing, it had better be true that $\frac{3}{1} + \frac{2}{1}$ $= \frac{5}{1}$, or for any whole numbers p and r that $\frac{p}{1} + \frac{r}{1} = \frac{p+r}{1}$. Our intuition, based on the arithmetic of whole numbers, also strongly suggests that three things added to two of the same things ought to be five of these things. So $\frac{3}{7} + \frac{2}{7}$ "should be" $\frac{5}{7}$, or in general $\frac{p}{q} + \frac{r}{q} = \frac{p+r}{q}$. The less obvious decision is what to do with fractions with unlike denominators, such as $\frac{3}{4} + \frac{2}{7}$. Here we take advantage of the fact that these fractions have other names. We list some of the names for the fractions $\frac{3}{4}$ and $\frac{2}{7}$:

$$\text{Names for } \frac{3}{4}: \quad \frac{3}{4}, \frac{6}{8}, \frac{9}{12}, \frac{12}{16}, \frac{15}{20}, \frac{18}{24}, \frac{21}{28}, \frac{24}{32}, \cdots$$

$$\text{Names for } \frac{2}{7}: \quad \frac{2}{7}, \frac{4}{14}, \frac{6}{21}, \frac{8}{28}, \frac{10}{35}, \frac{12}{42}, \frac{14}{49}, \frac{16}{56}, \cdots$$

If we handle matters properly, the problem $\frac{3}{4} + \frac{2}{7}$ should give the same answer as the problem $\frac{21}{28} + \frac{8}{28}$. Once the original problem is replaced by one with equivalent fractions having a common denominator, we simply add the numerators as we did in the previous example, this time getting 29/28.

Each of these problems is illustrated by an area model in Figure 5-7. In the first two problems, we are merely combining like objects directly. In part (a) each region is one unit, so we read off the answer as a total of five units, or 5/1. In part (b) each region is 1/7, so we read off the answer as a total of five 1/7's, or 5/7. In part (c) the horizontal lines are drawn in to show that 3/4 is equivalent to 21/28 and that 2/7 is equivalent to 8/28. Then we read off the answer as a total of 29 1/28's, or 29/28. Finding a common denominator for the two fractions is done by taking the product of the given denominators. Geometrically this means that cutting fourths into seven like pieces yields the same result as cutting sevenths into four like pieces.

When adding fractions with unlike denominators, we capitalize on their having alternate representations. To give a definition for adding fractions, we need only tell how to add fractions with common denominators, for we can always convert a problem involving the addition of fractions into one in which the denominators are the same.

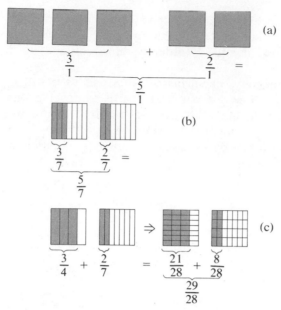

FIGURE 5-7

☐ Definition for Adding Fractions

If $\frac{p}{q}$ and $\frac{r}{q}$ are fractions, then $\frac{p}{q} + \frac{r}{q}$ is called their **sum** and is defined to be $\frac{p + r}{q}$.

It may seem at first that little is accomplished by replacing $\frac{p}{q} + \frac{r}{q}$ by $\frac{p + r}{q}$. The point is that the "new" idea of having a plus sign between fractions is explained in terms of the "old" idea of having a plus sign between whole numbers.

We will now look at some examples, including several at a level beyond what is usually expected in elementary school mathematics.

EXAMPLE 5-4

Perform the following additions:

(a) $\frac{5}{8} + \frac{3}{4}$ (b) $\frac{1}{6} + \frac{2}{5} + \frac{3}{4}$ (c) $\frac{2}{153} + \frac{5}{204}$

(d) $\dfrac{1}{2^5 \times 3^6 \times 11^8} + \dfrac{1}{2^3 \times 3^{17} \times 7^2 \times 11}$

SOLUTION

(a) Common denominators are easily recognizable. We could use 8, the LCM of 8 and 4; or we could use 32, the product of 8 and 4; or for that matter we could use 16 or 64 or many others. Using 8, we have $\dfrac{5}{8} + \dfrac{3}{4} =$ $\dfrac{5}{8} + \dfrac{6}{8} = \dfrac{5+6}{8} = \dfrac{11}{8}$.

(b) When we have three or more fractions, it is easiest to find one common denominator for all the fractions. In this case LCM $(6, 5, 4) = 60$ is an easy-to-find common denominator. Thus $\dfrac{1}{6} + \dfrac{2}{5} + \dfrac{3}{4} = \dfrac{1 \times 10}{6 \times 10} +$ $\dfrac{2 \times 12}{5 \times 12} + \dfrac{3 \times 15}{4 \times 15} = \dfrac{10}{60} + \dfrac{24}{60} + \dfrac{45}{60} = \dfrac{10 + 24 + 45}{60} = \dfrac{79}{60}$.

(c) One common denominator for 2/153 and 5/204 is the LCM of 153 and 204. Since $153 = 3^2 \times 17$ and $204 = 2^2 \times 3 \times 17$, LCM $(153, 204) =$ $2^2 \times 3^2 \times 17 = 612$. So $\dfrac{2}{153} + \dfrac{5}{204} = \dfrac{2 \times 4}{153 \times 4} + \dfrac{5 \times 3}{204 \times 3} = \dfrac{8}{612} + \dfrac{15}{612}$ $= \dfrac{8 + 15}{612} = \dfrac{23}{612}$. Alternatively, we could use the product of the denominators as a common denominator. Then $\dfrac{2}{153} + \dfrac{5}{204} =$ $\dfrac{2 \times 204}{153 \times 204} + \dfrac{5 \times 153}{204 \times 153} = \dfrac{408}{31212} + \dfrac{765}{31212} = \dfrac{408 + 765}{31212} = \dfrac{1173}{31212}$. This answer is satisfactory, but may be reduced by a common factor of 51 to $\dfrac{23}{612}$.

(d) Again we can use the LCM $(2^5 \times 3^6 \times 11^8, 2^3 \times 3^{17} \times 7^2 \times 11) =$ $2^5 \times 3^{17} \times 7^2 \times 11^8$. Therefore,

$$\frac{1}{2^5 \times 3^6 \times 11^8} + \frac{1}{2^3 \times 3^{17} \times 7^2 \times 11}$$

$$= \frac{3^{11} \times 7^2}{2^5 \times 3^{17} \times 7^2 \times 11^8} + \frac{2^2 \times 11^7}{2^5 \times 3^{17} \times 7^2 \times 11^8}$$

$$= \frac{3^{11} \times 7^2 + 2^2 \times 11^7}{2^5 \times 3^{17} \times 7^2 \times 11^8}.$$

In our more careful look at the arithmetic of fractions, we should be aware of a few concerns. We saw when adding whole numbers that the sum is necessarily a whole number, but when subtracting whole numbers that many problems (such as $2 - 6$) are undefined. This suggests that we ought to check when our rule for adding fractions is defined. We admit as a fraction any expression which is a pair of whole numbers a/b where b is not 0. This means that in our definition p, q, and r are whole numbers and that q isn't 0. Our rule says that the sum is $\dfrac{p + r}{q}$. Is this always a fraction? Certainly q is an acceptable denominator, since it is the denominator of the given fractions. The numerator $p + r$ is the sum of the two whole numbers and hence must be a whole number. Therefore $\dfrac{p + r}{q}$ is of the desired form and we can safely say that the sum of two fractions is a fraction; or briefly, that the set of fractions is closed under addition.

There is a second concern. Our definition applies to any two fractions having a common denominator. But there are many choices of common denominators for adding two arbitrary fractions. Will it matter which one we select? An illustration of this appeared in Example 5-4(c): $\frac{2}{153} + \frac{5}{204} = \frac{23}{612}$ when a common denominator of 612 is used, but $\frac{2}{153} + \frac{5}{204} = \frac{1173}{31212}$ when a common denominator of 31212 is used. Since $\frac{1173}{31212} = \frac{23 \times 51}{612 \times 51} = \frac{23}{612}$, the sums in this case are equivalent. We are asking now if we can depend on getting a well-defined sum for all choices of common denominators in each problem we do. To answer this question, we show first that the sum of two fractions using any common denominator is the same as the sum using the lowest common denominator. We use the fact that all common denominators are multiples of the lowest common denominator. (See Problem 16.) Suppose we begin with any two fractions, which when expressed in terms of a lowest common denominator are p/q and r/q. Let $\frac{p \times n}{q \times n}$ and $\frac{r \times n}{q \times n}$ be representations of these fractions with any other common denominator. We wish to show that the sum given by $\frac{p}{q} + \frac{r}{q}$ is equivalent to the sum given by $\frac{p \times n}{q \times n} + \frac{r \times n}{q \times n}$. Let's compute the second sum and show that it is the same as the first:

$$\frac{p \times n}{q \times n} + \frac{r \times n}{q \times n} = \frac{p \times n + r \times n}{q \times n} \qquad \text{Definition for adding fractions.}$$

$$= \frac{(p + r) \times n}{q \times n} \qquad \text{Distributive property (for whole numbers)}$$

$$= \frac{p + r}{q} \qquad \text{Reducing fractions principle}$$

$$= \frac{p}{q} + \frac{r}{q} \qquad \text{Definition for adding fractions}$$

This shows that when the definition is applied to two fractions using any common denominator we get the same result as when it is applied using the lowest common denominator. It follows that all choices of common denominator yield the same result. To say that we get the same sum regardless of choice of representation is to say that addition of fractions is well-defined.

Now that we see that our definition guarantees that all sums of fractions are defined (and well-defined), we can investigate for other properties. Since our definition applies only to fractions having a common denominator, we will assume that the fractions we are adding are in this form. This is not an unreasonable assumption, since we have just shown that the way in which the common denominator is selected does not alter the sum.

One property we can easily check is commutativity: Does the order in which we add affect the sum? For given fractions p/q and r/q, does $\frac{p}{q} + \frac{r}{q} = \frac{r}{q} + \frac{p}{q}$? According to the definition for adding fractions, this is the same as asking whether $\dfrac{p + r}{q} = \dfrac{r \times p}{q}$. But this is a simple consequence of the commutative property for adding *whole numbers*, so we are done. If you prefer, this could be written out in this form:

$$\frac{p}{q} + \frac{r}{q} = \frac{p + r}{q} \qquad \text{Definition for adding fractions}$$

$$= \frac{r + p}{q} \qquad \text{Commutative property for adding whole numbers}$$

$$= \frac{r}{q} + \frac{p}{q} \qquad \text{Definition for adding fractions}$$

It should not be surprising that the commutative property for adding fractions depends on the commutative property for adding whole numbers, since addition of fractions is defined in terms of addition of whole numbers.

Another thing to check is whether there is an identity element for addition in the set of fractions, a member of the set which when added to any fraction gives that fraction as the sum. We know that 0 is the identity for adding whole numbers, so the likely candidate among fractions is 0/1, a fraction that corresponds to the whole number 0. We find that for any fraction p/q we have $\dfrac{p}{q} + \dfrac{0}{1} = \dfrac{p}{q} + \dfrac{0 \times q}{1 \times q} = \dfrac{p}{q} + \dfrac{0}{q} = \dfrac{p + 0}{q} = \dfrac{p}{q}$. Since we know addition of fractions is commutative, we also have $\dfrac{0}{1} + \dfrac{p}{q} = \dfrac{p}{q}$, so (since it has the desired property whether added on the right or on the left) 0/1 is an identity for adding fractions. Notice that in saying $\dfrac{p + 0}{q} = \dfrac{p}{q}$ we invoked the identity property for whole numbers, so again a property for fractions depends on the corresponding property for whole numbers.

Three properties for adding fractions which are analogs of properties of adding whole numbers — closure, commutativity, and identity — have been mentioned so far. Can you think of any other properties that might exist? Do you see a pattern developing? Once we establish a definition for addition of fractions in terms of addition of whole numbers, all the "new" properties are simple consequences of the "old" ones.

This highly desirable feature of our work encourages us to define subtraction of fractions in a similar way: express the given fractions in terms of a common denominator and then define $\dfrac{p}{q} - \dfrac{r}{q} = \dfrac{p - r}{q}$. Examples:

$$\frac{3}{4} - \frac{1}{4} = \frac{3 - 1}{4} = \frac{2}{4}$$

$$\frac{7}{10} - \frac{4}{10} = \frac{7 - 4}{10} = \frac{3}{10}$$

$$\frac{1}{2} - \frac{1}{3} = \frac{3}{6} - \frac{2}{6} = \frac{3 - 2}{6} = \frac{1}{6}$$

$$\frac{1}{8} - \frac{7}{8} = \frac{1 - 7}{8} \text{ is undefined, since } 1 - 7 \text{ is undefined.}$$

Something else is inherited from whole number arithmetic! Since we cannot subtract a larger whole number from a smaller one (and get a whole number answer), neither can we subtract a larger fraction from a smaller one (and get a fraction for an answer). Thus $\frac{p}{q} - \frac{r}{q}$ is defined only when $\frac{p}{q} \geq \frac{r}{q}$. Since it is not always possible to subtract one arbitrary fraction from another, we say that the set of fractions is *not* closed under subtraction. (Recall that the whole numbers are not closed under subtraction, either.)

What about other properties for subtraction of fractions? We will investigate the existence of an identity and let you decide for yourself about the others. Again we get a clue from whole number arithmetic, where we found that 0 is an identity "on the right" (for instance, $17 - 0 = 17$) but not "on the left" ($0 - 17$ is undefined). We try 0/1 as a candidate for the identity. As we might expect, for an arbitrary fraction $\frac{p}{q}$, $\frac{p}{q} - \frac{0}{1} = \frac{p}{q} - \frac{0 \times q}{1 \times q} = \frac{p}{q} - \frac{0}{q} = \frac{p - 0}{q} = \frac{p}{q}$, so it serves the purpose on the right, but $\frac{0}{1} - \frac{p}{q} = \frac{0 \times q}{1 \times q} - \frac{p}{q} = \frac{0}{q} - \frac{p}{q} = \frac{0 - p}{q}$, which is not defined unless p is 0. Since it fails to work on the left, 0/1 is not an identity element for subtraction. Actually, the restriction on the definition (that larger fractions cannot be subtracted from smaller ones) eliminates the possibility of a two-sided identity. For instance, if a/b is the identity we must have (among other things) $\frac{1}{2} - \frac{a}{b} = \frac{1}{2}$ and $\frac{a}{b} - \frac{1}{2} = \frac{1}{2}$. But if $\frac{1}{2} - \frac{a}{b}$ is defined, a/b must be no more than 1/2, and if $\frac{a}{b} - \frac{1}{2}$ is defined, a/b must be no less than 1/2. The only possibility is that $a/b = 1/2$, in which case $\frac{1}{2} - \frac{a}{b} = \frac{1}{2}$ fails.

Both addition and subtraction of fractions can be represented on the number line with a few modifications of what we did for the whole numbers.

EXAMPLE 5-5

Represent each of these on the number line:

(a) $\frac{3}{7} + \frac{2}{7}$ (b) $\frac{3}{4} + \frac{2}{3}$ (c) $\frac{3}{4} - \frac{1}{4}$

SOLUTION

(a)

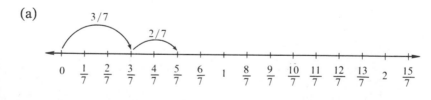

(b) To display this problem, it is easiest to use first our knowledge of equivalent fractions to express $\frac{3}{4} + \frac{2}{3}$ in terms of a common denominator as $\frac{9}{12} + \frac{8}{12}$, and then to mark off the number line in twelfths.

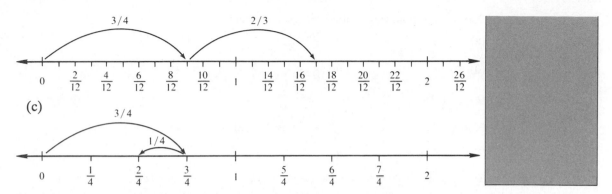

(c)

We summarize this section by noting that addition and subtraction of fractions are defined in terms of addition and subtraction of whole numbers, using the fact 'that fractions can be expressed in terms of common denominators. The fractions inherit all the properties the whole numbers possess with respect to addition and lack the properties the whole numbers lack with respect to subtraction. A few properties remain to be checked in the problems.

EXERCISES AND PROBLEMS 5-2

DEFINITION

1. Give three different common denominators for each pair of fractions:

   (a) $\dfrac{2}{3}, \dfrac{5}{6}$ (b) $\dfrac{4}{5}, \dfrac{7}{9}$ (c) $\dfrac{p}{q}, \dfrac{r}{s}$

2. Tell in each case whether the " $+$ " refers to the addition of fractions or to the addition of whole numbers: (a) $\dfrac{p + r}{q}$ (b) $\dfrac{p}{q} + \dfrac{r}{s}$ (c) $\dfrac{p}{q + s}$

3. Perform the following additions:

   (a) $\dfrac{3}{7} + \dfrac{1}{7}$ (b) $\dfrac{1}{2} + \dfrac{1}{4}$ (c) $\dfrac{1}{6} + \dfrac{2}{7} + \dfrac{3}{8}$

   (d) $\dfrac{9}{21} + \dfrac{1}{39}$ (e) $\dfrac{3}{10} + \dfrac{7}{100}$ (f) $\dfrac{1}{10} + \dfrac{31}{1000}$

   (g) $\dfrac{7}{869} + \dfrac{2}{237}$ (h) $\dfrac{1}{2^3 \times 3^7} + \dfrac{1}{2^5 \times 3^2}$

   (i) $\dfrac{1}{2^3 \times 3^{20} \times 7^{11}} + \dfrac{1}{3^4 \times 5^3 \times 7^{15}}$

4. Display the problem $\dfrac{3}{4} + \dfrac{2}{5}$ using (a) an area model.   (b) a number line.

5. The discussion about the sum of two fractions says that "the sum of two fractions is a fraction." Yet $\dfrac{1}{4} + \dfrac{3}{4} = 1$, so the sum of two fractions is sometimes a whole number. Explain. (Four words should be sufficient.)

6. Perform the following subtractions (when possible):

(a) $\dfrac{3}{7} - \dfrac{1}{7}$ (b) $\dfrac{1}{2} - \dfrac{1}{4}$ (c) $\dfrac{2}{91} - \dfrac{1}{39}$

(d) $\dfrac{1}{39} - \dfrac{2}{91}$ (e) $\dfrac{7}{10} - \dfrac{3}{100}$ (f) $\dfrac{1}{10} - \dfrac{31}{1000}$

(g) $\dfrac{1}{8051} - \dfrac{1}{13,363}$

7. Find a value of b such that $\dfrac{1}{10} - \dfrac{963}{b}$ is defined. Find a value of a such that $\dfrac{1}{10} - \dfrac{a}{8}$ is defined.

8. Split this set into two sets so that the sums of the fractions in the two sets are the same.

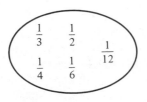

PROPERTIES

9. We found that addition of fractions satisfies closure, commutative, and identity properties. Name one or more other possible properties and check to see if they hold, giving evidence to support your answer.

10. 0/1 is an identity for adding fractions. Are there any others? How many different *numbers* are there that serve as an identity for the addition of fractions?

11. How does the answer obtained when applying the definition of subtracting fractions to $\dfrac{a \times n}{b \times n} - \dfrac{c \times n}{b \times n}$ compare with the answer obtained when the definition is applied to $\dfrac{a}{b} - \dfrac{c}{b}$?

12. Formulate a "missing addend" description for the definition of subtraction. Show that it is equivalent to the definition given.

13. We found that subtraction of fractions lacks the closure and identity properties. Name one or more other possible properties and check to see if they hold, giving evidence to support your answer.

14. Sometimes we do arithmetic with "mixed numbers," such as 2⅜.
    (a) Give a definition for expressions of this type.
    (b) Give a definition for addition of mixed numbers. Verify that the sum obtained by your definition agrees with the sum obtained by using the definition $\dfrac{p}{q} + \dfrac{r}{q} = \dfrac{p + r}{q}$.

15. Suppose we defined addition of fractions by $\dfrac{p}{q} \oplus \dfrac{r}{s} = \dfrac{p + r}{q + s}$. (We use the symbol "$\oplus$" to distinguish it from ordinary addition of fractions.) By this definition $\dfrac{1}{2} \oplus \dfrac{3}{4} = \dfrac{4}{6}$.
    (a) Is $\oplus$ defined for all fractions?
    (b) Is it well-defined? (Do we get an equivalent answer when fractions are replaced by equivalent fractions?)

(c) Does it agree with the arithmetic of whole numbers? (For instance, does $2 + 3$ still equal 5 when interpreted as fractions?)

(d) Does $\oplus$ satisfy a commutative property?

(e) Associative property?

(f) Identity property?

(g) Bill calls this operation "baseball addition." Why? (Hint: Think of "hits" and "at bats.")

16. Show that every common denominator is a multiple of the lowest common denominator. (Hint: See Problem 18, Section 4-3.)

MATERIALS AND CALCULATORS

17. To illustrate $\frac{1}{3} + \frac{1}{2}$ using Cuisenaire rods (see Problem 31, Section 5-1), which single rod should be used to represent

(a) 1?   (b) 1/3?   (c) 1/2?

(d) Explain how to get the answer in terms of the rods. (Be sure to give the answer!)

18. Explain how Cuisenaire rods might be used to illustrate subtraction of fractions.

19. Consult several elementary school mathematics series (texts). Identify which ones use area models for fractions; number line models.

20. Suppose a child writes "$\frac{2}{3} + \frac{4}{5} = \frac{6}{8}$." How can you convince him this is incorrect?

P21. Write programs to do the following for fractions, giving *exact* answers. (For example, for $\frac{1}{2} + \frac{1}{3}$ the program gives 5/6, not a decimal approximation.) The answers need *not* be in lowest terms.

(a) the sum of two fractions

(b) the difference of two fractions

P22. Write programs to generate

(a) the geometric series of Problem 27

(b) the harmonic series of Problem 28.

PROBLEM SOLVING EXTENSIONS

23. Find the largest fraction that has a denominator of 17 and when added to 1/3 gives an answer less than 1.

24. (a) Express each of the following as a simple fraction:

$$\frac{1}{1}, \quad \frac{1}{1 + \frac{1}{1}}, \quad \frac{1}{1 + \frac{1}{1 + \frac{1}{1}}}, \quad \frac{1}{1 + \frac{1}{1 + \frac{1}{1 + \frac{1}{1}}}}$$

(b) What are the next three simple fractions in the sequence?

25. (a) The divisors of 6 are 1, 2, 3, and 6. Compute $\frac{1}{1} + \frac{1}{2} + \frac{1}{3} + \frac{1}{6}$.

(b) The divisors of 28 are 1, 2, 4, 7, 14, and 28. Compute $\frac{1}{1} + \frac{1}{2} + \frac{1}{4} + \frac{1}{7} + \frac{1}{14} + \frac{1}{28}$.

*(c) Recall from Problem 23 in Section 4-1 that 6 and 28 are "perfect numbers." Will a similar result hold for other perfect numbers? Explain.

*26. In ancient times, only **unit fractions** (fractions with numerators of 1) like $\frac{1}{2}$, $\frac{1}{3}$, and $\frac{1}{8}$ were used. Other fractions were expressed as sums of different unit fractions. Examples: $\frac{2}{3} = \frac{1}{2} + \frac{1}{6}$; $\frac{3}{10} = \frac{1}{4} + \frac{1}{20}$; $\frac{5}{7} = \frac{1}{2} + \frac{1}{5} + \frac{1}{70}$. Express each of the following as sums of different unit fractions:

(a) $\frac{3}{4}$ (b) $\frac{6}{11}$ (c) $\frac{2}{7}$ (d) $\frac{4}{13}$ (e) $\frac{53}{87}$

27. The unending series $\frac{1}{1} + \frac{1}{2} + \frac{1}{4} + \frac{1}{8} + \frac{1}{16} + \ldots$ is an example of an infinite **geometric series**, one in which each term is a fixed multiple (in this case 1/2) of the previous term. The sum of the first three terms is $\frac{1}{1} + \frac{1}{2} + \frac{1}{4} = \frac{7}{4} + 1\frac{3}{4}$.

(a) Find the sum of the first four terms, first five terms, first six terms.
(b) Guess the sum of the unending series.
(c) Guess the sum of $\frac{9}{10} + \frac{9}{100} + \frac{9}{1000} + \frac{9}{10000} + \ldots$

*28. The unending series $\frac{1}{1} + \frac{1}{2} + \frac{1}{3} + \frac{1}{4} + \frac{1}{5} + \ldots$ is called the **harmonic series**. The sum of the first three terms is $\frac{1}{1} + \frac{1}{2} + \frac{1}{3} = \frac{11}{6} = 1\frac{5}{6}$.

(a) Find the sum of the first four terms, first five terms, first six terms.
(b) Guess the sum of the unending series.
(c) Note the following.

$$\frac{1}{1} + \frac{1}{2} = 1\frac{1}{2}$$

$$\frac{1}{1} + \frac{1}{2} + \frac{1}{3} + \frac{1}{4} > \frac{1}{1} + \frac{1}{2} + \frac{1}{4} + \frac{1}{4} = 2$$

$$\frac{1}{1} + \frac{1}{2} + \frac{1}{3} + \frac{1}{4} + \frac{1}{5} + \frac{1}{6} + \frac{1}{7} + \frac{1}{8}$$

$$> \frac{1}{1} + \frac{1}{2} + \frac{1}{4} + \frac{1}{4} + \frac{1}{8} + \frac{1}{8} + \frac{1}{8} + \frac{1}{8} = 2\frac{1}{2}$$

Show that the sum of the first 16 terms exceeds 3.
(d) Guess the sum of the unending series in light of part (c).

5-3
MULTIPLICATION AND DIVISION OF FRACTIONS

So far in our extension of the whole numbers to the fractions we have proceeded straightforwardly and encountered no difficulties. We have gained the ability to divide one whole number by another (non-zero) whole number, which is one of the chief reasons for inventing fractions, without encumbering the addition and subtraction processes. The remaining task is to develop satisfactory methods for multiplication and division of fractions. Our approach will closely parallel what we did in the preceding section, with a few important new ideas introduced along the way.

To introduce multiplication and division of fractions we will once again call upon area models. Just as the product 3×4 is the number of square units (or area) in a rectangle whose dimensions are 3 units by 4 units, we can interpret $\frac{2}{3} \times \frac{5}{7}$ as the number of square units (of area) in a rectangle whose dimensions are 2/3 units by 5/7 units, as shown in Figure 5-8.

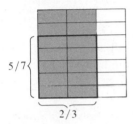

FIGURE 5-8

We see that if we use vertical lines to divide the original unit square into three like pieces and take two of these pieces, we have a (shaded) rectangle with a width of 2/3. If we use horizontal lines to divide the shaded rectangle into seven like pieces and take five of these pieces, we have (inside the heavy line) a rectangle whose dimensions are 2/3 by 5/7. It is easy to determine what fraction of the unit area this (heavy line) rectangle represents. It contains 2×5 of the smallest pieces, while there are 3×7 of these pieces in the entire unit square. Thus its area is $\frac{2 \times 5}{3 \times 7}$, so in terms of our area model $\frac{2}{3} \times \frac{3}{7} = \frac{2 \times 3}{3 \times 7}$. Since we have taken *part* (5/7) of the shaded area, which is *part* (2/3) of the original square, we can think of the product of fractions in terms of a "part-of-part" model.

Only slight modification is needed when one or both of the fractions exceed 1.

Represent the product $\frac{3}{2} \times \frac{7}{5}$ using an area model.

EXAMPLE
5-6

To show 3/2, we need more than one unit. Since we are going to build a rectangle with a base of 3/2, we place two unit squares as shown.

SOLUTION

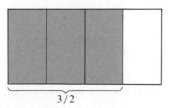

To show a height of 7/5, we need to extend the shaded rectangle upward by adding two more unit squares.

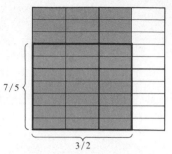

Now we have inside the heavy line a rectangle with dimensions 3/2 by 7/5. Each unit square has been cut up into 2×5 pieces. In all, we have 3×7 of these pieces. Thus the area of the rectangle (inside the heavy line) is the fraction $\dfrac{3 \times 7}{2 \times 5}$. Our model suggests that $\dfrac{3}{2} \times \dfrac{7}{5} = \dfrac{3 \times 7}{2 \times 5}$. From this it seems natural to define the product of two arbitrary fractions p/q and r/s by $\dfrac{p}{q} \times \dfrac{r}{s} = \dfrac{p \times r}{q \times s}$.

This product is defined for all fractions p/q and r/s, for if p and r are whole numbers, so is $p \times r$; and if q and s are non-zero whole numbers, so is $q \times s$. Is it well-defined — namely, do we get the same answer regardless of representation? First let's try $\dfrac{3}{5} \times \dfrac{2}{5}$. By our new definition, $\dfrac{3}{5} \times \dfrac{2}{5} = \dfrac{3 \times 2}{5 \times 5} = \dfrac{6}{25}$. Applying this definition to the equivalent problem, $\dfrac{6}{10} \times \dfrac{4}{10} = \dfrac{6 \times 4}{10 \times 10} = \dfrac{24}{100} = \dfrac{6}{25}$, so at least it is agreeable for this example. This is quite easy to show in the general setting. First we show that the product of any two fractions is equivalent to the product of their reduced representatives. Suppose p/q and r/s are reduced fractions and that $\dfrac{p \times m}{q \times m}$ and $\dfrac{r \times n}{s \times n}$ are respective equivalent fractions. Then we begin by applying the definition to the unreduced representatives and show that this is equivalent to the product determined by the reduced fractions:

$$\frac{p \times m}{q \times m} \times \frac{r \times n}{s \times n} = \frac{(p \times m) \times (r \times n)}{(q \times m) \times (s \times n)} = \frac{(p \times r) \times (m \times n)}{(q \times s) \times (m \times n)}$$

$$= \frac{p \times r}{q \times s} = \frac{p}{q} \times \frac{r}{s}$$

Since each representation gives an answer equivalent to the result when the product is written in terms of reduced fractions, it follows that all representations give the same answer.

Since this definition of multiplying fractions is defined for all fractions, yields equivalent results for equivalent problems, and agrees with our area model (in the typical examples we have investigated), we are persuaded to adopt it.

Definition for Multiplying Fractions ☐

If $\frac{p}{q}$ and $\frac{r}{s}$ are fractions, then $\frac{p}{q} \times \frac{r}{s}$ is called their **product** and is defined to be $\frac{p \times r}{q \times s}$.

Observe that once again a "new" idea (multiplying fractions) is defined in terms of an "old" idea (multiplying whole numbers). This will make the questions of commutativity, associativity, and identity for multiplying fractions easy to deal with.

Another old friend, distributivity, can also be probed. Does multiplication distribute over addition? As before, we can safely assume that the fractions being added have the same denominator, as the process of changing to a common denominator has no bearing on the results. Recall the distributive law for whole numbers a, b, and c:

$$a \times (b + c) = a \times b + a \times c$$

The analog for fractions p/q, r/s, and u/s is:

$$\frac{p}{q} \times \left(\frac{r}{s} + \frac{u}{s}\right) = \frac{p}{q} \times \frac{r}{s} + \frac{p}{q} \times \frac{u}{s}$$

Our technique will be to evaluate both sides of this equation and compare. We begin with the expression on the left side and apply the definition for adding fractions (which the parentheses indicate is to be done first) followed by the definition for multiplying fractions:

$$\frac{p}{q} \times \left(\frac{r}{s} + \frac{u}{s}\right) =$$
$$\frac{p}{q} \times \frac{r + n}{s} \quad =$$
$$\frac{p \times (r + u)}{q \times s}$$

We arrive at a fraction whose numerator and denominator are expressed in terms of sums and products of whole numbers. Evaluating the right side of the original expression involves first multiplying, then adding:

$$\frac{p}{q} \times \frac{r}{s} + \frac{p}{q} \times \frac{u}{s} =$$
$$\frac{p \times r}{q \times s} + \frac{p \times u}{q \times s} =$$
$$\frac{p \times r + p \times u}{q \times s}$$

We again arrive at a fraction whose numerator and denominator are expressed in terms of sums and products of whole numbers. How do the fractions $\frac{p \times (r + u)}{q \times s}$ and $\frac{p \times r + p \times u}{q \times s}$ compare? Since they have the same denominator, they will be equivalent if their numerators are equal; namely, if $p \times (r + u) = p \times r + p \times u$. But this is merely a statement of the distributive property for whole numbers, so the fractions are clearly equal.

This completes our proof that multiplication distributes over addition. The distributive property for fractions is seen to depend on the distributive property for whole numbers, still another example of the mathematical structure underlying arithmetic.

Recapping our treatment so far, we see that introducing fractions gains the advantage of being able to divide one whole number by another (non-zero) whole number and that these fractions themselves can be added, subtracted, and multiplied according to new rules which are consistent with the old rules governing whole numbers. The final challenge is to arrange for division of fractions to fit reasonably into the scheme.

The usual approach of inverting the divisor and multiplying can be obtained by directly paralleling the alternative definition for dividing whole numbers. Recall the missing factor interpretation for division of whole numbers:

If a and b are whole numbers (and b is not 0), then the quotient of a and b is the (whole number) answer to the question $b \times \square = a$.

If we rewrite this in terms of fractions, we have:

If p/q and r/s are fractions (and r/s is not 0), then the quotient of p/q and r/s is the (fraction) answer to the question $\frac{r}{s} \times \square = \frac{p}{q}$.

First we'll do a specific example involving numbers. Consider the problem $\frac{2}{3} \div \frac{4}{5} = \square$. It is equivalent to the problem $\frac{4}{5} \times \square = \frac{2}{3}$. We now show that the solution is $\frac{2}{3} \times \frac{5}{4}$.

$$\frac{4}{5} \times \boxed{\frac{2}{3} \times \frac{5}{4}} = \frac{4}{5} \times \frac{2 \times 5}{3 \times 4}$$

$$= \frac{4 \times (2 \times 5)}{5 \times (3 \times 4)}$$

$$= \frac{2 \times (4 \times 5)}{3 \times (4 \times 5)}$$

$$= \frac{2}{3}$$

This shows that $\frac{2}{3} \times \frac{5}{4}$ is precisely the solution to $\frac{2}{3} \div \frac{4}{5} = \square$.

We now proceed to show that $\frac{p}{q} \times \frac{s}{r}$, which is obtained from $\frac{p}{q} \div \frac{r}{s}$ by inverting the divisor, is precisely the quantity that satisfies $\frac{r}{s} \times \square = \frac{p}{q}$, or, in other words, satisfies $\frac{p}{q} \div \frac{r}{s} = \square$. Let's fill in $\frac{p}{q} \times \frac{s}{r}$ for $\square$ and evaluate $\frac{r}{s} \times \square$.

$$\frac{r}{s} \times \boxed{\frac{p}{q} \times \frac{s}{r}} = \frac{r}{s} \times \frac{p \times s}{q \times r} \qquad \text{(Definition for multiplying fractions)}$$

$$= \frac{r \times (p \times s)}{s \times (q \times r)} \qquad \text{(Definition for multiplying fractions)}$$

$$= \frac{p \boxed{\times (r \times s)}}{q \boxed{\times (r \times s)}} \qquad \text{(Commutative and associative properties for multiplying whole numbers)}$$

$$= \frac{p}{q} \qquad \text{(Reducing fractions principle)}$$

This shows that $\frac{p}{q} \times \frac{s}{r}$ is the desired quotient according to the missing factor interpretation, which we applied to division of fractions. It leads to the

Definition for Dividing Fractions □

> If $\frac{p}{q}$ and $\frac{r}{s}$ are fractions (and $\frac{r}{s}$ is not 0), then $\frac{p}{q} \div \frac{r}{s}$ is called their **quotient** and is defined to be $\frac{p}{q} \times \frac{s}{r}$.

This definition tells us that to divide one fraction by another we can invert (the second fraction) and multiply (by the first fraction). So long as r/s is a fraction different from 0, s/r will be a fraction and $\frac{p}{q} \times \frac{s}{r}$ will be defined. This tells us that $\frac{p}{q} \div \frac{r}{s}$ is defined for all fractions p/q and non-zero fractions r/s. Since multiplication of fractions has been shown to yield an unambiguous answer regardless of choice of representation, we are guaranteed that $\frac{p}{q} \div \frac{r}{s}$ is also well-defined.

The fraction s/r obtained by inverting r/s is called the **reciprocal** or **multiplicative inverse** of r/s. Notice that the reciprocal of r/s is the fraction which when multiplied by r/s gives 1:

$$\frac{r}{s} \times \frac{s}{r} = \frac{r \times s}{s \times r} = \boxed{\frac{r \times s}{r \times s}} = \frac{1}{1} = 1$$

Some examples of reciprocals are:

Number	Reciprocal
2/3	3/2
6	1/6
0	does not exist

0 has no reciprocal, since there is no number which can be multiplied by 0 to give 1. All other fractions do have reciprocals.

This chapter concludes with a brief discussion of arithmetic with so-called mixed numbers, numbers like $2\frac{3}{4}$. If we interpret $2\frac{3}{4}$ as two whole units plus $\frac{3}{4}$ of another unit,

we can convert it to an ordinary fraction by thinking of everything in terms of fourths.

Then, $2\frac{3}{4}$ is easily recognizable as $\frac{11}{4}$.

Given a problem involving mixed numbers, we can readily convert it to one involving ordinary fractions. For instance, to add $2\frac{3}{4} + 5\frac{2}{7}$ we can first rewrite $2\frac{3}{4}$ as $\frac{11}{4}$ and rewrite $5\frac{2}{7}$ as $\frac{37}{7}$. Then:

$$
\begin{aligned}
2\frac{3}{4} + 5\frac{2}{7} &= \frac{11}{4} + \frac{37}{7} \\
&= \frac{77}{28} + \frac{148}{28} \\
&= \frac{77 + 148}{28} \\
&= \frac{225}{28} \\
&= 8\frac{1}{28}
\end{aligned}
$$

In practice it is not necessary when adding (or subtracting) mixed numbers to change to fractions. Another way of doing this problem is to think of $2\frac{3}{4}$ as $\frac{2}{1} + \frac{3}{4}$ (or simply $2 + \frac{3}{4}$) and to think of $5\frac{2}{7}$ as $\frac{5}{1} + \frac{2}{7}$ (or simply $5 + \frac{2}{7}$). Then:

$$
\begin{aligned}
2\frac{3}{4} + 5\frac{2}{7} &= 7 + \left(\frac{3}{4} + \frac{2}{7}\right) \\
&= 7 + \frac{29}{28} \\
&= 7 + 1\frac{1}{28} \\
&= 8\frac{1}{28}
\end{aligned}
$$

It is always true that to add mixed numbers we can add the whole number parts and add the fractional parts and form a new mixed number.

To multiply or divide mixed numbers, it is usually easiest to convert them to ordinary fractions. For example, to find $3\frac{2}{5} \div 4\frac{3}{7}$ we change these mixed numbers to $\frac{17}{5}$ and $\frac{31}{7}$ respectively:

$$
\begin{aligned}
3\frac{2}{5} \div 4\frac{3}{7} &= \frac{17}{5} \div \frac{31}{7} \\
&= \frac{17}{5} \times \frac{7}{31} \\
&= \frac{17 \times 7}{5 \times 31} \\
&= \frac{119}{165}
\end{aligned}
$$

Since we can readily think of mixed numbers as ordinary fractions, they are worthy of no further discussion. Once again we are able to dispense with a new form of arithmetic in terms of something mastered earlier. In fact, the next example illustrates a whole chain of converting given problems to easier ones.

Problem	*Type*
$3\frac{2}{5} \div 4\frac{3}{7}$	Division of mixed numbers
$\frac{17}{5} \div \frac{31}{7}$	Division of fractions
$\frac{17}{5} \times \frac{7}{31}$	Multiplication of fractions
$\frac{17 \times 7}{5 \times 31}$	Multiplication of whole numbers

In the next chapter we will consider ratios, decimals, and percents, all of which are closely related to fractions. Following that, we will continue extending our system of numbers to remedy other deficiencies.

EXERCISES AND PROBLEMS 5-3

DEFINITION

1. Perform the following operations:

(a) $\frac{2}{3} \times \frac{5}{8}$

(b) $\frac{3}{10} \times \frac{7}{100}$

(c) $\frac{5}{9} \times \frac{3}{7} + \frac{5}{9} \times \frac{4}{7}$

(d) $\frac{2}{3} + \frac{4}{5} \times \frac{6}{7}$

(e) $\frac{2}{3} \times \frac{4}{5} + \frac{6}{7}$

(f) $\frac{2}{3} \times \left(\frac{4}{5} + \frac{6}{7}\right)$

(g) $3\frac{1}{8} \times 6\frac{2}{3}$

(h) $\frac{2}{3} \div \frac{5}{6}$

(i) $2\frac{3}{7} \div 3\frac{4}{11}$

(j) $\frac{13}{10} \div \frac{7}{100}$

2. Expressions of the form $\dfrac{p/q}{r/s}$, called **complex fractions**, occur occasionally in arithmetic. They can be changed to ordinary fractions as follows:

$$\frac{\dfrac{p}{q}}{\dfrac{r}{s}} = \frac{\dfrac{p}{q} \times q \times s}{\dfrac{r}{s} \times q \times s} = \frac{p \times s}{r \times q}$$

Example:

$$\frac{\dfrac{2}{3}}{\dfrac{5}{7}} = \frac{\dfrac{2}{3} \times 3 \times 7}{\dfrac{5}{7} \times 3 \times 7} = \frac{2 \times 7}{5 \times 3} = \frac{14}{15}$$

Express each of these as ordinary fractions:

(a) $\dfrac{\dfrac{5}{8}}{\dfrac{3}{7}}$ (b) $\dfrac{1\dfrac{2}{3}}{5\dfrac{3}{4}}$

3. Find reciprocals of (a) 9/10   (b) 11.

4. Which fraction(s) have no reciprocal?

5. (a) Find the reciprocal of the reciprocal of 5/8.
   (b) Find the reciprocal of the multiplicative inverse of 5/8.

6. (a) Does $1\dfrac{2}{3} + 4\dfrac{5}{6} = 1\dfrac{5}{6} + 4\dfrac{2}{3}$? Explain.

   (b) Does $1\dfrac{2}{3} \times 4\dfrac{5}{6} = 1\dfrac{5}{6} \times 4\dfrac{2}{3}$? Explain.

7. Determine the following, answering in mixed numbers reduced to lowest terms.

   (a) $6\dfrac{1}{5} + 4\dfrac{2}{3}$ (b) $6\dfrac{1}{5} - 4\dfrac{2}{3}$ (c) $6\dfrac{1}{5} \times 4\dfrac{2}{3}$ (d) $6\dfrac{1}{5} \div 4\dfrac{2}{3}$

PROPERTIES

8. Suppose for the fractions $\dfrac{p}{q}$ and $\dfrac{r}{s}$ that $\dfrac{p}{q} < \dfrac{r}{s}$. What can you say about the order of their reciprocals?

9. Is multiplication of fractions
   (a) commutative?   (b) associative?
   (c) Is there a (two-sided) identity?

10. Is division of fractions
    (a) commutative?   (b) associative?
    (c) Is there a (two-sided) identity?

11. Are fractions closed under
    (a) addition?   (b) subtraction?
    (c) multiplication?   (d) division?

12. Are the positive fractions closed under
    (a) addition?   (b) subtraction?
    (c) multiplication?   (d) division?

13. Display $\frac{2}{5} \times \frac{3}{4}$ using an area model. Do the same for $\frac{9}{7} \times \frac{5}{8}$.

14. Supply reasons for each statement in this proof of the distributive property for fractions:

$$\frac{p}{q} \times \left(\frac{r}{s} + \frac{u}{s}\right) = \frac{p}{q} \times \left(\frac{r+u}{s}\right)$$
$$= \frac{p \times (r+u)}{q \times s}$$
$$= \frac{p \times r + p \times u}{q \times s}$$
$$= \frac{p \times r}{q \times s} + \frac{p \times u}{q \times s}$$
$$= \frac{p}{q} \times \frac{r}{s} + \frac{p}{q} \times \frac{u}{s}$$

15. The usual distributive law is referred to by saying "multiplication (of fractions) distributes over addition (of fractions)." Which of these forms of the distributive law holds for arbitrary fractions?
   (a) multiplication over subtraction
   (b) multiplication over division
   (c) addition over multiplication
   (d) division over addition

16. Does the following distributive property hold for fractions? Explain why.

$$\frac{p}{q} \div \left(\frac{r}{s} + \frac{u}{s}\right) = \left(\frac{p}{q} \div \frac{r}{s}\right) + \left(\frac{p}{q} \div \frac{u}{s}\right)$$

17. Suppose a, b, c, d, e, and f are all positive whole numbers. Write $\frac{a}{b} \times \left(\frac{c}{d} + \frac{e}{f}\right)$ as a single fraction involving these six letters.

18. Extending the whole numbers to include the fractions makes division (except by 0) possible. Can you anticipate what will be accomplished by extending later to include negative numbers?

19. The positive fractions satisfy a property not satisfied by the whole numbers. What is this property?

MATERIALS AND CALCULATORS

20. We wish to illustrate the division problem $\frac{3}{5} \div \frac{1}{2}$ using Cuisenaire rods. (See Problem 31, Section 5-1.)
   (a) Which single rod should we use to represent 1? Why?
   (b) Which single rod should we use to represent 1/2? Why?
   (c) How do we represent 3/5?
   (d) Finish explaining how to use the rods to solve $\frac{3}{5} \div \frac{1}{2}$, giving the answer to the problem and telling how to get the answer with the rods.

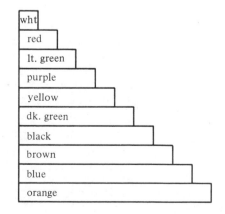

wht
red
lt. green
purple
yellow
dk. green
black
brown
blue
orange

C21. If we use a calculator to multiply fractions by first converting them to decimals, is the answer usually exact or usually approximate? Give an example of each.

P22. Write programs to do the following for fractions giving *exact* answers, *not* decimal approximations (the answers need *not* be in lowest terms):
(a) the product of two fractions   (b) the quotient of two fractions

PROBLEM SOLVING EXTENSIONS

23. Gwen multiplies her fractions like this:

$$\frac{1}{3} \times \frac{2}{3} = \frac{2}{3} \qquad \frac{1}{2} \times \frac{1}{3} = \frac{3}{6} \times \frac{2}{6} = \frac{6}{6} = 1 \qquad \frac{1}{4} \times \frac{3}{8} = \frac{2}{8} \times \frac{3}{8} = \frac{6}{8} = \frac{3}{4}$$

(a) What would you expect her to get for the problem $\frac{1}{6} \times \frac{2}{3}$?

(b) Why do you think she multiplies fractions this way?
(c) How can you help her?

24. (a) What is Jennifer's error in the work shown below? Describe the error pattern.

$$\begin{array}{cccc} 6\frac{7}{9} & 8\frac{1}{9} & 15\frac{2}{7} & 7\frac{1}{10} \\ -3\frac{2}{9} & -2\frac{4}{9} & -8\frac{6}{7} & -2\frac{3}{10} \\ \hline 3\frac{5}{9} & 5\frac{7}{9} & 6\frac{6}{7} & 4\frac{8}{10} = 4\frac{4}{5} \end{array}$$

(b) What would you expect her to get for this problem?

$$\begin{array}{c} 12\frac{1}{8} \\ -7\frac{5}{8} \\ \hline \end{array}$$

(c) Make up another problem she'd probably get right.
(d) How can you help her?

25. Ms. Kazee had a student who divided $\frac{1}{6}$ by $\frac{1}{2}$ as follows:

$$\frac{1}{6} \div \frac{1}{2} = \frac{1 \div 1}{6 \div 2} = \frac{1}{3}$$

(a) Was the student just lucky, or is it always true that $\frac{p}{q} \div \frac{r}{s} = \frac{p \div r}{q \div s}$?

(b) Is this process most like the way we add, subtract, or multiply fractions?
(c) Is this way of dividing fractions well-defined? (Do we get the same answer regardless of choice of representation?)

26. By multiplying the sun protection factor (SPF) of a suntan lotion by one-half, you can determine how many hours you are protected from the sun. For example, if a lotion has an SPF of 4 you can lie in the sun for two hours.
(a) What should the SPF be if you want to spend 1½ hours in the sun with one application of lotion?
(b) If you use lotion with a SPF of 6, how many times must you apply the lotion to be protected for eight hours?

27. If a box of laundry detergent contains 20 cups, how many loads can be washed if each load requires three-quarters of a cup? (Before working the problem, estimate whether your answer should be more or less than 20.)

28. A certain outboard motor requires that a half-pint of oil be mixed with each gallon of gas. How much oil should be mixed with 3½ gallons of gas?

29. (a) Two adults and a child took a round-trip flight together between Columbus, Ohio, and Wilkes-Barre, Pennsylvania. Each adult paid full fare, and the child paid two-thirds fare. If the total (round-trip) fare was $264, how much of the fare was for the child?

(b) The flight between Columbus and Pittsburgh took 30 minutes. After a plane change, the Pittsburgh to Wilkes-Barre flight took 40 minutes. What portion of the (one-way) flight does the Columbus to Pittsburgh leg represent?

(c) The airlines deprived the child of a seat on an overbooked flight (asking that he share a seat with a parent) on the return trip from Pittsburgh to Columbus. The travelers sought a refund for the child's part of the fare for the Pittsburgh to Columbus flight. To how much refund were they entitled?

*30. Fred and Minnie Hill are each 90 years old. Joe Smith, on the other hand, is half again as old as he was when he lacked 20 years of being eight-ninths as old as he is now. How old is Joe Smith?

*31. Find the smallest positive fraction which is exactly divisible (a whole number of times) by both
(a) 4/15 and 6/25   **(b)** 2/3 and 5/8   **(c)** $\dfrac{2^3 \times 3 \times 5^9}{7^9 \times 11^3}$ and $\dfrac{3^6 \times 5^2}{7^4 \times 11}$.

32. Fractions of the form $2 + \dfrac{1}{3 + \dfrac{1}{4 + \dfrac{1}{5}}}$ are called **continued fractions**.

(a) Show that the given continued fraction has a value of $\dfrac{157}{68}$. Evaluate the following continued fractions:

(b) $1 + \dfrac{1}{1 + \dfrac{1}{1 + \dfrac{1}{1}}}$ **(c)** $5 + \dfrac{1}{4 + \dfrac{1}{3 + \dfrac{1}{2 + \dfrac{1}{1}}}}$

33. An ordinary fraction such as 21/16 can be expressed as a continued fraction where all the numerators are 1's, as follows:

$$\frac{21}{16} = 1 + \frac{5}{16} = 1 + \frac{1}{\frac{16}{5}} = 1 + \frac{1}{3 + \frac{1}{5}}$$

Another example:

$$\frac{157}{41} = 3 + \frac{34}{41} = 3 + \frac{1}{\frac{41}{34}} = 3 + \frac{1}{1 + \frac{7}{34}} = 3 + \frac{1}{1 + \frac{1}{\frac{34}{7}}} = 3 + \frac{1}{1 + \frac{1}{4 + \frac{6}{7}}}$$

$$= 3 + \frac{1}{1 + \frac{1}{4 + \frac{1}{\frac{7}{6}}}} = 3 + \frac{1}{1 + \frac{1}{4 + \frac{1}{1 + \frac{1}{6}}}}$$

Express each of the following as a continued fraction where the numerators are 1's:
(a) 5/6   **(b)** 41/33   **(c)** 131/15

34. A man stipulated that upon his death one-half of his camels be given to his oldest child, one-third be given to his second child, and one-ninth be given to his youngest child. When he died, he had 17 camels. His lawyer, a clever woman, borrowed a camel from a neighbor to make a total of 18. She then distributed them as follows:

$$
\begin{array}{lll}
\text{Oldest child} & \dfrac{1}{2} \times 18 = & 9 \\[2ex]
\text{Second child} & \dfrac{1}{3} \times 18 = & 6 \\[2ex]
\text{Youngest child} & \dfrac{1}{9} \times 18 = & \underline{2} \\
\text{Total} & & 17
\end{array}
$$

She then returned the borrowed camel, and everyone was satisfied except the local arithmetic teacher. Aside from the fact that she got no camels, what bothered her?

35. If there are four quarter notes in one beat of music, how many eighth notes are there in
(**a**) 1 beat?   (**b**) 3 beats?   (**c**) 1½ beats?

36. When playing the Horn Trio of Brahms (Opus 40), Virginia, Bill, and Jim noticed this rhythm:

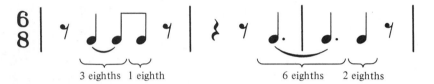

They noticed how the lengths of the notes were doubled. This is an example of **augmentation**, a process in which lengths of notes are multiplied, usually by 2. Another process is **diminution**, in which lengths of notes are decreased in value.

Tell what kind of note results when the length of
(**a**) a half note is multiplied by 2.
(**b**) a quarter note is multiplied by 2.
(**c**) an eighth note is multiplied by 2.
(**d**) a quarter note is multiplied by 3.
(**e**) a half note is multiplied by 1/2.
(**f**) a quarter note is multiplied by 1/2.

37. If microwaves lose half their energy for each 2 cm of food they penetrate, what fraction of the original energy will reach the bottom of a meatloaf 10 cm thick?

38. A certain cookbook recommends that when doubling a recipe for a microwave oven, the cooking time be multiplied by 1½. For example, if doubling a recipe requiring 10 minutes' cooking time, the new time is 1½ × 10 = 15 (minutes). Tell how long to cook something if we
(**a**) double a recipe which requires 7 minutes' cooking time.
*(**b**) triple a recipe which requires 12 minutes' cooking time.
(**c**) Will this use of fractions vanish with calculators and the metric system?

Ratio and Proportion; Decimals and Percents

6-1
RATIO AND PROPORTION

Examples of ratio and proportion are plentiful in a range of disciplines including music and mechanics, ecology and economics, geometry and geography. When discussing our own field of education, we speak of teacher-pupil ratios and the ratio of black students to white students, just to name a few of the numerous examples. In addition to the countless direct applications of ratio and proportion to situations in the real world, familiarity with these concepts is helpful in strengthening mathematical problem solving skills.

If set A has p members and set B has q members, then we say that the **ratio** of A to B is $p:q$ (read "p to q"). For example, the ratio of X's to Y's in the figure

$$X \quad X \quad X$$
$$Y \quad Y \quad Y$$
$$Y \quad Y \quad Y$$

is $3:6$. The ratio of Y's to X's is $6:3$. Since there is one X for every two Y's, we also say that the ratio of X's to Y's is $1:2$. Thus $3:6$ and $1:2$ are the same ratio, and in general we will agree that the ratios $p:q$ and $r:s$ are **equal** if p/q and r/s are equal as fractions. According to this definition we then see that we can write $3:6 = 1:2$ or, for that matter, $3:6 = 50:100$ or $3:6 = 19:38$. A statement that two ratios are equal is called a **proportion**. Thus $3:6 = 1:2$ (read "three is to six as one is to two") is a proportion. (Some books use the notation $3:6::1:2$ for what we have written $3:6 = 1:2$.)

EXAMPLE 6-1

One day at the humane society there are 30 dogs, 15 cats, and 5 gerbils.
(a) What is the ratio of dogs to gerbils?
(b) What is the ratio of cats to gerbils?
(c) What is the ratio of dogs and cats to gerbils?
(d) What fraction of the animals are dogs?
(e) What fraction of the animals are cats?
(f) What fraction of the animals are dogs and cats?

SOLUTION

(a) There are 30 dogs and 5 gerbils, so the ratio of dogs to gerbils is $30:5$. Since $30/5 = 6/1$ (as fractions), we could also answer that the ratio of dogs to gerbils is $6:1$.

(b) $15:5$ or $3:1$ (c) $45:5$ or $9:1$

(d) 30 out of the 50 animals are dogs, so the fraction of the animals which are dogs is $30/50$ or $3/5$.

(e) $15/50$ or $3/10$ (f) $45/50$ or $9/10$

In the preceding example, we sometimes say that the ratio of dogs to gerbils is **higher** than the ratio of cats to gerbils (or that the ratio of cats to gerbils is **lower** than the ratio of dogs to gerbils). Note that in comparing the size of disjoint sets (as dogs and gerbils) we use a ratio, and when comparing the size of a subset of a set with the whole set (as dogs to the entire set of animals) we use a fraction.

Some elementary school mathematics texts introduce yet another term, **rate-pair**, to describe a situation like 2 pencils for 15¢, where the units are different. We will not concern ourselves with this distinction and will refer to this comparison between the (disjoint) sets of pencils and pennies as a ratio. For that matter, we have little reason to concern ourselves with the distinction between ratios and fractions, with the possible exception given in Example 6-2.

In Ms. Daley's class there are twice as many girls as boys. In Ms. Rucker's class there are three times as many girls as boys. Find the ratio of girls to boys in the two classes combined.

EXAMPLE 6-2

SOLUTION

The ratio of girls to boys is 2 : 1 in Ms. Daley's class and 3 : 1 in Ms. Rucker's class. When combining the classes, can we simply add the ratios to get 5 : 1? Since after combining the classes there cannot be more than three girls for each boy, 5 : 1 is not the answer. It turns out that we can say relatively little about the ratio in the two classes combined. To illustrate, suppose each class had 24 students. Then we would have:

	Ms. Daley		Ms. Rucker		Combined	
Girls	16	2 : 1	18	3 : 1	34	34 : 14
Boys	8		6		14	
Total	24		24		48	

so the ratio when the classes are combined would be 34 : 14. However, if the class sizes were 15 and 32 respectively, the ratio would be 34 : 13, as shown in the following chart:

	Ms. Daley		Ms. Rucker		Combined	
Girls	10	2 : 1	24	3 : 1	34	34 : 13
Boys	5		8		13	
Total	15		32		47	

Example 6-2 establishes that in general it is impossible to add ratios, as we often do with fractions. It also emphasizes that it is impossible to determine the exact numbers unless we are given the number of members in the whole set. For instance, in Ms. Daley's class there are twice as many girls as boys, but we can't tell from this information alone whether there are 16 girls or 10 girls or some other number of girls.

Examples 6-3 and 6-4 illustrate how we can use ratios to solve word problems.

**EXAMPLE
6-3**

A recipe for 20 cookies calls for (among other things) 1 cup of flour, 2/3 cup of butter, and 2 eggs. How much of each of these ingredients is needed to make 30 cookies?

SOLUTION

Since we are making 1½ times as many cookies, we will need 1½ times as much of each ingredient; namely, 1½ cups of flour, 1 cup of butter (1½ × 2/3 = 3/3 = 1), and 3 eggs.

A more general way to solve this problem, which may be easier to use when the numbers are not as convenient, is to set up proportions:

Let f be the amount of flour required. Then

$$f : 30 = 1 : 20 \qquad \text{(write a proportion)}$$
$$\frac{f}{30} = \frac{1}{20} \qquad \text{(ratios are equal if equal as fractions)}$$
$$20f = 30 \qquad \text{(definition of equal fractions)}$$
$$f = \frac{30}{20} \qquad \text{(divide both sides by 20)}$$
$$f = 1\frac{1}{2} \qquad \text{(reduce)}$$

Let b be the amount of butter required. Then

$$b : 30 = 2/3 : 20$$
$$\frac{b}{30} = \frac{2/3}{20}$$
$$20b = 20$$
$$b = 1$$

Let e be the number of eggs required. Then

$$e : 30 = 2 : 20$$
$$\frac{e}{30} = \frac{2}{20}$$
$$20e = 60$$
$$e = 3$$

**EXAMPLE
6-4**

If 10 miles is about 16 kilometers, how many miles are there in 30 kilometers?

SOLUTION

Let m be the number of miles in 30 kilometers. Then

$$m : 30 = 10 : 16 \qquad \text{(write a proportion)}$$
$$\frac{m}{30} = \frac{10}{16} \qquad \text{(ratios are equal if equal as fractions)}$$
$$16m = 300 \qquad \text{(definition of equal fractions)}$$

$m = \dfrac{300}{16}$ (divide both sides by 16)

$m = 18\dfrac{3}{4}$ (reduce)

$m = 19$ (round to nearest mile)

In setting up a proportion, as in Example 6-4, the *units* are helpful in checking whether the terms are in the correct order. Notice in writing "$m : 30 = 10 : 16$," we would have m (miles) : 30 (km) = 10 (miles) : 16 (km), or roughly "miles are to kilometers as miles are to kilometers." If we had incorrectly written "$m : 30 = 16 : 10$," we would have "miles are to kilometers as kilometers are to miles," suggesting that we had made an error.

EXERCISES AND PROBLEMS 6-1

DEFINITION

1. If the ratio of girls to boys in a class is $2 : 5$,
   (a) what is the ratio of boys to girls?
   (b) what fraction of the students in the class are girls?
   (c) how many girls are in the class?

2. Write a ratio based on the following information:
   (a) 80% of those surveyed favored impeachment.
   (b) This year's fuel supply may be only 80% of last year's.
   (c) There are six times as many girls as boys in math class.
   (d) Six out of every seven students in math class are girls.
   (e) Your savings account earns 5% interest.
   (f) You spend 20% of your income on rent.

3. Suppose in Example 6-2 that Ms. Daley has 420 students and Ms. Rucker has 80 students. (They lecture at the university.) What is the combined ratio of girls to boys? (Other information is given in Example 6-2.)

4. (a) If you know that the ratio of girls to boys in a class is $7 : 3$, can you tell exactly how many girls are in the class?
   (b) What *can* you tell about the number of girls in the class?

*5. Suppose the ratio of girls to boys in Ms. Daley's and Ms. Rucker's class is respectively $2 : 1$ and $3 : 1$. If the classes each contain the same number of students, what can you tell about the number of girls in Ms. Daley's class?

6. If Jim was 12 when he finished sixth grade, how old do you think he was when he finished third grade?

APPLICATIONS — SPORTS

7. Tom Pierson of Sweden won a marathon race in Columbus, Ohio, running the 26.2-mile course in 2 hours 11 minutes. At this rate, (a) what was his average speed in miles per hour?   (b) What was the average time it took him to run 1 mile?

8. The pressure on a scuba diver at the surface is one atmosphere (14.7 pounds per square inch, abbreviated 14.7 psi). In salt water, one additional atmosphere of pressure is experienced for every 33 feet of depth. For example, the pressure at 33 feet is 29.4 psi, at 66 feet it is 44.1 psi, etc.
   (a) What is the pressure at 99 feet?
   (b) What is the pressure at 150 feet?
   (c) At what depth is the pressure 88.2 psi?
   (d) At what depth is the pressure 100 psi?

APPLICATIONS — CONSUMERS

9. (a) If your car goes 18 miles on one gallon of gas, how far will it go on three gallons?
   (b) If 200 grams of candy cost 80¢, how much can you buy for $2?
   (c) If a 15-liter radiator requires 4 liters of antifreeze, how much antifreeze will a 22-liter radiator require?
   (d) If 3/4 cup of sugar is required to make 30 cookies, how much sugar is required to make 40 cookies?

10. (a) If 8 ounces of 7-Up contains 97 calories, how many calories are in a 12-ounce bottle? A 16-ounce bottle?
    (b) If 8 ounces of beer contains 104 calories, how many calories are in a 12-ounce bottle?
    (c) If 10 average-size potato chips contain 114 calories, how many calories are there in 25 average-size potato chips?
    (d) If a 20-slice loaf of white bread contains 1240 calories, how many calories are there in 5 slices?

11. Which is the better buy (in terms of cost per ml)?
    (a) 48 ml for 59¢ or 64 ml for 69¢?
    (b) 16 ml for 23¢ or 12 ml for 18¢?
    (c) 32 ml for 89¢; 48 ml for $1.29, or 40 ml for 99¢?

12. A consumer group determined that a specific list of groceries costs $25.86 now, while the same items cost $20.00 two years ago. At this rate, how much would it cost to purchase groceries which cost $50.00 two years ago?

13. The directions for making orange juice from frozen concentrate call for three cans of water for each can of concentrate. How much orange juice can be made from a 12-ounce can of concentrate?

14. Is the cost of driving a car proportional to the number of miles driven?

15. A power and light company in Ohio advertised that 98% of the electricity used by its customers was produced by power plants that burn coal. They gave the following examples of the approximate amount of coal used each year for the operation of typical appliances:

Refrigerator	One ton
Electric water heater	Two tons
Clothes dryer	A half-ton

At that rate, how much coal is needed to
(a) run a refrigerator for 10 years?
(b) run a refrigerator for half a year?
(c) use an electric water heater for a month?
(d) use all three for a year?
(e) use all three since you were born?
(f) use all three for your entire lifetime?

16. Long ago, Mildred and Claire were selling apples to passers-by. Mildred sold 3 apples for a penny; Claire sold her apples 2 for a penny. One day, when they each had 30 apples left, Mildred and Claire decided to take the rest of the day off. They asked a friend to sell the 60 apples at 5 for 2¢. If Mildred and Claire had sold their apples separately they would have made 25¢ between them. At 5 for 2¢ only 24¢ was earned. Were Mildred and Claire cheated by their friend? What happened to the one penny?

17. According to *U.S. News and World Report* (Dec. 22, 1980), the hours of work time necessary to purchase certain goods in the U.S. and U.S.S.R. compare as follows:

	U.S.	*U.S.S.R.*
Stockings	.25	2
Vodka (half-liter)	1	6
Men's shoes	8	33
Bicycle (inexpensive)	15	61
Refrigerator (medium)	54	323

According to these figures,
   (a) a Soviet worker works how many times as long as an American worker to purchase a pair of stockings?
   (b) on which item does the Soviet worker compare most favorably with the American worker? least favorably?
   (c) In the U.S., a refrigerator is worth 54 bottles of vodka. How many bottles of vodka is a refrigerator worth in the U.S.S.R.?

APPLICATIONS — MISCELLANEOUS

18. A sewing pattern for a skirt is given in a $1:4$ ratio. A width of 8 cm on the pattern corresponds to what width of material?

19. If 80 out of each 100 seeds planted germinate, how many seeds must be planted so that 200,000 seeds germinate?

20. Sue drove her car 13,000 miles in 1½ years. At this rate, what is the number of miles she drove in 1 year?

21. If it takes 15 minutes to saw a log into three pieces, how long would it take to saw it into four pieces? (Be careful!)

22. If she averaged 8 hours of sleep per 24-hour day, how many years of her life has a 72-year-old woman spent sleeping?

23. Some estimates of the ratio of rats to people in certain large cities are as high as $5:1$. If this ratio is accurate, how many rats are there in one of these cities with a population of 1,000,000? 500,000?

24. On a particular scale drawing, 1/4 inch represents one foot. How much would be represented by 3/4 inch? 2 inches? 30 feet would be represented on the drawing by how many inches?

25. If one inch on a map represents 15 miles, how many miles are represented by 2 inches? 5 inches? n inches? How far apart on the map are two cities which are 100 miles from each other?

26. A school district with 6000 students has a teacher-pupil ratio of $1:30$.
   (a) How many more (or fewer) teachers are required to achieve a teacher-pupil ratio of $1:25$?

(b) How much more (or less) will this cost the district per year if the expense per teacher is $9,000 per year?

(c) How much will this cost for each pupil in the district?

(d) Repeat parts (a), (b), and (c) for reducing a 1 : 30 ratio to 1 : 20.

27. IQ (Intelligence Quotient) is the ratio of mental age to chronological age expressed as a fraction and multiplied by 100. For instance, a 10-year-old who performs on an IQ test like an average 12-year-old would have an IQ of 120:

$$\frac{\text{Mental age}}{\text{Chronological age}} \times 100 = \frac{12}{10} \times 100 = 120$$

(a) Amy is 8 years old but performs on an IQ test as if she were 9 years old. Determine her IQ.

(b) Bobbie is 8 years old but performs on an IQ test as if he were 6½ years old. Determine his IQ.

(c) Six-year-old Kathleen has an IQ of 125. What is her mental age?

28. Compare the two thermometers.

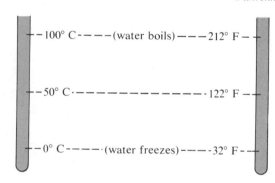

Celsius   *Fahrenheit*

−100° C −−−−(water boils)−−−212° F −

−50° C·−−−−−−−−−−−−−−·122° F −

−0° C −−−−·(water freezes)−−−·32° F −

(a) Change 25° C to degrees Fahrenheit.

(b) Change 50° F to degrees Celsius.

(c) Change 200° C to degrees Fahrenheit.

(d) Change 392° F to degrees Celsius.

29. Gear A has 18 teeth and gear B has 12 teeth.

(a) If gear A makes one turn, how many turns will gear B make?

(b) Fill in the chart:

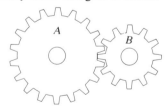

Number of turns made by gear A	1	2	6			100
Number of turns made by gear B				9	32	

(c) If gear A makes 100 revolutions (turns) per minute, how many revolutions per minute does gear B make?

(d) According to (c), which gear turns faster?

30. Repeat the previous problem for gears A and B having 20 and 15 teeth respectively.

31. The 1980 census showed Cleveland with a population of 572,532 compared to 751,000 in 1970. Estimate the population of Cleveland in the year 2000 assuming that the population continue to decline at (a) the same *number* of people per 10-year period. (b) the same *rate* per 10-year period.

32. Repeat the previous problem, estimating the population of Cleveland in the year 2020. Which answer makes more sense?

MATERIALS AND CALCULATORS

33. Problems like these can be found in sixth grade texts:

(a) Fill in: (b) Fill in:

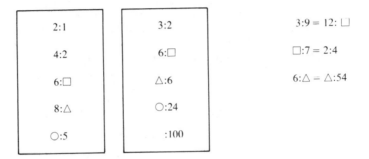

(c) Plot several values of □ and △ which make $8 : 12 = □ : △$ true. One is done for you. What do you notice?

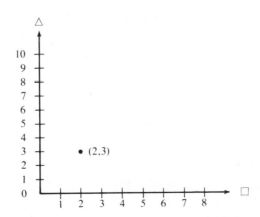

(d) An ant can lift about 50 times its own weight. If a person could do this, how much could a person lift if he weighed 60 kg? 80 kg? A grasshopper can jump 20 times its own length. If a person could do this, how far could he jump if his height was 120 cm? 170 cm? A sea otter can eat an amount of food equal to 1/5 its own weight in a day. How much could an equally voracious 60-kg person eat at this rate?

34. A **trundle wheel** (or **measuring wheel**) is a wheel with a handle attached to it, often designed to click once each time the wheel goes around. If one turn of the wheel is one meter, how much is six turns?

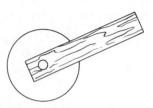

***L*35.** Use a trundle wheel to determine the dimensions of your classroom.

***P*36.** Write a program that converts
(a) degrees Celsius to degrees Fahrenheit.
(b) degrees Fahrenheit to degrees Celsius. (See Problem 28.)

GEOMETRY

*37. Our definition of ratio is stated in terms of the number of members in two disjoint sets. Since the number of members in a set is always a whole number, we have defined ratios only for whole numbers. Express the following as ratios (not necessarily using whole numbers). Can they be expressed in terms of whole numbers? (We will say more about this later.)
(a) The ratio of the circumference of a circle to its diameter.
(b) The ratio of the length of the diagonal of a square to the length of a side.
(c) The ratio of the length of the altitude (height) of an equilateral (all sides of equal length) triangle to the length of a side.

38. Two triangles are **similar** if their sides "are proportional." This means that there is a 1-1 correspondence between the sides of the first triangle and the sides of the second triangle so that the ratios of the corresponding lengths are equal. For example, $\triangle ABC$ and $\triangle DEF$ are similar:

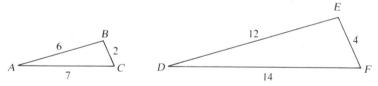

since in the correspondence   the ratios are respectively

$$\overline{AB} \quad \leftrightarrow \quad \overline{DE} \qquad\qquad 6:12 = 1:2$$

$$\overline{AC} \quad \leftrightarrow \quad \overline{DF} \qquad\qquad 7:14 = 1:2$$

$$\overline{BC} \quad \leftrightarrow \quad \overline{EF} \qquad\qquad 2:4 = 1:2$$

Given that $\triangle GHI$ is similar to $\triangle JKL$, find the length of (a) $\overline{GH}$ (b) $\overline{JL}$

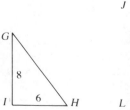
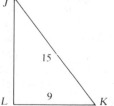

(c) Given that these two triangles are similar, find x.

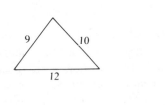

39.

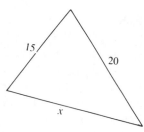

Fill in the following chart:

Object	Shadow Length	Height	Ratio
Flagpole	10 meters	8 meters	
Boy		152 centimeters	5:4
Shed	3 meters		
Fence	120 centimeters		

40. (a) If the ratio of the sides of two squares is 2:3, what is the ratio of their areas?

(b) If the ratio of the edges of two cubes is 2:3, what is the ratio of their volumes?

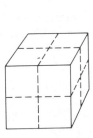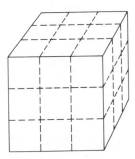

(c) If you double all the dimensions of a box, what happens to its volume?

6-2
DECIMAL NOTATION

With interest rates, finance charges, various taxes, and discounts so prevalent in today's society, people who do not understand decimals and percents are likely to pay dearly for their lack of expertise. Moreover, the advent of the metric system and the popularity of hand calculators make decimals more important than ever.

In this section and the next we will discuss notation, ordering, and arithmetic of ordinary decimals. In the last section of this chapter we will probe some interesting questions which arise as we explore the ties between common fractions and decimals, with emphasis on repeating decimals. We will discuss decimal notation first.

To begin with, the monetary system itself is based on decimals. We can think of $243 as

2 hundreds + 4 tens + 3 ones

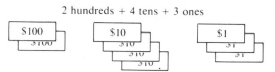

Similarly, we can think of $1.52 as

1 one + 5 dimes + 2 pennies

These examples involving money illustrate how the base ten place value system in which we have ones, tens, hundreds, etc., can be extended to include certain fractions. Since 10 dimes make a dollar, each dime is 1/10 of a dollar, and since 100 pennies make a dollar, each penny is 1/100 of a dollar. Thus in our base ten system we have a natural representation for tenths and hundredths: 1.52 represents $1 + 5/10 + 2/100$. Of course, the system employed here to indicate tenths and hundredths works equally well to represent certain other fractions.

Recall how the ten-for-one trading scheme discussed when we first introduced whole numbers (see Numeration, Chapter 2) was capable of representing large numbers easily. For instance, we saw in Figure 2-6 that our (Hindu-Arabic) numeral "365" was considerably briefer than the corresponding numeral

ꝯꝯꝯ∩∩∩∩∩∩|||||

in the Egyptian system. Much larger numbers, like the typical yearly U.S. Internal Revenue Department Receipts ($268,342,952,000) can still be written concisely in our base ten system. Even if this number were to grow a hundredfold, it could be written with a mere two additional digits.

The feature of our numeration system that permits us to write arbitrary large numbers is that each place to the *left* of the ones place represents ten times the value of the preceding place.

2 2 2 2 2
- 2 × 1
- 2 × 10   (10 = 10 × 1)
- 2 × 100   (100 = 10 × 10)
- 2 × 1000   (1000 = 10 × 100)
- 2 × 10000   (10000 = 10 × 1000)

We could say equivalently that each new place as we move to the *right* of the ten thousands place represents one-tenth the value of the preceding place.

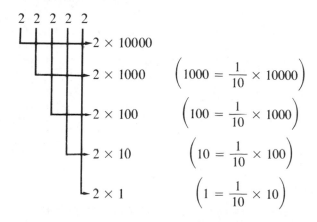

2 2 2 2 2
- 2 × 10000
- 2 × 1000 $\left(1000 = \dfrac{1}{10} \times 10000\right)$
- 2 × 100 $\left(100 = \dfrac{1}{10} \times 1000\right)$
- 2 × 10 $\left(10 = \dfrac{1}{10} \times 100\right)$
- 2 × 1 $\left(1 = \dfrac{1}{10} \times 10\right)$

Hence it is quite natural to extend this process to the right of the ones place by introducing what we call the **decimal point** and letting each successive place to the right represent one-tenth the value of the preceding place. Beginning with the tens place, we then would have this:

2 2.2 2 2
- 2 × 10
- 2 × 1 $\left(1 = \dfrac{1}{10} \times 10\right)$
- $2 \times \dfrac{1}{10}$ $\left(\dfrac{1}{10} = \dfrac{1}{10} \times 1\right)$
- $2 \times \dfrac{1}{100}$ $\left(\dfrac{1}{100} = \dfrac{1}{10} \times \dfrac{1}{10}\right)$
- $2 \times \dfrac{1}{1000}$ $\left(\dfrac{1}{1000} = \dfrac{1}{10} \times \dfrac{1}{100}\right)$

$$2\ ,\ 2\quad 2\quad 2\ ,\ 2\quad 2\quad 2\ ,\ 2\quad 2\quad 2\quad .\quad 2\quad 2\quad 2\quad 2\quad 2\quad 2$$

billions
hundred millions
ten millions
millions
hundred thousands
ten thousands
thousands
hundreds
tens
ones
decimal point
tenths
hundredths
thousandths
ten-thousandths
hundred-thousandths
millionths

FIGURE 6-1

By extending the process even further, we can express small amounts like the length of a grain of pollen (0.00005 meters) or the thickness of a parcel of hemoglobin in the blood (0.000002 meters).

Of course, there is no end to the process, as we can arbitrarily write large numbers by extending to the left of the decimal point or small numbers by extending to the right of the decimal point. A summary of the more commonly used place values is given in Figure 6-1. Notice that the suffix *-th* is used for all values to the right of the decimal point.

When saying "32,000" we simply say "thirty-two thousand" (rather than saying "three ten thousands and two thousands"). In the same manner, we read 0.0032 as "thirty-two ten-thousandths." Moreover, since

$$0.001892 = \frac{1}{1000} + \frac{8}{10000} + \frac{9}{100000} + \frac{2}{1000000}$$

$$= \frac{1000}{1000000} + \frac{800}{1000000} + \frac{90}{1000000} + \frac{2}{1000000}$$

$$= \frac{1892}{1000000}$$

we read "0.001892" as "one thousand eight hundred ninety-two millionths."

EXAMPLE
6-5

Write (a) 0.0005 and (b) 60.87219 in words.

SOLUTION

(a) $.0005 = \frac{5}{10000}$, so we say "five ten-thousandths."

(b) $60.87219 = 6 \times 10 + \frac{8}{10} + \frac{7}{100} + \frac{2}{1000} + \frac{1}{10000} + \frac{9}{100000}$

$= 60 + \frac{80000}{100000} + \frac{7000}{100000} + \frac{200}{100000} + \frac{10}{100000} + \frac{9}{100000}$

$= 60 + \frac{87219}{100000}$

so we say "sixty and eighty-seven thousand two hundred nineteen hundred-thousandths."

This idea of thinking of the entire fractional part of a number as having a single denominator is also helpful when *comparing* decimals. To compare decimals, we think of them as fractions; but with decimals it is trivial to find a common denominator to facilitate comparison.

Place in order (smallest to largest): 0.5, 0.55, 0.505.

EXAMPLE

6-6

$$0.5 = \frac{5}{10} \qquad \text{(don't reduce)}$$

$$0.55 = \frac{55}{100}$$

$$0.505 = \frac{505}{1000}$$

A common denominator is 1000, so we have

$$0.5 = \frac{5}{10} = \frac{500}{1000}$$

$$0.55 = \frac{55}{100} = \frac{550}{1000}$$

$$0.505 = \frac{505}{1000}$$

Since $500/1000 < 505/1000 < 550/1000$, we have $0.5 < 0.505 < 0.55$. (In retrospect we can compare the decimals directly by thinking of $0.5, 0.55$, and 0.505 as 0.500, 0.550, and 0.505 respectively.) It is apparent from this example that a given decimal has more than one name. For instance 0.5, 0.50, and 0.500 are all equivalent. This comes as no surprise, since fractions themselves have many names ($1/2 = 2/4 = 5/10 = 50/100$, etc.).

Of course, the whole number part of a decimal (in 59.325 the whole number part is 59) prevails in comparing decimals. For instance, $256.2 > 255.9$, even though the decimal part of the second number is greater.

There is a final question as to what to do with decimals when they have more decimal places than we want or need. What we do is **round off** to a decimal with the appropriate number of places. This amounts to dropping all places beyond the last one we are interested in and increasing the digit in this last place by one if the place *immediately* following it contains a 5, 6, 7, 8, or 9. To see why this is the way we round off, let's look at some specific examples:

(1) To round off 56.36 to the nearest tenth, we are essentially deciding whether to write 56.3 or 56.4. Recognizing 56.3 as 56.30 and 56.4 as 56.40, it is clear that 56.36 is closer to 56.40, so we round off 56.36 to 56.4.

(2) To round off 7.395 to the nearest hundredth, we must choose between 7.39 (7.390) and 7.40 (7.400). Now, 7.395 is exactly halfway between 7.390 and 7.400, so the usual agreement is to round *up* to 7.40. We write 7.40 rather than 7.4 or 7.4000 to show that 7.40 has been rounded to the nearest hundredth.

(3) In rounding off .02499 to the nearest hundredth, we must choose between .02 (.02000) and .03 (.03000). Because .02499 is slightly closer to .02000 than it is to .03000, we round off .02499 to .02. Note that though the last digits are 9's we round *down,* since the digit immediately following the 2 is a 4.

$400,000,000 Worth of Rounding Off!

"Pennies really can add up. The General Accounting Office — Congress's watchdog agency — is now recommending that Social Security benefit calculations be rounded off to the nearest penny rather than the next higher dime, as at present. Potential savings: 400 million dollars over a seven-year period."

(Source: *U.S. News & World Report,* Feb. 16, 1981, p.11)

EXERCISES AND PROBLEMS 6-2

DEFINITION AND ORDER

1. Fill in this chart.

Fraction	Decimal	Percent	Ratio
1/2	.5	50%	1:2
1/4			
	.75		
		20%	
	.002		
1/1000			
			3:10

2. Write out the following numbers:
   (a) six hundred eighty-two thousand
   (b) six hundred eighty-two thousandths
   (c) six hundred eighty-two millionths
   (d) six hundred eighty-two thousand and six hundred eighty-two thousandths

3. Write the following in words:
    (a) .0003   **(b)** 5600
    (c) .0056   **(d)** 13,000,000,000
    (e) .00000017

4. Place in order (smallest to largest):
    (a) .66, .089, .7   **(b)** 256.41, 246.87, 256.37   **(c)** 6.3, 6.03, 6.003

5. Evaluate:
    (a) 2.1_{four} **(b)** 2.3_{four} **(c)** 2.01_{five} **(d)** 31.003_{four}

6. Write as base eight "decimals":
    (a) 3/8   **(b)** $2\frac{5}{8}$ **(c)** $3\frac{5}{64}$
    (d) 7/16   ***(e)** 1/3

7. In base ten, 1/2, 1/4, and 1/5 are terminating decimals. Which of the decimals 1/2, 1/3, 1/4, 1/5, 1/6 are terminating decimals in base twelve?

8. Write a flowchart that shows how to compare two numbers each of which has one decimal place.

ROUNDING OFF

9. Round off each of these:
    (a) 8.46 to the nearest tenth
    (b) .85 to the nearest tenth
    (c) .0348 to the nearest hundredth
    (d) .0348 to the nearest tenth
    (e) .0498 to the nearest hundredth
    (f) 12345 to the nearest thousand
    (g) 487 to the nearest thousand

10. If "$862 \xrightarrow{100} 900$" means "862 rounded off to the nearest hundred is 900," then determine the following:
    (a) $241 \xrightarrow{100}$ **(b)** $8.23 \xrightarrow{.1}$
    (c) $7.486 \xrightarrow{.01}$ **(d)** $9.5489 \xrightarrow{.1}$

11. The attendance at a football game was 37,000 to the nearest thousand. What is the smallest number of people that could have been in attendance? The largest number?

12. A metal bar measures 8.375 to the nearest thousandth. What is its shortest possible length? Longest?

13. Write a flowchart that shows how to round off a decimal to the nearest tenth.
(See also Problem 17.)

MATERIALS AND CALCULATORS

14. Examine several elementary school mathematics texts, comparing the grade levels in which decimals are introduced. Is there greater emphasis on decimals or on fractions?

15. A certain calculator shows eight digits to the right of the decimal point. What is the smallest positive number that this calculator will display?

L16. Some squared paper is marked with heavy lines every ten small squares. On this kind of paper one "heavy" square contains $10 \times 10 = 100$ small squares.

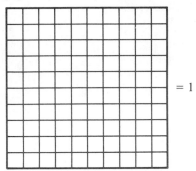 = 1

If a "heavy" square equals 1 unit, what is the value of (**a**) one small square? (**b**) a row of ten small squares? (**c**) three rows of ten small squares plus seven small squares? Tell how to use this kind of paper to represent (**d**) .6 (**e**) .04 (**f**) .64 (**g**) 2.03.

P17. Many calculators and computers have an "integer function" that drops the fraction part of a number like this:

$$\text{INTEGER}(5.6) = 5$$
$$\text{INTEGER}(8.1) = 8$$
$$\text{INTEGER}(11.99) = 11$$

Write a program that uses the integer function to round decimals to the nearest integer like this:

5.6 is rounded to 6

8.1 is rounded to 8

11.62 is rounded to 12

(Hint: Alter the decimal before using the integer function.)

6-3
OPERATIONS WITH DECIMALS; PERCENTS

When doing exercises involving decimals such as

$$.6 + .2,$$
$$.6 \times .2, \text{ and}$$
$$.6 \div .2,$$

our work resembles whole number arithmetic:

$$6 + 2 = 8$$
$$6 \times 2 = 12$$
$$6 \div 2 = 3.$$

The new feature of our work involves locating the decimal point in the answer:

$$.6 + .2 = .8$$

$$.6 \times .2 = .12$$

$$.6 \div .2 = 3$$

Probably the most confusing aspect in doing these exercises is understanding why the answer has one decimal place when we *add* .6 and .2, two decimal places when we *multiply* .6 and .2, and no decimal places when we *divide* .6 by .2. Along with illustrating how to work with percents, our chief goal for this section will be to develop meaningful rules for doing arithmetic with decimals, and in particular, for locating the decimal point when adding, subtracting, multiplying, and dividing decimals.

We will postpone the matter of determining decimal representatives for ordinary fractions and initiate a discussion of the arithmetic of decimals. We are going to develop techniques for doing arithmetic with terminating decimals (such as 0.125) and not concern ourselves with non-terminating decimals (such as 0.33333 . . .). The main theme recurring here will be that (terminating) decimals are merely representatives for fractions, so the rules for doing arithmetic with decimals have essentially been established in Chapter 5. Our objective will be to develop procedures for working with decimals which do not require converting back and forth to fractions every time we do a computation, though in fact the procedures will evolve from our knowledge of the arithmetic of fractions. Since computations with decimals so closely parallel our earlier work with fractions and whole numbers, we will relax matters a bit and generate our rules by examining typical examples.

All the rules we will develop are of course built into modern calculators. (There are certain cases where the calculator needs help. See, for example, Problems 28 and 29 at the end of this section.) Studying this section will benefit you as a teacher by increasing your understanding of how and why the rules apply.

Finding common denominators for decimals is simple, so addition and subtraction of decimals poses no problem. To add 5.1 + 0.149, we recognize 1000 as a common denominator, observing that

$$5.1 = 5\frac{1}{10} = 5\frac{100}{1000}$$

$$0.149 = \frac{149}{1000}$$

The sum 5.1 + 0.149 can then be regarded as $5\frac{100}{1000} + \frac{149}{1000} = 5\frac{249}{1000}$.

The same result can be achieved more directly by rewriting

$$\begin{array}{r} 5.1 \\ +\ .149 \end{array} \quad \text{as} \quad \begin{array}{r} 5.100 \\ +\ .149 \end{array} \quad \text{to get} \quad \begin{array}{r} 5.100 \\ +\ .149 \\ \hline 5.249 \end{array}$$

This essentially amounts to "lining up the decimal points," "filling in zeros to the right of the decimal point as necessary," and adding according to the algorithm for whole numbers.

<table>
<tr><td>EXAMPLE
6-7</td><td>Compute (a) $0.0052 + 8.3 + 9.02$ (b) $6.43 - 0.699$.</td></tr>
</table>

SOLUTION

$$
\begin{array}{ll}
\text{(a)} & \begin{array}{r} .0052 \\ 8.3000 \\ +9.0200 \\ \hline 17.3252 \end{array}
\end{array}
\qquad
\begin{array}{ll}
\text{(b)} & \begin{array}{r} 6.430 \\ -\ .699 \\ \hline 5.731 \end{array}
\end{array}
$$

Somewhat informally, we summarize our rules governing addition and subtraction of decimals. The term **decimal places** is used to mean places to the right of the decimal point.

☐ Procedure for Adding or Subtracting Decimals

> 1. Line up the decimal points.
> 2. Fill in zeros, so that all numbers have the same number of decimal places.
> 3. Add or subtract according to the rules for whole numbers.
> 4. Place a decimal point in the answer so that it has the same number of decimal places as the numbers in step 2.

Examining a typical example also suggests a method for multiplying decimals. We will compute 5.62×82.4 by changing the factors to fractions.

$$
\begin{aligned}
5.62 \times 82.4 &= 5\frac{62}{100} \times 82\frac{4}{10} \\
&= \frac{562}{100} \times \frac{824}{10} \\
&= \frac{463088}{1000} \\
&= 463.088
\end{aligned}
$$

We find the answer by computing 463088, the product of the whole numbers 562 and 824, and then inserting a decimal point. The decimal point is placed to show that we have 463,088 *thousandths*. The denominator 1000 arises in turn because the respective denominators that we multiply together are 100 and 10. The product has three decimal places because the *total* number of decimal places in the factors is three. Though we certainly haven't proven it by one example, this technique always works, so we have the following procedure.

☐ Procedure for Multiplying Decimals

> 1. Multiply the numbers as whole numbers (disregarding the decimal point).
> 2. Place a decimal point in the product so that it has as many decimal places as the sum of the number of decimal places in the factors.

Multiply $860 \times 0.04 \times 0.173$.

EXAMPLE

6-8

$860 \times 4 \times 173 = 595120$. The total number of decimal places in the factors is $0 + 2 + 3 = 5$, so the number of decimal places in the product is 5. The answer is 5.95120.

One kind of multiplication problem is particularly easy to do — a problem where one of the factors is 10, 100, 1000, or some other power of 10. It is easy to see that this kind of problem requires nothing more than shifting the decimal point, as in the following examples:

$0.9821 \ \times 1000 = 982.1000 = 982.1$ (move 3 places .982,1)

$0.00568 \times 10 \ \ \ = 0.05680 \ - 0.0568$ (move 1 place 0,0568)

$3.2 \times 100 \ = 320.0 \ \ \ \ = 320$ (move 2 places 3.20.)

This computational shortcut is reminiscent of our "multiplying by multiples of ten principle" of Section 3-5 and will be useful when we discuss division of decimals next.

From our rules for multiplying decimals, we can now write

(a) $.7 \times \ .09 = .063$

(b) $.003 \times \ .06 = .00018$

(c) $.6 \times \ \ \ 8 = 4.8$

(d) $.002 \times \ 900 = 1.800$

(e) $.8 \times \ 1.5 = 1.20$

(f) $4 \times \ .75 = 3.00$

Suppose we use a finger to cover up the second factors so that we have a "missing factor" in each problem. Then each of the multiplication problems suggests a corresponding division problem.

(a) $.7 \times$ $= .063$

(b) $.003 \times$ $= .00018$

(c) $.6 \times$ $= 4.8$

(d) $.002 \times$ $= 1.800$

(e) $.8 \times$ $= 1.20$

(f) $4 \times$ $= 3.00$

What can we tell about the missing factors?

In problem (a) it is clear that we need a missing factor of 9 with a decimal point inserted somewhere. The product (.063) has three decimal places, and the known factor (.7) has one. To satisfy the rules for multiplying decimals, the missing factor must have two decimal places (since 2 is what we must add to 1 to get 3). So the missing factor is .09, and we have solved the division problem:

$$.7 \overline{)\,.063}^{\;.09}$$

In problem (b) the missing factor is 6, again with a decimal point inserted somewhere. The product (.00018) has five decimal places, and the known factor (.003) has three. Hence, the missing factor must have $5 - 3 = 2$ decimal places. This tells us that the quotient is .06, and we have solved another division problem:

$$.003 \overline{)\,.00018}^{\;.06}$$

Multiplication problems (c) through (f) suggest the following division problems:

$$.6 \overline{)\,4.8}^{\;8} \qquad .002 \overline{)\,1.800}^{\;900} \qquad .8 \overline{)\,1.20}^{\;1.5} \qquad 4 \overline{)\,3.00}^{\;.75}$$

In all six cases, the number of decimal places in the quotient (missing factor) can be determined by subtracting the number of decimal places in the divisor (known factor) from the number of decimal places in the dividend (product). A familiar technique that helps locate the decimal point in the quotient involves the following procedure for dividing decimals.

☐ Procedure for Dividing Decimals

> 1. Move the decimal point in the divisor enough places to the right to make it a whole number, and move the decimal point in the dividend the same number of places to the right.
> 2. Divide the numbers using the usual scaffold algorithm (with decimals).

Let's take a closer look at what is happening when we move the decimal points according to step 1. Recall when discussing fractions that we saw when dividing two pizzas among three people that each person gets 2/3 of a pizza; namely, the answer to the division problem $2 \div 3$ is 2/3. If we can follow this interpretation when dividing decimals, we can change each division problem to a "fraction" whose numerator and denominator are decimals. For instance, we can think of $.063 \div .7$ (problem a) as .063/.7 and write

$$.063 \div .7 = \frac{.063}{.7} = \frac{.063 \times 10}{.7 \times 10} = \frac{.63}{7} = .63 \div 7.$$

This shows that $.063 \div .7$ is equivalent to $.63 \div 7$, or in other words that

$$.7 \overline{)\,.063} \qquad \text{is the same as} \qquad .7_\wedge \overline{)\,0_\wedge 63}$$

Similarly, in problems (b) and (c) we have

$$.00018 \div .003 = \frac{.00018}{.003} = \frac{.00018 \times 1000}{.003 \times 1000} = \frac{.18}{3} = .18 \div 3$$

$$4.8 \div .6 = \frac{4.8}{.6} = \frac{4.8 \times 10}{.6 \times 10} = \frac{48}{6} = 48 \div 6$$

Applying the scaffold algorithm to problems involving decimals (step 2) requires only one modification: the partial quotients may now be decimals. Problems (a) through (f) would look like this when we carry out step 2:

(a)
$$
\begin{array}{r}
7\overline{).63} \\
-.63 \\
\hline
q = .09
\end{array}
= .09 \times 7
$$

(b)
$$
\begin{array}{r}
3\overline{).18} \\
-.18 \\
\hline
q = .06
\end{array}
= .06 \times 3
$$

(c)
$$
\begin{array}{r}
6\overline{)48} \\
- 48 \\
\hline
q = 8
\end{array}
= 8 \times 6
$$

(d)
$$
\begin{array}{r}
2\overline{)1800} \\
-1800 \\
\hline
q = 900
\end{array}
= 900 \times 2
$$

(e)
$$
\begin{array}{r}
8\overline{)12.0} \\
- 8.0 \\
\hline
4.0 \\
-4.0 \\
\hline
q = 1.5
\end{array}
$$
$= 1.0 \times 8$

$= .5 \times 8$

(f)
$$
\begin{array}{r}
4\overline{)3.00} \\
-2.80 \\
\hline
.20 \\
-.20 \\
\hline
q = .75
\end{array}
$$
$= .70 \times 4$

$= .05 \times 4$

The solution to a more complicated problem is provided next.

Compute $1.2079 \div .235$.

EXAMPLE 6-9

SOLUTION

(1) $\ .235\overline{)\,1.207\,9}$

(2)
$$
\begin{array}{r}
235\overline{)1207.9} \\
-1175.0 \\
\hline
32.9 \\
-23.5 \\
\hline
9.4 \\
-9.4 \\
\hline
q = 5.14
\end{array}
$$
$= 5.0 \times 235$

$= .1 \times 235$

$= .04 \times 235$

Our final topic for this section is **percent**, which is simply a fraction (or ratio) in which the denominator of the fraction (or second number of the ratio) is 100. We use the symbol "%" to indicate this, and write 97% for 97/100, 2% for 2/100, etc. Furthermore, since 97/100 = .97 and 2/100 = .02, we can write 97% = .97 and 2% = .02. Solving problems involving percents is just another instance then of changing a new problem to something familiar. This, coupled with the convention that the word "of" in the expression "4% of 56" means "times" (multiply), are the most important ideas concerning percent. A few examples are provided to illustrate these ideas.

EXAMPLE
6-10

(a) Find 20% of $80.   (b) 36 is 40% of what number?

(c) 10 is what percent of 8?   (d) Compute 4% tax on $14.50.

(e) Determine 1½% per month finance charge on $120, for three months (not compounded).

(f) Estimate (mentally) a 15% discount on $48.39.

(g) The population of Hamlet used to be 400. If it increased 10% per year for two years, what is its population now?

SOLUTION

(a) 20% of $80 means .20 × $80 = $16. (Notice that 20% = 20/100 = 1/5, so this is simply 1/5 of $80, which is $16.)

(b) This effectively says 36 = .40 × □. This missing factor multiplication problem is really a division problem; namely, 36 ÷ .40 = □.

$$.40\overline{)36.00.} \\ \underline{-36\ 00} \quad = 90 \times 40 \\ q = 90$$

(c) This effectively says 10 = (□/100) × 8. Multiply both sides by 100 and divide both sides by 8 to get 1000/8 = □; namely, □ = 125. The answer is 125%.

(d) .04 × $14.50 = $.5800 = 58¢

(e) .015 × $120 × 3 = $5.400 = $5.40

(f) About $7.50. This is not difficult if we notice that 15% is 1½ times 10%, which is easy to compute. To get an estimate, think of $48.39 as a little less than $50.00. Now 10% of 50 is $5, so 15% of $50 = 1½ × $5 = $7.50. This discount ought to be a little less than $7.50. (Actually it is $7.26.)

(g) Is this a 20% gain? No! The first gain is 10% of 400, or 40, giving a population of 440. The second gain is 10% *of 440* or 44, giving a population of 484. This is a common pitfall in working with percent and you should watch for it in the problems.

EXERCISES AND PROBLEMS 6-3

COMPUTATIONS WITH DECIMALS

1. The multiplication problem .42 × 8.9 = 3.738 suggests what *two* division problems?

2. We can also locate the decimal point in the product 49.8 × 2.34 by estimating. Because 49.8 is about 50 and 2.34 is about 2, 49.8 × 2.34 must be about 50 × 2 = 100. In locating the decimal point in 116532 (the product of 498 × 234), we place it so that the answer will be as near as possible to 100; so 116.532 is the correct answer. Locate the decimal point in the following computations by estimating:

(a) $3.94 \times 6.01 = 236794$ (b) $22.37 \times 5.4 = 120798$
(c) $165.81 \times 29.71 = 49262151$

3. Multiply out $860 \times .04 \times .173$ *as fractions* to confirm the answer to Example 6-8.

4. (a) Show that $3.2 \div .8$ is equivalent to $32 \div 8$. (Provide all details.) Do the same for:
   (b) $1.800 \div .002 = 1800 \div 2$ (c) $1.20 \div .8 = 12.0 \div 8$

5. Which of the numbers a, b, or c is the largest?

$$a = .0000000000123456789 + .0000000000987654321$$

$$b = .0000000000123456789 \times .0000000000987654321$$

$$c = .0000000000123456789 \div .0000000000987654321$$

6. We saw that multiplying by 10, 100, 1000, or some other power of 10 shifts the decimal point to the right one, two, three, . . . places. Investigate multiplying by .1, by .01, by .001, etc.

7. Barb was adding and subtracting amounts of money (expressed in dollars and cents) on her calculator. When she got an answer of $124.525 she thought she must have made a mistake. Do you agree?

8. True or False? Support your answer. "If T is the set of all positive numbers whose decimal representation terminates (like $6 = 6.$ and $1/4 = .25$), then T is closed under multiplication."

PERCENTS

9. (a) Find 30% of 90.   (b) 40 is what percent of 25?
   (c) 25 is what percent of 40?   (d) Find 4% of $2400.
   (e) 15 is 30% of what number?   (f) 15 is 15% of what number?
   (g) 80 is 200% of what number?   (h) Find 0.5% of 2000.

10. Which of the following tax rates do you know?
    (a) sales tax in your state
    (b) city income tax in your city
    (c) state income tax in your state
    (d) state gasoline tax in your state
    (e) federal gasoline tax
    (f) tax on a package of cigarettes in your state
    (g) others

11. Which of the following do you know?
    (a) finance charges on any charge accounts you may have
    (b) interest rate on a savings account you may have
    (c) discounts you qualify for

12. Complete the 4% sales tax table for purchases from $.00 to $3.00:

If purchase is

from	to	tax is
.00	.12	.01
.13	.37	.02
.38		.03

Note: This table is based on rounding off the tax to the nearest cent. Not all tables are constructed in this way.

13. Suppose you pay federal income tax according to the following schedule:

Taxable Income		Tax	
Over—	But not over—		Of excess over
$500	$1,000	$70 + 15%	$500
$1,000	$1,500	$145 + 16%	$1,000
$1,500	$2,000	$225 + 17%	$1,500
$2,000	$4,000	$310 + 19%	$2,000
(e) □	$6,000	$690 + 21%	$4,000
$6,000	$8,000	$1110 + 24%	(f) □
$8,000	$10,000	$1590 + 25%	$8,000
$10,000	$12,000	(g) □ + 27%	$10,000
$12,000	$14,000	$2630 + 29%	$12,000
$14,000	$16,000	$3210 + □ (h)	$14,000
$16,000	$18,000	$3830 + 34%	$16,000
		etc.	

How much tax do you pay if your taxable income (after deductions) is
(a) $2,000?   (b) $3,000?   (c) $2,493?   (d) $487?
Fill in the missing entries in the table:
(e) _____   (f) _____   (g) _____   *(h) _____

14. A credit union advertises that its daily interest rate is .00032877 (simple interest). How much is saved by paying $100 ten days earlier?

15. The following **circle graph** (or **pie graph**) shows a family's relative expenditures on certain items.

If this is based on $20,000, how much is devoted to each item?

16. Make a pie graph showing the following expenditures:

Tuition and books	$1,000
Room and board	$3,000
Other	$2,000

17. On March 1 a store lowered its prices by 10%. On March 10 it raised its prices by 10% over the sale price. How did the March 10 prices compare with the prices before the sale?

18. A restaurant advertised a $5.50 value for $5.00, claiming a 10% savings. Comment.

19. A store advertised that all coats were up to 40% off. How much could you expect to pay for a coat which had a pre-sale price of $100?

20. Carl has $4; Bill has $5. Carl said, "I have 20% less than Bill." Bill replied, "I have 25% more than Carl." Who's right?

21. Mike Smith read that he could save 30% of the gas his car uses by driving slowly, 20% by making smooth starts and stops, 30% by keeping his engine tuned, 15% by keeping his tires properly inflated, and 10% by avoiding unnecessary idling. He concluded that if he filled his tank and drove home following all of these suggestions, the gas tank would be overflowing by the time he got there. Comment.

22. The previous five problems suggest certain misunderstandings that arise with percents. Do you have such a problem to contribute?

23. The price of a coat was reduced by 20% to $120. What was the original price of the coat?

24. Barb has 50% as many marbles as Betty. Betty has 80% as many marbles as Phyllis. Phyllis has _____% as many marbles as Barb. (Fill in.)

25. Brian noticed while traveling in Indonesia that he was charged 10% service and 10% tax on his hotel bills. Explain how this increased his bills 21% (rather than 20%).

MATERIALS AND CALCULATORS

26. Use the technique of Problem 4, Section 3-5, to represent these multiplication problems. (Hint: Let one "heavy" square equal 1 unit, as in Problem 14, Section 6-2.)
    (a) $.2 \times .3$ (b) $2 \times .3$ (c) $.2 \times 3$ (d) 2×3
    (e) 1×4.3 (f) 1.2×4 (g) 1.2×4.3

C27. Perform the following computations (without a calculator). Check your results with a calculator.
    (a) $.85 + .2$ (b) $.002 + .32 + 1.5$
    (c) $6.801 - .9999$ (d) $2.8 \times .49$
    (e) $.003 \times .002$ (f) $.048 \div 6$
    (g) $.048 \div .6$ (h) $.048 \div .06$
    (l) $.048 \div .000006$ (j) $.22459 \div .037$
    (k) $.015989 \div 5.9$

C28. A particular calculator gives .0000001 as the answer to the problem $.00037 \times .00054$.
    (a) What is the correct answer?
    (b) Is .0000001 the correct answer rounded off?
    (c) How can the calculator be used to help find the correct answer?
    (d) Another calculator gives an answer of $1.998 \ldots - 07$. Interpret this answer.

C29. Devise a way to determine the first six digits of 825396×548912. (Some calculators do this automatically, but you can do it without this feature.) Based on this, give an approximate answer.

C30. A particular piece of paper is 0.001 inches thick. How thick would it become if it could be folded 4 times? 7 times? 10 times? Estimate how many folds it would take to gain a thickness of 240,000 miles (the average distance to the moon).

C31. Many calculators have a "repeat add" feature: When you key in "3 ⊞ ⊟ ⊟ ⊟" the calculator displays "3, 6, 9, 12," etc. (Some calculators require that you key in "3 ⊞ ⊞ ⊟ ⊟ ⊟" to get this display.) Using a calculator with the repeat add feature, determine the display after each of the following:
    (a) $.1$ ⊞ ⊟ ⊟ ⊟   (b) $.01$ ⊞ ⊟ ⊟ ⊟ $\ldots$ ⊟   (c) $.02$ ⊞ ⊟ ⊟ ⊟ $\ldots$ ⊟
                                         40 times   20 times

*C*32. (a) Using a calculator with a "repeat multiplication" feature (see the previous problem), determine 1.12^4 by keying in "1.12 ⊠ ▤ ▤ ▤." (This number represents the effect of four years of inflation at 12%. For example, groceries now costing \$100 will cost $\$100 \times 1.12^4$ after four years of inflation at 12%.)
  (b) Determine $\$100 \times 1.12^4$.
  (c) At a 12% inflation rate, how many years will it take for costs to double?

PROBLEM SOLVING EXTENSIONS

33. Joe works consistently like this:

$$
\begin{array}{cccc}
2.6 & 1.3 & .84 & 8.1 \\
\underline{\times\ 5} & \underline{\times 1.7} & \underline{\times .86} & \underline{\times 4.2} \\
1.30 & 91 & 504 & 162 \\
 & \underline{13} & \underline{672} & \underline{324} \\
 & 22.1 & 7224. & 34.02
\end{array}
$$

  (a) Find his error and describe his error pattern.
  (b) What would you expect him to get for this problem?

$$
\begin{array}{c}
826 \\
\underline{\times .3}
\end{array}
$$

  (c) Make up another problem he'd probably get right.
  (d) How can you help him?

34. (a) How many quarters are there in \$3.50?
  (b) Find $3\frac{1}{2} \div \frac{1}{4}$.
  (c) Find $3.50 \div .25$.
  (d) Find $350 \div 25$.
  (e) When doing part (a) did you use method (b), (c), (d), or some other method? Which method do you think is easiest?

35. The phone company offered two rates for residential customers. "Unlimited" service cost the basic rate plus a flat \$3.20 per month regardless of the number of calls. "Measured" service cost the same basic rate plus 9¢ for each call after 30 calls per month. (The first 30 calls are included in the basic rate.) How many calls would a customer have to average each month before it would be more advantageous to buy unlimited service?

36. Fill in the box and the circle with 2 *different* symbols chosen from +, −, ×, and ÷ so that the equation is true.

$$9 \ \Box \ .9 = 9 \ \bigcirc \ .9$$

37. A gymnast scored a total of 19.14 in her event. If one of her scores was 9.59, what was her other score?

38. If a U.S. dollar is worth .43 British pounds,
  (a) how much is \$100 (U.S.) in British pounds?
  (b) how much is 100 British pounds in U.S. dollars?

39. Sam pays $1\frac{1}{2}$% interest on \$100 for one month rather than losing a month's interest on \$100 in his savings account, which pays 6% *per year*. How much does he gain or lose as a result of this maneuver?

40. A teacher's take-home income increased 7.1% while consumer prices increased 12.7%. His new purchasing power is what percent of his old purchasing power? (Hint: He has 1.071 times as much money to buy goods that cost 1.127 times as much.)

41. The following figures were reported for the 1980 census:

State	1980 Population	Change from 1970
Alabama	3,863,698	+12.2%
Alaska	400,331	+32.3%
Arizona	2,714,013	+52.9%
Arkansas	2,280,687	+18.6%
California	23,510,372	+17.7%
Colorado	2,877,726	+30.2%
Connecticut	3,096,951	+2.1%
Delaware	594,779	+8.5%
District of Columbia	635,233	−16.0%

(a) What was the population of Alabama in 1970?

(b) What was the population of the District of Columbia in 1970?

(c) Which state had more people in 1970, Arizona or Arkansas?

(d) If the same *rate* of growth continues, what will the population of Arizona be in 1990? In the year 2000?

(e) If the same *rate* of growth continues, which state will have a greater population in 1990, Alabama or Arizona?

42. These problems are based on actual figures:

(a) If factory output went down 4.5% one year and up 1.7% (of the new amount) during the next year, what was the change during the two-year period? (The answer is *not* "down 2.8%.")

(b) Repeat part (a) for consumer prices that went up 13.5% one year and up 10.7% during the next year.

(c) Repeat part (a) for profits that went down 2.2% one year and up 3.8% during the next year.

43. A statue of Buddha in Bangkok, Thailand, is made from 5½ tons of 18-carat (75% pure) gold. What is the value of this amount of gold (a) at $700 an ounce? (b) at current gold prices?

6-4

REPRESENTING FRACTIONS AS DECIMALS

Have you ever seen the bewilderment of children who when using a calculator are surprised by mysterious answers to seemingly simple problems like $1 \div 3$? Instead of a "nice" whole number answer, the entire display lights up with something like ".33333333". The aim of this section is to help you solve the mystery of these unending decimals. Thanks to the calculator, we can explore these interesting questions without being bogged down with tedious arithmetic.

To obtain the decimal expansion for 1/2, we know from our previous work that we need merely compute $1 \div 2$, expressing the answer as a decimal. This gives us the familiar decimal expansion .5. Let's do the same for several different fractions. Using a calculator with an eight-digit display, we get

$$\frac{1}{2} = .5$$

$$\frac{1}{3} = .33333333$$

$$\frac{1}{4} = .25$$

$$\frac{1}{5} = .2$$

$$\frac{1}{6} = .16666666$$

$$\frac{1}{7} = .14285714$$

$$\frac{1}{8} = .125$$

(There may be some variation in the display depending on the calculator. For 1/6 the display might be 0.16666 or .16666667, etc., depending on number of digits displayed, initial zeros, and rounding features.)

We see that 1/2, 1/4, 1/5, and 1/8 terminate, that 1/3 repeats in blocks of one digit, that 1/6 repeats in blocks of one digit after a delay of one digit, and that 1/7 appears to repeat in blocks of six digits. The decimal expansions for fractions like 1/2, 1/4, 1/5, and 1/8 are called **terminating decimals**, while the decimal expansions for 1/3, 1/6, and 1/7 are called **repeating decimals**. Can we predict in advance whether we will get terminating or repeating decimals (or perhaps neither) for 1/9, 1/10, 1/11, 1/12, and 1/13?

First, what is the property common to the fractions whose decimal expansions terminate? (Perhaps you already have some feeling for this from Problems 22 and 23 in Section 5-1.) Writing our terminating decimals as fractions with denominators of 10, 100, 1000, etc., we have

$$\frac{1}{2} = .5 = \frac{5}{10},$$

$$\frac{1}{4} = .25 = \frac{25}{100},$$

$$\frac{1}{5} = .2 = \frac{2}{10}, \quad \text{and}$$

$$\frac{1}{8} = .125 = \frac{125}{100}.$$

This suggests that

(1) fractions with terminating decimal expansions can be written with denominators which are powers of 10 (10, 100, 1000, etc.).

Next we observe that for 1/2, 1/4, 1/5, and 1/8 respectively,

2 is a factor of 10,

4 is a factor of 100,

5 is a factor of 10,   and

8 is a factor of 1000.

On the other hand, for fractions like 1/3, 3 is *not* a factor of 10, 100, 1000, or any other power of 10. This leads us to the observation that

(2) (reduced) fractions with terminating decimal expansions have denominators which are factors of powers of 10.

Finally, since

$$10 = 2 \times 5,$$

$$100 = 2^2 \times 5^2,$$

$$1000 = 2^3 \times 5^3, \text{ and in general,}$$

$$10^n = 2^n \times 5^n,$$

we see that

(3) the only possible factors of powers of 10 are numbers whose prime factorization consists entirely of 2's and/or 5's. (Of course, 1 is also a factor.)

Putting statements (1), (2), and (3) together, we have the following

Criterion for Terminating Decimals □

(Reduced) fractions with terminating decimal expansions have denominators whose prime factorization consists *entirely* of 2's and/or 5's.

To reinforce these ideas we offer some examples.

Which of the following fractions have terminating decimal expansions? Explain how you can tell. For those which terminate, tell how many places will be required.

(a) $\frac{7}{40}$ (b) $\frac{3}{64}$ (c) $\frac{2}{35}$ (d) $\frac{21}{120}$ (e) $\frac{3^4}{5^7}$

EXAMPLE 6-11

SOLUTION

(a) 7/40 does not reduce, so the 7 in the numerator is of no significance. The prime factorization of 40 is $2^3 \times 5$, which consists entirely of 2's and 5's, so the decimal expansion for 7/40 will terminate. We can predict from the $2^3 \times 5$ factorization that we will end up with a denominator of 10^3, or three decimal places:

$$\frac{1}{40} = \frac{1}{2^3 \times 5} = \frac{5^2}{2^3 \times 5^3} = \frac{5^2}{10^3} = \frac{25}{1000} = .025, \text{ as predicted.}$$

(b) The prime factorization of 64 is 2^6, which consists entirely of 2's, so the decimal expansion terminates. We can predict from the 2^6 factorization that we will end up with a denominator of 10^6, or six decimal places:

$$\frac{3}{64} = \frac{3}{2^6} = \frac{3 \times 5^6}{2^6 \times 5^6} = \frac{3 \times 5^6}{10^6} = \frac{46875}{1000000} = .046875, \text{ as predicted.}$$

(c) The prime factorization of 35 is 5×7, which does *not* consist entirely of 2's and/or 5's. Since no multiple of 10 contains a factor of 7, the decimal expansion will *not* terminate.

(d) At first glance we might wrongly conclude that since 120 contains a factor of 3, the decimal expansion for 21/120 will not terminate. However, 21/120 reduces to 7/40, which terminates as we saw in part (a).

(e) Since the prime factorization of the denominator consists entirely of 5's, the decimal expansion terminates. We can predict from the 5^7 factorization that we will end up with a denominator of 10^7, or seven decimal places.

With our analysis of terminating decimals completed we turn to repeating decimals. The behavior of the decimal expansion for 1/7 provides considerable insight. We show one form of the long-division process for $1 \div 7$:

```
        .142857
    7)1.000000
      7
      ─
      30
      28
      ──
       20
       14
       ──
        60
        56
        ──
         40
         35
         ──
          50
          49
          ──
           1
```

At this point we have 6 decimal places in the quotient and a remainder of 1 (or technically .000001). As the division continues we will get the same digits in the quotient. (Why?)

```
        .142857142857
    7)1.000000000000
      7
      ─
      30
      28
      ──
       20
       14
       ──
        60
        56
        ──
         40
         35
         ──
          50
          49
```

Part I

$$
\begin{array}{r}
10 \\
\underline{7} \\
30 \\
\underline{28} \\
20 \\
\underline{14} \\
60 \\
\underline{56} \\
40 \\
\underline{35} \\
50 \\
\underline{49} \\
1
\end{array} \Bigg\} \quad \text{Part II}
$$

Do you see the repetition in Part I and Part II? Since after a while we get the same remainders, we will also get the same digits in the quotient.

Observe that in dividing 1 by 7 the remainder at each step must be less than 7. The only possibilities are 0, 1, 2, 3, 4, 5, or 6. If 0 occurs as a remainder, the process terminates. If 0 does not occur as a remainder, one of the other remainders must recur within seven steps (since there are only six different possibilities). By a similar argument, in dividing any whole number p by a larger whole number q, we know that either a zero occurs as a remainder (and the process terminates) or one of the other remainders must recur within q steps (since there are only $q - 1$ possibilities).

In each of the following examples we indicate by an arrow the first place where a remainder recurs or equals the original dividend. We express 1/3, 1/6, 1/11, and 5/13 as decimals:

$$
\begin{array}{r}
.333 \\
3\overline{)1.000} \\
9 \\
10 \\
9 \\
\overline{10} \\
9 \\
\overline{1}
\end{array}
\qquad
\begin{array}{r}
.166 \\
6\overline{)1.000} \\
6 \\
40 \\
36 \\
40 \\
36 \\
\overline{4}
\end{array}
\qquad
\begin{array}{r}
.0909 \\
11\overline{)1.0000} \\
0 \\
1\,00 \\
99 \\
10 \\
0 \\
100 \\
99 \\
\overline{1}
\end{array}
\qquad
\begin{array}{r}
.38461538 \\
13\overline{)5.00000000} \\
3\,9 \\
1\,10 \\
1\,04 \\
60 \\
52 \\
80 \\
78 \\
20 \\
13 \\
70 \\
65 \\
50 \\
39 \\
110 \\
104 \\
\overline{6}
\end{array}
$$

Exactly at the point where the remainder recurs or equals the original dividend, the quotient necessarily begins to repeat.

With these results as examples we will introduce some convenient notation for repeating decimals. To show that the decimal for 1/7 repeats in blocks of six digits we will write

$$\frac{1}{7} = .\overline{142857}.$$

Similarly we can write

$$\frac{1}{3} = .\overline{3}$$

$$\frac{1}{6} = .1\overline{6}$$

$$\frac{1}{11} = .\overline{09}$$

$$\frac{5}{13} = .\overline{384615}$$

Note for 1/6 that the bar (called the **repetend bar**) over the 6 (but not over the 1) means that the 6 repeats but the 1 does not repeat. We provide some further experience with this new notation.

EXAMPLE 6-12

Write each of the following using bar notation:

(a) .85858585 . . .   (b) .0023232323 . . .   (c) .8333333333 . . .

SOLUTION

(a) .$\overline{85}$.

(b) Here only the "23" repeats (*not* the "00"), so we write .00$\overline{23}$.

(c) Here only the "3" repeats (not the "8"), so we write .8$\overline{3}$.

EXAMPLE 6-13

Write out the first ten (or more) decimal places of each of the following:

(a) .$\overline{846}$ (b) .1$\overline{8}$ (c) .$\overline{0528}$ (d) .0$\overline{528}$

SOLUTION

(a) The bar indicates that all three digits repeat, so we write .$\overline{846}$ = .846846846846 . . . .

(b) The bar indicates that only the "8" repeats, so we write .1$\overline{8}$ = .1888888888 . . . .

(c) .$\overline{0528}$ = .052805280528 . . . .

(d) .0$\overline{528}$ = .0528528528 . . . .

Parts (c) and (d) of this example show the importance of using the bar notation very carefully.

Given an arbitrary fraction like 7/24, what can we say about its decimal expansion? Since $24 = 2^3 \times 3$, its prime factorization does not consist entirely of 2's and/or 5's, so it does not terminate. But does it necessarily repeat? If we were to divide 7 by 24 we know that all remainders which occur must be less than 24, so within 24 steps a remainder would recur and the quotient would begin to repeat. Without performing any division we know that the decimal expansion for 7/24 re-repeats within 24 steps. Upon performing the division with a certain calculator we see obtain "0.2916666". We know this is not exact (since the decimal is non-terminating). Actually the answer is .291$\overline{6}$, so our expansion begins to repeat after only four places. The important thing is that we could predict that *it does repeat*.

By the same reasoning, the decimal expansion for

8/23 repeats within 23 places,

3/14 repeats within 14 places,

7/103 repeats within 103 places, and in general

p/q either terminates or repeats within q places.

This leads us to our second main conclusion of this section:

> The decimal expansion for a fraction p/q either terminates or repeats within q places.

Together with our criterion for terminating decimals, this gives us considerable information about decimal expansions for fractions. We can be more specific about patterns of repeating decimals, but it will be more fun for you to discover some of these specifics for yourself in the problems.

There are two more questions we do want to answer. We just found that every fraction has a decimal expansion which either terminates or repeats. It is easy to see that every terminating decimal can be expressed as a fraction. For example, .0008162 *means* 8162/10000000. Less obvious is the question of whether every repeating decimal can be expressed as a fraction. We will broach this question with some examples.

Express each of the following as fractions:

(a) $.\overline{43}$ (b) $.\overline{018}$ (c) $.2\overline{85}$

EXAMPLE
6-14

(a) Let $n = .\overline{43}$. Then $100n = 43.\overline{43}$. (How do we multiply a decimal by 100?) Subtracting gives us $99n = 43$, so finally $n = 43/99$. Using a calculator to check our work confirms that $43 \div 99 = .\overline{43}$. We usually organize our work like this:

$$100n = 43.\overline{43}$$
$$n = .\overline{43}$$
$$\overline{99n = 43}$$
$$n = \frac{43}{49}$$

SOLUTION

(b) Let $n = .\overline{018}$. This time we multiply by 1000. (Why?)

$$1000n = 18.\overline{018}$$

$$\underline{n = .\overline{018}}$$

$$999n = 18$$

$$n = \frac{18}{999} \quad \text{or} \quad \frac{2}{111}$$

(c) Let $n = .2\overline{85}$. We multiply by 100.

$$100n = 28.5\overline{85}$$

$$\underline{n = .2\overline{85}}$$

$$99n = 28.3$$

$$n = \frac{28.3}{99} = \frac{283}{990}$$

Note that we did *not* answer "28.3/99," since our definition of fractions requires whole numbers in the numerator and denominator. We simply multiplied numerator and denominator by 10.

This technique allows us to convert *any* repeating decimal to a fraction, so we have our third main conclusion of this section:

> Every repeating decimal can be expressed as a fraction.

Have we covered all possible decimals, or are there decimals which neither terminate nor repeat? Consider the decimal .101001000100001000001 . . . . Do you see that it is constructed by writing a 1 followed by a 0, then a 1 followed by two 0's, then a 1 followed by three 0's, etc.? Certainly this is a well-defined decimal in that it is possible to determine what each decimal place is. It clearly doesn't terminate. Neither does it repeat, for the pattern of 0's is never repeating. In Chapter 8 we will encounter several other important numbers which have non-terminating, non-repeating decimal expansions. Do you know of such numbers?

A mind-boggling fact is that mathematically *almost all* decimals are non-terminating, non-repeating, but this is content for another course. For now, we give you the opportunity to uncover some interesting patterns for repeating decimals.

EXERCISES AND PROBLEMS 6-4

EXPRESSING FRACTIONS AS DECIMALS

1. Write the following as four-place decimals:
   (a) 5/8   (b) 3/16   (c) 11/40   (d) 11/18.
   (In each case tell whether your answer is exact or approximate.)

2. Classify the following fractions according to whether their decimal expansions are terminating or repeating. For those which terminate, tell in how many places. Explain your reasoning.

(a) $\frac{2}{3}$ (b) $\frac{3}{4}$ (c) $\frac{1}{9}$ (d) $\frac{1}{10}$ (e) $\frac{1}{11}$ (f) $\frac{1}{12}$ (g) $\frac{1}{13}$

(h) $\frac{1}{21}$ (i) $\frac{1}{20}$ (j) $\frac{1}{60}$ (k) $\frac{1}{25600}$ (l) $\frac{11}{2^{17} \times 5^{29}}$ (m) $\frac{13}{7 \times 5^{23}}$

(n) $\frac{11}{5^4 \times 13^2}$

3. Find a fraction between .635 and .636 with a denominator of 489. Explain your method.

4. Determine which fraction in each pair is greater by changing each of them to a decimal.
   (a) 4/5 and 7/9   (b) 64/17 and 19/5
   (c) 4/13 and 7/23

5. Repeat Problem 4, using the method of Chapter 5.

6. Find the given decimal place (digit) for the decimal expansion of the given fraction.
   (a) 10th digit of 1/7 (answer: 8)
   (b) 29th digit of 1/7
   (c) 1053rd digit of 1/7
   (d) 1,000,000th digit of 1/7
   (e) 457th digit of 2/13
   (f) 840th digit of 4/19
   (g) 200,953rd digit of 1/99

7. If $7/17 = .\overline{4117647058823529}$, find the 1001st digit in the decimal expansion.

8. (a) Express 1/7, 2/7, 3/7, 4/7, 5/7, 6/7 as decimals. Find a pattern.
   (b) Do the same for 1/13, 2/13, 3/13, 4/13, . . . , 12/13.

9. (a) Find a way to get the 4th, 5th, and 6th digits of the decimal expansion for 1/7 by looking at the 1st, 2nd, and 3rd digits.
   (b) Can you find other fractions for which a similar thing happens?

10. Observing that $100 \times \frac{1}{59} = \frac{100}{59} = 1\frac{41}{59}$, what relationship exists between the decimal expansion of 41/59 and the decimal expansion of 1/59?

11. Tell whether the decimal expansion for 3/106106777711 is terminating, repeating, or non-repeating. Explain how you can tell without computing the decimal expansion.

12. Give an example of a common fraction whose decimal expansion (a) terminates in exactly four places. (b) repeats in blocks of exactly four digits (and in no less).

13. Which fractions have decimal expansions which (a) terminate in exactly four decimal places? (b) Repeat in blocks of exactly four digits?

14. Classify all (positive) fractions with decimal expansions which are (a) terminating   (b) repeating   (c) non-repeating.

15. (a) Find decimal expansions for 1/13, 1/17, 1/19, 1/23, 1/29, 1/31, 1/37, and 1/41. Since 1/13 repeats in blocks of six digits we say it has block size, or **period**, 6. Give the period for each of the other fractions.
    (b) What do the denominators of these fractions have in common?
    (c) Find a relationship between the period and the denominator of the fraction.
    (d) What would your answer to part (c) suggest about the period of 1/47?

16. Repeat parts (a), (b), and (c) of the previous problem for the fractions 1/26, 1/34, 1/38, 1/46, 1/58, 1/62, 1/74, and 1/82.

17. (a) Based on the previous two problems, guess at the periods of the decimal expansions for 1/52 and 1/68.

    (b) Now express 1/52 and 1/68 as decimals. What are the periods?

    (c) Guess at the period for the decimal expansion of $\dfrac{1}{2^3 \times 5^7 \times 13}$.

REPEATING DECIMALS

18. Write out the first ten (or more) decimal places of

    (a) $.\overline{216}$ (b) $.2\overline{16}$ (c) $.21\overline{6}$ (d) $.216$

19. Write each of the following using bar notation.

    (a) .66666 . . .   (b) .31313131 . . .   (c) .06060606 . . .
    (d) .35222222 . . .   (e) .75

20. If the decimal expansion for 1/43 is $.\overline{023255813953488372093}$, find a fraction whose decimal expansion is $.\overline{325581395348837209302}$.

21. Use the method of Example 6-14 to express each of the following as fractions:
    (a) $.7\overline{4}$ (b) $.8\overline{76}$ (c) $.9\overline{369}$
    (d) $.0\overline{89}$ (e) $.1\overline{63}$

*22. Use the method of Example 6-14 to change $.\overline{9}$ to an ordinary fraction. Can you explain the surprising result?

23. Find a common fraction whose decimal expansion is .163.

24. If $.\overline{1}$ = 1/9, what fraction is given by

    (a) $.\overline{2}$?   (b) $.\overline{3}$?   (c) $.\overline{4}$?   (d) $1.\overline{7}$?

25. If $.\overline{01}$ = 1/99, what fraction is given by

    (a) $.\overline{02}$?   (b) $.\overline{03}$?   (c) $.\overline{04}$?   (d) $.\overline{13}$?   (e) $.\overline{84}$?   (f) $1.\overline{97}$?

26. If $.\overline{001}$ = 1/999, what fraction is given by

    (a) $.\overline{002}$?   (b) $.\overline{003}$?   (c) $.\overline{004}$?   (d) $.\overline{019}$?   (e) $.\overline{524}$?

27. Use the method of the previous three problems to express each of the following as a fraction. (Compare with Problems 21 and 22.)

    (a) $.\overline{43}$ (b) $.\overline{74}$ (c) $.\overline{876}$ (d) $.\overline{9}$ (e) $.\overline{163}$

28. (a) Express the terminating decimal .5 as a repeating decimal.   (b) Can all terminating decimals be written as repeating decimals?   (c) Can all decimals be written as repeating decimals?

29. Solve the cryptarithm:

    $$\dfrac{EVE}{DID} = .\overline{TALK}$$

NON-REPEATING DECIMALS

30. (a) Write out the next ten digits of this non-repeating decimal:
        .12345678910111213141516 . . .

    (b) What is the 100th place in this decimal?

    (c) Can this decimal be expressed as a fraction?

31. Repeat the previous problem for the non-repeating decimal
.101001000100001000001000001 . . .

CALCULATORS

C32. Here is a list of what several different calculators display for $1 \div 6$. Tell what you think each would display for $8 \div 9$.
   (a) .16666666
   (b) 0.1666666
   (c) .16666667
   (d) 0.1666667
   (e) .17

C33. If a calculator display for the decimal expansion of a fraction shows 0.16666667, we'd probably assume that the correct expansion is $.1\overline{6}$. Yet it could conceivably be any of the following. Write out the first 20 digits of each.
   (a) $.1\overline{6}$
   (b) $.1\overline{666667}$
   (c) $.\overline{1666667}$
   (d) $.1666667$
   (e) $.1\overline{6666670}$

34. Find the fractions corresponding to the decimal expansions of Problem 33.

C35. Use a calculator to express 1/17, 2/17, 3/17, 4/17, and 5/17 to six places. There is enough information here to get *every* digit of 1/17. Can you do it?

C36. Convert 5/12 to a decimal, using a calculator. Is the last digit rounded off? (This varies with different calculators.) Round off your answer to a four-place decimal.

C37. Debbie wanted to find the decimal expansion for 3/13. Her calculator displayed "0.2307692" for $3 \div 13$. She noticed that one of the digits of her eight-digit display was used up by the zero at the beginning of the number, so she devised an easy way to get one more digit at the end of the number instead of the initial zero. How did she do it?

P38. Write a program to compute the decimal expansion of p/q, five digits at a time. (Hint: See Problem 31, Section 3-6.)

Integers

7-1
DEFINING INTEGERS

A teacher began his class one day by explaining why he wasn't prepared to give his students any examples of negative numbers. He had intended to go to the library and look up some examples, but everything seemed to go wrong.

It was a cold winter day with a temperature of $-5°$ F, and he was delayed because his car wouldn't start. He owed money after losing a bet because a certain elevation was below sea level and because a certain date was B.C. rather than A.D. Later he was embarrassed when he misplayed a hand of cards to go "down three," frustrated when the corporation he had invested in went into the red causing a stock fluctuation of -2 points per share, and disappointed when his favorite football team lost a game because there was a loss of one yard on a crucial play. After all these problems, he was too disgusted to try to think of any examples of negative numbers [24]!

In this chapter, we will take ideas like "below zero," "in the red," and "in the hole" and consolidate them into the single concept that we will call being "negative." These negative numbers seem to arise when the temperature *drops* below zero, when we *lose* more money than we have, and when points are *deducted* from our score. They typically occur when we *subtract* a larger number from a smaller one: a temperature of 3° drops 8°; we have $4 and lose a $10 bet; or our score is 0 and then 3 points are deducted. We are going to extend the whole numbers to a new set called integers, which (unlike the whole numbers) will be closed under subtraction. The arithmetic of whole numbers will need to be expanded to accommodate the newly added integers. This task will not be difficult, since our extension from the whole numbers to the integers will closely parallel our previous extension from the whole numbers to the fractions.

Recall that fractions were introduced to solve certain division problems for which the whole numbers were inadequate. We created 2/3 so we would have an answer to $2 \div 3$, as when dividing two pizzas equally among three people. The fractions 5/8, 1/7, and 8/1 arose from the division problems $5 \div 8$, $1 \div 7$, and $8 \div 1$. Now we wish to introduce numbers so that $2 - 3$ will have a solution, as when having $2 and owing $3. This set of numbers should also contain the solutions to other subtraction problems like $5 - 8$, $1 - 7$, and $8 - 1$.

Our real-life experiences suggest that the solution to $2 - 3$ ought to be -1. If we have $2 and need to pay $3, we give up our $2 and *owe* $1. If the thermometer reads 2° and the temperature drops 3°, it will be 1° below zero. The subtraction problems $2 - 3$ and $5 - 8$ are illustrated on a thermometer in Figure 7-1. This method of illustrating subtraction is actually familiar. In case you don't recognize it, move the page so that the words "Drop of 3°" in Figure 7-1 are on top. We easily see the thermometers to be number lines, not unlike the ones we referred to many times when discussing the whole numbers and the fractions, except that they contain numbers "below zero." In fact, some mathematics educators have suggested that number lines be introduced in a vertical position to children, so that they more closely resemble thermometers and other number lines with which children are familiar.

FIGURE 7-1

So far, we have seen that the subtraction problems $2 - 3$ and $5 - 8$ suggest the need for certain numbers "below zero." We need the numbers we have called -1 and -3 to take care of those particular problems, and to take care of similar problems we introduce the entire set of **negative integers**, $\{-1, -2, -3, -4, -5, -6, \ldots\}$. The union of the negative integers and the whole numbers is called the **integers** and is usually listed like this: $\{\ldots, -3, -2, -1, 0, 1, 2, 3, \ldots\}$.

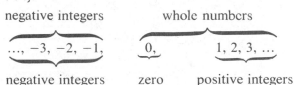

FIGURE 7-2

We see that integers are of two types, negative integers and whole numbers. It is often convenient to divide whole numbers into two classes, **positive integers** and zero. This classification scheme partitions the integers into three classes instead of two. Both schemes are shown in Figure 7-2.

If we let

$$Z = \{\ldots, -3, -2, -1, 0, 1, 2, 3, \ldots\},$$
$$N = \{-1, -2, -3, -4, \ldots\},$$
$$P = \{1, 2, 3, 4, \ldots\}, \text{ and}$$
$$W = \{0, 1, 2, 3, \ldots\},$$

then we can write

$$Z = N \cup W,$$
$$W = \{0\} \cup P,$$
$$Z = N \cup \{0\} \cup P,$$
$$N \cap W = \{\ \}, \text{ and}$$
$$N \cap P = \{\ \},$$

to show some of the relationships among the sets.

It is common in many elementary school texts to write "+3" rather than "3" to indicate 3, especially when first introducing integers. This symbolism is usually dropped soon after it is introduced. Writing +3 to emphasize that 3 is an integer is analogous to writing 3/1 to suggest that 3 is a fraction.

We are told by D. E. Smith in *History of Mathematics* [43] that about 2000 years ago the Chinese recorded credits and debits using red rods and black rods. As a modification of this procedure, we use black chips to represent credits and white chips to represent debits in giving a set model for integers. Then +4 and −7 can be represented as follows:

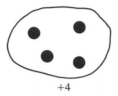   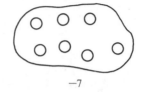

+4   −7

If we agree that each black chip cancels a white chip, we can represent 4 and −7 (or any other integer) in many ways. One way to represent each number is shown below:

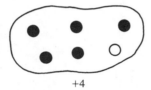   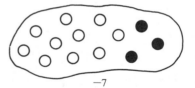

+4   −7

The usefulness of this model will be seen in the next section when we add and subtract integers.

Another useful model is the number line, which will be extremely helpful in ordering and doing arithmetic with integers. We do this by first pairing 0 with any point on the line, calling this point the **origin.** Then we arbitrarily pair 1 with any point to the right of the origin. Letting the piece of the line from 0 to 1 be our unit, we now have but one choice for assigning each of the other integers. We assign 2 to the point two "units" to the right of the origin. The integers −1 and −2 are assigned to the points one and two units to the left of the origin, respectively. Any other counting number p is paired with the point p units to the right of the origin, and the negative integer $-p$ is paired with the point p units to the left of the origin. The numbers 1 and −1, 2 and −2, and p and $-p$ are called **opposites** of one another. For example, the opposite of 13 is −13, and the opposite of −13 is 13. (The opposite of 0 is 0 itself.)

EXAMPLE 7-1

Find the opposite of the opposite of −7.

SOLUTION

The opposite of −7 is 7, whose opposite is −7.

The symbol " − " takes on still another meaning besides "minus" and "negative." It is also used to mean "opposite." We write " − (− 7)" to mean the "opposite of negative seven." Notice that the first " − " is read "opposite (of)" and the second " − " is read "negative." The symbol " − 4" could mean either "negative four" or "the opposite of (positive) four." But since the opposite of (positive) four is negative four, the two interpretations are equivalent.

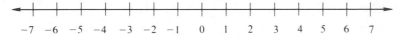

As on a thermometer, the points associated with a number and its opposite mirror one another. For instance, − 5 is located five units to the left of the origin and 5 is located five units to the right of the origin. We say that each of the numbers − 5 and 5 has an **absolute value** of 5, which describes the fact that each is located five units from the origin. The symbolism " $|-5|$ " is read "the absolute value of negative five," and " $|5|$ " is read "the absolute value of five." Each integer is completely identified by its absolute value and its sign. Zero has an absolute value, but it has no sign since it is neither positive nor negative. The sign of a positive integer is understood and often is not written.

Find the absolute value and sign of

(a) − 7   (b) 3   (c) 0   (d) − 84,327.

EXAMPLE
7-2

SOLUTION

(a) − 7 is located seven units to the left of the origin, so $|-7| = 7$. The sign of − 7 is negative.

(b) 3 is located three units to the right of the origin, so $|3| = 3$. Its sign is understood to be positive.

(c) 0 is located 0 units to the right (or left) of the origin, so $|0| = 0$. It has no sign.

(d) Even without a picture, it is clear from the way we have designed the number line that − 84,327 is located 84,327 units to the left of the origin, so $|-84,327|$ is 84,327, and the sign of − 84,327 is negative.

Unlike an actual thermometer, our number line is assumed to extend indefinitely in both directions.

Ordering the integers has essentially been done by the method with which we placed them on the number line. As was the case with whole numbers, for any two integers p and q,

$p < q$ if p is located to the left of q on the number line,
$p > q$ if p is located to the right of q on the number line,
$p = q$ if p and q are located at the same point on the number line.

Some typical cases are provided in Example 7-3.

EXAMPLE
7-3

Fill in the square with the appropriate symbol $<$, $=$, or $>$.

(a) 3 □ 5   (b) -6 □ -6 (c) -8 □ -6 (d) 2 □ -4

(e) 0 □ -7 (f) $|-5|$ □ 5

SOLUTION

(a) 3 and 5 are located respectively three and five units to the right of the origin, so 3 is located to the left of 5 and we have $3 < 5$. Whole numbers compare as expected.

(b) $-6 = -6$

(c) -8 is located eight units to the left of the origin and -6 is located six units to the left of the origin, so $-8 < -6$. This example shows how negative integers are located in *reverse order* (of their opposites).

(d) 2 is located to the right of the origin and -4 is located to the left of the origin, so 2 is clearly located to the right of -4 and we write $2 > -4$.

(e) 0 is located at the origin and -7 is located to the left of the origin, so $0 > -7$. These last two examples illustrate how each whole number is greater than every negative integer.

(f) Since $|-5|$ is five units from the origin, we have $|-5| = 5$.

We have introduced the integers but have yet to show how to do arithmetic with them, especially to substantiate our claim to have a set closed under subtraction. In the problems, you will have a chance to investigate the ideas developed so far.

EXERCISES AND PROBLEMS 7-1

DEFINITION

1. (a) List the examples of negative numbers you can find in the second paragraph of this section.
   (b) Add several examples of your own to the list.

2. Some elementary teachers write "⑥" to mean "six in the hole."
   (a) What number do you think this represents?
   (b) What do you think of the idea?
   (c) Do you have any innovations of your own?

3. (a) Is 0 an integer? A positive integer? A negative integer? Which of these are integers?
   (b) $+5$ (c) -5 (d) $|5|$ (e) $|-5|$
   (f) 1/2   (g) $-1/2$ (h) $576 + 293$

4. Use the black and white chips set model to represent each of these numbers three different ways: (a) 5   (b) -2 (c) 0.   (d) If you had an unlimited supply of chips, how many ways could you represent -7?

5. Find the opposite of
   (**a**) 7   (**b**) -3 (**c**) x (**d**) 0
   (**e**) $|5|$ (**f**) $|-5|$ (**g**) $576 + 293$

6. Is $-p$ positive or negative if p is
   (**a**) positive?   (**b**) negative?   (**c**) 0?

NUMBER LINES AND ORDER

7. Name some everyday "number lines" other than the thermometer. Are they horizontal or vertical?

8. Suppose you were making a number line, starting with an unmarked line. Describe all the steps involved in locating points corresponding to -2, -1, 0, 1, and 2.

9. Fill in the square with the appropriate symbol $<$, $=$, or $>$.
   (**a**) $-9 \square 7$ (**b**) $7 \square -2$ (**c**) $2 \square -7$ (**d**) $0 \square -5$
   (**e**) $4 \square -4$ (**f**) $-8 \square -6$ (**g**) $-8999 \square -9000$

10. If we are to put $-2/3$ and $-1/2$ on our number line, would $-2/3$ be to the left or the right of $-1/2$?

11. In the next section, we are going to show how to do problems like the ones below. Use a number line or other methods to try to explore solutions.
    (**a**) $(-4) + (-3)$ (**b**) $7 - 11$ (**c**) $(-8) - (-5)$
    (**d**) $(-3) + 5$ (**e**) $(-12) \times (-4)$ (**f**) $(-12) \times 4$
    (**g**) $(-8) \div (-2)$ (**h**) $(-8) \div 2$

OPPOSITES AND ABSOLUTE VALUE

12. Write out in words (use *negative, opposite, minus,* etc.)
    (**a**) $6 - 4$
    (**b**) -4 (There are two possible answers, but they are equivalent.)
    (**c**) $-(-2)$ (**d**) $-(+5)$ (**e**) $6 - (-(-4))$
    (**f**) $-x$ (where x is any *integer*)
    (**g**) -0

13. Evaluate
    (**a**) $|6|$ (**b**) $|-9|$ (**c**) $|0|$ (**d**) $|12|$
    (**e**) $|-5|$ (**f**) $|8 - 6|$ (**g**) $|8| - |6|$

14. Find an integer p such that
    (**a**) $|p| > p$ (**b**) $|p| = p$ (**c**) $|p| < p$
    (**d**) Give a rule that determines which condition will hold for a given integer.

15. We can also define absolute value for integers this way:

$$|p| = \begin{cases} p, & \text{if } p \text{ is a whole number} \\ -p, & \text{if } p \text{ is a negative integer} \end{cases}$$

Determine $|8|$, $|-8|$, and $|0|$ by this definition. Do the results agree with the interpretation in terms of distance from the origin?

RELATIONSHIPS WITH WHOLE NUMBERS AND FRACTIONS

16. (**a**) Is there a smallest whole number? Integer? Positive integer? Negative integer?
    (**b**) Is there a largest whole number? Integer? Positive integer? Negative integer?

17. By our definitions, is the number 3 a fraction? Is the number -3 a fraction?

18. Are the integers an extension of the whole numbers or of the fractions (or both or neither)?

19. Using the definition given in this section, *list* the members of
    (a) Z (b) N (c) P
    (d) $N \cup P$ (e) $N \cap P$ (f) $W \cap P$

20. Which of the sets Z, N, P, and W are subsets of Z? Of N? Of P? Of W?

21. Find a 1-1 correspondence between
    (a) N and P (b) P and W *(c) W and Z

22. The division problems $2 \div 3, 4 \div 6, 6 \div 9$, etc. (among whole numbers), all give rise to some fraction. Are there different subtraction problems (among whole numbers) which give rise to the integer -1?

23. We said for fractions that "$p/q < r/s$ (as fractions) if $p \times s < r \times q$ (as whole numbers)." Write an analogous statement about integers which is as much like the statement involving fractions as possible.

CALCULATORS

C24. Start with the number 10 and repeatedly subtract 1. After subtracting 1 ten times you arrive at 0. Continue subtracting 1's. What sequence of numbers is displayed on the calculator for the next ten steps?

APPLICATIONS

25.

Geographic Extremes

Feature	Name	Location	Meters	Feet
Highest mountain (world)	Mt. Everest	Nepal/Tibet	8848	29,028
Highest mountain (U.S.)	Mt. McKinley	Alaska	6194	20,320
Lowest land point (world)	Dead Sea	Israel/Jordan	*400	*1312
Lowest land point (U.S.)	Death Valley	California	*86	*282
Deepest ocean	Pacific Ocean	Mariana Trench	*11,034	*36,198

*Indicates depth or below sea level

Which differs more from sea level, the top of Mt. Everest or the bottom of the Mariana Trench?

26. Find the difference in meters of each of the following:
    (a) world land extremes (Mt. Everest and Dead Sea)
    (b) U.S. land extremes
    (c) highest mountain and deepest ocean

27. Do the previous problem substituting "feet" for "meters."

28. (a) The earth's diameter is approximately 12,756 kilometers (7926 miles). The height of Mt. Everest is what percent of the diameter?
    (b) If the diameter of a globe is 30 centimeters (about 12 inches), how "high" is Mt. Everest on the same scale?
    (c) How does your answer to (b) compare with the thickness of a page of this book?

29. (a) Driskill Mountain is the highest point in Louisiana, with an elevation of 535 feet. New Orleans is the lowest, with an elevation of 5 feet below sea level. Calculate the difference in elevations of these two places; namely, the range of the elevation.

(b) Do the same for Mt. Whitney (14,494 feet) and Death Valley (−282 feet) in California.

30. (a) On January 22, 1943, Spearfish, South Dakota, recorded an official temperature of −4° F at 7:30 a.m. and a temperature of 45° F two minutes later (due to Chinook winds)! What was the temperature change?

(b) The record-low temperature in the U.S. is −80° F, recorded in Alaska in 1971. The lowest in the contiguous states is −70° F, recorded at Rogers Pass, Montana, in 1954. How much colder is the Alaska temperature than the Montana temperature?

(c) How much colder is the Alaska temperature than the U.S. record high of 134° F, recorded in 1913 in Greenland Ranch, California, which has an elevation of −178 feet?

(d) The record low in Hawaii is 14° F (1961). The record low in Florida is −2° F (1899). How much lower is Florida's record low?

(e) The world-record high and low are 136° F in Libya, Africa, and −127° F in Vostok, Antarctica. What is the range (difference between the two) of world temperatures?

31. A strong wind has the effect of making temperatures seem much colder. A wind-chill factor shows the combined effects of wind and temperature as equivalent temperatures in still air. For example, the wind-chill table below shows in the circled entry that if there is a 30 mile-per-hour wind and the temperature is 20° F, the cooling effect is equivalent to −18° F on a calm day.

Find the wind-chill factor (equivalent temperature on a calm day) of a day with the following conditions:
(a) wind 10 mph, temperature 30°
(b) wind 30 mph, temperature 30°
(c) wind 20 mph, temperature 20°
(d) Which effect is colder: 10 mph wind with 15° temperature, or 30 mph wind with 30° temperature?

Wind Chill
Equivalent Temperatures (°F)

Calm	35	30	25	20	15	10	5	0	−5	−10
5	33	27	21	16	12	7	1	−6	−11	−15
10	21	16	9	2	−2	−9	−15	−22	−27	−31
15	16	11	1	−6	−11	−18	−25	−33	−40	−45
20	12	3	−4	−9	−17	−24	−32	−40	−46	−52
25	7	0	−7	−15	−22	−29	−37	−45	−52	−58
30	5	−2	−11	(−18)	−26	−33	−41	−49	−56	−63
35	3	−4	−13	−20	−27	−35	−43	−52	−60	−67
40	1	−4	−15	−22	−29	−36	−45	−54	−62	−69
45	1	−6	−17	−24	−31	−38	−46	−54	−63	−70
50	0	−7	−17	−24	−31	−38	−47	−56	−63	−70

Wind speed (mph)

32. As you travel by plane higher in the upper levels of air, the temperature drops as shown in the following chart:

Feet	Meters	Fahrenheit	Celsius
Sea level	Sea level	59°	15°
1000	300	56°	13°
5000	1500	41°	5°
10,000	3000	23°	−5°
15,000	4500	5°	−15°
20,000	6000	−15°	−26°
30,000	9000	−47°	−44°

Find the change in Fahrenheit temperature as you go from sea level to (a) 10,000 feet   (b) 20,000 feet   (c) 30,000 feet.

33. Find the change in Celsius temperature in the previous problem as you go from sea level to (a) 3000 meters   (b) 6000 meters   (c) 9000 meters.

34. Greenwich Mean Time (during daylight savings time) is given below for several cities:

London	+1
Frankfurt	+2
Singapore	+7½
Jakarta	+7
Hong Kong	+8
Los Angeles	−7
Honolulu	−10

For example, if it is 1 P.M. in London, it is 2 P.M. in Frankfurt, 7:30 P.M. in Singapore, and 5 A.M. in Los Angeles. (It is 1 hour past noon in London and 7 hours before noon in Los Angeles.) If it is 1 P.M. in London, what time is it (a) in Hong Kong?   (b) in Honolulu?

35. (a) Use the information from the previous problem to find the time in each of the other six cities if it is 9 A.M. in London. (Note: If the time for London is 7 A.M. on Monday, the time for Honolulu will be for Sunday evening.)
   (b) Explain why it is Sunday evening in Honolulu.

36. All times given are "local time," the time in that city.
   (a) A flight leaves Honolulu at 12:20 P.M. and arrives in Los Angeles at 8:30 P.M. How long does the flight take? (Don't forget the time change! See Problem 34.)
   (b) Repeat part (a) for a flight leaving Singapore at 9 P.M. on Saturday and arriving in Frankfurt at 11:20 A.M. on Sunday.
   (c) An airline flight (on a 747 aircraft) leaves Singapore at 1:30 P.M. and arrives Los Angeles at 8:30 P.M. the same day. Along the over-9000-mile trip there are two stops totaling 2½ hours. How long does the flight take (including the stops)? (Is your answer reasonable? The 747 flies less than the speed of sound, which is about 750 miles per hour.)

7-2
OPERATIONS WITH INTEGERS

Our task for this section was mentioned earlier. We need to develop the arithmetic of the integers and, in particular, to show that the set is closed under subtraction. We will derive a few results quite carefully, sketch others, and let you establish some on your own.

As usual, we start with addition. Since a significant portion of the integers are whole numbers, part of the job is already done. If we are to add two integers that happen to be whole numbers, we add them as whole numbers. This is not only very easy to do, but it ensures that our results will be consistent with what we've done before. The sum $2 + 3$ will be 5 whether we think of 2 and 3 as whole numbers or as integers.

The set model for integers involving black chips and white chips presented in the previous section provides a concrete way of viewing addition and subtraction of integers. It will be sketched briefly here. The interested reader can find a thorough discussion of this model in "A Concrete Approach to Integer Addition and Subtraction" by Albert B. Bennett, Jr., and Gary L. Musser [63]. Figure 7-3 illustrates several of the cases for adding integers. Subtraction of integers will be presented later.

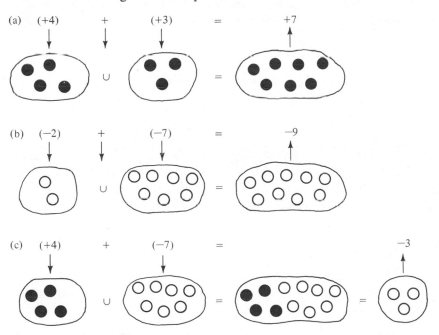

FIGURE 7-3

We can also use our extended number line, which now includes the negative integers, as a model for addition of integers. Adding two positive integers will be done exactly as it was for whole numbers. First we show the sum of $+2$ and $+3$.

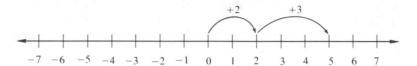

Next let's add two negative integers. Our practical experience suggests that if we "add debt to debt" we have even more debt. This is confirmed by our number line model. Suppose we add $(-4) + (-2)$. We start at the origin and make a jump of -4. Notice that a jump of -4 is a jump to the *left*. (In working

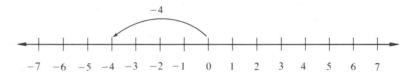

with children, you may prefer to call these steps "backward" and jumps to the right steps "forward.") Now from that point we make a jump of -2, which is two units to the left. Clearly, the result is -6. Geometrically, this says if we

move 4 units to the left and then 2 units to the left we will have moved a total of 6 units to the left. This merely involves adding $4 + 2$ as usual while recording that the moves are to the left. This will be true for any two negative integers: simply add their absolute values to get (the absolute value of) the sum, and remember that the sum is negative. Picturing the number line makes this quite simple to remember. Summarizing our work so far, we have the following:

☐ Adding Two Integers with Like Signs

> Add the absolute values and preface with the common sign.

We already know that $p + 0 = p$ and $0 + p = p$ for any whole number p. Similarly, we define $n + 0 = n$ and $0 + n = n$ for any negative integer n. It remains to define the sum of a positive integer and a negative integer. A special case is a pair of opposites like 5 and -5. The sum $5 + (-5)$ would be shown on the number line as a jump five units to the right of the origin followed by a jump five units to the left. These opposite jumps effectively offset one another,

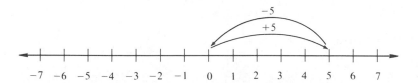

resulting in a return to the origin (just as a gain of $5 and a loss of $5 balance out). This prompts us to write $5 + (-5) = 0$. Similarly, $(-5) + 5 = 0$. For that matter, we can see the sum of any number and its opposite to be 0.

A more general case is one like $(-2) + 5$, where the numbers are not opposites. Again this particular problem is easy to solve on the number line, where positive numbers are taken as jumps to the right, and negative numbers

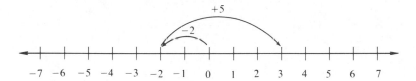

as jumps to the left. Notice that after jumping 2 to the left of the origin, the jump of $+5$ takes us to the right of the origin. We can picture this by replacing the jump of $+5$ in the first sketch by a jump of $+2$ (to get back to the origin)

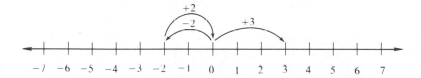

followed by a jump of $+3$. The geometric solution shown on the number line can also be written out arithmetically:

We know that $5 = 2 + 3$, so instead of $(-2) + 5$ we can write $(-2) + [2 + 3]$. Assuming that we have the associative property for adding integers, this can be rewritten as $[(-2) + 2] + 3$, which is $0 + 3$, or 3. The steps then are

$$(-2) + 5 = (-2) + [2 + 3]$$
$$= [(-2) + 2] + 3$$
$$= 0 + 3$$
$$= 3$$

The essence of the approach to adding numbers with unlike signs is that part of the number which is larger (in absolute value) is spent canceling out the effect of the other number, and what is left is the *difference* of the absolute values. This difference may, however, be negative, as in Example 7-4.

EXAMPLE
7-4

(a) Find the sum $2 + (-6)$ arithmetically.

(b) Check the result geometrically.

SOLUTION

(a) Part of the -6 will be spent offsetting the 2. We split -6 into $(-2) + (-4)$.

$$
\begin{aligned}
2 + (-6) &= 2 + [(-2) + (-4)] \\
&= [2 + (-2)] + (-4) \\
&= 0 + (-4) \\
&= -4
\end{aligned}
$$

(b)

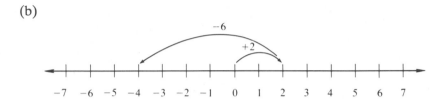

It should be clear that if we start at the origin and make a positive jump (to the right) and a negative jump (to the left) in either order, we will end up to the right or the left of the origin, according to which of the jumps was greater. Arithmetically, this means that the sign of the sum of a positive integer and a negative integer is the same as the sign of the one which is larger (in absolute value). (If the numbers are opposites, the sum is 0.) Because the jumps associated with adding a positive number and a negative number (in either order) are in opposite directions, the final distance from the origin will be equal to the *difference* of the lengths of the jumps. These observations can be summarized as follows:

☐ Adding Two Integers with Unlike Signs

1. If they are opposites, the sum is 0.
2. Otherwise, the sum is the difference of their absolute values prefaced with the sign of the term which has the larger absolute value.

EXAMPLE
7-5

Find these sums.

(a) $4 + (-4)$ (b) $(-7) + 5$
(c) $5 + (-7)$ (d) $(-231) + 846$
(e) $(-4561) + (-823)$
(f) $(-2) + (-5) + 8 + 11 + (-3)$

SOLUTION

(a) These numbers are opposites, so the sum is 0.

(b) The signs differ, so find the difference $7 - 5 = 2$. Since the larger term (in absolute value) is *negative* seven, the sum will be *negative* two; namely, -2.

(c) The signs differ, so find the difference $7 - 5 = 2$. Since the larger term (in absolute value) is *negative* seven, the sum will be *negative* two; namely, -2. This is, of course, the same answer as for (b), as the order of the factors is irrelevant.

(d) The signs differ, so find the difference $846 - 231 = 615$. Since the larger term (in absolute value) is *positive* 846, the sum will be *positive* 615.

(e) These numbers are both negative, so find the sum simply by adding and affixing a negative sign: $(-4561) + (-823) = -5384$.

(f) In a case with more than two numbers, it is easiest to add all the positive terms, add all the negative terms, and then add the two partial sums. (Notice that we are assuming the ability to regroup and reorder; namely, the associative and commutative properties.)

$$(-2) + (-5) + 8 + 11 + (-3) = [(-2) + (-5) + (-3)] + [8 + 11]$$
$$= (-10) + 19$$
$$= 9$$

We have rather freely applied the associative and commutative properties of addition whenever convenient. We emphasize that they have *not* been established for adding integers, so it should not be assumed that they hold automatically. Fortunately both properties do hold, but to establish them algebraically would require the consideration of several cases, especially for the associative property, which involves three numbers. These cases arise depending on whether the individual terms are positive or negative (or zero). You may wish to investigate some or all of the cases for each property, but we choose to omit the proofs here. In lieu of any proofs, we offer an example which we strongly emphasize is *not* a proof.

EXAMPLE

7-6

(a) Verify that the associative property for the addition of integers holds for the particular sum $(-2) + (-5) + 3$.

(b) Sketch the results on the number line.

SOLUTION

(a) We are to group the terms in these two different ways:

$$[(-2) + (-5)] + 3 = (-7) + 3 = -4$$
$$(-2) + [(-5) + 3] = (-2) + (-2) = -4$$

(b)

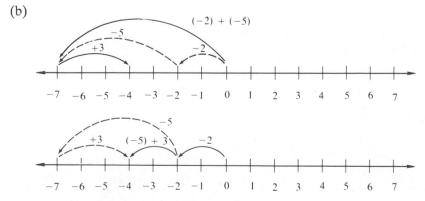

We have said without giving proofs that addition of integers is commutative and associative. Even more basic perhaps is the matter of whether or not we have arranged things so that the sum of every pair of integers is uniquely defined and so that the sum is necessarily an integer. We have given definitions for adding two integers covering each of the following possibilities:

1. Both integers are whole numbers.
2. Both integers are negative.
3. One integer is negative; the other is zero.
4. One integer is negative; the other is positive.

Certainly the cases are exhaustive; that is, all possibilities are accounted for. (Into which case does adding a positive integer to zero fall?) Hence the sum is always defined. Also the cases are mutually exclusive; that is, each possibility falls into no more than one case. Moreover, each case produces a single answer. The fact that we write both $+4$ and 4 to represent the same integer has no bearing on determining the sum. (With fractions, we had to check whether $1/2$ and $2/4$ would act the same when adding.) Since a single rule applies to finding the sum of any two particular integers regardless of their representation, and since this single rule produces exactly one answer, we can say that the sum is well-defined. Finally, we check if this sum is necessarily an integer. Case 1 always yields a whole number (which is an integer), and cases 2 and 3 always yield a negative integer. In case 4 the answer is determined by subtracting a smaller absolute value from a larger one (which gives a whole number, since absolute values of integers are whole numbers), and making the answer a negative integer if the term with the larger absolute value is negative. In any event, case 4 gives an integer as do the other cases, and we can remark that the integers are closed under addition.

To illustrate subtraction of integers, we return to the set model referred to earlier. Using the take-away description for subtraction, problems like $(+4) - (+3)$ and $(-7) - (-3)$ are straightforward, as we see in Figure 7-4. Problems

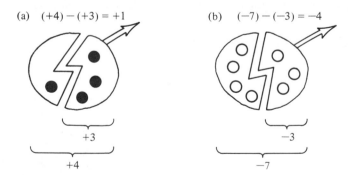

FIGURE 7-4

like $(+4) - (+6)$ are not difficult if we use an alternate representation for $+4$ containing 6 black chips:

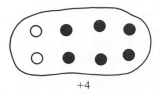

+4

The problem is illustrated in Figure 7-5. To do $(+5) - (-3)$ we represent $+5$ in a way that contains 3 white chips, as shown in Figure 7-6.

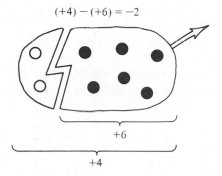

$(+4) - (+6) = -2$

+6

+4

FIGURE 7-5

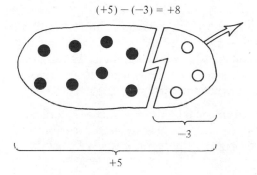

$(+5) - (-3) = +8$

−3

+5

FIGURE 7-6

A closer look at the last problem suggests a convenient shortcut for subtracting integers. The problem $(+5) - (-3)$ in terms of the set model asks us to take away 3 white chips from a set of 5 black chips. To solve the problem we put in 3 white chips and 3 black chips, and take away 3 white chips. The net effect is to put in 3 black chips.

Suppose in general we have a set of p chips (of either color) and we wish to take away q white chips. To solve the problem we put in q white chips and q black chips, and take away q white chips. The net effect is to put in q black chips. We see that taking away q white chips has the same effect as *adding q* black chips. This suggests that subtracting a negative integer is equivalent to adding its opposite.

By a similar argument we can see that taking away q black chips has the same effect as adding q white chips. In terms of numbers this suggests that subtracting a positive integer is equivalent to adding its opposite.

In either case we see that subtracting an integer is equivalent to adding its opposite. Recalling that the opposite of q is denoted "$-q$" we write this in form of a definition:

☐ Definition for Subtracting Integers

> Given integers p and q, we define the **difference** $p - q$ to be $p + (-q)$.

Here the distinction between the "$-$" signs is significant. The definition says that (for integers p and q) "p minus q" is "p plus the opposite of q." Once again, we change a new problem to a familiar one when we replace the difference $p - q$ by the sum $p + (-q)$.

EXAMPLE 7-7

Compute

(a) $8 - 2$ (b) $2 - 8$ (c) $(-3) - (-5)$ (d) $0 - (-8)$

(e) $(-3) - 5$

SOLUTION

(a) By our definition for subtracting integers, instead of subtracting 2 we add the opposite of 2, which is -2. Thus $8 - 2 = 8 + (-2) = 6$. Of course, it is easier just to subtract $8 - 2$ as whole numbers. The fact that the newly introduced definition is compatible with the corresponding definition for whole number is what matters.

(b) $2 - 8 = 2 + (-8) = -6$. We replace 8 by its opposite, -8, and add. This is the object of our extension to the integers, to be able to subtract a larger number from a smaller one.

(c) $(-3) - (-5) = (-3) + 5 = 2$

(d) $0 - (-8) = 0 + 8 = 8$

(e) $(-3) - 5 = (-3) + (-5) = -8$

Our definition for subtraction of integers essentially tells us that to subtract an integer we can add its opposite. Notice how this closely parallels what we said for dividing fractions:

To subtract integers, add the opposite; namely, $p - q$ means $p + (-q)$.

To divide fractions, multiply by the reciprocal; namely, $\frac{p}{q} \div \frac{r}{s}$ means $\frac{p}{q} \times \frac{s}{r}$.

We can also display this relationship, as we did earlier in Figure 3-38:

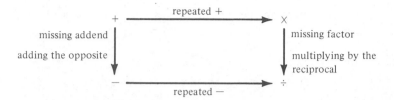

Continuing with the comparison between subtraction of integers and division of fractions we see that (1) in extending from the whole numbers to the integers we arrive at a system closed under subtraction, and (2) in extending from the whole numbers to the fractions we arrive at a system closed under division (except when dividing by 0).

Closure for subtraction of integers is an immediate consequence of closure for addition of integers, since every subtraction problem can be viewed as an addition problem. Would it also follow that integer subtraction is commutative, since integer addition is commutative? Let's check a typical example. Does $(-2) - 5 = 5 - (-2)$? Evaluating each gives:

$$(-2) - 5 = (-2) + (-5) = -7$$

$$5 - (-2) = 5 + 2 = 7$$

Since $(-2) - 5$ and $5 - (-2)$ convert to significantly *different* addition problems, we get different answers. One counter-example is enough to prove that subtraction of integers is not commutative. Several other queries about subtracting integers are suggested in the problems.

In discussing multiplication of integers, we will see how we must define products like $5 \times (-3)$ in order to maintain consistency with our previous work.

To define the product of two integers, our definition must again be applicable to all these possibilities:

1. Both integers are whole numbers.
2. Both integers are negative.
3. One integer is negative; the other is zero.
4. One integer is negative; the other is positive.

Cases 1 and 3 are simple in light of how we handled addition. You are asked to deal with these in the problems. We will do case 4 in detail, which should suggest to you a way to do case 2.

In case 4 we have two integers, one negative, the other positive. $5 \times (-3)$ is such a problem. The most reasonable answer seems to be -15, for if we owed five people each $3 our combined indebtedness would be $15. There is a nice method to show that $5 \times (-3)$ must be -15 if multiplication (and addition) of integers satisfies all the properties that multiplication (and addition) of whole numbers satisfied. If so, we can apply the distributive property to $5 \times (-3) + 5 \times 3$ to get

$$5 \times (-3) + 5 \times 3 = 5 \times [(-3) + 3].$$

Evaluating the right side gives

$$5 \times [(-3) + 3] = 5 \times 0 = 0.$$

But since 5×3 is 15, evaluating the left side gives

$$5 \times (-3) + 5 \times 3 = 5 \times (-3) + 15.$$

Equating these two results gives

$$5 \times (-3) + 15 = 0,$$

so $5 \times (-3)$ must be the opposite of 15, which is -15. In general, for positive integers p and q we have

$$p \times (-q) + p \times q = p \times [(-q) + q]$$
$$= p \times 0$$
$$= 0$$

so $p \times (-q)$ must be the opposite of $p \times q$, where $p \times q$ is known to be a positive integer. This says that a positive (integer) times a negative (integer) is a negative (integer); namely, we multiply as whole numbers and take the opposite of the product to make it negative. If integer multiplication is to be commutative, then $(-q) \times p$ must equal $p \times (-q)$, which is negative. This says that a negative (integer) times a positive (integer) is a negative (integer). Again we multiply as whole numbers and take the opposite.

Division of integers (without fractions) is about as tractable as division of whole numbers. An example like $(-8) \div (-2)$ suggests what happens. Let $(-8) \div (-2) = \square$. This is equivalent to $(-2) \times \square = -8$. Clearly, the answer is 4. In general, if p and q are positive integers, then $(-p) \div (-q) = \square$ is equivalent to $-q \times \square = -p$. The number $\square$ must be positive and we can conclude the familiar rule "negative divided by negative is positive." Other rules can be determined by similar arguments. Problems like $2 \div 3$ and $(-2) \div (-3)$ and $(-2) \div 3$ have no solutions in the integers.

The problems give you the opportunity to develop the remaining rules for doing arithmetic with integers. You may assume when doing the problems that the usual properties (closure, commutative, associative, identity, distributive over addition) hold for multiplication of integers.

This chapter has presented our second extension of the whole numbers. In Chapter 8, we will embed both the integers and the fractions in a single system called the rational numbers.

EXERCISES AND PROBLEMS 7-2

DEFINITION

1. Show each of these sums on a copy of the number line:
   (a) $5 + 2$ (b) $(-5) + (-2)$ (c) $(-3) + 0$
   (d) $(-4) + 4$ (e) $7 + (-2)$ (f) $(-6) + 3$

2. Find these sums.
   (a) $8 + (-8)$ (b) $246 + (-389)$ (c) $(-841) + (-224)$
   (d) $(-5) + 6 + 5 + (-12) + (-11) + 17$

3. Evaluate each sum in the two given ways.
   (a) $8 + [(-2) + 4]$ and $[8 + (-2)] + 4$
   (b) $(-7) + (-2)$ and $(-2) + (-7)$
   (c) $(-5) + (-2) + 3 + 4 + (-7)$ and $[3 + 4] + [(-5) + (-2) + (-7)]$

4. A statement in this section says "the sign of the sum of *a positive integer and a negative integer* is the same as the sign of the one which is larger (in absolute value)." Would this statement still be true if the italicized words were changed to "any two integers"?

5. Four cases for adding two integers were given on page 240. Into which case does adding a positive integer to zero fall?

6. What is the sum of $3 + 5$ (a) as whole numbers?   (b) as integers?   (c) as fractions?

7. Compute the following using the method of Figures 7-3 through 7-6, giving a sketch for each.
   (a) $(-5) + (-6)$ (b) $(+8) + (+2)$ (c) $(-2) + (+6)$
   (d) $(+8) - (+5)$ (e) $(-5) - (-1)$ (f) $(-2) - (-6)$
   (g) $0 - (-3)$ (h) $(-6) - (-4)$

8. Show the solutions to Example 7-7 on the number line.

9. Compute:
   (a) $2 - 5$ (b) $(-2) - (-5)$ (c) $(-8) - 5$
   (d) $2 - (-4)$ (e) $0 - (-6)$

10. Compute:
   (a) $(-2) \times 11$ (b) $7 \times (-9)$ (c) $(-8) \times (-3)$
   (d) $0 \times (-13)$ (e) $(-6) \div 3$ (f) $(-12) \div (-2)$
   (g) $8 \div (-4)$ (h) $0 \div (-5)$

11. Explain how to compute the product of two integers when:
   (a) both integers are whole numbers
   (b) one integer is negative; the other is zero
   (c) both integers are negative.
   (d) Show that there is only one possible answer for $(-4) \times (-2)$ by invoking the distributive property. (Hint: Use the method presented for finding the product of a positive integer and a negative integer.)

12. Compute:
   (a) $(-6) \times (-3) + (-5)$ (b) $(-6) \times [(-3) + (-5)]$
   (c) $(-4) + (-2) \times (-6)$ (d) $(-4) + [(-2) \times (-6)]$
   (e) $|(-5) - (-3)|$ (f) $(-2)^2 + (-5)^3$
   (g) $12 \div (-2) \times 3$

13. Do the following problems from Section 7-1:
   (a) 11   (b) 29   (c) 30

PROPERTIES

14. Is integer subtraction associative? Support your answer.

15. Is it always true for integers p and q that $p - q$ and $q - p$ are opposites?

16. Give additive inverses for each, where p and q are integers:
   (a) 6   (b) -5 (c) 0   (d) p
   (e) $-p$ (f) $p + q$ (g) $p + (-q)$

17. (a) What is the identity for multiplying integers?
    (b) Does the set of integers contain an additive inverse for each of its members? A multiplicative inverse?
    (c) Argue that multiplication of integers is commutative.

18. The sum of two positive integers is a positive integer. The sum of a positive integer and a negative integer may be positive, negative, or zero. We abbreviate these rules in the following sign chart:

Add	+	−
+	+	?
−		

    (a) Complete the addition chart.
        Make similar charts for
    (b) subtraction   (c) multiplication   (d) division.

19. Let

$$W = \{0, 1, 2, 3, \ldots\}$$

$$N = \{-1, -2, -3, -4, \ldots\}$$

$$Z = \{\ldots, -3, -2, -1, 0, 1, 2, 3, \ldots\}$$

$$F = \text{the set of fractions (as defined on pages 151-152)}$$

    Which of these sets are (is) closed under   (a) addition?   (b) subtraction?
    (c) multiplication?   (d) division?   (e) addition, but not multiplication?
    (f) multiplication, but not addition?

    Which of these sets contain(s) a solution to (g) $\square + 2 = 0$?   (h) $3 - 17 = \square$?

20. Suppose integer addition were defined by $p + q = |p| + |q|$. Would there be
    (a) closure?   (b) commutativity?   (c) an identity (for addition)?   (d) an additive inverse for the integer 53?

21. Let A be a set which is closed under subtraction. Suppose 3 and 7 belong to A. Show that each of these must be in A.
    (a) 4   (b) −4   (c) 0   (d) 10
    (e) 6   (f) 11   (g) 1   *(h) 59
    *(i) List *all* members of A.

*22. (a) Repeat Problem 21(i) given instead that 3 and 6 are in A.
     (b) Generalize the results of Problems 21 and 22(a).

23. Find integers p, q, and r such that
    (a) $p < q$ and $p + r < q + r$
    (b) $p < q$ and $p + r > q + r$
    (c) $p < q$ and $pr < qr$
    (d) $p < q$ and $pr > qr$
    (e) $p < q$ and $pr = qr$
    (Hint: Some answers may be "impossible.")

24. Do the following statements hold for all integers a, b, and c? Explain.
    (a) "If $a < b$, then $a + c < b + c$."
    (b) "If $a < b$, then $ac < bc$."
    (c) "If $ac < bc$, then $a < c$."

25. If possible, find integers p and q such that
   (a) $|p + q| < |p| + |q|$ **(b)** $|p + q| = |p| + |q|$
   (c) $|p + q| > |p| + |q|$
   (d) Give a rule that determines which condition holds for a given pair of integers.

*26. True or False? Support your answer. "If a set is closed under subtraction, then it is closed under addition."

MATERIALS AND CALCULATORS

27. Examine several elementary school texts to see how they show that a negative times a negative is positive. In what grade is this done?

C28. (a) Start with zero and add 3 ten times to arrive at 30 (which is 10×3). Now start with zero and subtract 3 ten times. What multiplication problem (and answer) does this computation suggest?
   (b) How many 4's need to be added on the calculator to get 48? This suggests that $48 \div 4 =$ ____? How many -4's need to be added to get -48? What division problem (and answer) does this computation suggest?

PROBLEM SOLVING EXTENSIONS

29. On a grade 8 mathematics assessment test 22% of the responders answered "14" for "$(-5) + (-9) =$ ____."   **(a)** What error did they make?   **(b)** Why do you think they made this error?

30. The following question appeared on the same grade 8 test:

> The air temperature on the ground is 31°. On top of a nearby mountain, the air temperature is $-7°$. How many degrees difference is there between these two temperatures?
>
>   A. $-24°$
>
>   B. 24°
>
>   C. 38°
>
>   D. 39°
>
>   E. I don't know

In one county more pupils picked a particular incorrect response than the correct response. Tell which response you think they picked and why.

31. After 20 minutes of playing a certain card game four children had these scores:

Betsy	$+23$
Meg	-4
Greg	$+11$
Steve	-13

Make up and solve two different exercises based on this information. Make your two exercises as different from each other as you can.

32. p is an element of $\{-2, -1, 0, 1, 2, 3, 4, 5\}$. q is an element of $\{-4, -3, -2, -1, 0, 1\}$. Find the *smallest* and *largest* values of

   (a) $p + q$ **(b)** $p - q$ **(c)** $p \times q$ **(d)** $|p \times q|$ **(e)** $|p + q|$

33. Recall that 10^3 means $10 \times 10 \times 10$. The notation 10^{-3} is used to mean $1/10^3$, or $1/1000$. Also, 10^0 is defined to be 1. This allows us to write

$$564 = 5 \times 10^2 + 6 \times 10^1 + 4 \times 10^0$$

$$\text{and } .407 = 4 \times 10^{-1} + 7 \times 10^{-3}$$

This is called **expanded notation**. Write each of these in expanded notation:
(a) 247   (b) .512
(c) 1,000,000   (d) .000000000000007

34. It is possible to write any decimal as a number between 1 and 10 (inclusive) times a power of ten. (Many calculators express certain numbers in this way.) Some examples of this **scientific notation** are given below.

$$597 = 5.97 \times 10^2$$

$$.00081 = 8.1 \times 10^{-4}$$

$$53.01 = 5.301 \times 10^1$$

$$.5614 = 5.614 \times 10^{-1}$$

$$93,000,000 = 9.3 \times 10^7$$

$$5.21 = 5.21 \times 10^0$$

Write each of the following in scientific notation:
(a) 43   (b) 8004   (c) 9,000,000   (d) .03
(e) .00007   (f) 60000.0003   (g) 12×10^{15} (h) 8.602

35. Compute the value of each expression. Answer in scientific notation.
(a) $(3 \times 10^3) \times (4 \times 10^{12})$ (b) $(6.5 \times 10^{-4}) \times (2.4 \times 10^5)$
(c) $(3.4 \times 10^{-7}) \times (4.1 \times 10^{-29})$ (d) $(6.2 \times 10^{-6}) \div (3.1 \times 10^3)$
(e) $(2 \times 10^{-3}) \div (4 \times 10^{-7})$

36. (a) Translate into words (especially each "$-$"), given that x is an integer:
$(-x) - (-2) = 5$
(b) Determine the value of x.
(c) Is $-x$ positive or negative?

37. Find an integer x which satisfies
(a) $-x = 2$ (b) $x + (-2) = -9$
(c) $(-6) - x = -11$ (d) $x = -x$

Some Fields

8-1
RATIONAL NUMBERS

We have seen that the set of whole numbers is "big enough" to accommodate addition and multiplication but that the set has to be extended to permit arbitrary subtraction and division. By extending to the integers we can subtract one whole number from another, and by extending to the fractions we can divide one whole number by another (except by 0).

Now we set out to find the smallest extension of the whole numbers that allows both subtraction and division among all its members. Unfortunately, we can never quite accomplish this, because division by 0 cannot be defined satisfactorily. However, we can readily find a set that does enable us to do all additions, subtractions, multiplications, and divisions except division by 0.

The integers alone do not suffice, since they do not contain the solutions to division problems like 2 ÷ 3. Neither do the fractions alone suffice, since they do not contain the solutions to subtraction problems like 2 − 3. Any candidate for a set which permits both operations necessarily contains all the integers and all the fractions. (See Problem 3.)

The smallest set which contains all the integers and all the fractions would contain those numbers and no other numbers. This is precisely the union of the integers and the fractions; let's call it S. Some typical members of S are shown in Figure 8-1.

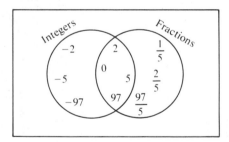

FIGURE 8-1

Some typical sums of members of S are these:

$$(-5) + 2 \qquad \text{(both integers)}$$

$$\frac{1}{5} + \frac{2}{5} \qquad \text{(both fractions)}$$

$$(-5) + \frac{2}{5} \qquad \text{(an integer and a fraction)}$$

We check to see if S contains solutions to these three problems:

$$(-5) + 2 = -3$$

$$\frac{1}{5} + \frac{2}{5} = \frac{3}{5}$$

$$(-5) + \frac{2}{5} = \, ?$$

(We might like to answer $-23/5$ to the last problem, but this does not belong to S.) How does S fare when doing subtraction? Some typical subtraction problems are these:

$$(-5) - 2 \qquad \text{(both integers)}$$
$$\frac{1}{5} - \frac{2}{5} \qquad \text{(both fractions)}$$
$$(-5) - \frac{2}{5} \qquad \text{(an integer and a fraction)}$$

Only the first of these three problems has a solution in S. (The tentative solutions $1/5 - 2/5 = -1/5$ and $(-5) - 2/5 = -27/5$ are not available to us in S.) S is still not big enough.

Let's interpret the troublesome problems among those given above on the number line. We can show $(-5) + 2/5$ like this:

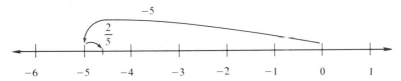

The solution is $2/5$ of a unit closer to the origin than -5 is. This is a point $5 - 2/5$ or $4^3/_5$ or $23/5$ units to the left of the origin. In the sense of "opposites" as described in Chapter 7, it is the opposite of $23/5$. According to our number line model, we'd like to be able to write $(-5) + 2/5 = -23/5$.

The natural solution to the subtraction problem $1/5 - 2/5$ as suggested by the number line seems to be $-1/5$:

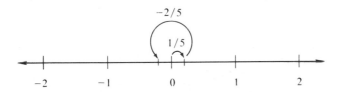

For the problem $(-5) - 2/5$, the apparent solution is $-27/5$:

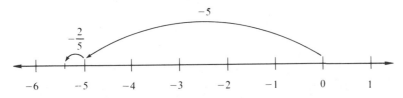

The numbers lacking in set S when doing addition and subtraction seem to be the opposites of the fractions.

This suggests that our next contender for a set closed under the four basic operations should be the fractions extended to include their opposites. We will call this set the **rational numbers** (or the "**rationals**," for short) and use Q to represent it. (The letter R is reserved for another set.) Figure 8-2 shows the relationships among the whole numbers, the fractions, and the rational numbers. It shows that the whole numbers are a subset of the fractions, which are in turn a subset of the rationals. A few typical members of the three sets are also displayed. The figure indicates that 7 is a whole number, a fraction, and a rational number, and that −7 is a rational number but not a fraction or a whole number.

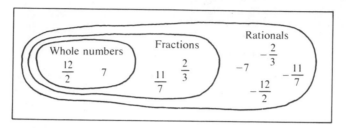

FIGURE 8-2

Recall that fractions have many different representations: 3, 3/1, 6/2, 9/3, 12/4, and 300/100 all represent the same fraction. This also applies to rational numbers. When doing integer division we know that $(-3) \div (-1) = 3$, which prompts us to write $(-3)/(-1) = 3$. Also, $(-6) \div (-2) = 3$, so we write $(-6)/(-2) = 3$. Hence, 3, 3/1, $(-3)/(-1)$, 6/2, $(-6)/(-2)$, etc., are all used to represent the rational number 3. Similarly, 2/3 can be represented by $(-2)/(-3)$, 4/6, $(-4)/(-6)$, etc. Rational numbers which are opposites of fractions, like $-(4/5)$, also have other representations, like $(-4)/5$ and $4/(-5)$. In fact, every rational number can be represented in the form p/q, where p and q are *integers* (q not 0). We will call this the **quotient of integers form**. A study of the various cases should also convince you that there is always a way to do this so that the denominator is a positive integer.

EXAMPLE 8-1	Write each number in the quotient of integers form:
	(a) $-\dfrac{3}{5}$ \qquad (b) $-\dfrac{-4}{7}$ \qquad (c) $-\dfrac{-2}{-3}$
SOLUTION	(a) $-\dfrac{3}{5} = \dfrac{-3}{5}$ \qquad (b) $-\dfrac{-4}{7} = \dfrac{-(-4)}{7} = \dfrac{4}{7}$
	(c) $-\dfrac{-2}{-3} = \dfrac{-(-2)}{-3} = \dfrac{2}{-3} = \dfrac{-2}{3}$ (To see that $\dfrac{2}{-3} = \dfrac{-2}{3}$, note that by extending our reducing fractions principle (page 152), $\dfrac{2}{-3} = \dfrac{2 \times (-1)}{-3 \times (-1)} = \dfrac{-2}{3}$.)

Our usual course of action after discussing notation for a new set of numbers is to decide how to order them and, in particular, how to tell when two of them are equal. In this section, we offer instead a series of problems designed to let you determine the criteria for ordering the rational numbers and continue our investigation of whether we now have a set of numbers that is closed under the four basic operations.

Of course, before we can discuss the closure properties, we have to clarify how to do arithmetic with rational numbers. The method for adding rational numbers is a combination of the methods used to add integers and to add fractions:

To Add Rational Numbers □

1. Write the numbers in the quotient of integers form so that they have a common denominator.
2. Add the numerators using *integer* addition, writing the sum over the common denominator.

Finding a common denominator in the first step is like what we do when adding fractions; the second step involves adding integers.

Find these sums:

(a) $\frac{2}{3} + \frac{4}{5}$ (b) $\frac{5}{8} + \frac{-3}{4}$ (c) $\left(-\frac{7}{9}\right) + \left(-\frac{8}{9}\right)$

(d) $\frac{3}{-5} + \frac{2}{5}$ (e) $\frac{2}{7} + \frac{-3}{7} + \frac{5}{-7} + \frac{-4}{-7}$

EXAMPLE 8-2

(a) $\frac{2}{3} + \frac{4}{5} = \frac{10}{15} + \frac{12}{15} = \frac{10 + 12}{15} = \frac{22}{15}$ (This problem is solved exactly as if we interpret this as addition of fractions.)

(b) $\frac{5}{8} + \frac{-3}{4} = \frac{5}{8} + \frac{-6}{8} = \frac{5 + (-6)}{8} = \frac{-1}{8}$

(c) $\left(-\frac{7}{9}\right) + \left(-\frac{8}{9}\right) = \frac{-7}{9} + \frac{-8}{9} = \frac{(-7) + (-8)}{9} = \frac{-15}{9}$

(d) $\frac{3}{-5} + \frac{2}{5} = \frac{-3}{5} + \frac{2}{5} = \frac{(-3) + 2}{5} = \frac{-1}{5}$

(e) $\frac{2}{7} + \frac{-3}{7} + \frac{5}{-7} + \frac{-4}{-7} = \frac{2}{7} + \frac{-3}{7} + \frac{-5}{7} + \frac{4}{7}$

$= \frac{2 + (-3) + (-5) + 4}{7} = \frac{6 + (-8)}{7} = \frac{-2}{7}$

SOLUTION

As with integers, we change every subtraction problem to an addition problem:

To Subtract Rational Numbers □

For any rational numbers $\frac{p}{q}$ and $\frac{r}{s}$, define $\frac{p}{q} - \frac{r}{s}$ to be $\frac{p}{q} + \frac{-r}{s}$.

$\left(\text{Notice that } \frac{-r}{s} \text{ is the same rational number as } -\frac{r}{s}.\right)$

EXAMPLE 8-3

Find these differences:

(a) $\dfrac{5}{8} - \dfrac{1}{4}$ (b) $\dfrac{1}{3} - \dfrac{1}{2}$

(c) $\left(-\dfrac{5}{8}\right) - \left(-\dfrac{4}{5}\right)$ (d) $\dfrac{-7}{52} - \dfrac{2}{39}$

SOLUTION

(a) $\dfrac{5}{8} - \dfrac{1}{4} = \dfrac{5}{8} + \dfrac{-1}{4} = \dfrac{5}{8} + \dfrac{-2}{8} = \dfrac{5 + (-2)}{8} = \dfrac{3}{8}$

This is the same answer as if we interpret this as subtraction of fractions, so it is preferable to solve it this way:

$$\dfrac{5}{8} - \dfrac{1}{4} = \dfrac{5}{8} - \dfrac{2}{8} = \dfrac{3}{8}$$

(b) $\dfrac{1}{3} - \dfrac{1}{2} = \dfrac{1}{3} + \dfrac{-1}{2} = \dfrac{2}{6} + \dfrac{-3}{6} = \dfrac{2 + (-3)}{6} = \dfrac{-1}{6}$

(c) $\left(-\dfrac{5}{8}\right) - \left(-\dfrac{4}{5}\right) = \dfrac{-5}{8} + \dfrac{4}{5} = \dfrac{-25}{40} + \dfrac{32}{40} = \dfrac{7}{40}$

(d) $\dfrac{-7}{52} - \dfrac{2}{39} = \dfrac{-7}{52} + \dfrac{-2}{39} = \dfrac{-7}{4 \times 13} + \dfrac{-2}{3 \times 13} = \dfrac{(-7) \times 3}{4 \times 13 \times 3}$

$+ \dfrac{(-2) \times 4}{3 \times 13 \times 4} = \dfrac{-21}{3 \times 4 \times 13} + \dfrac{-8}{3 \times 4 \times 13} = \dfrac{-29}{156}$

Multiplication of rational numbers follows a procedure much like the one used for addition:

☐ To Multiply Rational Numbers

1. Write the numbers in the quotient of integers form.
2. Multiply the numerators and denominators using *integer* multiplication.

EXAMPLE 8-4

Find these products:

(a) $\dfrac{2}{3} \times \dfrac{4}{5}$ (b) $\dfrac{-2}{5} \times \dfrac{7}{11}$ (c) $\dfrac{-3}{7} \times \dfrac{-9}{13}$

(d) $\dfrac{-4}{5} \times \dfrac{7}{3}$ (e) $\dfrac{2}{3} \times \dfrac{17}{-5} \times \dfrac{-3}{2} \times \dfrac{-10}{9}$

SOLUTION

(a) $\dfrac{2}{3} \times \dfrac{4}{5} = \dfrac{2 \times 4}{3 \times 5} = \dfrac{8}{15}$ (as with fractions)

(b) $\dfrac{-2}{5} \times \dfrac{7}{11} = \dfrac{(-2) \times 7}{5 \times 11} = \dfrac{-14}{55}$

(c) $\dfrac{-3}{7} \times \dfrac{-9}{13} = \dfrac{(-3) \times (-9)}{7 \times 13} = \dfrac{27}{91}$

(d) $\dfrac{-4}{5} \times \dfrac{7}{3} = \dfrac{(-4) \times 7}{5 \times 3} = \dfrac{-28}{15}$

(e) $\dfrac{2}{3} \times \dfrac{17}{-5} \times \dfrac{-3}{2} \times \dfrac{-10}{9} = \dfrac{2 \times 17 \times (-3) \times (-10)}{3 \times (-5) \times 2 \times 9}$

$= \dfrac{1020}{-270} = \dfrac{34 \times 30}{-9 \times 30} = \dfrac{34}{-9} = \dfrac{-34}{9}$

You can check your understanding by seeing if you can state the procedure for dividing rational numbers.

Our main concern now is whether Q is closed under addition, subtraction, multiplication, and division (except dividing by 0). To learn if Q is closed under addition, we must check to see if the sum of any two members of Q is a member of Q. As with fractions, any two members of Q can be represented with a common denominator (such as the product of their denominators). Let p/q and r/q be any two rational numbers expressed in this form. Then, by the definition for addition of rational numbers,

$$\frac{p}{q} + \frac{r}{q} = \frac{p+r}{q}$$

where the addition on the right is integer addition. Because p and r are integers and because the integers are closed under addition, $p + r$ must be an integer. Hence $(p + r)/q$ is a rational number, since it is expressed in the quotient of integers form. We can conclude that since the sum of two rational numbers is a rational number, the rational numbers are closed under addition.

For subtraction, again let p/q and r/q be any two rational numbers. Then:

$$\frac{p}{q} - \frac{r}{q} = \frac{p}{q} + \frac{-r}{q} \qquad \text{(Definition for subtraction of rationals)}$$

$$= \frac{p + (-r)}{q} \qquad \text{(Definition for addition of rationals)}$$

Here again $p + (-r)$ is the sum of two integers, so the answer is in quotient of integers form, and thus is a rational number.

Showing that Q is closed under multiplication can be done easily for arbitrary rational numbers p/q and r/s. Closure for division is also easy to show, provided r/s is not 0.

A summary of the most important properties which hold for the rational numbers Q is given in Figure 8-3.

Properties of Addition	*Properties of Multiplication*
1. Q is closed under $+$.	6. Q is closed under $\times$.
2. $+$ is commutative in Q.	7. $\times$ is commutative in Q.
3. $+$ is associative in Q.	8. $\times$ is associative in Q.
4. There is an identity for $+$ in Q.	9. There is an identity for $\times$ in Q.
5. Each element of Q has an additive inverse (opposite) which belongs to Q.	10. Each element of Q (except 0) has a multiplicative inverse (reciprocal) which belongs to Q.
11. $\times$ distributes over $+$ in Q.	

FIGURE 8-3   Properties of Q, the Rational Numbers

A set with addition and multiplication operations which satisfies these 11 properties is called a **field**. This is quite an important idea in mathematics, as the field properties summarize what is needed for arithmetic to behave nicely. The list of properties is deliberately displayed quite concisely so that you can see the relationships among the properties. Notice how most of them appear in pairs. Observe that these are the properties which have kept recurring in our development.

While all the properties are familiar to you by this time, some deserve a few extra remarks. To say that there is an identity for addition in Q (Property 4) means that there is one fixed element of Q; namely 0, which satisfies $\frac{p}{q} + 0 = \frac{p}{q}$ and $0 + \frac{p}{q} = \frac{p}{q}$ for every element $\frac{p}{q}$ of Q. Similarly, Property 9 says that we have the fixed element 1 for which $\frac{p}{q} \times 1 = \frac{p}{q}$ and $1 \times \frac{p}{q} = \frac{p}{q}$ for every element $\frac{p}{q}$ in Q. Property 5 is tantamount to saying that Q is closed under subtraction, for to subtract in Q we add the opposite. This property ensures that an opposite is always available for this purpose. Property 10 is tantamount to saying that Q is closed under division (except by 0), for to divide in Q we multiply by the reciprocal. Unlike the identity, which is fixed, each element of Q has a different opposite and each element of Q has a different reciprocal. Property 11 is the familiar distributive property, which says that for rational numbers a, b, and c, $a \times (b + c) = a \times b + a \times c$.

These properties so well describe the rational numbers that any set (with at least two members and for which addition and multiplication are defined as usual) that satisfies these 11 properties necessarily contains *every* rational number! (See Problem 31.)

EXERCISES AND PROBLEMS 8-1

DEFINITION

1. Do the following problems according to the rules for the arithmetic of rational numbers:

   (a) $\frac{3}{4} + \frac{2}{3}$ (b) $\frac{-5}{8} + \frac{3}{8}$ (c) $\frac{-4}{7} + \frac{-5}{6}$

   (d) $\left(-\frac{8}{9}\right) + \frac{2}{3}$ (e) $\frac{2}{33} + \frac{-7}{55}$ (f) $\frac{6}{11} - \frac{2}{11}$

   (g) $\frac{4}{7} - \frac{6}{7}$ (h) $\frac{1}{4} - \frac{1}{3}$ (i) $\frac{-2}{3} - \frac{-5}{6}$

   (j) $\frac{-1}{9} - \frac{1}{3}$ (k) $\left(-\frac{4}{7}\right) - \left(-\frac{-2}{7}\right)$ (l) $\frac{5}{68} - \frac{7}{51}$

2. Do the following problems according to the rules for the arithmetic of rational numbers:

   (a) $\frac{5}{7} \times \frac{6}{5}$ (b) $\frac{-4}{9} \times \frac{3}{-2}$

   (c) $\left(-\frac{2}{3}\right)^2$ (d) $\frac{2}{7} \times \frac{-3}{5} \times \frac{4}{-3} \times \frac{-5}{1}$

   (e) $\left(-\frac{2}{3}\right) \times \left(-\frac{4}{5}\right)$ (f) $\frac{3}{34} \times \frac{85}{9}$

(g) $\dfrac{5}{9} \div \dfrac{2}{7}$

(h) $\dfrac{6}{11} \div \dfrac{-2}{3}$

(i) $\dfrac{-6}{11} \div \dfrac{2}{3}$

(j) $\dfrac{-6}{11} \div \dfrac{-2}{3}$

(k) $\left(-\dfrac{6}{11}\right) \div \left(-\dfrac{2}{3}\right)$

(l) $\dfrac{-39}{22} \div \dfrac{6}{143}$

(m) $\dfrac{1}{5} \times \left(\dfrac{-5}{3} + \dfrac{4}{3}\right)$

(n) $\dfrac{(-2) \times 3 \times 4}{5 \times (-6) \times (-7)}$

(o) $\dfrac{-1}{2} + \left(\dfrac{-3}{4} \times \dfrac{-5}{6}\right)$

(p) $\dfrac{-1}{2} + \dfrac{-3}{4} \times \dfrac{-5}{6}$

3. What problem involving whole numbers is impossible if the integer -19 does not exist? If the fraction 5/11 does not exist?

4. (a) Which of the following are representations for -5?

$$\dfrac{5}{1}, \dfrac{-5}{1}, \dfrac{5}{-1}, \dfrac{-5}{-1}, -\dfrac{5}{1}, \dfrac{-5}{1}, -\dfrac{5}{-1}, -\dfrac{-5}{-1}$$

(b) Which of the following are representations for 2/3?

$$\dfrac{-2}{3}, \dfrac{2}{-3}, \dfrac{-2}{-3}, -\dfrac{2}{3}, -\dfrac{-2}{3}, -\dfrac{2}{-3}, -\dfrac{-2}{-3}$$

(c) Develop a rule for determining (by counting the "$-$" signs) when such a number is positive and when it is negative.

5. Fill in the missing entries in this chart:

	Rational Number	Sign	Absolute Value
	$-\dfrac{2}{3}$	negative	$\dfrac{2}{3}$
(a)	$\dfrac{5}{8}$	————	————
(b)	————	negative	$\dfrac{4}{9}$
(c)	————	none	————
(d)	————	————	0

6. Do you know any numbers that should be placed *outside* the set of rationals in Figure 8-2?

ORDER

7. Make a copy of Figure 8-1 and insert the following numbers in the right positions:
   (a) 5/8   (b) -11 (c) 19   (d) 6/1   (e) 10/2

8. Make a copy of Figure 8-2 and insert the following numbers in the right positions:
   (a) 5/8   (b) 200/100   (c) $-(8/5)$ (d) -1 (e) 0

9. Decide which rational number of each pair is located more to the left on a number line:
   (a) 2 or 3
   (b) -2 or -3
   (c) 0 or 3
   (d) 0 or -3
   (e) 2 or -3
   (f) -2 or 3
   (g) 1/3 or 1/4
   (h) $-1/3$ or $-1/4$
   (i) $-1/3$ or 1/4
   (j) 1/3 or $-1/4$
   (k) $-3/4$ or $-4/5$
   (l) $-5/7$ or $-8/11$

10. Write "<", "=", or ">" between each pair of numbers given in Problem 9.

11. Devise a general rule for deciding for arbitrary rational numbers p/q and r/s whether $p/q < r/s$, $p/q = r/s$, or $p/q > r/s$.

12. Place in order, smallest to largest:
    (a) 0, 5, 6, 1/5, 1/6, -5, -6, $-1/5$, $-1/6$
    (b) 3/13, 4/17, $-3/13$, $-4/17$

13. Find a rational number between 4/15 and 3/11.

PROPERTIES

14. Find $Z \cap F$ where Z is the set of integers and F is the set of (non-negative) fractions.

15. Which of the following problems have solutions in the set S described in this section?
    (a) $(-5) \times 2$ (b) $1/5 \times 2/5$ (c) $(-5) \times 2/5$
    (d) $(-5) \div 2$ (e) $1/5 \div 2/5$ (f) $(-5) \div 2/5$

16. Which integers have multiplicative inverses that are integers? Which (non-negative) fractions have additive inverses that are (non-negative) fractions?

17. Find additive inverses (opposites) for the following numbers:
    (a) 3   (b) -2 (c) 1/3   (d) $-3/4$ (e) 0

18. Find multiplicative inverses (reciprocals) for the numbers given in the previous problem.

19. (a) Show that Q is closed under multiplication.
    (b) Show that $Q \backslash \{0\}$ is closed under division.

20. Find the smallest set which contains 1 and is closed under
    (a) addition   (b) multiplication
    (c) subtraction   (d) division
    (e) addition and multiplication
    (f) addition and subtraction
    (g) addition, subtraction, and multiplication
    (h) addition, subtraction, multiplication, and division

21. Find the smallest set which contains 3 and is closed under the operations listed in Problem 20.

22. Is it true that if the sum of any two members of a set is in the set, then the sum of any three members of the set is in the set?

23. (a) Find the reciprocal of the opposite of $-4/9$.
    (b) Find the opposite of the reciprocal of $-4/9$.

24. Which element in the following table is the identity?

*	r	s	t
r	s	t	r
s	t	r	s
t	r	s	t

25. It was stated that Property 5 is tantamount to saying that Q is closed under subtraction, for it ensures that we always have an opposite. How do we know that when we "add the opposite" the answer will be in Q?

26. (a) One of the properties of multiplication has an exception included in its statement. Which one?

(b) Is the distributive property a property of addition or multiplication (or both or neither)?

27. Which elements of Q are
(a) additive identities?
(b) additive inverses?
(c) multiplicative identities?
(d) multiplicative inverses?

28. Which of these distributive properties hold in Q? For those that don't, give counter-examples.
(a) $(a + b) \times c = a \times c + b \times c$
(b) $a + (b \times c) = (a + b) \times (a + c)$
(c) $(a \times b) + c = (a + c) \times (b + c)$
(d) $a \times (b - c) = a \times b - a \times c$
(e) $a \div (b + c) = (a \div b) + (a \div c)$
(f) $(a + b) \div c = (a \div c) + (b \div c)$

29. Which field property fails if we remove each of the following numbers (and no others) from Q?
(a) 0   **(b)** 1   **(c)** -59 **(d)** 1/59   **(e)** 59, -59, 1/59, and $-1/59$

30. Suppose addition and multiplication are defined as usual for the set $\{-1, 0, 1\}$. Which field properties are satisfied?

31. Assume that M is a set containing at least two elements, that addition and multiplication are defined as usual, and that all the field properties are satisfied. Show that each of these numbers is in M (two examples are given):
Examples: 1 is in M by Property 9.
             2 is in M by Property 1, since $1 + 1 = 2$.
(a) 3   **(b)** 4   **(c)** 12   **(d)** -1
(e) -2 **(f)** -24 **(g)** 1/3   **(h)** 2/3
(i) $-2/3$ *(j)** $-9/17$
(k) Is there any rational number that is not in M?
(l) What might happen if M did not contain at least two elements?

32. Show that the positive rationals with the operations $+$ and $\times$ do *not* satisfy all the field properties.

33. Let W be the whole numbers,
       F be the (non-negative) fractions,
       Z be the integers,
       N be the negative integers, and
       Q be the rationals.
List *all* the sets with the given property. Write "none" if appropriate.
(a) -1 belongs to the set.
(b) $-2/3$ belongs to the set.
(c) 7 belongs to the set.
(d) The set has an additive identity.
(e) The set has a multiplicative identity.
(f) Each member of the set has an additive inverse.
(g) Each member of the set has a multiplicative inverse.
(h) The set is closed under addition.

(i) The set is closed under subtraction.

(j) The set is closed under multiplication.

(k) The set is closed under division.

34. We know that "every rational number can be expressed in the form p/q where p and q are integers (q not 0)." Is the following statement true? "Every rational number can be expressed in the form $p - q$ where p and q are fractions."

35. When a set has an operation that satisfies Properties 1-5 in Figure 8-3 (like the rationals with addition), it is called a **commutative group**. Which of the following are commutative groups? (If not, tell why.)

(a) the whole numbers with addition

(b) the integers with addition

(c) the whole numbers with multiplication

(d) the fractions with multiplication

(e) the fractions, other than 0, with multiplication

(f) the even whole numbers with addition

(g) the even whole numbers with multiplication

(h) the odd whole numbers with addition.

*36. Complete the commutative group table below, using the commutative and associative properties. Show all computations.

*	I	A	B	C	D
I	I	A	B	C	D
A	A	C	I	D	B
B	B				
C	C				
D	D				

Hint: B * A = A * B and D * A = A * D by the commutative property. Then compute B * B * A in two ways to find B * B. By the associative property

$$(B * B) * A = B * (B * A)$$

$$= B * I$$

$$= B$$

We now have (B * B) * A = B, so B * B is the element which, times A, gives B. But D * A = B, so B * B = D. Now evaluate (B * D) * A similarly to find B * D.

37. Using W, F, Z, and Q as in Problem 33, give a problem involving only *whole* numbers and the operations $+$, $-$, $\times$, or $\div$ which

(a) has a solution in F but not in W.

(b) has a solution in Z but not in W.

(c) has a solution in Q but not in F or in I. (Hint: Use three numbers and two operations.)

CALCULATORS

C38. (a) Use a calculator to determine 2^{20} by repeated multiplications. (Watch the display as successive powers are generated.) Do successive powers of 2 increase or decrease in size?

(b) Do the same for $(0.2)^{20}$.

(c) Experiment with the calculator to determine for which (positive) numbers successive powers increase and for which (positive) numbers successive powers decrease.

(d) Find two numbers that differ by 0.2, one for which the successive powers increase and the other for which the successive powers decrease.

(e) Investigate what happens when you compute successive powers of negative numbers.

8-2
REAL NUMBERS

After our success in developing a system of numbers closed under the four basic operations (except for division by 0), it would seem reasonable to conclude that all numbers have been accounted for. In this section, we will go through considerable effort to show this is not the case. We do this to complete the story of the real numbers, since numbers that are not rational numbers do appear in rather simple settings. We also do this because it ties together a variety of topics, such as factoring whole numbers into primes and finding areas of squares.

The Greeks knew and understood the rational numbers two thousand years ago, but some of the ideas in this section were not clarified until a few hundred years ago. This reflects the subtlety of some of the concepts and suggests why we will not be able to delve deeply into the ideas in this brief presentation. We can, however, still arrive at some significant results.

Many interesting problems that we will investigate can be displayed on a geoboard, an instructional device made simply by pounding nails (usually smooth, brass ones) into a board in a square array, as shown in Figure 8-4. We usually show a top view, as in Figure 8-5. The smallest possible square is considered to have an area of one unit. The areas of some other typical geoboard figures are shown in Figure 8-6.

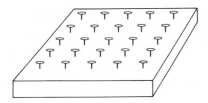

FIGURE 8-4   Geoboard

What is the area of the geoboard figure in Figure 8-7? Do you see that it consists of four small (1/2 unit) triangles like the one in Figure 8-6? This tells us that its area is two units. We will use this square a little later.

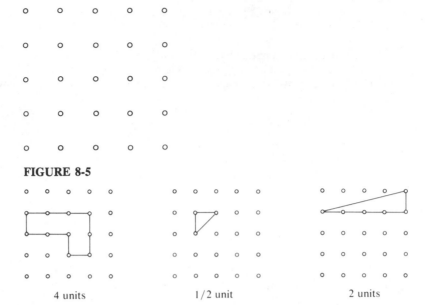

FIGURE 8-5

4 units   1/2 unit   2 units

FIGURE 8-6

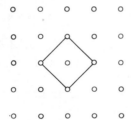

FIGURE 8-7

One useful mathematical concept that we want to have available in our discussions is the "square root" of a number. The name is actually quite descriptive, as we shall soon see. Recall that the *square* of a number is the product of that number and itself. Notice how "the square of 3" can be interpreted geometrically as 9 in Figure 8-8. If you take the square whose side is 3 units long, then it will contain $3 \times 3 = 9$ unit squares. Here we call 3 "the square root of 9." The symbol $\sqrt{}$ is used to indicate square root and we write $\sqrt{9} = 3$ to say "the (non-negative) square root of 9 is 3." Similarly, we see in Figure 8-9 that $\sqrt{4} = 2$ and $\sqrt{16} = 4$. In general, we say that the **square root** of a number p is that number which, when multiplied by itself, gives p. Notice

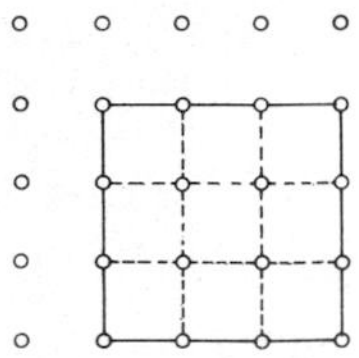

FIGURE 8-8

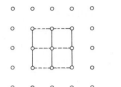

FIGURE 8-9

by this definition that 9 has *two* square roots, for 3 × 3 = 9 and (−3) × (−3) = 9. Here 3 is called the **non-negative square root** of nine or the **principal square root** of nine.

The distinction between square roots and principal square roots, with regard to notation, is a trouble spot for many students. The reason is that while a number may have two square roots, the symbol "$\sqrt{}$" means "the principal square root." The following series of statements may help clarify matters. These statements are all correct:

9 has two square roots, 3 and −3. 9 has one principal square root, 3. $\sqrt{9} = 3$.

To say "$\sqrt{9} = -3$" is wrong, since −3 is not the *principal* square root of 9.

True or False?

(a) $\sqrt{16} = 4$ (b) $\sqrt{16} = -4$

(c) $\sqrt{-16} = 4$ (d) $\sqrt{-16} = -4$

(e) 4 is a square root of 16.   (f) −4 is a square root of 16.

(a) True, since 4 is non-negative and 4 × 4 = 16.

(b) False, since −4 is negative.

(c) False, since 4 × 4 ≠ −16.

(d) False, since (−4) × (−4) ≠ −16.

(e) True, since 4 × 4 = 16.

(f) True, since (−4) × (−4) = 16.

EXAMPLE 8-5

SOLUTION

According to the definition of square root, we saw that 9 had two square roots, 3 (the principal one) and −3. Notice as well by this definition that −4 has *no* square roots, for no number multiplied by itself gives a negative product. A highly non-trivial question is whether 2 has any square roots.

In Figure 8-7 we saw a geoboard square with area 2. Geometrically, the length of its side is $\sqrt{2}$. Algebraically, we have defined $\sqrt{2}$ to be the number which when multiplied by itself gives 2. According to our geoboard problem, there ought to be such a number, but is it contained in the rationals? After all, the integers didn't contain the answer to $2 \div 3 = \square$, and the fractions didn't contain the answer to $2 - 3 = \bigcirc$, so how do we know the rationals contain the answer to $\triangle \times \triangle = 2$ (where both triangles must be filled in with the same number)?

We will temporarily assume that $\sqrt{2}$ exists and start looking for it by trial and error among the rationals: 1 is too small since $1 \times 1 < 2$ and 2 is too big since $2 \times 2 > 2$, so we know that the number we are searching for lies between 1 and 2, and we write (assuming that $\sqrt{2}$ exists) $1 < \sqrt{2} < 2$. Geometrically, we see that a "1 square" is too small and a "2 square" is too big. (Its area is 4.)

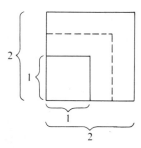

Next we try numbers between 1 and 2:

$$1.5 \times 1.5 = 2.25 \qquad \text{(too big)}$$

$$1.4 \times 1.4 = 1.96 \qquad \text{(too small)}$$

Hence, $1.4 < \sqrt{2} < 1.5$. Geometrically we show that the "1.4 square" is too small and the "1.5 square" is too big.

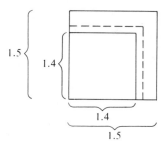

We can continue this process, getting this at the next step:

$$1.45 \times 1.45 = 2.1025 \qquad \text{(too big)}$$

$$1.42 \times 1.42 = 2.0164 \qquad \text{(too big)}$$

$$1.41 \times 1.41 = 1.9981 \qquad \text{(too small)}$$

Hence $1.41 < \sqrt{2} < 1.42$. With the help of a calculator with a square root feature, we can obtain $1.4142135 < \sqrt{2} < 1.4142136$.

Notice that even though we have been unable so far to find a rational number whose square is 2, we have initiated a process that determines a decimal accurate to as many places as we have the ambition and technology to carry out the computations (provided such a decimal exists). We know since $1.4142135 < \sqrt{2} < 1.4142136$ that as a decimal, $\sqrt{2}$ starts off "1.414213." If we wanted the next few decimal places, we could get them if we were willing to work at it. Assuming $\sqrt{2}$ can be written as a decimal, this process (at least theoretically) determines all its decimal places. This leads us to say that the decimal defined in this way is a "number," but we have yet to determine whether this number is a rational number or if we have again enlarged the number system by introducing $\sqrt{2}$.

We now focus on this issue and show that $\sqrt{2}$ is *not* a rational number. Because of the amount of discussion devoted to this one question, we label this section "optional." A helpful review of the important Unique Factorization Theorem is included in this optional section.

$\sqrt{2}$ Is Not a Rational Number (Optional Discussion)

To show this result, we will use the Unique Factorization Theorem (Fundamental Theorem of Arithmetic) developed in Chapter 4. It tells us that every whole number greater than 1 is either prime or that it can be factored into primes in exactly one way (except for the order of the factors). Some examples are given below:

$$6 = 2 \times 3$$
$$8 = 2^3$$
$$12 = 2^2 \times 3$$
$$13 \text{ is prime}$$
$$60 = 2^2 \times 3 \times 5$$
$$6327 = 3^2 \times 19 \times 37$$

Notice what happens if we find the prime factors of the square of each of these numbers:

$$36 = 2^2 \times 3^2$$
$$64 = 2^6$$
$$144 = 2^4 \times 3^2$$
$$169 = 13^2$$
$$3600 = 2^4 \times 3^2 \times 5^2$$
$$40030929 = 3^4 \times 19^2 \times 37^2$$

Every prime factor appears twice as often in the square of a number as it did in the number itself; namely, for any whole number p (greater than 1), when the square of p is factored into primes, every prime factor appears an *even* number of times.

Tell whether 2 appears as a factor an even number of times or an odd number of times (p is any whole number greater than 1):

(a) 2^5 (b) 2^8 (c) $2^4 \times 3^5$ (d) $2^5 \times 3^4$

(e) $7^5 \times 11^2$ (f) p (g) p^2 (h) $2p^2$

(a) 2 appears 5 times, which is odd.

(b) 2 appears 8 times, which is even.

(c) 2 appears 4 times, which is even.

(d) 2 appears 5 times, which is odd.

(e) 2 appears 0 times as a *factor*, which is even.

(f) We cannot tell without knowing more about p. If p were 2^2, we would answer "even," but if p were 2^3 we would answer "odd."

(g) Since p^2 is the square of a whole number, 2 must appear as a factor an even number of times.

(h) 2 appears as a factor an even number of times in p^2. It appears one extra time in $2p^2$, so altogether it appears an odd number of times. (One more than an even number is an odd number.)

Arguments like those in Example 8-6 will be used in this discussion. Our strategy will be to show that if $\sqrt{2}$ is a rational number, then there is also a whole number that can be factored into primes in more than one way. According to the Unique Factorization Theorem, there is no such whole number, so $\sqrt{2}$ cannot be a rational number.

Suppose $\sqrt{2}$ is a rational number. Then $\sqrt{2} = p/q$, for some integers p and q. We can assume p and q are whole numbers, since $\sqrt{2}$ is positive. Squaring both sides, we get $2 = p^2/q^2$, and multiplying both sides by q^2 we get $2q^2 = p^2$. Now 2 appears an *odd* number of times in the factorization of $2q^2$ and an *even* number of times in the factorization of p^2. But $2q^2$ and p^2 are the same whole number, so this says that this whole number factors two different ways. Since the assumption that $\sqrt{2}$ is a rational number leads to this contradiction of the Unique Factorization Theorem, the assumption must be false; namely, $\sqrt{2}$ is not a rational number.

As an example of this argument using prime factors, let's assume $\sqrt{2} = 14/10$ (since we know that $\sqrt{2}$ is about 1.4) and show that this assumption leads to the existence of a whole number that factors into primes in two ways. Our argument will be like the general argument just given, where p is 14 and q is 10. If "$\sqrt{2} = 14/10$," then squaring both sides gives "$2 = 196/100$" and multiplying both sides by 100 gives "$200 = 196$." Factoring 200 and 196 into primes gives "$2 \times 2 \times 2 \times 5 \times 5 = 2 \times 2 \times 7 \times 7$." (Of course, all the statements in quotation marks are false since the initial assumption that $\sqrt{2} = 14/10$ is false.) Notice how the statement "$2 \times 2 \times 2 \times 5 \times 5 = 2 \times 2 \times 7 \times 7$" says that a number has exactly three (an odd number) factors of 2 and at the same time that it has exactly two (an even number) factors of 2 — a contradiction to the

Unique Factorization Theorem. A similar contradiction to the Unique Factorization Theorem will occur for any whole numbers p and q, for we will always get two factorizations of a whole number, one with an odd number of 2's and the other with an even number of 2's.

We have shown the existence of a number that occurs in geometry (the length of the side of a square whose area is 2), which can be written out as a decimal (1.414213 . . .) yet is *not* a rational number. Notice that $\sqrt{2}$ can be interpreted in another way, as the length of the diagonal of the geoboard square whose side is 1 unit:

What we need is a number for each possible length that can occur. It turns out there is an abundance of such numbers beyond the rationals required to describe all possible lengths. We shall assume from now on that there is a number associated with each possible length. The collection of all such numbers together with their opposites will be called the **real numbers**. Some lengths (like 2, 79, and 3/4) can be represented by rational numbers, and others (like $\sqrt{2}$) cannot be represented by rational numbers. Those real numbers which are *not* rational numbers are called **irrational numbers**.

A few other famous irrational numbers are $\sqrt{3}$, π, and e. It can be shown that $\sqrt{3}$ is irrational by an argument much like the one used to show that $\sqrt{2}$ is irrational. The number π (about 3.14159) occurs as the length of the circumference of a circle whose diameter is 1; however, it is beyond the scope of this book to show that π is irrational. The number e (approximately 2.7182818284) is widely used in mathematics, science, statistics, and economics. It is named in honor of Leonhard Euler (1707-1783), who was prolific in the areas of mathematics, physics, astronomy, chemistry, geography, and navigation. His collected work comprises 74 volumes, much of it published while he was totally blind. Euler was prolific in another sense of the world — he married and fathered 13 children [41].

Since by our assumption there is a number corresponding to every possible length, there is a number associated with every point to the *right* of the origin on the number line. This number is precisely the length of the piece of the number line between the origin and the point. For example, the point $\sqrt{2}$ units to the right of the origin is paired with the number $\sqrt{2}$. We will further assume that each real number associated with a length has an opposite. If we are given a point to the *left* of the origin, we will pair it with the opposite of the number which is the length of the piece of the number line between the point and the origin. For example, the point 8 units to the left of the origin is associated with -8, and the number $\sqrt{2}$ units to the left of the origin is associated with $-\sqrt{2}$. For every point on the line, there is one real number that corresponds to it.

But we also know that the converse is true — that for every real number there is a point on the line that corresponds to it. The number 0 corresponds to the origin, the number $\sqrt{3}$ corresponds to the point $\sqrt{3}$ units to the right of the origin, the number $-\pi$ corresponds to the point π units to the left of the origin, etc. The statements that there is a real number corresponding to each point (previous paragraph) and a point corresponding to each real number (this paragraph), taken together, say that there is a one-to-one correspondence between the real numbers and the points on a line. The real number that corresponds to a given point is called the **coordinate** of that point.

We will now comment briefly on ordering the real numbers and on the arithmetic of the real numbers. We will assume throughout that each real number has a unique decimal expansion. (There are some pathological difficulties here. See, for example, Problem 22, Section 6-4.)

To compare numbers like π and $\sqrt{10}$, we look at their decimal representations to decide that $\pi < \sqrt{10}$:

$$\pi = 3.14159\ldots$$

$$\sqrt{10} = 3.16227\ldots$$

A blown-up picture of the number line shows the relative positions of π and $\sqrt{10}$. The larger of two numbers always lies to the right on the number line:

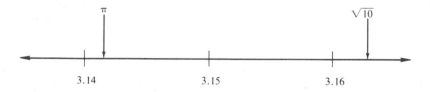

It is not at all easy to write down rules for doing arithmetic with real numbers. An article appeared in the Mathematical Association of America *Monthly* [21] which showed how it is possible to know every decimal place of one number and every decimal place of another number and not know even one decimal place of their sum! This, of course, is a non-routine example conjured up to prove a point, but it does illustrate the difficulty in providing universally applicable rules governing the arithmetic of real numbers. Fortunately, this poses little difficulty in most problems we confront in our everyday lives.

We usually work with rational numbers, and we have developed workable methods for doing arithmetic with rational numbers. In cases where we must deal with irrational numbers like $\sqrt{2}$ or π, we can use decimal approximations that allow us to get arbitrarily close to the actual answers. For example, using $\sqrt{2} \doteq 1.4$ and $\pi \doteq 3.1$ to conclude that $\sqrt{2} + \pi \doteq 4.5$ might suffice in the unlikely event that we ever needed to know this sum. Moreover, the field properties apply to real numbers, enabling us to do things like $2\pi + 6\pi = 8\pi$ (using the distributive property), and certain rules of algebra permit us to perform computations like $\sqrt{2} \times \sqrt{3} = \sqrt{6}$.

One final example is provided to show how arithmetic with irrational numbers can be "squeezed" between problems involving rational numbers.

Given that $1.4 < \sqrt{2} < 1.5$ and $3.1 < \pi < 3.2$, write similar expressions for

(a) $\sqrt{2} + \pi$ (b) $\pi - \sqrt{2}$ (c) $\pi \times \sqrt{2}$

EXAMPLE
8-7

SOLUTION

(a) Since $1.4 < \sqrt{2}$ and $3.1 < \pi$, then $1.4 + 3.1 < \sqrt{2} + \pi$; namely, $4.5 < \sqrt{2} + \pi$. Similarly, $\sqrt{2} < 1.5$ and $\pi < 3.2$, so $\sqrt{2} + \pi < 1.5 + 3.2$; namely, $\sqrt{2} + \pi < 4.7$. Hence $4.5 < \sqrt{2} + \pi < 4.7$.

(b) The answer to a subtraction problem is smallest when the number we are subtracting is as big as possible and the number we are subtracting *from* is as small as possible. Hence the smallest value occurs when we subtract 1.5 (the upper value for $\sqrt{2}$) from 3.1 (the lower value for π). Then we get $3.1 - 1.5 < \pi - \sqrt{2}$. The largest value occurs when we subtract 1.4 (the lower value for $\sqrt{2}$) from 3.2 (the upper value for π). Then we get $\pi - \sqrt{2} < 3.2 - 1.4$; namely, $\pi - \sqrt{2} < 1.8$. Hence $1.6 < \pi - \sqrt{2} < 1.8$.

(c) We can picture this by using an area model. The product $\pi \times \sqrt{2}$ can be interpreted as the area of a rectangle with sides π and $\sqrt{2}$.

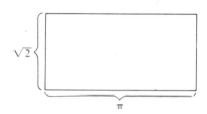

But $3.1 < \pi < 3.2$ and $1.4 < \sqrt{2} < 1.5$, so the area of this rectangle will be greater than the area of a rectangle with sides 3.1 and 1.4 and less than that of a rectangle with sides 3.2 and 1.5.

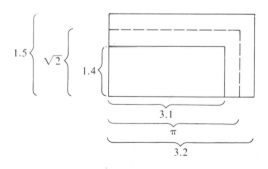

Hence $3.1 \times 1.4 < \pi \times \sqrt{2} < 3.2 \times 1.5,$

or $4.34 < \pi \times \sqrt{2} < 4.80$

With better approximations for π and $\sqrt{2}$, we could get better approximations for $\sqrt{2} + \pi$, $\pi - \sqrt{2}$, and $\pi \times \sqrt{2}$.

With our brief introduction to real numbers, we have extended our number system for the last time. We are satisfied to have a complete set of numbers, one for each point on the line.

What a Memory!

"In Japan Hideaki Tomoyori has learned to carry the mathematical formulation pi to 20,000 places, putting to shame his own earlier record of 15,151 places." (*Time*, June 18, 1980, page 88.) Care to challenge him?

EXERCISES AND PROBLEMS 8-2

SQUARE ROOTS

1. Which numbers have
   (a) two square roots?   (b) one square root?
   (c) no square root?   (d) two principal square roots?
   (e) one principal square root?   (f) no principal square root?

2. For what values of p is each statement true?
   (a) $\sqrt{p} = 9$ (b) $\sqrt{p} = -9$ (c) $\sqrt{-p} = 9$ (d) $\sqrt{-p} = -9$
   (e) $\sqrt{p} \geq 0$ (f) $\sqrt{p} > 0$ (g) $\sqrt{p} < 0$ (h) $\sqrt{p} \leq 0$

3. Square roots are defined for all fractions (but not for negative numbers). Notice in the figure that the shaded square is 1/4 of the unit square and that each side of the square has length 1/2. Hence $\sqrt{1/4} = 1/2$.

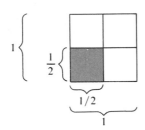

   (a) Find $\sqrt{1/9}$. Include a sketch.
   (b) Find $\sqrt{4/9}$. Include a sketch.
   (c) Find $\sqrt{9/4}$. Include a sketch.

4. Tell whether 3 appears as a factor an even number of times or an odd number of times (p is any whole number greater than 1).
   (a) 3^4 (b) 3^3 (c) $3^4 \times 5^3$ (d) $2^3 \times 5^3 \times 7^3$
   (e) p (f) p^2 (g) $2p^2$ (h) $3p^2$
   (i) $9p^2$

5. Show that there are whole numbers p and q for which assuming that $\sqrt{4} = p/q$ does *not* lead to a contradiction of the Unique Factorization Theorem.

6. Give an argument based on prime factorization to show that $\sqrt{3}$ is not a rational number.

7. Give an argument based on prime factorization to show that $\sqrt{6}$ is not a rational number.

8. Give an argument based on prime factorization to show that $\sqrt{12}$ is not a rational number.

*9. If n is a whole number and $\sqrt{n}$ is a rational number, then $\sqrt{n} = p/q$ for some whole numbers p and q, so $n = p^2/q^2$ and $n \times q^2 = p^2$. Use the Unique Factorization Theorem to characterize n; namely, when is $\sqrt{n}$ rational?

10. One of the most important results in all of geometry is the **Pythagorean theorem**. It tells us that in a triangle with a right angle, the square of the length of the longest side (**hypotenuse**) equals the sum of the squares of the other two sides (**legs**). For example, in the right triangle shown, $3^2 + 4^2 = 5^2$.

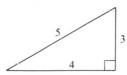

Section 11-2 is devoted to the Pythagorean theorem. For now, we offer a few exercises. Find x in each right triangle (not to scale):

(a)
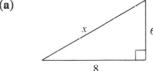

(b)
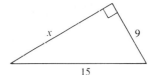

(c)
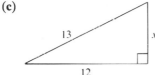

(d)

(e)
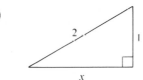

(f)
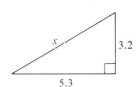

11. People have made up mnemonics for the digits of π. Here is one made up by a student:

    How I wish I could eliminate my energy bills now

    3 .1 4 1 5   9   2   6   5   3

    Make up a mnemonic of your own for the first several digits of
    (a) $\pi \doteq 3.14159265358979323846$
    (b) $\sqrt{2} \doteq 1.414213562373$

12. We said that π is irrational. Does $\pi = 22/7$?

13. We know that if C is the circumference of a circle and d is its diameter, then $C = \pi d$ or $\pi = C/d$. Does this mean π is rational? Explain.

14. What field property is being employed to write $2\pi + 6\pi = 8\pi$?

15. Long ago the approximation $\pi^2 = 10$ was used.
    (a) Taking π as 3.14159, determine π^2.
    (b) Compute $10 - \pi^2$.
    (c) Compute $(10 - \pi^2) \div \pi^2$ (the *relative error*) expressing your answer as a percent.

ORDER

16. Place in order, smallest to largest: e, 2.71828, $2.71\overline{828}$. (Use $e = 2.7182818284$.)

17. Give a reason for each statement:
    (a) $\sqrt{5} < \sqrt{11}$ **(b)** $-\sqrt{101} < 2$ **(c)** $3.14 < \pi$
    (d) $\pi < 22/7$ **(e)** $-\sqrt{7} < -\sqrt{6}$

18. Given that $\sqrt{3} \doteq 1.732051$, fill in this sequence of inequalities:
    (a) $1.7 < \sqrt{3} < 1.8$
    (b) $1.73 < \sqrt{3} < \underline{\hspace{1cm}}$
    (c) $\underline{\hspace{1cm}} < \sqrt{3} < 1.733$
    (d) $\underline{\hspace{3cm}}$
    (e) $\underline{\hspace{3cm}}$
    (f) $1.732051 < \sqrt{3} < 1.732052$

ARITHMETIC WITH REAL NUMBERS

19. Concepts such as absolute value are extended to include all the real numbers. Determine each of the following:
    (a) $|\pi|$ **(b)** $|-\pi|$ **(c)** $-|\pi|$ **(d)** $-|-\pi|$
    (e) $|\sqrt{2}|$ **(f)** $|-\sqrt{2}|$ **(g)** $-|\sqrt{2}|$ **(h)** $-|-\sqrt{2}|$

20. If $3.1 < \pi < 3.2$ and $1.7 < \sqrt{3} < 1.8$, give similar expressions (as in Example 8-7) for
    (a) $\pi + \sqrt{3}$ **(b)** $\pi - \sqrt{3}$ **(c)** $\sqrt{3} - \pi$ **(d)** $\pi \times \sqrt{3}$
    (e) 2π **(f)** $-\pi$ **(g)** $\pi \div \sqrt{3}$

21. If $2.7 < e < 2.8$ and $3.1 < \pi < 3.2$ and $2.2 < \sqrt{5} < 2.3$, give similar expressions (as in Example 8-7) for
    (a) $e + \pi + \sqrt{5}$ **(b)** $e \times \pi \times \sqrt{5}$ **(c)** $e \times (\pi + \sqrt{5})$
    (d) $e \times (\pi - \sqrt{5})$ **(e)** $e - (\pi - \sqrt{5})$

22. Draw an area model for Problem 20(d).

*23. Suppose in the following figure that $OA = 1$, $OC = \sqrt{2}$, and $OB = \pi$ and that $\triangle OAC$ is similar to $\triangle OBD$. Then

$$\frac{OD}{OC} = \frac{OB}{OA},$$

$$\frac{OD}{\sqrt{2}} = \frac{\pi}{1},$$

$$OD = \pi \times \sqrt{2}.$$

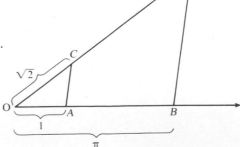

Draw similar figures that show how to get each of the following lengths (assuming that lengths of 1, $\sqrt{2}$, and π are given):

(a) π^2 (b) $\pi \div \sqrt{2}$ (c) $1/\pi$

APPLICATIONS

24. Delta Air Lines explained in its 1980 System Route Map that the distance you can see in clear weather is given by

$VK = 3.56 \sqrt{A}$, where VK is the distance in kilometers and A is the altitude in meters,

or by

$VM = 1.22\sqrt{A}$, where VM is the distance in miles and A is the altitude in feet.

(In Chapter 10 we will ask you to derive these formulas.)

For example, at an altitude of 10,000 meters (32,808 feet),

$$VK = 3.56 \sqrt{10,000} \doteq 356 \text{ kilometers, and}$$

$$VM = 1.22 \sqrt{32,808} \doteq 221 \text{ miles.}$$

(a) Find VK and VM (to the nearest whole number) to fill in this table:

Height in Meters	View in KM	Height in Feet	View in Miles
1,000		3,281	
3,000		9,842	
5,000		16,404	
10,000	356	32,808	221
12,000		39,370	

(b) At what height would you be able to see 500 km (311 miles)?

25. (a) The "f-stop" on a camera depends on the size of the lens opening: the bigger the number the *smaller* the lens opening. Common f-stops are 1.4, 2, 2.8, 4, 5.6, 8, 11, and 16. This may appear to be a rather unusual sequence of numbers. Write the following sequence of numbers, approximating those which are not whole numbers to one decimal place each and compare with the f-stop numbers:

$$\sqrt{2}, \quad 2, \quad 2\sqrt{2}, \quad 4, \quad 4\sqrt{2}, \quad 8, \quad 8\sqrt{2}, \quad 16, \ldots$$

(b) Find the next number in the sequence.
(c) Express your answer to part (b) to one decimal-place accuracy.

MATERIALS

26. Find areas for these geoboard figures:

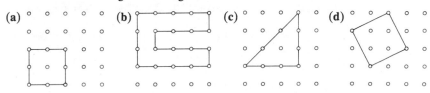

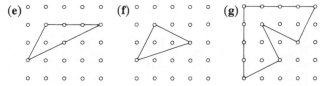

27. Sketch the construction of *squares* with the following areas on the geoboard:
     (**a**) 1   (**b**) 4   (**c**) 9   (**d**) 2

L28. Which of the following size squares can be constructed on a geoboard? For those which can, show the solution.
     (**a**) area 3   (**b**) area 5   (**c**) area 6   (**d**) area 7   (**e**) area 8

L29. *Determining π by Measuring*
     (**a**) Describe a procedure for approximating π using various round objects available to you.
     (**b**) Fill in the chart summarizing approximations for π after measuring three different objects.

Object	Measurements	Approximation for π

     (**c**) From the approximations obtained (rather than what you previously knew about π), what is your best estimate of π? How did you arrive at this answer?
     (**d**) Tell to how many significant digits you measured your round objects. To how many significant digits should your estimate of π be given? What is the accepted value of π to the same precision? How do you account for this error (if any)?

CALCULATORS

C30. (**a**) Verify on a calculator that $7.68 < \sqrt{59} < 7.69$ by computing 7.68^2 and 7.69^2.
     (**b**) Use trial and error (and not a square root key) to locate $\sqrt{73}$ between two decimals which differ by .01 (as in part a). Record the results of your trial and error process like this:

$$8.5^2 = 72.25 \quad \text{(too small)}$$
$$8.7^2 = 75.69 \quad \text{(too big)}$$
$$8.6^2 = 73.96 \quad \text{(too big)}$$
$$8.55^2 = 73.1025 \quad \text{(too big)}$$

     (**c**) Repeat part (b) for $\sqrt{137}$.
     (**d**) Repeat part (b) for $\sqrt{343}$.

C31. (**a**) Using π = 3.141592654 and 7926.41 miles as the diameter of the earth, compute the circumference of the earth. (Use a calculator with ten-digit display or use the technique of Problem 17, Section 3-5.) (**b**) How much does the value of the circumference change if the value of π is changed by .000000001? (**c**) Express your answer to part (b) in inches. (**d**) An Englishman named Shanks spent 20 years determining π to 707 places (of which 527 were correct). Comment in light of parts (a), (b), and (c).

C32. e is the "limit" of the expression $\left(1 + \frac{1}{n}\right)^n$ as n grows without bound. Use a scientific calculator to find the value of $\left(1 + \frac{1}{n}\right)^n$ when n is

     (**a**) 1   (**b**) 10   (**c**) 100   (**d**) 1000   (**e**) 10,000

P33. In 1732 the great mathematician Leonhard Euler, discussed in the conclusion to this section, disproved the conjecture that numbers of the form $2^{2^n} + 1$ are primes by showing it to be false when n is 5.   (a) For $n = 5, 2^{2^5} + 1 = 2^{32} + 1$. Compute $2^{32} + 1$.
(b) Write a program to factor this number, thus proving it isn't prime. (See also Problem 28, Section 4-2.)

8-3
CLOCK ARITHMETIC

This section provides a change of pace from the previous one. While the development of the real numbers is quite deep, clock arithmetic is easily accessible for elementary school children. Its value in providing insights into doing arithmetic together with its appeal as a fresh, enjoyable topic make clock arithmetic excellent enrichment material for the elementary school mathematics curriculum.

We start with examples of how we do arithmetic on an ordinary clock. For instance, if it is 10 o'clock, what time will it be 4 hours later? Simply adding 10 + 4 to get 14 is obviously not what is done here. By picturing a clock, we see that 4 hours after 10 o'clock is 2 o'clock, or in some sense that $10 \oplus 4 = 2$. (We use "$\oplus$" to denote that this addition is taking place on a clock.) Similarly,

$$9 \oplus 6 = 3$$
$$2 \oplus 4 = 6$$
$$8 \ominus 3 = 5$$
$$2 \ominus 5 = 9$$

The fact that no number exceeds 12 is one of the nice features of the system.

After motivating the topic with the familiar twelve-hour clock, we can switch to other clocks to do arithmetic as well. A five-hour clock is a suitable size for what we wish to do in most of our illustrations. Notice how the "5" is replaced by "0" in our version of the clock. One reason for this is that adding 5 on a five-hour clock is like adding 0. For instance, 5 hours after 2 o'clock is again 2 o'clock (on a five-hour clock).

In the elementary school classroom, these clocks can be constructed out of cardboard. (The round cardboard commonly used by restaurants to serve pizza is ideal for this.) The children put the numbers on the clock (evenly spaced) and add a cardboard hand with a metal fastener. Then, to show $2 \oplus 4$ on their

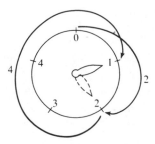

five-hour clock, they position the hand at "2" and then count 4 units (clockwise) to reach "1." This is like doing addition on the number line except that the line "wraps around" to where it started. Similarly, we can show (assuming five-hour clock arithmetic throughout)

$$3 \oplus 2 = 0$$
$$4 \oplus 3 = 2$$
$$4 \ominus 1 = 3$$
$$2 \ominus 4 = 3$$
$$0 \ominus 1 = 4$$

Now let's do a multiplication problem on a five-hour clock. To do $3 \otimes 2$, we would start at 0 (the "origin") and make three jumps of 2 to arrive at 1.

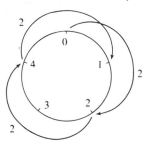

In five-hour clock arithmetic, we have $3 \otimes 2 = 1$. Similarly, we could show

$$4 \otimes 3 = 2$$
$$2 \otimes 4 = 3$$
$$3 \otimes 3 = 4$$

Is it possible to do $3 \oplus 4$ in five-hour clock arithmetic? At first glance, this seems impossible since we have no fractions. We do know that the problem $3 \oplus 4 = \square$ is equivalent to $4 \otimes \square = 3$. In this system, there are only five possibilities for the number $\square$, so it is a simple matter to try them all:

$$4 \otimes \boxed{0} = 0$$
$$4 \otimes \boxed{1} = 4$$
$$\boxed{4 \otimes \boxed{2} = 3}$$
$$4 \otimes \boxed{3} = 2$$
$$4 \otimes \boxed{4} = 1$$

We see that $4 \otimes \square = 3$, or equivalently $3 \ominus 4 = \square$, does have a solution in this system; namely, $\square = 2$.

This is truly a remarkable system! We can do $2 \ominus 4$ without negatives and $3 \oplus 4$ without fractions. We can figure out the answers on a clock made out of a cardboard pizza plate, and even if we guess, there are only five guesses to make. Are we so fortunate with all the arithmetic? We'll initiate an investigation into this question here and finish it in the problems.

Since there are only 5 numbers, there are only 25 possible addition problems in the entire system. All the solutions are given in this addition table:

$\oplus$ 5	0	1	2	3	4
0	0	1	2	3	4
1	1	2	3	4	0
2	2	3	4	0	1
3	3	4	0	1	2
4	4	0	1	2	3

Every problem has a solution which is one of the numbers 0, 1, 2, 3, or 4. This shows that this system is closed under addition. A study of the table also shows that it is commutative. Associativity is less obvious, but it also holds in this system. Zero is clearly the identity. Notice also that every number has an opposite (additive inverse) in that

$$0 \oplus 0 = 0$$

$$1 \oplus 4 = 0$$

$$2 \oplus 3 = 0$$

$$3 \oplus 2 = 0$$

$$4 \oplus 1 = 0$$

— namely, for any number in the system there is always a number in the system which when added to it gives zero, the identity.

We can even write out a complete subtraction table, where the numbers across the top are being subtracted *from* the numbers on the left. For example, the entry $2 \ominus 4 = 3$ is underlined.

$\ominus$ 5	0	1	2	3	4
0	0	4	3	2	1
1	1	0	4	3	2
2	2	1	0	4	<u>3</u>
3	3	2	1	0	4
4	4	3	2	1	0

Every subtraction problem is possible and yields an answer from among the numbers 0, 1, 2, 3, and 4. This means that the set is closed under subtraction. It is easy to see how subtracting a number is like adding its opposite. "Subtracting 2" means "jumping 2 counterclockwise," which will certainly give the same result as "jumping 3 clockwise." In other words, to subtract a number we can add the opposite of the number, just as we did with integers.

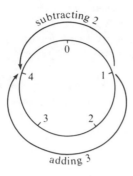

Skeletons of multiplication and division tables are shown in Figure 8-10. You are asked to supply the rest of each table.

$\otimes$ 5	0	1	2	3	4		$\div$ 5	0	1	2	3	4
0				0			0	*		0		
1		1					1					
2	0			1			2			1		
3							3	*				2
4				2	1		4					

FIGURE 8-10

We can see by looking at the completed table that every number (except 0) has a reciprocal (multiplicative inverse). The reciprocal of 2 is 3, since $2 \otimes 3 = 1$. The reciprocal of 4 is 4, since $4 \otimes 4 = 1$. Is it true that to divide by a number we can multiply by its reciprocal as we did with fractions?

An amazing result is that the system consisting of the set {0, 1, 2, 3, 4} and the operations $\oplus$ and $\otimes$ satisfies all 11 properties of a field. Contrast this with the results of Problem 31 in Section 8-1, where any set (having at least two elements) with ordinary addition and multiplication which satisfies the 11 field properties necessarily contains every rational number!

Clock arithmetic has many interesting and useful applications. It is at the heart of "casting out nines," a technique for checking computations based on nine-hour clock arithmetic. Even without its applications, the material presented in this section is highly appropriate for enrichment programs in the elementary schools.

EXERCISES AND PROBLEMS 8-3

COMPUTATIONS

1. (a) $1 \oplus 2$ (b) $3 \ominus 1$ (c) $2 \otimes 2$ (d) $4 \div 2$
       5   5   5   5

(e) $4 \div 3$ (f) $2 \ominus 3$ (g) $5 \otimes 6$ (h) $5 \oplus 4$
       5   5   7   7

2. Draw a sketch showing the solutions for the previous problems on the appropriate "clocks."

3. Complete the tables in Figure 8-10.

4. Write out complete tables for the following:
   (a) $\oplus$ (b) $\ominus$ (c) $\otimes$ (d) $\oplus$
       3   3   3   3
   (e) $\oplus$ (f) $\ominus$ (g) $\otimes$ (h) $\oplus$
       7   7   7   7

5. (a) Write out a complete table for $\otimes$.
                                        6
   (b) How does this table differ from the table for $\otimes$ and $\otimes$ in terms of patterns?
                                                       5   7

6. Add 4 and 3 in
   (a) five-hour clock arithmetic.   (b) base five.
   (c) Compare your results.

7. Find the opposite of 2 on the following clocks:
   (a) three-hour   (b) four-hour   (c) five-hour   (d) six-hour.

8. Find the reciprocal of 2 on the following clocks:
   (a) three-hour   (b) four-hour   (c) five-hour   (d) six-hour.

9. In five-hour clock arithmetic, what is the reciprocal of
   (a) 1?   (b) 3?   (c) 0?

10. Find the opposite and the reciprocal of each number in seven-hour clock arithmetic.

11. Repeat Problem 10 for six-hour clock arithmetic.

12. Answer these questions based on five-hour clock arithmetic.
    (a) Which numbers are their own opposites?
    (b) Which numbers are their own reciprocals?
    (c) Find a number whose opposite is also its own reciprocal. Are there other numbers with this property?

13. Repeat the previous problem based on seven-hour clock arithmetic.

14. The figure below is a *part* of a multiplication table for a certain clock arithmetic. What system is it? *Explain your reasoning.*

$\otimes$?	1	2	3	4	5
1	1	2	3	4	5
2	2	4	6	8	10
3	3	6	9	0	3
4	4	8	0	4	8
5	5	10	3	8	1

PROPERTIES

15. In five-hour clock arithmetic, is it true that we can divide by a number by multiplying by its reciprocal?

16. Under which of the following operations is {0, 1, 2, 3, 4} closed? When not, give a counter-example.
    (a) $\oplus$ (b) $\ominus$ (c) $\otimes$ (d) $\oplus$
        5   5   5   5

17. (a) Show that the distributive property holds in this example:
$$2 \underset{5}{\otimes} (4 \underset{5}{\oplus} 3) = (2 \underset{5}{\otimes} 4) \underset{5}{\oplus} (2 \underset{5}{\otimes} 3)$$

(b) Show that the associative property for multiplication holds in this example:
$$(3 \underset{5}{\otimes} 4) \underset{5}{\otimes} 2 = 3 \underset{5}{\otimes} (4 \underset{5}{\otimes} 2)$$

(c) Do these examples *prove* that the respective properties hold throughout the system?

18. (a) Fill in the following chart:

Type of Clock Arithmetic	Numbers That Have Reciprocals
2	1
3	1, 2
4	1, 3
5	1, 2, 3, 4
6	
7	
8	
9	
10	
11	
12	

(b) In which systems do all candidates (except 0) have reciprocals? Generalize.

(c) In those systems which lack reciprocals, which ones are lacking? Generalize.

(d) According to your findings, would you predict that 56 has a reciprocal in 100-hour clock arithmetic? In 70-hour clock arithmetic? In 93-hour clock arithmetic?

19. Suppose we agree to order the numbers in five-hour clock arithmetic as follows: $0 < 1 < 2 < 3 < 4$.

(a) Does the transitive property for $<$ hold?

(b) We know $2 < 4$. Is $2 + 1 < 4 + 1$ (in five-hour clock arithmetic)?

(c) Show that the "greatest common divisor" of 2 and 3 is *not* 1 (in five-hour clock arithmetic).

(d) Show that the "least common multiple" of 2 and 4 is *not* 4 (in five-hour clock arithmetic).

(e) According to our definitions, which is greater (in five-hour clock arithmetic), 1/4 or 3? (Use $1 \oplus 4$ for 1/4.)

(f) Suppose we define a "prime" five-hour clock arithmetic number as one whose only factors are itself and 1. Which numbers are "prime" according to this definition?

*20. (a) Solve the equation $y^2 - 5y = 0$ in the real numbers by factoring. How many solutions are there?

(b) Solve the corresponding equation in six-hour clock arithmetic ($y^2 \underset{6}{\ominus} 5y = 0$, where y^2 means $y \underset{6}{\otimes} y$ and where $5y$ means $5 \underset{6}{\otimes} y$) by substituting each of the numbers

0, 1, 2, 3, 4, 5 to see which ones make the statement true. How many solutions are there?

(c) Show that $y^2 \ominus 5y$ factors in two completely different ways.
$$6$$

MATERIALS AND CALCULATORS

L21. (a) Make a five-hour clock as described in this section. Use it to solve the appropriate parts of Problem 1.

(b) Repeat part (a) for a seven-hour clock.

P22. Write a program to determine (a) opposites   (b) reciprocals in clock arithmetic for any prime hour clock p.

PROBLEM SOLVING EXTENSIONS

23. If March 14 is a Thursday, what day is
   (a) March 21?   (b) March 29?   (c) April 1?
   (d) April 3?   (e) April 19?

24. Some primes can be written as the sum of two squares (of whole numbers); some cannot.

   $2 = 1^2 + 1^2$ 3 cannot $5 = 1^2 + 2^2$

   7 cannot   11 cannot $13 = 2^2 + 3^2$

   (a) Extend the list to include all primes less than 60.
   (b) Classify those which can. (Hint: Divide each number by 4.)
   (c) Which of the following primes would you predict can be written as the sum of two squares? 61, 67, 97, 101, 103, 107, 211, 2311.
   (d) Express 65 as the sum of squares in two ways.

Geometry

9

9-1

PROBLEM SOLVING IN GEOMETRY

To many, geometry has a "bad name" because of inappropriate experience with the subject in school. Actually geometry is a highly useful subject, which — if approached properly — can be exciting and interesting to learners.

We will introduce geometry through problem solving. For example, we will ask (in fact, we already have asked) questions about squares before we define squares formally. Once again we move from the concrete to the abstract, from the informal to the more formal. In terms of the "van Hiele levels" described by Alan Hoffer in the *Mathematics Teacher* [27], we probe geometry first at the levels of recognition and analysis and later at the levels of deduction and rigor.

Since we will be using the same problem solving strategies introduced in Chapter 1 (which we hope you have used throughout the first eight chapters), this section essentially reinforces earlier ideas within the context of geometry. In fact, a number of the problems of Chapter 1 were themselves taken from geometry.

We will pose six problems for you to solve. You are strongly urged to try to solve the problems *before* studying the solutions that follow.

Problem 1. How many squares can be found on an 8 × 8 checkerboard?

Problem 2. The students of Townsend School are curious to know if they can tile the floor of their multi-purpose room with different-colored square tiles so that the entire floor from wall to wall will be covered with "T's," where each "T" is made from five tiles of the same color and the "T's" can face any of four directions:

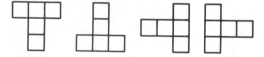

(They understand that the "T's" along the walls may be cut off.) Can it be done? If so, what is the smallest number of colors needed to make the "T's" stand out from each other? (Hint: Use graph paper or dot paper.)

Problem 3. Two quarters touch each other as shown in Figure 9-1. The lower quarter remains stationary and the upper quarter is rotated around it. Which

FIGURE 9-1

way will George be looking when the upper quarter is rotated three-fourths of the way around the stationary quarter?

Problem 4.   Figure 9-2 shows 32 points, each of which is connected to every other point by one line segment. How many segments are there connecting the 32 points?

Problem 5.   The area of a rectangle is equal to the product of its length and width. The length is *increased* by 30% and the width is *decreased* by 25%. What effect does this have on the area?

Problem 6.   What size squares can be constructed on a 5 × 5 geoboard or, equivalently, what size squares can be drawn on 5 × 5 dot paper so that the vertices ("corners") of the squares are located on the dots?

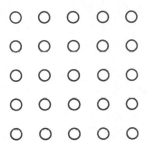

FIGURE 9-2

Before reading on, see how many of the six problems you can solve. The solutions are presented in Examples 9-1 through 9-6 respectively.

(Problem 1)

EXAMPLE
9-1

SOLUTION

We employ the strategies *don't make unwarranted assumptions, solve a simpler problem, draw a sketch, systematically account for all possibilities*, and *look for a pattern*. (If you haven't solved the problem so far, try again using these strategies before reading on.)

If you answered 64 you made an *unwarranted assumption* (that only "small squares" were to be counted). It is possible to have squares of size 1 × 1, 2 × 2, 3 × 3, . . . , 8 × 8. Since this is fairly involved, we first *solve a simpler problem.*

Let's consider checkerboards of size 1 × 1, 2 × 2, and 3 × 3. We *draw a sketch* of each

1 × 1   2 × 2   3 × 3

and in each case *systematically account for all possibilities*:

1×1 *checkerboard:*   1 square of size 1×1

2×2 *checkerboard:* $4 = 2^2$ squares of size 1×1

$\underline{1 = 1^2}$ square of size 2×2
5   squares altogether

3×3 *checkerboard:* $9 = 3^2$ squares of size 1×1

$4 = 2^2$ squares of size 2×2

$\underline{1 = 1^2}$ square of size 3×3
14   squares altogether

We *look for a pattern* and observe the following:

Size of board	Number of squares
1×1 checkerboard	$1^2 = 1$
2×2 checkerboard	$1^2 + 2^2 = 1 + 4 = 5$
3×3 checkerboard	$1^2 + 2^2 + 3^2 = 1 + 4 + 9 = 14$

This suggests an answer for the 8×8 checkerboard of

$$1^2 + 2^2 + 3^2 + 4^2 + 5^2 + 6^2 + 7^2 + 8^2 =$$

$$1 + 4 + 9 + 16 + 25 + 36 + 49 + 64 = 204.$$

It is easy to verify that 1, 4, 9, 16, 25, 36, 49, and 64 represent the number of 8×8, 7×7, 6×6, 5×5, 4×4, 3×3, 2×2, and 1×1 squares respectively, so 204 is the correct answer.

EXAMPLE 9-2

(Problem 2)

SOLUTION

Here we *identify a subgoal, draw a sketch* and *systematically account for all possibilities* — blended with a generous amount of *guess and check*. Use these hints if you haven't already solved the problem.

First we search for a way to place two T's together so that the spaces around them can be completely filled in. This is our *subgoal*.

Some attempts which fail are these:

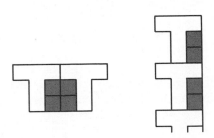

In each case, by *systematically accounting for all possibilities*, it can be seen that it is impossible to cover all of the four shaded squares. A more promising start is

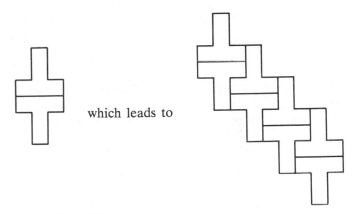

which leads to

and finally to Figure 9-3, colored in just three colors.

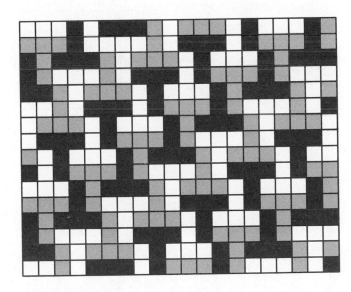

FIGURE 9-3

<table>
<tr><td>EXAMPLE
9-3</td></tr>
</table>

(Problem 3)

SOLUTION

This problem could fool you if you fail to *check your answer*. When the quarter on top rolls halfway around, points A and B will be touching, which means George will be right side up. Again we *draw a sketch:*

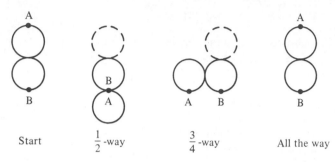

| Start | $\frac{1}{2}$ -way | $\frac{3}{4}$ -way | All the way |

At the 3/4-way mark George will be upside down and therefore looking to the right. Of course, the simplest way to do the problem is to *act it out*, but this assumes you have 50¢ — and we didn't want to make an *unwarranted assumption!*

<table>
<tr><td>EXAMPLE
9-4</td></tr>
</table>

(Problem 4)

SOLUTION

Can you *think of a similar problem?* If not, let's *try some simpler problems, make a table,* and *look for a pattern.*

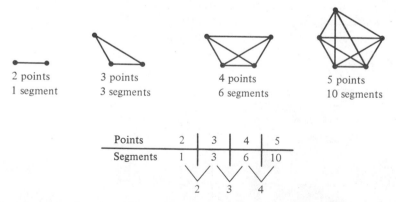

By examining the differences (see Problem 38, Section 3-3) we see a clear pattern which suggests that six points will result in 15 segments. Indeed, the addition of a sixth point gives us five new segments in addition to the ten segments we already had. By the same argument the pattern clearly continues **indefinitely**. We see that for 32 points we will get 496 lines.

If we successfully *think of a similar problem* we see this is the familiar handshake problem of Section 1-1. Still another way to view it is as $\binom{32}{2} = \dfrac{32 \times 31}{2 \times 1} = 204.$ (See Problem 43 of Section 2-1 and Problem 14 of Section 3-4.)

(Problem 5)

The results of this problem may surprise you. We use the strategy *write an open sentence.* If the original rectangle has length L and width W, its area will be LW. If the length increases by 30%, the new length will be $1.30L$. The new width, after a 25% decrease, will be $.75W$, so the new area becomes $A = (1.30L)(.75W) = .975LW$. Thus the area actually *decreases* despite the fact that the increase in length is greater than the decrease in width. We can *check the answer* if we (carefully) *sketch* an example on squared paper.

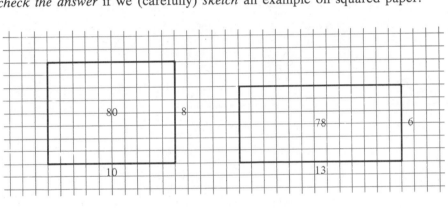

(Problem 6)

Once again we must be careful not to make any *unwarranted assumptions.* (The sides of the squares need *not* be horizontal or vertical.) Most people are quick to find squares of size (area) 1, 4, 9, and 25 and may miss the squares of size 2, 5, 8, or 10 shown below. If we *systematically account for all possibilities* by considering all possible values of a and b, we see that squares

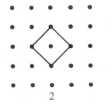

2

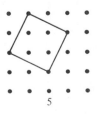

5

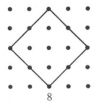

8

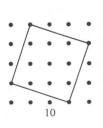

10

of size 3, 6, 7, 11, etc., are impossible to draw. (Some squares, like squares of size 13 and 17, are possible on larger geoboards.)

Once again we provide some problems for you to try.

EXERCISES AND PROBLEMS 9-1

PROBLEM SOLVING

1. How many *rectangles* can be found on **(a)** a 3 × 3 checkerboard?   **(b)** an 8 × 8 checkerboard? (All squares are rectangles.)

2. Count how many triangles are in the following figures:

(a)   **(b)**

3. Repeat the floor tile problem (Example 9-2) using each of the following:

(a)   **(b)**   **(c)**

4. Move as few coins as possible to make the triangle point down instead of up:

5. It takes three points to determine the three vertices of a triangle. How many different triangles are determined **(a)** by five points, using three at a time?   **(b)** by the 32 points of Figure 9-2, using three at a time?

6. How many quadrilaterals are determined by the 32 points of Figure 9-2 using four at a time?

7. What happens to the area of a rectangle if its length and width are each
(a) doubled?   **(b)** tripled?   **(c)** halved?

8. The volume of a box is equal to the product of its (inside) length, width, and height. What happens to the volume if length, width, and height are each (a) doubled? (b) tripled?   (c) halved?

9. Find all squares which can be constructed on geoboards of the following sizes: (a) 6 × 6 (namely, 36 nails)   (b) 8 × 8   (c) 10 × 10

10. Show how to construct squares of size 13 and of size 17 on a 10 × 10 geoboard.

11. Can an equilateral triangle (a triangle whose sides are all the same length) be constructed on a 5 × 5 geoboard? Give details.

12. Fold an equilateral triangle from an ordinary sheet of paper. (Use no other tools.)

13. A basketball player 2 meters tall is looking into a mirror mounted on the wall 3 meters away. How long is the mirror if it is exactly long enough to show his image from head to toe (and no more)?

14. The lawn in Debbie's front yard is approximately 32 meters by 24 meters. In her back yard it is approximately 32 meters by 42 meters. If her mower cuts a path about 3/4 of a meter wide, about how far does she walk each time she cuts her lawn?

9-2
GEOMETRY OF SHAPES

The photographs on the chapter opening page give a small sample of the geometric shapes that surround us. Our sampling includes tall buildings and lowly water mains, functional bridges and artistic sculpture.

In this chapter we will elaborate on some of the topics from geometry already introduced and develop some new geometric concepts. Just as geometry permeated our earlier discussions of numbers, so will certain number concepts illuminate our treatment of geometry. This is consistent with our overall goal of stressing the relationships between the various branches of mathematics.

Earlier, we saw how the notion of set was fundamental to defining numbers and subsequently to comparing them and adding them (along with other operations). Again we will use sets — this time in describing geometric figures. We will de-emphasize the set notation in our treatment so as not to distract from the concepts themselves, but the concepts involving sets will nevertheless underlie what we do. Before reading further, can you recall any of the vocabulary of sets that is used in a geometric sense?

We will use the idea of a **point** as our building block. Any set of points will be called a **geometric figure**. Two well-known types of geometric figures are **lines** and **planes**, though we will not attempt to define lines or planes (or points). Instead these concepts will provide a starting point or basis for subsequent definitions.

Certain assumptions we make about points, lines, and planes provide some insight into how they are related:

(1) Two points determine one line. (Namely, given two points, precisely one line can be drawn which contains both points.)
(2) Two intersecting lines determine one point.
(3) A line and a point not on the line determine one plane.

Just as it is assumed that the two points in (1) are distinct (different), so it is assumed that the two lines in (2) are distinct.

We will use the most common method of naming points, lines, and planes. Points will be named by capital letters, (like "A" or "P"), lines by pairs of capital letters (like "$\overleftrightarrow{AB}$" or "$\overleftrightarrow{PQ}$," which we read as "line AB" and "line PQ," respectively), and planes by triples of capital letters (like "plane ABC" or "plane PQR"). Sometimes lines and planes will be named by single lowercase letters (like "line m" or "plane p"). Statements (1), (2), and (3) and the naming of these figures are illustrated next:

(1)    Points R and S determine $\overleftrightarrow{RS}$.

(2) 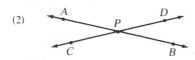 $\overleftrightarrow{AB}$ and $\overleftrightarrow{CD}$ determine point P.

(3) 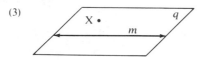   Line m and point X determine plane q.

Other geometric figures can be described in terms of points, lines, and planes. The subset of a line consisting of two points and all the points between them is called a **line segment**. ("Between" is another undefined term for us.) We write "$\overline{EF}$" to indicate the segment consisting of the two points E and F (called **endpoints**) and all the points between them. Point K is on $\overline{EF}$, but J and L are not. Why?

Any point on a line (such as E) separates the line into two pieces called **half-lines**. Specifically, point E separates $\overleftrightarrow{EF}$ into two half-lines, one containing J and one containing K (and F). These half-lines are symbolized by $\overset{\circ}{\longrightarrow}{EJ}$ and $\overset{\circ}{\longrightarrow}{EK}$ respectively. The open dot in the symbol indicates that the point E itself does not belong to either of the half-lines. $\overset{\circ}{\longrightarrow}{EK}$ and $\overset{\circ}{\longrightarrow}{EF}$ are precisely the same half-line, so it makes sense to write $\overset{\circ}{\longrightarrow}{EK} = \overset{\circ}{\longrightarrow}{EF}$. (The equal sign here indicates that $\overset{\circ}{\longrightarrow}{EK}$ and $\overset{\circ}{\longrightarrow}{EF}$ are equal sets, just as we wrote earlier that $\{A, B, C\} = \{C, B, A\}$.) The set made up of $\overset{\circ}{\longrightarrow}{EJ}$ together with point E is called "**ray EJ**"

and is denoted $\vec{EJ}$. E is called the **endpoint** of $\vec{EJ}$. We see that $\overleftrightarrow{EJ}$ and $\vec{EJ}$ are the same, except that $\vec{EJ}$ contains point E while $\overleftrightarrow{EJ}$ does not. It would be correct to say that $\overleftrightarrow{EJ} \subseteq \vec{EJ}$, but we choose here to minimize such symbolism.

Earlier, when we spoke of "intersecting" lines, we had an example of the way in which the language of sets appears quite naturally. (The intersection of two lines, each of them a set of points, is what they have in common.) Now we use the union of sets. We can describe an **angle** as the union of two (distinct) rays which have a common endpoint. The rays are called the **sides** of the angle. The common endpoint is called the **vertex** of the angle. (The plural of vertex is **vertices**.) When it is unambiguous, we can name an angle by its vertex. Otherwise, we name the angle by three points, one on each ray with the vertex always listed between the other two. Thus the angle shown below can be

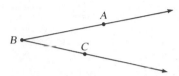

correctly named $\angle B$ (read "angle B"), $\angle ABC$, or $\angle CBA$. Names such as $\angle ACB$ or $\angle C$ do not name the angle shown. Just as the name "Scott" would not be sufficient to distinguish among several Scotts in the same room, $\angle R$ does not sufficiently distinguish among $\angle ORP$, $\angle PRQ$, and $\angle ORQ$ in the figure shown here:

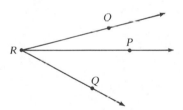

We will now explore our development so far through several examples.

Give concise names for the following:

(a) $\overleftrightarrow{RS} \cap \overrightarrow{WV}$ (b) $\overleftrightarrow{RS} \cap \overrightarrow{VW}$

(c) $\overleftrightarrow{RS} \cap \overleftrightarrow{TV}$ (d) $\overleftrightarrow{RS} \cap \vec{TV}$

(e) $\angle STV \cap \angle RTW$

(f) $\angle STV \cap \angle PTR$

(g) $\vec{TR} \cup \vec{TP}$ (h) $\vec{TR} \cup \vec{TS}$

EXAMPLE 9-7

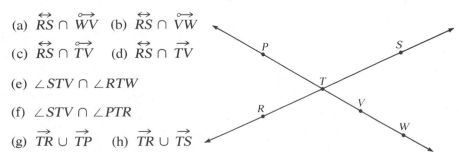

SOLUTION

(a) $\{T\}$, but we usually just write T.   (b) $\{\ \ \}$

(c) $\{\ \ \}$. Note that T does not belong to $\overrightarrow{TV}$.

(d) T (e) $\overrightarrow{TW}$ (f) T (g) $\angle RTP$ (or $\angle PTR$)

(h) $\overleftrightarrow{RS}$ (assuming that R, T, and S are **collinear**; namely, that they lie on the same line)

EXAMPLE 9-8

How many ways are there to denote the given line using the given letters?

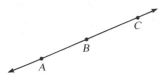

SOLUTION

We name a line by two capital letters. There are three ways to choose the first letter and then two ways to choose the second one. In all, there are $3 \times 2 = 6$ ways to make the choices. This can easily be verified by listing them: $\overleftrightarrow{AB}$, $\overleftrightarrow{AC}$, $\overleftrightarrow{BA}$, $\overleftrightarrow{BC}$, $\overleftrightarrow{CA}$, $\overleftrightarrow{CB}$.

An important ingredient in understanding geometry is the ability to visualize various relationships among geometric figures.

EXAMPLE 9-9

Show all possible intersections of a line and an angle.

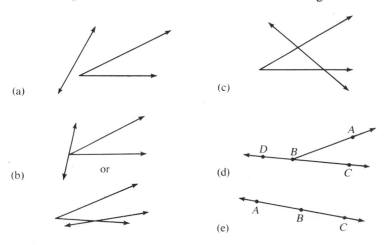

SOLUTION

(a) The "smallest" possible intersection is $\{\ \ \}$.

(b) In these two cases, the intersection is one point.

(c) Perhaps the most obvious case, the intersection is two points.

(d) $\angle ABC \cap \overleftrightarrow{DC} = \overrightarrow{BC}$. The intersection is a ray.

(e) $\angle ABC \cap \overleftrightarrow{AC} = \overleftrightarrow{AC}$. The intersection is a line.

The possible intersections of a line and an angle are { }, a point, two points, a ray, and a line. That it would have been quite easy to overlook one or more of these possibilities suggests the care required in such problems.

Our next category of geometric figures is called **curves**. A careful definition of curve requires advanced concepts like continuity, which we cannot address in this brief treatment. We will agree that a curve is a set of at least two points that can be traced (as with the tip of a pencil) from a starting point to a finishing point without "skipping." In this book, we will also require that a curve lie in a plane. The examples below should help to clarify the meaning of curve:

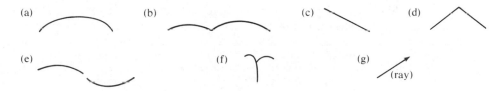

(a), (b), (c), (d), and (f) are curves.
(e) is not, since it cannot be traced without skipping.
(g) is not, since it lacks a finishing point.

A curve that ends where it starts and that otherwise can be drawn without retracing any of its points is called a **simple closed curve**. Observe that in defining simple closed curves we do allow the starting point and finishing point to coincide, but we do not allow any additional overlapping.

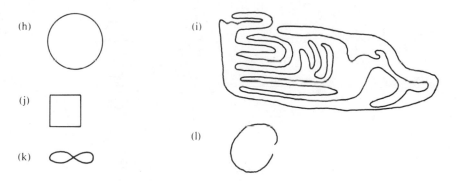

(h), (i), and (j) are simple curves.
(k) is not a simple closed curve, since to trace it involves more overlapping than the starting point and finishing point. (It is not "simple.")
(l) is a curve, but not a simple closed curve, since it does not end where it starts. (It is not "closed.")

Each simple closed curve separates the plane into two regions called the **interior** and **exterior**. (You will have the opportunity to supply definitions for these two terms in the exercises.) A simple closed curve is called a **convex curve** if each segment formed by connecting two points on the curve does *not* intersect the exterior of the curve.

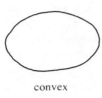

convex

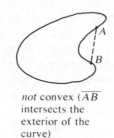

not convex ($\overline{AB}$
intersects the
exterior of the
curve)

Any simple closed curve that is the union (of a finite number) of segments
is called a **polygon**. Polygons are further classified according to the number of
"sides" (minimum number of segments) that make up the polygon. The more
common types are shown in Figure 9-4. A polygon with a greater number of

Number of Sides	Name	Example
3	Triangle	
4	Quadrilateral	
5	Pentagon	
6	Hexagon	
7	Heptagon	
8	Octagon	
9	Nonagon	
10	Decagon	

FIGURE 9-4

sides is commonly called an **_n_-gon**, where _n_ is the number of sides. For example, the figure below is a 13-gon:

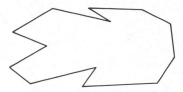

In specifying polygons, it is conventional to list the vertices consecutively. Thus we speak of "triangle _ABC_" (denoted $\triangle ABC$). It could also be named $\triangle CAB$, $\triangle ACB$, etc. The quadrilateral shown might be named "quadrilateral _WXYZ_" (abbreviated "quad. _WXYZ_") or quad. _XYZW_ or quad. _XWZY_, etc., but _not_ quad. _XZYW_, etc.

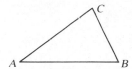 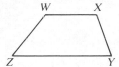

The union of a polygon and its interior is called a **closed polygonal region**. The interior alone is called an **open polygonal region**. ("Polygonal" is pronounced "po-LIG-on-al.") It can also be named according to the particular type of polygon involved. For instance, this polygonal region is a **triangular region:**

So far, all the figures named have been what we call **plane figures**, because they are subsets of the plane. Figures which are not subsets of the plane are called **space figures**. The set of all points is called **space**. A number of important plane figures and space figures will be defined after a bit more of our geometry is developed. Do you know, for instance, what concepts are needed to give a definition for "square"?

Other definitions are given in Problems 11, 12, and 32.

EXERCISES AND PROBLEMS 9-2

LINES, ANGLES, PLANES

1. Give other examples of geometric shapes we see in our everyday lives besides the ones given in the introductory paragraph of this section.

2. Give examples showing how the following language about sets is used in geometry:
   (a) intersection   (b) union   (c) empty set   (d) subset

3. (a) Look up the definition of *point* in a dictionary. What basic concepts are assumed in the definition given?
   (b) Do the same for *line*.

4. Why don't points J and L belong to $\overline{EF}$? Does E belong to $\overline{EF}$?

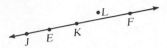

5. Give two other names for $\angle A$, using the letters given. In how many ways can it be (correctly) named using three of the given letters?

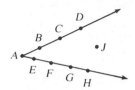

6. Would you say $\overleftrightarrow{AB}$ and $\overleftrightarrow{CD}$ intersect? Why or why not?

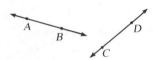

7. These poorly drawn figures falsely suggest some of the possible intersections of a line and an angle. Correct the figures to show the correct number of points of intersection in each case:

(a)

(b)

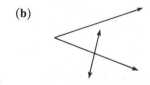

(c)

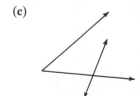

(d)

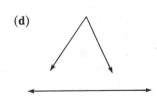

8. Sketch two angles whose intersection is
   (a) exactly 0 points   (b) exactly 2 points   (c) exactly 3 points
   (d) exactly 4 points   (e) more than 4 points.

9. Give concise names for the following. ($\overleftrightarrow{MN}$ and $\overleftrightarrow{QP}$ are straight lines.)

(a) $\overleftrightarrow{MN} \cap \overleftrightarrow{QP}$ (b) $\overleftrightarrow{QP} \cap \overleftrightarrow{MN}$ (c) $\overline{MN} \cap \overline{QP}$

(d) $\overleftrightarrow{TN} \cap \overleftrightarrow{QP}$ (e) $\overline{TN} \cap \overline{QP}$ (f) $\angle OSP \cap \overleftrightarrow{MN}$

(g) $\angle OSP \cap \angle MOQ$ (h) $\angle NTS \cap \angle MOQ$ (i) $\angle OSP \cap \overleftrightarrow{TP}$

(j) $\angle OSP \cap \overrightarrow{TP}$ (k) $\angle OSP \cap \overrightarrow{PT}$ (l) $\angle OSP \cap \overline{PT}$

(m) $\angle OSP \cap \angle PON$ (n) $\angle QON \cap \{S\}$ (o) $\overrightarrow{OM} \cap \overrightarrow{ON}$

(p) $\overleftrightarrow{OM} \cap \overleftrightarrow{ON}$ (q) $\overleftrightarrow{OM} \cap \overrightarrow{ON}$ (r) $\overrightarrow{OM} \cup \overrightarrow{ON}$

(s) $\overrightarrow{SO} \cup \overrightarrow{ST}$ (t) $\overleftrightarrow{SO} \cup \overrightarrow{ST}$

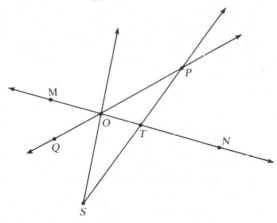

10. A point on a line separates it into two half-lines.
  (a) What is the intersection of these half-lines?
  (b) What is the union of these half-lines?
  (c) What is the union of these half-lines together with the point that separates them?

11. (a) Develop the notion of half-plane as in the previous problem.
   (b) Do the same for half-space.
  *(c)** Define the **interior of an angle** in terms of the intersection of certain half-planes. Will an exception need to be made for **straight angles** (angles whose opposite rays are collinear)?

12. Certainly a line "goes on without an end"; it has no "last point." If you remove the endpoints of a segment, will what is left (called an **open segment**) have a last point?

13. What figure is described by the following? "The union of two points A and B, all points P between A and B, and all points Q such that B is between A and Q."

14. What figure is described by the following? "The union of two points A and B, all points P between A and B, all points Q such that B is between A and Q, and all points R such that A is between B and R."

15. Suppose we try to generate a plane according to statement (3) on page 292 that a plane is determined by a line and a point not on the line.

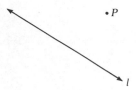

Consider all possible lines that are determined by P and the points on l, such as $\overleftrightarrow{PA}$, $\overleftrightarrow{PB}$, $\overleftrightarrow{PC}$, etc.

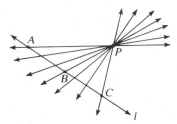

What points (if any) of the plane would not be on any of the lines?

16. (Theorem of Pappus of Alexandria, c. 300 A.D.) Draw two lines m and n. Choose points A, B, C, D, E, and F alternately on m and n (so that A, C, and E are on m and B, D, and F are on n). (a) Find $G = \overleftrightarrow{AB} \cap \overleftrightarrow{DE}$, $H = \overleftrightarrow{BC} \cap \overleftrightarrow{EF}$, and $J = \overleftrightarrow{CD} \cap \overleftrightarrow{AF}$. (Redraw your figure if necessary.) (b) What seems to be true about G, H, and J?

17. Draw three lines l, m, and n, which all meet at O. Draw $\triangle PQR$ and $P'Q'R'$ so that P and P' are on l, Q and Q' are on m, and R and R' are on n. (a) Find $S = \overleftrightarrow{PQ} \cap \overleftrightarrow{P'Q'}$, $T = \overleftrightarrow{PR} \cap \overleftrightarrow{p'R'}$, and $U = \overleftrightarrow{QR} \cap \overleftrightarrow{Q'R'}$. (b) What seems to be true about S, T, and U?

COUNTING PROBLEMS

18. Count the number of angles in each figure:

(a)

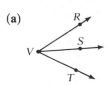

(b)

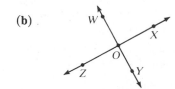

(c)

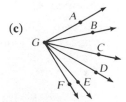

19. In how many ways can each line be named using the given letters?

(a)

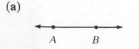

(b)

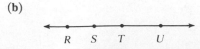

20. Determine all possible intersections (as in Example 9-9) of
(**a**) two lines   (**b**) two rays
(**c**) a line and a ray   (**d**) a half-line and an angle
(**e**) two angles.

21. Find the maximum number of lines determined by (**a**) 6 points (**b**) 10 points (**c**) 1000 points.

22. Use Pascal's triangle to find the maximum number of lines determined by (**a**) 7 points (**b**) 8 points.

23. What is the maximum number of points determined by (**a**) 3 lines? (**b**) 4 lines? (**c**) 8 lines? (**d**) 1000 lines?

CURVES, POLYGONS, REGIONS

24. Which of the following are curves?

(**a**)    (**b**) [rectangle]   (**c**) [line with arrows]
                                                                        (line)

(**d**) [segment]   (**e**) [curve]   (**f**) [curve]
(segment without
its endpoints)

25. (**a**) Which capital letters of the alphabet are curves? (Assume block letters without serifs — "L" not "L," etc.)

(**b**) Which are simple closed curves?

26. Given that *A*, *B*, and *C* are collinear, is this polygon a hexagon or a heptagon?

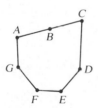

27. According to our definition, which of the following are polygons?

(**a**) [figure]   (**b**) [figure]   (**c**) [figure]

(**d**) [circle]   (**e**) [figure]   (**f**) [figure]

(**g**) [hexagon]   (**h**) [figure]   (**i**) [figure]

(**j**) [figure]   (**k**) [figure]

(**l**) Bill found when he interviewed young children that many of them thought Figure (j) was a triangle and Figure (k) was not. Can you account for this?

28. (a) Tell whether the indicated points are interior or exterior points of the simple closed curve.

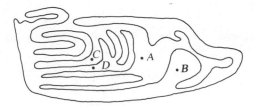

   (b) Can you do the same here, where part of the simple closed curve is hidden? Be careful!

29. Give a technique for distinguishing between the interior and exterior of a simple closed curve without using words like *inside* or *outside*.

30. Which of the polygons in Figure 9-4 are convex?

31. Is the following definition of convex curve equivalent to the one given on page 295? "A simple closed curve is convex if no line intersects it at more than two points."

32. A set that contains the line segment joining any two of its points is called a **convex set**. If set *S* is the closed curve shown below together with its interior, then *S* is a convex set. Remove *as few points as possible,* so *S* will *not* be convex. Tell what is removed and explain why the new set is not convex.

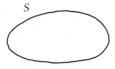

33. Set *T* is the pentagon *ABCDE* shown together with its interior. Describe the largest subset of *T* that contains *B* and is convex.

34. Technically, an angle is the union of two rays. But we refer to the **angles of a polygon** as the union of two sides (segments) of the polygon having a common endpoint. Thus we say that a triangle has three angles, and so on. How many angles do the following polygons have?
   (a) pentagon   (b) decagon   (c) nonagon   (d) heptagon
   (e) hexagon   (f) octagon   (g) 19-gon   (h) *n*-gon

35. Assuming that the "in bounds" part of each of the following is a quadrilateral region, which are open and which are closed?
   (a) football field   (b) basketball court
   (c) tennis court   (d) volleyball court

36. Suppose R is the region consisting of the interior of rectangle $ABCD$ together with side $\overline{AB}$. **(a)** Is this a closed region? **(b)** Is this an open region?

37. What concepts are prerequisite to defining a square? A circle?

38. A simple closed curve drawn in a plane separates it into two regions (besides the curve itself).
   (a) What are the names of these regions?
   (b) Into how many regions does a simple closed curve drawn on the surface of a sphere (like a table tennis ball) separate the surface?
   (c) Repeat (b) for the surface of a torus (doughnut).

MATERIALS

39. For each of these terms give one or more examples of physical models which could be found in an ordinary classroom:
   (a) point   **(b)** line   **(c)** line segment   **(d)** plane
   (e) angle   **(f)** curve   **(g)** simple closed curve **(h)** polygon
   (i) triangle   **(j)** quadrilateral **(k)** hexagon

40. Make a **hexaflexagon** as shown on pages 75-79 of *Patterns and Puzzles in Mathematics* [50] (or another source).

41. Examine an elementary school mathematics series to determine the grade level at which each of the following terms is introduced:
   (a) triangle   **(b)** rectangle   **(c)** parallelogram
   (d) angle   **(e)** quadrilateral **(f)** line segment

9-3
CONGRUENCE; POLYGONS AND CIRCLES

A favorite activity with fifth or sixth graders involves **polyominoes**, shapes formed by cutting along the lines of squared paper. In these grades polyominoes can be used to introduce the important topic of congruence. We will sketch the idea here.

Let's suppose that a sixth grade class is trying to find different **tetrominoes** (polyominoes made from four squares) and that there is a question whether Melissa's tetromino is the same as Scott's:

Melissa's
tetromino

Scott's
tetromino

The issue is settled when one of the children shows that the two tetrominoes are the same by turning Scott's tetromino halfway around to look like Melissa's. Figure 9-5 shows the complete set of tetrominoes found by the class.

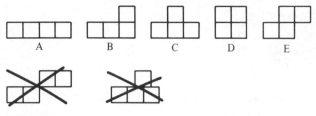

FIGURE 9-5

Shapes like those crossed out are not considered to be polyominoes. Other candidates that may appear to be different tetrominoes are the same as those of Figure 9-5. For example, do you see how these shapes are the same as C and E respectively?

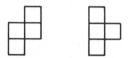

In this scenario we saw how polyominoes provided an experience in which certain concepts of geometry were made meaningful to sixth grade children. We will follow this natural approach to define congruence. We will say that two geometric figures are **congruent** when they can be made to coincide as a result of performing rigid motions. We will discuss rigid motions in some detail in Section 11-3, relying for now on our intuitive understanding (much like the children as they compare polyominoes by turning them as in our example, or by sliding them or flipping them).

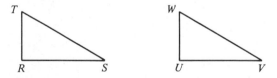

FIGURE 9-6

Figure 9-6 shows two congruent triangles. We write $\triangle RST \cong \triangle UVW$, which indicates not only that the triangles are congruent, but that if they were made to coincide, R would coincide with U, S with V, and T with W. This may seem a bit picky, but indicating this 1-1 correspondence between the vertices helps to identify which parts of the triangles are respectively congruent. For example, from $\triangle RST \cong \triangle UVW$ we can correctly write $\overline{RS} \cong \overline{UV}$, $\overline{RT} \cong \overline{UW}$, $\angle R \cong \angle U$, $\angle S \cong \angle V$, etc., without looking at the sketch.

For two triangles to be congruent it is *necessary* that all of their **corresponding parts** (corresponding sides and corresponding angles) be respectively congruent. This is clear if we expect two triangles to coincide. But there will be times when we wish to conclude that two triangles are congruent without actually verifying that all three sides and all three angles are respectively congruent. Thus the question arises as to what conditions are *sufficient* to show two triangles are congruent. Since this will be an excellent question to explore when we study constructions, we postpone it until Section 11-1. However, we will state two criteria, each of which is sufficient to ensure congruent triangles.

SSS Criterion

If three sides of one triangle are respectively congruent to three sides of another triangle, then the triangles are congruent.

SAS Criterion

If two sides and the *included* angle of one triangle are respectively congruent to two sides and the *included* angle of another triangle, then the triangles are congruent.

To clarify, an angle "included" between two sides is the angle whose rays contain these sides. For example, in $\triangle ABC$ below, $\angle A$ is included between $\overline{AB}$ and $\overline{AC}$, $\angle B$ is included between $\overline{BA}$ and $\overline{BC}$, and $\angle C$ is included between $\overline{CA}$ and $\overline{CB}$:

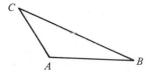

To further distinguish between necessary and sufficient conditions we will test the condition that "two sides of one triangle are respectively congruent to two sides of another triangle." Certainly it is *necessary*, since to have congruent triangles *all* the corresponding parts must be congruent. But clearly it is not *sufficient* to ensure congruent triangles, since we can have $\overline{DE} \cong \overline{GH}$ and $\overline{DF} \cong \overline{GI}$ without having congruent triangles:

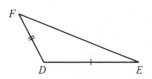 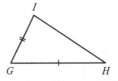

Congruence is an important concept in classifying shapes. For example, to determine whether a quadrilateral is a square, we compare the lengths of its sides and compare the measures of its angles. When considering the sides, we don't really have to know their lengths in centimeters, inches, or other units. All we need to know is that all the sides are the *same* length. An analogous statement is true for the angles. This is much like the matching idea from Section 2-1, page 20, where we could compare the number of students in one set with the number of seats in another set, without knowing the actual number in either set.

We will now use the concept of congruence to define several common geometric figures. Polygons that have all their sides congruent are called **equilateral**. Some equilateral polygons are shown in Figure 9-7. An equilateral quadrilateral is called a **rhombus**. Convex polygons that have all of their angles

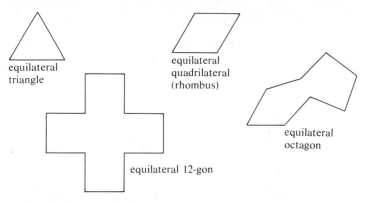

FIGURE 9-7

congruent are called **equiangular**. Figure 9-8 shows some equiangular polygons. A **rectangle** is an equiangular quadrilateral. Note that according to our definition, an equiangular polygon must be convex. In particular, the 12-gon of Figure 9-7 is not considered equiangular, even though all of its angles are congruent.

FIGURE 9-8

Polygons that are both equilateral and equiangular are called **regular**. The most common regular polygons are shown in Figure 9-9. Now we can define a **square** as a regular quadrilateral. More will be said about regular polygons after we clarify a few more preliminary concepts.

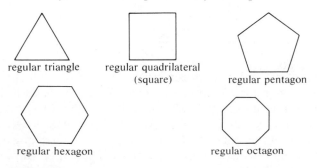

FIGURE 9-9

Figure 9-10 shows a regular **dodecagon** (12-sided polygon). At a glance it looks much like a circle. Figure 9-2 shows a design made by joining each of 32 evenly spaced points to the other points with white thread. Though it is actually a 32-gon (together with its diagonals), it appears to be a circle. In this respect, circles are closely related to polygons and we discuss them next.

FIGURE 9-10

Given a point O and a segment $\overline{OB}$, the set of all points P (in a plane) such that $\overline{OP} \cong \overline{OB}$ is called the **circle** with **center** O and **radius** $\overline{OB}$.

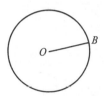

Note that according to this definition, B is a point of the circle (since $\overline{OB} \cong \overline{OB}$), but O, the center, is *not* a point of the circle. Any segment that has its endpoints on the circle is called a **chord**, and any chord that contains the center is called a **diameter**. (When we measure circles later on, the radius and diameter will also refer to the *lengths* of these segments.) Analogous to what we said for polygons, a circle together with its interior is called a **circular region**.

Identify the points and segments in the accompanying figure using the vocabulary for circles.

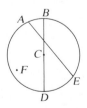

EXAMPLE
9-10

SOLUTION

Point C is the center of the circle.

Points A, B, D, and E are points of the circle.

Points C and F are not points of the circle. They are interior points. (A circle is surely a simple closed curve.)

$\overline{AE}$ and $\overline{BD}$ are chords.

$\overline{BD}$ is a diameter.

$\overline{BC}$ and $\overline{CD}$ are radii.

Important to our later work with compass and straightedge constructions will be the intersection of two circles.

EXAMPLE
9-11

Find all possible intersections of two circles.

SOLUTION

We offer several sketches to show the various possibilities.

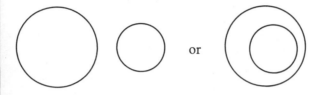

The intersection is empty (no points).

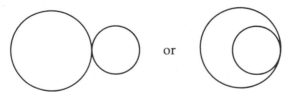

Externally tangent circles.   Internally tangent circles.

The intersection is one point, in which case we say the circles are **tangent**.

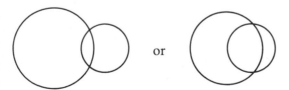

The intersection is two points.

It is impossible to draw two different circles which intersect in three points. In fact, we will find later that given three points (not on the same line) it is possible to draw the unique circle that contains them. We will also investigate other topics related to this section, such as the conditions that tell us when two triangles are congruent.

EXERCISES AND PROBLEMS 9-3

POLYGONS

1. List common examples of shapes that are regular polygons.

2. Most nuts (nuts and bolts type) are shaped like one of these:

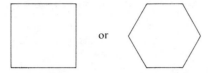

But the controls on certain fixtures (like those on some fire hydrants and natural gas valves outside the house) are shaped like this:

Give the most descriptive name for each shape. Why do you think each shape is used?

3. (a) Which of the polygons in Figure 9-7 are equiangular?
   (b) Which of the polygons in Figure 9-8 are equilateral?
   (c) Draw (if possible) an equiangular triangle which is not equilateral.
   (d) Draw (if possible) an equilateral hexagon which is not equiangular.

4. (a) List three properties of a square.
   (b) For each property you listed in part (a), give an example of a geometric figure that satisfies this one property but is *not* a square.
   (c) We defined a square as a regular quadrilateral. Give several other acceptable definitions.

5. A **scalene** triangle has no sides congruent. An **isosceles** triangle has two sides congruent. If *RSTU* is a square, (a) find two scalene triangles contained in the figure. (b) Find two isosceles triangles contained in the figure.

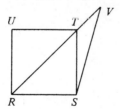

6. Ten bowling pins are placed in the usual pattern. Paint each pin either white or black so that no three pins of the same color will form the vertices of an equilateral triangle.

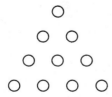

CIRCLES

7. (a) Which is a better physical model for a circle, a wedding band or a cardboard pizza plate?
   (b) Which is a better model for a circular region?

8. (a) Draw a circle which has a radius $\overline{AB}$, a chord $\overline{AC}$, and a diameter $\overline{CD}$. With regard to this circle, what is (b) $\overline{AD}$? (c) $\overline{DB}$?

9. Find all possible intersections of (a) a circle and a line (b) a circle and an angle (c) a circle and a rectangle.

10. In how many points does each of the following intersect a circle?
    (a) one of its diameters   (b) one of its radii
    (c) one of its chords   (d) its center
    (e) an angle with its vertex at the center of the circle
    (f) a smaller circle with the same center

11. The three circles shown intersect at four points. (a) Show with a sketch the least number of points at which three circles can intersect. (b) The greatest number. (c) Show a sketch for each of the remaining possible number of intersections.

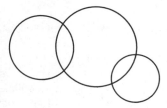

CONGRUENCE

12. Assume that each pair of figures is congruent. Write a mathematical sentence expressing the fact. List the letters in corresponding order.

      **Example**

trapezoid $ABDC \cong$ trapezoid $SRUT$

(a)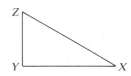

(b)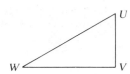

(c)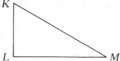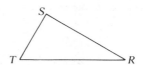

(d)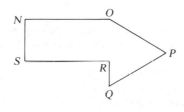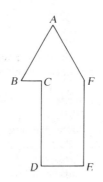

13. Laura and Janet were trying to find different ways to cut a cake into two congruent pieces. How many ways can you find
    (a) so that you cut along the dashed lines of Figure A?
    (b) Find several ways to do this where *none* of the cuts is along the dashed lines.

Figure A   Figure B   Figure C

Note: The possibilities shown in Figures B and C are considered to be the same solution, since the pieces of Figure B are congruent to the pieces of Figure C.

14. David, Carla, Sandy, and Larry want to cut Figure A of the previous problem into four congruent pieces. With this change, repeat parts (a) and (b) of the previous problem.

15. After watching Laura and David and the others, Paul wanted to divide the figure shown into four congruent pieces by cutting along dashed lines. He found two substantially different ways. Can you? Can you find a third way?

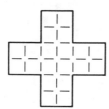

16. A couple bequeathed a parcel of land shaped like this figure

(three-fourths of a square) to their four children. They requested that the land be divided into four congruent pieces (pieces with the same size and shape). How can this be done?

17. (a) Write out in full the sentence abbreviated SSS.
    (b) Write out in full the sentence abbreviated SAS.
    (c) Name the angle included between $\overline{RQ}$ and $\overline{QT}$.
    (d) $\angle P$ of $\triangle MNP$ is included between which two sides?
    (e) For which of the following triangles is the marked angle included between the marked sides?

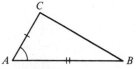  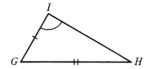

In the remaining parts tell whether the given conditions are examples of SSS, SAS, or neither.
    (f) In $\triangle JKL$ and $\triangle MNO$ we have $\overline{JK} \cong \overline{MN}$, $\overline{KL} \cong \overline{NO}$, and $\angle K \cong \angle N$.
    (g) In $\triangle PQR$ and $\triangle STU$ we have $\overline{PQ} \cong \overline{ST}$, $\overline{PR} \cong \overline{TU}$, and $\angle P \cong \angle T$.
    (h) In $\triangle VWX$ and $\triangle YZA$ we have $\overline{VW} \cong \overline{YZ}$, $\overline{VX} \cong \overline{YZ}$, and $\overline{WX} \cong \overline{YZ}$.

18. Prove that the angles opposite the congruent sides of an isosceles triangle are congruent. (Hint: Draw the median to the base of the isosceles triangle and use SSS.)

COUNTING PROBLEMS

19. A segment whose endpoints are vertices of a convex polygon is called a **diagonal** of the polygon provided it is not a side. For example $\overline{AD}$ is a diagonal of pentagon $ABCDE$, but $\overline{DE}$ is not a diagonal. How many diagonals are there in each of the following (convex) polygons?
    (a) triangle   (b) quadrilateral   (c) pentagon   (d) hexagon
    (e) decagon   (f) 20-gon   (g) n-gon

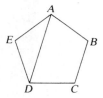

MATERIALS

20. Is the geoboard figure   **(a)** 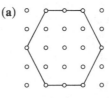   **(b)**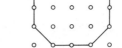

a regular hexagon?   a regular octagon?

*L*21. Make the following figures on a geoboard (if possible):
    (a) rhombus   **(b)** pentagon   *(**c**) equilateral triangle

22. **(a) Pentominoes** are polyominoes consisting of five squares. Find as many different pentominoes as you can. (Two of them are shown below.) Save your set of pentominoes for later reference.
    (b) Hexominoes are polyominoes consisting of six squares. Find ten different hexominoes. (Two of the 35 possibilities are shown below.)

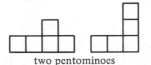 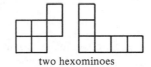

two pentominoes   two hexominoes

23. Cut a strip of paper 2 cm by 15 cm. Tie a single overhand knot (like the first step of tying a shoelace), drawing it taut while keeping it flat. Cut off the ends which protrude from the knot. What regular polygon is formed?! (Do you see why?)

24. Consult an elementary mathematics series to find out at what grades the following topics are introduced:
    (a) square   **(b)** rectangle   **(c)** circle   **(d)** right angle
    (e) congruence

25. There are several rather bad "jokes" based on geometric terms. For example, "polygon" is "what you say after someone steals your parrot," and "coincide" is "what you do when it's raining outside." Can you add one of your own? (It could hardly be worse than these!)

9-4
GEOMETRIC RELATIONS

In our study of number concepts we found several important relations among numbers, such as "equals" and "is less than." In the previous section we introduced congruence, a key geometric relation. In this section we will present more geometric relations and some of their consequences.

To see the connection between relations among numbers and relations among geometric figures we will first compare the relations *equality* for fractions and *congruence* for triangles. To highlight our comparison we list certain features with an example of each:

$= for\ Fractions$ $\cong\ for\ Triangles$

1. Some fractions are $=$.

$$\frac{2}{4} = \frac{9}{18}$$

1. Some triangles are $\cong$.

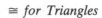
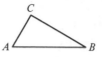

2. Some fractions are not $=$.

$$\frac{2}{4} \ne \frac{4}{16}$$

2. Some triangles are not $\cong$.

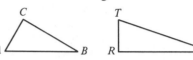

3. Every fraction is $=$ to itself. (Reflexive property of $=$.)
$$\frac{2}{4} = \frac{2}{4}$$

3. Every triangle is $\cong$ to itself. (Reflexive property of $\cong$.)
$$\triangle ABC \cong \triangle ABC.$$

4. If a fraction is $=$ to a second fraction, then the second fraction is $=$ to the first. (Symmetric property of $=$.)
If $\frac{2}{4} = \frac{9}{18}$, then $\frac{9}{18} = \frac{2}{4}$.

4. If a triangle is $\cong$ to a second triangle, then the second triangle is $\cong$ to the first. (Symmetric property of $\cong$.)
If $\triangle ABC \cong \triangle DEF$, then $\triangle DEF \cong \triangle ABC$.

5. If a fraction is $=$ to a second fraction, and if the second fraction is $=$ to a third fraction, then the first fraction is $=$ to the third fraction. (Transitive property of $=$.)
If $\frac{2}{4} = \frac{9}{18}$ and $\frac{9}{18} = \frac{50}{100}$, then $\frac{2}{4} = \frac{50}{100}$.

5. If a triangle is $\cong$ to a second triangle, and if the second triangle is $\cong$ to a third triangle, then the first triangle is $\cong$ to the third triangle. (Transitive property of $\cong$.)
If $\triangle ABC \cong \triangle DEF$ and $\triangle DEF \cong \triangle GHI$, then $\triangle ABC \cong \triangle GHI$.

Though equality is a relation among numbers and congruence is a relation among geometric figures, they both are reflexive, symmetric, and transitive. (Relations that are reflexive, symmetric, and transitive are called **equivalence relations**. The relation "$<$" among numbers is *not* an equivalence relation since it is neither reflexive nor symmetric — though it is transitive. See Problem 23 at the end of this section.)

Lines can be related in two very special ways. Two lines l and m (in the same plane) are called **parallel lines** if they do not intersect. Two lines that intersect to form congruent adjacent angles are called **perpendicular lines**, and the angles formed are called **right angles**. To indicate that lines l and m are parallel we write "$l \parallel m$." To indicate that lines m and n are perpendicular we write "$m \perp n$." We can also indicate in a figure that lines l and m are parallel by using arrowheads (other than on the ends) and that lines m and n are perpendicular by using a box as follows:

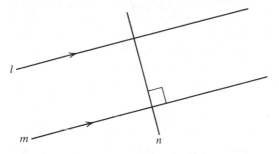

Occasionally we may also say that *segments* are parallel (or perpendicular) if the lines containing them are parallel (or perpendicular). We will comment on the history of the parallel relation and then develop some useful terminology that grows out of a discussion of congruence, parallelism, and perpendicularity.

Most of the geometry presented in this book was known by Euclid around the year 300 B.C. He made a rather cumbersome statement about parallel lines tantamount to saying that given a line l and a point P not on the line, there is exactly one line containing P which is parallel to l. Geometries which include this result about parallel lines are referred to as **Euclidean geometries**.

Euclid referred to his statement about parallel lines as a **postulate** (a statement accepted without proof), but there was considerable doubt whether this conclusion was a postulate or a **theorem** (a statement that can be deduced from the other postulates). The controversy remained unresolved for thousands of years until the nineteenth century, when it was reported independently by Gauss of Germany, Bolyai of Hungary, and Lobatchevsky of Russia that Euclid's statement about parallel lines could not be proved from the other postulates. The coincidence that after two thousand years three people announced the results at about the same time led to considerable suspicion of plagiarism. The record is so controversial it even prompted mathematician-humorist Tom Lehrer to write a song about it in the 1950s.

Parallel Postulate

Given a line and a point not on it, there is exactly one line which contains the point and which is parallel to the line.

To show that this parallel postulate could not be proved from the others, mathematicians invented geometries that satisfied all the postulates *except* the parallel postulate. By showing that the parallel postulate may or may not hold while all the other postulates were satisfied, they proved that the parallel postulate was independent. These other geometries, which did not satisfy the parallel postulate, became known as **non-Euclidean geometries**. Given a line *l* and a point *P* not on *l*, in these new geometries there were either no lines containing *P* and parallel to *l* or there were *many* lines containing *P* and parallel to *l*. These non-Euclidean geometries later proved to be very useful in fields like Einstein's theory of relativity and space travel. In fact, though Euclid's geometry is quite appropriate for ordinary plane geometry, it is not suitable for certain problems that must take the curvature of the earth into account. Thus the controversy about whether a certain statement was a postulate or a theorem back in Euclid's time led to results that proved useful in modern-day space travel. This is only one of many examples of how mathematics considered at one time to be purely abstract later proved to have practical applications.

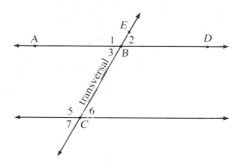

FIGURE 9-11

Having completed our excursion through time and space, we now return to some basic ideas. When two parallel lines are cut by a third line, usually called a **transversal**, certain pairs of angles are congruent and are given names as follows (for simplicity, we will refer to $\angle ABC$ in Figure 9-11 as $\angle 3$, illustrating another way of naming angles):

$$\angle 2 \cong \angle 3 \qquad \textbf{vertical angles}$$

$$\angle 3 \cong \angle 7 \qquad \textbf{corresponding angles}$$

$$\angle 1 \cong \angle 5 \qquad \textbf{corresponding angles}$$

$$\angle 3 \cong \angle 6 \qquad \textbf{alternate interior angles}$$

$$\angle 2 \cong \angle 7 \qquad \textbf{alternate exterior angles}$$

Except for vertical angles, which are formed any time two lines intersect, the terminology listed above is based on having two lines cut by a transversal.

To see that vertical angles $\angle 2$ and $\angle 3$ are congruent, imagine rotating $\angle ABC$ about point *B* until $\overrightarrow{BA}$ coincides with $\overrightarrow{BD}$ (half of a complete turn). Under this rigid motion $\overrightarrow{BC}$ will also rotate half of a complete turn about *B*, so that $\overrightarrow{BC}$ will coincide with $\overrightarrow{BE}$. Thus $\angle ABC$ will coincide with $\angle DBE$. It is always true that the vertical angles formed by intersecting lines are congruent.

The result concerning the congruence of corresponding angles is usually summarized as follows:

> If two parallel lines are cut by a transversal, the corresponding angles are congruent.

The converse is true as well; namely:

> If two lines are cut by a transversal so as to form congruent corresponding angles, then the two lines are parallel.

The statements also hold if "corresponding" is replaced by "alternate interior" or "alternate exterior." Some of the proofs for the statements are considered in the exercises and problems.

A couple of practical problems motivate our next definitions. Suppose we wish to hang a picture at a certain height midway between two windows. To locate the place to hang our picture, we might first determine the correct height, as shown by $\overline{AB}$ in Figure 9-12, and then find the *midpoint M* of this segment. The **midpoint** of $\overline{AB}$ is the point which separates $\overline{AB}$ into two congruent segments. We also say that the midpoint **bisects** the segment.

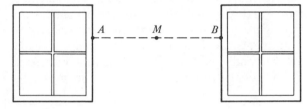

FIGURE 9-12

Our second practical problem is to tell how to cut a pie into eight congruent pieces. To do this, we might first cut it into halves, then fourths, then eighths. When cutting the fourths into eighths, we would be bisecting the angles we had

previously. We use the terminology **bisect an angle** to describe the forming of two new angles from a given angle by positioning a ray that begins at the vertex of the given angle and lies in the interior of the angle in such a way as to form two congruent angles. This new ray is called the **angle bisector**, as shown in the accompanying diagram. $\overrightarrow{BD}$ bisects $\angle ABC$ since $\angle ABD \cong \angle DBC$, and $\overrightarrow{YW}$ bisects $\angle XYZ$ since $\angle XYW \cong \angle WYZ$.

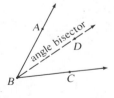 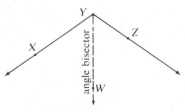

Sometimes we combine the ideas of *perpendicular* and *bisector* and refer to the **perpendicular bisector** of a segment. The perpendicular bisector of a segment $\overline{PQ}$ is the line perpendicular to $\overline{PQ}$ that contains the midpoint of $\overline{PQ}$ as shown:

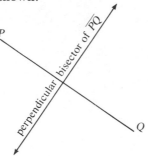

The terms "angle bisector" and "perpendicular bisector" often arise in connection with triangles. The terms "midpoint" and "perpendicular" lead to two further definitions: The segment drawn from a vertex of a triangle to the midpoint of the side opposite the vertex is called the **median** to that side. The segment drawn perpendicularly from a vertex of a triangle to (the line containing) the side opposite the vertex is called the **altitude** to that side. Each of these ideas is illustrated in Figure 9-13. Note the special markings to show congruent angles, congruent segments, and perpendicular lines. Also note that the angle bisector is a ray, the perpendicular bisector is a line, and the median and altitude are segments. Finally observe that an altitude may lie *outside* the triangle, as for $\triangle RST$.

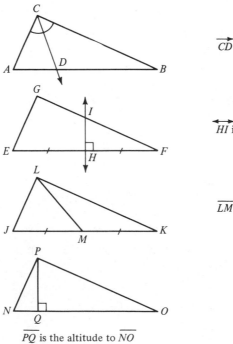

$\overrightarrow{CD}$ is the angle bisector of $\angle ACB$

$\overleftrightarrow{HI}$ is the perpendicular bisector of $\overline{EF}$

$\overline{LM}$ is the median to $\overline{JK}$

$\overline{PQ}$ is the altitude to $\overline{NO}$

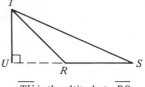

$\overline{TU}$ is the altitude to $\overline{RS}$

FIGURE 9-13

EXERCISES AND PROBLEMS 9-4

PARALLEL AND PERPENDICULAR LINES

1. A quadrilateral with exactly two sides parallel is called a **trapezoid**. A quadrilateral with two pairs of parallel sides is called a **parallelogram**.

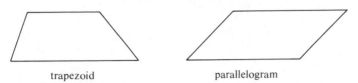

trapezoid   parallelogram

Classify the following as trapezoids, parallelograms (or both or neither):

(a) (rectangle)   (b) (rhombus)

(c) (square)   (d) (regular hexagon)

(e)   (f)   (g)

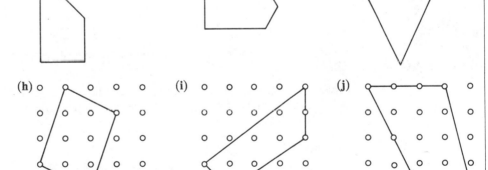

(h) (geoboard figure)   (i) (geoboard figure)   (j) (geoboard figure)

(k) Give your idea of a definition for an **isosceles trapezoid**.

2. In the accompanying figure, name a pair of
   (a) alternate interior angles
   (b) alternate exterior angles
   (c) vertical angles
   (d) corresponding angles.

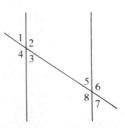

3. Assume $\overleftrightarrow{RY}$, $\overleftrightarrow{UW}$, and $\overleftrightarrow{XZ}$ are straight lines, and that $\overline{RS} \cong \overline{ST}$, $\overleftrightarrow{RS} \parallel \overleftrightarrow{UW}$. Make no other assumptions. Which angles of the figure are necessarily congruent to $\angle R$? Give a reason in each case.

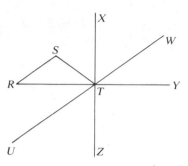

4. Draw a circle with diameter $\overline{XY}$. Pick any point Z on the circle and draw $\angle XZY$. Do this several times and look for a conclusion.

5. Suppose lines j and k lie in the same plane and are each perpendicular to line m. (a) Make a conjecture about lines j and k. (b) Prove your conjecture.

6. Is the following definition for perpendicular lines equivalent to the definition given earlier? "Two lines are perpendicular if their union contains a right angle."

7. Given a line and a point, how many lines can be drawn (in that same plane) which contain the point and are perpendicular to the line if
(a) the point is on the line?   (b) the point is not on the line?

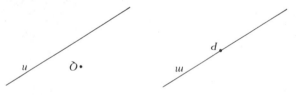

FIGURE 9-14

8. How many times between noon and midnight do the hands of a clock form a right angle? (See Figure 9-14.)

9. We proved that vertical angles are congruent. Assume (without proof) that "if two parallel lines are cut by a transversal, then the corresponding angles are congruent." Use these results to prove that
(a) if two parallel lines are cut by a transversal, then the alternate interior angles are congruent.
(b) if two parallel lines are cut by a transversal, then the alternate exterior angles are congruent.

BISECTORS, ALTITUDES, MEDIANS, AND MIDPOINTS

10. Draw a large triangle, $\triangle RST$.
(a) Sketch the altitude to side $\overline{RS}$ and label it a.
(b) Sketch the median to side $\overline{ST}$ and label it m.
(c) Sketch the perpendicular bisector of side $\overline{RT}$ and label it p.
(d) Sketch the angle bisector of $\angle S$ and label it b.
(e) Which of these are lines? rays? segments?

11. **(a)** Draw △XYZ so that the altitude to $\overline{XY}$ lies inside the triangle and the altitude to $\overline{YZ}$ lies outside the triangle.
(b) Where does the altitude to $\overline{XZ}$ lie, inside or outside the triangle?

12. **(a)** Repeat the previous problem (both parts) so that the answer to (b) is different.
(b) Can a median, altitude, angle bisector, or perpendicular bisector of a triangle ever lie on a side of the triangle? Give examples of the possibilities.

13. Draw any quadrilateral. Connect the midpoints of the sides (in order) to form a new quadrilateral.
(a) What seems to be true about this quadrilateral?
(b) Test your conclusion on several more examples.

14. Show by a sketch that the requirement that the angle bisector lie in the interior of the angle is necessary if we desire an angle to have only one angle bisector.

*15. It is easy to find three or four nails on a geoboard which have the property that among all segments having a pair of these nails as endpoints, no segment has a midpoint located at a nail. Is it possible to find five such nails? (Hint: Coordinatize the geoboard and consider whether the coordinates of the points selected are even or odd.)

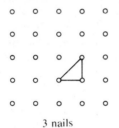

3 nails

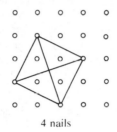

4 nails

PARALLEL POSTULATE

16. Suppose we say that vertical lines are lines which pass through the center of the earth. Are two vertical lines parallel according to this definition?

17. **Finite Geometries**. We will now consider a geometry having precisely four points, which we will denote A, B, C, and D. In this geometry, there are no other points. Each set of two points will be called a line. For example, {A, B} and {D, B} are lines.

Lines having a point in common will be called intersecting, while lines having no points in common will be called parallel. For example, {A, B} intersects {D, B} at B, while {A, B} and {D, C} are parallel. The set consisting of all four points will be the only plane in this finite geometry.

Answer the following questions, based on the above assumptions.
(a) Are {A, B} and {B, A} the same line or different lines?
(b) Name all the lines. How many are there?
(c) Find all lines that contain D and are parallel to (do not intersect) {A, B}.
(d) Which of conditions (1), (2), and (3) from page 292 hold in this geometry?
(e) Does the parallel postulate hold in this geometry?
*(f) Devise a seven-point geometry that satisfies (1), (2), and (3) from page 292. (Use three points per line.) How many lines are there in this geometry? Does the parallel postulate hold?
*(g) Repeat part (f) for nine points.
*(h) Find a finite geometry with five points per line that satisfies (1), (2), (3), and the parallel postulate.

18. Suppose our geometry is restricted to all points in this closed square region, where "lines" are defined to be segments with (both) endpoints on the polygon. Thus in this geometry, $\overline{AB}$ and $\overline{CD}$ are "lines."

If we define two "lines" to be "parallel" if they do not intersect, then is $\overline{AB}$ "parallel" to $\overline{CD}$? Does the parallel postulate hold?

19. Assume that the by-laws for the Salamander Lodge contain the following rules:

   (1) Every committee shall have at least two members.

   (2) Every member shall be on at least two (different) committees.

   (3) Given a committee and a member not on the committee, there is exactly one committee that has this member and none of the members of the given committee.

   (a) Find the smallest number of members (other than 0) so that rules (1) and (2) are satisfied. Answer by listing all the members and the committees to which they belong.

   (b) Find the smallest number of members (other than 0) so that rules (1), (2), and (3) are all satisfied.

20. Show that the commutative and associative properties are in general *independent* of one another by finding (a) a set S and an operation $*$ such that $*$ is both associative and commutative on S, *and* (b) a set T and an operation $\#$ such that $\#$ is associative but not commutative.

*21. Find a set U and an operation $\circ$ such that $\circ$ is commutative but not associative.

PROPERTIES OF RELATIONS

22. A relation is called **reflexive** if for every member b of the replacement set, b is related to b. For example, the relation "equals" is reflexive since for every number b, $b = b$. A relation is called **symmetric** if whenever b is related to c, then c is related to b. For example, the relation "equals" is symmetric since whenever $b = c$, then $c = b$.

   A relation is called **transitive** if whenever b is related to c and c is related to d, then b is related to d. For example, the relation "equals" is transitive since whenever $b = c$ and $c = d$, then $b = d$.

EXAMPLE
9-12

Is "$<$" for the set of whole numbers reflexive? symmetric? transitive?

SOLUTION

"$<$" is not reflexive. 2 is a whole number, but "$2 < 2$" is false.
"$<$" is not symmetric. $2 < 3$, but "$3 < 2$" is false.
Transitive holds. If $b < c$ and $c < d$, then $b < d$. For example, given $2 < 3$ and $3 < 5$, $2 < 5$ is true.

Tell whether each of the following is reflexive, symmetric, and transitive. Use the indicated replacement set for both variables.

(a) "less than or equals" for the set of whole numbers
(b) "does not equal" for the set of whole numbers
(c) "is taller than" for the set of all people
(d) "lives within a mile of" for the set of all people
(e) "is the sister of" for the set of all people
(f) "is the spouse of" for the set of all people
(g) "matches" for the set P, where $P = \{ \{a, b, c\}, \{a, b\}, \{a, c\}, \{b, c\}, \{a\}, \{b\}, \{c\}, \{ \ \} \}$
(h) "is a subset of" for the set P as in part (g)
(i) "is a proper subset of" for the set P as in part (g)
(j) "is disjoint with" for the set P as in part (g)
(k) "divides" for the set of whole numbers
(l) "is parallel to" for the set of lines in a plane
(m) "intersects" for the set of lines in a plane
(n) "is perpendicular to" for the set of lines in a plane

MATERIALS

(In Problems 23-26, "draw" means using compass and straightedge.)

23. Draw any angle with vertex V. Now draw a circle with V as center. Label the points where the circle intersects the angle A and B. Now draw a circle with center A and radius $\overline{AV}$ and another circle with center B and radius $\overline{BV}$. These last two circles intersect at V and some other point. Label this point W and draw $\overrightarrow{VW}$. What have you constructed?

24. Let $\overline{CD}$ be any segment. Draw a circle with center C and radius $\overline{CD}$. Draw a second circle with center D and radius $\overline{DC}$. Now draw the line joining the two points where these circles intersect. What have you constructed?

25. Draw a line m and a point P not on m. Draw a circle with center P so that it intersects line m at two points, J and K. Draw the circles with centers J and K and radii $\overline{JP}$ and $\overline{KP}$ respectively. These two circles intersect at P and some other point. Label this point Q and draw $\overline{PQ}$. What have you constructed?

26. Draw a line n and a point G on n. Draw a circle with center G so that it intersects n at two points, E and F. Draw the circles with centers E and F and radii $\overline{EF}$ and $\overline{FE}$ respectively. Now draw the line joining the two points where these circles intersect. What have you constructed?

Measurement

10-1
LENGTH AND PERIMETER

Few, if any, topics have as many practical applications as measurement. Time, temperature, length, weight, and capacity are just a few of the things we commonly measure. These concepts and others involving measurement are commonly found in elementary school mathematics and science books. In this text we have already encountered measurement in a deeper setting when using number lines and area models to motivate the definitions for addition and multiplication, which suggests measurement's ties to other mathematical concepts. In fact, even counting is a simple form of measurement.

A fairly unsophisticated example of measurement may provide us with some insight into the concept. Let's say Roger is camping in a Canadian wilderness. In pitching his tent, he observes that he needs to cut two poles as tall as his shoulder. In "measuring" the desired amount, he compares his sticks to a given unit, in this case the distance from the ground to his shoulder. His own body provides him with a set of references for making various comparisons. The water is "ankle deep," the grass is "knee high," etc. This is not unlike using a meter stick marked off in centimeters or a yardstick marked off in inches. In each case, the measurement is essentially a comparison to some known unit.

The fact that **measurement** is a comparison to some known unit will be taken as our working definition. In practice this may be quite obscured, as in the measurement of temperature. We indirectly learn the temperature from a thermometer because the mercury in the thermometer "rises" and "falls" consistently according to temperature. In this section we will emphasize straightforward measurements of things like length, area, and volume.

We begin with length. The way in which length, congruence, and real numbers are related to each other is interesting, but a full discussion of these ideas is not possible in this brief treatment. We will be content now to review the sequence in which these topics have been developed in this text, with emphasis on the geometry involved.

Let's reexamine the steps in marking coordinates on a number line. Arbitrarily select two points on a (horizontal) line and label them 0 and 1, with 0 to the left of 1. The segment with endpoints 0 and 1 now becomes our unit of measure.

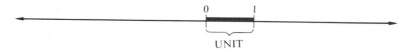

Mark off copies of the unit to the right along the line and label the points we obtain in this way 2, 3, 4, 5, ...

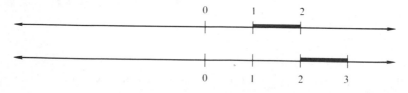

Subdivide the resulting segments into congruent pieces to determine the points corresponding to 1/2, 3/2, 5/2, 7/2, ...

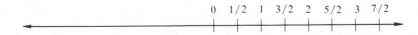

Using the same technique, mark off points corresponding to 1/3, 2/3, 4/3, 5/3, . . . and the other fractions.

Once all fractions are obtained in this manner, flip the line using a perpendicular line through the origin as the "mirror" and mark off all the points corresponding to the negative numbers. A few typical points are labeled in this figure:

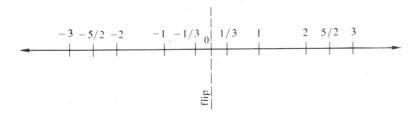

By this process, we obtain all points on the line that correspond to rational numbers. Between these points are other points corresponding to irrational numbers like $\sqrt{2}$ and π and their opposites. We found in Section 8-2 that irrational numbers like these have decimal expansions which define for them unique positions on the number line that we can approximate as closely as we like by rational numbers.

To measure an arbitrary segment $\overline{AB}$, we use rigid motions to position it on the number line with A at the origin and B lined up with some other point (call it P) to the right of the origin. The (positive) real number associated with P is what we refer to as the **length** of $\overline{AB}$. We will use the notation "$\overline{AB}$" to refer to the segment and "AB" to refer to the length of the segment. Thus "$\overline{AB}$" is a set of points while "AB" is a number. The length AB is also called the **distance** from A to B.

There is an important property of measurement that we wish to discuss next. Assume that you are planning to drive from Chicago to Louisville and wish to know the distance. Suppose you consult a mileage chart included on a map of the eastern United States and learn that it is 285 kilometers (177 miles) from Chicago to Indianapolis and 182 kilometers (113 miles) from Indianapolis to Louisville. Then you could *add* the distances and deduce that it is about 467 kilometers (290 miles) from Chicago to Louisville via Indianapolis. This additive property of measure is indeed useful.

It is not hard to see that application of the additive property of measure has certain conditions imposed on it. It would be quite misleading, for instance, to add the distance between Chicago and Boston to the distance between Boston and Louisville to obtain the distance from Chicago to Louisville, unless of course you planned to travel via Boston. The reason it works for Indianapolis but not for Boston is that Indianapolis is "between" (at least as far as driving is concerned) Chicago and Louisville while Boston is not. We state the

☐ Additive Property for Lengths

> If B is between A and C, then $AB + BC = AC$.

Sometimes it is useful to find the **perimeter** of a polygon, the sum of the lengths of its sides. For example, we may wish to know how much weatherstripping is needed to go around a (rectangular) door. To determine this, we would probably measure two unlike sides, add, and double the results.

Though it doesn't make sense to talk about the "sum of the lengths of the sides" of a circle, we can still give meaning to the term *perimeter* in that context. For example, if we used a piece of string to represent a circle we could cut it and lay it out to form a segment.

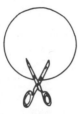

The segment would, of course, have a length. This length corresponds to the "perimeter" of the circle and is called the **circumference**.

Another way to view the circumference of a circle is in terms of the perimeters of regular polygons that closely approximate the circle. We saw in Figures 9-2 and 9-10 how the 32-gon and the dodecagon closely approximated circles. Using this idea, the circumference of a circle can be "squeezed" as narrowly as we like between the known perimeters of certain polygons.

We can obtain a crude approximation for the circumference of a circle as follows: Suppose we have a circle whose radius has length r. (From now on we say that "the radius of the circle is r," adopting the common practice of referring to both the *segment* joining a point of the circle to its center and the *length* of this segment as the "radius." Similarly, the term "diameter" will refer to both a segment and a length.) We inscribe a regular hexagon in the circle as shown in Figure 10-1(a) and observe that the circumference of the circle is slightly more than the perimeter of the hexagon, which can be shown to be $6r$.

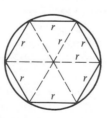

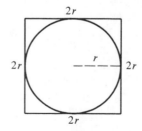

FIGURE 10-1(a)   **FIGURE 10-1(b)**

Next we circumscribe a square around the circle, as shown in Figure 10-1(b), and observe that the circumference of the circle is less than $8r$, the perimeter of the square. Letting C denote the circumference of a circle with radius r, we have

$$6r < C < 8r, \text{ or}$$

$$3 \times 2r < C < 4 \times 2r.$$

Since the diameter is twice the radius, we can replace $2r$ by d and write

$$3d < C < 4d.$$

Thus the circumference of a circle is between 3 and 4 times the diameter. The actual value is called π, or **pi**, and can be shown to be approximately 3.14.

More exact values of π can be obtained by refining the process of using perimeters of regular polygons or by other methods, for π occurs in many significant ways other than as the ratio of circumference to diameter in a circle. In Section 12-1 we will see that π can be approximated by pitching pennies!

We close this section with a closer look at similar triangles, which were mentioned briefly in the problems of Section 6-1. Recall that similar triangles are triangles whose corresponding angles are congruent and whose corresponding sides are proportional.

While it is *necessary* that all three pairs of corresponding angles be congruent and that corresponding sides be proportional, it is *sufficient* that two pairs of corresponding angles be congruent.

AA Criterion

If two angles of one triangle are respectively congruent to two angles of another triangle, then the triangles are similar.

The AA criterion gives us a powerful tool in solving problems, best illustrated by a few examples.

Find the unknown side x, where angles are congruent as indicated.

EXAMPLE
10-1

(a)

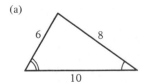

(b)

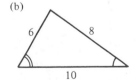

(a) We wish to write a proportion involving x and some of the known quantities. We write our first ratio in terms of x, the unknown side, and 10, the side corresponding to x in the other triangle. We recognize x and 10 as corresponding sides because each is opposite the "unmarked"

angle in its respective triangle. The other known side of the small triangle is 2, which is opposite the "single-marked" angle, so its corresponding side in the big triangle is 6, since it is also opposite the "single-marked" angle. This gives us

$$\frac{x}{10} = \frac{2}{6}, \text{ or } 6x = 20, \text{ or } x = \frac{20}{6} = 3\frac{1}{3}.$$

Our proportion takes this form:

$$\frac{\left(\begin{array}{c}\text{side opposite } \textit{unmarked angle} \\ \text{of } \textit{small} \text{ triangle}\end{array}\right)}{\left(\begin{array}{c}\text{side opposite } \textit{unmarked angle} \\ \text{of } \textit{big} \text{ triangle}\end{array}\right)} = \frac{\left(\begin{array}{c}\text{side opposite } \textit{single-marked} \\ \text{angle of } \textit{small} \text{ triangle}\end{array}\right)}{\left(\begin{array}{c}\text{side opposite } \textit{single-marked} \\ \text{angle of } \textit{big} \text{ triangle}\end{array}\right)}$$

(b) This time our corresponding sides are x and 8 (each opposite the "double-marked" angle) and 7 and 10, each opposite the "unmarked" angle. Our proportion is

$$\frac{x}{8} = \frac{7}{10}, \text{ so } 10x = 56, \text{ or } x = 5.6.$$

Note that in Example 10-1 we used "side" to refer to both a segment and its length, just as we use "diameter" to refer to both a segment and a length.

Sometimes it is a bit more difficult to identify the similar triangles, as in the next example.

EXAMPLE
10-2

Find x in this figure, given that ABC is a right triangle with altitude $\overline{CD}$.

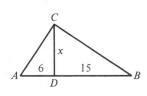

It may be helpful to isolate the three triangles involved. We label $\angle A$ with one mark and $\angle B$ with two marks, and mark the right angles according to the given information.

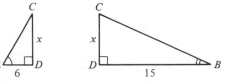

We have $\triangle ACD \sim \triangle ABC$ and $\triangle CBD \sim \triangle ABC$ by the AA criterion. This entitles us to conclude that $\angle ACD$ of the first triangle is congruent to $\angle ABC$ of the third triangle (by our *necessary* condition for similar triangles) and also that $\angle BCD \cong \angle BAC$. (In the next section we will prove a general theorem that will allow us to conclude this directly.) What we have so far is shown in this sketch:

 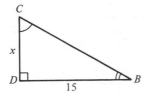

We write a proportion, beginning with x of the first triangle. Being opposite the "single-marked" angle, it corresponds to 15 of the second triangle. Moreover, the 6 of the first triangle corresponds to the x of the second triangle. This gives us

$$\frac{x}{15} = \frac{6}{x}, \text{ or } x^2 = 90, \text{ or } x = \sqrt{90} \doteq 9.5.$$

Many interesting and valuable activities about similar triangles can be done in the middle school grades. A few examples will be presented in the problems.

EXERCISES AND PROBLEMS 10-1

LENGTH

1. Draw a sketch locating points A, B, and C so that $PQ = 10$, $QR = 12$, and $PR =$
   (a) 22   (b) 2   (c) 11.

2. (a) What is wrong with this statement? "If B is between A and C, then $\overline{AB} + \overline{BC} = \overline{AC}$."
   (b) Find two different ways to correct the statement.

3. Knowing the distance from Chicago to Boston and the distance from Boston to Louisville does tell you a little about the distance from Chicago to Louisville. What does it tell you?

4. Sketch all triangles each of whose sides has length 1, 2, 3, 4, or 5. The triangles may be scalene, isosceles, or equilateral. Two examples are given:

 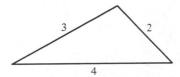

5. An amusement park has installed a system of railings to organize the long lines waiting to ride. Riders can either enter at A to board the ride at B or enter at C to board the ride at

D. Find dimension *x* so that the length of the dashed lines will be the same. (Assume all openings are 1 meter wide and that the path is centered between the rails.)

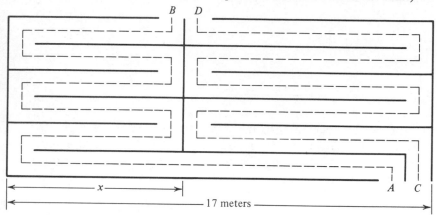

PERIMETER

6. Find the perimeter of each:
   (a) a rectangle with length 8 and width 5
   (b) a square with side 7
   (c) an isosceles triangle with base 5 and (congruent) sides 7
   (d) a regular pentagon with side 11

7. Find the perimeter of each:

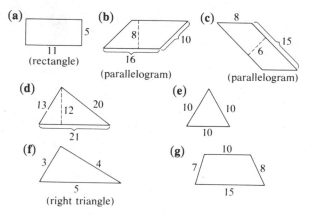

(a) 5, 11 (rectangle)
(b) 8, 10, 16 (parallelogram)
(c) 8, 15, 6 (parallelogram)
(d) 13, 12, 20, 21
(e) 10, 10, 10
(f) 3, 4, 5 (right triangle)
(g) 10, 7, 8, 15

8. A certain frame material is 1 inch wide. How long a piece of this frame material is needed to go around a 5″ × 7″ picture? (Be careful!)

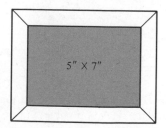

5″ × 7″

9. Lake Temagami in Ontario is shaped something like this. It is up to 5 miles wide and has a very jagged shoreline and many islands. One resort brochure said it has over 3000 miles of shoreline. Is this possible? Explain.

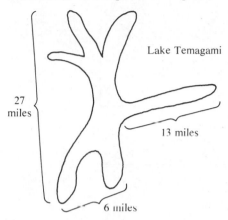

Lake Temagami

27 miles

13 miles

6 miles

10. Find all triangles whose sides have lengths which are whole numbers and whose perimeter is 19.

CIRCLES

*L*11. Draw a circle with diameter 10 cm. Measure its circumference, explaining your method.

12. Find the exact circumference (in terms of π) of
   (a) a circle with diameter 6   **(b)** a circle with radius 10.

13. Find the exact radius (in terms of π) of
   (a) a circle with circumference 20
   (b) a circle with circumference 15π
   (c) a circle with diameter 18.

14. A can is just large enough to hold three tennis balls. Which is greater, its height or its circumference?

15. A Costa Rican lumberman sometimes needs to know the diameter of a tree before deciding whether to cut it down. He does this by wrapping a string completely around the tree and then folding it a whole number of times to estimate the diameter.
   (a) How many times does he fold it?
   (b) What is the lumberman's estimate for the diameter of a tree if the string around it measures 270 centimeters?

16. Do the following problems about π from Section 8-2:
   (a) 11   **(b)** 12   **(c)** 13   **(d)** 14   **(e)** 15   **(f)** 31

17. (a) Pick any point P inside a circle. Draw any four chords $\overline{AB}, \overline{CD}, \overline{EF}$, and $\overline{GH}$ which contain P. Measure the eight segments $\overline{AP}, \overline{BP}, \overline{CP}, \ldots , \overline{HP}$. Compare $AP \times BP$, $CP \times DP$, $EP \times FP$, and $GP \times HP$ and describe your results.
   (b) What unit of measure (inches, centimeters, millimeters) is most appropriate for this problem?

*18. Find a 1-1 correspondence between the points (in a plane) outside a circle and the points inside the circle other than the center. (Hint: Using the radius of the circle as 1 unit, form a ratio of distances from the center of the circle.) Notice that even for a tiny circle we can match all the points in the plane outside the circle with a proper subset of points inside!

SIMILAR TRIANGLES

19. Find x and y.

(a)

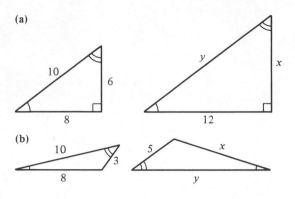

(b)

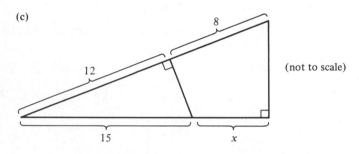

(c)

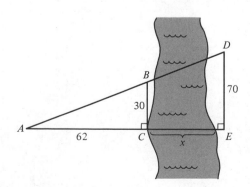

(not to scale)

20. Do Problem 38, Section 6-1.

21. Do Problem 39, Section 6-1.

22. To determine the width of a river, Mrs. Waters and her eighth grade class sighted right triangles ABC and ADE and made the following measurements: $BC = 30$ meters, $DE = 70$ meters, $AC = 62$ meters.
   (a) Set up a proportion involving x, the length of $\overline{CE}$ (the width of the river at C).
   (b) Find x.

23. (a) How many ways are there to fill in four blanks with the numbers 1, 2, 3, and 6, one number per blank?
    (b) If the blanks are arranged to form a proportion, how many of the ways will result in a correct proportion? (Show them.)

MATERIALS

24. Do Problem 29, Section 8-2.

25. Jan's eyes are 150 centimeters above the ground. She sees the tip of a tree in a mirror which is lying on the ground and makes the measurements shown. How high is the tree?

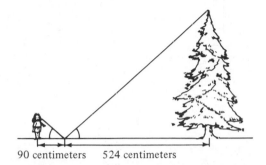

90 centimeters   524 centimeters

26. A sixth grade class found that Tony's shadow was 134 centimeters long, while a telephone pole cast a shadow 751 centimeters long. Tell what you can about the height of the pole.

27. A **stadia device** is a primitive instrument capable of measuring lengths. It can be fashioned from a cardboard mailing tube, sealed off at one end (except for a pinhole) and fitted with two parallel threads at the other end. It is convenient to make the length 100 times the distance between the parallel threads. Then a team determines the length "cut off" on a ruler by the threads as it is sighted through the stadia device. By similar triangles we see that the distance from the viewer to the ruler is 100 times the length "cut off" on the ruler.

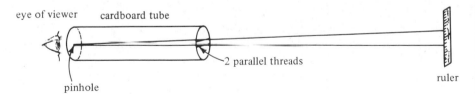

eye of viewer   cardboard tube

2 parallel threads

pinhole

ruler

    (a) If 12 centimeters is "cut off" on the ruler, how far away is it from the viewer? (Answer in appropriate units.)
    (b) Label the triangles and prove they are similar. What are the assumptions? (You may wish to draw in the altitude from the pinhole to the ruler.)
    (c) Make a stadia device and try it!

28. A **hypsometer** is another primitive instrument. It is capable of measuring heights. It can be fashioned from a piece of cardboard, a piece of squared paper, a straw, some string,

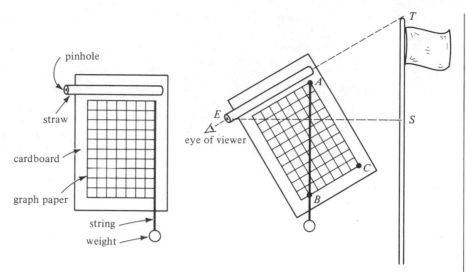

Figure A   Figure B

and a weight (Figure A); it is inclined to sight a point T as shown in Figure B.
(a) If $AC = 10$ units, $BC = 6$ units, and $ES = 12$ meters, find TS.
(b) Is this the height of a flagpole? Explain.
*__(c)__ Prove that $\triangle ABC \sim \triangle ETS$.
(d) Make a hypsometer and try it!

10-2
ANGLE MEASURE

While length, area, and volume go a long way to describe the size of various geometric figures, there is still another important way to measure certain figures. This is angle measurement. The techniques are much the same in that we measure an angle by seeing how many unit angles will "fit" in its interior, but there are some striking differences.

In elementary work, the most common unit of measure for angles is the **degree**. It is the angle formed by rotating a ray 1/360 of a complete turn. Since the amount of rotation is so small, it is difficult to distinguish the two rays unless they are drawn quite long. The symbol for one degree is "1°." Since 90 of these

l° angle

1° angles will fit in the interior of a right angle, we say that a right angle has measure 90°. Some other typical measurements are shown in Figure 10-2.

Of course, angles may lie in a variety of positions. The important thing to remember is that according to our approach, an angle is measured by seeing

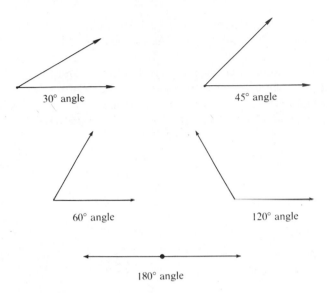

FIGURE 10-2

how many unit angles fit "side by side" in its *interior*. Thus $\angle ABC$ has a
measure of 72° since 72 1° angles would fit in its interior. We denote this

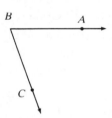

$m(\angle ABC) = 72°$. In this book and in most others where an angle is defined as
the union of two rays, its measure is not 288°, even though 288 1° angles would
fit in its *exterior*. This way of measuring angles means that angles never exceed
180° in measurement. Figure 10-3 shows that when we consider angles of 160°,

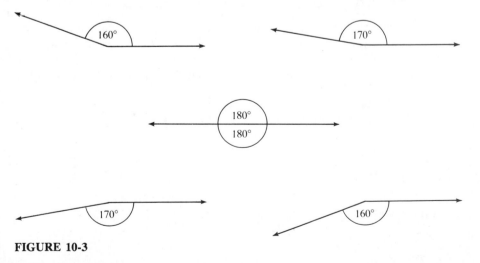

FIGURE 10-3

170°, 180°, "190°," etc., what we might consider to be a "190° angle" is actually a 170° angle since its *interior* contains 170 1° angles. (Note also that a 180° angle can be measured either of two ways with the same result.) Unlike measuring the lengths of segments or the areas of polygons, there is a limit on how large angle measures can get (180°) when we measure using the method described.

Next we seek the analog to the additive property for lengths. Note that in Figure 10-4 we have $m(\angle AOB) = 130°$ and $m(\angle BOC) = 70°$, but $m(\angle AOC)$ is 160° (as in Figure 10-3). Thus $m(\angle AOB) + m(BOC) \neq m(\angle AOC)$. The

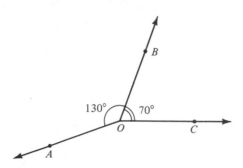

FIGURE 10-4

difficulty arises because $\overrightarrow{OB}$ lies in the *exterior* of $\angle AOC$. Hence for additivity we require that the common side $\overrightarrow{OB}$ of the two given angles lie in the *interior* of the angle formed by $\overrightarrow{OA}$ and $\overrightarrow{OC}$. This is analogous to saying, in terms of the additive property for lengths, that B is *between* A and C. This gives us the

☐ Additive Property for Angle Measure

> If $\overrightarrow{OB}$ lies in the interior of $\angle AOC$, then $m(\angle AOB) + m(\angle BOC) = m(\angle AOC)$.

As you probably know, the instrument commonly used to measure angles is the **protractor**, one version of which is shown in Figure 10-5. To use the protractor to measure an angle, position the bottom of the arrow at the vertex of the angle and align the protractor so that one ray lies along the "zero edge" and the other

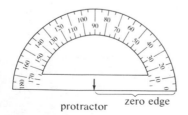

protractor   zero edge

FIGURE 10-5

ray lies somewhere between the 0 and the 180 marks. Figure 10-6 shows the
measurement of a 135° angle and a 50° angle.

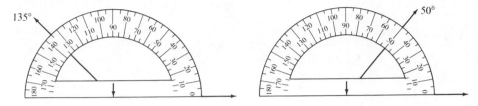

FIGURE 10-6

There is a common classification scheme for angles and triangles based on
angle measure. As mentioned earlier, right angles have a measure of 90°.
Angles whose measures are less than 90° are called **acute angles**, and angles
whose measures exceed 90° are called **obtuse angles**. Triangles are classified in
much the same way. Triangles that contain a right angle are called **right
triangles**. Triangles that contain an obtuse angle are called **obtuse triangles**.
Triangles with all three angles acute are called **acute triangles**.

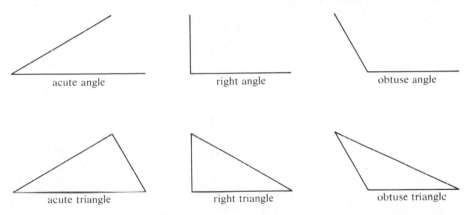

In right triangles, the side opposite the right angle is called the **hypotenuse**, and
the other two sides are called the **legs**. Thus in right $\triangle ABC$, $\overline{AB}$ is the
hypotenuse, while $\overline{AC}$ and $\overline{BC}$ are the legs.

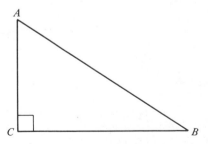

Our main goal in this section is to find the sum of the measures of the
angles of a triangle. This is an easy consequence of our results concerning

parallel lines. We start with any triangle $\triangle ABC$ and draw $\overleftrightarrow{DE}$ through B parallel to $\overline{AC}$, as shown in Figure 10-7.

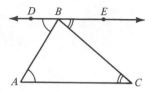

FIGURE 10-7

Then $\angle A \cong \angle DBA$ and $\angle C \cong \angle CBE$ (Why?). Since congruent angles have equal measures, we have for the sum of the measures of the angles of $\triangle ABC$,

$$m(\angle A) \quad + m(\angle ABC) + m(\angle C) =$$
$$m(\angle DBA) + m(\angle ABC) + m(\angle CBE) =$$
$$m(\angle DBE) = 180°$$

(Do you see where we used the additive property for angle measure?) We summarize this important theorem:

> The sum of the measures of the angles of a triangle is 180°.

Problem 16 suggests a graphic way of illustrating this idea. It is worth noting that this theorem depends on the parallel postulate. In non–Euclidean geometries the sum of the measures of the angles of a triangles isn't 180°. See, for example, Problem 26 of Section 10-4, where the sum exceeds 180° in a geometry that has no parallel lines.

As a corollary to our main theorem we have the following:

> If two angles of one triangle are respectively congruent to two angles of another triangle, then the third angles are also congruent.

The study of angle measure will be revisited in Section 11-1 when we do compass and straightedge constructions.

EXERCISES AND PROBLEMS 10-2

DEFINITIONS

1. A **scalene** triangle is one with no two sides congruent. With this and our other definitions, we can classify triangles according to both sides and angles. Sketch an example of each of the following, or write "impossible" if appropriate.
   (a) scalene triangle
   (b) isosceles scalene triangle
   (c) isosceles obtuse triangle
   (d) isosceles right triangle
   (e) obtuse right triangle
   (f) equilateral acute triangle
   (g) equilateral obtuse triangle
   (h) equilateral right triangle
   (i) scalene right triangle
   (j) acute right triangle

2. Two angles are **complementary** if the sum of their measures is 90°. Two angles are **supplementary** if the sum of their measures is 180°. What is the measure of an angle complementary to an angle with measure
(a) 42°? (b) 88°? (c) x°?

3. Answer the previous question when *complementary* is replaced by *supplementary*.

4. One of two supplementary angles has a measure three times the other one. How large are the angles?

5. An **exterior angle** on a triangle is an angle formed by one side of the triangle and the extension of another side. Thus $\angle CAD$ is an exterior angle of $\triangle ABC$. Prove that $m(\angle CAD) = m(\angle B) + m(\angle C)$.

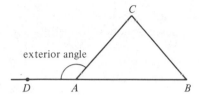

ANGLES IN POLYGONS

6. One acute angle of a right triangle measures 60°. Find the measure of the other acute angle.

7. Give all possible answers in each case:
(a) The measure of one angle of an isosceles triangle is 100°. What are the measures of the other angles?
(b) The measure of one angle of an isosceles triangle is 20°. What are the measures of the other angles?

8. $\triangle PQR$ has an exterior angle with measure 107° and an interior angle with measure 62°. Find the measure of angle Q.

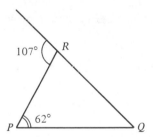

9. Find the sum of the measures of the angles of a (convex)
(a) quadrilateral (b) pentagon (c) hexagon (d) 20-gon.

10. What is the sum of the measures of the angles of this non-convex polygon?

11.

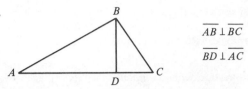

$$\overline{AB} \perp \overline{BC}$$

$$\overline{BD} \perp \overline{AC}$$

(a) How many right triangles are contained in the figure? Name each of them.
(b) Which two triangles contain $\angle A$ and a right angle?
(c) What are the third angles of these two triangles?
(d) Are the third angles congruent? Why or why not?

ANGLES AND PARALLEL LINES

12. Parallel lines m and n are cut by a transversal t.
(a) If $m(\angle 1) = 70°$, find the measures of the other angles.
(b) Name a pair of congruent angles.
(c) Name a pair of complementary angles.
(d) Name a pair of supplementary angles.

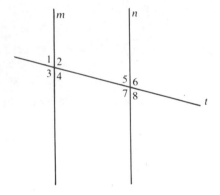

13. (a) If $\angle RVL \cong \angle WLV$, then which of the lines (if any) must be parallel?
(b) If $\angle ABD \cong \angle CDE$, then which of the lines (if any) must be parallel?

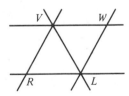

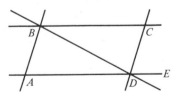

14. l_1, l_2, l_3, and l_4 are straight lines. Are any of the lines parallel? How can you tell?

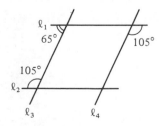

15. Why is $\angle A \cong \angle DBA$ in Figure 10-7?

MATERIALS AND CALCULATORS

*L*16. Draw several different-shaped (rather large) triangles on separate sheets of paper. Tear off the "corners" and tape them together as shown to determine the sum of the angles. Comment on your observation.

NOTE: The diagram is drawn inaccurately.

 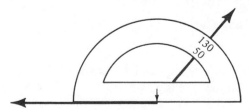

*C*17. In a right triangle, the ratio of the leg opposite a given acute angle to the leg adjacent to a given angle is called the **tangent** of the angle. For example, in the triangle shown, the tangent of $\angle A$ is 3/4 = .75. Use a calculator with a tangent key (usually $\boxed{\text{TAN}}$) to find the tangent of the following angles: **(a)** 45°   **(b)** 30°   **(c)** 40°   **(d)** 52°

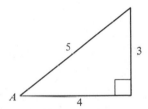

*C*18. Use the results of the previous problem to draw on graph paper angles with (approximately) the given measures.

19. Prove that AAS ("two angles and non-included side criterion") follows from ASA ("two angles and included side criterion").

*20. Starting with three congruent squares, we form angles *X*, *Y*, and *Z* as shown. Prove $m(\angle X) + m(\angle Y) = m(\angle Z)$.

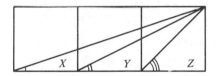

21. John's protractor has two sets of numbers. He can't tell whether the angle shown is 50° or 130°. How do you help him?

10-3
AREA

Besides showing how to find areas of many common figures, this section will culminate in an example that will bring together geometric ideas, number concepts, and problem solving strategies. Even our derivation of basic area formulas will illustrate the strategy *think of a simpler problem*. We will first define area and then solve a simple problem (so that we'll have one to think of).

In order to decide on a definition of area, we recall that measurement is a comparison to a known unit. What should this unit be? When we measured length our unit was a fixed segment. For area measure, we define our unit to be a square with the unit segment as its side. This will lead to the usual convenient way for measuring area. We call this unit for measuring area a **square unit** and define the area of a polygon to be the number of square units that will fit inside the polygon. (We are implicitly assuming that the number of square units is not restricted to whole numbers.)

Now let's do our simple problem.

EXAMPLE
10-3

Find (without using any formulas) the area of a rectangle with sides of (a) 3 and 7   (b) 3½ and 7   (c) $\sqrt{10}$ and 7.

SOLUTION

(a) We *draw a sketch* and observe that a row of 7 squares will fit along the bottom and that 3 such rows will fit inside the rectangle. Thus the area is $3 \times 7 = 21$ (square units).

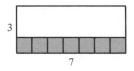

(b) After fitting in 3 rows of 7 square units, we see that the remaining portion of the rectangle can be filled by 7 pieces, each one-half of a square unit. Thus the area is $3 \times 7 + \frac{1}{2} \times 7$ or, using the distributive property, $3½ \times 7 = 24½$ (square units).

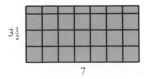

(c) Since $\sqrt{10}$ is between 3.1 and 3.2, we can use the method of part (b) to conclude that the area is between $3 \times 7 + .1 \times 7 = 3.1 \times 7$, and $3 \times 7 + .2 \times 7 = 3.2 \times 7$. By pinching $\sqrt{10}$ between 3.16227766016 and

3.16227766017 we can again use the method of part (b) to conclude that the area is between $3 \times 7 + .16227766016 \times 7 = 3.162277660016 \times 7$ and $3 \times 7 + .16227766017 \times 7 = 3.16227766017 \times 7$. This kind of squeezing process leads us to conclude that the actual area is exactly $\sqrt{10} \times 7$.

We have freely used similar ideas in our area models for developing multiplication for whole numbers, fractions, and real numbers respectively, so the preceding discussion may seem a bit stilted; however, we have presented it here to stress how the familiar formula for the area of a rectangle applies to (non-negative) real numbers — not just to whole numbers or just to fractions. Calling the two known sides of our rectangle the **base** and the **height**, we now have the formula for the **area of a rectangle**:

$A = bh$, where b is the base and h is the height.

Areas of many other common polygons are easy to determine if we assume that the area of the polygon is unchanged when we cut up and reassemble it. For instance, we can see that the area of a parallelogram with base b and height h is the same as the area of a rectangle with these dimensions, since a parallelogram can be cut up and reassembled into a rectangle as shown below.

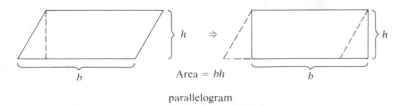

parallelogram

Note that we use the height of the parallelogram and not the other side. In the figure below, the area is 40 square units, *not* 50 square units.

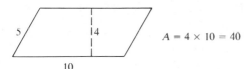

$A = 4 \times 10 = 40$

To determine the area of a triangle, observe that a triangle with base b and height h has one-half the area of a parallelogram of the same dimensions.

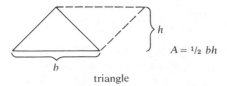

$A = \frac{1}{2} bh$

triangle

Sometimes we find the area of a polygon by splitting it into (disjoint) pieces and summing the area of the pieces, which is essentially the **additive property for areas.**

EXAMPLE

10-4

Find the area of

(a) polygon *ABCDEF*

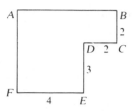

(b) geoboard figure *RSTU*

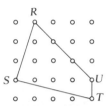

SOLUTION

(a) Split the figure into two rectangles and find the area of each. $AB = FE + DC = 4 + 2 = 6$

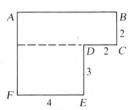

$$\text{Area} = 6 \times 2 + 4 \times 3 = 12 + 12 = 24$$

(b) Split the figure into three triangles, $\triangle RWS$, $\triangle RWU$, $\triangle SUT$, and find the area of each. Each triangle is half a rectangle:

$$\triangle RWS: A = \frac{1}{2} \times 1 \times 3 = \frac{3}{2}$$

$$\triangle RWU: A = \frac{1}{2} \times 3 \times 3 = \frac{9}{2}$$

$$\triangle SUT: A = \frac{1}{2} \times 4 \times 1 = 2$$

Hence area figure $RSTU = 3/2 + 9/2 + 2 = 8$.

So far we have found the area of a triangle in terms of the area of a parallelogram, and we have found the area of a parallelogram in terms of the area of a rectangle, illustrating once again the strategy *think of a simpler problem*. In the problems, you will have the opportunity to apply this principle to find the area of a trapezoid.

We can use a similar technique to find the area of a circle, closely approximating a circle by regular polygons as in Figure 10-1. We show a circle with radius r inscribed in a regular hexagon with side s.

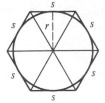

Then the area of the circle is roughly equal to the area of the hexagon. (Is the area of the circle more or less than the area of the hexagon?) But the area of the hexagon is the sum of the areas of the six triangles. Summarizing (and applying a few number properties along the way) we have

$$\left(\begin{array}{c}\text{area of}\\ \text{circle}\end{array}\right) \doteq \left(\begin{array}{c}\text{area of}\\ \text{hexagon}\end{array}\right) = 6 \times \left(\begin{array}{c}\text{area of}\\ \text{triangle}\end{array}\right) = 6 \times \frac{1}{2}\, sr = \frac{1}{2}\, r \times 6s.$$

But $6s$ is the perimeter of the hexagon, so we have

$$\left(\begin{array}{c}\text{area of}\\ \text{circle}\end{array}\right) \doteq \frac{1}{2}\, r \times \left(\begin{array}{c}\text{perimeter}\\ \text{of hexagon}\end{array}\right).$$

The approximation gets better if we use a regular polygon with 10 or 100 sides in place of the regular hexagon. As we increase the number of sides, the area of the regular polygon gets closer to the area of the circle. Meanwhile the perimeter of the polygon gets closer to the circumference of the circle. This leads to the *exact* expression for the area of a circle,

$$A = \frac{1}{2}\, r \times C.$$

But since $C = 2\pi r$, we have $A = \dfrac{1}{2}\, r \times 2\pi r = \pi r^2$. Thus the formula for the **area of a circle** is

$$A = \pi r^2.$$

Problem 19 shows a physical embodiment of this idea using paper and a scissors.

We now return to our friends the polyominoes, which were introduced in Section 9-3. Do you remember meeting the Pentomino family? We showed pictures of two of the family members in Problem 22 of Section 9-3 and asked you to find more. (Did you find all twelve pentominoes?) Starting with a set of twelve pentominoes, it's a challenging puzzle to build a rectangle using each pentomino exactly once. This puzzle has entertained countless people and even has been sold commercially. We mention it here for its entertainment value, but — more important — for its instructional value.

The first question we might ask is "What size rectangles should we *try* to build from a set of twelve pentominoes?" Since each pentomino has an "area" of 5 square units, any rectangle must have an area of 60 square units. Should we attempt to build a rectangle with one side of length 8? Is it physically possible to use the pentominoes to build a rectangle with one side of length 2?

Even when we see which rectangles are worth attempting, the actual building of a rectangle with twelve pentominoes isn't especially easy. A solution found by a sixth grade class is shown in Figure 10-8, but don't be surprised if it takes you 30 minutes to find another of the thousands of solutions. After attempting this you will be in a better position to appreciate Problem 22 and its solution. Our next example reviews a useful tool for solving problems.

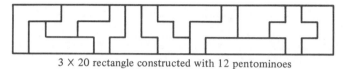

3 × 20 rectangle constructed with 12 pentominoes

FIGURE 10-8

EXAMPLE 10-5

Build a rectangle using all of the five distinct tetrominoes. (See Figure 9-5.)

SOLUTION

Can you *think of a similar problem?* See if you can before reading on. A rectangle made of five tetrominoes will necessarily have area 20 square units. The factors of 20 are 1, 2, 4, 5, 10, and 20, so the only possible rectangles will have dimensions 2 × 10 or 4 × 5. If we color each of these

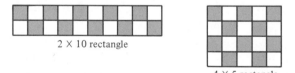

2 × 10 rectangle   4 × 5 rectangle

rectangles like a checkerboard, each will have ten dark squares and ten light squares. (Beginning to sound familiar?) Four of the tetrominoes will cover an *even* number of dark squares. We call these the *even tetrominoes*.

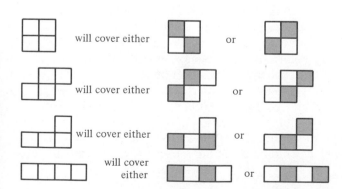

The fifth tetromino will cover an *odd* number of dark squares, so we call it an *odd tetromino*.

 will cover either or

Since the sum of four even numbers and one odd number is odd, the five pentominoes together will cover an *odd* number of dark squares. Thus it is impossible for the five tetrominoes to cover the ten dark (and ten light) squares, so we needn't even try! Do you remember using this technique in Chapter 1?

Looking back, we see how the polyominoes raised questions which led to discussions involving congruence, rigid motions, area, factors, and adding odd and even numbers. Not bad for something that has been sold commercially for its entertainment value!

EXERCISES AND PROBLEMS 10-3

POLYGONS

1. Find the area of each of the figures of Problem 7, Section 10-1.

2. (a) Tell how to find the area of the trapezoid shown.
   (b) Can you find a second way of doing this problem?

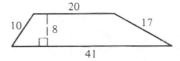

3. A parallelogram has sides of length 5 and 8. Find
   (a) the largest possible area   (b) the smallest possible area.

4. Derive formulas for the areas of each.
   (a) square with side s

   (b) trapezoid with bases b_1 and b_2 and height h

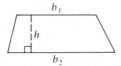

5. If the ratio of corresponding sides of two similar polygons is $2:3$, what can you say about the ratio of their (a) perimeters?   (b) areas?

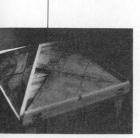

6. The table in Goethe's house in Frankfurt, Germany, shown in Figure 10-9 opens to form a bigger table as shown below:

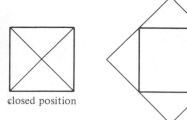

closed position

open position

FIGURE 10-9

(a) How much does this increase the area of the table top?

(b) If the table top in the closed position is 1 meter on a side, what are the dimensions of the table top in the open position?

7. Ancient Babylonians used the formula

$$A = \frac{(a + c)(b + d)}{4}$$

to find the area of a quadrilateral with successive sides a, b, c, d. The formula is inscribed on the tomb of Ptolemy, who died in 51 B.C. Is the formula correct? Defend your answer.

8. We know that two segments of the same length are congruent and that two angles with the same measure are congruent. Prove or disprove: "Two rectangles with the same area are congruent."

9. Find all rectangles whose sides have lengths which are whole numbers and whose area is
(a) 13   (b) 15   (c) 20   (d) 25   (e) 60
(f) 7,000,000. (Just tell how many — don't list them for part f.)

10. Find all rectangles whose areas and perimeters are numerically the same.

11. Draw a figure similar to a checkerboard, 8 squares by 8 squares. What is its area in square units? Cut it as shown. Arrange the pieces to form a 5 × 13 rectangle. What is its area in square units? Is there more area? Can you account for what happened?

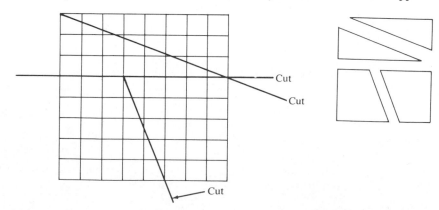

*12. Let $ABCD$ be a square with perimeter 90 and let $AEGH$ be a rectangle with perimeter 90.

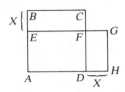

(a) Why does $BE = DH$? Call this length x.

(b) How long is $\overline{AB}$?

(c) How long is $\overline{AE}$ (in terms of x)?

(d) How long is $\overline{AH}$ (in terms of x)?

(e) Find the exact area of the square.

(f) Find the area of the rectangle (in terms of x).

(g) Compare the areas. Which is greater? Why?

(h) A farmer wants to make a rectangular pen using 100 feet of fencing. What dimensions should the pen have in order to have the largest area?

CIRCLES

13. Using $A = \pi r^2$, the formula for the area of a circle with radius r, find the area (in terms of π) of a circle with **(a)** radius 6   **(b)** diameter 10   **(c)** circumference 100

14. Find the area.

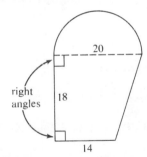

15. If the circle inscribed in square $ABCD$ has radius 10, find the shaded area.

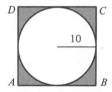

16. Find the shaded area between the circles of radius 1 which touch as shown.

(a)   (b)

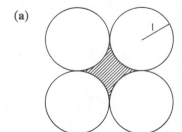
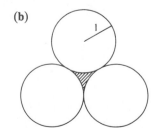

17. If an 8-inch (round) pizza serves two, how many should two 12-inch pizzas serve?

MATERIALS

18. (Area of Lake Erie.) The map showing Lake Erie has been traced on squared paper. The side of each square is 20 miles.

   (a) What is the area of each square?

   (b) Count all the squares that are *entirely* over water. How many squares? How many square miles?

   (c) Count all the squares that cover *any* water. How many squares? How many square miles? What do you know about the area of Lake Erie?

   (d) Next draw lines midway between the grid lines already on the map. What is the area of each square?

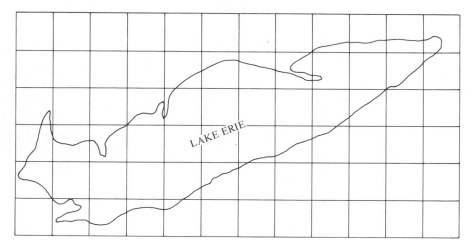

   (e) Count all these small squares that are *entirely* over water. How many squares? How many square miles?

   (f) Count all the squares that cover *any* water. How many squares? How many square miles?

   (g) Now what do you know about the area of Lake Erie? What is your best estimate of its area? How could you improve your estimate?

L19. Cut up a circle and reassemble it as shown. (Tape it to your paper.)

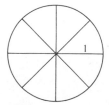 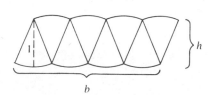

   (a) The new shape resembles which kind of quadrilateral?

   (b) Estimate the lengths b and h, given that the circle has circumference 2π and radius 1.

   (c) Express the area in terms of π.

20. Sketch ten different hexominoes, no two of which are congruent.

21.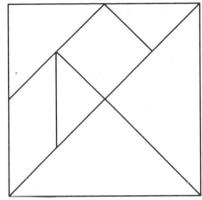

(Tangrams.) This 4000-year-old puzzle originated in China and is said to have helped Napoleon pass time while in exile. To make the puzzle cut a square piece of cardboard or wood into seven pieces as shown. Then reassemble the pieces to form (**a**) a triangle (**b**) a parallelogram (which is not a rectangle)   (**c**) a hexagon   (**d**) the original square.

22. (Pentominoes.)

  (**a**) Which rectangles have sides whose measures are whole numbers and whose area is 60 square units?

  (**b**) Of these, the 1×60 rectangle can be eliminated as a rectangle tiled by the twelve pentominoes. Can any others be eliminated?

  *(**c**) Using the twelve pentominoes each once, find a way of tiling a 3×20 rectangle other than the one given in Figure 10-8. (The U-shaped piece cannot be on the end.)

  *(**d**) Find a way of tiling a different rectangle (not 3×20).

23. There are 35 distinct hexominoes, 24 "odd" and 11 "even." (See Example 10-5.)

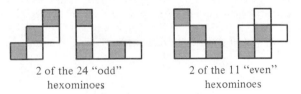

2 of the 24 "odd"   2 of the 11 "even"
    hexominoes   hexominoes

  (**a**) Which rectangles are candidates to be tiled by the 35 distinct hexominoes (using each hexomino exactly once)?

  (**b**) How many dark squares will be in each of these rectangles?

  (**c**) How many dark squares will be covered by the 24 odd hexominoes?

  (**d**) How many dark squares will be covered by the 11 even hexominoes?

  (**e**) Which rectangles do you think can be tiled by the 35 hexominoes (using each hexomino exactly once)?

MOSTLY PROBLEM SOLVING

24. Try this quiz on the areas of states.

  (**a**) Name the three states with the largest area.

  (**b**) Name the three states with the smallest area.

  (**c**) Name a pair of states consisting of a state east of the Mississippi River which has more area than a state west of the Mississippi River.

25. The following questions appeared on a grade 8 mathematics assessment test with students responding as indicated:

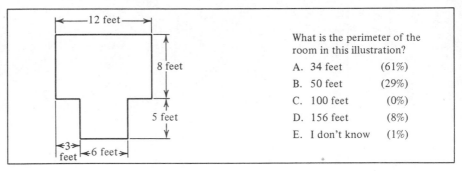

(a) Which response is correct? **(b)** Can you account for why students often chose one of the incorrect responses?

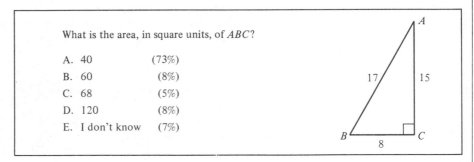

(c) Which response is correct? **(d)** Can you account for why students often chose "A"?

26. The area of an ellipse is given by $A = \pi ab$, where a and b are the semi-major and semi-minor axes as shown. **(a)** Find the area of the ellipse in front of the White House in Washington, D.C., if $a = 536$ feet and $b = 454$ feet. **(b)** Suppose we think of a circle as an ellipse where $a = b = $ radius. Rewrite the formula $A = \pi ab$, substituting r for a and for b.

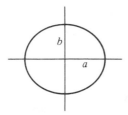

27. Debbie is cutting out cards for a game from a large sheet of cardboard. How many 2×3 rectangles can be cut from a 10×14 sheet? Include a sketch of how to do it.

28. A square cake is frosted on top and on all four sides. Can it be cut into nine pieces so all contain the same amount of cake and frosting?

29. A rectangle with dimensions 64×100 is divided by parallel lines into 6400 unit squares. A diagonal of this rectangle passes through how many vertices of these squares?

10-4
SPACE FIGURES AND THEIR MEASURE

No, we aren't going to be discussing spaceships, planets, or stars. We have in mind different kinds of "space figures." These figures are in fact quite "down to earth." Many of them are well known to children. After a soccer game a child may enjoy an ice cream cone or a cool drink of water with lots of ice cubes. The soccer ball, the cone, and the cubes are all examples of the kind of space figures we *will* be discussing.

When Sue teaches her third grade class the names of the geometric solids, she incorporates the names into the daily activity. It becomes a game in which the children delight in filling a *cylinder* with water and ice *cubes* before their imaginary journey around the *sphere* (world) to the *pyramids* of Egypt. Our goal in this section will be to introduce the space figures and their names and then describe ways of measuring them.

Analogous to a polygon in the plane will be what we call a **polyhedron** in space. While a polygon consists of segments joined together in a special way, a polyhedron consists of closed polygonal regions joined together in a special way. The polygonal regions are called **faces**; the intersections of the faces are called **edges**; and the points where three or more edges intersect are called **vertices** (plural of **vertex**). Polygons are classified according to the number of sides; polyhedra are classified according to the number of faces:

Number of Faces	Name
4	tetrahedron
6	hexahedron
8	octahedron
12	dodecahedron
20	icosahedron

tetrahedron

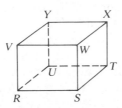

hexahedron

The tetrahedron shown has

4 faces: polygonal regions $\triangle ABC$, $\triangle ABD$, $\triangle BCD$, $\triangle ACD$

6 edges: $\overline{AB}$, $\overline{AC}$, $\overline{AD}$, $\overline{BC}$, $\overline{BD}$, $\overline{CD}$

4 vertices: A, B, C, D

The hexahedron has 6 faces, 12 edges, and 8 vertices.

A polyhedron with one face a polygon and whose other faces (called **lateral faces**) are triangles with a common vertex is called a **pyramid**. Pyramids are further classified according to the polygon which constitutes the **base**. The rectangular pyramid shown has 5 faces, 8 edges, and 5 vertices. The hexagonal pyramid has 7 faces, 12 edges, and 7 vertices.

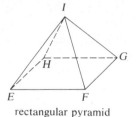

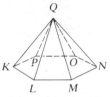

rectangular pyramid   hexagonal pyramid

A **prism** is a polyhedron with two congruent bases which are polygons lying in parallel planes and whose other faces (called **lateral faces**) are parallelograms formed by joining corresponding vertices of the bases. As with pyramids, prisms are further classified according to their bases. The triangular prism shown in Figure 10-10 has 5 faces, 9 edges, and 6 vertices. The hexagonal prism has 8 faces, 18 edges, and 12 vertices. A **cube** is a prism made up of 6 square faces.

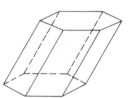

triangular prism   hexagonal prism

FIGURE 10-10

After this barrage of definitions, can you think of any more important geometric figures yet to be defined? There are just a few, including one of the first shapes you ever learned. Can you think of it?

The most important measures of space figures are surface area and volume. Surface area refers to the sum of the areas of each of the faces of the solid. Volume refers to a measure of the number of cubic units it would take to "fill" the solid.

As an example of surface area, the surface area of the triangular prism of Figure 10-10 is the total area of its five faces, which is the total area of three rectangles (the lateral faces) and two triangles (the bases). The surface area of the hexagonal prism is the total area of six parallelograms (the lateral faces) and two hexagons (the bases).

Determining volumes will require another type of unit of measure. We begin with our basic unit of length and build a cube using this unit as the length of its side. To measure the volume of a polyhedron, we then see how many "cubic units" fit inside the given polyhedron. Rectangular prisms whose lateral edges meet the bases at right angles are called **right rectangular prisms**. As an easy example, suppose we have a right rectangular prism with edges of length 4,

3, and 2. Then to fill it up with cubic units, we would need two layers each 4 × 3 units; namely, $V = 4 \times 3 \times 2$.

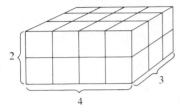

In general, the **volume of a right rectangular prism** is given by

$V = lwh$, where l is the length, w is the width, and h is the height.

Notice that the "lw" in the formula is precisely the area of the base, which in this case is a rectangle. A similar result holds for *any* prism; namely, the **volume of a prism** is given by

$V = Bh$, where B is the area of the base and h is the height.

You might guess that since triangles are involved, a pyramid has one-half the volume of a prism with the same base and height. To see that this is *not* the

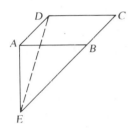
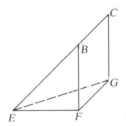
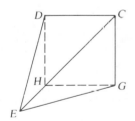
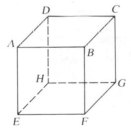

FIGURE 10-11

case, see Figure 10-11, where a prism with all edges of length 1 (a cube) is split into three square pyramids, all with the same size base and the same height:

Pyramid	Base	Height
ABCDE	Square ABCD	AE = 1
BCGFE	Square BCGF	FE = 1
DCGHE	Square DCGH	HE = 1

Together these three pyramids make up the entire prism, so each must have one-third the volume of the prism. A generalization of this is that the **volume of a rectangular pyramid** is given by

$$V = \frac{1}{3}\,lwh, \text{ where } l \text{ and } w \text{ are the length and width of the base}$$
$$\text{and } h \text{ is the height.}$$

Still more general, the **volume of *any* pyramid** is given by

$$V = \frac{1}{3}\,Bh, \text{ where } B \text{ is the area of the base}$$
$$\text{and } h \text{ is the height.}$$

The space figures involving circles are the **cylinder** (analogous to the prism), the **cone** (analogous to the pyramid), and the **sphere**. The volume formulas for the cylinder and the cone are thus closely related to those of the prism and pyramid. In fact, the **volume of a cylinder** is given by

$$V = Bh, \text{ where } B \text{ is the area of the base}$$
$$\text{and } h \text{ is the height,}$$

and the **volume of a cone** is given by

$$V = \frac{1}{3}Bh, \text{ where } B \text{ is the area of the base}$$
$$\text{and } h \text{ is the height.}$$

Archimedes (c. 287-212 B.C.) knew of an interesting relationship among the volumes of the cylinder, cone, and sphere, which is taken up in Problem 10.

EXERCISES AND PROBLEMS 10-4

DEFINITIONS

1. Sketch **(a)** a pentagonal pyramid   **(b)** a pentagonal prism.

2. **(a)** Is a tetrahedron necessarily a pyramid?
   (b) Is a hexahedron necessarily a prism?

3. Tell whether the condition given is characteristic of a pyramid or a prism (or both or neither).
   (a) It has one base.
   (b) It has two bases.
   (c) Its lateral faces are parallelograms.
   (d) Its lateral faces are triangles.
   (e) It has the same number of faces as vertices.
   (f) It can have as few as three faces.
   (g) It can have as few as four faces.
   (h) It can have as few as five faces.
   (i) One or more of its faces might be a parallelogram.
   (j) It always has an even number of vertices.
   (k) It always has an even number of edges.
   (l) It always has an even number of faces.
   (m) The shape of a pup tent (closed on both ends). (See figure.)
   (n) The shape of a "house." (See figure.)

(m)

(n)

4. **(a)** What kind of pyramid is an octahedron?
   (b) What kind of prism is an octahedron?

5. Count the number of faces (F), edges (E), and vertices (V) for each of the following:

	F	E	V
(a) dodecahedron		30	20
(b) cube	6		
(c) rectangular prism			
(d) tetrahedron			
(e) pentagonal pyramid			

6. In the previous problem, compute $F + V$ in each case and compare it with E. Write a formula involving F, V, and E based on your observation.

7. **(a)** A pyramid whose base is a 13-gon has how many vertices? edges? faces?
   (b) A prism whose bases each are 13-gons has how many vertices? edges? faces?

8. Give an example of a polyhedron which has
   (a) 7 faces, 12 edges, 7 vertices
   (b) 4 faces, 6 edges, 4 vertices
   (c) 7 faces, 15 edges, 10 vertices
   (d) 9 faces, 16 edges, 9 vertices.

VOLUMES

9. Some space figures involving circles are identified below along with the formulas for their volumes.

sphere

$$V = \frac{4}{3}\pi r^3$$

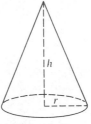

(right circular) cone

$$V = \frac{1}{3}\pi r^2 h$$

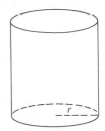

(right circular) cylinder

$$V = \pi r^2 h$$

Find the volume of each of the following. (Answer in terms of π.)
   (a) sphere with radius 6
   (b) cone with radius 4 and height 11
   (c) cylinder with radius 4 and height 11

10. Suppose you have a sphere, a cone, and a cylinder all with radius r and all the same height.
   (a) What is this height?
   (b) Determine the volume of each (in terms of π).
   (c) Add the two smaller volumes, and look for a conclusion.

11. Find the volume of each:
   (a) square pyramid with base edge 6, lateral edge 5, and height 4
   (b) square prism with base edge 6, lateral edge 4, and height 4
   (c) a pyramid whose base is a 3-4-5 right triangle and whose height is 7
   (d) the trough as sketched

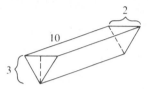

12. Consider the following geometric figures: pyramid, prism, cone, cylinder. If B is the area of the base, h is the height, and V is the volume, then for which of the figures does
   (a) $V = Bh$?   **(b)** $V = (1/2)\ Bh$?   **(c)** $V = (1/3)\ Bh$?

13. Find the volume of the "ice cream cone" consisting of a **hemisphere** (half of a sphere) with radius 2 resting on a base of an inverted right circular cone with height 10.

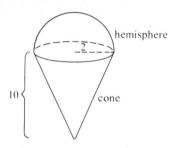

14. Find the approximate volume of a cylindrical piece of a tree with a *circumference* of 270 centimeters and a height of 5 meters. (See Problem 15, Section 10-1.)

15. Invent an additivity property for volumes patterned after the additivity property for areas.

RATIOS

16. What happens to the area of a square when its side is
   (a) doubled?   **(b)** tripled?   **(c)** halved?

17. What happens to the volume of a cube when its edge is
   (a) doubled?   **(b)** tripled?   **(c)** halved?

18. Assume that the apparent size of a gem is proportional to its area, while its cost is proportional to its volume. What happens to cost if apparent size is doubled?

19. A can of corn is 1½ times as tall and 1½ times as wide as another can. Its volume is how many times as great as the volume of the smaller can?

20. A cone-shaped cup has a mark halfway up the side.
   (a) The cup filled to the mark contains what portion of the total volume of the cup?

   (b) How far from the bottom should the mark be placed to indicate half-full?

MOSTLY PROBLEM SOLVING

21. Two lines are called **skew** if they do not lie in the same plane. In the sketch below, imagine that certain edges of a block of wood are extended to form lines. Then $\overleftrightarrow{AE}$ is parallel to $\overleftrightarrow{BF}$ (denoted $\overleftrightarrow{AE} \parallel \overleftrightarrow{BF}$)

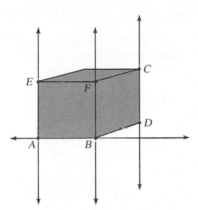

and $\overleftrightarrow{AE} \parallel \overleftrightarrow{DC}$, while $\overleftrightarrow{AB}$ and $\overleftrightarrow{DC}$ are skew. Though it may appear in the sketch that $\overleftrightarrow{AB}$ and $\overleftrightarrow{DC}$ meet, it is understood that $\overleftrightarrow{DC}$ is "behind" $\overleftrightarrow{AB}$.
   (a) Name another pair of skew lines in the figure.
   (b) Identify a pair of skew lines in your clasroom.

22. A shed is pictured below. The outside is to be painted on all four walls together with the roof. What is the area to be painted?

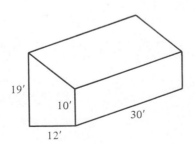

23. Which of the twelve pentominoes (see Figure 10-8) can be folded into a box (without a cover)? In each case, shade the square that becomes the bottom of the box. Examples:

                              cannot be folded into a box

                              can be folded into a box with
                                                  the shaded side as bottom

24. Two hexominoes are shown below. Each of them can be folded into a cube.

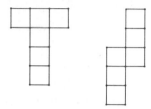

Draw several different hexominoes that can be folded into a cube.

L25. Get a set of geoblocks and find as many different polyhedra as you can, identifying each.

26. Consider the "triangle" ABC formed on the surface of the earth by connecting the North Pole with the equator at 0° longitude and 90° longitude as shown. Determine the measure of
(a) $\angle ACB$ (b) $\angle CAB$ (c) $\angle CBA$
(d) $\angle ACB + \angle CAB + \angle CBA$. Comment!

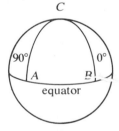

27. The surface area of a unit cube is 6 square units, since six faces each have area 1. The surface area of the prism formed by placing one cube on top of another is 10 square units.

Area = 6 square units   Area = 10 square units

Find the surface area (including the bottom) of these "towers":

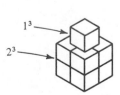

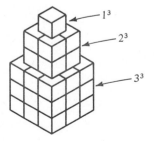

28. On a statewide assessment test, only 20% of the eighth graders who attempted the following problem got it correct. Can you do it?

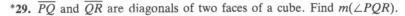

The radius of the inside of the pipe is 3 inches. The wall of the pipe is 1 inch thick. What is the diameter of the pipe?

A. 4 inches

B. 5 inches

C. 7 inches

D. 8 inches

E. I don't know.

Pipe

*29. $\overline{PQ}$ and $\overline{QR}$ are diagonals of two faces of a cube. Find $m(\angle PQR)$.

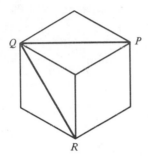

10-5
UNITS OF MEASURE: THE METRIC SYSTEM

We have seen that measurement is a comparison to some known unit. In this section, we will examine such units more closely, with special emphasis on the metric system.

It will be advantageous to require certain conditions for our units of comparison. Some desirable features for our units are that they be

(1) standardized,
(2) widely used,
(3) appropriate in size, and
(4) conveniently interrelated.

An illustration of each of these is given next. (1) It would not suffice to say that the width of a table is four "pencils," since pencils vary in length. (2) It would not help to know that a bottle holds four gills if we didn't know what a gill is. (3) It would be inconvenient to measure distances between cities in inches or our height in miles. (4) It isn't feasible to determine how much the water in a 20-gallon aquarium will weigh if we don't know the interrelationship between capacity and weight.

Increasing world trade together with improved transportation and communication have fostered more universally accepted systems of measurement. Dominant among these is the metric system, now the standard in nearly every country. A number of systems have units which share advantages (1) and (3) on the list above, but none can match the metric system with respect to points (2) and (4). More will be said about the interrelationships as the basic units of length, area, volume, weight, capacity, and temperature are discussed. Our emphasis throughout will be on the metric system.

The basic unit of length in the metric system is the **meter**. (It is abbreviated simply "**m**," without a period. Subsequent abbreviations will be written in parentheses following the word when it is first introduced.) If the meter is not already familiar to you, it is suggested that you examine a meter stick, which is simply a stick one meter long marked off into 100 equal parts. Each of these parts is called a **centimeter** (**cm**). Part of a meter stick is shown in Figure 10-12.

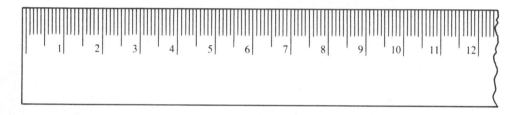

FIGURE 10-12

The entire meter stick would have 100 such units. If we need a smaller unit of measure we can use the **millimeter** (**mm**), which we obtain by dividing the centimeter into ten equal parts. (Consequently there are 1000 millimeters in a meter.) When we need larger units, we have the **kilometer** (**km**), which is equivalent to 1000 meters. We can summarize these units as follows:

$$1000 \text{ millimeters} = 1 \text{ meter}$$

$$100 \text{ centimeters} = 1 \text{ meter}$$

$$1000 \text{ meters} = 1 \text{ kilometer}$$

Some typical examples of measurements using these units are the following:

A chalk tray is often about a meter above the classroom floor.

The width of the fingernail on your little finger is probably about one centimeter.

The thickness of a dime is a little more than one millimeter.

Lake Michigan is about 100 kilometers wide.

The fact that one unit of length is derived from another by using factors of ten is highly desirable for at least two reasons. It is easy to remember (for example, there are 100 centimeters in a meter), and it is easy to convert from one unit to the other by using multiples of ten. Some comparisons with the English system make this quite graphic.

(a) Convert 5793 meters to kilometers. (b) Convert 5793 yards to miles.

EXAMPLE
10-6

(a) The conversion factor indicated by "kilo-" is 1000. Hence there are 5793 ÷ 1000 kilometers; namely, 5.793 kilometers.

(b) The conversion factor is 1760. Hence there are 5793 ÷ 1760 miles; namely, about 3.291477 miles.

To do (a) we merely divide by 1000 (an easy number to remember) by moving the decimal point three places to the left. (It doesn't even require a calculator.) To do (b) we must remember the less memorable number 1760 and perform the division 5793 ÷ 1760.

The compactness of the metric system becomes even clearer when we consider units of weight and capacity. The basic metric unit of weight is the **gram** (**g**). Other common units of weight are the **milligram** (**mg**) and the **kilogram** (**kg**). They are related to the gram as follows:

$$1000 \text{ milligrams} = 1 \text{ gram}$$

$$1000 \text{ grams} = 1 \text{ kilogram}$$

Some typical examples of measurements using these units are the following:

A nickel weighs 5 grams.
A vitamin C pill might weigh 250 milligrams.
A young woman of average height might weigh 50 kilograms.

The same prefixes occur when we discuss capacity. Here the basic unit is **liter** (**l**). It is slightly more than a quart in the English system. The liter and quart agree better than most units from the two systems. Another common unit of capacity is the **milliliter** (**ml**). Again the prefix "milli-" indicates that the milliliter is 1/1000 of the base unit, the liter. Namely,

$$1000 \text{ milliliters} = 1 \text{ liter.}$$

Typical examples of capacity in the metric system are these:

A full carafe of wine is commonly 1 liter.
A bottle of eye drops might contain 25 milliliters.

The three basic units meter, gram, and liter, together with the prefixes centi-, milli-, and kilo-, are sufficient for most of the common measurements involving length, weight, and capacity. Compare the few simple conversions needed in the metric system with those belonging to the English system:

$$12 \text{ inches} = 1 \text{ foot}$$

$$3 \text{ feet} = 1 \text{ yard}$$

$$1760 \text{ yards} = 1 \text{ mile}$$

$$16 \text{ ounces} = 1 \text{ pound}$$

$$3 \text{ teaspoonsful} = 1 \text{ tablespoonful (cooking)}$$
$$4 \text{ teaspoonsful} = 1 \text{ tablespoonful (medical)}$$
$$2 \text{ tablespoonsful} = 1 \text{ fluid ounce}$$
$$8 \text{ fluid ounces} = 1 \text{ cup}$$
$$2 \text{ cups} = 1 \text{ pint}$$
$$2 \text{ pints} = 1 \text{ quart}$$
$$4 \text{ quarts} = 1 \text{ gallon}$$
$$4 \text{ pecks} = 1 \text{ bushel}$$

With all these (and more) units and conversion factors to know, it is no wonder most of the world has gone to the metric system!

Another advantage of the metric system is the way in which it circumvents expressing measurements in fractions or mixed numbers. For instance, a height of 5′ 2½″ can be reported simply as 159 centimeters — no fractions, no mixed units.

EXAMPLE

10-7

Express each of the following in terms of a single unit with no fractions or decimals.

(a) 1.6 m   (b) 2 m 57 cm   (c) .042 m

(d) 2¼ km   (e) 1/3 kg

SOLUTION

(a) 1.6 m = 160 cm (To convert meters to centimeters, the conversion factor is 100. We multiply, rather than divide, since there will be more centimeters than meters.)

(b) 2 m 57 cm means 2m + 57 cm, which equals 200 cm + 57 cm, or 257 cm

(c) .042 m = 42 mm (multiply by 1,000)

(d) 2¼ km = 2.25 km = 2250 m (multiply by 1,000)

(e) 1/3 kg ≐ .333 kg = 333 g (This is approximate, but very close.)

In discussing area and volume, we derived the basic units from the basic unit of length. Thus our basic units of area and volume are square meters and cubic meters respectively. Be sure to note that a square meter is 100 centimeters by 100 centimeters, so that there are 10,000 (not 100) *square* centimeters in a *square* meter. this is analogous to the way there are 144 (not 12) square inches in a square foot.

Besides the ease with which it is possible to convert among the units of length (meters to centimeters, etc.), among the units of weight (grams to kilograms, etc.), and among the units of capacity (milligrams to grams, etc.), there is a useful interrelationship between length, weight, and capacity: under certain conditions (of temperature and pressure), a cube of water one centimeter on a side (length) weighs one gram (weight) and occupies a milliliter of space (capacity). Compare the problems in the next example.

EXAMPLE
10-8

(a) An aquarium holds 35 liters of water. How much does the water weigh?

(b) An aquarium holds 15 gallons of water. How much does the water weigh?

SOLUTION

(a) 35 liters = 35,000 milliliters, so the water weighs 35,000 g, or 35 kg.

(b) A gallon of water weighs 8.3453 pounds (according to an engineering handbook). Hence 15 gallons weighs $15 \times 8.3453 \doteq 125$ pounds.

We can also conclude from this example that a liter of water weighs a kilogram. This is handy for estimating weights of quantities of water as well as other liquids about as heavy as water, like milk, gasoline, and bleach.

Water also plays a role in defining the basic unit of temperature in the metric system. The temperature scale is based on **degrees Celsius** (°C), where the freezing and boiling points of water are taken to be 0° C and 100° C respectively. The range of temperatures between these two is divided up into 100 parts. On this scale, room temperature is about 20° C and normal body temperature is about 37° C.

It is usually recommended in the United States that young children be taught the metric system without reference to the customary system. However, it is also recommended that the relationships between the systems be incorporated in teaching those already familiar with the customary system. For example, a young child would be introduced to the liter without reference to the customary system, while an adult more familiar with the customary system would be told that a liter is approximately one quart. A summary of units most commonly used in the metric system is given in Figure 10-13.

A handy way to convert from one unit to another is shown in the examples below. It is a kind of bookkeeping device based on the idea that multiplying by one leaves the value of something unchanged.

EXAMPLE
10-9

(a) Change 8 feet to inches.

(b) Change 2 square meters to square centimeters.

(c) Change 60 miles per hour to feet per second.

(d) Change 80 kilograms to pounds, given that one kilogram is about 2.2 pounds.

SOLUTION

(a) $8 \text{ ft} = 8 \text{ ft} \times \dfrac{12 \text{ inches}}{1 \text{ ft}} = 96$ inches

(b) 2 square meters $= 2 \text{ m} \times \text{m} = 2 \text{ m} \times \text{m} \times \dfrac{100 \text{ cm}}{1 \text{ m}} \times \dfrac{100 \text{ cm}}{1 \text{ m}}$
$= 20,000$ square cm

(c) 60 miles per hour $= \dfrac{60 \text{ miles}}{1 \text{ hr}} = \dfrac{60 \text{ miles}}{1 \text{ hr}} \times \dfrac{1 \text{ hr}}{60 \text{ min}} = \dfrac{1 \text{ min}}{60 \text{ sec}} \times \dfrac{5280 \text{ ft}}{1 \text{ mile}}$

$= 88 \text{ ft per sec}$

(d) 80 kg $\doteq 80 \text{ kg} \times \dfrac{2.2 \text{ lbs}}{1 \text{ kg}} = 176 \text{ lbs}$

Type of Measure	Unit	Abbreviation	Conversion	Referent (approximate)	Customary Counterpart
LENGTH	meter	m	—	height of chalk tray above floor	a little more than a yard
	millimeter	mm	1000 mm = 1 m	thickness of a dime	—
	centimeter	cm	100 cm = 1 m	width of fingernail on adult's little finger	1 cm $\doteq$ 2/5 inch
	kilometer	km	1 km = 1000 m	Lake Michigan is about 100 km wide	1 km $\doteq$ .6 miles
WEIGHT	gram	g	—	nickel weighs 5 grams	1 g $\doteq$ 1/28 ounce
	milligram	mg	1000 mg = 1 g	vitamin C pill might weigh 250 mg	—
	kilogram	kg	1 kg = 1000 g	average young woman might weigh 50 kg	1 kg $\doteq$ 2.2 pounds
CAPACITY	liter	l	—	full carafe of wine	1 liter $\doteq$ 1 quart
	milliliter	ml	1000 ml = 1 l	bottle of eye drops might contain 25 ml	—
TEMPERATURE	degree Celsius	°C	—	water freezes 0° C room temperature 20° C water boils 100° C	0° C = 32° F 100° C = 212° F

FIGURE 10-13

So far in this section, we have stressed a particular system of measurement, the metric system, and its units. We close with a brief discussion of precision and errors in measurement which applies to any system of measurement.

The **precision** of a measurement is a technical term defined as the unit of measure used.

EXAMPLE 10-10

What is the precision of each of the following?

(a) 12 centimeters (measured to the nearest centimeter)

(b) 7 inches (measured to the nearest inch)

(c) 8½ inches (measured to the nearest 1/2 inch)

(d) 8½ inches (measured to the nearest 1/16 inch)

(e) 8½ inches

(a) 1 centimeter

(b) 1 inch

(c) 1/2 inch

(d) 1/16 inch. We are told the measurement was made to the nearest 1/16 inch, so this is our unit of measure. Since 8½ inches was given as the measure, the measurement was apparently nearer to 8½ ($8\frac{8}{16}$) than to $8\frac{7}{16}$ or $8\frac{9}{16}$.

(e) 1/2 inch. When no further information is given, we assume the measurement to have been made to whatever units it is reported in, in this case half-inches.

To say that a measurement is 12 centimeters to the nearest centimeter is to say that it is closer to 12 than to 11 or 13 centimeters. This means that it is at least 11½, but less then 12½, centimeters. Hence the greatest possible error is 1/2 centimeter. In general the **greatest possible error** of a measurement is one-half the unit of measure (precision) and is expressed in the same terms (centimeters, inches, etc.).

Find the greatest possible error for each of the measurements in the previous example.

EXAMPLE
10-11

SOLUTION

(a) 1/2 centimeter   (b) 1/2 inch   (c) 1/4 inch

(d) 1/32 inch   (e) 1/4 inch

Suppose the greatest possible error of a measurement were half a centimeter. Is this a large error or a small one? You should react cautiously to this question. In giving the distance from New York to Los Angeles, no one would quibble about 0.5 centimeter (or even know the difference). But to a patient undergoing surgery, this amount of error could prove fatal. The seriousness of the error is relative to what is being measured. In response to this question, something has been devised which helps to reflect the error in comparison to what is being measured. The relative error is defined to be the greatest possible error divided by the measurement. It is given independent of units, as the units "cancel out." Relative error is usually given in percent.

Find the relative error for each of the measurements in Example 10-10.

EXAMPLE
10-12

SOLUTION

(a) relative error $= \dfrac{\text{greatest possible error}}{\text{measurement}} = \dfrac{1/2 \text{ centimeter}}{12 \text{ centimeters}} =$

$\dfrac{1}{2} \div \dfrac{12}{1} = \dfrac{1}{2} \times \dfrac{1}{12} = \dfrac{1}{24}$, or about 4%

(b) relative error $= \dfrac{1/2 \text{ inch}}{7 \text{ inches}} = \dfrac{1}{2} \div \dfrac{7}{1} = \dfrac{1}{2} \times \dfrac{1}{7} = \dfrac{1}{14}$, or about 7%

(c) relative error $= \dfrac{1/4 \text{ inch}}{8\frac{1}{2} \text{ inches}} = \dfrac{1}{4} \div \dfrac{17}{2} = \dfrac{1}{4} \times \dfrac{2}{17} = \dfrac{1}{34}$,

or about 3%

(d) relative error $= \dfrac{1/32 \text{ inch}}{8\frac{1}{2} \text{ inches}} = \dfrac{1}{32} \div \dfrac{17}{2} = \dfrac{1}{32} \times \dfrac{2}{17} = \dfrac{1}{272}$,

or about .4%

(e) (same as c)

The types of measurements developed in this chapter can be supplemented by the statistical measures of central tendency and measures of dispersion, which will be developed in Section 12-2, to accommodate many, but by no means all, of the instances where we use measurements to describe our surroundings.

EXERCISES AND PROBLEMS 10-5

UNITS OF MEASURE

1. Select the most reasonable unit of measure or number from those listed:
   (a) The luggage limit per airline passenger is 40 __?__ . (kilograms, grams, milligrams)
   (b) The pool is 20 __?__ long. (kilometers, meters, centimeters, millimeters)
   (c) The injection contained 1 __?__ . (cubic kilometer, cubic meter, cubic centimeter, cubic millimeter)
   (d) The doctor prescribed 2 __?__ of eardrops per dose for the child's infection. (kiloliters, liters, milliliters)
   (e) The football player weighed 110 __?__ . (kilograms, grams, milligrams)
   (f) The basketball player was 2 __?__ tall. (kilometers, meters, centimeters, millimeters)
   (g) The distance between New York and Los Angeles is nearly 5000 __?__ . (kilometers, meters, centimeters, millimeters)
   (h) George got a speeding ticket for exceeding __?__ on the freeway. (10 kilometers per hour, 55 kilometers per hour, 100 kilometers per hour)
   (i) A sudden shower dumped 3 __?__ of rain. (kilometers, meters, centimeters, millimeters)
   (j) The bedroom carpet required 20 __?__ of carpeting. (square kilometers, square meters, square centimeters, square millimeters)
   (k) BJ went for a swim at the lake on a day when the temperature was __?__ . (10° C, 25° C, 60° C, 75° C, 100° C)
   (l) Marie averaged 12 __?__ in her new car. (liters per kilometer, kilometers per liter, kiloliters per kilometer, kilometers per kiloliter)

2. Express each of the following in terms of a single unit with no fractions or decimals.
   (a) 5.8 kg
   (b) 3.41 g
   (c) 7½ liters
   (d) 1 m 56 cm
   (e) 4 m 3 cm
   (f) .076 km

3. Use a *ruler* to find (by measuring) the three medians of this triangle. Which is easier to use, centimeters or inches?

4. Find *one-third* the length of $\overline{XY}$ **(a)** in inches   **(b)** in centimeters.   **(c)** Which is easier?

$$X \text{————————————————} Y$$

5. A **carat** is 200 milligrams.
   (a) How many carats in a gram?
   (b) A .8 carat diamond is how many milligrams?

6. The **gram calorie** is a measure of heat used in physics. It is the amount of heat needed to raise one gram of water one degree Celsius. The **kilogram calorie** is the common measure related to food intake. It is the amount of heat needed to raise one kilogram of water one degree Celsius. In terms of food, it is the amount of food able to produce this amount of energy.
   (a) Which represents more heat, a gram calorie or a kilogram calorie? How many times more?
   (b) An ice cream sundae containing 500 calories would contain enough heat to raise how many liters (kilograms) of water from the freezing point to the boiling point?

7. Moslems fast throughout their month of Ramadan. Nothing can be eaten or drunk from before dawn until after sunset according to the definition "before, and until after, a white hair and a black hair held at arm's length are indistinguishable." *What* is being measured according to this definition?

CONVERSIONS

8. Convert each of the following:
   (a) 2 kilometers to meters
   (b) 5682 grams to kilograms
   (c) 6 milliliters to liters
   (d) 20 centimeters to millimeters
   (e) 1 kilometer to centimeters
   (f) 54 kilograms to milligrams

9. The Sears Tower in Chicago is 442 meters tall. How many kilometers tall is it?

10. Tell how many
   (a) cubic millimeters in a cubic meter
   (b) cubic centimeters in a cubic meter
   (c) square meters in a square kilometer
   (d) square millimeters in a square centimeter.

11. 100 **hectares** = 1 square kilometer. How many square meters are there in a hectare?

12. Estimate the weight of the following:
   (a) 5 liters of gasoline   **(b)** 2 liters of fruit juice   **(c)** 1/2 liter of beer

13. (a) Marty weighs 90 kilograms and just barely floats in water. What is the approximate volume of his body in cubic centimeters?
    (b) Use your own weight to compute your volume.

14. Suzy's weight dropped a kilogram during a long tennis match on a hot day. What is this loss of water in terms of liters?

15. True or False? Explain your answer.
    (a) A cubic centimeter of lead weighs one gram.
    (b) A cubic centimeter of lead occupies one milliliter.

16. A large box of detergent contains 5 pounds 4 ounces. Express this in terms of a single unit.

17. Let's see how well you know the English system of measure:
    (a) (True Story.) I have two containers of shampoo. One says "net weight 5 ounces," the other "8 fluid ounces." Which is more?
    (b) How much does a gallon of water weigh?
    (c) How many furlongs in a mile?
    (d) How many gallons in a peck?
    (e) How many acres in a square mile?
    (f) How many cubic inches in a cubic foot?
    (g) How many cubic feet in a cord (of wood)?

18. Use the method of Example 10-9 to convert
    (a) 30 kilograms to milligrams
    (b) 30 milliliters to liters
    (c) 40 inches to centimeters, given that $1'' \doteq 2.54$ cm.
    (d) 6 kilometers to miles, given that 1 km $\doteq .62$ miles.
    (e) 10 cubic yards to cubic inches.
    (f) 1 cubic meter to cubic centimeters.
    (g) 40 kilometers per hour to meters per second.
    (h) 1 light-year (the *distance* light travels in one year) to miles, given that light travels 186,000 miles per second.
    (i) 32 feet per second per second (the acceleration due to gravity) to meters per second per second given that 1 meter $\doteq 39.37$ inches.

19. Do Problem 28, Section 6-1 (converting between Celsius and Fahrenheit degrees).

20. Jungfrau Mountain in Switzerland is 4157 meters high. How many feet is this? (Use 1 mile $\doteq 1.609$ kilometers $\doteq 5280$ feet.)

21. Bill converted $1000 to drachmas at 42.20 drachmas per dollar when he arrived in Greece. When he left Greece he converted his unused drachmas back to dollars at a rate of 42.80 drachmas per dollar and got $200 back.   (a) How many drachmas did he get for $1000 when he arrived in Greece?   (b) How many drachmas did he convert back to dollars when he left Greece?   (c) How much would he have saved if he had converted only the $800 he actually needed while in Greece?

22. How much would it cost to buy $500 worth of Indian rupees at 7.90 rupees per dollar and convert them back to dollars at 8.00 rupees per dollar?

23. Draw a segment of any length you wish. Define this length to be 1 "glunk." Divide your segment into four congruent parts. Define the length of each of these smaller parts to be 1 "glink."
    (a) Draw a unit which is 1 square glunk.
    (b) How many square glinks in 1 square glunk?
    (c) How many cubic glinks in 1 cubic glunk?

24. Repeat the previous problem, giving the unit the name of your choice and dividing your unit into six parts, again giving the smaller unit a name of your choice.

PRECISION, GREATEST POSSIBLE ERROR, RELATIVE ERROR

25. Find the precision of each of the following:
    (a) 50 g (measured to the nearest gram)
    (b) 50 g (measured to the nearest ten grams)
    (c) 50.00 g
    (d) 8¼ inches (measured to the nearest 1/4 inch)
    (e) 8¼ inches (measured to the nearest 1/32 inch)
    (f) 8¼ inches

26. Find the greatest possible error of the measurements of Problem 25.

27. Find the relative error of the measurements of Problem 25.

MATERIALS AND CALCULATORS

*L*28. Determine the following in metric units:
    (a) your height   (b) your weight
    (c) the dimensions of your classroom
    (d) the dimensions of this book
    (e) the weight of this book

29. (a) The thickness of a dime is a little greater than 1 millimeter. Describe a way to determine the thickness of a dime to the nearest *tenth* of a millimeter using a ruler marked off in millimeters (and as many dimes as you like).
    (b) Carry out the plan you described in (a). How thick is a dime, to the nearest tenth of a millimeter?

*L*30. (a) Use a balance scale to weigh 1 liter of water. Describe your procedure.
    (b) Measure the container and determine its volume (up to the 1-liter mark) in cubic centimeters.
    (c) Compare the capacity, the weight, and the volume. Explain any differences from what you expected.

*L*31. What are the dimensions of a red Cuisenaire rod?

32. Increasing use of the metric system should result in greater emphasis on decimals (compared with fractions) in the elementary school mathematics curriculum. Examine several elementary school mathematics series to see if they reflect this change. Which system of measurement seems to be emphasized?

*L*33. Use a roll of adding machine tape to make a tape measure 2 meters long. (Use a meter stick.) Use the measuring tape to make several measurements, including perhaps your waistline.

*L*34. Use a 1-meter trundle wheel (see Problem 34, Section 6-1)
    (a) to measure several distances inside the building
    (b) to measure several distances outside
    (c) to mark off 10 meters; 100 meters.

*L*35. Bring in customary measuring devices like measuring cups, pails, bathroom scales, etc., and calibrate them in the metric system.

*L*36. Use a balance scale and metric weights to weigh the following:
    (a) a dime   (b) a penny   (c) an eraser   (d) a pencil
    (e) a sheet of (tablet or notebook) paper   (f) a scissors

L37. Which weighs more, a dime or a sheet of (tablet or notebook) paper? How many times more? (Seeing is believing!)

L38. Determine the area of each of the following (in metric units):
(a) a dollar bill (b) a penny (c) this book cover (d) a table top

L39. (a) Determine the area of a sheet of (tablet or notebook) paper.
(b) Cut the paper into strips 1 cm wide and tape them together end to end to make one long strip 1 cm wide. How long is the strip?

L40. (Class Activity.) Each person measures the size of various objects (weight, length, capacity, volume, area, etc.), one measurement per object. It is labeled with masking tape. Form two teams. Conduct a metric "spelldown" where team members estimate the given measurement.

L41. (a) Obtain a map of your state or of several states including the one you are in. Use the scale to determine a distance of 100 km. (Convert from miles if necessary: 1 mile is about 1.61 km.) Use a compass to draw a circle on the map showing all places 100 kilometers from your city, 200 km, 300 km, etc.
(b) How far is it from your home town to your school?
(c) (Class Activity.) Summarize the information from part (b) for the entire class.
(d) Determine the mean, median, and mode of the data of part (c). (See Section 12-2.)
(e) Determine the standard deviation of the data of part (c). (See Section 12-2.)

L42. Consult the National Council of Teachers of Mathematics *A Metric Handbook for Teachers* [32] and other resources for additional activities involving the metric system.

43. (a) Divide part of a piece of paper 18 cm wide into 20 columns of equal widths by the following procedure:

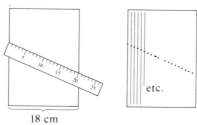

18 cm

Figure A   **Figure B**

Lay a centimeter ruler so that the "0 point" is on the left edge and the "20 point" is on the right edge as shown in Figure A. Place dots at each of the numbers 1, 2, 3, 4, 5, . . . , 19 and draw lines through the dots parallel to the (vertical) edges (as in Figure B).
(b) Tell how you would divide a piece of paper 28 cm wide into 20 columns of equal width.

P44. Write a program to convert
(a) degrees Celsius to degrees Fahrenheit.
(b) degrees Fahrenheit to degrees Celsius. (See Problem 28 of Section 6-1.)

MOSTLY PROBLEM SOLVING

45. Give an instance where you have recently measured each of these:
(a) distance (b) time (c) temperature
(d) length (e) weight (f) others

46. List several things which you measure besides length, area, volume, weight, capacity, and temperature.

47. Give a second illustration of each of the four desirable features of a unit listed at the start of this section.

48. A can is just large enough to hold three tennis balls each with diameter 7 cm. Find the volume of the can
   (a) in spherical "tennis balls."   **(b)** in cubic cm.

49. The earth is about 150,000,000 kilometers (93,000,000 miles) from the sun. If light travels at a speed of about 300,000 kilometers (186,000 miles) per second, how long does it take the light to travel from the sun to the earth?

50. (Source: Charlotte L. Wheatley, *School Science and Mathematics* [62].) The human heart pumps about 65 milliliters of blood per heartbeat. If the heart beats 68 times per minute (under normal conditions),
   (a) how much blood does it pump per minute?
   (b) per hour?
   (c) how long will it take to pump 1 liter?

51. Answer the previous question for a heartbeat of 145 times per minute (when running).

52. Determine your own pulse and answer the questions of Problem 50. Assume your heart pumps 65 milliliters of blood per heartbeat.

53. **(a)** A problem from an arithmetic book asks how much 2 pounds of meat will cost at 5 cents a pound. How old is the book?! **(b)** Another problem asks how many barrels of apples worth $5 per barrel are needed to pay for 4 barrels of flour at $10 per barrel. Solve the apple problem.

Further Topics
in Geometry

11

377

11-1
CONSTRUCTIONS

You won't need a hard hat for this construction project. The only tools you'll need are compass and straightedge, and the most dangerous thing around will be the point on your compass.

The appeal of this section may be a bit like the appeal of going somewhere on a bicycle instead of by car or growing your own vegetables instead of buying them. We leave behind our calculators, which will be of no use in this section (except perhaps if we use an edge to draw a straight line), and ask what we can do with compass and straightedge alone.

Before discussing the constructions themselves we offer a few comments about the construction implements. The term **construct** (unless otherwise indicated) refers to straightedge and compass. By **straightedge** we mean an instrument capable of guiding our pencil to draw a straight line through two given points. We assume it is long enough to join any two given points we wish to join. We further assume that it contains no marks as on a ruler, so if you are using a ruler as a straightedge you are *not* to use the markings for any purpose. By **compass** we mean an instrument capable of drawing a circle with a given center and a given radius. (In a pinch, we could use a piece of string.) We assume that we can adjust the compass to any given radius and that it maintains this radius even if picked up from the paper. (The ancient Greeks assumed a collapsing compass, one which would *not* maintain a given radius when picked up from the paper. It can be shown that a fixed compass setting can be transferred from one place to another even with a collapsing compass, so this does not alter the original question about what can be constructed. (See the "greasy compass" problem, Problem 4 at the end of this section.) In terms of our reference to going by bicycle instead of by car, we might say we're using a three-speed bicycle.

We urge you to *use a sharp pencil* and work very carefully. Constructions can be very unconvincing if technique is sloppy. Finally we recommend that you do not erase the lines and arcs you draw in making a construction (unless, of course, you make a mistake). These markings will indicate how you performed the construction.

Actually we sneaked in a few basic constructions in the problems for Section 9-4. Problems 23-26 gave the constructions for the angle bisector, perpendicular bisector, perpendicular to a point not on a given line, and perpendicular to a point on a given line respectively. (If you haven't done these problems, it's suggested you do them now.)

We will demonstrate two basic constructions and their justification and probe other questions in the problems.

EXAMPLE 11-1

(Copy a segment.)

Given a line $\overleftrightarrow{AB}$ and a segment $\overline{CD}$, construct a segment $\overline{AE}$ so that $\overline{AE}$ lies along $\overleftrightarrow{AB}$ and so that $\overline{AE} \cong \overline{CD}$.

Suppose $\overleftrightarrow{AB}$ and $\overline{CE}$ are given.

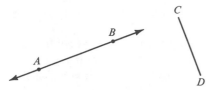

Using C as center, open the compass to radius $\overline{CD}$. Maintaining this setting, use A as center and draw an arc (part of a circle) with radius $\overline{AE}$ so that $\overline{AE} \cong \overline{CD}$, with E on $\overleftrightarrow{AB}$.

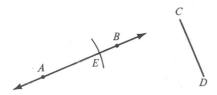

By our assumptions about the compass we have $\overline{AE} \cong \overline{CD}$ as desired.

SOLUTION

(Copy an angle.)

Given an angle $\angle HIJ$ and a ray $\overrightarrow{KL}$, construct an angle $\angle LKM$ so that $\angle LKM \cong \angle HIJ$.

**EXAMPLE
11-2**

Suppose $\angle HIJ$ and $\overrightarrow{KL}$ are given.

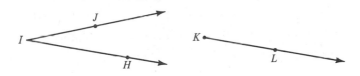

Step 1: Using I as center and $\overline{IH}$ as radius, draw an arc which intersects $\overrightarrow{IJ}$ at X. Step 2: Maintaining this setting, use K as center and draw the circle (or comparable arc) with radius $\overline{KY}$ so that $\overline{KY} \cong \overline{IH}$. Step 3: Using H as center, open the compass to radius $\overline{HX}$. Maintaining this setting, use Y as center and draw an arc with radius $\overline{YM}$ so that $\overline{YM} \cong \overline{HX}$. Step 4: Draw $\overrightarrow{KM}$. We now have $\angle LKM \cong \angle HIJ$ as desired.

SOLUTION

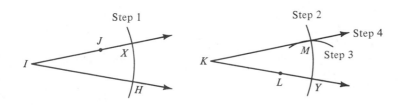

Justification for the construction of Example 11-2 depends on the fact that ∠*HIX* and ∠*YKM* are corresponding parts of congruent triangles △*HIX* and △*YKM*. (We can draw in $\overline{HX}$ and $\overline{YM}$.) The triangles are congruent by the SSS criterion (see page 305).

A similar argument can be given to show that the method of Problem 23, Section 9-4, gives us the angle bisector. Again we get corresponding angles of two triangles which are congruent by SSS. The justifications for some of the other constructions require a bit more, as Example 11-3 shows.

EXAMPLE
11-3

Give justification for the construction of the perpendicular bisector (Problem 24, Section 9-4).

SOLUTION

The construction looks like this, with the dashed lines added to show the triangles:

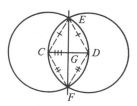

"By construction" we have $\overline{CE} \cong \overline{DE}$ and $\overline{CF} \cong \overline{DF}$. Also $\overline{EF} \cong \overline{EF}$. Thus △*CEF* ≅ △*DEF* by SSS. Since corresponding parts of congruent triangles are congruent, we have ∠*CEG* ≅ ∠*DEG*. Now look at △*CEG* and △*DEG*. We have $\overline{CE} \cong \overline{DE}$, ∠*CEG* ≅ ∠*DEG*, and $\overline{EG} \cong \overline{EG}$, so △*CEG* ≅ △*DEG* by SAS. Since the corresponding parts of congruent triangles are congruent, we have $\overline{CG} = \overline{DG}$ (so $\overleftrightarrow{EF}$ *bisects* $\overline{CD}$) and ∠*CGE* ≅ ∠*DGE* (so $\overleftrightarrow{EF}$ is *perpendicular* to $\overline{CD}$). Since $\overleftrightarrow{EF}$ bisects $\overline{CD}$ and is perpendicular to $\overline{CD}$, $\overleftrightarrow{EF}$ is the perpendicular bisector of $\overline{CD}$.

Our construction project will continue in the problems. We'll also do some "building on" in the next section.

EXERCISES AND PROBLEMS 11-1

BASIC CONSTRUCTIONS

1. (a) Draw an angle. Construct its bisector.
   (b) Draw a segment. Construct its perpendicular bisector.
   (c) Draw a line *m* and a point *P* on *m*. Construct a line that contains *P* and is perpendicular to *m*.
   (d) Repeat part (c) for *P* *not* on *m*.

(e) Draw a segment $\overline{AB}$ and a line n which does not intersect $\overline{AB}$. Copy $\overline{AB}$ on n.

(f) Draw an angle $\angle RST$ and a ray that does not intersect $\angle RST$. Copy $\angle RST$ using the ray as one side of the angle.

2. Given a line l and a point P not on l, construct a line through P which is parallel to l by constructing
   (a) congruent corresponding angles.
   (b) congruent alternate interior angles.
   (c) two lines perpendicular to the same line.
   (d) Can you find still another method?

3. ("Rusty Compass" Constructions.) Ralph's compass is rusty and will only work at a fixed setting. (It always draws the same-size circles.)
   (a) Name one or more constructions he can do even with this compass.
   (b) Name one or more constructions he can't do with this compass.

4. ("Greasy Compass" Constructions.) Ellen's compass is greasy and — though it draws perfect circles of any desired size — it collapses if she lifts it from the paper. Can you find a way that Ellen can construct a circle congruent to the circle with center O shown below, but so that the new circle has center P?

5. Explain how to bisect an arc of a circle.

6. (a) Draw an angle. Divide it into four congruent angles using compass and straightedge.
   (b) Explain how to divide an angle into 32 congruent parts. (You don't have to do the construction.)

7. Trisect a right angle.

8. Give justifications for the construction of
   (a) the perpendicular at a point on a line (Problem 26, Section 9-4).
   (b) the perpendicular from a point not on a line (Problem 25, Section 9-4).

TRIANGLES

9. Repeat Problem 10 of Section 9-4, replacing the word "sketch" by the word "construct."

10. Draw a fairly large triangle (preferably *not* a right triangle). Use this same triangle to do all of the following:
    (a) Construct the three medians. What happens?
    (b) Construct the three altitudes. What happens?
    (c) Construct the three angle bisectors. What happens?
    (d) Construct the three perpendicular bisectors. What happens?

11. The four parts of the previous problem determine four points: The point where the three medians intersect is called the **centroid**. Label it M. The point where the three altitudes intersect is called the **orthocenter**. Label it O. The point where the three angle bisectors intersect is called the **incenter**. Label it I. The point where the three perpendicular bisectors intersect is called the **circumcenter**. Label it C. Three of these four points lie on the same line (called the **Euler line**). Draw the Euler line.

12. **(a)** Use the circumcenter to draw a circle that contains the vertices of a triangle. **(b)** Use the incenter to draw a circle that touches ("is tangent to") the triangle at three points.

REGULAR POLYGONS

13.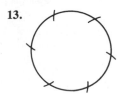

Johnny was playing with his compass. He noticed that if he marked off six arcs around the circle each the size of the radius he seemed to get back where he started. **(a)** Did he? **(b)** Was he just lucky or would this happen for any circle? Give evidence to support your conclusions.

14. Construct **(a)** an equilateral triangle **(b)** a right angle **(c)** a square **(d)** a regular hexagon **(e)** a regular octagon **(f)** a regular dodecagon.

MOSTLY PROBLEM SOLVING

15. In this activity we are going to test which conditions concerning sides and angles of pairs of triangles are sufficient to ensure that the triangles are congruent. $\triangle ABC$ is given. Your goal is to try in each case to *construct* a triangle, $\triangle DEF$, which satisfies the given conditions but is *not* congruent to $\triangle ABC$. In many cases, any triangle you construct that meets the conditions *will* be congruent to $\triangle ABC$, but there are one or more cases where non-congruent counter-examples can be found. If you can't find a counter-example, then construct a triangle which is congruent to the given triangle.

    (Given) $\triangle ABC$ **(a)** $\angle A \cong \angle D$, $\angle B \cong \angle E$, $\angle C \cong \angle F$ (AAA)

    (b) $\overline{AB} \cong \overline{DE}$, $\overline{BC} \cong \overline{EF}$, $\overline{CA} \cong \overline{FD}$ (SSS)

    (c) $\angle A \cong \angle D$, $\overline{AB} \cong \overline{DE}$, $\overline{CA} \cong \overline{FD}$ (SAS)

    (d) $\angle A \cong \angle D$, $\overline{AB} \cong \overline{DE}$, $\overline{BC} \cong \overline{EF}$ (SSA)

    (e) $\angle A \cong \angle D$, $\angle B \cong \angle E$, $\overline{BC} \cong \overline{EF}$ (AAS)

16. The five sets of conditions we have listed (AAA, SSS, SAS, etc.) represent five ways to fill three blanks _____ using A's and S's. List all possible ways of filling in three blanks with A's and/or S's. Circle those that ensure congruent triangles. Mark an "X" through those which don't. (Note that AAS and SAA are equivalent. Why? Which others are equivalent?)

17. Draw a triangle on a piece of cardboard. Construct the centroid. Cut out the triangle and balance it so that the centroid is resting on the point of your compass.

18. Draw two points on a piece of paper. Draw five different circles that contain both of these points. What can you say about the centers of these circles?

19. A group of archaeologists has come to you with the tracing of a piece of a small circular plate they found on a dig. Knowing your expertise in constructions, they expect you to construct the circle. Can you do it?

20. Problem 12(a) shows that three points (not on the same line) determine a circle. How many circles are determined by eight points? (Hint: See Example 9-4.)

21. (Dividing a segment into five congruent parts using compass and straightedge.) We wish to divide $\overline{AB}$ into five congruent parts.

Step 1.   Draw $\overrightarrow{AC}$ and mark off five congruent segments starting at A. Label these points R, S, T, U, and V.

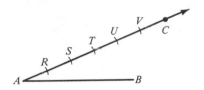

Step 2.   Draw $\overline{VB}$.

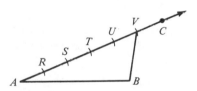

Step 3.   Construct $RW \parallel VB$, by constructing congruent alternate interior angles.

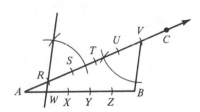

Step 4.   On $\overline{AB}$ mark off $\overline{WX}$, $\overline{XY}$, $\overline{YZ}$ congruent to $\overline{AW}$.

(a) We constructed AR equal to 1/5 of AV. Why is AW equal to 1/5 of AB?
(b) Draw a segment $\overline{JK}$ and trisect it using compass and straightedge.
(c) Use compass and straightedge to divide a given segment into seven congruent parts.
(d) Construct $\overline{MN}$ so that $MN:PQ = 8:3$.

$P\text{————————}Q$

11-2
THE PYTHAGOREAN THEOREM

It is generally agreed that the theorem named in honor of Pythagoras was known long before his time, but Pythagoras is usually credited with being the first to *prove* the theorem (Figure 11-1). There are literally hundreds of proofs, dramatizing how there may be many ways to establish a truth. In fact, *The Pythagorean Proposition* [29] contains 256 different proofs.

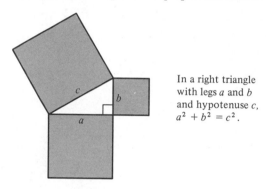

In a right triangle with legs a and b and hypotenuse c, $a^2 + b^2 = c^2$.

FIGURE 11-1   Pythagorean Theorem

Though it's not known exactly which proof Pythagoras gave, he probably gave a proof based on comparing areas of two figures such as those in Figures 11-2 or 11-3.

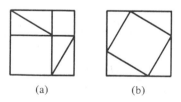

(a)   (b)

FIGURE 11-2

Figure 11-2(a) shows four copies of the right triangle and the two squares whose sides are the legs of the triangle; Figure 11-2(b) shows four copies of the right triangle and the square whose side is the hypotenuse of the triangle. (How can we be sure that the inside figure is a square?) Subtracting the areas of the four triangles from each figure gives the result.

(a)   (b)

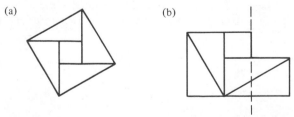

FIGURE 11-3

Another proof is given in Figure 11-3(a), which shows four copies of the right triangle and a small square whose side is the difference between the legs. Together they form a square whose side is the hypotenuse. These same pieces are reassembled to form Figure 11-3(b). The dashed line separates Figure 11-3(b) into two squares, which can be seen to be the squares of the legs. (See Problem 10 at the end of this section.)

In an effort to highlight the elegance of these proofs, we have been quite terse. This will also give you the opportunity to become more involved as you fill in the details which are discussed in the problems.

We offer still another proof which illustrates quite a different approach.

Use the fact that $\triangle RST$, $\triangle RTU$, and $\triangle TSU$ are similar to prove the Pythagorean theorem.

EXAMPLE 11-4

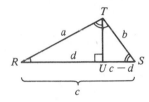

(First we note that methods of Example 10-2 can be used to establish that the triangles are indeed similar.)

$\triangle RTU \sim \triangle RST$, so $\dfrac{a}{c} = \dfrac{d}{a}$, or $a^2 = cd$.

$\triangle TSU \sim \triangle RST$, so $\dfrac{b}{c} = \dfrac{c - d}{b}$, or $b^2 = c^2 - cd$.

Adding gives $a^2 + b^2 = c^2$.

SOLUTION

A sample of yet a different approach is given in Problem 11 at the end of this section, where we present a proof due to James A. Garfield (1831-1881), twentieth president of the United States [29].

In our next example we present a few straightforward applications. Later we will give an example of where the need to use the theorem is disguised.

Find x in each figure.

EXAMPLE 11-5

(a)

(b)

(c)

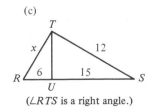

($\angle RTS$ is a right angle.)

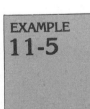

(d)

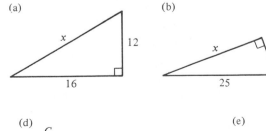

($\angle ACB$ is a right angle.)

(e)

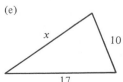

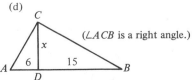

SOLUTION

(a) The hypotenuse is x, so we write

$$16^2 + 12^2 = x^2$$
$$256 + 144 = x^2$$
$$400 = x^2$$
$$x = 20$$

(b) The hypotenuse is 25, so we write

$$x^2 + 7^2 = 25^2$$
$$x^2 + 49 = 625$$
$$x^2 = 576$$
$$x = 24$$

(c) In $\triangle RST$, $\overline{RS}$ is the hypotenuse. Since $RS = 6 + 15 = 21$, we can write

$$x^2 + 12^2 = 21^2$$
$$x^2 + 144 = 441$$
$$x^2 = 297$$
$$x = \sqrt{297}$$

(d) This is precisely Example 10-2, which is easier to solve using similar triangles. $x = \sqrt{90}$.

(e) We are not given a right triangle, so the Pythagorean theorem does not apply. Not enough information is given to solve this problem. (What can you say about x?)

It is worth emphasizing that the Pythagorean theorem applies only to *right* triangles. In fact, we can test whether a triangle is a right triangle by what we call the **converse of the Pythagorean theorem:**

If in a triangle with sides a, b, and c we have $a^2 + b^2 = c^2$, then the triangle is a right triangle.

EXAMPLE 11-6

Which of the following triangles are right triangles?

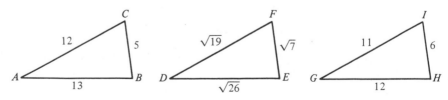

In each case we check to see if the sum of the squares of the shorter sides equals the square of the longer side. In $\triangle ABC$ we have

$$12^2 + 5^2 = 144 + 25 = 169 = 13^2,$$

so $\triangle ABC$ is a right triangle. In $\triangle DEF$ we have

$$(\sqrt{7})^2 + (\sqrt{19})^2 = 7 + 19 = 26 = (\sqrt{26})^2,$$

so $\triangle DEF$ is a right triangle. In $\triangle GHI$ we have

$$6^2 + 11^2 = 36 + 121 = 147 \neq 12^2,$$

so $\triangle GHI$ is *not* a right triangle.

Our last example provides an application of the Pythagorean theorem.

Find the area of an equilateral triangle with side 2.

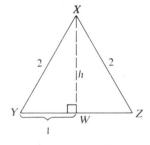

We need to know h, the height of the triangle. We observe that the dashed line splits the equilateral triangle $\triangle XYZ$ into two right triangles, $\triangle XYW$ and $\triangle XZW$. Applying the Pythagorean theorem yields

$$1^2 + h^2 = 2^2$$
$$1 + h^2 = 4$$
$$h^2 = 3$$
$$h = \sqrt{3}$$

Therefore, the area of $\triangle XYZ$ equals $\frac{1}{2} \times 2 \times \sqrt{3}$, which equals $\sqrt{3}$.

EXERCISES AND PROBLEMS 11-2

COMPUTATIONS

1. Find x in each triangle.

(a)

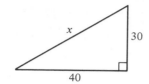

(b)

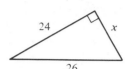

(c)

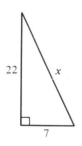

(d)

(e)

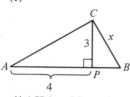

($\angle ACB$ is a right angle.)

(f)

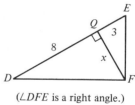

($\angle DFE$ is a right angle.)

(g)

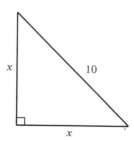

(h)

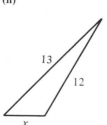

(i) Which of the following are right triangles?

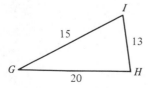

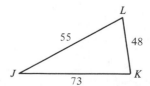

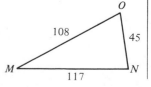

2. Find AC and BC in Example 10-2.

3. What *can* you say about x in part (e) of Example 11-5?

4. Do Problem 10, Section 8-2.

5. (Streetcar Problem.) A streetcar track is made from two pairs of rails each 1 mile (5280 feet) long. On a hot day it expands so that each piece is 5281 feet long, causing the track to buckle as shown. (a) Guess at the value of h. (b) Find h.

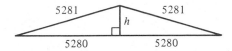

6.

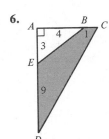

(a) Find the area of quadrilateral $BCDE$.
(b) Find the perimeter of quadrilateral $BCDE$.

7. Find x in Example 11-5(d) without using similar triangles. (Hint: Let $AC = y$ and let $BC = z$ and set up several equations.)

8. Find the area of an equilateral triangle with side
(a) 4   (b) 10   (c) 5   (d) 1   (e) s

9. Give the details to show that $HIJK$ is a square. (See Figure 11-2b.)

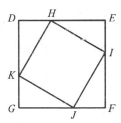

PROOFS AND CONVERSES

10. Let a be the longer leg, b be the shorter leg, and c be the hypotenuse of a given right triangle.

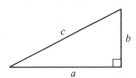

(a) Express the side of the small square in Figure 11-3(a) in terms of a and b.

Find the following dimensions of Figure 11-3(b), using the given triangle:
(b) w **(c)** x **(d)** y **(e)** z **(f)** $w \times x + y \times z$

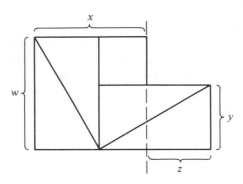

11. According to mathematics historian Howard Eves [40], President Garfield's proof of the Pythagorean theorem is based on this figure. Find the proof.

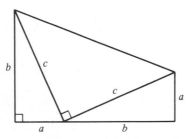

12. Reassemble the eight pieces of squares a^2 and b^2 to fit into square c^2.

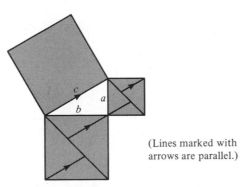

(Lines marked with arrows are parallel.)

13. True or False? Support your claim with a proof (if it is true) or a counter-example (if it is false). "The (area of the) semicircle on the hypotenuse of a right triangle equals the sum of the (areas of the) semicircles on the legs."

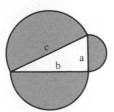

14. The **converse** of a statement is the statement obtained by interchanging the "if" part with the "then" part. (See Appendix.) For example, the converse of "If a figure is a square, then it is a rectangle" is "If a figure is a rectangle, then it is a square." As is often the case, the converse of the original true statement is false. State the converse of each of the following and tell whether the converse is true or false:
   (a) If an angle has measure 42°, it is acute.
   (b) If two sides of a triangle are congruent, then the angles opposite these sides are congruent.
   (c) For any whole numbers a and b, if $a = b$, then $a^2 = b^2$.
   (d) For any integers a and b, if $a = b$, then $a^2 = b^2$.
   (e) All whole numbers are integers.
   (f) All cats are mammals.

PROBLEM SOLVING EXTENSIONS

15. The ancient Egyptians are said to have used a rope knotted at even intervals to form right angles in their construction projects. (a) How do you think they did this? (b) If the length of the segment between consecutive units is taken to be one unit, what is the smallest (whole number) of units the rope could have?

16. $ORQS$ is a rectangle with O at the center of the circle containing Q. Which is longer, $\overline{ST}$ or $\overline{PQ}$?

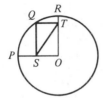

17. Find the shaded area between the circles of radius 1 which touch as shown.

18. (a) Given a segment of length 1, construct (using compass and straightedge) segments of length $\sqrt{2}$, $\sqrt{3}$, $\sqrt{4}$, $\sqrt{5}$, $\sqrt{6}$. (Hint: Use $\sqrt{2}$ to get $\sqrt{3}$.)
    (b) Can a segment of length $\sqrt{n}$ be constructed for every positive whole number n?

19.

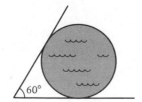

Chris wanted to measure the diameter of a circular pond without getting wet, so she walked away from the pond until it occupied 60° of her vision. She then made a simple measurement and calculated the diameter. How did she do it?

20. (a) A right rectangular prism has edges of length 3, 16, and 24. Find the length of a diagonal of the prism; namely, find *AB*.

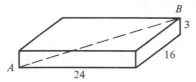

(b) The answer to part (a) is a whole number. Find at least two more prisms, each of whose edges and diagonal are whole numbers. (At least one of your answers should have the property that the GCD of the three edges is 1.)

*21. Let *P* be any point inside an equilateral triangle $\triangle RST$. Find $a + b + c$ in terms of *d*, the length of $\overline{RS}$. Surprisingly, it doesn't depend on which point *P* we choose! (Hint: Draw $\overline{PR}, \overline{PS}$, and $\overline{PT}$ and find the areas of $\triangle RSP$, $\triangle RTP$, and $\triangle STP$ in terms of *a, b, c,* and *d*, the side of the equilateral triangle.)

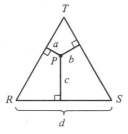

22. (a) Derive the formula for the distance we can see from a given altitude. (See Problem 24, Section 8-2.) (Hint: This formula is an approximation obtained by rounding-off one of the numbers which occurs.) **(b)** Use your formula to determine how far one can see (under clear conditions) from atop the Sears Tower, 1454 feet high.

23. A ball with a diameter 26 cm rests on the open end of a pipe whose inside diameter is 10 cm. How high is the top of the ball above the top of the pipe?

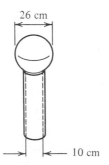

24. (From *NCTM/MAA Sourcebook* [14], p. 162.) Two round bars are placed next to each other so that they touch along their length. A third bar is put on top as shown.
(a) If the diameter of each bar is 2 cm, what is the height *h* of the stack of three pipes?
(b) Repeat part (a) for a stack of ten pipes.

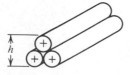

25. How large a square beam may be cut from a perfect log 40 centimeters in diameter and 10 meters long? (See Figure 11-4.)

FIGURE 11-4

11-3
SYMMETRY AND TRANSFORMATIONS

Have you ever tried to open the door of a building by pushing on one side only to find that you should be pushing on the other side? The appeal of symmetry, which seems to be stronger than the appeal of practicality, has resulted in the design of doors that have fooled nearly all of us at one time or another.

On a more positive note, the Taj Mahal, considered by many to be the most beautiful building in the world (see Figure 11-5), provides an outstanding example of symmetry. Besides the obvious horizontal (left and right) symmetry, there are reflecting pools that provide vertical symmetry as well.

FIGURE 11-5

So strong was this desire for symmetry in building the Taj Mahal that, according to one source, an entire building was created on account of it. A guide at the Taj Mahal related the following information to the author: The Taj Mahal itself was built by 20,000 workmen between 1631 and 1653 as a monument to Mumtaz Mahal by her husband, Emperor Shah Jahan. Also built on one side of the approach to the Taj Mahal was a mosque. To maintain the balance, a building identical to the mosque was built directly across from the mosque on the other side of the approach. As a perfect "mirror image" of the mosque, it faced the opposite way. Since a mosque must always face Mecca, the second building could not be used as a mosque even though it was identical. Thus its only purpose was to maintain the symmetry! (See Figure 11-6.)

The symmetry we see in the design of a modern door or in the Taj Mahal is symmetry with respect to a line. One half of the figure is congruent to the other half by a flip in this line, as shown in Figure 11-7. When the paper on which the A is printed is folded on the line of symmetry, the two halves of the A coincide.

FIGURE 11-6

Before folding   After folding

FIGURE 11-7

Another way of viewing this to imagine that the entire paper is rigidly flipped about the line of symmetry. The figure would then coincide with the original figure (though of course the paper would be turned over). This kind of symmetry is called a **folding symmetry** and is just one kind of symmetry.

Figure 11-8 does *not* have a folding symmetry, but it does have a **turning symmetry** or **rotational symmetry**. When the figure is turned 180° around its center, the result will coincide with the original figure.

FIGURE 11-8

Still another type of symmetry is shown in Figure 11-9, where it is understood that the sawtooth figure continues indefinitely in the same pattern. This figure will coincide with itself when we slide it so that one tooth moves to the next. This is an example of a **sliding symmetry** or **translational symmetry**.

FIGURE 11-9

The symmetries are specific instances of the idea of congruence. As in our original example of congruence involving polyominoes in Section 9-3, we have discussed symmetries in terms of rigid motions. This is natural and intuitive. If a child were asked to select one of two peppermint sticks, he or she might place them side by side to determine which is longer. If you were asked right now to take out a sheet of paper and cut it into two pieces of equal size, you might fold it to obtain matching halves. The processes of sliding and turning the peppermint sticks or folding the paper are representative of what we call **rigid motions** or **transformations**.

Each of the three basic rigid motions will now be illustrated. Figure 11-10 shows a **flip** (or **reflection**) of $\triangle XYZ$ about line m. Notice how $\triangle XYZ$ and $\triangle X'Y'Z'$ appear to be mirror images of one another with respect to the

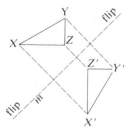

FIGURE 11-10

"mirror," line m. You can imagine this reflection to be the result of copying $\triangle XYZ$ on tracing paper and folding it along line m so that X moves to X', Y moves to Y', and Z moves to Z'. Figure 11-11 shows another flip, this time showing what happens when two of the vertices of the triangle are on opposite sides of the flip line, while the third is on the flip line. Observe that points "change sides" with respect to the flip line *n*, and points that are on the flip line (like point *F*) don't move at all. (*F* and *F'* are the same point.)

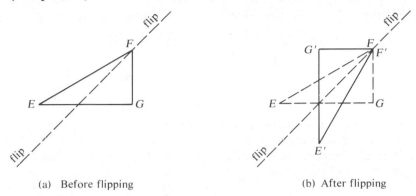

(a) Before flipping   (b) After flipping

FIGURE 11-11

Figure 11-12 shows a **turn** (or **rotation**) of △*RST* about point *P* to position *R'S'T'*. You can picture this rotation as what would happen if you were to copy △*RST* on tracing paper and then swing the tracing paper a quarter of a (clockwise) turn while holding point *P* fixed by the tip of a pencil. This would move *R* to *R'*, *S* to *S'*, and *T* to *T'*.

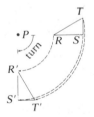

FIGURE 11-12

Figure 11-13 shows a **slide** (or **translation**) of △*ABC* to position *A'B'C'*. You can think of this translation as what would happen if you were to copy △*ABC* on tracing paper and then slide the tracing paper so that *A* moves to *A'*, *B* moves to *B'*, and *C* moves to *C'*.

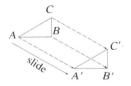

FIGURE 11-13

We can summarize the important features of these three basic rigid motions as follows:

Basic Rigid Motions

Informal Name	Formal Name	Defined in Terms of
Flip	Reflection	Flip line
Turn	Rotation	Center and (clockwise) angle measure
Slide	Translation	Direction and distance

As a result of a rigid motion, each point P of the plane is paired with another point in the plane called its **image** and denoted P'. The image of a point is not necessarily distinct from the original point, as in Figure 11-11, where F and F' are the same point.

EXAMPLE
11-8

Find the image of P for each of the following rigid motions:

(a) a flip in line l

(b) a 60° (clockwise) turn about point O

(c) a slide from R to S.

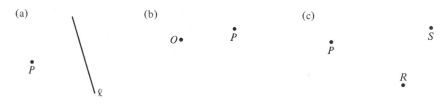

SOLUTION

(a) From P we construct m, the line perpendicular to l, labeling point A as shown. On line m (on the opposite side of l) construct $\overline{P'A} \cong \overline{PA}$. (Figure 11-14a.)

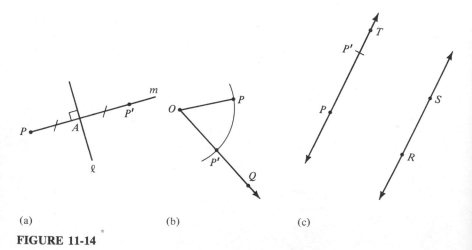

FIGURE 11-14

(b) Construct $\overrightarrow{OQ}$ so that $m(\angle POQ) = 60°$ (using the fact that the measure of each angle of an equilateral triangle is 60°). There are two choices. We choose $\overrightarrow{OQ}$ so that the rotation is *clockwise*. On $\overrightarrow{OQ}$, construct $\overline{OP'} \cong \overline{OP}$. (Figure 11-14b.)

(c) Draw $\overleftrightarrow{RS}$. Construct $\overleftrightarrow{PT} \parallel \overleftrightarrow{RS}$. Construct $\overline{PP'}$ on $\overleftrightarrow{PT}$ so that $\overline{PP'} \cong \overline{RS}$ (and P' and S are on the same side of $\overleftrightarrow{PR}$). (Figure 11-14c.)

We list three reasons for introducing rigid motions:

(1) They provide an intuitive basis for understanding congruence.
(2) They provide the opportunity to explore and discover interesting mathematical relationships.
(3) They provide a setting to reinforce important mathematical properties.

We have already dealt with item (1) in Section 9-3 and now briefly illustrate the remaining two points.

At least two approaches can be used in the elementary school to (2) provide the opportunity to explore and discover interesting mathematical relationships through rigid motions. Figure 11-15 shows the **Mira**, a device which acts like a transparent mirror, permitting the user to see a figure and its image simultaneously. It can be used to construct bisectors, perpendiculars,

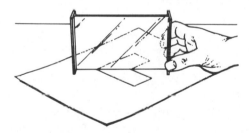

FIGURE 11-15   Mira

and parallels. The Mira can be used in the primary grades to test for (folding) symmetry and in the intermediate grades to establish congruences. Third graders might use the Mira to determine which letters of the alphabet have folding symmetry or which figures are congruent. Sixth graders might use the Mira to determine the rigid motions that establish a congruence or to construct parallel lines.

A second concrete approach to rigid motions is **paper folding**. Relationships such as congruence, perpendicularity, and parallelism can be investigated through paper folding. The traditional Japanese art of **origami** involves intricate and often fascinating figures formed by paper folding, including flowers and animals — even birds with flapping wings [54]!

Next we illustrate using rigid motions to (3) provide a setting to reinforce important mathematical properties. First we will define a new operation and then discuss its properties. When one rigid motion is followed by another, we call this the **product** of the rigid motions. For example, a clockwise turn of 30° about a point O *followed by* a clockwise turn of 60° about a point O is equivalent to a 90° clockwise turn about O. The words "followed by" indicate the "product" of the two turns. Notice that the product of two turns about the same point is a turn about this point.

For now we will restrict our discussion to the **symmetry motions**, those rigid motions for which the image of a given equilateral triangle is the equilateral triangle itself. Given equilateral $\triangle ABC$ in Figure 11-16 we see that

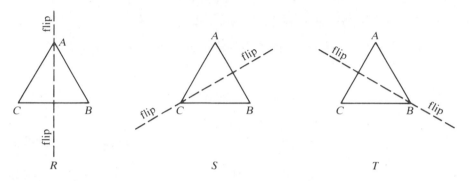

FIGURE 11-16

the image of $\triangle ABC$ after a flip in the altitude to point A is again $\triangle ABC$. As a result of this flip, which we will call R, the image of A is A, the image of B is C, and the image of C is B. We denote this as follows:

$$A \rightarrow A$$
$$B \rightarrow C$$
$$C \rightarrow B$$
$$R$$

We also have S (a flip in the altitude to C) and T (a flip in the altitude to B). We see that R, S, and T describe the three folding symmetries of equilateral $\triangle ABC$.

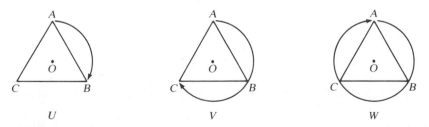

FIGURE 11-17

The triangle also has three turning symmetries, as shown in Figure 11-17. The motion labeled "U" turns the triangle 1/3 of a complete, clockwise revolution about point O. (A goes to B, B goes to C, C goes to A.) The motion labeled "V" turns the triangle 2/3 of a complete, clockwise revolution about point O. The motion labeled "W" turns the triangle one complete clockwise revolution about point O. As a result of motion W, A moves all the way around back to A, B moves to B, and C moves to C. Each point of the triangle is transformed back to itself. It should not be surprising that this motion, where each point is transformed to itself, is called the **identity** transformation.

When describing these transformations, we are usually more interested in the result of the transformation than in how it was done. For instance, motion V is equivalent to turning the triangle 1/3 of a complete *counter*-clockwise revolution about point O, or for that matter, 5⅔ clockwise revolutions about point O. Though there are an unlimited number of rotations that move A to B, B to C, and C to A, we speak of them collectively as a single transformation. Thus, there are in all six symmetries for an equilateral triangle — three folding symmetries and three turning symmetries.

Figure 11-18 tells exactly what happens to each vertex under the six motions. If we were to perform movement U twice, we would have effectively rotated the triangle 2/3 of a revolution, which is the same as doing movement V.

$A \rightarrow A$	$A \rightarrow B$	$A \rightarrow C$
$B \rightarrow C$	$B \rightarrow A$	$B \rightarrow B$
$C \rightarrow B$	$C \rightarrow C$	$C \rightarrow A$
R	S	T
$A \rightarrow B$	$A \rightarrow C$	$A \rightarrow A$
$B \rightarrow C$	$B \rightarrow A$	$B \rightarrow B$
$C \rightarrow A$	$C \rightarrow B$	$C \rightarrow C$
U	V	W

FIGURE 11-18

Hence we write $U \cdot U = V$. Similarly, U followed by V is equivalent to W, so we write $U \cdot V = W$. We can also string together flips. If we perform R twice, the triangle returns to its original position, which is equivalent to doing W. Hence $R \cdot R = W$. Next let's try to determine the effect of doing $R \cdot U$. We do so by recording what happens to each of the vertices:

$$A \longrightarrow A \longrightarrow B$$
$$B \longrightarrow C \longrightarrow A$$
$$C \longrightarrow B \longrightarrow C$$
$$\quad R \qquad\quad U$$

FIGURE 11-19

This diagram says, for instance, that A remains fixed when we do R, and then A moves to B when we do U. The net effect of $R \cdot U$ is

$$A \longrightarrow B$$
$$B \longrightarrow A$$
$$C \longrightarrow C$$

This is recognized to be S, so we write $R \cdot U = S$.

So far, the "product" of two rigid motions (symmetries) of the equilateral triangle has been another rigid motion (symmetry) of the equilateral triangle. This suggests that perhaps the set of these six rigid motions is **closed** with respect to the "product" of performing one transformation after another;

namely, the product of two of these transformations is one of these transformations. This is significant because it indicates that we can discuss closure in the absence of numbers. The closure idea is present not only when adding or multiplying numbers, but even when moving certain geometric figures.

We have discussed closure and identities for rigid motions. Are there commutative and associative properties for transformations? Are there inverses for transformations? We encourage you to probe these non-trivial questions in the problems. In an attempt to arouse your curiosity, we advise you that of the five properties (closure, commutativity, associativity, identity, and inverse), exactly four hold. Can you find the exception?

It may help to organize into a table the results of doing successive transformations. Such a table is started for you in Figure 11-20. The products we have determined so far are shown as entries in the table. For example, the circled entry is $R \cdot U = S$.

	R	S	T	U	V	W
R	W			(S)		
S						
T						
U					V	W
V						
W						

first {

FIGURE 11-20

All in all, the study of symmetry and rigid motions in geometry has practical and aesthetic value. It may even help to open new doors to us.

EXERCISES AND PROBLEMS 11-3

SYMMETRY

1. Count the number of folding symmetries and turning symmetries for each:
   (**a**) equilateral triangle   (**b**) square   (**c**) regular pentagon
   (**d**) regular hexagon   (**e**) figure (e)

(e)

2. Notice how the regular 18-gon $ABCD \ldots R$ resembles a circle. How many symmetries does the 18-gon have? How many would the circle have?

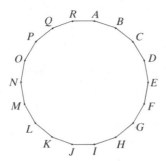

3. (From a third grade text.) In how many ways can you fold each figure so that one half exactly matches the other half?

4. Which capital letters of the alphabet have (**a**) folding symmetry? (**b**) turning symmetry? (**c**) sliding symmetry?

5. You wish to tear a piece of paper exactly in half. Explain how to do it. How is congruence involved here?

6. We mentioned earlier that the Costa Rican lumberman measures the circumference of a tree using a piece of string and that he then folds it to get an approximation for the radius. Explain how he does this.

7. How could a folding symmetry be used in sewing clothes?

8. "TOT," "RADAR," and "DAD" are word **palindromes**, words which are the same spelled backwards and forwards. (**a**) Find several more words which are palindromes. (**b**) What is "Able was I ere I saw Elba" spelled backwards? Can you make up a phrase or sentence which is a palindrome? (**c**) 828 and 4774 are number palindromes. How many three-digit number palindromes are there? (The first digit cannot be 0.) (**d**) How many six-digit palindromes are there? (**e**) Are there more seven-digit or eight-digit palindromes?

9. (**a**) A university marching band spells OHIO facing the fans in the west stands. What change do they need to make to spell OHIO facing the fans in the east stands?
   (**b**) Figure 11-21 shows a sign in front of a hotel in Italy when viewed from the north. How does it appear when viewed from the south?

10. Symmetry plays a role in microwave cooking. According to one cookbook, if you are cooking several items and place one item in the center and the others around it, the outside will attract the microwave energy first and keep the one in the center from being cooked. It sug–gests the following placement for up to five items:

FIGURE 11-21

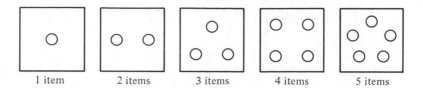

1 item   2 items   3 items   4 items   5 items

(a) Draw a sketch to show how six items should be placed.

(b) Which would cook more evenly, a round meatloaf or a rectangular one? What does this have to do with symmetry?

RIGID MOTIONS

11. (a) A right-handed person using a pair of rubber gloves usually wears out the right glove before the left. When a left glove is turned inside out, it becomes a right glove. Thus the life of two pairs of gloves can be extended. Is this congruence being accomplished through a reflection, a rotation, or a translation?

(b) Assuming a perfectly matched pair of shoes, is a right shoe congruent to a left shoe?

12. Show the image of △*JKL* for each transformation. In each case *K′*, the image of *K*, is given.

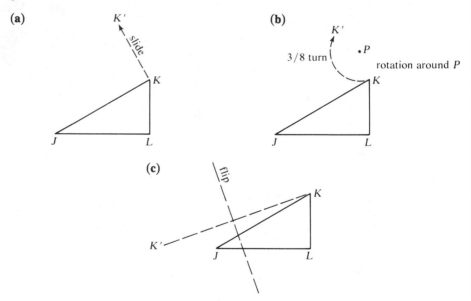

(a)

(b)

(c)

13. Copy this sketch on another piece of paper. Fold the paper on line *n* to determine the image of trapezoid *ABCD*.

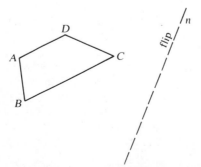

14. $\overline{RS} \cong \overline{TV}$. Describe a sequence of rigid motions that will move $\overline{RS}$ to $\overline{TV}$.

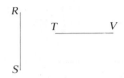

15. (a) Show the image of $\triangle PQR$ after a flip about m followed by a flip about n.

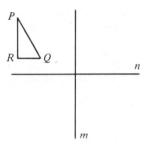

   (b) Describe a single motion which has the same effect as the two flips described in part (a). Give the details.

16. Which points are **invariant** (do not move) when doing
   (a) a slide?   **(b)** a flip?   **(c)** a turn?

17. Ms. Muscle moved her refrigerator two feet sideways by herself, using a series of turns about the corners of the base, since it was too heavy to slide directly. What is the least number of rotations she could have made to do this? (She used the fact that a translation can be accomplished as a product of __?__ .)

18. (a) What is the inverse of motion R (Figure 11-16)? Namely, what transformation can be applied following R to return the triangle to its original position?
   (b) What is the inverse of U (Figure 11-17)?

19. Complete the following products, following the procedure shown in Figure 11-19:
   (a) $S \cdot S$ **(b)** $S \cdot W$ **(c)** $T \cdot U$

20. (a) Complete the table given in Figure 11-20. (See also Problem 19.)
   *****(b)** Find out which one of the five properties (closure, commutativity, associativity, identity, and inverse) fails. Give evidence.

*****21.** Make a table similar to Figure 11-20 for the symmetries of the square.

22. (a) Suppose O and Q are two distinct points. What is the product of a half-turn (turn of 180°) about O followed by a half-turn about Q? Be specific.
   (b) What is the product of half-turns about three distinct non-collinear points O, P, and Q? Be specific.

23. We know that (a) below is a magic square (all rows, columns, diagonals total 15). Complete magic square (b), using the numbers 1 through 9.

  (a)   (b)

24. Ernst Krenck published *Twelve Little Pieces*, Op. 83, in 1939 [74]. The music is based on the twelve-tone technique in which each of the twelve chromatic tones (C, C#, D, etc.) is used exactly once in the original theme. (**a**) How many orders of twelve different tones are possible? (**b**) The twelve pieces use various combinations of an original theme and three forms of it. The original theme and three forms are shown below:

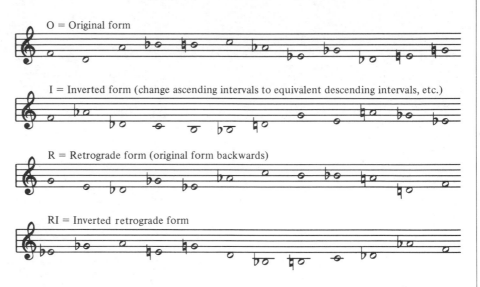

Is RI formed by playing R upside down or by playing I backwards? (**c**) Describe each of the forms as a reflection, rotation, or translation. Be specific, telling *what kind* of reflection, etc. (**d**) The twelve pieces use different combinations of O, I, R, and RI:

1. O: Dancing Toys
2. I: Peaceful Mood
3. R: Walking on a Stormy Day
4. RI: The Moon Rises
5. O + I: Little Chessmen
6. O + R: A Boat, Slowly Sailing
7. O + RI: Streamliner
8. I + R: Glass Figures
9. I + RI: The Sailing Boat, Reflected in the Pond
10. O + R + RI: On the High Mountains
11. O + I + R: Bells in the Fog
12. O + I + R + RI: Indian-Summer Day

Explain how the sailing boat is "mathematically" reflected in the pond. (**e**) How many combinations of O, I, R, and RI (in which we use one or more of these forms) are possible? (**f**) Which ones are *not* used by the composer?

25. Tell how to hit a billiard ball located at *A* so that it will bounce off three cushions and strike a ball located at *B*, given that the angle a ball rebounds from a cushion is congruent to the angle it strikes the cushion. (Hint: *Try a simpler problem.*)

Given condition

26. (Absent-minded Schoolboy Problem.) A boy starts out from his home at *H* and walks to school at *S*. Being absent-minded, he continues walking in the same direction until he walks twice as far as he should. He then spots a movie theater, *M*, and walks in that direction, again twice as far as necessary. The same thing happens again when he sees *I*, the ice cream parlor. All this is shown in the figure. Upon reaching point *P* he again heads for school, but in his absent-minded way he walks double the necessary distance to school, then the movie, then the ice cream parlor. (a) Accurately complete the given figure to find out where he is. (b) Repeat the problem for any other choice of points *H, S, M,* and *I* (with no three of these points collinear). *(c) Can you explain why this happens?

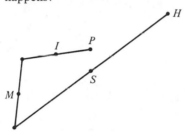

27. (From *NCTM/MAA Sourcebook* [14], p. 281.) In bookbinding, often several pages are printed on a large sheet which is folded and trimmed to form a section (a "signature") of the book. For example, a signature with four leaves (eight pages) can be obtained as follows:

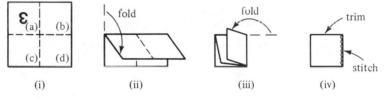

(i)   (ii)   (iii)   (iv)

If page 3 is printed (upside down) in position (a), tell which pages should be printed in positions (b), (c) and (d) (and whether each is upside down or not) so that when the paper is folded and stitched as shown, the pages will be in the right order and right side up.

MATERIALS

*L*28. Use a Mira to complete each word or picture of Figure 11-22.

FIGURE 11-22

L29. **(a)** Show where to place the Mira so that the dot on Space Ship SS-7 is reflected into the
dot of the R-1 Rocket in Figure 11-23. Do the same for the Flying Saucer and the R-2
Rocket.

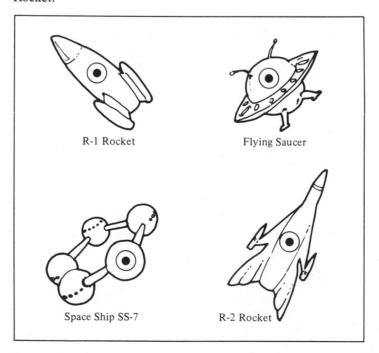

R-1 Rocket   Flying Saucer

Space Ship SS-7   R-2 Rocket

FIGURE 11-23

(b) The Mira line is an important line with regard to the segment joining SS-7 and R-1. What is it?

30. Use a Mira to construct
    (a) the perpendicular bisector of a given segment
    (b) the bisector of a given angle
    (c) a line parallel to a given line through a point not on the line
    (d) a line perpendicular to a given line through a point not on the line
    (e) a line perpendicular to a given line through a point on the line.

31. Repeat Problem 30 by paper folding.

32. Use a folding symmetry to cut out a Valentine heart.

33. Use paper folding to (a) illustrate the fraction 1/8 (b) illustrate that the diagonals of a parallelogram bisect each other (c) locate the center of a given circle (d) construct a square (without using any of the original edges of the paper) (e) construct an equilateral triangle.

34. Read a book on origami [54] and fold some figures. (Special paper is recommended.)

Probability and Statistics, Graphs and Functions

12-1
PROBABILITY

It might appear at first that in discussing probability, often associated with gambling and games of chance, we are going from a practical realm to something almost frivolous. In fact, though probability *is* an exciting and enjoyable topic, it is also quite useful.

Weather forecasting and predicting election results are two familiar examples of the occurrence of probability (and statistics) in practical situations. Saying that "there is a 10% chance of rain tomorrow" conveys considerably more information than "there is a chance of rain tomorrow." Careful sampling of returns in a presidential election gives early insight into the likely outcome. (However, shoddy sampling techniques have been known to yield misleading predictions, as in the celebrated case of the Truman vs. Dewey campaign of 1948.)

Some contemporary information related to probability and statistics is given in *The Odds on Virtually Everything* [34]. It is difficult to determine the accuracy of the following information, but you may find it interesting. (The **odds** of a certain event occurring is the ratio of the likelihood it will happen to the likelihood it will not happen.)

*The odds of becoming a millionaire are 1:423.

*The odds of being killed in a crash by a regularly scheduled commercial plane are, based on

number of passengers	1:603,930
hours in the air	1:21,772
passenger miles	1:8,959,000

*The odds, based on the contraceptive method used, that a woman will become pregnant are

rhythm	1:52
foam/cream/jelly	1:70
diaphragm	1:91
condom	1:109
IUD	1:280
pill	1:603

Less obvious applications of probability occur in such areas as insurance and educational research. Should you buy a $50-deductible or a $100-deductible car insurance policy? What does it mean if some day as a teacher you read that "students who were taught reading by Method A did significantly better (at the .05 level) than students who were taught reading by Method B"?

Besides its practical applications, teaching probability in the elementary schools motivates and reinforces the arithmetic of fractions, decimals, and percents; it encourages critical thinking; and it fosters investigation and exploration in mathematics by elementary school children.

To get a feeling for the concept of probability, consider the following example:

EXAMPLE 12-1

Juan loves black jelly beans. His older sister, Maria, showed him the contents of the two bags illustrated below and offered him the choice of picking one jelly bean (with his eyes closed) from either bag A or bag B. Which bag should Juan select to have the greatest chance of drawing a black jelly bean?

 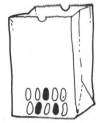

Bag A contains
3 black jelly beans
7 white jelly beans

Bag B contains
1 black jelly bean
1 white jelly bean

SOLUTION

Juan opted for bag A, since it contained more black jelly beans. Was he right? His chances for "success" for bag A are 3 out of 10, so he could expect success about 3/10 of the time. His chances for bag B are 1 out of 2, so he could expect success about 1/2 (or 5/10) of the time. Thus his chances for success were actually better for bag B, though it contained *fewer* black jelly beans.

In the spirit of this example, probability can be viewed as a comparison between the number of ways a particular thing may happen to the number of possibilities. If someone thinks of a letter of the alphabet, the probability of your guessing it in one try is 1/26, since there is one correct choice out of 26. Yet without clarification of this definition, someone could argue that the probability of guessing the correct letter of the alphabet is 1/2: either you guess it or you don't. The difficulty here is that there is one way to guess correctly but 25 ways to guess incorrectly. Implicit in the definition of probability is the idea that the possibilities are **equally likely**; that is, one possibility is as likely to occur as any other.

To tighten up the definition of probability we first introduce some vocabulary. Any activity such as drawing lots or flipping coins is called an **experiment**. Any set S for which each outcome of the experiment corresponds to exactly one member of S is called a **sample space**. Any subset of a sample space is called an **event**. Recalling that "$n(A)$" means "the number of members in set A," we can now define probability for any experiment which has a finite number of equally likely outcomes:

☐ Definition of Probability

> In any experiment with a finite number of equally likely outcomes given by a sample space S, the **probability of an event E** occurring is given by
> $P(E) = n(E)/n(S)$.

EXAMPLE 12-2

An ordinary die (singular for "dice") with faces numbered 1, 2, 3, 4, 5, and 6 is rolled. (a) Show *two* possible sample spaces. (b) List the event "an odd number is rolled" for each sample space. (c) Find the probability the event occurs using each sample space.

SOLUTION

(a) Remembering the sample space is a *set*, we can write $S = \{1, 2, 3, 4, 5, 6\}$. Clearly each outcome corresponds to one member of S, so S is a sample space. Another sample space is $T = \{odd, even\}$. To confirm that T is a sample space, note that each of the possible outcomes corresponds to exactly one member of T. (1, 3, and 5 correspond to "odd" and 2, 4, and 6 correspond to "even.")

(b) For $S = \{1, 2, 3, 4, 5, 6\}$, the event "an odd number is rolled" is the subset $E = \{1, 3, 5\}$. For $T = \{odd, even\}$, the event is simply $F = \{odd\}$.

(c) Using S as a sample space, we have $n(S) = 6$ and $n(E) = 3$, so $P(odd) = 3/6$. Using T as a sample space, we have $n(T) = 2$ and $n(F) = 1$, so $P(odd) = 1/2$ (which of course equals 3/6).

EXAMPLE 12-3

A letter is selected randomly from the 11 letters of the word "commutative." What is the probability it is (a) a "t"? (b) a vowel? (c) an "n"?

SOLUTION

(To understand what we mean by "selected randomly," imagine that the 11 letters are written one each on 11 identical slips of paper and shuffled in a hat. If we draw one without looking at it, it will be selected randomly. Also note that each slip of paper is equally likely to be chosen. We can think of the (set of) 11 slips of paper as our sample space.)

(a) Of the 11 slips of paper, 2 will contain t's, so $P(t) = 2/11$.

(b) Of the 11 slips of paper, 5 will contain vowels (a, e, i, o, u), so $P(\text{vowel})$ $= 5/11$.

(c) Of the 11 slips of paper, *none* will contain an n, so $P(n) = 0/11$ or 0.

As problems get more complicated, we can use the techniques for counting developed earlier. We will also make use of **tree diagrams,** illustrated in the examples that follow.

A coin is flipped twice. Find the probability of obtaining (a) both heads (b) a head and a tail (in either order) (c) a tail followed by a head.

EXAMPLE 12-4

SOLUTION

(a) We draw a tree diagram, signifying "heads" by H and "tails" by T.

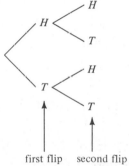

first flip   second flip

This tree diagram suggests the sample space $\{HH, HT, TH, TT\}$. Of the four possibilities only the choice HH is included in the event "both heads," so $P(\text{both heads}) = 1/4$.

(b) Both HT and TH are included in the event "a head and a tail (in either order)," so $P(\text{a head and a tail}) = 2/4$ or 1/2.

(c) Only HT is included in the event "a tail followed by a head," so $P(\text{a head followed by a tail}) = 1/4$.

A setting familiar to most people that generates an abundance of examples is determining the probabilities of making various selections out of an ordinary deck of cards. Familiarize yourself with an ordinary deck of 52 cards if necessary in preparation for the examples that follow.

EXAMPLE

12-5

One card is drawn from an ordinary deck of 52 cards. Determine the probability that it is

(a) a red card   (b) a king   (c) *not* a king

(d) a king *or* a queen

(e) a king *and* a red card (in other words, a red king)

(f) a king *or* a red card   (g) a heart

(h) a heart, if we are also given that the card is red

SOLUTION

(a) 26 of the 52 cards (half of them) are red, so $P(\text{red}) = 26/52$. Since $26/52 = 1/2$, we can alternatively write $P(\text{red}) = 1/2$. It would be quite correct in this case to say that since there are two *equally likely* colors, $P(\text{red}) = 1/2$.

(b) $P(\text{king}) = 4/52$, because there are 52 possibilities of which four are kings.

(c) $P(\text{not a king}) = 48/52$, because there are 52 possibilities of which 48 are *not* kings. Note that $P(\text{king}) + P(\text{not a king}) = 1$.

(d) Four of the cards are kings and four are queens, so eight of the cards are kings or queens. Hence $P(\text{king or queen}) = 8/52$.

(e) There are four kings of which two are red. The number of "favorable" outcomes is then two, and we have $P(\text{king and red}) = 2/52$.

(f) Four of the cards are kings, 26 are red cards, but only 28 (not 30) are kings or red cards. Why? Hence $P(\text{kings or red}) = 28/52$.

(g) Looking at this as choosing from 52 *cards,* we have 13 hearts out of 52, so $P(\text{heart}) = 13/52$. Looking at it as choosing one of four equally likely *suits*, we have $P(\text{heart}) = 1/4$. This is quite agreeable, for in fact $13/52 = 1/4$.

(h) Since we know the selection is red, it is one of 26 possibilities. Of these 26 possibilities 13 are hearts, so $P(\text{heart given red}) = 13/26 = 1/2$.

EXAMPLE

12-6

Two cards are drawn from an ordinary deck of cards, one after the other without replacement. (The term "without replacement" means that the second card is drawn before the first card is replaced in the deck.) Determine the probability of drawing

(a) two kings   (b) two red cards

(c) a king, then a queen   (d) a king and a queen in any order

(e) at least one ace

(a) First we count the ways of getting two kings. There are four ways to draw the first king. For each of the four kings that might be drawn first, there are three kings that can be drawn second; so we have 4×3 ways of drawing two kings. In all, there are 52 choices for the first card and, once it is selected, 51 choices for the second card. Thus there are 52×51 possible choices of any two cards, so

$$P(2 \text{ kings}) = \frac{4 \times 3}{52 \times 51} = \frac{1 \times 1}{13 \times 17} = \frac{1}{221}.$$

Note: In multiplying 13×17 we can use the shortcut of Problem 23, Section 3-5.

(b) There are 26 red cards to start with and 25 after the first one is selected, so the number of ways of drawing two red cards is 26×25. As in part (a), there are 52×51 possible outcomes:

$$P(2 \text{ reds}) = \frac{26 \times 25}{52 \times 51} = \frac{1 \times 25}{2 \times 51} = \frac{25}{102}.$$

(c) There are four ways to draw a king. For each of these four choices, there are four ways remaining in which to draw a queen. Thus

$$P(\text{king then queen}) = \frac{4 \times 4}{52 \times 51} = \frac{1 \times 4}{13 \times 51} = \frac{4}{663}.$$

(d) We can get either a king followed by a queen or a queen followed by a king. We have already seen that there are $4 \times 4 = 16$ ways to select a king followed by a queen. Similarly, there are $4 \times 4 = 16$ ways to select a queen followed by a king. In all there are $16 + 16 = 32$ ways to select a king and a queen in any order. Thus

$$P(\text{king and queen in any order}) = \frac{32}{52 \times 51} = \frac{8}{13 \times 51} = \frac{8}{663}.$$

(e) The event "at least one ace" and the event "no aces" together account for all of the possibilities, so it can easily be shown that

$$P(\text{at least 1 ace}) + P(\text{no aces}) = 1, \text{ or}$$

$$P(\text{at least 1 ace}) = 1 - P(\text{no ace}).$$

Since there are 48 cards which are *not* aces,

$$P(\text{no ace}) = \frac{48 \times 47}{52 \times 51} = \frac{4 \times 47}{13 \times 17} = \frac{188}{221}, \text{ so}$$

$$P(\text{at least 1 ace}) = 1 - \frac{188}{221} = \frac{33}{221}.$$

Part (e) can be generalized as follows (see also Problem 61):

Probability of Complementary Events

P(event E will occur) $= 1 - P$(event E will not occur).

As another example, suppose a coin is flipped five times. There will be $2^5 = 32$ possible outcomes, so

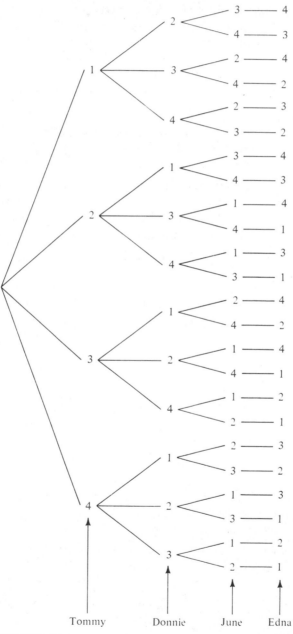

FIGURE 12-1

$$P(\text{at least 1 head}) = 1 - P(\text{no heads})$$
$$= 1 - P(\text{all tails})$$
$$= 1 - \frac{1}{32}$$
$$= \frac{31}{32}.$$

Next we consider examples where one event may depend on another.

Tommy, Donnie, June, and Edna decide to draw lots to see which two have to do the dishes. Edna places four slips of paper numbered 1 to 4 respectively into a hat and mixes them up. In the order named, they each draw a slip of paper and keep it. The two with the lowest numbers will have to do dishes. Find the probability that

EXAMPLE

12-7

(a) Tommy, who draws first, will have to do dishes.

(b) Edna, who must take the slip left over after the others have drawn, will have to do dishes.

(c) Edna will have to do dishes if Tommy shows her that he got a 1.

(d) Edna will have to do dishes if the boys tell her (truthfully) that the sum of their numbers is at least five.

There are different ways to solve this problem. The tree diagram shown in Figure 12-1 can be used to answer all four questions.

SOLUTION

(a) Tommy does dishes if he draws a 1 or a 2. It can be seen from the diagram that this condition is satisfied in the first 12 of the 24 branches, so $P = 12/24$ or $1/2$. Another approach is to see that he has four equally likely draws (1, 2, 3, or 4) and he does dishes in two of these cases (1 or 2), so $P(\text{Tommy does dishes}) = 2/4$ or $1/2$.

(b) Edna must take the number left over. Since each number is equally likely to be left over, her probability is the same. (Non-believers can count that each of the numbers 1, 2, 3, and 4 appears six times as a choice for Edna in the 24 branches of the tree diagram.)

(c) Since Tommy got a 1, we can restrict ourselves to the first six branches of the tree diagram. Of these six equally likely outcomes, Edna washes dishes in two cases (the branches 1-3-4-2 and 1-4-3-2), so $P = 2/6$ or $1/3$. Another approach is to see that she now has three equally likely draws (2, 3, or 4) and she does dishes in one of these cases (2), so $P = 1/3$.

(d) Figure 12-2 shows the branches that satisfy the condition that "the sum of the boys' numbers is at least five" (marked with an "x"). Of these 16 equally likely outcomes, Edna does dishes in 10 cases (marked with a "√"), so $P = 10/16$ or $5/8$.

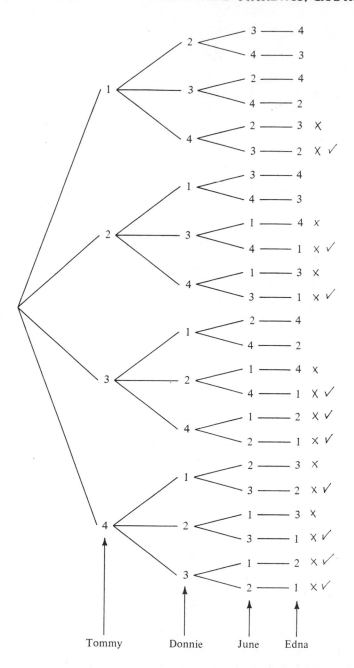

FIGURE 12-2

We can see from part (c) of this example that if Tommy draws a 1, indicating that he must do dishes, the probability that Edna must do dishes decreases from 1/2 to 1/3. The same would be true if Tommy drew a 2. On the other hand, if Tommy drew a 3 or a 4, the probability that Edna does dishes increases. Since the draw for Edna depends on the draw made by Tommy we speak of these as **dependent** events. Another way of viewing dependent events is given in Problem 65.

Sometimes we are interested in the probability of one event occurring (such as the event that Edna draws a 1 or a 2) in light of another event occurring (such as the event that Tommy draws a 1). The probability that one event will occur, given that another event has occurred, is called **conditional probability**. The next two examples illustrate this idea.

We spin the two spinners shown below each once. Find the probability that (a) spinner B shows a 3. (b) the sum of the spins is 6.

Spinner A   Spinner B

EXAMPLE
12-8

Once again we draw a tree diagram:

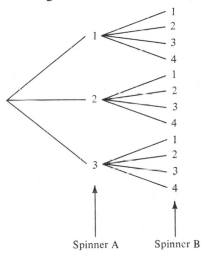

Spinner A   Spinner B

(a) Of the 12 branches, we see that spinner B shows a 3 in three branches, so P(B shows 3) = 3/12 or 1/4. (Since only spinner B is involved in this part, it would be quite correct to consider the sample space {1, 2, 3, 4} for spinner B and conclude P(B shows 3) = 1/4).

(b) The 12 branches of the tree diagram show the 12 equally likely outcomes of the sample space. Of these, there are two branches (2 + 4 and 3 + 3) for which the event "the sum of the spins is 6" occurs, so P(sum is 6) = 2/12 = 1/6.

Repeat the previous example, given that spinner A shows a 3.

EXAMPLE
12-9

SOLUTION

Since we are given that spinner A shows a 3, we can limit our consideration to only this part of the tree diagram:

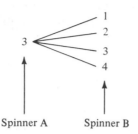

Spinner A   Spinner B

(a) Of the four branches being considered, spinner B shows a 3 in one case, so P(B shows 3, given A shows 3) = 1/4.

(b) Of the four branches being considered, the sum is 6 in one case, so P(sum is 6, given A shows 3) = 1/4.

Note that the outcome of spinner A does not affect the outcome of spinner B, while the outcome of spinner A does affect the sum.

All the examples so far are illustrations of what is **mathematical** (or *a priori*) **probability**, characterized by the ability to determine the exact probability from given information prior to actually drawing any cards, etc. By contrast, saying that the chances that a given unborn infant will be a boy are slightly better than one-half, or that there is a 10% chance of rain tomorrow are examples of **experimental** (or *a posteriori*) **probability**, in that these probabilities are estimated by considering what has happened in similar situations in the past.

An example of experimental probability popular in elementary school mathematics is the tossing of thumbtacks on a hard surface. The tacks can land with either "point up" ($\perp$) or "point down" ($\wedge$). For example, if we have tossed a tack 50 times and recorded that it landed "point up" 27 times and "point down" 23 times, we say the experimental probability of "point up" is $P = 27/50$.

To further contrast mathematical probability with experimental probability we provide an example involving both.

EXAMPLE
12-10

Given two dice, determine (a) the mathematical probability (b) the experimental probability of rolling a pair.

SOLUTION

(a) The *mathematical* probability is computed from certain assumptions about the dice. Imagine that we roll the dice and look first at one die, then the other. There are six possible outcomes for the first die (1, 2, 3, 4, 5, or 6) and six possible outcomes for the second die, so there are 6 × 6 possible outcomes for the two dice. To have a pair, there are six choices for the first die and then only one choice for the second die, since the second die must match the first. Thus $P(\text{pair}) = (6 \times 1)/(6 \times 6) = 6/36$ or 1/6.

(b) The *experimental* probability is observed by actually rolling two dice. At the time of writing, the author actually rolled two dice 100 times with the following results:

1,3	6,3	2,6	1,2	5,2	5,4	2,5	3,5	6,5	2,3
3,5	5,6	5,4	2,6	2,1	3,1	4,6	1,5	5,3	6,2
6,6	3,6	1,6	1,3	2,5	2,6	3,5	3,6	6,4	6,5
3,1	2,5	1,2	2,3	6,2	3,5	4,6	4,5	2,8	2,6
5,2	2,4	1,1	5,2	2,4	1,5	1,5	1,3	2,4	4,6
3,1	6,5	2,1	4,6	4,6	4,6	2,6	1,2	5,1	2,4
5,4	4,4	6,5	5,6	5,6	3,6	2,6	4,5	5,5	3,5
3,1	2,4	4,2	6,5	4,6	5,4	4,5	5,5	1,1	3,1
5,5	4,5	3,5	4,4	3,2	2,2	6,5	4,6	5,5	6,4
6,3	5,2	2,1	6,3	6,4	3,5	6,3	3,6	3,5	2,2

By actual count a pair appeared 11 times in 100 trials so $P(\text{pair}) = 11/100$.

Since the mathematical probability of getting a pair is 1/6, we would expect about 1/6 of the 100 trials, or about 16, to be pairs. The actual count was 11, a bit lower. Another 100 trials would probably yield a different result, but we would expect the results to contain about 16 pairs.

Our reason for drawing attention to the distinction between mathematical probability and experimental probability is to attempt to dispel a common misconception about probability. Let's consider an example which, though hypothetical, discusses a typical instance of this misconception.

Luke has tossed a fair coin five times and has gotten five heads. "Fair" means that heads and tails are equally likely. What is the probability that a sixth toss will be heads?

EXAMPLE
12-11

Some people would argue that since the coin is "running" heads, the next flip has a probability of more than one-half of being heads. Others might contend that since it is very unlikely that the same thing would happen six times in a row, the "law of averages" suggests that the next toss would probably be tails. They are both basing judgment on what has already happened (*a posteriori*), when in fact this is irrelevant (so long as the coin is fair). The probability that any given toss is heads remains one-half. (Certainly the tossed coin doesn't know whether it is "supposed to" land heads or tails!)

SOLUTION

Further examples are offered for your consideration in the problems.

EXERCISES AND PROBLEMS 12-1

BASIC PROBLEMS

1. A bag contains three white, five blue, and six red marbles. One marble is drawn. Find the probability it is
   (a) white   (b) white or blue   (c) red

2. If you choose any whole number 1 to 10 (including 1 and 10) what is the probability that it is
   (a) prime?   (b) even?

3. The dial of a spinner is divided into three colors — red, white, and blue. If $P(\text{red}) = 1/2$ and $P(\text{white}) = 1/4$, what is the probability of blue?

4. The six faces of an ordinary (hexagonal) pencil have been painted — two of them red, one white, three blue. The pencil is rolled on a flat surface and stops with one of the faces on top. Find the probability it is
   (a) red   (b) white   (c) blue

5. A die has six faces numbered 1, 2, 3, 4, 5, and 6. If the die is rolled once, find the probability of
   (a) getting a 2   (b) *not* getting a 2
   (c) getting a 2 or greater   (d) getting an even number
   (e) What are the *odds* of getting a 2?

6. A card is drawn from an ordinary 52-card deck. Determine the probability it is
   (a) a black card   (b) a club
   (c) an ace   (d) a picture card (king, queen, or jack)
   (e) a black ace   (f) an ace or a black card (or both)
   (g) neither an ace nor a black card
   In the remaining parts, we are given that the card drawn is black. Find the probability it is
   (h) a club   (i) a heart   (j) a king

7. It is known that the king of clubs is missing from a deck of cards. (No other cards are missing.) Repeat the previous problem with this modified deck.

8. Two cards are drawn without replacement from an ordinary deck of 52 cards. Determine the probability of drawing
   (a) two jacks   (b) two clubs
   (c) two black cards   (d) no black cards
   (e) a black card followed by a red card
   (f) cards of different colors
   (g) cards of different suits (hearts, clubs, etc.)
   *(h) a heart followed by a king

9. Repeat the previous problem given that the first card *is* replaced before drawing the second.

10. It is known that the king of clubs is missing. (No other cards are missing.) Repeat Problem 8 with this modified deck.

11. Three cards are drawn without replacement from an ordinary deck. Find the probability of drawing
    (a) three jacks   (b) three clubs

(c) three black cards   (d) cards of three different suits
(e) a black card followed by two red cards
(f) a black card and two red cards in any order
*(g) a red card followed by a heart followed by a king

12. A box contains nine slips of paper numbered 1 through 9 respectively. Two slips are drawn (without replacement). Find the probability that both contain odd numbers.

13. If the probability of rain on Monday is 50% and of rain on Tuesday is 50%, what is the probability of rain
    (a) on both days?   (b) on at least one of the days?

14. Two dice are thrown. Find the probability of obtaining
    (a) a total of seven   (b) a pair   (c) an even sum

15. (a) Show that if three coins are flipped, the probability of getting all heads or all tails is 1/4.
    (b) What (if anything) is wrong with the following argument? If three coins are flipped, two must land the same way. The chances that the third one will agree are, therefore, 1 out of 2, so the probability of getting all heads or all tails is 1/2.

16. A baby was given these three blocks to play with:

Her parents were convinced that she was a genius when she lined them up to spell "CAT" (even though all the letters were not right side up).
    (a) What is the probability that if she lined them up at random the letters would be in sequence "C-A-T"?
    (b) What is the probability that she would spell "CAT" *and* all the letters would be right side up?

17. A man who won a million dollars in the state lottery said he knew he was going to win, having told several of his friends in advance. Argue that he did or did not have psychic powers. (Could anything else explain what happened?)

18. Suppose a thousand people around the country claim to be "seers" (prophets). Suppose further that each of them is asked to pick in advance one day in the year in which the year's most tragic event will occur. About how many would you expect to be right just by guessing? Suppose two of the thousand actually named the right day. Would this be convincing evidence that they had special powers?

19. *Any* two whole numbers are chosen at random. (These might be 8,587,003,816,925 and 746,829,222,817,314,414,732,996,824; we aren't limiting this to numbers like 3 and 7.) Find the probability they are
    (a) both divisible by 2   (b) not both divisible by 2
    (c) both divisible by 3   (d) not both divisible by 3

*20. Urn I contains one white marble and nine black ones. Urn II contains five white marbles and one black one. An urn is chosen at random, and then a marble is selected from this urn. If it is white, what is the probability it came from urn I?

21. Repeat Example 12-1 given that bag A is unchanged and bag B contains
    (a) two black and three white jelly beans.
    (b) one black and two white jelly beans.

22. A bag contains five white marbles and four black marbles. If three marbles are drawn (without replacement), find the probability that *at least* one is white.

23. In Example 12-7, find the probability that
    (a) both boys have to do dishes.
    (b) Edna will have to do dishes if the boys tell her (truthfully) that the sum of their numbers is at least six.

24. Repeat Example 12-7 if there are five children (add Vivian to the list) and a fifth slip of paper numbered 5.

25. In the experiment of Example 12-8, find the probability that spinner B shows a 3, given that sum of the spinners is six.

26. Solve the problem of Example 12-10(a) using a tree diagram.

PASCAL'S TRIANGLE

27. Pascal's triangle is the following configuration of numbers (first alluded to in Problems 40-44, Section 2-1):

$$
\begin{array}{ccccccc}
1 & 1 \\
1 & 2 & 1 \\
1 & 3 & 3 & 1 \\
1 & 4 & 6 & 4 & 1 \\
1 & 5 & 10 & 10 & 5 & 1
\end{array}
$$

    (a) Fill in the next five rows and save for future reference.
    (b) Describe as many patterns as you can.

28. Pascal's triangle is useful in doing certain probability problems. We will illustrate it here by considering the number of heads obtained when flipping coins.

    If we flip one coin, we get either tails or heads. Thus we get either 0 heads or 1 head; moreover, there is just one way of getting 0 heads and one way of getting 1 head.

    If we flip two coins, we get (using *H* for heads and *T* for tails) *TT, HT, TH,* or *HH*. Thus we get either 0 heads (1 way: *TT*), 1 head (2 ways: either *HT* or *TH*), or 2 heads (1 way: *HH*).

    If we flip three coins, we get 0 heads (1 way: *TTT*), 1 head (3 ways: *HTT, THT, TTH*), 2 heads (3 ways: *HHT, HTH, THH*), or 3 heads (1 way: *HHH*).

    Did you notice that we seem to be generating Pascal's triangle?

$$
\begin{array}{lcccc}
\text{one coin:} & 1 & 1 \\
\text{two coins:} & 1 & 2 & 1 \\
\text{three coins:} & 1 & 3 & 3 & 1
\end{array}
$$

We will now try to get some feeling for why this is happening by looking at one of the entries in the diagram. Suppose we wish to know how many ways there are to get three heads with four coins. The sequences of *H*'s and *T*'s that qualify are: *HHHT, HHTH, HTHH,* and *THHH*. Notice that if the fourth toss is tails, all the first three tosses must be heads (*HHHT*), which, as we saw *when considering three coins,* can occur in only one way (*HHH*). But if the fourth toss is heads, the first three tosses must result in exactly two heads (<u>HHTH</u>, <u>HTHH</u>, or <u>THHH</u>), which we saw *when considering three coins* can occur in exactly three ways (*HHT, HTH,* or *THH*). Thus the number of ways to get three heads in four tosses equals the sum of the number of ways of getting either three heads or two heads *when tossing three coins*.

Use Pascal's triangle to help find the probability of getting exactly
(a) 0 heads when tossing three coins
(b) 1 head when tossing three coins
(c) 2 heads when tossing three coins
(d) 3 heads when tossing three coins
(e) 0 heads when tossing four coins
(f) 1 head when tossing four coins
(g) 3 heads when tossing four coins
(h) 4 heads when tossing six coins
(i) 10 heads when tossing ten coins
(j) 9 heads when tossing ten coins

29. Suppose you guess at every item on a true-false quiz, filling in each item with either T or F. Find the probability of getting
(a) all the questions right on a three-question quiz
(b) all the questions right on a five-question quiz
(c) exactly four questions right on a five-question quiz
(d) at least four questions right on a five-question quiz
(e) at least 70% right on a ten-question quiz

30. A coin is flipped five times to see if it is fair. What is the probability that a fair coin would land heads all five times? How many times should the coin be flipped so that the probability of all heads is less than 1/1000?

EXPECTED VALUE

31. A state lottery advertises that if you correctly pick three digits in order (like 122 or 509) you are paid $500 for every $1 you spend. On the average, how much can you expect to get back for each $1 you spend?

32. The probability of winning the sweepstakes sponsored by a radio station is given to be 1/500,000. If it costs 20¢ to mail in your entry, how much should the prize be to make it mathematically worthwhile?

33. Suppose at a roulette table the probability of selecting the winning number is 1/38 and that the winner gets $30 (plus the original dollar) for each $1 bet. (a) About how much would you expect to be ahead or behind after 38 $1 bets? (b) Based on part (a), on the average how much can you expect it to cost (in terms of anticipated wins or losses) to make a $1 bet? This amount is called the **expected value**. (c) If $10,000 is bet at a given table in one night, how much will "the house" (the casino) expect to win or lose?

34. A game is played in which the house pays the player $2 for every $1 bet if he gets 0, 1, 4, or 5 heads on 5 tosses of a fair coin.
(a) Find the probability the player wins on any given play.
(b) Find the probability the house wins on any given play.
(c) How much profit (or loss) does the house make on the average for every $10 which is bet?
(d) Simulate the game yourself ten times, recording your winnings (or losses).

APPLICATIONS

35. A sampling is made of the output of machines A and B, the results of which are shown below:

	Number of Acceptable Pieces	Number of Defective Pieces	Total
Machine A	60	15	75
Machine B	24	1	25
Total	84	16	100

One of the 100 pieces is selected at random. What is the probability
(a) it came from machine A?
(b) it is defective?
(c) it came from machine A if it is defective?
(d) it came from machine A if it is acceptable?
(e) it is defective, if it came from machine A?

36. How many questions should a true-false quiz have so that the chance of passing (with a score of 70% or better) just by guessing at the answers will be less than 0.05? Note: The "0.05" of this problem is similar to the 0.05 level of significance referred to when discussing the reading experiment at the beginning of this section.

37. When weather forecasters say, "There is a 10% chance of rain tomorrow," they mean that under similar conditions in the past it has rained the next day about 10% of the time. Suppose that after predicting a 10% chance of rain, it rains. Was the weather forecaster wrong?

38. A weather forecaster says that the chance of rain today is 60%. You look outside and it is raining. Is the weather forecaster wrong?

39. In making election predictions, past records are checked to see how the early votes of selected states (or other subdivisions of the total population) matched the final results. Some areas are designated as "good predictors." (Have you heard the saying "As Maine goes, so goes the nation"?) Can you think of a situation in which one candidate might be leading in the early returns, yet the prediction might favor the other candidate?

40. $50-deductible insurance means that the insurance company pays all damages over $50, while the policyholder pays the first $50. Suppose $50-deductible auto insurance costs $20 more per year than $100-deductible. (It costs *more* because you collect more if you have an accident.) Which would be a better buy if you expected to have exactly one accident (assume the damages are in excess of $100) once each
(a) year?   (b) two years?   (c) three years?
(d) What other factors might be taken into consideration?

41. A supermarket manager wants to determine a service charge for cashing checks for the sole purpose of offsetting the cost of bad checks. He finds that about 1 out of every 200 checks cashed is bad, averaging $50 apiece. What service charge should he assess? What other factors might be involved?

42. Ron has two alarm clocks, each of which works 80% of the time. Find the probability that he gets up on time if he
(a) sets one alarm. (He is on time if it works.)
(b) sets both alarms and gets up as soon as one of them goes off. (He is on time if either one works.)
(c) sets both alarms and gets up when the second one goes off. (He is on time only if they both work.)

43. A dance studio reputedly once offered a lesson to anyone who had a "lucky dollar." They said a bill was a "lucky dollar" if its serial number included a 2, 5, or 7.

(a) What is the probability that a given *digit* is a 2, 5, or 7?

(b) What is the probability that a given *digit* is *not* a 2, 5, or 7?

(c) There are eight digits in the serial number of a dollar bill. What is the probability that all eight digits will *not* be "lucky" ones?

(d) Out of 100 dollar bills, how many do you think will be lucky ones?

44. A businesswoman has flown a million miles as an airline passenger without an accident. Is she more susceptible to being in an accident on her next flight than a woman who will be flying for the first time? (Suppose they get on the same plane.)

45. From 1820 through 1960 inclusive, every U.S. President elected in a year divisible by 20 died in office. What does this say about the likelihood of a President elected in 1980 dying in office?

46. Freddy is a compulsive gambler. He bets only on races which have exactly seven horses (his lucky number), but he admits he just guesses at which horse will win. Having lost ten consecutive times when trying to pick the winner, he now feels "due" to win. Estimate his probability of picking the winner.

47. According to the odds given in the introduction to this section, what is the *probability* that

(a) a given person will become a millionaire?

(b) a passenger will die during a two-hour flight?

(c) a woman will inadvertently become pregnant while taking contraceptive pills?

48. A major manufacturer of beer once advertised that an extremely small percentage of people surveyed could distinguish among its beer served from cans, from bottles, and from kegs. About what fraction of the people ought to distinguish correctly simply by guessing (even if they don't taste it)?

*49. (Steve Viktora Birthday Problem.) In Ghana, children are often named according to the day of the week on which they are born. Find

(a) the probability that both of two children were born on the same day of the week.

(b) the probability that at least two children were born on the same day if there are three children. (Hint: First find the probability that all three children were born on different days.)

(c) the number of children necessary to make the probability of at least two being born on the same day more than 1/2.

(d) the number of children necessary to make it absolutely certain that two were born on the same day.

*50. (Classic Birthday Problem.) Suppose there are r people in a room. Find the probability that at least two of these people have the same birthday for each value of r given below. Assume that all years have 365 days and that all birthdays are equally likely. (Hint: In each case first consider the probability that each two people have a *different* birthday.)

(a) $r = 2$ (b) $r = 3$ (c) $r = 4$

(d) *Guess* how many people would have to be in the room so that the chances are that at least two have the same birthday.

51. If 12 children are separated into three teams of four each, what is the probability that two particular children will be on the same team?

52. By one estimate, for each 5000 eggs laid by a salmon, 100 live to be fish. With predators and other hazards it is estimated that ten of these fish reach the spawning ground. According to these estimates, what is the probability that a given egg (a) develops into a fish? (b) develops into fish which reaches the spawning ground?

53. (True Story.) A third grade teacher noticed that one of her pupils' homework papers was written in the pupil's handwriting for the first three items and in someone else's handwriting for the rest of the items. When asked to explain, the pupil said that she did the first three items and then fell asleep. When she awoke the rest was done, but she didn't know who did it. What is the probability . . . ?

54. In a modified version of *Kauda*, a game played by the children of Nepal, eight shells are tossed so that they land either "up" or "down." (Figure 12-3 shows two shells "up" and six shells "down.") The winner is determined according to the number of shells landing up:

Player	Wins with
Chauka	0, 4, or 8 up
Panja	1 or 5 up
Chhakka	2 or 6 up
Tiya	3 or 7 up

Assuming that each shell is equally likely to land "up" or "down," find the probability that (a) Chauka will win. (b) Compute the probability for the other players. (c) Use nutshells or seashells to determine the experimental probability that a shell lands "up," describing your method. (d) Would the results of part (a) be the same in light of the experimental probability you found in part (c)? Explain.

FIGURE 12-3

MATERIALS

*L*55. (a) Toss a thumbtack onto a hard surface 30 times. Record the results for each toss according to whether the point of the tack is "up" or "down."
    (b) Estimate from your data the probability of getting an "up" on a single toss.

56. (Class Activity.) Flip a coin ten times. As a class, summarize your results. (How many got four heads? five heads? etc.) Graph the results.

57. The grid in Figure 12-4 is four squares by eight squares, where the side of each square is equal to the diameter of a penny.

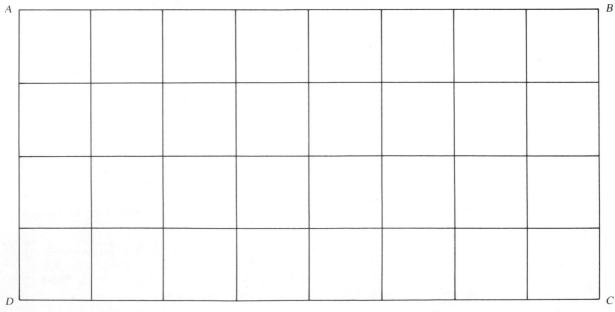

FIGURE 12-4

(a) Make a grid four squares by four squares, where the side of each square is equal to *twice* the diameter of a penny.

(b) Toss a penny (no other coin will do) onto your grid 40 times. (Use only the tosses where the entire penny is inside of the boundaries of the grid.) Count how many times the penny lands in a position touching one of the grid lines. Estimate from your data the probability of touching a grid line.

*(c) Compute the mathematical probability of touching a grid line. (Hint: Suppose the center of the penny lies on or in a given square. Consider those points inside that square for which the penny will touch the grid vs. all the points inside the square.)

58. (a) Toss a *penny* (no other coin will do) on the grid of Figure 12-4 40 times (only the tosses where the entire penny is inside of rectangle *ABCD*). Count how many times a *vertex* of one of the squares is covered by the penny. Estimate from your data the probability of covering a vertex.

(b) The mathematical probability can be shown to be π/4. How close did you come? Account for the difference.

*(c) Show that the probability is π/4. (See the hint in the previous problem.)

*59. (**Monte Carlo Method**.) Suppose we throw darts at the figure shown, a circle with radius 1 inside of a square with side 4. We count the darts landing inside the circle and compare with the number landing inside the rectangle, ignoring those that miss the rectangle. (a) Assuming it is equally likely for a dart to hit any of the points inside the rectangle, what fraction of the throws that hit the rectangle would you expect to land in the circle? (b) Explain how dart throwing could be used to estimate π. (c) Explain how dart throwing could be used to find the area of an irregular shape.

DEFINITIONS

60. The odds of a certain event occurring is the ratio of the likelihood it will happen to the likelihood it will not happen. Examples: A die has six faces, 1, 2, 3, 4, 5, 6. Suppose a die is thrown once.

> The odds in favor of getting a 3 are 1 : 5.
> The odds against getting a 3 are 5 : 1.
> The odds in favor of getting 5 or greater are 2 : 4 (or 3 : 1).

A die is thrown. What are the odds (**a**) in favor of getting a 2?   (**b**) against getting a 2? (**c**) in favor of getting a 2 or greater?

A coin is flipped. What are the odds (**d**) in favor of getting heads?   (**e**) in favor of getting tails?

Two coins are flipped. What are the odds (**f**) in favor of getting two heads? (**g**) against getting two heads?

61. Recall that an event is a subset of a sample space *S*. Some additional terms frequently used when discussing probability are these:

If an event consists of precisely one member of *S*, it is called a **simple event**. Otherwise it is called a **compound event**. If *E* is an event, then those members of the sample space which are not in *E* form a set called the **complementary event**.

For example, tossing a die is an experiment. The possible outcomes are 1, 2, 3, 4, 5, and 6. One sample space is {1, 2, 3, 4, 5, 6}. The event "getting a 3" is written {3} and is a simple event. The event "getting an odd number" is written {1, 3, 5} and is a compound event. The complementary event to {1, 3, 5} is {2, 4, 6}; namely, "getting an even number." The probability of getting an odd number is $P(\{1, 3, 5\}) = n(\{1, 3, 5\})/n(\{1, 2, 3, 4, 5, 6\}) = 3/6 = 1/2$.

Write out the vocabulary as was done in this example for the following problems:
(**a**) 2(a)   (**b**) 2(b)   (**c**) 14(a)   (**d**) 14(b)

62. Two events E and F are called **mutually exclusive** if $E \cap F = \{\ \}$. When rolling a die, are the following pairs of events mutually exclusive?
(**a**) getting a 3 and getting an odd number
(**b**) getting a 3 and getting an even number
(**c**) getting an odd number and getting an even number
(**d**) When does $P(E) + P(F) = P(E \cup F)$?
(**e**) Relate part (d) to addition of whole numbers.

63. (True Story.) A waitress knew that three people in a party of four ordered coffee but couldn't remember which three. When she brought the coffee she didn't ask who wanted coffee. She found out with a question that was easier for the group to answer. (**a**) What was her question? (**b**) Relate this story to one of the concepts presented in this section.

64. In Example 12-2, tell which of the following sets are sample spaces:
$U = \{$less than 3, more than 4$\}$
$V = \{$more than 3, less than 4$\}$
$W = \{$more than 2, less than 5$\}$
$X = \{1,$ more than 1$\}$

65. One way to view independent events is as follows: Events A and B are **independent** if $P(A$ given $B) = P(A)$. In other words, the probability of event A occurring is the same whether we are given that event B has occurred or not. Use this definition to test whether the events A and B are independent by computing $P(A$ given $B)$ and $P(A)$ for each of the following. In each case the experiment consists of rolling a pair of dice, one red and the other green.
(**a**) $A = \{$red die is odd$\}$ $B = \{$green die is odd$\}$
(**b**) $A = \{$red die is odd$\}$ $B = \{$total of both dice is 7$\}$
(**c**) $A = \{$red die is odd$\}$ $B = \{$total of both dice is 12$\}$
(**d**) $A = \{$red die is odd$\}$ $B = \{$total of both dice is 4$\}$
(**e**) $A = \{$red die is more than 4$\}$ $B = \{$total of both dice is 7$\}$
(**f**) $A = \{$red die is more than 4$\}$ $B = \{$total of both dice is 9$\}$

12-2
STATISTICS

Expensive Statistics!

"Federal statisticians have been counting themselves lately. They found that some 29,000 workers in more than 100 agencies are assigned to produce statistics for the myriad of government programs. Cost to taxpayers: About 1 billion dollars a year." (Source: *U.S. News & World Report,* July 14, 1980, page 12.)

Statistics have become an important aspect of the American way of life — at least in the federal government! In another article we read that a 14-year study of 265,000 Japanese men and women reported in the *British Medical Journal* concluded that a husband who smoked 20 cigarettes a day doubled a non-smoking wife's chance of dying of lung cancer (*Time*, January 26, 1981, p. 57). These statistics could be a matter of life and death!

Like probability, statistics is an extremely useful subject which, though worthy of considerable study, we will only briefly introduce in this book. In a broad sense, the field we call **statistics** is the study of methods of obtaining and analyzing quantitative data.

Statistics has several branches. Carefully drawing conclusions about how an entire population will vote based on knowing how a sample of that population is planning to vote is an example of what is called **statistical inference**. Describing the results of an exam for a class by stating the highest and lowest scores, the average score, how many scores were above 90%, etc., is an example of what is called **descriptive statistics**. Even the techniques for sampling (when engaging in statistical inference) comprise a branch of statistics, appropriately called **sampling statistics**. In our limited exposure to this topic, we will consider only descriptive statistics.

In Section 12-3 we will discuss the use of graphs and charts to represent data. Besides using graphs and charts, we can also describe data in other ways. For instance, considerable information about the results of a test is rapidly transmitted by saying that out of 100 possible points, the median (described below) was 76, the high was 98, and the low was 57. Two often useful things to know about a set of test scores are the average or middle score and the extent to which the scores are spread out. This also applies to data other than test scores, and in general we classify statistical measures which summarize a set of data into two types — measures of central tendency and measures of dispersion.

The common **measures of central tendency** are the mean, the median, and the mode. The **mean** is what is usually intended when the word *average* is used. Given a set of n numbers (not necessarily different), the mean is the sum of the numbers divided by n. Thus the mean of 12, 13, and 17 is $(12 + 13 + 17)/3 = 14$. The **median** of a set of numbers (not necessarily different) is the middle number when they are arranged in order of size. Thus the median of 12, 13, and 17 is 13. There are different methods for determining the median in a case like 1, 2, 10, 14, where there is no one middle number. A natural way to handle this is to pick the number halfway between the middle numbers. For example, the median for 1, 2, 10, 14 is 6, since 6 is halfway between 2 and 10. Finally, the **mode** of a set of numbers is the most frequently occurring number. For instance, if more people got 100 than any other score on a test, then 100 would be the mode. For a set of data like 1, 2, 10, 14, each number occurs once; so there is no one mode. The mean, median, and mode are each referred to as "statistics" of a given set of data.

Determine (a) the mean, (b) the median, and (c) the mode for the following set of quiz scores: 8, 9, 5, 3, 9, 7, 7, 10.

EXAMPLE 12-12

SOLUTION

(a) The sum of the eight scores is 58, so the mean is 58/8 = 7.25.

(b) To determine the median, we arrange the scores in order (3, 5, 7, 7, 8, 9, 9, 10) and pick the middle one. There is no middle score. The middle lies between 7 and 8, so we say it is 7.5.

(c) The most frequently occurring scores are 9 and 7, each of which occurs twice. There are two modes, 9 and 7. (This set of data is described as **bimodal**.) In practice we probably wouldn't report the mode for so few numbers, since it is hardly distinguishable from the others.

Notice that the mean, median, and mode(s) were different.

Our next example shows the need for other measures to characterize different sets of data.

EXAMPLE 12-13

Determine the mean, median, and mode for data sets A and B.

Data Set A	Data Set B
10	0
10	10
10	10
10	10
10	20

SOLUTION

Mean of A = 50/5 = 10; mean of B = 50/5 = 10. Median of A = median of B = 10. Mode of A = mode of B = 10.

Each of these two quite different sets of data has a mean, median, and mode of 10. These three statistics fail to distinguish between the two sets of numbers in any way. The essential difference (somewhat exaggerated in this example) is that the scores in set A are "bunched up" (in fact, they are the same) while the scores in set B are "spread out." Statistics that identify the degree to which scores are "bunched up" or "spread out" are called **measures of dispersion**.

The simplest measure of dispersion is the range, the difference between the highest and lowest scores. The range of data set A of Example 12-13 is 10 − 10 = 0. The range of data set B is 20 − 0 = 20.

EXAMPLE 12-14

Find the range of the set of test scores 89, 52, 100, 96, 83, 74, 64, 81, 74, 88.

SOLUTION

The highest score is 100; the lowest is 52. The range is 100 − 52 = 48.

Now suppose the scores were 100, 100, 100, 52, 100, 100, 100, 100, 100, 100. Again the range would be 48 for this vastly different set of data. This time the scores are actually tightly bunched together with one exception, but the range doesn't indicate this. We see that the range is heavily influenced by an extreme score or two and fails to tell us much about the other scores.

What we need is a measure of dispersion which takes into account all the data. Such measures do exist, but they are a bit more complicated to compute. Our next task is to develop the two most common measures of this type, the variance and the standard deviation.

The essential ingredient of these measures is to compare each item of data with the average of all of the data. When scores are bunched, they will not deviate much from the average; when the scores are spread, deviations will be greater. To illustrate how we do it, let's carry out the computations for a simple example using the numbers 10, 12, 12, and 18. We are going to calculate the **deviations from the mean**, so we start by determining the mean. We readily see it to be 52/4, or 13. Then we have

Number	Mean	Deviation from Mean
10	13	3 (below the mean)
12	13	1 (below the mean)
12	13	1 (below the mean)
18	13	5 (above the mean)

Our next step is to square each of the deviations:

Number	Mean	Deviation from Mean	Deviation Squared
10	13	3 (below the mean)	9
12	13	1 (below the mean)	1
12	13	1 (below the mean)	1
18	13	5 (above the mean)	25

The **variance** is now the average of all of the squares of the deviations from the mean:

$$\text{Variance} = \frac{9 + 1 + 1 + 25}{4} = \frac{36}{4} = 9$$

In summary:

Procedure for Computing Variance □

1. Calculate the mean.
2. Find the individual deviations from the mean.
3. Square these individual deviations.
4. Calculate the average of the squares of the deviations.

EXAMPLE 12-15

Compute the variance for the numbers 1, 4, 10, 12, and 18.

SOLUTION

1. Calculate the mean:

$$\text{Mean} = \frac{1 + 4 + 10 + 12 + 18}{5} = \frac{45}{5} = 9$$

Number	Mean	2. Deviation from Mean	3. Deviation Squared
1	9	8 (below)	64
4	9	5 (below)	25
10	9	1 (below)	1
12	9	3 (above)	9
18	9	9 (above)	81

4. Calculate the average of the squares of the deviations:

$$\text{Variance} = \frac{64 + 25 + 1 + 9 + 81}{5} = \frac{180}{5} = 36$$

The most important measure of dispersion is the **standard deviation**, the (positive) square root of the variance. In the first example above we found the variance to be 9, so the standard deviation is 3. (Recall that 3 is the positive "square root" of 9 since $3^2 = 9$.) In Example 12-15, the variance is 36, so the standard deviation is 6. In practice you are likely to encounter numbers with square roots that are not so easy to determine. For instance, if the variance is 10, then the standard deviation is $\sqrt{10}$, which is *approximately* 3.16228 (obtained using a calculator).

A useful application of standard deviation is in standardizing test results. Given a test score, we can translate it into a standardized score called a **z-score** by determining how many standard deviations it is away from the mean. Scores below the mean are prefaced with a minus sign. For example, suppose a test had a mean of 70 and a standard deviation of 6. A score of 76 would be one standard deviation (6 points) above the mean, so it would be equivalent to a z-score of 1. A score of 82 would be two standard deviations (12 points) above the mean, so it would be equivalent to a z-score of 2. A score of 64 would be one standard deviation (6 points) *below* the mean, so it would be equivalent to a z-score of −1. Further illustrations are given below.

EXAMPLE 12-16

The following scores were made on a test with a mean of 70 and a standard deviation of 6. Complete the table.

Name	Raw Score	Z-score
Ali	76	1.0
Brenda	64	−1.0
Ching	79	1.5

David	82	
Ellen	67	
Fernando	70	
Glenda		2.5
Harry		−3.0
Irene	55	

David's 82 is 12 points above the mean. This is two standard deviations, so his z-score is 2.

Ellen's 67 is 3 points below the mean. This is a half of a standard deviation *below* the mean, so her z-score is −.5.

Fernando's score equals the mean. Since it differs from the mean by 0 standard deviations, his z-score is 0.

Glenda's z-score is 2.5, so her raw score must be 2.5 standard deviations (15 points) above the mean, which is $70 + 15 = 85$.

Harry's score is three standard deviations (18 points) *below* the mean so his raw score is $70 − 18 = 52$.

Irene's score is 15 points below the mean. This is 2.5 standard deviations *below* the mean, so her z-score is −2.5.

SOLUTION

To illustrate the value of standard scores, we will now examine a hypothetical case where inequities occur because of a failure to account for dispersion. Mr. Knight and Mr. Bishop each teach a section of the same course, but at different hours. They give different tests and compare results. Because the mean for each class turns out to be 70 and because the instructors rate the classes about equal in ability, they decide to grade using the same criteria. The instructors overlook the fact that the scores on Mr. Knight's test are quite "bunched up," with a standard deviation of only 5, while the scores on Mr. Bishop's test are comparatively "spread out," with a standard deviation of 20. Bobby's grade was 80, the highest score on Mr. Knight's test. Joey, who is in Mr. Bishop's class, also got 80, but in this class 80 was just a bit above average. In grading by common standards, both students got a B. Moreover, no one in Mr. Knight's class got an A or an F, though there were many A's and F's in Mr. Bishop's class. Of course, it is possible that all this is quite fair and appropriate, but it is more likely that the performances varied because of the different tests being administered. Z-scores for Bobby and Joey would have been 2.0 and .5 respectively, more accurately reflecting each individual's performance on the particular test administered in comparison with that of the others who took that test. In practice, the same phenomenon can occur even with a single instructor administering several different tests.

Important testing instruments, particularly when given to large numbers of people, are often standardized. Another method (besides z-scores) used is to scale the test so the mean becomes 500 and the standard deviation becomes

100. Then, a score two standard deviations above the mean is 700 and a score one standard deviation below the mean is 400, etc.

Volumes can be written about statistics (and in fact have been). Since educators are often heavy users of statistics, you may wish to investigate this topic beyond the brief discussion provided in this section.

EXERCISES AND PROBLEMS 12-2

BASIC COMPUTATIONS

1. Find the mean, median, and mode for each group of data:
   (a) 4, 5, 6, 9, 11
   (b) 2, 6, 6, 6
   (c) 3, 5, 5, 7, 8, 11
   (d) 1, 12, 2, 0, 2, 0, 10, 5, 0 (see Problem 2, Section 12-3)
   (e) 1.0, 5.2, 1.5, .4, 30.1, 39.4, 9.5, 19.2, .7

2. In each part, find a set of data with the given characteristics:
   (a) The mean equals the median.
   (b) The mean is greater than the median.
   (c) The mean is less than the median.
   (d) The mean is 20 and the median is 20.
   (e) The mean is 20 and the median is 25.
   (f) The mean is 25 and the median is 20.

3. When is the mean of a set of numbers a member of the set?

4. Find the variance and standard deviation for each set of data. (Hint: In these carefully selected examples, the standard deviation is always a whole number.)
   (a) 4, 6, 6, 12   (b) 5, 7, 7, 13
   (c) 0, 2, 3, 4, 6   (d) 10, 13, 19, 21, 27
   (e) 0, 3, 4, 6, 12   (f) 0, 3, 3, 5, 5, 6, 6

5. Find the mean and standard deviation for each set of data. Look for patterns in parts (a)-(e) and (f)-(j).
   (a) 0, 3, 4, 6, 12   (b) 1, 4, 5, 7, 13
   (c) 2, 5, 6, 8, 14   (d) 3, 6, 7, 9, 15
   (e) 10, 13, 14, 16, 22   (f) 0, 3, 4, 6, 12 (same as a)
   (g) 0, 6, 8, 12, 24   (h) 0, 9, 12, 18, 36
   (i) 0, 12, 16, 24, 48   (j) 0, 300, 400, 600, 1200
   (k) What effect does adding the same amount to each item of data have on the mean and the standard deviation?
   (l) What effect does multiplying each item of data by the same amount have on the mean and the standard deviation?
   (m) On the basis of your answer to (k), determine indirectly the mean and standard deviation for the numbers 4, 7, 8, 10, 16. Verify by computing directly.
   (n) On the basis of your answer to (l), determine indirectly the mean and standard deviation for the numbers 0, 15, 20, 30, 60. Verify by computing directly.
   *(o) Suppose a given set of data has a mean of m and a standard deviation of s. What will be the mean and standard deviation if you triple each data item and then add 6? If you add 6 to each data item and then triple the result?

6. Convert the scores of Example 12-16 to standard scores with mean 500 and a standard deviation of 100. (Hint: Ali's score would be 600; Brenda's would be 400.)

7. Which of the following is most affected by one exceptionally low score?
   (a) mean, median, or mode?   (b) range or standard deviation?

8. We can check the computation of the mean of a set of numbers by seeing if the total amount of deviations above the mean equals the total amount of deviations below the mean. The mean for 4, 5, 8, 9, and 14 is 8.

Score	Deviation
4	4 below ⎫ total 7 below
5	3 below ⎭
8	
9	1 above ⎫ total 7 above
14	6 above ⎭

   (a) Find the mean of 1, 4, 8, 8, 20, and 25 and use the method illustrated above to check it.
   (b) Repeat (a) for the numbers $122,000, $122,200, $122,200, $122,600, $123,000.
   (c) Why does this work?

APPLICATIONS

9. A professor gives four exams, each graded with a maximum of 100 points. She likes to give more preference to the grades a student earns as the semester advances. She uses what is called a **weighted mean**, or **weighted average**, counting the second score twice as much as the first, the third three times as much as the first, and the last five times as much. Joan got scores of 80, 90, 70, and 60 so her weighted average was

$$\frac{80 + 180 + 210 + 300}{1 + 2 + 3 + 5} = \frac{770}{11} = 77$$

   Compute weighted means for the following students:
   (a) Archie 60, 70, 80, 90   (b) Brian 70, 70, 70, 70
   (c) Cornelius 90, 86, 77, 93

10. The president of a company draws a salary of $200,000 per year. The eight people working in sales and management each earn $40,000 per year; four foremen (or is it forepersons?) each earn $20,000 and twelve laborers each earn $10,000.
    (a) The president claims the average employee of the company earns $28,800. Is he right?
    (b) The union claims the average working man for the company earns $10,000. Are they right?
    (c) Statistically describe the wages from an impartial viewpoint.

11. In the opening of this section the word *quantitative* was used to describe data.
    (a) What is the difference between *quantitative* and *qualitative*?
    (b) In chemistry, compounds are sometimes analyzed to determine what chemicals are present, and other times they are analyzed to determine how much of a known chemical is present. Which is quantitative? Which is qualitative?

12. Students in a class had the following scores on an exam: 99, 96, 95, 93, 91, 90, 89, 89, 87, 86, 85, 82, 82, 80, 78, 77, 77, 77, 76, 75, 73, 72, 70, 70, 63.
    (a) Find the mean, median, and mode.
    (b) Group the data into intervals 60-64, 65-69, 70-74, 75-79, etc., indicating how many scores fall into each group.

13. We are bombarded in advertising with statements like "America's most popular brand" or "used by more people than any other brand."
    (a) Does being most popular necessarily mean something is better or even preferable? Support your answer.
    (b) An item of graffiti once stated (roughly), "Eat garbage —3 billion flies can't be wrong." Comment in light of your answer to part (a).

14. A student has scores of 72, 80, 65, 78, and 60 on her first five 100-point tests. What must she get on the next 100-point test to get an average of (a) 70?   (b) 80?

15. A newspaper article reports that there will be an estimated 72,000 rapes in a certain city during an average woman's lifetime, and that "consequently, with the city's population of 290,000 women, 1 out of 4 will be raped." Assume the estimates of 72,000 rapes and the 290,000 women are accurate. Do you agree with the analysis? Explain.

SAMPLING

16. Four hundred trout are netted in a pond, tagged, and released unharmed. Several weeks later 100 trout are netted in the same pond, of which 40 are found to be tagged. (a) Estimate the total number of trout in the pond, explaining your method. (b) What assumptions are being made?

17. One hundred sparrows in a preserve are captured, tagged, and released unharmed. Several weeks later 200 sparrows are captured in the same preserve, of which 40 are found to be tagged. (a) Estimate the sparrow population of the preserve, explaining your method. (b) What assumptions are being made?

18. In the first 2000 digits in the decimal representation for π, the digits 0 through 9 occur with the following frequency:

Digit	0	1	2	3	4	5	6	7	8	9
Frequency	182	212	207	189	195	205	200	197	202	211

    (a) About how many times would you expect each digit to occur if the digits occur with equal frequency?
    (b) What is the maximum "error" (discrepancy from the expected value) which occurs?
    (c) Express this "error" as a relative error.
    (d) Does the evidence seem to confirm or deny the contention that all digits occur with equal frequency?
    (e) A digit is chosen at random from the first 2000 digits in the decimal representation for π. What is the probability it is a 2?

19. (a) Suppose a coin is flipped a million times. About how many times do you think it would come up heads?
    (b) Suppose a coin is flipped once. About how many times do you think it would come up heads?
    (c) In which case is it easier to estimate what will happen?

20. (Class Activity.) Take surveys, one or more, on issues in your class. Use secret ballot and summarize the results. Some possible issues:
    (a) abortion
    (b) draft registration
    (c) religion
    (d) smoking
    (e) drinking
    (f) drugs
    (g) Do blondes have more fun?

MATERIALS AND CALCULATORS

21. Describe an activity using brown bags and colored chips (or bags of M&M's) which could be used with sixth graders to simulate the trout and sparrow problems (Problems 16 and 17).

*L*22. Determine the average reaction time for a group of students in your class as follows: Form a circle and join hands. Everyone closes his or her eyes. One person starts a stopwatch and squeezes the hand of the person to the right. Each person in succession "passes on" the squeeze in a circle back to the original person, who stops the watch. Divide the total elapsed time by the number of reactions. What kind of average is this (mean, median, or mode)?

23. Examine several elementary school mathematics series. Which concepts from this section are introduced? In what grades?

*C*24. Use a calculator with a square root key to determine the standard deviation for the following sets of data.
    (a) 2, 3, 5, 14   **(b)** 13, 18, 19, 25, 36, 39

12-3
GRAPHS

In considering methods for describing data, we certainly do not wish to overlook graphing, a descriptive yet simple way of conveying information. Consider this clever elementary introduction to graphing, attributed to the authors of the Nuffield Project, an activity-based program initiated in England's elementary schools. Pupils in the early grades are asked whether they walk to school, take the bus, or travel by other means. Those who walk are asked to place their math books in one pile, those who come by bus to place their books in another pile, and the rest to place their books in a third pile. (See Figure 12-5.) A "graph" that readily facilitates comparisons vividly comes to life through a direct contribution by each child. This is likely to be the first graph these children ever encounter, but one they will long remember!

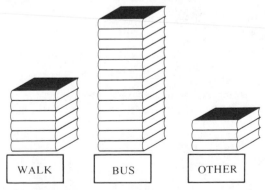

WALK   BUS   OTHER

FIGURE 12-5

After concrete experiences like the one just described, similar graphs can be made on paper. We could show the same information as with the books by drawing a graph like Figure 12-6. Such a diagram is called a **bar graph**. It is

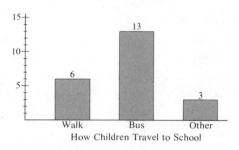

How Children Travel to School

FIGURE 12-6

constructed simply by making bars (vertical or horizontal) whose lengths are proportional to the amounts they represent (just as the areas of the respective parts of the circle graph given in Problem 15, Section 6-3, are proportional to the amounts they represent).

A slight modification of the bar graph, in which we place the bars contiguously ("touching") — especially to show data grouped in intervals — is called a **histogram**. The information from the 1976 *CBS News Almanac* given in Figure 12-7(a) is portrayed in a histogram in Figure 12-7(b).

U.S. Family Income: 1970

Family Income	% of Families
Under $5,000	18.4%
$5,000–$9,999	29.7%
$10,000–$14,999	26.9%
$15,000–$24,999	19.5%
$25,000 and over	5.3%

FIGURE 12-7(a)   **FIGURE 12-7(b)**

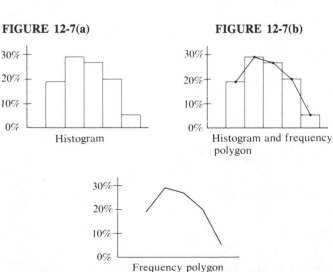

Histogram   Histogram and frequency polygon

Frequency polygon

FIGURE 12-8

When the upper ends of the (vertical) bars at the middle of the intervals are connected by line segments, the resulting figure is called a **frequency polygon**. (In Figure 12-8 the income levels are the same as in Figure 12-7.)

Similar graphs (though not necessarily constructed from histograms) are often used to show trends, as in Figure 12-9. We can see that they have the capability of comparing two different sets of data on the same graph. (Source: U.S. Public Health Service.) A glance at this graph tells us that the marriage rate in the United States from 1910 to 1980 fluctuated between about 8 and 12 marriages per thousand people while the divorce rate increased quite steadily from about 1 per thousand to about 5 per thousand.

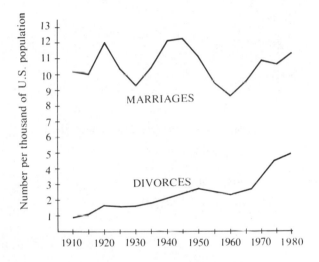

FIGURE 12-9

The circle graph (or pie graph), first mentioned in Problem 15 of Section 6-3, is illustrated again in Figure 12-10. Observe how useful it is in showing parts of a whole. (Source: U.S. Dept. of Commerce.) The circle graph is just one of many graphs we may see any time we pick up a newspaper.

1980 Government Transfer Payments (Federal, State, Local)

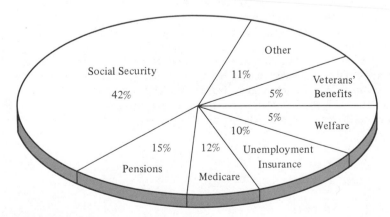

FIGURE 12-10

EXERCISES AND PROBLEMS 12-3

GRAPHS

1. Children in a kindergarten class were asked to cut out a shape of their choice from colored paper. The class then tabulated the number of children who cut out various shapes:

$$
\begin{array}{ll}
\text{triangles} & — \; 2 \\
\text{rectangles} & — \; 7 \\
\text{trapezoids} & — \; 1 \\
\text{hexagons} & — \; 1 \\
\text{circles} & — \; 3 \\
\text{others} & — \; 8 \\
\end{array}
$$

(a) Draw a bar graph depicting this data.

(b) Draw a circle graph depicting this data.

(c) Make up three vastly different problems based on this information. (Perhaps one could involve geometry, another fractions, etc.)

2. The following chart summarizes certain data concerning the planets in our solar system.

Planet	Natural Satellites ("Moons")	Distance from Sun in Astronomical Units	Diameter
Earth	1	1.0	1.0
Jupiter	12	5.2	11.2
Mars	2	1.5	0.53
Mercury	0	0.4	0.38
Neptune	2	30.1	3.8
Pluto	0	39.4	0.47
Saturn	10	9.5	9.4
Uranus	5	19.2	3.7
Venus	0	0.7	0.95

(a) Draw a bar graph showing the number of natural satellites ("moons") for each planet.

(b) The distance from the sun is given in comparison to the earth's average distance from the sun (about 93,000,000 miles). For example, Jupiter is 5.2 times as far from the sun, which is about $5.2 \times 93{,}000{,}000 = 480{,}000{,}000$ miles (using two-digit accuracy throughout). How many miles is Mars from the sun? How many miles is Mercury from the sun? Draw a bar graph showing the distance each planet is from the sun in astronomical units.

(c) The diameter is given in comparison to the earth's diameter (about 8,000 miles). Which planet is about the same size as earth? Neptune's diameter is how many times as great as Mercury's? Which is the biggest planet? Which is the smallest planet?

(d) Draw a bar graph showing the diameter of each planet in the units given. Draw a bar graph showing the diameter of each planet in miles. Compare the graphs.

3. (a) An avocado seed was potted on January 9. It sprouted on January 22 and was measured on certain days afterward. (This is actual data.) Graph this data in the most appropriate way. Suggestion: Use the actual height in millimeters.

Date	Height
January 9	0 millimeters
January 21	0 millimeters
January 22	8 millimeters
January 23	14 millimeters
January 24	20 millimeters
January 25	26 millimeters
January 26	34 millimeters
January 28	49 millimeters
January 29	63 millimeters
January 30	78 millimeters
February 4	160 millimeters

(No measurements were made January 27 or 31 or February 1-3.)

(b) To promote branching, it was cut to a length of 84 mm (about 3¼ inches) on February 5. Two weeks later, it was still 84 mm tall. No further measurements were taken until 10 months later, when it reached a height of 75 cm (750 mm). What was its average rate of growth per day during the 300-day period beginning February 5? Compare this to the rate of growth from January 21 to February 4.

4. (a) In Figure 12-7(a) are all possible incomes accounted for? Specifically, is an income of $9999.86 accounted for?

(b) Incomes have been divided into different brackets: under $5,000, $5,000-$9,999, etc. Do all intervals cover the same extent of income?

(c) In reading the graph, it appears that there are more people earning from $15,000 to $24,999 than from $0 to $5,000. How do you suppose the results would come out if each income bracket covered a $5,000 range (so there would be brackets from $15,000 to $19,999 and from $20,000 to $24,999)?

(d) What is the sum of the percentages given in Figure 12-7(a)? What should the total be? What happened?

5. Do Problems 15 and 16 of Section 6-3 concerning circle graphs.

6. Find several examples of different kinds of graphs in newspapers and magazines.

7. Make one graph which shows all the following average U.S. retail food prices (in cents) for selected years.

	1924	1934	1944	1954	1964	1974
(a) One pound of bread:	8.9	8.3	8.8	17.2	20.7	34.5
(b) One pound of chuck roast:	21.6	17.5	28.8	51.4	56.8	102.1
(c) One pound of butter:	52.2	31.5	50.0	72.4	74.4	94.6

Add more recent data if you have it. (Consult an almanac.)

8. A graph comparing the population of several large cities in 1970 is presented like this:

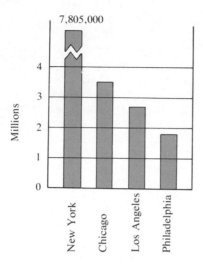

It would appear at first glance by looking at the bars that New York has a population about how many times as great as Chicago? Actually it is how many times as great? Redraw the graph to show the relative sizes more accurately.

9. The following graph appeared in a publication called *Road Maps of Industry* (No. 1758, March, 1975).

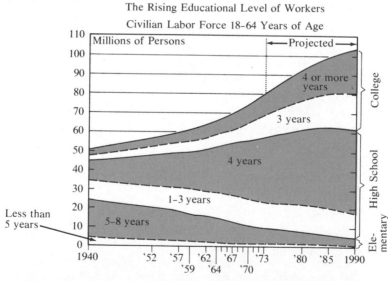

(a) About how many workers in 1940 had an eighth grade education or less? How many in 1973? How many workers in 1990 are projected to have an eighth grade education or less?

(b) The graph indicates that about 15 million workers in 1940 had finished four years of high school. (Notice that out of about 50 million workers, about 35 million did *not* finish high school.) About how many workers in 1973 had finished four years of high school?

(c) There are six groups of workers indicated in the graph: less than 5 years of elementary school, 5-8 years of elementary school, 1-3 years of high school, etc. Which groups are growing? Staying about the same? Diminishing?

10. (a) Collect data about the preferences of at least 15 people regarding their favorite popular singer, sport, TV program, book, food, or category of your choice. Summarize the data in (b) a table (c) a bar graph (d) a circle graph.

11. Graph "service charges" vs. "number of checks" for each of the three categories of Problem 22, Section 12-4, placing all three graphs on the same axes.

12-4
RELATIONS AND FUNCTIONS

Throughout this book, we have been pointing out relationships among different mathematical concepts. In conclusion, we will look back over our development and highlight relations and functions and ways of depicting them.

In Section 9-4 we examined certain relations in geometry. Quite a different example of a relation is given in Figure 12-11, an excerpt from a list of selected parks and facilities in Michigan. The chart indicates certain activities that can be done at the facilities. For instance, we read that Bald Mountain Recreation Area has camping but not riding.

	Camping	Cabins	Picnicking	Hiking	Boating	Fishing	Riding	Swimming	Winter Sports
Bald Mountain Recreation Area	X	X	X	X	X	X		X	X
Brighton Recreation Area	X		X	X	X	X	X	X	
Holland	X		X			X		X	
Interlochen	X		X	X	X	X		X	
Mackinac Island				X	X				
Pinckney Recreation Area	X		X	X	X	X	X	X	
Porcupine Mountains	X	X	X	X	X	X		X	X
Tahquamenon Falls	X		X	X	X	X		X	
Isle Royale National Park	X	X	X	X	X	X			

FIGURE 12-11

In general, a **relation** is an ordered pairing between the members of two sets. In the example of Figure 12-11, the relation can be expressed as "has the activity," and the two sets are the set of activities and the set of parks.

We consider next the relation "is less than" for the set $\{1, 2, 3, 4\}$. Here the two sets mentioned in the definition of relation are the same. Figure 12-12 uses

	1	2	3	4
1		X	X	X
2			X	X
3				X
4				

FIGURE 12-12

a chart similar to the one in Figure 12-11 to show the relationship between the sets. The chart says that "1 is less than 2," "1 is less than 3," etc. It also says "1 is not less than 1," "2 is not less than 1," etc. Note the importance of the order.

The usual convention for picturing a relation involving numbers is to list them as in Figure 12-13. We write the numbers in increasing size from left to right and from bottom to top. We use dots to indicate the ordered pairs which belong to the relation. In the relation "y is less than x," the values for y appear vertically and the values for x appear horizontally. We indicate the members of the pairs by giving the x value, then the y value. Hence $(2, 1)$ is one of our ordered pairs, while $(1, 2)$ is not. The picture which displays all of the ordered pairs, in this case Figure 12-13, is called the graph of the relation.

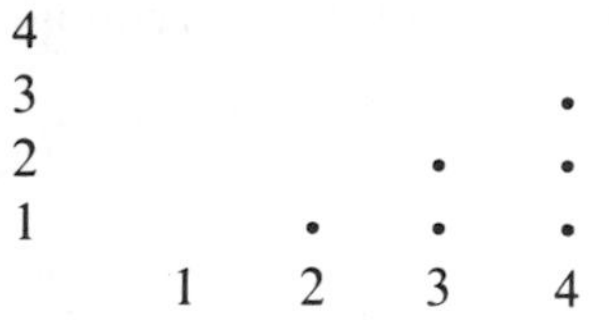

```
4
3                    •
2               •    •
1          •    •    •
      1    2    3    4
```

FIGURE 12-13

Our next example of a relation, like the preceding one, appears early in the elementary school curriculum — though less formally, of course. It is the relation "y is one more than x" (a predecessor to addition), which we show for the sets $\{1, 2, 3, 4, 5, 6\}$ and $\{1, 2, 3, 4, 5\}$ in Figure 12-14. Unlike the previous examples, this relation is one in which for any value of x, there is exactly one value of y. Such a relation is called a **function**. In each pair of numbers (x, y), the first number is called the x-coordinate and the second number is called the

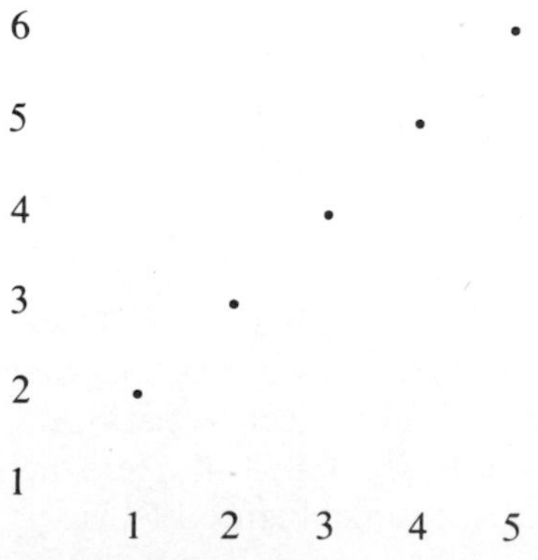

```
6                    •

5               •

4          •

3     •

2  •

1
      1    2    3    4    5
```

FIGURE 12-14

y-coordinate. For example, in the pair (1, 2), 1 is the *x*-coordinate and 2 is the *y*-coordinate.

By using number lines as in Figure 12-15 we can show the relation "*y* is one more than *x*" for the set of all real numbers. The solid line here is merely a set of points. Among these points are the pairs (1, 2), (2, 3), (3, 4), (4, 5), and (5, 6). Only this time the line indicates many other pairs like (0, 1), (−1, 0), (1/2, 3/2), (√2, √2 + 1), etc. Since for each first number there is exactly one second number, this too is a function.

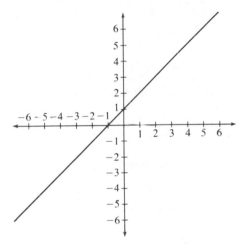

FIGURE 12-15

Which of the following are graphs of functions?

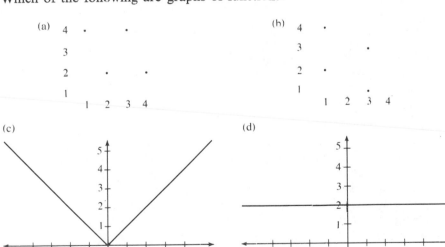

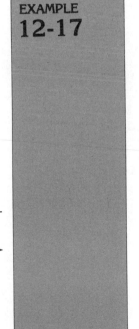

SOLUTION

(a) Yes, it doesn't matter that different x values are paired with the same y values, like (1, 4) and (3, 4).

(b) No, there are two y values associated with 1. We have (1, 2) and (1, 4); also (3, 1) and (3, 3).

(c) Yes. This is the absolute value function $(x, |x|)$. Note that every number has exactly one absolute value associated with it. (See Section 7-1 for a discussion of absolute value.)

(d) Yes. This is what is called a **constant** function. All first numbers are paired with the same second number.

There is another way to describe relations and functions besides graphs (or listing all the pairs). This is to write what is called an open sentence. Open sentences have appeared earlier in this book. Figure 12-16 lists some examples.

(a) $2 + \square = 6$ Section 3-3

(b) $3 \times \square = 12$ Section 3-6

(c) $\frac{4}{5} \times \square = \frac{2}{3}$ Section 5-3

(d) $6 : \triangle = \triangle : 54$ Section 6-1

(e) $8 : 12 = \square : \triangle$ Section 6-1

(f) $\square \times (-2) = 8$ Section 7-2

(g) $\triangle \times \triangle = 2$ Section 8-2

(h) $3 \underset{5}{\oplus} 4 = \square$ Section 8-3

FIGURE 12-16

These are statements which are true or false depending on the values which are substituted. The sentence $2 + \square = 6$ is true when $\square$ is replaced by 4, but not when $\square$ is replaced by 5. The sentence "$6 : \triangle = \triangle : 54$" is true when both $\triangle$'s are replaced by 18 (or -18) and false otherwise. If a symbol appears more than once it is understood that it must take on the same value throughout the sentence. ("$6 : 12 = 27 : 54$" would not be permitted as a replacement for "$6 : \triangle = \triangle : 54$." In sentences where two different symbols are used, like "$8 : 12 = \square : \triangle$," we may consider replacements for $\square$ and $\triangle$ using the same or different values. One solution to this sentence is to replace $\square$ by 2 and $\triangle$ by 3.

The symbols $\square$ and $\triangle$ are examples of what are called **variables**. The set of all values which may be considered for substitution for a variable is called the **replacement set** for that variable, and the set of those values which make the statement true is called the **solution set**. In the open sentence $3 \times \square = 12$, the replacement set for $\square$ was understood to be the whole numbers, since we were discussing whole numbers at the time. The solution set is {4}, since 4 is the only whole number which makes the sentence true. Using this new terminology, the relation "is one more than" as given in Figure 12-14 can be described like this:

□ = △ + 1 is the open sentence

{1, 2, 3, 4, 5} is the replacement set for △

{1, 2, 3, 4, 5, 6} is the replacement set for □

{(1, 2), (2, 3), (3, 4), (4, 5), (5, 6)} is the solution set

While the format $4 + □ = 6$ is excellent for young children and adequate for some of our purposes, there are open sentences where this notation is awkward. Perhaps using an intermediate form like $4 + \boxed{x} = 6$ will wean our students to symbolism like $4 + x = 6$, which is much easier to use in statements like $y = x^2 - 5x + 6$. However, the idea is no different. This last equation represents a set of ordered pairs including (0, 6), (2, 0), and (5, 6).

A very convenient notation for function is illustrated next. The symbolism $f(x) = x + 2$ is equivalent to the open sentences $y = x + 2$ or $□ = △ + 2$. The advantage is that it provides an easy way to write down ordered pairs which belong to the function. To show that 7 is the value paired with 5 for the function f, we simply write $f(5) = 7$. Similarly, $f(0) = 2, f(19) = 21$, and $f(-8) = -6$.

If $f(x) = 3x + 6$ and $g(x) = x^2$, find

(a) $f(9)$ (b) $g(3)$ (c) $f(-5)$ (d) $f(p)$ (e) $f(g(3))$

EXAMPLE 12-18

(a) $f(9) = 3(9) + 6 = 27 + 6 = 33$

(b) $g(3) = 3^2 = 9$

(c) $f(-5) = 3(-5) + 6 = -15 + 6 = -9$

(d) $f(p) = 3p + 6$

(e) $f(g(3)) = f(9)$ (from part b)

$= 33$ (from part a)

SOLUTION

In closing, we illustrate how functions might be used to approach concepts in the elementary school curriculum. Figure 12-17 shows an activity in which a third grade class is making a table to show the relationship between the number of fingers and the number of hands. Do you see how the number of fingers is a function of the number of hands? The purpose of the activity in the classroom was to introduce multiplication, and functions were not mentioned. But at a higher level we recognize that the information in the table describes a function and write

$$f = 5h,$$

where f is the number of fingers and h is the number of hands. The activity provides a concrete approach to multiplication while laying the foundation for the concept of function.

This last illustration serves both to reflect on what we have done and to look ahead. It reflects on higher mathematics (the concept of function) as

FIGURE 12-17

relevant to the elementary school curriculum (whole number multiplication), showing children who are involved in problem solving (making a table). For many of you, it looks ahead to the classroom, where as a teacher you will have the opportunity to affect the lives of future generations.

EXERCISES AND PROBLEMS 12-4

GRAPHS

1. Graph the following relations using the replacement set $\{1, 2, 3, 4, 5\}$ for both x and y.
   (a) $y = x$ (b) $y \neq x$ (c) $y > x$
   (d) $y = x + 1$ (e) $y = 2x$ (f) $y = 2x - 1$

2. Graph the relations of Problem 1 using the real numbers as the replacement set.

3. Graph all ordered pairs of real numbers (x, y) which satisfy $x + y = 6$.

4. (a) Plot the points (x, y) such that for whole numbers x and y, the fraction y/x is equivalent to 2/3. For example plot $(3, 2)$, $(6, 4)$, etc. Plot at least five points. What do you notice? (b) On the same axes, plot the fractions y/x equivalent to 3/4. (c) Use the graphs you have drawn to add $2/3 + 3/4$.

FUNCTIONS AND RELATIONS

5. Which of the graphs of Problem 1 are functions?

6. Which of the graphs of Problem 2 are functions?

7. Which of the following are graphs of functions?

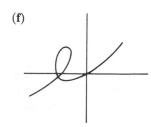

8. (a) Are all functions relations? (b) Are all relations functions? (c) Give an example of a relation that is also a function. (d) Give an example of a relation that is *not* a function. (e) Give an example of a function that is not a relation.

9. (a) Find two examples of functions which appear in this text *before* this chapter. (b) Give two more examples as in part (a), this time for relations.

10. (a) When writing $\square \times \square = 16$, can the $\square$'s be filled in with two different numbers, like this: "$\boxed{2} \times \boxed{8} = 16$"?
    (b) When writing $\square \times \triangle = 16$, can the $\square$ and the $\triangle$ be filled in with the same number, like this: "$\boxed{4} \times \boxed{\triangle} = 16$"?

11. If $f(x) = 5 - x$ and $g(x) = 3x$, find
    (a) $f(6)$ (b) $g(2)$ (c) $f(g(2))$ (d) $g(f(2))$
    (e) $f(w)$ (f) $f(3w)$ (g) $f(w + 5)$

12. The **operations** addition and multiplication (for whole numbers) can be thought of as functions with pairs of whole numbers as input and single whole numbers as output. Complete this chart.

Input	Function	Output
2, 3	+	5
4, 9	+	—
6, —	+	11
—, —	+	0
5, 6	×	—
4, 71	×	—
—, 13	×	52

13. Based on the pattern of the given examples, guess the output for the remaining entries. (Note: This can be used as a classroom game with children, where they make up their own examples.)

	Input	Output		Input	Output
(a)	2, 3	7	(b)	2, 3	4
	5, 7	36		5, 7	11
	8, 8	65		8, 8	15
	9, 1	10		9, 1	9
	11, 2	—		11, 2	—
	4, 9	—		4, 9	—
(c)	2, 3	7	(d)	2, 3	1
	5, 7	32		5, 7	4
	8, 8	72		8, 8	0
	9, 1	82		9, 1	64
	11, 2	—		11, 2	—
	4, 9	—		4, 9	—
(e)	2, 3	3	(f)	2, 3	3
	5, 7	7		5, 7	7
	8, 8	8		8, 8	8
	9, 1	1		9, 1	9
	11, 2	—		11, 2	—
	4, 9	—		4, 9	—

14. Given that f and g are functions, let $f \circ g$ be the function which is defined by $f \circ g(x) = f(g(x))$. For example, using the functions of Problem 11, $f \circ g(x) = f(g(x)) = f(3x) = 5 - 3x$.

    (a) Compute $f \circ g(7)$.   **(b)** Determine $g \circ f(x)$.

    (c) Compute $g \circ f(7)$.

    (d) Are $f \circ g$ and $g \circ f$ the same function?

    (e) Does the commutative property for "$\circ$" applied to functions hold in this example?

15. Let $f(x) = x + 2$, $g(x) = 5x$, $h(x) = x - 6$.

    (a) Determine $f \circ g(x)$.   **(b)** Determine $g \circ h(x)$.

    (c) Determine $(f \circ g) \circ h(x)$.   **(d)** Determine $f \circ (g \circ h)(x)$.

    (e) Are $(f \circ g) \circ h$ and $f \circ (g \circ h)$ the same function?

    (f) Does the associative property for "$\circ$" applied to functions hold in this example?

16. Solve (find the solution set for) each of the open sentences of Figure 12-16 using the following replacement sets:

$$\square \in \{1, 2, 3, 4, \ldots, 10\}$$

$$\triangle \in \{1, 2, 3, 4, \ldots, 20\}$$

17. Solve the open sentence $5 + \square = 2$ for the replacement set

    (a) whole numbers   **(b)** integers

18. Find the solution set for $x^2 - 2x - 8 = 0$, where $x \in \{0, 1, 2, 3, 4, 5\}$.

19. The numbers of five-hour clock arithmetic are 0, 1, 2, 3, and 4. (See Section 8-3.) Suppose we plot pairs of such numbers ($\square$, $\triangle$) on the following graph:

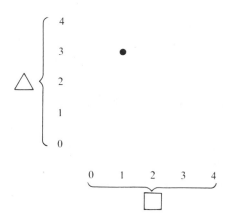

The dot indicates the pair $(1, 3)$ — that is, the pair obtained when $\square$ is replaced by 1 and $\triangle$ is replaced by 3.

On separate graphs, graph all pairs ($\square$, $\triangle$) using 0, 1, 2, 3, and 4 that satisfy the relation

    (a) $\square = \triangle$

    (b) $\square = \triangle \oplus 1 \atop 5$

    (c) $\square = \triangle \ominus 4 \atop 5$

    (d) $\square = \triangle \oplus 2 \atop 5$

APPLICATIONS

20. Elizabeth uses the following formula to determine the *maximum* limit for exercise in teaching physical education:

$$\left(\begin{matrix} \textit{maximum} \text{ number of} \\ \text{heartbeats per minute} \end{matrix}\right) = 220 - \text{age in years}$$

According to this formula,
(a) What is the maximum number of heartbeats per minute for a 20-year-old?
(b) Joyce reached her limit with 185 heartbeats per minute. How old is Joyce?

21. Elizabeth uses the following formula to determine the *recommended* number of heartbeats:

$$\left(\begin{matrix} \textit{recommended} \text{ number of} \\ \text{heartbeats per minute} \end{matrix}\right) = 220 - \left(\begin{matrix} \text{number of heartbeats} \\ \text{per minute at rest} \end{matrix}\right) - \text{age}$$

Joe's normal pulse is 72 beats per minute. How many heartbeats are recommended for Joe?

22. A bank offers the following rates for checking: "If you maintain an average balance during a statement month of $300 or more, you will have no service charges on your checking account and you need read no further. If your average balance during a statement month is between $200 and $300, you are entitled to ten free transactions that month. Each additional transaction will cost $.10. If your average balance is under $200 during a statement month, there is a $1 service charge on your account. That entitles you to ten free transactions. Each additional transaction that month will cost $.10."

Find service charges for the following customers:

Customer	Average Balance	Number of Checks
Mr. Allen	$142	18
Ms. Baker	$257	24
Miss Chase	$482	17
Dr. Davis	$214	18
Mrs. Edwards	$189	11

23. A package of shoelaces contains the following information about lengths of laces for regular shoes:

	inches	cm
1 and 2 pairs eyclets	18	46
3 pairs eyelets	21	53
4 pairs eyelets	24	61
5 and 6 pairs eyelets	27	69

What length do you think is given for shoes with 7 and 8 pairs of eyelets? (a) in inches? (b) in centimeters?

24. According to *National Wildlife* magazine (June-July, 1976) the snowy tree cricket's chirp is a function of the temperature; namely, the number of chirps every 15 seconds, c, is given by $c = t - 39$ where t is the temperature in degrees Fahrenheit. According to this,
(a) How many chirps does the cricket make every 15 seconds if the temperature is 70° F? 50° F?
(b) What is the temperature if the cricket chirps 40 times in 15 seconds? 30 times?

25. Collect additional examples of charts like Figure 12-11 which depict relations. (You might consult newspapers, magazines, advertising brochures, catalogues, etc.)

MATERIALS AND CALCULATORS

*C26. The deepest ocean is the Pacific, which is 11,034 meters (36,198 feet) in the Mariana Trench. An almanac gives its location as 11° 21′N, 142° 12′E. Use a map or globe to find the nearest land to this point.

27. Read about Target K in "Instructional Games with Calculators" in the *Arithmetic Teacher* [56]. What is the function discussed in the example? If someone guesses "20," what value does this function take on?

*C28. (a) The "**sine**" (abbreviated "**sin**") is a function which gives the ratio of the side opposite an angle to the hypotenuse of a right triangle. For example, the sine of 30° is 1/2 and we write sin 30° = .5, as in triangles *ABC* and *DEF*.

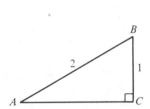
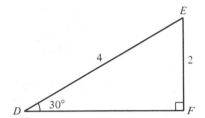

Use a scientific calculator to find the sine of 0°, 10°, 20°, . . . , 90° and graph the results. (Check that the calculator is in the "degree mode" by finding sin 30°, which should be .5.)

(b) Repeat part (a) for the cosine function. Use cos 60° = .5 as a check.

(c) Repeat part (a) for the tangent function. Use tan 45° = 1 as a check. (See page 343.)

(d) Use the results of part (a) to find the length of the side opposite a 70° angle in a right triangle with hypotenuse of length 10.

(e) We have defined the "sine" function only for angles between 0° and 90°. How can the definition be extended to angles of more than 90°?

(f) Use your scientific calculator to graph the sine function for 0°, 10°, 20°, . . . , 400°.

29. You've done a lot of work so far, so here is something a bit different. We have the numbers 876, 4293, 41, 7, and 324. This is a fine list of numbers just as they are, so you have nothing to do.

Appendix
Logic and Proof

Throughout the text we find arguments in support of many of the mathematical claims we make. This Appendix provides a framework for these arguments by examining certain underlying ideas in the reasoning process. It presents some of the language of mathematics by reinforcing several significant concepts such as "commutativity" and "associativity" and by clarifying the important distinction between "necessary" and "sufficient" conditions.

Logic describes the relationships among **statements,** sentences which are either true or false (but not both). Some examples of statements are

(1) "Canada borders the United States,"
(2) "Beethoven became deaf,"
(3) "2 + 3 = 7," and
(4) "All spiders have six legs."

Of course the first two statements are true and the last two are false. "Raise the flag" and "How much money do you have?" are *not* statements, since they cannot be considered true or false.

We can form a new statement from a given statement by **negation.** The negations of statements (1) through (4) are, respectively,

(1′) "Canada does not border the United States,"
(2′) "Beethoven did not become deaf,"
(3′) "2 + 3 ≠ 7," and
(4′) "Not all spiders have six legs."

Note that the first two statements are false and the last two are true. In general, the negation of a true statement is false, and the negation of a false statement is true. This can be summarized by a **truth table,** where we use *"p"* to represent a statement, ~*p"* to represent its negation, and "T" and "F" to represent "true" and "false" respectively:

p	$\sim p$	
T	F	Truth Table for Negation
F	T	

The truth table covers the only two possibilities: either p is true or p is false. If p is true, then $\sim p$ is false. If p is false, then $\sim p$ is true.

We will say that any two expressions which have the same truth values are **logically equivalent.**

Show by a truth table that $\sim\sim p$ is logically equivalent to p.

EXAMPLE
A-1

SOLUTION

We show construction of the truth table in three steps, beginning with both possible truth values for p.

p
T
F

p	$\sim p$
T	F
F	T

p	$\sim p$	$\sim\sim p$
T	F	T
F	T	F

Step 1   Step 2   Step 3

Since the truth values for p are the same as those for $\sim\sim p$, we say that p and $\sim\sim p$ are logically equivalent.

Two statements can be joined together to form compound statements in several ways. If p is the statement "All dogs are mammals" and q is the statement "All butterflies are insects," then we can form the compound statement "All dogs are mammals and all butterflies are insects" by inserting "and" between the original statements. This new statement can be represented **"$p \wedge q$"** and is called a **conjunction.** The conjunction of two statements is considered to be true when both statements are true, as shown in the following truth table:

p	q	$p \wedge q$
T	T	T
T	F	F
F	T	F
F	F	F

Truth Table for
Conjunction

Note that if p is true, then q can be either true or false. Similarly if p is false, then q can be either true or false. This gives rise to the four possibilities listed in the table.

In conjunctions the order of two statements is immaterial; namely, $p \wedge q = q \wedge p$. We say that conjunction of statements is **commutative,** just as we say that addition of whole numbers is commutative. Similarly, in conjunctions the grouping of statements is immaterial; namely, $(p \wedge q) \wedge r = p \wedge (q \wedge r)$. We say that conjunction of statements is **associative.**

By inserting "or" between two statements we obtain another type of compound statement. Using p and q as above we have an example, "All dogs are mammals or all butterflies are insects." This is represented **"$p \vee q$"** and is called a **disjunction.** The disjunction of two statements is considered to be true when either (or both) of the statements is true:

p	q	$p \vee q$
T	T	T
T	F	T
F	T	T
F	F	F

Truth Table for
Disjunction

Next we show a relationship between conjunction and disjunction. If we negate the conjunction $p \wedge q$ we are saying that it is *not* the case that both p and q are true. Then either p is false or q is false (or perhaps both are false). To negate $p \wedge q$ we write $\sim(p \wedge q)$. To say p is false or q is false, we write $\sim p \vee \sim q$. A truth table confirms that these two expressions are logically equivalent.

Show by a truth table that $\sim(p \wedge q)$ is logically equivalent to $\sim p \vee \sim q$.

EXAMPLE
A-2

SOLUTION

We fill in the columns with T's and F's in the order shown:

p	q	$\sim$	(p $\wedge$ q)	$\sim$p $\vee$ $\sim$q
T	T	F		F
T	F	T		T
F	T	T		T
F	F	T		T
(1)	(2)	(3)		(4)

Since these truth values are identical, $\sim(p \wedge q)$ and $\sim p \vee \sim q$ are logically equivalent.

An extremely useful type of compound statement is the **implication** or **conditional,** represented **"$p \Rightarrow q$"** and read "If p, then q" or "p implies q." p is called the **hypothesis** and q is called the **conclusion.** For example, letting p be "2 is a factor of 6" (the hypothesis) and letting q be "2 is a factor of 30" (the conclusion), then $p \Rightarrow q$ represents "If 2 is a factor of 6, then 2 is a factor of 30," or "2 is a factor of 6 implies that 2 is a factor of 30."

Thinking of $p \Rightarrow q$ as "If p is true, then q is true" suggests the following truth table:

p	q	$p \Rightarrow q$	
T	T	T	
T	F	F	Truth Table for
F	T	T	Implication
F	F	T	

The first two lines of the truth table are evident, for if p is true, then the implication will be satisfied according to whether q is true or false. What about the last two lines of the truth table? In a sense "If p is true, then q is true" doesn't say *anything* about the case where p is false. In this case the implication is defined to be true. To see why this is the natural definition, consider the following illustration.

Suppose a tax law says that "If someone earns $1000 or more, then he/she must file a tax return." There are four possibilities:

	Earned $1000 or more?	Filed tax return?	Law satisfied?
(1)	yes	yes	yes
(2)	yes	no	no
(3)	no	yes	yes
(4)	no	no	yes

The only way the law is *not* satisfied is if someone does earn $1,000 or more and does *not* file a tax return. Similarly, the only way $p \Rightarrow q$ is false is if p is true and q is false, which is precisely what the truth table for implication says.

An important question is whether implication is commutative.

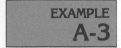

Show that implication is *not* commutative.

We construct truth tables for $p \Rightarrow q$ and for $q \Rightarrow p$.

p	q	$p \Rightarrow q$	$q \Rightarrow p$
T	T	T	T
T	F	F	T
F	T	T	F
F	F	T	T

In the cases where p and q have opposite truth values, the truth tables disagree. To illustate, the statement "If you live in San Diego, then you live in California" is true, but the statement "If you live in California, then you live in San Diego" is not necessarily true.

The statements $p \Rightarrow q$ and $q \Rightarrow p$, which we just illustrated, are called **converses** of each other. We have illustrated by our San Diego example that the converse of a true statement is not necessarily true. Of course, there are cases for which a conditional statement and its converse both are true. For example, both the conditional statement "If you live in New York City, then you live in the most populated city in the United States" and its converse "If you live in the most populated city in the United States, then you live in New York City" are true. When an implication holds in both directions we call it a **biconditional.** Specifically, a biconditional is denoted "$p \Leftrightarrow q$" and has the following truth table:

p	q	$p \Leftrightarrow q$
T	T	T
T	F	F
F	T	F
F	F	T

Truth Table for Biconditional

Note that $p \Leftrightarrow q$ is true when p and q have the same truth values and is false otherwise.

In practice, biconditionals often take the form "p if and only if q." For example, the single statement "You live in New York City if and only if you live in the most populated city in the United States" combines a conditional statement and its converse into a single biconditional statement. Another example of a biconditional is the statement "An integer is even if and only if it is divisible by 2." It says both "If an integer is even, then it is divisible by 2" and "If an integer is divisible by 2, then it is even."

The words **"necessary"** and **"sufficient"** are often used in connection with conditionals and biconditionals. Let's return to our earlier example, "If you live in San Diego, then you live in California," a statement of the form $p \Rightarrow q$. To live in California (q), it is *sufficient* to live in San Diego (p), but is is *not necessary*. In short, p is sufficient (but not necessary) for q. On the other hand, to live in San Diego (p) it is *necessary* to live in California (q), but it is *not sufficient*. In short, q is necessary (but not sufficient) for p.

These relationships can readily be shown by a diagram (called an **Euler diagram**) as follows:

$p \Rightarrow q$
p is sufficient for q.
q is necessary for p.

It is understood that region p is contained in region q. To be in region q it is sufficient (but not necessary) to be in region p. To be in region p it is necessary (but not sufficient) to be in region q.

In the case of biconditionals, $p \Leftrightarrow q$ means that we have both $p \Rightarrow q$ and $q \Rightarrow p$. From $p \Rightarrow q$ we have that p is sufficient for q. From $q \Rightarrow p$ we have that p is necessary for q. Summarizing, in the biconditional $p \Leftrightarrow q$, p is both necessary and sufficient for q.

EXERCISES AND PROBLEMS—APPENDIX

1. Negate the following statements:
   (a) All birds can fly.
   (b) Barb wore a blue dress.
   (c) x is less than 7.
   (d) Triangle ABC is isosceles.

2. Let m be the statement "Joyce got married" and let b be the statement "Joyce had a baby."
   (a) What statement is given by $m \wedge b$?
   (b) What statement is given by $b \wedge m$?
   (c) Are these two statements logically equivalent?

3. Is $\sim(p \vee q)$ logically equivalent to $\sim p \wedge \sim q$? Confirm your answer using a truth table.

4. Test whether each of the following is commutative: (a) $\vee$ (b) $\Leftrightarrow$

5. Test whether each of the following is associative: (a) $\vee$ (b) $\Rightarrow$ (c) $\Leftrightarrow$

6. (a) Does $\wedge$ distribute over $\vee$—namely, is $p \wedge (q \vee r)$ logically equivalent to $(p \wedge q) \vee (p \wedge r)$? (Include a truth table.)
   (b) Does $\vee$ distribute over $\wedge$? (Include a truth table.)
   (c) Does $\vee$ distribute over $\Rightarrow$? (Include a truth table.)

7. We know that a truth table with one variable has two lines, and a truth table with two different variables has four lines. How many lines are there in a truth table with **(a)** three different variables? **(b)** four different variables? **(c)** ten different variables?

8. Use truth tables to test whether the two expressions are logically equivalent.
    (a) $p \Rightarrow q$ and $\sim p \vee q$
    (b) $p \Rightarrow q$ and $\sim(p \wedge \sim q)$
    (c) $\sim(p \vee q)$ and $\sim p \vee \sim q$
    (d) $\sim(p \wedge q)$ and $\sim p \wedge \sim q$
    (e) $p \Rightarrow q$ and $(p \vee q) \Leftrightarrow q$
    (f) $p \Rightarrow q$ and $\sim p \Rightarrow \sim q$ **(inverse)**
    (g) $p \Rightarrow q$ and $\sim q \Rightarrow \sim p$ **(contrapositive)**

9. Which of the following are *necessary* conditions for the statement "Laura lives in New York State" to be true? Which are *sufficient* conditions?
    (a) Laura lives in the United States.
    (b) Laura lives in East Aurora, N.Y.
    (c) Laura is a gymnast.
    (d) Laura lives in a state which borders Canada at Niagara Falls.
    (e) Laura lives East of the Mississippi River.
    (f) Laura doesn't live in New York City.

10. Assuming that the given statements are true, what conclusion (if any) follows:
    (a) If Hank diets, he will lose weight. If Hank loses weight, he will look better.
    (b) Olga has black hair or Olga has blonde hair. Olga doesn't have blonde hair.
    (c) If the levy passed, then the teachers got a raise. The levy didn't pass.
    (d) If Ruth got a raise, then she bought a new car. Ruth didn't buy a new car.
    (e) If it rains, we'll go to the movies. If it doesn't rain, we'll take a walk.

11. Let p be the statement "x belongs to set P" and let q be the statement "x belongs to set Q."
    (a) Write out in full the statement represented by $p \wedge q$. Can you express the statement $p \wedge q$ in terms of set unions or intersections? **(b)** Repeat part (a) for the statement $p \vee q$.
    (c) P is a subset of Q is the analog for which compound statement involving p and q?

12. A **universal quantifier** refers to all members of a set. For example, the italicized words in the following statements are universal quantifiers:
    All insects have six legs.
    For *any* whole numbers a and b, a + b = b + a.
    For *each* positive number b, there is a number c such that $bc = 1$.
    An **existential quantifier** refers to one or more members of a set. For example, the italicized words in the following statements are existential quantifiers:
    Some birds can fly.
    Given any prime number, *there exists* a larger prime number.
    For each positive number b, *there is* a number c such that $bc = 1$.
    Identify the universal and existential quantifiers in the following statement:
    (a) All children need love.
    (b) Some villains wear white hats.
    (c) For any positive numbers a and b, there is a positive integer n such that $a < nb$.
    (d) No wise man ever wishes to be younger.
    (e) Every man is a friend to him that giveth gifts (Solomon).

13. To prove that a statement involving a universal quantifier is false, we need only display a single counter-example. For instance, to show that "All birds can fly" is false we need only offer the penguin as a counter-example. Give a counter-example to show that each of the following statements is false.

(a) All birds can fly. (Give a different counter-example.)
(b) No mammals lay eggs. (Hint: Think Australia.)
(c) If the sum of the digits of a number is divisible by 7, the number is divisible by 7.
(d) For every integer n, $\sqrt{n^2} = n$.
(e) All primes are odd.
(f) All U.S. Supreme Court Justices have been men.
(g) All Americans are millionaires.

14. We can represent conjunction and disjunctions by circuits as shown here.

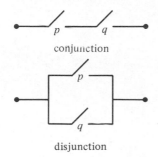

conjunction

disjunction

Note that current flows through the conjunction circuit only if switches p and q are both closed, and that current flows through the disjunction circuit if either switch p or q (or both) is closed. What compound statement is represented by each of the following circuits?

(a)

(b)

(c)

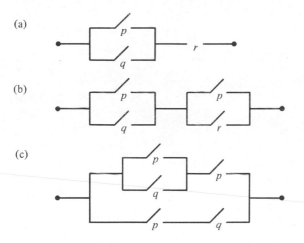

15. (a) Simplify circuit (b) of Problem 14 so that it has only three switches.
(b) Simplify circuit (c) of Problem 14 so that it has as few switches as possible.

Selected Answers and Hints

Note: Units are not given when clear from context.

1. 144   **3.** 28   **4.** 2, 2, and 9

Section 1-2

3.(a) 100 or 676   **5.** 19   **7.** 88   **9.(a)** 322   **10.** Hint: M = 1, S = 9 or 8.
11. 5, 9, and 8   **13.** 1,000,000   **15.(b)** 25   **17.** no   **22.** (9 + 9) ÷ .9

Section 2-1

2. (There are 6.)   **3.(a)** none   **(b)** 60   **4.(a) 2**   **(c)** 24   **6.** yes;
no.   **8.** no; no.   **9.** No, I will always get $1.   **10.(e)** and
(f) impossible   **11.** yes, 0; no   **12.** 3,628,800   **17.** color and size
19. readiness to die, fanaticism, enthusiasm, etc.   **20.** Dukas' *The Sorcerer's
Apprentice*, etc.   **21.(a)** size and shape   **(c)** shape and position
23.(a) {positive odd whole numbers less than 12} **(c)** {whole numbers less than 2}
24.(a) the 2-member set containing 101 and 102, or the 1-member set containing
101102   **25.(a)** no   **(c)** yes   **26.** yes   **27.** all except {1, 2}   **28.(a)** {x}, {y}
(b) impossible   **29.(a)** true   **(c)** true   **(e)** true   **(g)** true   **(i)** false
(k) false   **(m)** true   **30.** true; true   **31.(a)** finite, n is 5   **(c)** finite, n is 91
(e) infinite   **(g)** finite   **32.** the third one   **33.** the second one   **35.(a)** <
(c) =   **(e)** ?   **(g)** <   **36.** A proper subset of P matches Q.
37. { }, {a}, {b} (all proper) and {a, b}   **38.(a)** 1   **(c)** 4   **(e)** 16
40. 1 4 6 4 1 is next row   **41.(a)** 1   **(b)** 3   **42.** $(x + y)^3 = x^3 + 3x^2y + 3xy^2 + y^3$ **43.(b)** tenth row begins 1 9 36 84   **44.(a)** 15   **(c)** 120 = 36 + 84
45. 56   **47.** 26

Section 2-2

1.(a) 7   **(b)** 3   **2.(a)** numeral   **(c)** number   **5.(a)** 16   **(c)** 81
(e) 10,000   **6.(a)** 5×10^1 **(c)** $9 \times 10^2 + 5 \times 10^1 + 8 \times 1$ **(g)** 329
(i) 8,000,305   **7.** unite, duplex, tripod, etc.   **8.(a)** 9   **(b)** septet, octopus,
etc.   **9.(a)** 15   **(c)** sex   **(e)** 8   **(g)** 9   **(i)** decillion   **(k)** 33

(m) 19   **10.(a)** one billion   **(d)** twenty-three quintillion   **11.** 3,250,000,000
12.(a) 6247   **13.(a)** $82 - 59$ **14.(a)** 4, 0, 6; 3, 9, 16   **16.** $100p + 10q + r$
17. 1,000,000   **18.(a)** 8   **(c)** 1982   **(e)** XLIII   **(g)** mixture of 5 for 1
and 2 for 1   **20.(a)** 3   **(c)** 15   **(e)** $2^{64} - 1$ **21.(a)** four billion, nine
hundred million   **(e)** one trillion   **22.(c)** 210_{five} **23.(a)** true   **(c)** true
25. 15   **27.(a)** 69   **(c)** 116   **28.(a)** 10020_{three}, 73_{twelve} **29.(a)** 8
30.(a) 180   **(b)** 11.5   **31.(c)** 65   **34.(a)** 2:37 and 4 seconds
35.(b) 1021_{three} **36.** 3012   **38.(b)** 46_{eight} **(d)** 123_{five} **40.(b)** 324_{five}
41. 1024 and 1,048,576   **42.** 4000   **43.** about 6 trillion   **44.(a)** 2025
(b) 2197   **45.(a)** 1021   **46.** 3   **47.** house numbers   **48.(a)** 27   **(c)** 200
(Hint: write out the numbers in words.)   **49.(b)** about 167 hours   **(d)** 200
hours

☐ Section 3-1

1. 1   **2.(a)** $\{1, 2, 3, 4, 5, 6, 7\}$ **(c)** $\{1, 5, 7\}$ **6.(a)** when A is a subset of B
9. false   **10.** no   **11.** $V = \{1, 2, 3, 4, \ldots, 127\}$, $W = \{1001, 1002, 1003,$
$1004, \ldots, 1562\}$ **12.(a)** $D = E = \{a\}$ **(c)** impossible   **13.(a)** true
(c) false   **14.(a)** yes   **(c)** no   **(e)** yes   **(g)** yes   **15.(a)** no
(b) yes   **(c)** no   **16.(a)** closure for $+$ **(c)** associative for $+$
17. associative and commutative for $+$ **21.** yes   **24.(c)** multiplication
(d) Yes, it generates rows of the multiplication table   **25.(b)** Hint: identify a
subgoal.

☐ Section 3-2

1. neither (add columns)   **2.** Hint: J = O, A < 5.   **6.(a)** 3   **(c)** 43_{five}
(e) 1241_{five} **7.** 103_{six} **9.** seven   **14.(b)** 5050   **(d)** 10,000   **(f)** 2870
15. fish sandwich $+$ f.f. $+$ ch. shake, etc.   **16.** A1 512   **17.(b)** Ann 101,
Cora 99   **(c)** place value and addition; second or third grade   **20.(a)** first row;
9, 2, 7   **(b)** first row: 23, 12, 1, 20, 9   **21.(a)** Rotate 90° counterclockwise
22.(d) 5050   **23.(c)** 199; 100^2 **24.(b)** 55^2

☐ Section 3-3

1.(a) take-away   **(b)** missing addend   **(c)** comparison   **(d)** addition
2.(a) $\{b, c, d\}$ **(c)** {books which are not dictionaries}   **(e)** 21   **3.** $\{c, a, m,$
$e, r, a\} \setminus \{c, a, r\} = \{m, e\}$, etc.   **5.** $7 - 5 = 2$, $7 - 2 = 5$ missing addend
6.(a) A **(b)** 7   **8.** $7 - 3$ and $11 - 8$ are basic facts.   **12.** B   **13.** no;
no; no   **14.(a)** $a \geq b$ and $a - b \geq c$ **(c)** yes   **16.** 7, 9, 9, 13
17. Hint: E = 9, A = 4   **19.(b)** no   **20.(a)** 4175   **22.(a)** 1   **(c)** 32_{five}
(e) 134_{five} **23.(a)** 4   **(c)** 19_{twelve} **24.** 9   **31.(a)** 0   **32.** John 362
34. Mrs. Jones (she is the farmer)   **35.** 2:48   **36.** 9   **37.** missing addend

☐ Section 3-4

1. Area model generalizes best   **2.(a)** true   **(c)** false   **(e)** false
3.(a) $\{(1, r), (1, s), (1, t)\}$ **(d)** $\{\ \}$ **4.(a)** $R = \{a, b\}$, $S = \{d, e\}$, etc., or

$R = \{w, x, y, z\}$, $S = \{v\}$, etc.   **5.(a)** 1   **(c)** impossible   **(e)** 0
6.(a) no   **(b)** no   **(c)** yes   **7.(a)** no   **(b)** no   **(c)** using ordered triples
9.(a) 12   **(b)** $4 \times 3 = 12$ **(c)** Cartesian product   **10.(a)** 24; Cartesian
product   **11.** 23   **12.(a)** \$15.75   **13.(a)** 256   **(c)** 56   **(e)** 8
(g) 192   **15.(a)** 2,598,960   **(b)** nearly 5 years dealing 24 hours per day
16. closure: 2×3 is a whole number, etc.   **17.** $6 \times 3 = 3 \times 6$: commutative
property for $\times$ **20.(a)** yes   **(d)** no   **(g) yes**   **21.(a)** No, $2 + 3 = 5$.
(b) yes   **22.** $(5, 1)$; $(q, 5 - p)$ **25.(a)** no   **(b)** yes
26. $4 \times (2 + 3) = 4 \times 2 + 4 \times 3$ **28.** 1000×9827637 **30.(a)** yes
(c) yes   **34.(b)** the powers 2, 4, 8, 16, 32, . . .   **35.(a)** 0   **(b)** 1

Section 3-5 □

1.(a) 812   **(c)** 16420   **(e)** 10120   **(g)** 1600   **2.** estimate 9000; 738,
912180, etc., obviously wrong; low; high   **3.** Hints: $L \neq 0, 1$, so $A > N$ and
$A > L$.   **5.(a)** All find 2×3, though units differ.   **8.** place value,
distributive, place value, associative for $\times$, etc.   **10.** 5, 6, 2, 3
13.(a) 220_{five} **(c)** 2144_{five} **(e)** 1110_{four} **(g)** $41T6_{\text{twelve}}$ **14.(c)** 36
(g) 7×28 or 37×28, so by estimate must be 37×28 **15.** 371, etc.
17.(a) 4824   **(c)** 6598   **18.** Art 828   **19.** $9 \times 8 \times 7 \times \ldots \times 1$
20.(a) 8000   **22.(a)** 6   **(b)** 120   **(c)** 5040   **23.(a)** 23×27, etc.
(b) 23×26, etc.   **24.(a)** 54   **25.** 1, 121, 12321, etc.   **26.(a)** 25
(c) no   **27.(a)** 15, 21, 28   **(c)** pool   **(d)** 25, 36, 49   **(f)** 36
28.(a) $13^2 + 14^2$

Section 3-6 □

4. $5 \div 0$ and $0 \div 0$ **6.** $q4r3$, $q3r7$, $q2r11$, etc.; 5 answers possible
8. 7 (including 0)   **9.** trichotomy property for comparing whole numbers
11.(a) $q2r1$ **(b)** $q0r2$ **13.** quotient will be less than 10; more than 10
14. 2 hours 24 min.   **15.(b)** over 11 days   **16.(a)** $4 - 2 = 2$
(b) $2 \times 2 = 4$ **(c)** $2 + 2 = 4$ **17.** none   **18.** first row: yes, yes,
yes; last row: all yes   **19.(a)** $200 \div 50 = 4$ **20.(a)** $q27r4$ **21.(a)** 209
22.(a) $q32_{\text{five}} r3$ **(c)** $q1033_{\text{five}} r20_{\text{five}}$ **(e)** $q401_{\text{six}} r14_{\text{six}}$ **28.(a)** Use
repeated subtraction.   **30.(a)** $7 + 7 + 7 + 7 + 7$ **(c)** $7 + 7 = \div 7 =$
32.(a) 1533   **33.(a)** omitted place-holder 0   **(c)** yes   **(d)** misplaced
place-holder 0   **(f)** no   **34.(a)** C   **35.** 621 miles   **36.(a)** 100 mg
(c) 80,300 mg   **37.(a)** 14   **(c)** 8   **(e)** 1   **38.** $2^6 \div 2^2 = 2^4$; it checks
41. Hint: find missing factor by guess and check.   **42.(a)** 10^7
(c) impossible   **43.(a)** 2^3

Section 4-1 □

1.(a) true   **(c)** true   **(e)** false   **2.(a)** $c = 24$ **(c)** $c = 2^{11} \times 3^8 \times 5^6 \times 13^{87}$
(g) $c = 2 \times 4$ **3.** 1, 2, 3, 4, 6   **4.(a)** last digit is 6   **(b)** 43
(c) yes; $c = 2$ **5.(a)** 1, 2, 3, 6, 13, 26, 39, 78   **(c)** 1, 2, 7, 14, 19, 38,
133, 266   **(e)** 6   **6.(a)** 60   **7.(a)** false   **(c)** false   **(e)** true
8.(a)   \$14,004   **9.(a)** Use sum of digits.   **(c)** Use last 2 digits.
10.(a) by 3 and 9, not by 4   **(c)** by 3, 4, and 9   **13.(a)** true   **(b)** false
14.(a) $1(2)(3)/6 = 1$ **(c)** $3(4)(7)/6 = 1 + 4 + 9$ **15.** Hint: "factor out"

ABC using the distributive property.   **17.(a)** no   **(b)** no   **(c)** no
18.(a) Think $15 \times 18 = 3 \times 5 \times 18 = 3 \times 90$.   **19.** associative
20.(a) true; $c = 4!$ **(c)** false   **(e)** false   **(g)** true; $c = 49!$
21.(a) 0   **(c)** 1   **(e)** 2   **(g)** 24   **22.** Hint: the amount is divisible by 8
and by 9.   **23.(a)** 28   **(b)** 496, etc.   **(d)** no

Section 4-2

1.(a) 6, 10, etc.   **(b)** They are multiples of 2.   **(d)** 11; note $11^2 > 100$.
3. divisibility of a sum   **4.(a)** 2   **(b)** There is none.   **(c)** 97
5.(a) p(3) = 47; p(4) = 53   **(b)** no   **6.(a)** $f(0) = 11$, $f(1) = 13$, etc.;
$f(10) = 121 = 11 \times 11$ **9.(a)** $2 \times 3 \times 11$ **(c)** $3 \times 3 \times 17$
10.(a) 210   **(c)** 100,000   **11.** primes, 13   **12.(a)** 11×13 **(b)** prime
15.(a) infinitely many   **(b)** none   **16.** 72 has 12 divisors.   **17.** 72 and
two others; 30 and four others   **18.(a)** $3 \times 2 = 6$ **(c)** $3 \times 4 = 12$
19.(a) 1   **(c)** 4   **(e)** 16   **(g)** 64   **20.(a)** primes   **(c)** form p^4, where
p is prime   **21.** 211   **22.** false   **25.(a)** 2311   **26.(a)** 04   **(c)** 16
(e) 04   **(g)** 3   **(i)** 7   **29.(a)** 13×17 **(c)** 29×31
(e) 109×911 **30.** 3 and 5, 17 and 19, etc.   **31.** no others
32.(a) $14 = 7 + 7$, $16 = 5 + 11$, etc.   **33.** no   **36.** no

Section 4-3

2.(a) 2   **(c)** 1   **(e)** 29   **3.** 1   **4.(a)** 6   **(c)** 45   **(e)** 35   **(g)** 76
5.(a) 14   **(c)** 156   **7.(a)** 60   **(c)** 882   **(e)** 42   **(g)** 28   **9.** true
10.(a) when the only common factor is 1   **(c)** when a = 1 and b = 1
11.(a) 5   **12.(a)** 6   **(c)** 59   **(e)** 18   **16.(a)** 2, 5
19.(b) $a \times b = $ GCD $(a, b) \times$ LCM (a, b)   **20.(a)** 6409   **(c)** 9581
22. 1, 5, 7, 11, etc.   **23.(a)** associative   **(b)** closure   **24.** all   **25.(a)** red
(b) 3 purples or 2 dark greens   **27.(a)** 168   **30.(a)** 83   **(c)** 17
(e) 1   **31.(a)** 3 3-lb on *B*   **(d)** 1 5-lb on *A*, 2 3-lb on *B*   **32.(a)** impossible

Section 5-1

3. none   **7.(a)** ½   **(c)** ⅕   **8.** both   **9.** $^{12}/_2$, $^{18}/_3$, etc.; $^6/_{16}$, $^9/_{24}$, etc.
11.(a) yes   **(c)** no   **13.** check writing   **14.** $^4/_6$ and $^6/_9$ **15.** $^4/_4$ and $^6/_6$
16. $^6/_9$, $^8/_{12}$, etc.   **17.(a)** ¾   **(c).** $^4/_9$ **(e)** $^4/_5$ **(g)** $^2/_9$ **18.** 3 ways
19.(a) $^{19}/_{23}$ **20.** yes; no   **21.** $^{49}/_{98}$, $^{11}/_{22}$, etc.   **22.(a)** $^2/_{10}$ **(c)** $^{16}/_{100}$
(e) impossible   **(g)** impossible   **(i)** $^{75}/_{1000}$ **(k)** $^5/_{100}$ **24.(a)** $^9/_{11}$ **25.(a)** $^1/_6$,
$^1/_5$, ¼   **(c).** $^2/_7$, $^5/_{17}$, $^3/_{10}$ **26.(a)** $^{631}/_{1000}$, etc.   **(c)** $^{351}/_{420}$, etc.   **27.(a)** yes
(b) yes   **31.(a)** ¼   **(c)** $^5/_4$ **32.(a)** $^1/_6$ **33.(a)** $^1/_{10}$ **34.(b)** blue
35.(a) $^{243}/_{534}$ **(c)** neither   **38.** Hint: C < 3 and C ≠ 1.   **39.(a)** 32
41.(d) $(1 + 3 + 5 + 7 + 9)/(11 + 13 + 15 + 17 + 19)$; yes

Section 5-2

1.(a) 6, 12, 18, etc.   **(c)** *qs, 2qs, 3qs*, etc.   **2.(a)** whole numbers
(b) fractions   **3.(a)** $^4/_7$ **(c)** $^{139}/_{168}$ **(e)** $^{37}/_{100}$ **(g)** $^{43}/_{2607}$

(h) $247/2^5 \times 3^7$ **5.** Whole numbers are fractions.   **6.(a)** $^2/_7$
(c) not yet defined   (e) $^{67}/_{100}$ **8.** One set is $\{^2/_{12}, {}^6/_{12}\}$.   **10.** $^0/_1$, $^0/_2$, $^0/_3$,
etc., are all names for the same number.   **11.** same   **15.(a)** yes   **(b)** no
(c) no   **(d)** yes   **17.(a)** dark green   **(c)** light green   **23.** $^{11}/_{17}$
24.(a) $^1/_1$, $\frac{1}{2}$, $\frac{2}{3}$, etc.   **25.(a)** 2   **27.(a)** $^{15}/_8$, $^{31}/_{16}$, $^{63}/_{32}$

Section 5-3 □

1.(a) $^5/_{12}$ **(c)** $^5/_9$ **(e)** $^{146}/_{105}$ **(g)** $20^5/_6$ **(i)** $^{187}/_{259}$ **2.(a)** $^{35}/_{24}$
3.(a) $^{10}/_9$ **4.** 0   **5.** $^5/_8$ **6.(a)** yes   **(b)** no   **7.(a)** $10^{13}/_{15}$
(c) $28^{14}/_{15}$ **8.** Order is reversed.   **9.(a)** yes   **(c)** yes   **10.(a)** no
(c) no   **11.(a)** yes   **(b)** no   **(c)** yes   **(d)** no   **14.** definition adding
fractions, definition multiplying fractions, etc.   **15.(a)** yes   **(c)** no
16. no   **18.** will gain closure for subtraction   **19.** closure for division
20.(a) orange   **(c)** dark green   **21.** approximate   **23.(a)** $\frac{2}{3}$ **24.(b)** $4\frac{3}{4}$
25.(a) always true   **(c)** yes   **26.(a)** 3   **27.** 26   **29.(a)** $^2/_8$
(c) about \$14   **32.(b)** $^5/_3$ **33.(a)** $1/(1 + {}^1/_5)$ **35.(a)** 8   **(c)** 12
36.(a) whole   **(c)** quarter   **(e)** quarter   **37.** $^1/_{32}$ **38.(a)** $10\frac{1}{2}$

Section 6-1 □

1.(a) 5:2   **(b)** $^2/_7$ **(c)** cannot be determined   **2.(a)** 4:5   **(c)** 6:1
(e) 1:20   **3.** 17:8   **4.(a)** no   **6.** probably 9   **7.(a)** 12   **(b)** 5 minutes
8.(a) 4 atmospheres   **(c)** 165   **9.(a)** 54   **(c)** about 6   **10.(a)** 145.5;
194   **(c)** 285   **11.(a)** 64 ml   **(c)** 40 ml   **12.** \$64.65   **14.** no
15.(a) 10 tons   **(c)** $^1/_6$ ton   **17.(a)** 8   **(c)** 54   **19.** 250,000   **21.** 22.5
minutes   **23.(a)** 5,000,000   **25.** 30; 75; 15n; $^{100}/_{15}$ inches   **26.(a)** 40 more
27.(a) 112.5   **28.(a)** 45°   **(b)** 10°   **29.(a)** $^3/_2$ **(c)** 150   **(d)** B
31.(a) 215,596   **(b)** 332,751   **38.(a)** 10   **(c)** $^{50}/_3$ **39.** flagpole: 5:4; boy:
190 cm   **40.(a)** 4:9   **(c)** times 8

Section 6-2 □

1. $\frac{1}{4}$, .25, 25%, 1:4, etc.   **2.(a)** 682,000   **(c)** .000682   **3.(a)** three
ten-thousandths   **(d)** thirteen billion   **4.(a)** .089, .66, .7   **5.(a)** $2\frac{1}{4}$
(c) $2^1/_{25}$ **6.(a)** $.3_{eight}$ **(c)** 3.05_{eight} **7.** all except $^1/_5$ **9.(a)** 8.5
(c) .03   **(e)** .05   **(g)** 0   **10.(a)** 200   **(c)** 7.49   **11.** 36,500; 37,499
15. .00000001   **16.(a)** .01   **(c)** .37   **(e)** 4 small squares
17. Hint: add .5, then compute INTEGER.

Section 6-3 □

1. 3.738 ÷ .42 and 3.738 ÷ 8.9   **2.(a)** 23.6794   **(c)** 4926.2151   **5.** c
6. Decimal point shifts left   **7.** yes   **8.** true   **9.(a)** 27   **(c)** 62.5%
(e) 50   **(g)** 40   **12.** from .38 to .62, from .63 to .87, etc.   **13.(a)** \$310
(c) \$403.67   **(e)** \$4000   **(g)** \$2090   **14.** 33¢   **17.** 99%   **18.** saving is
9%   **19.** from \$60 to \$100   **20.** both   **23.** \$150   **27.(a)** 1.05
(c) 5.8011   **(e)** .000006   **(g)** .08   **(i)** 8000   **(k)** .00271

28.(a) .0000001998   **30.** 44 folds   **32.(b)** $157.35   **33.(b)** 2.478
34.(a) 14   **(c)** 14   **36.** × in box; − in circle   **37.** 9.55
39. loses $1   **41.(a)** 3,443,581   **(c)** Ark.   **(e)** Ala.
42.(a) 2.9% decrease   **43.(a)** $69,300,000 (use troy weight)

☐ Section 6-4

1.(a) .6250 (exact)   **(c)** .2750 (exact)   **2.(a)(c)(e)(g)** repeating
(i) terminates in 2 places   **3.** $^{311}/_{489}$ **4.(a)** $^{4}/_{5}$ **(c)** $^{4}/_{13}$ **6.(c)** 2   **(e)** 1
(g) 0   **8.(a)** $.\overline{142857}$, $.\overline{285714}$, $.\overline{428571}$, etc. (same pattern of digits)
9.(a) Subtract from 9.   **10.** same digits "moved over"   **11.** repeating
12.(a) $^{1}/_{16}$, etc.   **(b)** $^{1}/_{101}$, etc.   **14.(a)** all reduced fractions with
denominators whose prime factors are entirely 2's and 5's   **(c)** There are none.
15.(a) $^{1}/_{17}$ has period 16, $^{1}/_{31}$ has period 15.   **(b)** primes   **17.(b)** Periods are
6 and 16.   **18.(a)** .2162162162   **(c)** .2166666666   **19.(a)** $.\overline{6}$ **(c)** $.\overline{06}$
(e) $.75\overline{0}$ **20.** $^{14}/_{43}$ **21.(a)** $^{74}/_{99}$ **(c)** $^{1041}/_{1111}$ **(e)** $^{9}/_{55}$ **23.** $^{163}/_{1000}$
24.(a) $^{2}/_{9}$ **(c)** $^{4}/_{9}$ **25.(a)** $^{2}/_{99}$ **(c)** $^{4}/_{99}$ **27.(a)** $^{43}/_{99}$ **(d)** 1
28.(a) $.4\overline{9}$ **(b)** yes   **(c)** no   **29. Hint:** $\overline{TALK}$ = TALK/9999
30.(a) 1718192021   **(c)** no   **31.(a)** 0000000100   **(c)** no
32.(a) .88888888   **(c).** .88888889   **(e)** .89   **33.(a)** .166666, etc.
(c) .16666671666667166666   **34.(a)** $^{1}/_{6}$ **(c)** 1666667/9999999   **35. Hint:**
look for patterns.   **36.** .4167   **37.** She computed $^{30}/_{17}$.

☐ Section 7-1

1.(a) −5° temperature, owing money, etc.   **2.(a)** −6   **3.(a)** yes; no; no
(c) yes   **(e)** yes   **(g)** no   **5.(a)** −7   **(c)** −x **(e)** −5
(g) −869   **6.(a)** negative   **(b)** positive   **(c)** neither   **7.** ruler, etc.
9.(a) <   **(c)** >   **(e)** >   **(g)** >   **10.** left   **11.(a)** −7   **(c)** −3
(e) 48   **(g)** 4   **12.(a)** six minus four   **(c)** the opposite of negative two
(f) the opposite of x (*not* negative x)   **13.(a)** 6   **(c)** 0   **(e)** 5   **(g)** 2
14.(a) −3, etc.   **(c)** impossible   **15.** 8, 8, 0; yes   **16.(a)** yes; no; yes;
no   **(b)** no; no; no; yes   **17.** yes; no.   **18.** whole numbers
19.(a) $\{. . . , -3, -2, -1, 0, 1, 2, 3, . . .\}$ **(c)** $\{1, 2, 3, 4, . . .\}$ **(e)** $\{\ \ \}$
20. of Z: Z, N, P, W; of N: N **21.(a)** Match −n with n.   **22.** 0 − 1,
1 − 2, 2 − 3, etc.   **24.** −1, −2, −3, . . ., −10   **25.** bottom of Mariana
Trench   **26.(a)** 9248   **(c)** 19,882   **27.(b)** 20,602   **28.(a)** about .07%
29.(a) 540   **30.(a)** 49°   **(c)** 214°   **31.(a)** 16°   **(c)** −9°
32.(a) −36°   **(c)** −106°   **33.(b)** −41°   **34.(a)** 8 P.M.   **(b)** 2 A.M.
35.(a) Frankfurt, 10 A.M.; Singapore, 2:30 P.M.   **36.(a)** 5 hours 10 minutes

☐ Section 7-2

2.(a) 0   **(c)** −1065   **3.(a)** 10   **(c)** −7   **4.** yes   **5.** Case 1
6.(a) 8   **(b)** +8 or 8   **(c)** $^{8}/_{1}$ or 8   **9.(a)** −3   **(c)** −13   **(e)** 6
10.(a) −22   **(c)** 24   **(e)** −2   **(g)** −2   **11.(a)** Multiply as whole
numbers.   **(c)** Sign is positive, absolute value is product of absolute values.
12.(a) 13   **(c)** 8   **(e)** 2   **(g)** −18   **14.** no   **15.** yes   **16.(a)** −6

(c) 0   (e) p (g) $-p + q$ **17.(a)** 1   **(b)** yes; no   **19.(a)** W, N, Z, F
(c) W, Z, F (e) N (g) N, Z **20.(a)** yes   (c) no   **21.(a)** $7 - 3 = 4$
(c) $7 - 7 = 0$ (e) $0 - 3 = -3$ and $3 - (-3) = 6$ (g) $4 - 3 = 1$
23.(a) Use any integers.   (c) Use r positive.   (e) $r = 0$ **24.(a)** yes
(c) no   **25.(a)** $p = 2, q = -3$, etc.   (c) impossible
28.(a) $- 10 \times 3$ **29.(a)** The sum of 2 negatives is a positive.
(b) confusion with multiplication   **30.** 38°   **32.(a)** $-6, 6$ (c) $-20, 8$
(e) $0, 6$ **33.(a)** $2 \times 10^2 + 4 \times 10^1 + 7 \times 10^0$ (c) 1×10^6
34.(a) 4.3×10^1 (c) 9×10^6 (e) 7×10^{-5} (g) 1.2×10^{16}
35.(a) 1.2×10^{16} (c) 1.394×10^{-35} (e) 5×10^3 **36.** Opposite of x
minus negative two equals five   **37.(a)** -2 (c) 5

Section 8-1 ☐

1.(a) $^{17}/_{12}$ (c) $-^{59}/_{42}$ (e) $-^1/_{15}$ (g) $-^2/_7$ (i) $^1/_6$ (k) $-^6/_7$
2.(a) $^6/_7$ (c) $^4/_9$ (e) $^8/_{15}$ (g) $^{35}/_{18}$ (i) $-^9/_{11}$ (k) $^9/_{11}$ (m) $-^1/_{15}$
(o) $^1/_8$ **3.** $0 - 19$, etc.; $5 \div 11$ **4.(c)** Those with an odd number of $-$
signs are negative.   **5.(a)** positive; $^5/_8$ **(b)** $-^4/_9$ (c) $0; 0$ **6.** $\sqrt{2}, \pi$,
etc.   **9.(a)** 2   (c) 0   (e) -3 (g) $^1/_4$ (i) $-^1/_3$ (k) $-^4/_5$
10.(a) $<$ (c) $<$ (e) $>$ (g) $>$ (i) $<$ (k) $>$
12.(a) $-6 < -5 < -^1/_5 < -^1/_6 < 0 < ^1/_6 < ^1/_5 < 5 < 6$
13. $^{441}/_{1650}$, etc.   **14.** W.   **15.(a)** yes   **(b)** no   **16.** $1, 0, -1; 0$
17.(a) -3 (c) $-^1/_3$ (e) 0   **18.(a)** $^1/_3$ (c) 3   (e) impossible
20.(a) positive integers   (c) integers   (e) positive integers   (g) integers
21.(a) $\{3, 6, 9, 12, \ldots\}$ **(b)** $\{3, 9, 27, 81, \ldots\}$
(c) $\{\ldots, -6, -3, 0, 3, 6, \ldots\}$ **22.** yes   **23.(a)** $^9/_4$ **(b)** $^9/_4$ **24.** t
25. because Q is closed under addition   **26.(a)** property 10   **(b)** both
27.(a) 0   **(b)** all of them   **28.(a)** yes   (c) no   (e) no
29.(a) property 4   (c) property 5   (e) property 1   **30.** all except
property 1   **31.(b)** Hint: use part (a).   (c) Hint: use property 6.
(d) Hint: use property 5.   **33.(a)** Z, N, Q (c) W, F, Z, Q
(e) W, F, Z, Q (g) none   (i) Z, Q **34.** yes   **35.(a)** no
(c) no   (e) yes   (g) no   **37.(a)** $2 - 3$, etc.   (c) $0 - 2 \div 3$, etc.
38.(a) increase   (c) increase if > 1, decrease if < 1
(e) signs alternate $+$ and $-$

Section 8-2 ☐

1.(a) positive numbers   **(b)** 0   (c) negative numbers   **(d)** none
(e) non-negative numbers   **(f)** negative numbers   **2.(a)** 81   **(b)** none
(c) -81 (e) non-negative numbers   (g) none   **3.(a)** $^1/_3$ (c) $^3/_2$
4.(a) even   (c) even   (e) depends on p (g) even   **5.** $^2/_1$
10.(a) 10   (c) 5   (e) $\sqrt{3}$ **11.(b)** I want a date, so I say please, etc.
12. no   **13.** No, C and d cannot both be integers.   **14.** distributive
15.(a) 9.869587728   (c) about 1%   **16.** $2.71828 < 2.7\overline{1828} < e$
17.(a) $\sqrt{5} < 3 < \sqrt{11}$ **(b)** $-\sqrt{101} < 0 < 2$ (c) $3.14 < 3.141 < \pi$
18.(b) 1.74   (c) 1.732   **19.(a)** π (c) $-\pi$ (e) $\sqrt{2}$ (g) $-\sqrt{2}$
20.(a) $4.8 < \pi + \sqrt{3} < 5.0$ (c) $-1.5 < \sqrt{3} - \pi < -1.3$
(e) $6.2 < 2\pi < 6.4$ **21.(a)** $8.0 < e + \pi + \sqrt{5} < 8.3$

24.(a) 1000, 113, 3281, 70 (first row)   **25.(a)** 1, 4, 2, 2.8, etc.
26.(a) 4   **(c)** $^9/_2$ **(e)** 3   **(g)** 9   **28.(a)** no   **(c)** no   **(e)** yes
30.(a) 58.9824, 59.1361   **(c)** $11 < \sqrt{137} < 12$, $11.1 < \sqrt{137} < 11.2$, etc.
31.(a) 24901.55143   **(b)** .00001   **(c)** .6   **32.(a)** 2
(c) 2.7048138   **33.(a)** 4,294,967,297

☐ Section 8-3

1.(a) 3   **(c)** 4   **(e)** 3   **(g)** 2   **6.(a)** 2   **(b)** 12_{five} **7.(a)** 1
(b) 2   **8.(a)** 2   **(b)** none   **9.(a)** 1   **(b)** 2   **(c)** none
10. opposites: 0, 6, 5, 4, etc.; reciprocals: none, 1, 4, 5, etc.   **12.(a)** 0
(c) 2, 3   **14.** 12   **15.** yes   **16.(a)** yes   **(b)** yes   **17.(a)** 4 = 4
(c) no   **18.(a)** 6: 1, 5; 7: 1, 2, 3, 4, 5, 6   **(b)** prime clocks
(d) 100-hour; no   **19.(a)** yes   **(b)** no   **(c)** It is 4.   **23.(a)** Thursday
(c) Monday   **24.(a)** $13 = 2^2 + 3^2$; $17 = 1^2 + 4^2$; 19 cannot, etc.
(c) 61, 97, etc.

☐ Section 9-1

1.(a) 36   **2.(a)** 13   **5.(a)** 10   **7.(a)** multiplied by 4   **8.(a)** multiplied by
8   **9.(a)** 1, 2, 4, 5, 8, 9, 10, 13, 16, 17, 25   **10.** "over 3 up 2" for 13
11. no   **13.** 1 m   **14.** 2816 m

☐ Section 9-2

2.(a) intersection of points   **(c)** set of points common to parallel lines
4. J is not between E and F, 1 is not on $\overleftrightarrow{EF}$; yes   **5.** $\angle DAH$ and $\angle HAD$; 24
6. Yes, extend $\overleftrightarrow{AB}$.   **8.(c)** (Show vertex of 1 angle on a side of the other)
(e) (Show a common side.)   **9.(a)** 0   **(c)** 0   **(e)** { }   **(g)** 0
(i) $\overrightarrow{SP}$ **(k)** $\overrightarrow{SP}$ **(m)** P, O, T **(p)** { }   **(r)** $\overline{MN}$ **(t)** $\angle OST$
10.(a) { }   **(c)** the line   **11.(a)** 2 half-planes intersect in the empty set, *etc.*
12. no   **13.** $\overrightarrow{AB}$ **16.(b)** They are collinear.   **18.(a)** 3   **19.(a)** 2
20.(a) { }, a point, or a line   **(c)** { }, a point, or a ray   **(e)** 0, 1, 2,
3, or 4 points; or segment and 0 or 1 point; or ray and 0 or 1 point; or angle
21.(a) 15   **22.(a)** 21   **23.(a)** 3   **(c)** 28   **25.(a)** all of them, though
some require retracing   **(b)** D and O   **26.** hexagon   **27.(a), (f), (g)**
28.(a) A and C are exterior   **30.** triangle, quadrilaterial, hexagon, decagon
31. No, consider a square.   **32.** Remove any interior point.   **33.** (Extend
$\overline{BC}$ to meet $\overline{ED}$.)   **34.(a)** 5   **(c)** 9   **(e)** 6   **(g)** 19   **35.(a)** open
(c) closed   **36.(a)** no   **(b)** no   **38.(a)** interior and exterior
39.(a) center of clock, etc.   **(c)** edge of rectangular picture

☐ Section 9-3

1. stop sign, head of bolt, floor tile, etc.   **3.(a)** triangle, 12-gon
(c) impossible   **4.(a)** 4 sides, all sides congruent, all angles congruent, etc.
5.(a) $\triangle RSV$ and $\triangle TSV$ **6.** impossible   **7.(a)** wedding band

8.(b) chord   **9.(a)** 0, 1, or 2 points   **10.(a)** 2   **(c)** 2   **(e)** 2
12.(a) $\triangle EFG \cong \triangle ZYX$ **(c)** $\triangle KLM \cong \triangle TSR$ **13.(a)** There are at
least 6 ways.   **16.** (Cut 4 "L's".)   **17.(c)** $\angle RQT$ **(e)** $\triangle ABC$ and
$\triangle DEF$ **19.(a)** 0   **(c)** 5   **(e)** 35   **(g)** $n(n - 3)/2$ **20.(a)** no

Section 9-4 □

1.(a) parallelogram   **(c)** parallelogram   **(e)** trapezoid   **(g)** neither
(i) neither   **2.(a)** 2 and 8, etc.   **(c)** 1 and 3, etc.   **3.** $\angle RTS$,
$\angle RTU, \angle WTY$ **4.** It is a right angle.   **5.(a)** They are parallel.   **6.** yes
7.(a) 1   **8.** 22   **10.(e)** perpendicular bisector is a line, angle bisector
is a ray, others are segments   **11.(b)** outside   **12.(a)** impossible
13.(a) parallelogram   **16.** no   **17.(a)** same   **(c)** $\{C, D\}$ **(e)** yes
18. yes; no   **19.(a)** 3   **20.(a)** addition of whole numbers   **(b)** Let x #
$y = x$, for all whole numbers x and y.   **22.(a)** reflexive, transitive
(c) transitive   **(e)** none   **(g)** all three   **23.** angle bisector
25. perpendicular from P to m

Section 10-1 □

1.(a) (Q is between P and R.)   **(c)** (R is not on $\overleftrightarrow{PQ}$.)   **2.(a)** We don't add
segments.   **3.** The sum is an upper limit for the distance.   **6.(a)** 26
(c) 19   **7.(a)** 32   **(c)** 46   **(e)** 30   **10.** 32″ (unless the material is
"reversible")   **12.(a)** 6π **13.(a)** $10/\pi$ **14.** circumference
15.(a) 2 times (into 3 congruent parts)   **17.(a)** Products should be equal.
19.(a) 9 and 15   **(c)** 1   **22.(a)** $(x + 62) : 70 = 62 : 30$ **23.(a)** 24
25. about 873 cm   **27.(a)** 12 m   **28.(a)** 7.2 m

Section 10-2 □

1.(e), (g), (h), and **(j)** are impossible.   **2.(a)** 48°   **(c)** $(90 - x)°$
3.(a) 138°   **4.** 45° and 135°   **6.** 30°   **7.(a)** 40°   **(b)** 80°, or 20° and
140°   **8.** 45°, 62°, or 73°   **9.(a)** 360°   **(c)** 720°   **11.(a)** 3: $\triangle ABC$,
$\triangle ABD, \triangle BCD$ **(d)** yes   **12.(a)** $\angle 1 = \angle 4 = \angle 5 = \angle 8 = 70°, \angle 2 =$
$\angle 3 = \angle 6 = \angle 7 = 110°$ **(c)** There are none.   **13.(a)** $\overleftrightarrow{RV}$ and $\overleftrightarrow{LW}$
14. no   **15.** They are alternate interior angles formed by parallel lines.
17.(a) 1   **(c)** about .839

Section 10-3 □

1.(a) 55   **(c)** 90   **(e)** $25\sqrt{3}$ **2.** (area is 244)   **3.(a)** 40   **4.(a)** s^2
5.(a) 2 : 3   **(b)** 4 : 9   **6.(a)** doubles it   **7.** no   **8.** (disprove)
9.(a) 1×13 **(c)** 1×20 or 2×10 or 4×5 **10.** For example, 3×6.
11. 64; 65; no, there is a gap in the rectangle.   **13.(a)** 36π **(c)** $2500/\pi$
14. $50\pi + 306$ **15.** $400 - 100\pi$ **17.** 9   **18.(a)** 400   **(b)** 10; 4000
19.(a) parallelogram   **(c)** π **22.(a)** $1 \times 60, 2 \times 30, 3 \times 20$, etc.
(b) 2×30 **23.(a)** $3 \times 70, 5 \times 42, 6 \times 35$, etc.   **(b)** 105
(c) an even number   **25.(a)** B **(c)** B   **24.(a)** Alaska, Texas, California

(b) Rhode Island, Delaware, Connecticut   **26.(a)** 243,344π
(b) $A = \pi r^2$ **27.** 23   **28.** yes   **29.** 5

☐ Section 10-4

2.(a) yes   **(b)** no   **3.(a)** pyramid   **(c)** prism   **(e)** pyramid
(g) pyramid   **(i)** both   **4.(a)** heptagonal pyramid   **5.(a)** 12
(c) 6, 12, 8   **(e)** 6, 10, 6   **6.** $F + V = E + 2$ **7.(a)** 14, 26, 14
8.(a) hexagonal pyramid   **(c)** pentagonal prism   **9.(a)** 288π   **(c)** 176π
10.(a) 2r   **(c)** volume of sphere + volume of cone = volume of cylinder
11.(a) 48 **(c)** 14   **12.(a)** prism and cylinder   **13.** 56π/3   **14.** 3 cubic
meters   **16.(a)** times 4   **17.(a)** times 8   **18.** times $2\sqrt{2}$ **19.** ²⁷/₈
20.(a) ⅛   **21.(a)** $\overleftrightarrow{AE}$ and $\overleftrightarrow{BD}$ etc.   **22.** 1668   **26.(a)** 90°   **(c)** 90°
27. (left) 28   **28.** D

☐ Section 10-5

1.(a) kg   **(c)** cubic cm   **(e)** kg   **(g)** km   **(i)** cm   **(k)** 25° C
2.(a) 5800 g   **(c)** 7500 ml   **(e)** 403 cm   **5.(a)** 5   **6.** A kg calorie is
1000 times more.   **7.** time   **8.(a)** 2000   **(c)** .006   **(e)** 100,000
9. .442   **10.(a)** 1,000,000,000   **(c)** 1,000,000   **11.** 10,000   **12.(a)** 5 kg
(c) 500 g   **13.(a)** 90,000   **14.** 1   **15.(a)** false   **(b)** true   **16.** 84
ounces   **17.(a)** probably 8 fluid ounces   **(b)** about 8.3 pounds   **(c)** 8
(d) 2   **(e)** 640   **(f)** 1728   **(g)** 128   **18.(a)** 30,000   **(c)** about 100
(e) 466,560   **(h)** about 6 trillion   **20.** 13,641 feet   **21.(a)** 42,200
(b) 8560   **(c)** $2.84   **23.(b)** 16   **25.(a)** 1 g   **(c)** .01 g   **(e)** ¹/₃₂ inch
26.(a) .5 g   **(c)** .005 g   **(e)** ¹/₆₄ inch   **27.(a)** 1%   **(c)** .01%
(e) .2%   **31.** 2 cm × 1 cm × 1 cm   **38.(a)** about 100 square cm
46.(a) age, density, voltage, time, shoe size, etc.   **48.(a)** 3   **(b)** about 800
cubic cm   **49.** about 8 minutes   **50.(a)** 4420 ml   **(b)** 265.2 liters
(c) 13 to 14 seconds   **53.(a)** published in 1877   **(b)** 8

☐ Section 11-1

3.(a) Bisect angle, etc.   **5.** (Construct perpendicular bisector of chord.)
10.(a) They meet at a point.   **11.** M, O, and C are on the Euler line.
13.(a) yes   **15.** Construct counter-examples for **(a)** and **(d)**.   **18.** They lie
on a line.   **19.** Find intersection of perpendicular bisectors of 2 chords.
20. 56

☐ Section 11-2

1.(a) 50   **(c)** $\sqrt{533}$ **(e)** ¹⁵/₄   **(g)** $\sqrt{5}$ **2.** $AC = \sqrt{126}$, $BC = \sqrt{315}$
3. $0 < x < 27$ **5.** over 100 feet!   **6.(a)** 24   **(b)** 28   **8.(a)** $4\sqrt{3}$
(c) $25\sqrt{3/4}$ **10.(a)** $(b - a)^2$ **(c)** a   **(e)** b   **13.** true   **14.(a)** If an
angle is acute, then it has measure 42°; false   **(c)** For any whole numbers a
and b, if $a^2 = b^2$, then $a = b$; true   **(d)** false   **(e)** All integers are whole
numbers; false   **15.(b)** 12   **16.** neither   **17.** $3 - \pi/2$ **18.(b)** yes

20.(a) 29   **22.(b)** 46.5 miles   **23.** 25   **24.(a)** $2 + \sqrt{3}$ **25.** about 28 cm $\times$ 28 cm $\times$ 10 m

Section 11-3 □

1.(a) 3 of each   **(c)** 5 of each   **(e)** 2 of each   **2.** 36; infinitely many
3. 4 for the square   **4.(a)** A, H, I, M, etc. (vertical); B, C, D, E, etc.
(horizontal)   **(c)** none   **8.(a)** BIB, DUD, MOM, NOON, etc.   **(c)** 90
(e) neither   **10.(b)** round   **11.(a)** reflection   **16.(a)** none   **(b)** the flip
line   **(c)** a point, the center of the rotation   **17.** 2 (but probably at least 3);
rotations   **18.(a)** R **(b)** V **19.(a)** W **(c)** R **20.(a)** top row is
WUVSTR   **22.(a)** a slide, twice as long as a slide from O to Q **23.** Turn
square (*a*) 90° counterclockwise.   **24.(a)** 12!   **(b)** either one   **(c)** I is a
reflection about the pitch F; RI = R followed by I (or I followed by R)
(e) 15   **25.** Hint: use a reflection to solve for one cushion.   **26.(a)** home
27. page 6 (upside down), page 2, page 7   **29.(b)** perpendicular bisector of
segment

Section 12-1 (Answers are reduced.) □

1.(a) $^3/_{14}$ **(c)** $^3/_7$ **2.(a)** $^2/_5$ **3.** $\frac{1}{4}$ **4.(a)** $\frac{1}{3}$ **5.(a)** $\frac{1}{6}$ **(c)** $^5/_6$
(e) 1 : 5   **6.(a)** $\frac{1}{2}$ **(c)** $^1/_{13}$ **(e)** $^1/_{26}$ **(g)** $^6/_{13}$ **(i)** 0   **7.(a)** $^{25}/_{51}$
(c) $^4/_{51}$ **(e)** $^2/_{51}$ **(g)** $^8/_{17}$ **(i)** 0   **8.(a)** $^1/_{221}$ **(c)** $^{25}/_{102}$ **(e)** $^{13}/_{51}$
(g) $^{13}/_{17}$ **9.(a)** $^1/_{169}$ **(c)** $\frac{1}{4}$ **(e)** $\frac{1}{4}$ **(g)** $\frac{3}{4}$ **10.(a)** $^2/_{425}$ **(c)** $^4/_{17}$
(e) $^{13}/_{51}$ **(g)** $^{13}/_{17}$ **11.(a)** $^1/_{5525}$ **(c)** $^2/_{17}$ **(e)** $^{13}/_{102}$ **12.** $^5/_{18}$
13.(a) $\frac{1}{4}$ **14.(a)** $\frac{1}{6}$ **16.(a)** $\frac{1}{6}$ **19.(a)** $\frac{1}{4}$ **(b)** $\frac{3}{4}$ **21.(a)** B
23.(a) $\frac{1}{6}$ **28.(a)** $\frac{1}{8}$ **(c)** $\frac{3}{8}$ **(e)** $^1/_{16}$ **(g)** $\frac{1}{4}$ **(i)** $^1/_{1024}$
29.(a) $\frac{1}{8}$ **(c)** $^5/_{32}$ **30.** $^1/_{32}$; 10   **31.** 50 cents   **33.(a)** behind $7
(b) $7.38   **(c)** $1842   **34.(a)** $\frac{3}{8}$ **35.(a)** $\frac{3}{4}$ **(c)** $^{15}/_{16}$ **(e)** $\frac{1}{5}$
36. 13.   **40.(a)** $50   **(c)** $100   **42.(a)** $^4/_5$ **43.(a)** $^3/_{10}$ **44.** no
46. $\frac{1}{7}$ **47.(a)** $^1/_{424}$ **48.** $\frac{1}{6}$ **52.(a)** $^1/_{50}$ **54.(a)** $^9/_{32}$ **60.(a)** 1 : 5
(c) 5 : 1   **(e)** 1 : 1   **(g)** 3 : 1   **62.(a)** no   **(c)** yes
63.(a) "Who didn't order coffee?"   **64.** V and X **65.(a)** independent
(c) dependent   **(e)** independent

Section 12-2 □

1.(a) 7, 6, no single mode   **(c)** 6.5, 6, 5   **2.(a)** 4, 5, 6, etc.   **(c)** 1, 5, 6,
etc.   **(e)** 5, 25, 30, etc.   **4.(a)** 9, 3   **(c)** 4, 2   **(e)** 16, 4
5.(a)–(e) 16, 4   **(k)** Mean increases by same amount, standard deviation
is unchanged.   **6.** Ching 650, David 700, Ellen 450, Fernando 500, etc.
7.(a) mean   **(b)** range   **8.(a)** mean is 11; 23 below, 23 above   **9.(a)** $^{890}/_{11}$
10.(a) yes   **14.(a)** 65   **16.(a)** 1000   **18.(a)** 200   **(c)** 9%
(e) $^{207}/_{2000}$ **19.(a)** 500,000   **24.(a)** about 4.7

Section 12-3 □

2.(b) Mars: about 140,000,000 miles   **(c)** Venus; 10; Jupiter; Mercury
3.(b) 2.22 mm; 11.4 mm   **4.(a)** No; for example, $9999.86.   **(b)** no

8. 1½ times; 2 times   **9.(a)** about 25 million; 12 million; 8 million
(b) 55 million

☐ Section 12-4

4.(a) They lie along a line.   **5.** (a), (d), (e), and (f) are functions
6. (a), (d), (e), (f)   **7.** (a), (b), (d)   **8.(a)** yes   **(b)** no   **(c)** $y = x$
(d) $y > x$ **(e)** impossible   **9.(a)** square root, area, etc.   **(b)** "is a divisor
of," perpendicular, etc.   **10.(a)** no   **(b)** yes   **11.(a)** -1 **(c)** -1
(e) $5 - w$ **(g)** $-w$ **12.** 13, 5, 0, 0, 30, 284, 4   **13.(a)** 23, 37
(c) 123, 25   **(e)** 2, 9   **14.(a)** -16 **(c)** -6 **(e)** no
15.(a) $5x + 2$ **(c)** $5x - 28$ **(e)** yes   **16.(a)** $\{4\}$ **(c)** $\{\ \}$
(e) $\{(2, 3), (4, 6), (6, 9), (8, 12), (10, 15)\}$ **(g)** $\{\ \}$ **17.** (a) $\{\ \}$
(b) $\{-3\}$ **20.(a)** 200   **(b)** 35   **22.** Allen \$1.80, Baker \$1.40, Chase \$0
23.(a) 30   **(b)** 76   **24.(a)** 31; 11   **(b)** 79; 69

☐ Appendix

1.(a) "Not all birds can fly," or "Some birds can't fly."   **2.(c)** yes   **3.** yes
4.(a) yes   **5.(a)** yes   **6.(a)** Yes   **(c)** yes   **7.(a)** 8   **(c)** 1024
8.(a) true   **(c)** false   **(e)** true   **9.(a)** necessary   **(c)** neither
(d) both   **10.(a)** If Hank diets he will look better.   **(c)** none
12.(a) "all" is universal   **13.(a)** ostrich, emu, etc.   **14.(a)** $(p \vee q) \wedge r$

Bibliography

PROBLEM SOLVING AND APPLICATIONS

1. Butts, Thomas. *Problem Solving in Mathematics.* New York: John Wiley & Sons, forthcoming.
2. deBono, Edward. *PO: Beyond Yes and No.* Middlesex, England: Penguin Books, 1973.
3. Fujimura, Kobon. *The Tokyo Puzzles.* New York: Charles Scribner's Sons, 1978.
4. Gardner, Martin. *Mathematical Puzzles and Diversions.* New York: Simon & Schuster, 1959.
5. Gardner, Martin. *New Mathematical Diversions.* New York: Simon & Schuster, 1966.
6. Graening, Jay. "Induction: Fallible but Valuable." *Mathematics Teacher,* Feb. 1971.
7. Graham, L. A. *Ingenious Mathematical Problems and Methods.* New York: Dover Publications, 1959.
8. Krulik, Stephen, and Jesse A. Rudnick. *Problem Solving: Handbook for Teachers.* Boston: Allyn and Bacon, 1980.
9. Lester, Frank. "Ideas about Problem Solving: A Look at Some Psychological Research." *Arithmetic Teacher,* Nov. 1977.
10. Meiring, Steven P. *Problem Solving—a Basic Mathematics Goal.* Columbus: Ohio Department of Education, 1980.
11. National Council of Teachers of Mathematics. *Applications in School Mathematics* (1979 Yearbook). Reston, Va.: NCTM, 1979.
12. National Council of Teachers of Mathematics. *Mathematical Challenges.* Reston, Va.: NCTM, 1965.
13. National Council of Teachers of Mathematics. *Problem Solving in School Mathematics* (1980 Yearbook). Reston, Va.: NCTM, 1980.
14. National Council of Teachers of Mathematics. *A Sourcebook of Applications of School Mathematics.* Reston, Va.: NCTM, 1980.
15. Polya, G. *How To Solve It.* 2d ed. Princeton, N.J.: Princeton University Press, 1973.
16. Polya, G. *Mathematical Discovery.* 2 vols. Princeton, N.J.: Princeton University Press, 1954.
17. Wickelgren, Wayne A. *How To Solve Problems.* San Francisco: W. H. Freeman & Co., 1974.

NUMBER CONCEPTS

18. Beiler, Albert H. *Recreations in the Theory of Numbers.* 2d ed. New York: Dover, 1966.
19. Davis, Philip J. *The Lore of Large Numbers.* New York: Random House, 1961.

20. Gardner, Martin. "A Short Treatise on the Useless Elegance of Perfect Numbers and Amicable Pairs." *Scientific American,* March, 1968.
21. Myhill, John. "What Is a Real Number?" MAA *Monthly.* Aug.-Sept. 1972.
22. Nivan, Ivan. *Mathematics of Choice.* New York: Random House, 1965.
23. Ore, Oystein. *Invitation to Number Theory.* New York: Random House, 1967.
24. Schultz, James E. "Why I Don't Have Any Examples of Negative Numbers." *Arithmetic Teacher,* May 1973.
25. Shoemaker, Richard W. *Perfect Numbers.* Reston, Va.: NCTM, 1973.

GEOMETRY AND MEASUREMENT

26. Coxeter, H. S. M. *Introduction to Geometry.* New York: John Wiley & Sons, 1961.
27. Hoffer, Alan. "Geometry Is More Than Proof." *Mathematics Teacher,* Jan. 1981.
28. Kerr, Donald R., Jr. *Transformational Geometry.* Reading, Mass.: Addison-Wesley, 1976.
29. Loomis, Elisha Scott. *The Pythagorean Proposition.* Reston, Va.: NCTM, 1968 (originally published in 1940).
30. National Council of Teachers of Mathematics. *Geometry in the Mathematics Classroom* (36th Yearbook). Reston, Va.: NCTM, 1973.
31. National Council of Teachers of Mathematics. *Measurement in School Mathematics* (1976 Yearbook). Reston, Va.: NCTM, 1976.
32. National Council of Teachers of Mathematics. *Metric Handbook for Teachers.* Reston, Va.: NCTM, 1974.

PROBABILITY AND STATISTICS

33. National Council of Teachers of Mathematics. *Teaching Statistics and Probability* (1981 Yearbook). Reston, Va.: NCTM, 1981.
34. Scammon, Richard. *The Odds on Virtually Everything.* New York: G. P. Putnam's Sons, 1980.
35. Tanur, Judith M., et al. *Statistics: A Guide to the Unknown.* San Francisco: Holden-Day, 1972.

HISTORY

36. Beckmann, Petr. *A History of Pi.* New York: St. Martin's Press, 1971.
37. Bodley, R. V. C. *The Messenger.* Garden City, N.Y.: Doubleday, 1946.
38. Bronowski, Jacob. *Ascent of Man.* Boston: Little, Brown, 1973.
39. Dorrie, Heinrich. *100 Great Problems of Elementary Mathematics.* New York: Dover, 1965.
40. Eves, Howard W. *In Mathematical Circles.* Boston: Prindle, Weber, & Schmidt, 1969.
41. Kline, Morris. *Mathematical Thought from Ancient to Modern Times.* New York: Oxford University Press, 1972.
42. National Council of Teachers of Mathematics. *Historical Topics for the Mathematics Classroom* (31st Yearbook). Reston, Va.: NCTM, 1969.
43. Smith, David Eugene. *History of Mathematics.* Vol. 2. Boston: Ginn, 1925.
44. Smith, D. E., and Jekuthiel Ginsburg. *Numbers and Numerals.* Reston, Va.: NCTM, 1953.

ACTIVITIES

45. Abbott, Janet S. *Learn to Fold—Fold to Learn*. Franklin Mathematics Series. Chicago: Lyons and Carnahan, 1970.
46. Abbott, Janet S. *Mirror Magic*. Franklin Mathematics Series. Chicago: Lyons and Carnahan, 1970.
47. Bennett, Albert B. "Star Patterns." *Arithmetic Teacher*. Jan. 1978.
48. Biggs, Edith, and James R. MacLean. *Freedom to Learn: An Active Learning Approach to Mathematics*. Don Mills, Ontario: Addison-Wesley (Canada), 1969.
49. Hoffer, Alan R. *Mathematics Resource Project*. Palo Alto, Calif.: Creative Publications, 1977.
50. Horne, Sylvia. *Patterns and Puzzles in Mathematics*. Chicago: Lyons and Carnahan, 1970.
51. Johnson, Donovan A. *Paper Folding*. Reston, Va.: NCTM, 1957.
52. Kuenzi, N. J., and Bob Prielipp. *Cryptarithms and Other Arithmetical Pastimes*. Indiana, Pa.: School Science and Mathematics Assoc., 1979.
53. Mira Math Company. *Mira Math Activities for Elementary School*. Canada: Mira Math Company, 1973.
54. Randlett, Samuel. *The Art of Origami*. New York: Dutton, 1961.
55. Winner, Carol. *Make It Take It Math Games*. Rancho Santa Fe, Calif.: Carol Winner, 1978.

CALCULATORS

56. Judd, Wallace. "Instructional Games with Calculators." *Arithmetic Teacher*, Nov. 1976.
57. Lappan, Glenda, and Mary Jean Winter. "A Calculator Activity That Teaches Mathematics." *Arithmetic Teacher*, Apr. 1978.
58. National Council of Teachers of Mathematics. *Calculators—Readings from the Arithmetic Teacher and the Mathematics Teacher*. Reston, Va.: NCTM, 1979.
59. Rade, Lennart, and Burt A. Kaufman. *Adventures with Your Hand Calculator*. St. Louis, Mo.: CEMREL, Inc., 1977.
60. Schultz, James E. "Using A Calculator to Do Arithmetic in Bases Other Than Ten." *Arithmetic Teacher*, Sept. 1978.
61. Schultz, James E. "How Calculators Give Rise to a New Need for Skills in Algebra." *School Science and Mathmetics*, Feb. 1978.
62. Wheatley, Charlotte L. "Calculator Use in the Middle Grades." *School Science and Mathematics*, Nov. 1980.

TEACHING METHODS

63. Bennett, A. B., and G. L. Musser. "A Concrete Approach to Integer Addition and Subtraction." *Arithmetic Teacher*, May 1976.
64. Freudenthal, H. *Mathematics as an Educational Task*. Dordrecht, Holland: Reidel Publishing Co., 1973.
65. Holt, John. *How Children Fail*. New York: Dell, 1964.
66. National Council of Teachers of Mathematics. *An Agenda for Action*. Reston, Va.: NCTM, 1980.
67. Sobel, Max A., and Evan M. Maletsky. Teaching Mathematics: *A Sourcebook of Aids, Activities, and Strategies*. Englewood Cliffs, N.J.: Prentice-Hall, 1975.

68. Steen, Lynn Arthur, and Donald J. Albers, eds. *Teaching Teachers, Teaching Students: Reflections on Mathematical Education*. Boston: Birkhauser, 1981.
69. Williams, Elizabeth, and Hilary Shuard. *Elementary Mathematics Today: A Resource for Teachers Grades 1-8*. Menlo Park, Calif.: Addison-Wesley, 1970.

GENERAL

70. Bennett, A. B., and L. T. Nelson. *Mathematics—an Informal Approach*. Boston: Allyn and Bacon, 1979.
71. Bergamini, David. *Mathematics*. New York: Time-Life Books, 1972.
72. Dubisch, Roy. *Basic Concepts of Mathematics*. 2d ed. Reading, Mass.: Addison-Wesley, 1981.
73. Hoffer, Eric. *The True Believer: Thoughts on the Nature of Mass Movements*. New York: Harper & Row, 1966.
74. Miller, William Hugh. *Everybody's Guide to Music*. Radnor, Pa.: Chilton Book Company, 1961.

Index